Conversations
with Anne

**Other Books By Anne Bogart
Available From TCG**

The Viewpoints Book:
A Practical Guide to Viewpoints and Composition
by Anne Bogart and Tina Landau

Conversations with Anne

TWENTY-FOUR INTERVIEWS

Anne Bogart

THEATRE COMMUNICATIONS GROUP
NEW YORK
2012

Conversations with Anne is published by Theatre Communications Group, Inc., 520 Eighth Avenue, 24th Floor, New York, NY 10018-4156.

The publication of *Conversations with Anne* through TCG's Book Program is made possible in part by the New York State Council on the Arts with the support of Governor Andrew Cuomo and the New York State Legislature.

TCG books are exclusively distributed to the book trade by Consortium Book Sales and Distribution.

CIP data information is on file at the Library of Congress, Washington, D.C.

ISBN: 978-1-55936-375-4

Book design and composition by Lisa Govan
Cover design by Mark Melnick

First Edition, March 2012

Conversations with Anne has been in the making since early 2003 and it is impossible to adequately thank the numerous individuals who made the book possible. Many thanks go to the artists who so generously shared their personal stories and artistic journeys. Heartfelt thanks also go to the countless people who helped organize and manage the twenty-four interviews for *Conversations with Anne,* including the SITI Company administration led by Megan Wanlass, the ongoing help of the SITI Company interns, the many artist assistants and staff who helped with getting approvals, edits and proofreading, the practical support of SITI Company board members and the TCG publications staff for their dedicated work over the years with the realization of this book. Thanks also to the staff at the University of Chicago who arranged the conversation with Mary Zimmerman, and the American Repertory Theater who hosted the conversation with Robert Woodruff.

Contents

Introduction

By Anne Bogart

After 9/11, I noticed that people were gravitating with gusto toward one another to converse, to consider, to listen and to discuss substantive issues. People gathered in town halls, church basements and empty theaters. There seemed to be a need for mutual exchange under standard light, without artifice or the separation of stage and audience. The communities that formed shared an appetite for thinking together, musing together and considering the future in relation to the past, to the present and to recent events.

In this spirit I began an initiative in SITI Company's studio entitled *Conversations with Anne.* I invited colleagues who I admire and respect, one by one, to engage in a public conversation with me. Because the response was universally positive, we continued organizing these conversations throughout the past decade. At times *Conversations with Anne* happened in other cities, including Chicago, Boston and Baltimore. The transcripts of these conversations appear here and I am happy to share them with a larger community who might benefit from the reflections of these singular individuals captured in a moment in time in the midst of their distinct journeys.

Conversations
with Anne

Richard Foreman

As an undergraduate at Bard College I was part of a posse of theater students who organized the "I Hate Richard Foreman Club." We were zealous in our dislike for the man and his work. It was the early nineteen seventies and we often made journeys to New York City to see the work of the Open Theater, the Living Theatre, The Manhattan Project, the Performance Group, Peter Brook's Théâtre des Bouffes du Nord and Richard Foreman's Ontological-Hysteric Theater. We relished our hate for Foreman's work.

When Bard's film department invited Richard to speak with film students, we rounded up the "I Hate Richard Foreman Club" to face him down. Much to our surprise, no film students showed up, which left us to face and accuse him directly: "You use actors like props!" At the time, we were all highly influenced by Jerzy Grotowski's brand of actor-centric "poor theater," and Richard's auteur theater seemed heretical to us. Much to our frustration, Richard not only agreed that he treated actors as props, but then he abandoned us to watch a video of his production *Sophia Equals Wisdom*. We seethed.

In 1974, freshly out of college, I moved into a cheap loft on Grand Street in New York City, only a block away from Richard's theater on Broadway near Spring Street. Each and every evening that I had nothing else planned, I made my way to Richard's theater to watch a rehearsal or performance. Inevitably I left at the end of the evening hating the man and his work even more. But then I would return. I returned again and again. After about a year, I realized that not only did I not hate Richard Foreman, but also that he had taught me more than any other director. I finally saw that his work is perhaps the closest descendent to Bertolt Brecht's, and that Richard was developing Brecht's ideas forward.

Richard grew up in Westchester County, near New York City, graduated from Brown University in 1959, and went on to receive an MFA in playwriting from Yale School of Drama. Unhappy with the general state of theater and playwriting, he began to direct his own plays in New York City, often working with nonprofessionals and filmmakers as actors. Since then, he has produced and directed almost sixty of his own plays with his company the Ontological-Hysteric Theater. He also received a great deal of acclaim for his productions of Brecht's *Threepenny Opera* at Lincoln Center; Suzan-Lori Parks's *Venus* and plays by Václav Havel and Botho Strauss at the Public Theater; *Woyzeck* at Hartford Stage Company; Molière's *Don Juan* at the Guthrie Theater; Kathy Acker's *Birth of the Poet* at the Brooklyn Academy of Music; and Gertrude Stein's *Dr. Faustus Lights the Lights* at the Autumn Festivals in Berlin and Paris. He collaborated as librettist and director with composer Stanley Silverman on eight music-theater pieces produced by The Music Theater Group and The New York City Opera. He also wrote and directed the feature film *Strong Medicine*. In opera he directed *Die Fledermaus* at the Paris Opera, *Don Giovanni* at the Opéra de Lille, Philip Glass's *Fall of the House of Usher* at the American Repertory Theater and The Maggio Musicale in Florence.

Five of Richard's own plays received Obie Awards for Best Play of the Year, and he received four other Obie Awards for directing and one for "sustained achievement." He has also received the Literature Award from the American Academy and Institute of Arts and Letters, a "Lifetime Achievement in the Theater" Award from the National Endowment for the Arts, the PEN American Center Master American Dramatist Award, a MacArthur Fellowship and, in 2004, he was elected officer of the Order of Arts and Letters of France. He received an honorary doctorate from his alma mater, Brown University. New York University recently acquired his archives. Seven collections of his plays have already been published, and books studying his work have been published in New York, Paris, Berlin and Tokyo.

March 31, 2003

AB: Let me start by telling my personal story with Richard. When I was an undergraduate at Bard College in upstate New York, I was part of a company, Via Theater, which was very influenced by Grotowski. We used travel to New York in a van and we would see things that really rocked our worlds as twenty-one year olds. Peter Brook would do these workshops, and we would see the Open Theater and the Living Theatre and the Performance Group—and there was Richard Foreman. I hated Richard Foreman. I just thought he was awful. We formed the "I Hate Richard Foreman Club." This was 1973. We saw a sign at school saying that Richard Foreman was coming to visit the film students—because Richard used to work with film students as actors. So the "I Hate Richard Forman Club" all went to torture him, but none of the film students showed up. So, Richard came in, and we said, "You treat actors like props!" And Richard said, "Yeah."

So, I moved to New York, to Grand Street and Crosby, where I had a loft in 1974 for three hundred and twenty-five dollars per month for three people. Richard had a theater which was just a room on Broadway. Every time I had a free night I'd say, "What do I want to do tonight? Well, I'm going to go to Richard Foreman's and watch what he's doing." I'd go over and watch either a performance or an open rehearsal, and I'd leave afterward going, "I hate this, I hate that, I hate Richard Foreman." And then the next free night, "What am I going to do? I think I'll go see Richard Foreman." And after a year I realized that, in fact, I'd learned more from Richard than from anyone else and that I'm actually more influenced by Richard than anyone else. That's how I came up with the theory, which I hope is true, that Richard is actually the actor version of Bertolt Brecht.

Carrying on with this theme of hate, there was a huge installation at Exit Art this summer, and Richard's was "Ten Things I Hate About Theatre." Maybe we could start with this issue of hate.

RF: This is a raw moment to start with that issue because obviously we all hate George Bush.

I've always been ambivalent about the theater. I got into the theater as a kid because I was shy. I was an actor originally. I started doing my own shows in grade school. By the time I was well ensconced in junior high school, I realized that I thought more interesting things were going on in other art. It's very perverse that I've been in theater and that I've been able to continue. When I was a teenager, my friend and I would come into New York every Saturday and would see everything—everything—and I would invariably walk out of the theater, hits and so forth, and say, "John, it's hopeless. If that's what they think is good, how can I be a success?"

I don't trust any group human response. To me, group human response is what makes nazis. To me, the task of serious art is to make everybody really understand that they don't belong to a group. It doesn't work. The group response is just a return to some animalistic level, which we all have, which can make us feel good for a moment but really denies what I consider the truth of the human being, which is the potential for some kind of real lonely spirituality. When we started rehearsing our play this year, *Panic!*, I by accident came across this quote from Glenn Gould: "The purpose of art is not the momentary ejection of adrenaline, but rather the lifelong construction of a state of wonder and serenity."

I'm a little less articulate about it than I sometimes am because I have been thinking for the last two days something new about what's happening in my work and why it doesn't belong in the theater. After I graduated from Yale Drama School, I was writing plays. I was writing an imitation Brecht play, an imitation Giradoux. And one day I said to myself, "What would I really like to see if I walked into the theater right now?" I sat back at my desk, closed my eyes, and about in that much time I had this image—and that's what I've been working on these last thirty-five years. That image came from a not very good production that I had just seen at the Circle in the Square, José Quintero's production of *The Balcony*. I saw Shelley Winters standing and, I think it was Lee Grant, standing on the other side of the stage. There was a pause, and they were just sort of standing there looking at each other. That image about blew my mind—a static image.

I began writing these plays in which actors sort of just sat there and didn't move very much or repeated each other: "My arm's heavy on the table." "Oh yes." "Is my arm heavy?" "My arm's heavy." It was based upon this static, nothing happening, and on the physical presence on stage of the actor. In the early days the actors used to just stare at the audience saying their lines as if they were taking dictation on the blackboard or something, because I really wanted just the sheer physical presence of what was there to be the center of the theater, instead of looking through that and trying to see the intentions of the actor or trying to see a story that was theoretically taking place somewhere else. Of course, all this was relevant to what was happening in other arts in those days. Painting in those days started talking a lot about the presence of the canvas and the presence of flatness, getting back to the basic grammar of your art.

In the play I'm doing now, the actors all trudge on stage to loud music and then it stops and they sort of look at each other, sort of move off; there's a statement, then one actor grabs another and embraces her and she pushes him away, and he looks at something else, and then the play develops—it's not as static as my early plays were. But I realized it was a return to this notion that I want a laboratory where things come from—this moment of presence. Eric Bogosian said that what really turned his head around about my theater was that the present moment, what was really there physically on stage, took precedence over any allusions to story, to the elsewhere, to being transported.

Now, most of the theater still, even if it's more athletic in the Grotowski sense, or your sense, makes a lot of allusions to someplace else. I'm not against being entertained by that on occasion, but it does not interest me as something to work on. What I've been thinking was I started with this physical presence of just the dumb actor—I mean dumb in a high sense. In the early days, I was writing plays and directing so that there was just a registering of what was going on physiologically in the body—not trying to have complex psychology, not trying to have complex motives, just continual reassertions. In those days, most of the audience would walk out after twenty minutes. And we were proud: "Ha, ha! Great art! People don't appreciate it. This proves it's great." But at a certain point, I'd had it. So for various reasons, including what was happening with post-structuralist thought and a lot of mystical religious thought and so forth, the language started getting much more developed and aphoristic and a kind of repartee—complex language. But I realized just the other day that the body is there, the body is present. The actors are still pretty much staring at the audience, saying, in effect, "This is going on. Well what do you make of it?" The plays were designed to say continually to the audience, "What do you make of it?"

Okay, the body, present. Next stage: What the plays started to reflect was the chatter that goes through your head as you're just there. This relates a little bit to the way I have always written, which is sort of lying on my couch every day writing a few sentences, maybe a page, maybe just three sentences of dialogue. This sort of picks up, in an almost Gertrude Steinian sense, the chatter that is continually going on in the brain. Now, the chatter going on in my brain is the chatter of a person who feels very involved with reading and thinking, "Heidegger says such and such." "Yes, I'm here because I like being here, but it's bigger." "What's bigger?" "I don't know what's bigger; everything's bigger." This chatter, units of that chatter that came from this present body, developed the kind of text that became very verbally oriented.

I wanted to prove to people that I could write because so many people said, "Oh, he's a good director, but his texts can be a bit nonsense. They don't mean anything." I thought, no the texts are pretty smart, so I really tried to write interesting plays, and I was gratified because people started giving me awards for being a playwright. Then, two years ago, all of a sudden, I'd had enough good writing. So I started doing these plays where just a couple of pithy phrases on tape, processed by the tape, echoed themselves. I thought of them as phrases dropped down a well where they would reverberate, and each phrase would seem to have associations that were implied and doubled by tape, by music, by gonks and pings. The actors would be moving in relation to that dropped phrase. The actors say a few things, but very, very minimal.

But what I realized in the last couple of days is that it isn't so much that I was sick of good writing; it was rather that this still-present lethargic or frozen body is now in my work reflecting just what's in the air, what is language and thought, to present the possibility of discourse. This play this year starts out, "He goes where no man has dared to go." The next phrase is: "I will not enter this tomb." Each of these phrases must have the possibility of suggesting multiple interpretations. You could write a play about, "He goes where no man has dared to go." But is that because he's stupid, because he's daring? Is that because it's embarrassing to go to that place? Very many possibilities. And the phrases must suggest that both possibilities are specifically not developed. I agree with a French philosopher, Renan, who said—and other people have said—that he doesn't believe in development, because when you take a thought, when you take an impulse, when you take the seed of a story, and you develop it, you are automatically trapped by the conventions of the ways we've been trained to think, the way things logically must happen. So the lightning flash of a complex and contradictory idea has it all, and to develop it becomes the trap. Through that technique, not allowing the audience to feel, "Oh yeah, we all share that feeling," you are left alone with just moment by moment the raw possibility of, "Yes, things could different. Yes, things are like this now, but the world is so vast. The world is so complex."

It's not a question of hate or not hate. It's a question of total disorientation. I think it's therapeutic. A great American philosopher, Morse Peckham, wrote a book in which he defined art as providing a disorientation massage. We all know what makes us cry. We all know what we love. The purpose of art, I think, in these troubled times, is to provide that disorientation massage that makes you realize, "Well, things are confused. Things don't have to be this way. I don't know how they could be, but I can be lucid and feel enlightened even though it's all a mess." There has to be an organization that is rigorous that allows you to have that feeling of lucidity in the midst of, as John Keats said, the negative capability of not having this irritability reaching out after facts.

What do you think this organization is based on for you?

Essentially it's based upon trying to make everything—this isn't going to make any sense, but—totally dense and totally lucid. Everything is very precisely organized in continual punctuations and framings of all these things that might say, "What does that mean?" But that moment, "what does that mean," is framed so carefully by a gesture, a noise, a change of light, a surge of music. I'd like to think that organization into a total minuet of all these disturbing elements, this aesthetic organization, the arc, the composition, suggests a paradise of artistic lucidity. The materials of this artistic lucidity are incumbent on an uncluttered mind.

Do you think about it as a platonic sense, or do you start to organize it, and then react to it and change it?

Well, of course, I react to it and change it because all of my ideas are stupid. Hemingway said the artist needs a good built-in shit detector, and I think I have a very good built-in shit detector, but we rehearse a long time and I have millions of ideas and ninety percent of them are stupid.

So what is—I'm getting at something in the organization—not stupid?

When there's a tension. When I see it, I become tense. I work very intuitively. I do not work thinking about theory or what I'm trying to achieve. I wait until it coheres and I can recognize it.

When you first started working with actors, you worked with filmmakers, and then after a while worked with actors, sometimes with fantastic actors, sometimes with amateur actors. Will you talk about that process?

In the fifties every American play was about how we're having the terrible problem, but, you know what? If we only loved each other . . . And that was the performance, too, I felt. The actor out on stage, even if they're going through agony, the performer wanted to be loved, wanted to reach out to the audience. Perhaps because I'm adopted and I did not feed at my mother's breast, I am a person who does not respond to that too well, even in life. I'm a reserved person. Part of the aesthetic of my theater I'm sure is derived from my particular personality structure. You make art from your position, from what you have been given. I wanted to make a theater in touch with another level of reality. So, I used non-actors. In those days, I was fascinated by the beginnings of underground film, and that's where all my friends were. So my actors mostly were filmmakers, but they were overly awkward people who, instead of knowing how to move, be dramatic, would come out on stage, say a line. It was this physically present reality.

Then, quite by accident, I met my second wife, Kate Manheim, who became my leading actress for many years. She became an actress in my plays through great misunderstanding. Her father was a translator, Ralph Manheim, and when I first met her I said, "Oh, are you related to Ralph Manheim?" and she was very impressed and said she'd be in my play. But the truth was I was thinking of a famous German sociologist, Karl Mannheim. I accidentally said Ralph. She was not an actress, but she developed on her own this very electrifying, strong technique. For a lot of the period in this country after the war the actor's technique was basically centered on trying to find a way to relax inside yourself so that things could come through. Kate's technique was quite the opposite. It all came through tension, much as, I suppose, a classical ballet dancer operates in tension. But she developed this technique, and there was an imbalance with the non-actors. We started using actor-actors to balance off of her. That really was the transition.

For a long time they said, "Oh, he uses his actors like puppets." Well, it's true, even these days. I do choreograph the pieces. I think there are more directors now who work that way. To boost my ego, I like to refer to one actor I had in France who said, "You know, Richard, it's very strange. Every one of your plays, it's like you keep me in a very narrow corridor, but within that corridor somehow I feel freer than I've ever felt." I'd like to believe that's true. Some directors will say, "Well, Anne, this scene has to do with your mother." I want to say, "Anne, think whatever the hell you want; invent your own internal stuff, but don't hold your wrists like that. Put your two hands on your knees." So, it's where you exercise that degree of control, and all directors have the same degree of control and put it in different places.

I sometimes think you can see a director's body on stage. If you think of Bob Wilson—all angular and distant, a little bit cold. Or you think of Brook—"We're all so human here." I always thought with you it was like, "My foot hurts."

Absolutely. Because as a kid I was very shy and I felt very awkward and I still basically do. So the basis of a lot of my theater is stumbling over things.

What do you like in an actor? What appeals to you?

Well, obviously I don't like performances that reach out trying to gain love, and nobody likes actors who indicate, of course. I'm always telling the actors, in essence, do less. I was very influenced by the films of Robert Bresson, who used non-actors. He called them models. He didn't even refer to them as actors because he felt that if they didn't use their habits, some other force would speak through them. Bresson happened to be Jansenist Catholic and so was interested in invoking some other spiritual level. I also thought about the early performances of Yvonne Rainer, who was doing dances with non-dancers—who was, again, looking for a very physical presence of body without intention.

I want to make a play that has a poetic strategy, and the strategy of poetry is that words rhyme with other words. Words have associations with other words in the line or the next line, and you're supposed to be able to pick up on all that interaction—as opposed to a classical novel where you're supposed to look through the words and see that they happen. If the actor is playing intention or emotion too clearly—we are empathetic creatures, so we get hooked by that and block out the association of the way his arms are and how that would relate to the way her arms are, or the way it looks against the light and set and music.

One thing that I used to tell actors all the time—you're going to get my repertoire of things actors are not allowed to do. Very often when an actor is going to come on stage he's getting sort of psyched up and comes on stage with a certain energy to carry him through the scene, and I always tell him, "No, no, no, you can't jump on stage like that. You've got to come on stage and there's broken glass around you or there are hidden mines, but every moment you're under threat, and you must never let the energy of your motive carry you through the scene."

I also tell the actors: I want you to assume that everything you're saying, even if it's stupid, placed where it is, it's the most brilliant thing that could be said at that point—but you also have to have the feeling that that brilliance is being delivered only to the one or two people in the audience who will get it. You must assume that most of the other people are too dumb. It's like, "Just for you, here it is—not for the rest of you." Because, for me, what's exciting in art is the feeling that I'm watching something where I want to poke Anne. "Did you notice that?" We savor that, and we feel alert and energized by our noticing as opposed to everybody obviously noticing because it's being presented on this silver platter.

I remember Kate Manheim's performances which I saw many, many times. She does something with her eyes where you think she's looking only at you. It was uncanny.

In the play we're doing now, probably the most experienced actress is Elina Löwensohn. She has a great presence, but she would try to show too much her intentions and what she was thinking. It interfered with what's most exciting for me in the performer—just the arrogant fact of their presence is electrifying. I think Chris Walken's a great actor, and what I admire is that arrogance. In the beginning I didn't quite get him. I thought he seemed very stiff, but that stiffness was a kind of arrogance. I always feel that young actors have a tendency to try too hard and try and convince you.

You don't go see much theater anymore. I'm interested in the issue of influence from the inside and outside. When you were younger you went to see everything, right? And now you're extremely selective.

Well, not selective. I only go if a good friend is twisting my arm. I have too many good friends. When I was younger, I went to see everything because as Brecht, and I'm sure other people, said: You go see what you can steal. But even when I was young, almost everything I used to hate and walk out of, with a few exceptions. I always like things that are not successful. There were twenty productions I saw that had a profound affect on me: Joan Littlewood's *Oh! What a Lovely War*, Faulkner's *Requiem for a Nun* with Ruth Ford, *Camino Real*, Kazan's original production—which I was horrified to see that he sort of disowned in his book saying, "Well, we did it too realistic; it should have been more imaginative." My God, what was so great about it was the play was poetic, imaginative, and he did it like this down-to-earth, real thing. I've seen other directors try to be more poetic and imaginative and it's terrible. Those three shows—and there are others, but off the top of my head I can't remember—oriented me toward what I felt was alive in the theater. The only one of three of those that was successful was *Oh! What a Lovely War*. But I do like the low-down sort of pop elements, that are vulgar in the right way, which Joan Littlewood always was.

I began realizing in the other arts I saw things that I thought were much more rigorous and profound. Martha Graham influenced me a great deal then. Then at a certain point I just disappeared into my work, as

I think many artists do. Now I'm still trying to see influence, but from things I can encounter in my home: art magazines, video tapes, CDs, books—mostly books. I'm terribly influenced. I think of myself as a person who simply skims the cream off the top of this big pot of everything in our culture that is available to me.

And what happens to that cream?

Well, it gets put on a surface, where it dries, it coagulates, into little beads and then I arrange those beads in ways that please me.

Let's talk a little bit about the difference between directing your own work and directing other people's work. You have done Suzan-Lori Parks's *Venus*, the really acclaimed *Threepenny Opera* with Raul Julia, Bothos Strauss, Büchner, Molière . . .

The best thing I did, outside of my own work, was Molière's *Don Juan*, which I first did at the Guthrie, then did [with the Public Theater] in the park.

My own work I can treat as garbage. That's very freeing. I can change it. I don't have to respect it. When I do another play I do try to respect it. But I approach plays through the discourse, through the language, rather than through the characters. I'm listening for the writer's voice, and what does that imply? Take *Woyzeck*. I did *Woyzeck* with David Patrick Kelly in Hartford. That text is fragmentary and can be rearranged in different ways because he never really finished it. Woyzeck is a sort of schizoid guy, and it was written about the same time that Rimbaud was around. So I thought, well, maybe that is the voice that this play is really about, this wounded Rimbaud who doesn't have an arena where he can develop into this epic-making twentieth-century poet.

For me, it was Büchner's language in a translation. I always like the translation that seems the most wooden. When we did the Havel play, Tom Stoppard had made a translation and I thought, "Oh, it's so elegant and so phony," and so we took the original translation that had been made for Tom Stoppard and used that, because its woodenness, its awkwardness, seemed to me to relate more to what I am interested in, which is the raw material.

Cocteau once said if you want to be really avant-garde, just try to be as classical as possible and your own idiosyncratic nature will come through. So that is pretty much the way I work. I don't think too much. I know directors who will go through and make notes with their dramaturg and they'll have thousands of things written down. I don't. I'll read it once or twice casually and then with the actors. What is there to think about? I know I'm smart. So, that's not going to be a problem. I just have to be there, carefully watching, picking up on things and discovering through rehearsal. "Oh, yeah, when this actress says this line, it suggests this, and that connects to the way that this actress answers her." Just dealing with the text, it's not the same because, when she says the line, the line has a different weight and it suggests a different direction than if we had cast someone else in the part. So I wait.

That means you're listening.

That built-in shit detector—that means that you're always going to be sniffing, at every moment.

Joan MacIntosh, who did *Three Acts of Recognition*, described when she'd leave for dinner break you'd be staring at the stage. And she'd go out for two hours and come back, and you'd be in the exact same position, staring at the stage, hunched over, tense. What are you thinking?

It's not tense so much. It's not wanting to get out of the mood of the play. You go out to lunch, come back, forget the first half hour. You're carrying your lunch back with you. I want focus. In life, generally, I lie around the house and I become extremely lethargic, so lethargic I think I must be sick. But when I get into rehearsal I get extremely focused and awake and alert to what's happening. I grew up in a family of lawyers who used to have long discussions around the dinner table, and I was trained to be able to speak articulately the way a lawyer would speak. I began to realize that using that kind of sharp focus was not really productive. I wanted to be focused with a wide-angled vision. I was there waiting to see what would pop out of me from this total feel of what was going on on stage.

Tom Nelis [SITI Company member; performed in Foreman's *Pearls for Pigs*, 1997]: I felt that you purposefully set up a paradox for the actors where you have to become focused at being unfocused, be off-balanced. When we were in Hartford, you were away for a week, and you came back. You called everybody into the hallway and said, "You know, I'm sorry, it's been great working with you all, but it's horrible." You said, "You look like some absurdist Polish theater troupe. You nailed everything. You put everything on the music; it's all very tight and sharp, and it shouldn't be like that at all."

It should be tight and sharp, but it has to be syncopated. It has to be off the beat.

TN: I would make my first entrance in a full frog-man outfit with a spear gun and a monocle. The stage is littered with chairs and tables and heads, severed heads, and I'd work at making this entrance articulate, and then Richard would say, "Do we have any bigger flippers? Because Tom's too smooth out there." That became the aesthetic.

AB: "My foot hurts!"

You were playing the clown. You were great, but, you know, specifically you were supposed to be as ludicrous as possible.

TN: I didn't know!

Well, no. If I had told you to be ludicrous, you would play ludicrous.

AB: Antonioni says, if an actor says, "What are you looking for?" he makes something up because if he says what it is, then he'll get that, and that's never interesting.

That's true. Sometimes I can't resist, to prove I'm smart. I remember reading an interview with Mike Nichols—and I think Antonioni was the more interesting director—but Mike Nichols said, "Oh God, Antonioni will actually place the actor's hand in a certain position on the table. Horrors!" Well, for Mike Nichols's way of working, of course, but there are all different kinds of ways to work.

AB: Musicals and opera—you do a lot.

Well, not as much as I would like to. It's the same thing. I mean, my plays have so much music. I haven't done that many classic operas. I've done a number of contemporary operas with composers that I've worked with. I've really only done two classic operas so far: *Fledermaus* at Paris Opera and *Don Giovanni*, which is the greatest opera, so why do anymore? The big shock for me doing *Don Giovanni*—it was really an aesthetic problem. I like things to be very dense and very busy, so for an aria I have twenty ideas, and we rehearse, put in these twenty ideas, it's great. Then, "Oh my God, are they still going to sing that aria for five more minutes?" I mean, it just does go on. Also, the thing that I enjoy most in my own work, and even in classical texts which are not operas, I must admit, is discovering the way to rhythmically articulate and to keep changing the rhythms. It's like composing or editing film. Obviously if you're doing a classic opera, you can't do that because you are controlled by the music as written. You can learn from that and it can be interesting. I'd like to do more opera, but I do find that a big problem—that somebody else is waving the baton, and I am not.

AB: And when you say you'd like to do more—why?

Oh, vacation, glamour, ego trips. There are some operas that interest me. I was about to do [Weill and Brecht's *The Rise and Fall of*] *Mahagonny*, which is, for me, the greatest twentieth-century opera. The whole production was planned in France, in the same place I did *Don Giovanni*; it was all cast. And, two months before, the city of Lille had big political turmoil. They closed down the opera. That was a great tragedy for me because that's the piece I had wanted to do for twenty-five years, ever since I did *Threepenny*. After we did *Threepenny*, Joe [Papp] said to me, "What do you want to do next?" I said, "*Mahagonny*." "Okay, I'll get the record and I'll listen to it." And the next day he said, "Well, it's not as good as *Threepenny*." But that's the one piece that I really am still hungry to do. I have a great production in mind. Of course, it's controlled by the music. But the music changes so rapidly and is so much more gestural in terms of theatrical shape that it's easier to think of doing.

AB: Were you designing that?

Yes. I only worked with designers for the first ten years or so. For *Fledermaus* at the Paris Opera, the sets were done by Sally Jacobs, who was at that time Peter Brook's main designer. We worked very well together, but I really understood after that experience that as I'm thinking about directing I'm changing the set in my head all the time, and I'm making models myself and drawings. They're very sloppy, but it can fall down and that can give me an idea. Sally was open to anything I would say, but it gets translated into words and somehow it cuts out other impulses that come when I'm just with my hot glue dripping on my finger. It's like finger-painting or working with mud pies. A more primal you is at work, and I think in all art you have to get that primal you into the equation.

AB: I was in San Diego listening to NPR in the car, and there was an interview with you. You were doing a Kathy Acker play at BAM with David Salle. The interviewer said, "Richard, how's the collaboration?" And then you said, "It's not a collaboration. It's a collision!"

I think that in a good sense. I love Kathy Acker's work. In her novels I don't quite understand what she's doing, and yet I know there's a rigor there that's tremendous. So Peter Gordon, whose music I liked in those days, said, "Let's do an opera," I said, "Fine. But if I write it, it'll be too far out." Peter said, "Who do you want to write it?" I said, "Well, I'm really interested in Kathy Acker's work." And Peter said, "Oh, that's my ex-wife." So we asked Kathy. Kathy wrote—or rearranged because Kathy collages things sort of like I do—this obscene text, a big, gigantic production. And we said, "Well, nobody's ever going to put up the money to do this." So, I have an idea. Kathy was very much in the art world. "Kathy, do you know either Julian Schnabel or David Salle?"—both of whom were the big painters in those days, and maybe if they painted the scenery, we could then sell the scenery, and we could get enough money. So, "Yeah, I know David better, I'll ask him." He said, "Sure, I'd love to work with you. The only rule is, I don't want to work in a normal theater way. I'll design what I think is right for each scene, and that's what you have to work with." I said, "That's fine with me." I liked the idea of that kind of collision. There was a scene, very apropos for now, of these Iranians saying all kinds of obscene things, and David decided it should be set on a basketball court and all the Iranians are wearing big diapers. It worked magnificently. The first scene was a take on George Kaiser's expressionist play *Gas*, where a factory's about to explode. And David saw that in a chic Soho loft. That was harder to make work. But it was a great experience.

I made a list a couple of years ago of the fifteen great scandals I was involved with in the theater, including *Fledermaus* at the Paris Opera with the nude dancers, which was front page headlines for two days, a horrible mess. *The Birth of the Poet* was a huge scandal at BAM. After the first ten minutes the whole audience was screaming out back at the stage, as obscenity would follow obscenity, and people were walking out, throwing their programs at the stage.

AB: I want to go back to this "disorientation massage" and the world we live in now.

In a funny way, I think this proves my point that I've been making for like twenty-five years. Back in the sixties, when everything was starting to break a little, people were saying, "Well, it's not art. What is the political content?" I said that, and I've said since then, that it seemed to me that the forces of reaction in America come from people whose character structure is such that they cannot stand ambiguity. They want to know: Is this person good or bad? Left or Right? Black or white? I said then what could help America is anything that tries to create a character structure where people could accept living amidst ambiguity and knowing that you can still be lucid and gentle even though things seem complex and confusing. This administration clearly is run by the people around Bush who have decided that we've got to clean up the world. We have this situation which is going to, of course, bring more danger and ambiguity. I think of my art as therapy.

My whole life I've been very ambivalent about America. I know there are certain good things, but I've always felt very uncomfortable. I almost moved permanently to France back in the very late seventies, early eighties. Then I suddenly realized something that I'd never understood. When I was young man, I read Henry Miller. He talked about how much he hated America and how rich and wonderful life was in France and Greece, and then as he got to be older he came back to America. What happened? I realized at a certain point in France that I was an American, and some of the things that I hate about America were in me too. And I had to come back and fight my battles here. This is what I am. I'm a stupid adolescent as we all are.

Audience: Richard, you mentioned Gertrude Stein. What are your thoughts reading her and its influence on you?

From the time I was fifteen to the time I was thirty-six I thought there was only one person in the whole history of the theater who wrote decent plays, and that was Brecht. I don't feel that way anymore. I think Molière is the greatest of all writers in theater, but that being said: Brecht, and then Gertrude Stein, who I discovered through some of the filmmakers that I was working with. With Gertrude Stein, it's a question of this meditative state of being in the present. Gertrude Stein's homily that in writing you begin again, begin again, begin again, rather than getting into the flow and letting things develop. People accuse me of being surrealist, which in a sense I'm happy to be accused of because I think surrealism is one of the great liberating movements of the twentieth century, but I felt that surrealist art tended to ride the horse of that over a hilly landscape. Gertrude Stein kept getting off the horse to begin again, begin again. Its implication for being in a continual present was very important for me.

I did one Gertrude Stein production back in the late seventies in France, stupidly enough, in French. We translated *Dr. Faustus Lights the Lights*. It was the hardest thing I've ever done. It's very, very hard dealing with all that repetition.

I must admit, I'm not a person that can sit down and read *The Making of Americans* from beginning to end, or *Tender Buttons*. I can dip into them, just like I can dip into *Finnegan's Wake*, but I can't sit down and read it from beginning to end. I think I have a musical sensibility of a certain sort, but I listen to an entire Bach piece, I can't follow the score. I make an effort and I can hear what's going on, and then my mind drifts and I return and say, "I've got to pay attention and listen to how these lines work." And I drift out again, just like I would do reading Joyce, reading Gertrude Stein. I think that there aren't too many people creating that kind of art today. I think it is vitally important to create that kind of art, that maybe everybody's going to drift out. People have come to my plays and said, "I enjoyed it; it washes over me, and then I sort of drift out for awhile and then I come back to it." And maybe when a person originally said that to me I was thinking kind of negative thoughts like, "Oh, if you're not smart enough to stay with it," but no. I think it's terribly important that people have always made structures that are better and more rigorous and more demanding than we as an audience can live up to for every single moment. Serious art should be better than you are. I think my plays are more lucid, more rigorous, than I, Richard, am in my life. I'm a stumble bum like all the rest of us. Create art that is better than you are able to manifest in normal life.

Audience: What gives you pleasure working as the director?

Well, I'm basically a Puritan; I'm suspicious about pleasure. I think that's ego gratification, but I do know that I get the most pleasure from just getting up and making people start to move around. I guess it's sort of like General Patton. I get turned on to doing that with the real people that I'm dealing with.

Audience: Do you tend to write starting with a concept?

I have stacks of pages, and so I will look at a play three years from now. "Okay, what am I going to do? Oh this page looks interesting." It says, "my basic 1959, people pose, balcony, face." Hey, maybe there's a play in a big balcony and a face looking out. What other page could relate to this? Oh here's a play about a person whose tooth hurts. Well maybe that could be the head. So I put these pages that come from different years, different sources, together and try to articulate some sort of—not a narrative so much as a theme and variation, a ceremony, an event focused on certain controlling issues.

The play that I'm doing this year, *Panic!*, is a little different. These last two years I've just been writing a series of aphorisms, and that's different. I have written from beginning to end. It changes a lot in rehearsal, but I did sit down and write, over two days, forty aphorisms. This year I shuffled it a little bit more, got things from other places.

AB: What made you decide not to use body mikes in *Panic!*?

Well, first of all, I'm so sick of buying mikes because they're always breaking and it's a big hassle. I do not like projected voices. I like when the actors seemed much more intelligent, razor-like. Last year I did a play where no one spoke, and so I got rid of the mikes, literally. This year I felt would be the same thing, but as we were rehearsing, I got ideas that people would say a few things. Next year we're going to be saying more, but we're not going to use body mikes. Maybe I've broken into the real theater!

Audience: Why did you entitle your exhibit "The Ten Reasons Why I Hate Theatre"?

Well, because I do hate so much about the theater: actors trying to sell, narrative. I profoundly believe stories hide the truth. They set you down the groove of normal development and normal expectation. I know a story is supposed to have an arc and then conclude this or tell you something, but I figure it hides the real truth, which, perhaps in my terms, is more of a psychological truth or more spiritual truth. What is really vibrating inside of you? We should not have invaded Iraq because the whole world is going to hate us because the result is going to be more casualties. Okay, a plot could illuminate that truth, but in going down that road I think it hides the deeper, more universal, more potent truth that as we do what we have to do to get our guns or march for peace, at the same time, it's: "I'm cold," or "These people who are out here look stupid," or "Is this really going to work?" or "But I'm really thinking about that girl over there that I want to go to bed with tonight." Those things don't get shown. And I realized that the structure that was much more interesting to me and seemed to retain more of real life was that every moment there are all kinds of associations straying out like a river, many, many branches. I wanted to make an art which, instead of narrowing to a head in this final act, somehow branched out.

Audience: Have you been asked to teach in your life?

I have been asked occasionally. I have very mixed feelings about it. I could be good and turn people on. I also think it's a bit of an ego trip for me. But, basically, if I don't have to teach—and I don't—I would rather be involved in other things. Lately I've been thinking, Well, maybe that's selfish. I know from the way we rehearse now, people who are interns and so forth, on those infrequent occasions when we do start talking a lot, it seems to me that they're sort of turned on by the ideas, so maybe I have an obligation to do that, but I'm ambivalent about that.

AB: You actually inadvertently turned your theater into a school. A lot of people come through it very influenced by you. You make a space for them in your shows. Could you say something about the Blueprint Series?

We have a series where we give directors their first professionally done play in New York. Some of them are very talented. Ken Nintzel, who was my stage manager for a number of years, is, I think, very talented. My stage manager for many years was David Herskovits, who is now running Target Margin Theater. Robert Cucuzza, who's in my play now, has done some very interesting productions. So there are different people that pass through.

It's hard for them though. A lot of them think, We can do what Richard does. I'm not wealthy. I live not extravagantly, to be sure, but ten years before my father died, he started saying, "Well, son, one thing you know, you're not going to starve when I'm dead." So, I've always been able not to take any money from my theater, and when I do these operas and things I can put the money into my plays. I've been able to sustain this level of work for that reason. I don't know if I would have the guts or the courage to do that as rigorously as I have if I had not known I was not going to starve. A lot of young people who come to me are not in my extremely fortunate position, and I don't know what will happen. Some people have the gumption to do it—like Lee Breuer, whose work sometimes is wonderful and sometimes is awful, but he is crazier than I am as a person, and maybe feeding off of that craziness, he has been able to do that in a way that is commendable. Since I knew I would not starve, I felt an absolute obligation to try and do theater that maybe would send half the audience out after twenty minutes. Anything else in my position I think would be immoral.

Audience: You talked about the state of presence you're looking for—the actor just being present. Have you ever been interested in how an actor achieves that? Or is it more that you know it when you see it?

I don't unfortunately have any theory about acting. There are a lot of technical things the actors are doing in my plays these days. They're running around a lot, doing things. But it is still that presence at the center. There have been times in my career where I've had different ideas. In the beginning I was reading an early American psychoanalyst by the name of Trigant Burrow, whose theory was we have a false persona, and to get to the real self, the real persona, he trained people to have a different kind of tension, which meant that they no longer focused the tension like that, but were constantly registering things that were in their peripheral vision. I used to tell actors to do that, that that would create a kind of presence. But I haven't done that in years.

Very often we'll reach a place, at the end of a rehearsal period, a week before we're supposed to open the play, and I'll say, you know, "So and so, that's not right." They'll say, "But Richard, now I'm confused. I don't know what to do." I think it's difficult and then somehow, finally, it happens. But I don't know how. I'm not unhappy about not knowing. I think it has something to do with choosing the performer. Any director will tell you that nine-tenths of it is casting, and I think that is true. There are people who seem to belong in my world and people who don't. I'm sure I've made many mistakes. But you have that feeling.

Audience: What do you feel is the minimum time for a rehearsal period?

That's very hard to answer. I started working with nonprofessionals. We would rehearse until I thought it was ready. We'd only rehearse in the evening for four hours for three months. When I started doing productions for real theaters, I usually got eight weeks. And now—Equity has been very good to us. We have actors and people who don't speak. At a certain point some Equity people complained and Equity came down and took a careful look. Alan Eisenberg, head of Equity [at that point], came and concluded, "No, we want that you should be able to continue. This kind of work is okay. You have your main actors. As long as your extras have had no connection with Equity ever before this, then you can continue using them." What I'm not sure is if they know how long we rehearse. If we go under Equity contract, you're not allowed to rehearse for more than four weeks or something. But we rehearse fourteen weeks. That's because the process for me is like writing the play, rewriting the play. It's the only way that I can do these plays the way that I'm doing them now. The Wooster Group does the same thing over a long period of time. They don't rehearse every day, often, like we do when we're developing something. And they're not Equity. But if you think their work is good, it's because they use a similar lengthy period to evolve these works. I think that's the way you have to make art. You would not tell a novelist, "You've got eight weeks to write your novel." Some novelists work fast; other novelists may work on it for years, and what counts is the product. And I need that time to do what I'm doing now.

Audience: You seem to have this terrific blend of very opinionated views and self-honesty, so I do hope that one day you will be teaching more just to share that. Is there ever any conflict within yourself between your director half and your playwright half?

For a long time I felt I should not rewrite—like Kerouac, this is evidence of where you're at. So things that embarrassed me, things that seemed stupid, I would keep. I started off being shy about rewriting and changing things. Now I'm certainly just as critical at a certain stage as I am as a director. And I am opinionated, yes, but I know I'm a fool. I think that's absolutely necessary to function as an alert, awake human being. We're all mistaken. But we've all got to believe in what we're doing tremendously.

Peter Sellars

The hallmark of any talk by or with Peter Sellars is the shedding of tears. Usually everyone in the room ends up crying. Emotion or, perhaps more accurately, passion is the baseline of Peter's world. He embraces actors, audiences, friends, new acquaintances, difficult circumstances, political paradoxes and radical new ideas. Sellars clasps people, ideas and situations with his whole being, with his body, with his soul and with his mind. He often puts himself in the midst of challenging situations and then he talks until he has achieved his objective: communion.

Sometime during the eighties I was making a phone call at a public telephone booth at a Washington, D.C., airport and I found Peter on the phone next to me. Of course, it being Peter, we embraced warmly. "Peter," I asked him, "why do you direct opera more than theater these days?" He had two explanations. First, he said audiences in the United States come to the theater in a general state of bewilderment. With little understanding of the history of theater or any vocabulary to discuss it, there is little profundity or consequence. He appreciated that opera and dance audiences arrive equipped with contextual expectations and a shared language. Secondly, he noted that opera audiences are generally rich and powerful and have influence. They are the people who might in fact make significant changes in the world. Peter was interested in speaking directly through his work to audiences who have the power to impact the future.

Neither of Peter's explanations is entirely satisfying because the paradox in his own life trajectory is immediately apparent in his constant and prolific action in the world with communities that are not only powerful but include the disenfranchised and under-attended. Peter does make theater of intense political and democratic dimensions. Generations of theater artists feel his influence and inspiration.

Peter Sellars was born in 1957 in Pittsburgh. He studied at Harvard University, where his undergraduate productions are still legendary. Later he studied in Japan, China and India. He became the director of the Boston Shakespeare Company in 1983 and, at the tender age of twenty-six, was named director of the American National Theater in Washington, D.C. Since then he has supervised international festivals in Los Angeles, Austria and Australia. He has directed operas by Mozart, Messiaen, Hindemith, John Adams, Ligeti, Handel and Saariaho, in most of the major international opera houses. Recent theater productions include Aeschylus' *The Persians*, Shakespeare's *The Merchant of Venice* and Euripides' *Children of Herakles*. He collaborates regularly with such world-class contemporary artists as Mark Morris, Bill Viola and Esa-Pekka Salonen. All this and he also manages to be a professor of world arts and culture at UCLA, where he teaches Art as Social Action and Art as Moral Action.

April 21, 2003

AB: I would like to start with three little things that might provoke a conversation. One is: about ten years ago, in one of the Washington airports, I suddenly realized that Peter was on the phone next to me, and we started talking. I said, "What are you doing?" And he said, "Well, I'm not doing theater anymore!" And I said, "Why?" And he said, "Because I like doing opera. You know, the ballet and the opera have a language that people understand, but in the theater we don't. We don't really have a vocabulary. People go to the ballet or to the opera—they know what that language is. I am more interested in that."

Secondly: I saw *The Persians* in Paris in Bobigny about twelve, ten years ago, during the Gulf War. It was like a rock concert. I felt proud for the first time being an American in a European audience, because Peter and his company were critical of the Persian Gulf War. In L.A., people were walking out in droves. I'm interested in the issue of cultural difference, about how something that is politically engaging and critical of an American point-of-view is received in Europe and hated in this country. Peter is someone who mixes politics with art—a potent combination.

Lastly, he's doing *Idomeneo* at the Glyndebourne festival in England this summer, and he designed it two years ago as the American attack of Iraq.

Maybe taking *The Persians* to begin with, can you talk about how you engage in making art, how you choose what you do and what framework to put it in, and how it then meets an audience?

PS: First of all, it is so beautiful to be in this room with you, and there's a sense of community already. One of the biggest issues in theater is just remembering when you were together with certain people and that feeling of *we were all there at the same time, and we all heard the same thing, and we all saw the same thing*. Right now we are in the midst of so much official brainwashing: "You didn't see that," "This didn't happen," "This was a giant success," "We just finished a great war." In this world of spin, it's amazing to say, okay, we're not spinning. We're all in one place together, and we can remember the feeling.

Before, theater was about pumping everybody up; now it's about eliminating toxins from the system, finding a zone for peace, finding a zone of nonexaggeration. That's a very tricky thing. When I was growing up and doing my first show, people hired me and expected me to be marvelous. We didn't want to do anything marvelous because that was what the propaganda machine was doing. So you did something that was the opposite—and people thought, Well, there's nothing there. It's that whole question of public perception—who's receiving what based on what they are really looking for.

At the Mark Taper Forum with *The Persians* we lost seventy-five percent of the audience every night. But, once they actually left, that was easier. The hard thing was for the actors to go out every night and face a solid wall of human hatred. Theater is totally about reciprocity. Life is totally about reciprocity. The story is about what's happening between people—and what was happening between the audience and the actors was really horrible. There were nights the actors didn't want to go out there because they were facing that kind of hostility from the audience. John Ortiz, one of the actors in that show, had not done a whole lot of theater at that time and was mostly dealing with the protocol of the street in Bedford-Stuyvesant. He was going to punch somebody in the front row, and then he decided that he would leave, and I had to really convince him to go back. I said, "John, America is about none of us leaving the room. We all have to agree to stay in the room no matter how bad it gets, no matter how atrocious it is. As soon as you leave, you're not there. And every one of us has to somehow figure out a way to stay here, in this America, and not leave and go right back in with people who despise you, your existence, who look at you with that much contempt. You have to be there."

That whole question of staying in the room, is a big one. In L.A. it was kind of a beautiful thing because the audience would not just walk out. They would walk down the aisle, throw their program on the stage, then say, "I'll be in the restaurant!" There was this whole other show, which was the audience and people's reaction to it. Somebody would laugh and someone else would turn to them and say, "Shh, that's not funny!" There would be this incredible degree of disagreement within the audience every single night and you got the whole place stirring. The whole place had crazy, crazy energy. *The Persians* is—you know, it's boring. It was written before theater existed as dialogue, so there's just these really, really long monologues. The theatrical form of it was unrelenting. You had to focus on the issue.

You had an incredible design idea. You put three-quarters of your budget in the sound and every other seat had a speaker underneath it, and then there was a bare stage.

The sound designer Bruce Odland is a tremendous and subtle artist. The big thing was to actually give people the sound of the war, to be in the war sonically, because that is one thing your television really does not represent. We stopped the play at a few points to describe the different types of bombs that were being tested in the war: these bombs that suck your lungs out, that do all these things, so that the audience realizes that people died in a type of agony that is excruciating. It's that special thing in our weapons design that really started with napalm. Napalm means that you will die eventually, but the last two weeks you are in unbearable agony as your insides are burning. The cluster bomb is another example of it, where you don't just want to kill someone, you want to actually create agony. We described cluster bombs in great detail—how it worked, what happens and then followed that with the sound of the experience. The sound is terrifying. In fact, the sound source that Bruce used was New York City traffic. The audience had no idea. They heard it as the Gulf War and were terrified. But, in fact, the whole point is that if you are going to inflict this violence on the other half of the planet, do not think that you are exempt from it. That violence is part of every day of your life and you live in it.

We actually made that show with all of the violence that is right here. The big twist at the end of it is that the Saddam Hussein figure was a gang kid from East L.A. And the audience was really annoyed by that. For me, the big question was: What does it mean to be this person who lives only to defy the United States of America? John would walk out into the audience and look at the people and say, "You're scared of me. I know you are. You're scared of me with your breakfast every morning. You look at me on your TV and you're scared eating your Wheaties. I scare you. The fact that I exist scares you. I've won already." What does it mean to be willing to kill all your friends, like the gangs in East L.A., just to defy the United States of America? You know nobody in your neighborhood will live past the age of twenty-five, but you did defy the United States of America and, on your terms, won. What is that kind of sacrifice—or suicide or whatever you want to call it—about? The play was really trying to deal with the fact that the war is actually at home.

My favorite image that I will always cherish is Gordon Davidson, the artistic director of the theater, freaking out in the back row. The only way we could get the performance on, and I agreed with Gordon about this, was for me to go out and talk to the audience every night before the show, to calm them down and kind of apologize for what they were about to see. I was sitting with him in the back row of the theater and, as the first bombs fell on Baghdad, Joe Haj, the wonderful Palestinian actor, said something like, "I curse America." The audience was beside themselves, and Gordon Davidson said, "Peter! You can't have that in the show! That's a political statement—you can't have that! We've got to cut that!" I said, "Now, wait a minute, Gordon. You know, an F-16 from an Arab country flies over Santa Monica and bombs your house, and your wife, Judy, is smoldering in the ruins, what are you going to say about the people who did that? You will curse them. So, that's not a political statement; that is a human truth. Can we please deal at that level?" That was the fight every night—and to keep that show from being cut, because it was unbearably long.

It had been reviewed with enormous hostility by, interestingly, Sylvie Drake, in the *L.A. Times*. People don't know she was born in Cairo and, in fact, is from an Arab family. She attacked the production and said, "Doesn't Mr. Sellars realize that Saddam Hussein is a monster, and this kind of thing may go over in Europe where people are less sophisticated, but it will not play here." It is a very intense thing that this Arab American, whose name is Sylvie Drake, felt the necessity to make an incredible attack on all these issues. It's always the case when people write reviews that you don't know exactly what they are responding to. But that was a very extreme, like, slash-and-burn, scorched earth kind of review. We had just come from Paris where it was sold out and highly praised because, of course, the European position on the war was very different. And we were working in Bobigny, which is a suburb of Paris. Where in America we have the inner cities bombed out and gutted and then you force people who do janitorial work to live there, in Paris the whole idea is that anybody who is cleaning the metro, you don't want them in Paris. So, they've built these cities around the edges of Paris where all the immigrants are, all the Africans and Chinese and Arabs. We work at the Maison de Culture in Bobigny, which is one of those suburbs. The neighborhood is Arab, Chinese, Persian, African, and so that's already the vibe. If you are going to be in Paris and come to see the show, you have to be on the subway for forty-five minutes to get there. So, it's a self-selecting audience; people who came wanted to be there.

That's a really important thing: do people want to be there? Or did some marketing campaign convince them to go?

I'm curious how you handle mass exits—just emotionally. Does it not bother you? I don't know how you live with that.

This just goes so far back. It's been since I was, like, fourteen. Most of my shows in this country create mass exits. I am just so used to it. It's like a given. But it's unbelievably painful every single time. You just force yourself. I've always held this image of Mayakovsky seeing *The Bathhouse*, the last play he wrote. The Stalin era was beginning. The audience streamed out of the theater during the show. Mayakovsky would insist on standing in the audience and looking into the eyes of every person. And then took a long walk through Moscow and committed suicide, and that was his death. And you think—well, let's not do that. But when I did *The Persians* in Los Angeles, with just droves going out every night, I actually positioned myself in the central stairway and talked all night to people as they were leaving.

You are a courageous guy.

Again, it's this thing about America. Unless you're part of it, engage in it, then there is no conversation. So, you have to talk to people—even people who disagree with you. You can't say, "They're leaving. They must be stupid." You have to find out, well, okay, maybe they're not stupid and maybe they know something and maybe we could learn.

What is so amazing in this consumer culture, where one size fits none and yet there is only one size, is you have no idea what people are reacting to because there are so many complex vocabularies going around. What people assume is the given vocabulary that the work is going to occur in, inevitably isn't what you're doing—or in my case, it's not accidental. I am deliberately trying to make something that is anti-CNN or anti-what they're used to. So, of course it's going to be in a language that's difficult for them because they're trained to process things in a certain way, and this really disrupts that process. So I can't blame them because I set out to do that. I really have to engage with them and respect them. One of the most important things about audiences is respect. You have to respect every person in the room, and that's on stage, and that's in the audience. Every human being deserves respect, period, start there, end there. One of the biggest things about people leaving was getting over myself and how I wanted to run away. The performers are doing something difficult, and I can't go hide while they go out and fight the real battle. The sense of the liberation was not, first of all, hating the people who were leaving and taking it personally. We're not doing this as a popularity contest. You realize why you're not running for office and therefore you can say the sort of things you couldn't say if you were running for office. So go and have some difficult conversations. You usually get somewhere. Usually there are things that are very moving and surprising, and meanwhile people leave having had some real experience. But it's awfully painful.

I read recently two different things, one I'll bring up later. You said the reason you like creating opera in the opera world is that you like speaking to people who are in power. In other words, that you choose an audience that is actually the most powerful audience—politically and monetarily.

At Salzburg, the ticket price to get into a show that I directed is three hundred and fifty dollars or four hundred. Or there are tickets available for five hundred dollars apiece. I mean, I directed that show. Is that worth it? I'm very alarmed! At Glyndebourne, it's impossible to get in because it's the watering hole of the British upper class. Now they built a new theater, and you can actually get in. And now the British upper class are deserting it, I've been told, because it's not exclusive enough.

Two shows ago I did *Magic Flute* at Glyndebourne. Margaret Thatcher and John Major were both in the audience on different nights. The last show I did, *Theodora*, they were there. Michael Portillo, who was the minister of defense, brought Bill Cohen, the U.S. secretary of defense, to the show. That's a show about the U.S. army, so the idea that the secretary of defense is watching it is actually really interesting. That's to me a really important idea to work in those places—and, also, equally, that in the same year I am working in three housing projects in East Los Angeles. We have to demonstrate as artists that we are some of the few people in society that get to be in both places. We can be in a corporate boardroom, and we are working at the East L.A. Skills Center. Very few Americans have both things in their lives, so we are a few of the people who move across the society and actually begin to draw a picture that would never be drawn with, for and by each group. except that we're there. That's a very, very important responsibility. We are nomadic and we can move across these lines. So, not to work at these exclusive places would be, to me, a betrayal of those responsibilities.

As you said, I am about to do *Idomeneo* as the U.S. invasion of Iraq. You have to conceive of things much in advance in opera. If I could redo the costumes, I would love for them to be British soldiers and not all American because it's in England. On the other hand, that's perfectly in keeping with how we have treated the Coalition of the Willing. The Brits have been ripped off on every level and then never given any credit. When we wanted to stage pulling down that statue, we hired the thirty-two thugs that afternoon and said, "Hey, we'll give you ten bucks. Come here and pull down this statue with us." They put the American flag on the face of the statue before pulling it down. I don't know why they forgot the Micronesian flag, you know? So the British I am sure are used to being overlooked, but I hate to repeat that American insult next week.

In art one of the cool things we can do is cut across a lot of the assumptions about democracy. Democracy by itself needs to be really articulated, and at the moment isn't really working about anywhere in the world—like in either the major democracies or the dictatorships. At the moment that's the real question: what would a democracy look like? What really would it look like? Could we do that? That to me is the project of democracy that is always ahead of you. And one of the reasons we do theater is to hold in front of people where we are still going, that we haven't been there yet, but we're still trying to get there. You know, we're not finished with it. Let's deal with democracy.

There's also something really important about understanding and supporting certain types of elites, certain types of self-identified groups of people who do have common interests. One of the most beautiful things about the internet is you can locate people who have a really specific set of interests that are yours. It's not broadcasting; it's narrowcasting, and that is very cool. In a free world we have to make room for that. I am not talking about golf club memberships. I'm just talking about even making art. And recognizing certain things aren't for everyone—that's okay, they don't have to be. That's one of the real struggles we've had in America. We say, "Everybody has to get this, so if the average quote-unquote doesn't get this then we have to cut it." You know, my mother's an "average person," and she's fine with this.

One of the most liberating things I did was street theater. Instead of people telling you what the audience is, you're doing a performance in front of a shopping mall. Whoever comes is going to come, whoever walks on is going to walk on. All the assumptions about what people are interested in kind of all go away as soon as you start working in those conditions. I did a lot of that when I was a younger person.

You did something recently on the Anish Kapoor sculpture at the new Tate.

Anish is designing *Idomeneo*. Act One is actually set inside an internal organ, so there is no sky. There is only intense red. There is not a straight line anywhere. Everything is inside some body part, and it is terrifying and claustrophobic and relentless and lit from behind so it's warm and pulsing and moving. At the same time, the U.S. soldiers, the supply crew on the aircraft carrier wear distressed army fatigues and red T-shirts. Then we've overdyed that and stained them with different layers of blood which dried at different times, so there's old decayed dried blood, then fresher dried blood. So it's all this symphony of super intense reds. Jim Ingalls, the lighting designer, is using yellow-red across the spectrum to blood red.

I'm dizzy already.

There are these emotional shifts while the music of Mozart plays, which is, of course, the main thing that's missing from CNN—this image of national forgiveness. Mozart is the composer of forgiveness, the composer of compassion. Every one of his pieces is about forgiveness. He wrote *Idomeneo* when he was twenty-five and he completely doesn't know what he can't do, and so he is doing it all. The piece disobeys every rule. The first act is ninety minutes, the second act is an hour and the third act is two hours. It has dance. The opening image is an Arab-Asian woman (the original text is in Asia, but what that meant at that time, what part of the world that was, is complicated) standing in front of the massacred bodies of her father and brothers. She sings a ten-minute aria saying, "I must not hate the people who did this." Then the young man who's kind of the Mozart surrogate comes in and says, "I didn't do this, but I'm on the side of the people who are responsible, but please don't hate me." Four hours later the two of them are finally ruling the kingdom, and all the older generation had to abdicate. These will be the people who will carry the planet forward. The third character in the triangulation is Elektra, who's fresh from the *Oresteia*, where the issue of revenge was very real. Mozart makes it very clear. He has Ilia, the woman, sing the words "mercy" and "gratitude" like forty times in a row. And then Elektra comes on and sings revenge and hatred forty times in a row, and you get that that's the life choice. You can be this woman or that woman, and then you watch them try and deal with their lives.

Grace Paley said the other day at this June Jordan memorial, "You can either get involved or have a very unhappy life. At this moment in the world there's no choice; you can either be an activist or be miserable and angry every day."

Audience: Sometimes both.

The anger thing is a hard one. Something I've been doing in the past ten years is not staging anger, angry shows. My shows used to be shattering, at the end you couldn't speak and thought, Oh my God. That's horrifying. For ten years

I've done the opposite because there's enough horror every day when you watch television or read the newspaper. People do not need to know that the world is a bad place or a horrible place or that there's a lot of ugly stuff going on. You got that.

A few years ago, in the Newt Gingrich period, when they were kicking the shit out of country after country, they were going to abolish the NEA, I thought, What would it be like to live without any support for the arts of any kind? So I decided to go to Bangladesh. Americans complaining, that's one of the worst things on earth. It just drives you crazy. You want to say, "Please shut up!" So I thought, let's just go and be in a place where people aren't complaining all day. It's the poorest or the second poorest country on earth right now. There are in Dhaka, the capital, two hundred theater companies. Not one person is paid. There are two theaters, and your theater company has a night in one of those two theaters every three months or so. To say that they're not elaborately equipped is an understatement. It's just a shell where people can be together, essentially. The theater company that I was with has been in existence since 1976, which is a long time. They have fifty members. The youngest are sixteen and the oldest are in their eighties, and the company of fifty stays together. I thought, What is that? Of course, their company exists since 1976 because Bangladesh exists since 1975. These are people who fought as guerillas. Then they handed in their weapons and started a theater company because that was the only way they could continue trying to make the country they wanted to live in, to talk about issues of justice, to talk about what their hope is in their lifetime to see. And that's why over twenty-five years they all come to every rehearsal and that's what their plays are about. "Play" is a loose term. There's still some influence left over from the British, but a bunch of it is Bengali culture, which is sung. You'll be there and, in one afternoon's rehearsal, they just made up four songs. The sheer creativity pouring out is just incredible. I was seeing this one show, and I said to the person in the company that I was standing next to, "Well, you know, couldn't this be just a little more hard-hitting and really get right down into the problem?" And this person looked at me and said, "Peter, our audience already understands that life is difficult. The question is: What else can you tell them?"

I've been trying to stage things that are really illuminated from within and that don't leave you depressed and despairing and in a kind of cul-de-sac but that propose a forward momentum. If you watch television at all you just find yourself really, really depressed. That sense of despair is just so disempowering, so you disempower yourself from actually doing anything. You think, What can I do? and blah, blah, blah. But what can you do? Everything, so just do it.

AB: Nietzsche said there's two completely different possible experiences of life. One is from the point of view of being grateful, and the other is from the point of view of being ungrateful, and that's really stuck with me. The notion of a culture of complaint or Americans complaining—you can create an entire life from that point of view.

For me, one of the biggest lessons in that way is—and it is still hard to swallow, because the way you're brought up, it sticks in your throat—the African tradition of the praise song, that the African artist is there to praise. Did everybody see this movie they made of Salif Keita? You watch him sing this praise song to Moussa Traoré, who's like one of the all time mass murderers and you think, "Oh God."

I was reading—and actually I would recommend it to everybody, it's beautiful—these Persian epic novels from the twelfth century by Nizami. It's written in verse, it goes on forever, it's illustrated, usually, with a brush that has a single hair on it and somebody has drawn the detail on every insect so perfectly. The book itself is a vision and a whole performance just turning each page. The story of it is very cool, but the story doesn't begin till the eighth chapter. Chapter one is in praise of Mohammed; chapter two recounts Mohammed's night journey; chapter three says how the poet is personally grateful to be Muslim; chapter four is advice to his son; chapter five is in praise of the ruler who is some horrible Sultan chopping heads off; chapter six is about just rulers and how great just rulers are; chapter seven is a dedication to the just ruler on hand; and chapter eight is where the story begins. You get that it's better to praise somebody than to tell them you hate them, they're bad at what they do or they're monsters because you have to have a way to continue the conversation. Beginning the opposite way, there's not going to be a very long or interesting conversation. And, if you're in it for the length of a medieval Persian epic, then you better make sure that the conversation begins propitiously. Every human being has a whole lot going on. So, which side of someone are you going to address? Their best side or their worst side? Can you give them permission to show that side, and can you encourage and nurture that side?

The text itself is one of the most beautiful things, and I am kind of dying to stage it, but I don't know. It's stories of this young prince growing up, like those epics, fantastic hunting scenes. Then there are seven princesses waiting for him in seven pavilions in his palace. Each pavilion is a different color. Each princess in each pavilion is from a different part of the world. So the Chinese princess is in the black pavilion; the Arab princess is in the white pavilion; there's a Greek princess; there's an African princess. The known world—each has a pavilion and a color. Then he goes into each pavilion and each princess tells him a story, which is like an incredible moral teaching tale, but also just an amazing adventure. At the end of this amazing story, where among other things you finally realize how to live your life, the people in that story decide, in order to remember what has happened to them, to only wear clothing of that color for the rest of their lives. These colors and everything are all about alchemy and cosmology and the seven pavilions are the seven planets and it is all built around the inner and outer structure of the universe. It's a time when the main activity of the scientific world was in the Islamic world, and this was an interface with Islamic astronomy and understanding what the message of the planets were for your life.

And then, while he's been in these pavilions enjoying these lovely stories, his kingdom has gone straight to hell. Evil viziers have been running it in a corrupt and horrible manner, and the Mongols spot that and decide to invade while the kingdom is at its weakest. He's going to respond and he goes to the treasury and it's empty! And the army—they've all deserted. He has to leave in disgrace and go and live as a beggar for one year. A Kurdish shepherd teaches him all these life lessons, and he goes back to the kingdom and he says, "Okay, I'm king again." He opens the prison and takes seven prisoners out of the dungeon and has each of these prisoners tell their story of why they were arrested, tortured and condemned, and that gives him the wisdom to turn the kingdom around! Because, of course, you can find out what's wrong with a country by talking to its prisoners. The Mongols are repulsed, and the kingdom is prosperous forever. The idea that the wisdom of ruling comes from seven princesses and seven prisoners is a really intense and amazing image.

I just talk about it in terms of praise. It's all done as praise for the ruler to really beguile them. Let's begin with respect. Let's begin from that place. That's the African tradition as well. At first you think it's shallow and cheap, and later if you think about it a little more it's like Jesus saying, "Love your enemies," or Buddha talking about the eye of equality.

AB: What is the eye of equality?

Well, the eye of equality is actually an old Hindu thing. It's in the *Bhagavad Gita* and it finds its way into a bunch of Buddhist texts. I'm obsessed with it because we live in America and the thing that made America different from any country that came before us is this phrase "all men are created equal." What does that really mean if that's what our country is founded on? How do you prove it? How do you demonstrate that? How do you test that, how do you make it real and not an idea in your life?

I teach a class at UCLA called "Art as Moral Action." I did a semester on the eye of equality. For the final they had to write a fifteen-page paper: a portrait of somebody that you think that you are better than. Get real. But that's what we do in theater. That's why Mozart gave really great music to really terrible people, Shakespeare gave really great poetry to really horrible people. Yes, it's a terrible person doing something awful but, in fact, if you really look at it further, the Hindu thing is not recognizing it as good or evil. There is ignorance and awareness or enlightenment or however you want to put it, but it's not evil. It's ignorance. So you don't judge them. Then you can work with that and engage with that and not from a vantage point of superiority but some basis of equality. It's one of the most important things in working with actors and discussing character. That usually involves yin and yang handling skills because a lot of yin has to pile up over there and you have to make sure a bunch of yang will pile up over there. You have to constantly be adjusting to create and ensure equality.

AB: That brings me to the second shocking thing! In the program in Chicago for *The Merchant of Venice* you said you're not interested in virtuosity in acting now. I thought, That's all I think about in acting!

Well, the context for that—we're going to put two of Anne's comments together for sensation effect! One is my saying that opera and dance are far superior to theater and I'd rather work in that. In theater anyone can walk in and say, "Hey, I'm an actor," whereas, if you try that as an opera singer or as a dancer, forget it! There's just a basic level of skill that means the audience has to respect you, your moral right to say something, because you have sacrificed years of your life in order to be able to do this. That's impressive and that has a moral power.

On the other side, in theater, I was really campaigning against this idea that there is a way to speak Shakespeare. The nightmare for me is auditioning routinely, which I did for Shakespeare and just recently Euripides. I have to plead with people, "Please do this the way you would have done it before you went to Juilliard." Wait a minute and look at this and find some connection and go from there, rather than a presumed notion of what style is. One of the hardest things about that presumed idea of style is that you're trained to not actually look at the material but to say, "I know my moves," and then to execute those moves. I am really tired of watching most actors who earn their living by selling soap products on commercials having feelings they don't really have. Most American acting is very, very sophisticated and convincing—and actually in the service of something they know is simply not true. The whole veneer of that acting already leads me to some very false place, usually. I respect people who have that "technique" quote-unquote, but if you can cry for an AT&T commercial then what is the value of a human tear?

There's a Bill Viola show that I recently wrote an essay for, in the catalogue published by the Getty. A big section of it is about tears and what is inside certain tears. When your recite the Koran you're supposed to make people weep. What are the nature of those tears? And really differentiating among the different categories of tears—tears of self-pity, which are tears of total paralysis, refusing to change your life, wanting to just wallow in yourself but in fact totally indulging yourself, versus tears of repentance, which are the first steps toward changing your life. There are these amazing traditions about tears. Catherine of Siena wrote about tears. In my shows people cry all the time, and I want the audience to cry all the time, but what do those tears come from? Are those tears tangible evidence of a really deep and visible thing? Are those tears some way of going on record, even to yourself, that you have certain feelings and that you want to do certain things with your life? That's one of the biggest things about Koran recitation and stuff like that. You see something in your life and you can see your way through it—those tears. And also the tears of what you did wrong and the arrival of a type of knowledge or understanding, acknowledging you can't go back, and that now you must go forward.

AB: And then there are Spielberg tears, which are horrible.

It's the propaganda tears that Goebbels specialized in, to make everybody cry and feel that they are sensitive but not responsible. The tears of a certain kind of American melodrama of the early twentieth century, which gave everyone the strngth to go back cleansed into their sweatshops after a good cry. It was important to do that, to see *Bertha, the Sewing Machine Girl*, weep and weep, and then go back, cleansed, to your horrible sweatshop and sit at your sewing machine. That is why I love American melodrama—but they never really questioned the system enough for my taste, which is the difference between Dion Boucicault and Shakespeare. In Shakespeare there are the same tears, but it's also questioning the whole system. But Boucicault's plays are incredibly theatrical, fantastic.

AB: Have you done any of those?

I did Eugene O'Neill's father's version of *The Count of Monte Cristo* at the Kennedy Center with the American National Theater. That is truly some over-salted, over-buttered popcorn! The Dumas has some great things in it, but the adaptation is a little thin, and so I put in gigantic chunks of Byron and the Bible. Suddenly people found themselves in tears because the text really moved to this whole other level, and people were saying words that have this incredible, shocking power and people thought it was the melodrama—but it was an astonishing group of actors unleashed, declaring great spiritual truths.

Audience: For example, David Warrilow.

And, excuse me, David Warrilow is saying those words, or Richard Thomas, or Patti LuPone, or Roscoe Lee Browne. I gave him also all of Psalm thirty-seven in the middle of a tacky melodrama speech. Or Byron's poem on darkness, which is just terrifying, so intense! Also, I added a heap of music—Beethoven's opus ninety-five quartet, "Serioso" and the Schnittke Second Quartet.

AB: All this with a melodrama?

You want the texture to have all the moral force it can have. It was also audience deprivation. All our entertainments, all our news, everything is meant to flatter you and to flatter your worldview. Everything is designed to flatter you into buying. Most Americans have everything at their finger-tips. Dr. Maher Hathout, one of the founders of the Islamic Center of Southern California, speaking from experience said, you know, if you've been in an Egyptian prison and not had water for three days and on the third day you have a glass of water, you'll never forget the taste of water for the rest of your whole life. How do you get an American audience to taste water— for the first time? So I did a lot of the show turning the lights out so you couldn't see the action. Things were happening and you knew that because I put gravel on the stage and miked it. So you could tell that people were doing things—you just couldn't see them. Every once in a while the lights would come on and they would say one line and the lights would go off again for a while. On the one side, you put in everything you can think of, and you want it to be as rich as possible and full of texture, and on the other side you get to that point of necessity, which comes through absolute poverty and deprivation and which you only understand through poverty.

AB: For *The Children of Herakles* in Boston, you had one theatrical device for the entire evening, and the evening included an hour discussion before, then a coffee break, then the play, *Children of Herakles* by Euripides, and then dinner and then a film and literally one theatrical "effect," and when it came it was really shocking!

The way that theatrical effect was done was so simple. There's no slight of hand. It was just a woman in a white T-shirt who had a cereal bowl with fake blood in it. She was being sacrificed, and when her throat was cut she took the cereal bowl and poured it, and the red liquid went slowly down her front on her t-shirt and stained it. It dripped on the floor and there was this big piece of plastic and she was wrapped up in the plastic and carried away like it was a body bag, and the plastic was clear so you saw all this really scary crap in there like blood and stuff, her feet sticking through it. As a theater effect it was so utterly, utterly simple, and it was really, really honest in that you saw it coming.

AB: Actually dumb and beautiful.

In the age where Steven Spielberg has the special effects budget, it is really important that it's a cereal bowl and that you're pouring it on a T-shirt, that it's totally transparent. We are dealing with absolute transparency in what we are doing, and the image is powerful for other reasons. Now what are those other reasons? That interests me a lot. The other reasons are what we are really doing in theater, all the invisible stuff we do that isn't seen.

In *The Persians* we did the entire Iraq Army with one person, Martinus Miroto, who was the greatest refined dancer in central Java ten years ago. He also specializes in spirit possession dance. I was obsessed at the time with all the images of the war that Americans didn't see. In the first Gulf War, there was a photographer, Ken Jarecke, who worked for *Time* magazine. You may remember that the *Observer* in London published one of these photos and there was such a hue and cry it shut down the *Observer*. It was deemed antipatriotic. It was the same deal they went through with the Arab news channel: no question about, "How can you commit these atrocities?" Just, "How can you show them on television?" So Ken basically took all these photos up and down along the highway of death, and nobody would publish them. I got his number and said I'd love to use these photos in this performance. He gave us permission to use them. So I got these photographs, and these photographs are so shocking. I mean, you could see people dying, and you could see that their last moments were unbearable—a type of agony that is indescribable and horrifying. I couldn't use them. I couldn't. I mean, there's nothing you can do on a stage with that projected—it was obscene. So Miroto set up an altar in his dressing room and before each performance we would place a different photograph on the altar and pray to the soul of that person and try and contact that person who died that way and ask permission to dedicate the performance that night, to give some peace to their soul. He would channel that soul into his body, and then he would go out on stage and enact the person being hit by those bombs using only classical Javanese dance—not realistic but the opposite. That was the reason why the American audience felt so much closer to the Gulf War than all the television footage. They couldn't tell what it was that was bringing them so close to this war experience—they didn't know what that was. There's an emotional and spiritual level from inside that show because of the spiritual preparation that goes into it, and you can't possibly know about, and you're not supposed to.

AB: James Joyce calls that "the secret cause."

It's the ceremony. This is not a show that you clap or not clap at, you like or don't like, "loved him, hated her." We're here tonight to do a ceremony, to appreciate the spirits of the people who died and hope that people won't have to go through that again. It's what, in Tibetan tradition, are called dedications. It's what Orthodox Hebrew tradition is—you tie your shoe a certain way because you dedicate that action to people who are not present. When you do something the long, complicated way, it is because we are not being expedient; we're living in another way for invisible people based on a whole set of demands that we have to meet. You are making connections that are really deep, and so the simplest gestures on stage or in your life have incredible weight and consequence. Taking a cereal bowl full of blood and pouring it on a T-shirt is no big deal. By itself it's nothing. It's like in dance—move your hand this way, okay, so what? When does it become an empty gesture and when does it become a life-changing moment? That's the other side of the technique thing. Once you dedicate it that way, it removes your ego. It lets the performance rise to a whole other place because it's dedicated. Dedication is a really great word.

AB: Through the act of making theater, things happen and connections are made. Something happened to me when I was watching *The Children of Herakles*, and I told you about it after seeing it. There were some projections of text, and it completely opened up the experience to me like a flower, and I saw everything differently. The text that said something like, "God created Adam and Eve and they screwed it up; God created Moses and he screwed it up; God created . . ." and down the line about how we've screwed things up—behind a woman playing an extraordinary musical instrument. It might be worth sharing how that came about because it's a real thing that happened.

In the center of that production is a woman who is a musician, Ulzhan Baibussynova; she comes from Kazakhstan and she's twenty-eight years old and she is from one of the oldest shaman families in Central Asia. I wanted to connect this with Greek drama. The contemporary link is obvious. The ancient link is harder. What is it that speaks across the centuries? What is it that lets you know that this is the voice of your ancestors? This song—it's incredible because the whole history of humans' messing things up—God created Adam and Eve, Cain and Abel, then it goes to Moses, then it goes into Jesus, and then it goes into Mohammed—it covers a lot of territory. It literally handles all of the monotheistic religions, all of them, in one song. As you've said, it's an emotional moment. It's a moment of such shocking clarity. It goes past emotion into this real state of consciousness and recognition. That song was not in the show when it started. Ulzhan was singing that same music but with other words. We had a break before we went to Italy and France, and she went home to Kazakhstan, and she described the performance to elders. And they were really moved to know that this tradition was being passed forward. The songs had a new life in a certain way outside of Kazak tradition, were now a part of another tradition as well, connecting to Greek drama, connecting to theater in Europe and America in this moment. So it was a whole new world for her and particularly for the elders of Kazakhstan. Then one of the old men said to Ulzhan, "Come visit me next week," and she went, and he took from inside his breast pocket a little piece of paper. And he said, "These are the real words of this song; they haven't been revealed for one hundred fifty years, and it's now time to reveal them. You have permission to sing this song in this performance you are doing in the U.S., but only if the words are projected." And so what Anne saw was this one-hundred-fifty-year-old tradition that had been hidden, because in Kazakhstan they had to hide their real culture from each wave of invaders. Once again, the audience can feel it, but you can't put your finger on it. This is one of the biggest issues in theater: Can you feel, simulate, a moment of enlightenment, or can you create a moment of enlightenment? Are you acting like you are going to change your life, or are you going to change your life? How close can we get to making in the world the thing we want to actually happen so it's not just a simulacrum, it is the thing in itself, as Shakespeare would say.

Audience: When you are working in theater—not in opera but in theater—you essentially circumvent the actors and depend on Miroto or Ulzhan or other people who've been invited into the productions. What happens in a theater company like Anne's or a cast like *Merchant of Venice*, and suddenly you have to depend on the actors to achieve this? Where do we look for those actors that we don't have to work around?

What's interesting to me about actors is that actors are taking in stuff and are drawing out of a really deep place. How that place is accessed and how that place is discussed is, in my experience, not the same with any two performers. Then it's about creating collective structures where we're all part of something that's larger than any one of us.

Audience: But how do you identify the capacity for that response, that vibration, that they need?

It's tough. I hear you. Part of it is that I work with the same people over and over again. Part of it is—and I've gotten it wrong plenty of times—some people you know and you feel it and it's there. Auditions you can only run so much, so a lot of people I cast I've seen in something or somebody's told me this is an amazing person who will really go the distance. But once you are in rehearsal—for example, the first week of *Merchant of Venice*, we went through that play. Essentially the entire cast was quote-unqoute "people of color," who previously had never done Shakespeare and were only playing pimps and things on television. The question, "What is rhythm in Shakespeare?" is a really interesting thing to ask a young Panamanian or Brazilian actor, for whom rhythm is really interesting. Why am I going to listen to the Royal Shakespeare Company tell me what rhythm is when the British are the least rhythmic people? Let's ask a Jamaican about rhythm in Shakespeare. That's what I meant about received virtuosity. The first week of *Merchant of Venice* we went around the table and we would stop at every single line and every person in the room would share a personal experience that that line reminded them of. It took one week to read through the play once. But that meant that every single line had an association for every single person in the room, and every single person in the room was aware of how many other associations there also were. We were gradually creating our own collective lexicon of shared experience that we could then draw on in rehearsals to ground everything. The second week was reading the play again but within the room we had the Dhammapada, the Koran, Noam Chomsky, Manning Marable's *How Capitalism Underdeveloped Black America*—so that all the stuff that was going on in Shakespeare we were opening out into Eduardo Galeano. We created another lexicon that was not made up of our personal experiences, and we were also recognizing what Shakespeare was referring to and what the consequences of that were—discussion of the word "ghetto" and where it comes from.

Another strategy is learning from amazing performers. In the Greek plays I've cast a deaf actor named Howie Seago, who's really, really an amazing performer but also an amazing person. But everybody has to learn how to communicate with Howie, and just that act in rehearsal is one of the biggest tests. I invite a bunch of people into the room who can't have a conversation necessarily, and then the rehearsal process is about: Will a conversation be possible or not? We never start to make a show. It's always about: Can we test these issues with these people and see if communication is possible? Sometimes I am way off, and other times people have breakthroughs that astound me. *Peony Pavilion* is a really intense example of that, three actors playing each role in two different vocabularies. Hua Wenyi, the greatest living exponent of Chinese theater and kunqu, was partnered with Michael Schumacher from the Frankfurt Ballet. You were having two really different moving vocabularies. So I don't go around the actors, but I do try and create a total environment—something that is larger than just acting professionally.

Audience: What do you do with self-doubt or doubt and frustrations that arise? What's the place for that?

Be grateful for it. Doubt is a really, really important thing. Donald Rumsfeld doesn't doubt himself. If doubt has been sent into your life, it's a gift. My big lesson from my great master, Liz LeCompte, was that everything comes from what you don't know and can't say and don't understand, and that's the actual source of your most important work.

AB: She must have gotten that from Brecht.

Brecht was clear about that, that doubt is the gift. Doubt is where you find the sweet stuff because up until then it was merely "effective." I've always been trained to distrust effectiveness, which is why I like large portions of my shows to not be "effective." Everything on television is so effective, and Hollywood movies are effective, and I want to declare that we're not going to be effective for the next half hour. That doubt of yourself when you're in the noneffective zone is a really beautiful thing, and it is a gift. The doubt is your greatest empowerment as an artist. The key to your artistic identity is the nature of your doubt.

AB: Someone said if you look at any kind of certainty and you take it to its end point, it always ends in violence.

Wow. That's intense

Audience: You started out as a leader in theater at a very young age, and since you were speaking about trying to not to be better than anyone else I was wondering what that experience was like for you.

I started off as apprenticing at the Lovelace Marionette Theatre in Pittsburgh, Pennsylvania, when I was ten years old. When I went to high school it took too long to teach people how to work the puppets, so I started doing shows with people in them and started directing because someone had to organize stuff. When I was fourteen I made a conscious decision to only do what I love and what I care about every day, and the rest takes care of itself. So I never think of it as leadership. It was just trying to do something I really wanted to do and I need to do in order to exist. Like, you can't live in this country without saying certain things in public. I can't be an American and *not* say these things. I can't live every day and not try and make some noise about these questions. I'm not really looking around and saying, "Who can I lead?"

Because of my apprenticeship I've learned from a very young age to invite people much better, much more skilled, than I am into the room and so, by working with certain people like Miroto, by inviting certain artists, certain extraordinary things are going to happen. It's never about me . . . that's one of the reasons I moved to California. Living in New York, having to think about the American theater every day, would just drive me crazy. In L.A. I don't think about theater. If I choose to do theater, it always comes from something I want to say at a moment and am not saying it as a message or a piece of propaganda. It's just like I have to explore it and deal with it and invite really amazing people into a room and work through it, because I can't live unless I've made that commitment.

The show itself is the after-effect of the impulse, which is to try and solve something in life or deal with something in life, and then you figure out the show that will do that. Most shows it's usually the other way around. Norman Frisch told me to read *Children of Herakles* seven years ago, and he was right. I read it and was very moved by it, but it wasn't until after September 11 and America turned into this other thing that I said, "Well, we have to do *Children of Herakles*," because it was about responding to what America was doing.

AB: Norm said the most profound thing. I've quoted it. We were having dinner around *The Children of Herakles*, and I was working on *La Dispute* and this big prologue that wasn't working, and Norm said, "There's always something I wanted to tell directors, and it's the truth, and if they listened to me they'd be fine." And I said,

"Tell me!" And he said, "Yeah, but you'll never listen to me." And I said, "What?" And he said, "Do the play!" Very deep.

But it's a good place to process. If you are doing work you are about, then it is utterly unmistakable from anyone else's work, and so your artistic thumbprint or imprint kind of stands out—not because *you* want to stand out. So many people aren't working from their gift, and so they are doing this generalized thing. And if you're not actually speaking in your own voice, then no one is going to recognize that that's your voice, because it isn't. I would say search and keep looking, and you'll end up in a place that you didn't expect to end up in—in a great collaboration, nobody's fingerprints are on the material because you've created a genuine shared experience

Audience: You said that the most important thing is how you treat your collaborators, though earlier in the evening you talked about a lot of artists who I know for a fact treat their collaborators in the most offensive and hateful manner, artists that we both respect and love.

Respect anyway.

Audience: Obviously this is a contradiction.

One of the reasons I do old plays is that not much has changed in the history of the world. The other side is a lot has changed, and it's really important for each of us in our own lives to make certain vows that we are not going back there. There are some people—I see that every day—that, to make their work, they have to become horrible and hurt somebody. God knows, in the dance world it's like a rule. It is like any other addictive behavior. You have to see it, recognize it, analyze it and swear it off. It's also a message from our generation that we're not going to be that way. You don't have to be horrible to be an artist!

One of the most important things about working in this new period is reaffirming everything we do as a collective action, and recognizing there's no such thing as individual genius, and recognizing that the art of the twenty-first century is the creation of shared space. It's how many ways and how creatively we can share what we have and every one of us has some missing part of the picture. That's the image we have to give to politicians. It's the image we have to give to the media—that sophisticated adults have come together to work on something really complicated across lots of areas of agreement and disagreement but agree to share the space.

In this era of forced globalization, we have got to insist on shared space across borders and the real elimination of lots of offensive words and actions not through violence but through friendship. How do you deal with someone who hates you and wants to kill you? That's something America's got to deal with now, and we're not dealing well with that. These are not just nice Pollyannaisms of how I'd like to live. It's really the deepest issue of being an American in the twenty-first century. How do you behave with people who hate you and want to wipe you off the face of the earth? (First off, can you curtail some of your own presumptions and damaging behavior?) That is the issue for the next three generations: Can we find some type of response that is inclusive and create some basis for shared space that permits us to be face-to-face?

Charles L. Mee, Jr.

Chuck Mee is the closest I will ever come to having a mentor, guru, wise sage, counselor or muse. Or perhaps what we share is simply a remarkable friendship and love. Whenever I lose faith in the world, I call him up and ask if we might get together. Somehow by the end of any meal we share, my spirits are lifted and I am inspired to go back to my life with renewed gusto.

I often forget that Chuck is dependent upon two canes to get around. He somehow makes me forget this. I remember in 1991 driving around in a beat-up Toyota with Chuck and Annie Hamburger (the founder of En Garde Arts, a producing organization devoted to site-specific theater). We were looking for an appropriate site to stage Chuck's play *Another Person Is a Foreign Country*. At one point Annie pulled up to what looked like an enormous junk heap near the East River in Manhattan. Before I could even get out of the back seat of the car, Chuck had managed to climb to the top of the hill. I looked up to see his arms stretched wide, the width further extended by the line of his two canes, and he shouted down at us, "*Isn't this beautiful!*"

Beautiful indeed. Chuck finds delight and joy in much that he sees and experiences. He incorporates dance and music into the fabric of his plays. He chooses delight and love as his guiding principles. He once wrote three plays in a row about love: *First Love, Big Love* and *True Love*. He was of course, at the time, in love. When that love affair ended, he convinced himself that his life was finished. But Chuck, remaining ever open, next met the beautiful and talented Michi Barall, married her, his life completely renewed.

Chuck writes with a historian's perspective and he looks at the world with the eyes of a philosopher. Between 1972 and 1993 he wrote eleven books on world history and American international relations. He has four children from two marriages and for many years supported himself as an editor for the arts magazine *Horizon*. Chuck's work is now made possible by the generosity of Jeanne Donovan Fisher and Richard Fisher.

I am fortunate to be one of the directors with whom Chuck chooses to collaborate often. He is also a SITI Company member. Other directors he works with often are Robert Woodruff, Martha Clarke, Tina Landau, Ivo van Hove and Daniel Fish. His plays include adaptations of Greek plays: *Orestes 2.0, The Bacchae 2.1, Agamemnon 2.0, Trojan Women 2.0, Big Love, True Love* and *Iphigenia 2.0. Hotel Cassiopeia, bobrauschenbergamerica, Soot and Spit* and *Under Construction* each explore the work of a contemporary artist: Joseph Cornell, Robert Rauschenberg, James Castle, Jason Rhoades and Norman Rockwell, respectively. Other plays include *Queens Boulevard, Paradise Park, The Investigation of the Murder in El Salvador, Time to Burn, Full Circle, Summertime, First Love, Wintertime, Vienna Lusthaus, Limonade Tous Les Jours, Salome, A Perfect Wedding, Belle Epoque, Fetes de la Nuit, Mail Order Bride* and *Gone.* Chuck is the author of a beautiful memoir about his early years entitled *A Nearly Normal Life.*

September 29, 2003

AB: Chuck is, for me, a constant inspiration, and whenever I lose faith in the world, I end up in a conversation with him and gain it again. Years ago Chuck and I were doing a play called *Another Person Is a Foreign Country*. Annie Hamburger and En Garde Arts were producing it. We were looking for a site. It was a very complicated piece that involved a lot of people with various disabilities or abilities, and also it needed to be a very particular environment. We ended up doing it on 136th Street and Central Park West in an old, dilapidated building that was the first cancer hospital, Sloan-Kettering. We went to all kinds of places with Annie and her beat-up car to try and find where we were going to do this site-specifically. We got to one place with literally piles of junk—like mountains of garbage. It was somewhere near the East River. We got out of the car, and by the time I got out of the car, Chuck had already climbed the entire mountain and was standing on the top with his crutches in the air like sticks, going, "Isn't this beautiful?" That changed my life. What I understand is that he stands up on the detritus of our society and says, "Isn't this extraordinary? Isn't this amazing?" When I look around, I see junk, and I see things that make me really sad or discouraged or numb, but he just looks at it in ways that opens it up. So, Chuck: You're standing on this big mountain of junk, which is the world we're living in today. As a theater artist, what do you see?

CLM: I'm not sure I ever know what I see until I start making a play, really. I think I write plays half and half. Half, a story comes out in my head and the characters come out of my life and friends and stuff like that, the way most playwrights write. The other half comes out of plays that I've stolen. It always seems to me that it's not a hard thing to write a play. If you don't have an idea, then you steal—and then remake it, which is what the Greeks always did, and what Shakespeare always did.

You start by grabbing hold of *Iphigenia at Aulis*—Agamemnon is about to go to the Trojan War, and the gods won't give him a breeze to sail by until he sacrifices his daughter. You think, if you set it today, what does that mean? Then you think—I mean, I just make this up as I go along—Paul Wellstone, in1991, the first Persian Gulf War, got up and said on the floor of the Senate, when asked to vote in favor of the war, "I asked myself if I would send my own children to fight this war, and I wouldn't. So I can't vote to send any-body else's children to fight the war." You think of Agamemnon, you think it wasn't that the gods were saying, "We won't give you a breeze unless you hurt someone." What the gods were saying was, "You can't go to war to kill other people unless you're willing to take the person you love the most and kill her first. You make the first sacrifice, and then everybody else will go."

So it's so easy to take some story by one of the Greeks or by Shake-speare or Molière, some story that's been around a long time—and it's been around a long time because it speaks to everybody at almost every moment. Find in that what speaks to you in the moment. Bring it inside yourself and inside your own time and see how it comes out. And in see-ing how it comes out, you see what you notice about your own time. You see that you remember a speech by Paul Wellstone. You see that you remember looking at *Seventeen* magazine and how it socializes young women to do what Iphigenia volunteered to do for her father. "I will be sacrificed." She's a perfectly socialized young girl in Greece, just as young women today are perfectly socialized to fill a certain role. You start notic-ing stuff about the time that you live in. So, in a way, the theater is my guide to what I notice in the world.

I look at the world, I think it's too much. If you take the lens of a play and see it through that, you can actually see it better. But you take the next step, which is you eat the lens, and then you regurgitate something new.

That's a nice image. I say this to myself all the time, over and over—I believe Aristotle was right to say that human beings are social animals, which is to say they exist in relationship to one another and they don't otherwise exist. The horrible thing about Philoktetes—I mean, he's on an island, he's been abandoned because he has this horrible, loathsome wound, and it probably stinks. So they put him on an island. Then they come back to get him to fight in the Trojan War because they need his abil-ities as a killer. He's been spurned and despised and abandoned and dumped on this fucking island to die. Why would he go back? Because, the

Greeks believed, if you're not in relationship with human beings, then you're not a human being. You're an animal. So for him to live alone on a desert island was totally out of the question.

We find out who we are in our relationships with other people. That is to say, if we're cruel or kind or passionate or homicidal or vicious or backstabbing or devious—then that's who we are. The art form that reveals more clearly than any other art form what it is to be a human being is the theater because it's the art form of human relationships. In the theater is where you see what it is to be a human being, and what people can make in the theater is what is possible for human beings to be, what relationships exist and what relationships might exist. It's just infinite. The reason for working in new forms in the theater is exactly that. If you continue to cast human relationships in the forms that have been given to you, the forms of Ibsen—who was a great, playwright, but we know what he did—what could we find out? The way to find out is altering the form and the way of creating theater. The reason for avant-garde theater is to discover what else is possible for human beings to be. That's the only way I learn anything. The only way I know is by working.

Chuck was originally an historian, and moved through being an historian to being a playwright. If I had to equate you with any other playwright, I would say Heiner Müller. It's something about the way you sample history and use the detritus about you and reprocess it.

I graduated from college in 1960 and wrote for Off-Off-Off-Off-Off-Off-Off-Broadway. And then I got very caught up in anti–Vietnam War politics, got caught up with writing stuff, which led to writing stuff about the Cold War, which led to history—historical stuff about the Cold War. I began writing historical stuff about American foreign policy and America in the world. I did that for twenty years. I quit writing for the theater. I took this detour in life, which I never meant to do, and spent all that time dealing with history. It never felt like my real life, and it finally became kind of unbearable. I think the biggest reason it was unbearable and exhausting was that—and I think there are great historians, and I still enjoy reading historians who got past this problem in a way I never did—as a form history believes that it's possible to frame rational sentences and paragraphs that contain the reality of the world, even though the reality that's contained makes most people want to shriek and cry out and tear their hair out and run through the streets. It seemed fundamentally to me untrue. The theater, where you get to use your head *and* your heart, seems to me more likely to get at something that is actually the truth in a relationship. So that was why, I think, I was uncomfortable writing history rather than writing for theater.

But what I bring with me from writing history all those years is a belief, which other people have arrived at in different ways, which is that Freud is really a crock of shit. The discipline of psychology doesn't adequately describe what it is to be a human being. Human beings are not shaped only by the psychodynamics of early childhood, but also by history and culture and genetics and random accidents and all those other things that the Greeks knew—things like calls from the gods, fate, destiny, chance, wheel of fortune. The theater that I grew up in, theater from Ibsen to Arthur Miller, is a theater that believes all human behavior and activity can be reduced to psychological explanation. What strikes me as deeply mistaken about that idea—and pernicious—is that if there exists from the natural world a set of norms to which all human beings conform or are to be found deviant, abnormal, wanton, then you're trapped. You've already lost the game. You're already caught in somebody's totalitarian system that won't allow you to breathe. So I think even though people like Arthur Miller tried to be writing about politics, accepting the frame of understanding human beings as he did, which was so diminished from the understanding that the Greeks had, that Shakespeare had, that Molière had, that it made it impossible for him to ever actually write a political play. What he really wrote were psychodramas where people were bothered by politics and projected personal beliefs onto the situation.

Those restraints or shackles in a way are something that I learned from you, particularly working on _bobrauschenbergamerica_. It was hard for us as a company because we are very obsessed with discipline and doing things right and going deep and starting on time and working really hard. Your approach is, "Well, let's do what feels good." The last line of the play is, "That feels good to me." I think the reason that you chose Robert Rauschenberg is Rauschenberg's notion of freedom. Certainly I was irrevocably changed by working on this piece with you because you actually asked us to be in touch with what feels good. What feels good seems to release the restrictions of psychology in a way. Where did that come from?

It's part of what I learn from the Greeks and Shakespeare and history. So many systems of framing understanding are reductionist. I mean, there couldn't be mathematics if there weren't reductionists. It's a system of understanding relationships in a supremely, exactly distilled fashion. But for understanding of the world, human life, these reductionist systems just incapacitate people for getting through their daily lives and understanding what the fuck is happening to them and where they are. There was this wonderful thing when Oliver North appeared before the congressional subcommittee. Representative Dante Fascell from Florida asked the most wonderful question. He said to Oliver North, "I listened to everything you said, and it all sounds wonderful to me. And it seems that it must be true. And then I ask myself, 'Then why don't I feel good?'" I think how people feel really is how a lot of people settle. It's not a simplification. How you feel really is thinking and feeling with your reason and your instincts and your hunches and your childhood memories and what you had for lunch and your cells and your neurons and stuff. It's a very complicated system of understanding the world. It's immensely sophisticated. So that's a more likely way of really getting at something as complicated as human life.

Less so now, but you're never really afraid of using violence and inappropriate, sometimes politically incorrect, characters, situations, language—vicious language. Where does that come from in you? Can you talk about the uses of violence and where that's gone in your work?

Well, I think when my work was full of blood, violence and nastiness it came from a lot of personal rage, which I did feel with some intensity. I had polio when I was fifteen and immediately sort of settled that as an issue and decided that I had to figure out how to make my way in the world and had no time to think about that. I really set it aside. I did none of the emotional work of living through that experience for another ten or fifteen years—after I'd already drunk every form of alcohol available, had every drug available in the sixties, engaged in all sorts of high-risk, nasty, destructive to myself and others behavior. Some of those plays came out of the tail end of that, or they contained what much of the feeling of those years was. Now, it doesn't sort of consume my psyche.

I just got an email from Stephen Greenblatt. Stephen Greenblatt has to be the most brilliant Shakespeare scholar in the world. Aside from being incredibly sweet, adorable, funny, warm, he's unbelievably smart. We were talking a couple of years ago, and he said that it would be fun for him to watch me write a play. I said, "Stephen, you sit in a chair and watch my fingers go." So I said we could write a play together, and that would be really fun—take one of Shakespeare's lost plays and write it. So we've taken this lost play of Shakespeare's, which is really kind of interesting called *Cardenio*. It's taken from several chapters of *Don Quixote*. It seems kind of reliable that he wrote this play—and then the play disappeared. There's another play based on Shakespeare's called *The Second Maiden's Tragedy*. So between *Don Quixote* and *The Second Maiden's Tragedy*, you can kind of deduce what might have been Shakespeare's play. At least, you can deduce the story of it. He steals the story of *Don Quixote*. Everything he ever wrote—except *Midsummer*—he steals the storyline. Then you set it 2004 in Queens or something. So, we're about ready to commence to think about considering starting to work on this play. Stephen's in Berlin, at some advanced institute of something. He wrote me this email this morning. He said, "I haven't had time to think about the play, but I had this dream last night that feels as though I'm beginning to feel stirrings of anxiety." So he tells me this dream. And I think, "Right. No brainer. There's the first soliloquy for this piece." You take Shakespeare's storyline. You stick that dream in somewhere. You don't know how or where. And with that grain of sand in the oyster the play begins.

Robert Woodruff some years ago said that he loved to work with the designer George Tsypin because Tsypin always designed a set that you couldn't produce a play in. In trying to overcome the obstacle of the set design you're forced to do something smarter than you would have before. So always when I start out to work on a play, I take stuff at random that I throw in the middle of it, then you have to make it work. If you have to make it work, then you're forced to be resourceful in ways normally you wouldn't want to be. You'd rather be lazier. So I still throw into plays appropriated text—stuff I see online, *Seventeen* magazine, the *National Enquirer*, Arianna Huffington's speeches. You throw that in and then you have to figure out how to contain it. It forces you to be honest. You can't take everything from the real world and filter it through your own psyche, edit it, rewrite it, reconfigure it before you put in on the page. You have to rip it out and stick it down. You don't get to fuck with that. That goes verbatim. So you're forced to do bits and pieces of the world as it is today in whatever you're working on.

So what makes it yours?

Just the way you arrange it. We should talk about *bobrauschenbergamerica*, but the other person I've always thought about a lot is Max Ernst who, in a way, invented the collage toward the end of World War I. His idea initially was to take scissors and cut things up, newspapers and catalogues and stuff like that, paste it down on paper, then maybe add a little something—but to take the material of the real world, then to render it as hallucination. That's what all theater aspires to do—except theater is incredibly tedious—really replicating the real world in some fashion. But theater tries to take truly the material of our lives and render it as hallucination or nightmare or in some way that gives it another life above the floor on the stage that you can launch yourself into and live in. That frees you, so you can live in this world that isn't quite bound by the rules of the newspaper that Ernst cut it out of. That's how you connect yourself in a realm of freedom to explore who you can be.

Your intention is not to control, but to release—to make something smaller than you, but to bring in objects of text or whatever that actually mess you up and actually make you bigger. Then there's the issue of the big T word, which is hard to talk about because it affects everything, every choice we make about who we work with, how, our taste. One of the reasons I'm drawn to you is that your intentions are bigger than mine and your taste is somehow distasteful to me at times and at other times incredibly tasty. What are we doing, in rehearsal? Are we trying to control something, or are we trying to release something?

It's related to the idea that either you believe with Freud that there are a set of rules that govern behavior and those rules are rooted in nature itself and they are universal and eternal. Or you believe with Richard Rorty, who talked about how we don't really believe anymore, as Plato believed, that there's an ideal world and a real world, and that in a philosophical description, the closer you get to actually replicating the ideal, the truer your statement becomes, the truer your statement is. That there is this universal, eternal set of ideals, truths, and our job is to discover exactly what they are and model everything else on those. And Rorty says, obviously, we no longer believe this. So, if you no longer believe that, then what do you say when Hitler shows up, since you're no longer able to say, "Well, there's something fundamentally human that cries out against this"? We don't believe there is something fundamentally human. Where do you stand? What Rorty really says is what we're all engaged in is a creation of a world, the values, the relationships that we wish to be true, whether they were true in the past or not, this is what we aspire to now. So what we're doing is not discovering truth but creating truth for the society that we think is the society that feels best to us. In the theater what you're doing is discovering the possibilities of human relationships, then you hope that that discovery is an open process—not afraid of where it might take you, not already shutting off possibilities because you don't want to discover certain things, not already insisting that this is the final answer, but freely exploring and seeing where you might go—because this is a safe space to do that. If you freely explore what it is to be a human being by dropping shit on Iraq, actual people will die while you're finding out what international relationships can be. But in the theater, people don't die, usually. Sometimes they get sick and they vomit in the aisle while they're trying to get out, but they don't die. So it's a free ride to see, to open up and explore.

Stephen Greenblatt, the world's leading genius and my favorite thinker, has written a new book about Shakespeare, *Will in the World*. I was reading it this afternoon, and he talks about all the morality plays there were in Shakespeare's childhood and how confining they were, and how Shakespeare takes these plays—even names for his characters—and liberates them. Even if Falstaff ends up drunk and repudiated by Prince Hal, the lines of repudiation don't set it up as a moral tale. They set it up as two guys moving in different ways, so it remains open rather than a closed set of moral judgments. This is quite an amazing thing about Shakespeare, so deeply informed by these morality plays. He liberated them and opened up the exploration of what a new character might be. I don't remember where I read this, but the main thing Shakespeare did when he stole Thomas Lodge's novel *Rosalynd*, which Shakespeare made into *As You Like It*, was to remove the motivations of the characters so that what motivates people becomes deeply mysterious. And I forget who it was who said that with most playwrights, at the beginning of the play you don't know who the character is and by the end you know exactly who the character is, whereas with Shakespeare, you think you know who it is and by the end you realize you have no idea.

I feel that that's what wants to happen in *bobrauschenbergamerica* also. In the beginning these characters are stock characters. They all are recognizable. You think you know them. And at the end you don't. They're just widened. I learn from you to let yourself just not know the answers so easily. Could you talk about the genesis of the play?

Well, we'd been talking about doing stuff together for a long time. You and the SITI Company had done sort of a series of pieces about artists who are figures—Robert Wilson and Marshall McLuhan and now Virginia Woolf. There was a big retrospective of Rauschenberg's work at the Guggenheim five years ago. I think all of us live in the world Bob Rauschenberg made, which is to say we all live in a world of collage, whether we think about it or not. This is how society is made. You can hardly go to a coffee shop in Brooklyn without seeing walls decorated with collage. Television is collage. You're supposed to not notice that, but the reality is a story gets going, it gets interrupted, you have a commercial with a guy driving down the highway in California, then somebody's drinking a beer in Denver, and then somebody's skiing in Vermont, then you're back to the story. Rauschenberg had gone to Black Mountain College. He arrived in New York in the early fifties, and he just went out on the street and started collecting junk—not the stuff that other people had merely neglected or ignored or were indifferent to, but the stuff they had thrown away—that they were trying to get rid of. Rauschenberg gathered it up, brought it back to his studio and put it into new combinations that were amazing. So, you think about what he's doing and what he's saying—the sensibility of the artist being open to anything, to embrace it, to bring it back in. This is ferocious egalitarianism, the small-d democratic sentiment of inclusiveness, before anybody knew there was a word inclusiveness in Webster's Third International Dictionary. Let's put this together with a terrific sense of energy and optimism and joy and see how we feel. What we feel is incredibly liberated and happy. It feels like all the values we as Americans say we wish we had in this country. So he turns out to be kind of heroically an American artist—not by what he says, but by the content and structure of the stuff itself. It's really incredible and wonderful.

So we did this workshop down at the La MaMa basement space. Eight or ten people came in and we put some stuff together. They brought in fabulous stuff. Leon [Ingulsrud] had a piece about a truck driver who set out at five o'clock. You feel as though he's an American guy somewhere in Kansas getting in his truck and setting out across the country. I sort of put that together, then we took it up to Skidmore where SITI Company is teaching, and Anne basically made a curriculum for sixty people to create compositions based on this. It's a different kind of play. Instead of something like *Iphigenia at Aulis*, where there's a narrative line we follow through, when you think of somebody like Rauschenberg, the way you start to make the play is you look at his paintings. You think, What do I see over and over again? Chickens. Stuffed goats. Bathtub. Then you say, "Okay, what does that make me think of?" It makes me think of a couple of guys having a conversation about how they started in the chicken-raising business. Immediately you've got dialogue. You've got to talk about the stars. So we made these lists of some images, some text and some events that might occur. Then you hand these to the SITI Company, and Anne tells people to make compositions. They stick them together and you see what it makes. It's very cool. Anne and SITI Company members don't think in terms of, "Here's black, so there's white; here's yes so there's no." They think, "Here's purple, so there's thirty-two, this is X." And if it's thirty-three, it's not quite as good. So, the compositions are not simple juxtapositions of oppositions, but this very open, free, tossed-together stuff. The way of making the work is amazing. It had a sense of liberation in it at a cellular level.

I thought, watching this, Okay, what we've got so far is a lot of slosh, a lot of cool compositions, but how do we feel as though anything is going anywhere here? With a painting you can see the whole painting in detail at any moment you choose, so you could see any detail in context if you wanted. But with a work of art that occurs in time, you don't see the whole until the end. So somewhere in the middle you get a little bit anxious, just like an amoeba that can't see the light. If you feel not oriented, you feel anxious, whether you are an amoeba or a fruit fly or a deer at night. Since you don't want yourself, let alone an audience, to be so consumed by anxiety they can't pay attention to anything else, you need to give some orienting devices along the way. The most common form of orientation is a plotline: boy meets girl; there's a conspiracy to depose the king. Then you can go wherever you want to go. With the Greeks, you set up the plotline, then you have the chorus. The chorus is always riffing. But what the Greeks really understood is that if you get the plotline going, you can riff, and people are cool with that. What's mostly boring about plot-driven plays is that people have forgotten to riff, and it gets claustrophobic. It's why the Greeks are not claustrophobic. Shakespeare's dramaturgy could have been deduced by looking at a Greek play. Shakespeare just exploded the chorus and the individual voices. They have stories, too, and plotlines and relationships. So that's how you get this incredible richness. That's how in Shakespeare's plays you get these powerful stories going, but you also feel as though you're just deep in the human experience, going off in these digressions.

If you put together a piece that doesn't have a plotline, like the Rauschenberg piece, then how do you make this something other than stuff that sloshes? You don't want to stick a big plotline through it, but how about like a quilt, where you just stitch it a little here, stitch it a little there, and the stitching has just a little forward momentum, so it feels it's going somewhere. You get a bit of a break because we moved to another emotional place here. So that's boy meets girl, because that's a story that everybody understands. A little while later it's boy meets boy. A little while later the boy and girl are getting together. A little later, the boy and boy really get together. So these little things just kind of nudge it along.

We had trouble making transitions because there would be a scene, then a scene, then another scene. As a company, we usually spend huge amounts of time figuring out how to make transitions so it's really fluid. But it wasn't working. I said, "Chuck, how do we make these transitions?" He said, "Well, grout." The material between tiles. The transitions should be like grout. And that was very helpful. Something ends. There's a little space. Then something begins—as opposed to something lyrically connected or the end containing the beginning of the next thing. None of that actually held.

Yeah, transitions seem really tedious, and also so very unlike life. We so rarely have a transition in life.

Can you talk about what projects you are working on now?

I'm working on a piece, *Belle Epoque*, with Martha Clarke at Lincoln Center. I don't know if any of you saw *Vienna: Lusthaus*, which she and I did a number of years ago and was just revived at New York Theatre Workshop. We're doing a bunch of interminable workshops for that. Lincoln Center's put up a jillion dollars for these workshops. We've done eight weeks. Martha's incredibly inefficient and immensely expensive. We have five or six actors and a half dozen dancers and five musicians and a music director—Broadway musical prices for this piece that, you know, we'll see if Lincoln Center does it.

I'm doing a piece with Chen Shi-Zheng up at American Repertory Theater in Cambridge. Chen Shi-Zheng did *Peony Pavilion* up at Lincoln Center a few years ago, which was an unbelievably fabulous version of seventeenth-century Chinese opera. He did both a Mandarin production and an English-language version of *The Orphan of Zhao* this summer at the Lincoln Center Festival. He and I took a thirteenth-century Chinese play, *The Injustice Done to Tou-o*, and I set it in Queens this year. It's a story about a young woman who is systematically and horribly mistreated until finally she is unjustly found guilty of a murder and executed. In the original Chinese version she comes back as a ghost and her father, who is now in the government—he abandoned her back in the beginning of the play—in Beijing. She tells him what happened, and he comes back to the provinces and sets everything to rights, so that it's a happy ending. The moral being, if only the central government knew, everything would be okay. So, we cut that ending and I have her rise from the dead and murder everyone. But I did a fairly straight version of the storyline and wrote a bunch of songs and stuff. We took it into a workshop in May up at A.R.T., and Shi-Zheng said, "This is so linear and narrative, I can't even bounce a ball off it." I said, "Well, what do you want to do?" He said, "I think it should move vertically instead of horizontally." I said, "Great." So he went in and chopped it all up and rearranged it all. Now the moral of the story is more like, "Shit happens." It's this big nightmarish, violent thing with these crazy songs and people getting killed over and over and over again. Then maybe at the end you're able to put the whole story together. Or not. Shi-Zheng grew up in China. He was about seven years old when there was the cultural revolution and there was this big demonstration on the side of the street. He was on the sidewalk holding his mother's hand when she was shot and killed by a stray bullet. I think that this nightmarish, inexplicable, violent, horrible, chaotic piece replicates that event for him.

Then I'm doing a piece for Ivo van Hove for the Holland Festival. He took over the national theater in the Netherlands a few years ago. He came in and he took over this acting company of twenty people who were loyal to the previous artistic director—so they hate Ivo. They think he's an ass-hole. Or half of them hate him. He said to me, "You know, I think I need to get the whole company in one room so we can work together on a play and come out at the end a company. So, will you write a play for twenty actors?" So I said, "Cool." Now, I know these people. They did a play of mine a couple of years ago and I know these actors. I don't know if you know the Dutch, but they're very unromantic—very cynical and not into crap. So, this is a play about a wedding. It starts out with this young man and woman who are going to get married. Then there's confusion and a lot of consulting and stuff going on. He leaves the house, and then they all go out looking for him. Everybody's lost in the woods. The Radical Faerie wedding planners enter the story. Then the Priest, who has a checkered past, has come to marry these people. It gets very wild, and they end up calling it off and mud wrestling. Then, the Radical Faeries who planned the wedding feel so mortified that all their work is not coming off that even though they said they would never get married because it's for bourgeois people and it's crap, they decide that they'll get married because the wedding must take place. So, two Faerie wedding planners, two young women, decide to get married instead. Then the sister of the young woman who jilted this guy decides to marry him because she always loved him. They end up doing a big Bollywood dance number and living happily ever after. I'm forcing Ivo's company to get married—and it's an incredibly sentimental play.

And then there's Joseph Cornell.

And then there's Joseph Cornell, which we're doing. We're going to do a workshop of it at the end of October to start doing exactly what we did on the Rauschenberg piece, getting not just SITI Company, but other people to come into the workshop and start throwing stuff into the pot to make this piece.

Audience: What I'm hearing you say is that the world is so so crazily complex that your way of making it make some kind of sense is by writing a play about it. But it's also easy, when you write a play, to see that complexity in the play and you really could defeat your whole purpose once you get started. How do you go to your sources when you are engaging in that process?

I think that writing, and probably making a theater piece, is a test of character in the sense that you really want to leave stuff open to explore and to discover as much as you possibly can. Since you get incredibly lost and hopeless in this process and disoriented and think it's worthless and you don't know why you're doing it, the question always is: How brave can you be? How far can you go being lost in the wilderness before you start shutting down the possibilities so that you can just deal with it? That's always the thing. I came back from that June at Skidmore with this pile of stuff. There were sixty students. They went into groups of three. Each of them did three or four compositions. I came back with hundreds and hundreds and hundreds of ideas. I actually had this moment of total panic, thinking, What is this? This is nothing but people's random free associations when you say Rauschenberg. This is not a theater piece. So I thought, What would Rauschenberg do? I thought he would choose whatever he thought was cool. So I chose whatever I thought was cool. Then I did these little stitchings, and that was pretty much the piece. You have to have the confidence that it coheres just because somewhere you are a coherent person. If you trust that, which is what Rauschenberg trusted about himself, you're likely to have made something crazier that is more complex, full of honest contradictions, dark places, terror, sentimentality, pleasures, trivial interests, important thoughts, than if you try to think your way through it and arrive at a way of proceeding.

When Anne walks into a rehearsal room, it seems to me from being with her, that she doesn't walk in thinking, I know everything. I'm going to tell these people what to do. Rather she walks in thinking, Let's see what these amazing people bring into the room. Let's see what happens. Let's be open about the process, stay open as far as possible. As it goes along and as she sees stuff, somewhere she begins to think, I don't really like that. I don't think that's so amusing. That seems great. So that really what happens is that she exercises her taste, and she can't explain where her taste comes from or define it or describe it or surround it. So she has to trust that her taste, likewise, comes from a coherent person. If I do what I love, and Anne does what she loves, without thinking, What will the audience like (because nobody has a clue what the audience likes), then I have the confidence that since I'm not from Mars, somebody else might like it. So, it'll be an okay evening in the theater because I've done what I love and it comes from some kind of coherence I don't even understand. If I trust that coherence, rather than the panic and anxiety trying to create a form of coherence, then I'm likely to have gotten to something much more interesting and surprising, difficult and rewarding.

Audience: With the unique sort of collaborative process the SITI Company has, the role of the playwright has got to be a little bit more unique for you. How much are you involved once the rehearsal process has started? Does that differ if you were working with a different company?

The truth is that usually what I do as a playwright is that I write a play, I hand it to a director, and I say, "Have a good time. I'll see you on opening night." I believe that the actors and the director should be as free to do their thing as I was to do mine. I hope that they will discover their own production of that piece, rather than to imagine incorrectly that some definitive version of it exists in my mind. So I really give over—not out of some cuckoo, wonderful, altruistic, selfless idea, but out of a very selfish wish to have the play be wonderful, and knowing that everybody's going to do better work if they feel free and excited about what they're doing.

With *bobrauschenbergamerica* what was amazing was it's so much fun to be in the room with these people. I went to rehearsals more than I've ever done in my life before or since because it was so much fun—not because I did anything much in the room. I said a few things. But mostly I was just there to enjoy it. What's incredible about being in the room with SITI Company is that the lighting designer will make directorial remarks to the actor on stage, the actors will suggest scenic design elements, the sound designer will tell the actors what he thinks they ought to do. I mean, it's unbelievable the sort of open conversation that occurs among these people, which I've never seen the likes of in any rehearsal room ever. These people who have worked together all these years. I remember when we had the first read-through of the *bobrauschenbergamerica* script. People started reading and talking and reading and talking and they'd go so fast. These people know each other so well and are so smart that what would ordinarily be a thirty-minute conversation among actors to get from what this person said to some thought that came out of it, they go through in like a minute and a half. You're just amazed how fast these people are thinking, how much work they get through, that other people don't get through because they don't have that much time.

I think about the way Anne works. What most directors think they do is to take a script—in other words, literature—and they place it on the stage. What Anne thinks that she does is that she creates a three-dimensional event in time in which text has some place or places. It's a totally different way of making theater. It's really *the* way to make theater, I believe—to understand that a play is not staged literature. It really is this event that occurs. Playwrights don't make events. They provide text that can move inside an event. Truly, even when I'm writing plays that seem more like normal plays, I'm usually sort of thinking of what the event is and listening for where text comes out of that, in a way.

AB: The hardest thing we had with your script, our most difficult task, was that you asked us to do a moment of Viewpoints improvisation as the first event. And we tried and tried—and every fiber of all of our beings said, "NOOO!" It seemed anathema to do that. That was the hardest task you ever gave us.

Ellen Lauren (SITI Company Associate Artistic Director): Our whole thing was to be open and happy and energetic—and we're really usually really dark and setting things and panicking. I feel like you wrote it for us at a difficult time in our company— as you are doing for Ivo's company. It really brought us to a bright place, like Oz, like stepping from the black and white into color. It woke us up and we remembered how to just make each other laugh again.

Audience: I was thinking that Americans are often uncomfortable with intimacy and then you talk about the whole collage thing and it seems to me that that makes intimacy even more difficult. How do you as an American playwright think about intimacy and put it in your work all the time?

I think a lot about—partly because I worked as a historian for a long time—how the public world invades our private lives, how often our private imaginings are projected onto the world. It's the sort of thing you hope presidents and defense secretaries don't do, but they seem to project fantasies all the time. It's one of the reasons you don't like the world to be too uncivilized a place. I think about that continuing all the time in my plays and I think about the moving back and forth, crossing.

Audience: I'm wondering what our relationship is as art makers to the funding that we have. Normally we think of a big obstacle, we don't have enough money. We're always trying to get more money to pay the artists and to do our art. But you said that the project that you're working on at Lincoln Center, they're throwing so much money at it. Is that another obstacle that you can have?

I'm in a good position to speak about funding because I am completely supported by a patron who is fabulously generous. I have money so that I worry about nothing. I think about nothing except what I want to do. I spent most of my life working at a job and being incredibly hardworking and resourceful and devious and manipulative and shrewd to figure out how to make a living so that I could support myself to do the thing I actually wanted to do. So this is brand-new for me, for me to do what I actually want to do. The plays have a sort of arc in them—this stuff that was stored up for years has flowed out in them and I don't have time to censor them. I don't know that anybody really in the history of the arts has ever really suffered from the problem of too much money. You can suffer once you have the money from being an inadequate person, from not knowing what to do with it. But that's not the money's fault.

I think this is an interesting moment because I think that a lot of regional theaters are having funding difficulties, and I actually wish a lot of them would just go out of business because I think they're actually pretty boring. I take great hope when I sort of see what happens in New York on the "Lower East Side"—an awful lot of young companies and people who are making art with no money at all, just doing things together. That's really a more interesting group, people who don't have a lot of money. But it's also true that the kind of work that SITI Company does, which is incredibly expensive in the sense that here's a company that works together all the time, so that it's almost insupportable. It's quite common in Europe, and as a result you get companies like Pina Bausch's company, and Ivo's. They are able to make work together over a period of time, so you are able to make a different kind of work. With the kind of financial structure that operates in most theaters, you have three weeks of rehearsal time and then something goes up. It requires people not to be open in the rehearsal process. You have to have a finished script, so it's been workshopped to death, which is incredibly tedious, but commendable. Then you cast, and if the role calls for a thirty-three-year-old, five-foot-seven-inch blond woman, then that's who it has to be because nobody's guessing anymore, nobody's thinking that a six-foot-tall brunette could be interesting in this role because you can't afford to find out. There's a certain kind of financial structure that's very destructive.

André Gregory

André is a rebel, a cultural trickster and a director who breaks rules with visible glee. He is also a great storyteller. He revels in the act of speaking, as do those who are wrapped up in the listening.

When I was young, André seemed to me to be a romantic hero. I experienced his mythic production of *Alice in Wonderland* when it was revived during the mid-seventies in New York City. His company, the Manhattan Project, was by then already legendary. Soon afterward, I saw his gymnastic *Endgame*, his environmental *Seagull* and his enigmatic dark production of Wallace Shawn's *Our Late Night*. I loved the camaraderie of his company and the eccentricity and theatricality of the work. André's friendship with the writer Wallace Shawn proved to be remarkably fruitful over the years. He directed Wally's play *The Designated Mourner* and cast him as Vanya in *Vanya on 42nd Street*, a successful production that was also made into a movie. And then there were the mysterious journeys that André took to Poland to participate in the para-theatrical experiments of his close friend Jerzy Grotowski. These extraordinary adventures were chronicled in the highly successful independent film *My Dinner with André*, starring himself and Wally Shawn and directed by Louis Malle.

André was born in Paris in 1934 to Russian Jewish parents. In fleeing Hitler, the family finally arrived in New York City. After graduating from Harvard, André studied at the Neighborhood Playhouse and the Actors Studio. He then began to accept leadership positions in the regional theater movement, culminating in several instances where he was fired by a theater's board of directors. During André's subsequent international travels, the Berliner Ensemble in particular had an enormous influence upon his ideas about what theater could be. In 1968 he founded the Manhattan Project and he began to churn out the seminal productions that were so influential to everyone who came into contact with them. André, for a combination of personal, spiritual and professional reasons, has a habit of disappearing. Literally. He leaves his accustomed turf and no one knows where he goes. Often he journeys to far-flung places in the world, and then he returns with brilliant new ideas. In addition to his own creative projects, André has also worked as an actor with such icon-making directors as Peter Weir, Woody Allen, Brian De Palma and Martin Scorsese.

Many people who saw André's *Uncle Vanya* in an abandoned theater on 42nd Street, or later in the film based upon the production, suggested that his direction was minimal. Everything was meant to be casual, as if you were watching a rehearsal of Chekhov's play among friends. I saw the live production and realized afterward that, far from casual, this was the most intricately directed play that I had ever encountered. Every choice, from the rehearsal clothes to the hewn-wood rehearsal table was as deliberate and precise as any highly aesthetic production.

André's influence is slippery. He is an instigator of revolutions in small rooms. The impact of these revolutions is felt later in wider frameworks. I do not believe that *A Chorus Line* would ever have happened without the activity of André and the Manhattan Project (or without Joseph Chaikin and the Open Theater or Richard Schechner and the Performance Group). Audiences who never had the pleasure of being present at one of André's productions are nonetheless affected and influenced by his example.

November 17, 2003

AB: When I came to New York, I went and saw André's work a lot, and continue to, to this day—except sometimes it's hard to get a ticket—and he had a profound influence on me. I think of any artist working in the theater, he is the truest to his own interests—somehow his own development as a human being is closest reflected in the work. You can see the two work in parallel.

I used to be obsessed with knowing how he worked, so I talked to actors who had worked with him, or people who had known people who had worked with him. I said, "How does he do it, these amazing productions? I don't understand how he gets to where he's going." And people would tell me the most puzzling stories, like, "He never says anything. He just laughs or he doesn't laugh. We're guided by his laughter or his silence." Or then, "The rehearsals go for seven years." Or "They're in his living room." Or he left the theater for twelve years! And came back to it. He's gotten highly politicized lately. A directing student of mine at Columbia asked him, "How do you get off, doing what you do? How do you give yourself permission to do what it is you do?" Maybe that is a good place to start.

AG: When it comes to a political environment, I come from a very interesting background in the sense that my father left Russia a year before Stalin came to power, and went to Berlin. He left Berlin the day Hitler came to power, and went to Paris. He left Paris three days before the Germans invaded Poland, and he went to London. We were outfitted for gas masks as little kids. We crossed the Atlantic on two sister ships, and the other one was torpedoed, and we saw people drowning and picked up survivors. So my father went from Moscow to Berlin to Paris to London to

Scarsdale. He had this incredible nose for danger. He always got out in time. And in 1984, when he was eighty-four, he said to me, "You know, if I were young, I'd leave America."

He and I got along terribly. He never wanted me to be in the theater. He never wanted me to be an artist. He was a businessman. And we had one of our many fights when he was eighty-three. I must have been close to fifty. My wife went over to see him, and he said, "I don't understand why André always gets so upset with me. What's his problem?" And my wife said, "Well, I think he thinks sometimes you don't respect him." And he said, "Don't respect him? Of course I respect him! He would have been a great lawyer."

When Kennedy was assassinated, I went over to visit my father. He was watching television, and they had just arrested Oswald, and he said to me, "They won't leave him alive for forty-eight hours." And when Ruby killed Oswald, he said, "He'll never go to jail." They'll either kill him in jail, or they'll give him some kind of disease, but no one will ever find out what he has to say." I've always had a very strong sense of totalitarianism and fascism, and I strongly believe that, unless we save the next election, we will be going into something like the Greek junta, at the best.

When they were debating about going into Iraq, [Senator Robert] Byrd said, "I once heard that Hitler was nervous about going into Czech-oslovakia. And he said to [Hermann] Goering, 'I don't know if I should do it. I don't know if the German people will stand for it.' And Goering said, 'My Fuhrer, just give them an enemy to be afraid of, and they'll let you do anything.'"

I'm profoundly worried about where this country is going because I'm afraid we're going toward the totalitarianism of the Far Right. The question, what to do, and what can we do—was this what we're supposed to talk about?

It's going very well.

I saw *They Marched into Sunlight*. It's about October 1967 during the Vietnam War on the campus where they protested Dow Chemical and closed the campus down—and I realized everything radicals were saying about this country then is still true. Many—including myself—went to sleep after the Vietnam War and didn't realize that something profoundly loathsome was taking place in our system.

I'm just riffing here. Have any of you seen the film [*Blind Spot:*] *Hitler's Secretary*? This is one interview with the woman who was Hitler's secretary. Basically, she thought he was a charming old man. She never realized that the Jews were being sent to the concentration camps. She thought he was really trying very hard to save Germany from an outside enemy—and only ten years after Germany lost the war did she finally realize who he was, how she turned her eyes away. She had a nervous breakdown and finally started dealing with the shame of what it meant to be a German.

I am personally profoundly ashamed and nauseated to be a citizen of a terrorist country that has dropped the only nuclear weapon on other people, dropped more bombs on Vietnam and Cambodia than were dropped in the entire Second World War, that is involved now with a terrorist war in Iraq. We are the Axis of Evil. We are the terrorists. I am ashamed to be an American. The only thing that keeps me here is I cannot *not* be here—to try and find any way to stop the Christian Right and these fanatics that are in the White House from selling democracy down the river.

Now the question, of course, is, what to do? Noam Chomsky is somebody who is asking, "What do we do?" And he said there are two things we can do. He said we must stop the Bush people in the next election. You must give up whatever you are doing: Your main work is to stop the Bush people, because if they get in one more time, we have seen the end of democracy in this country. He said unless you have lived in a totalitarian country, you have no idea how truly terrible it is. He said we must stop Bush. And we've got to read. We've got to learn. He said, "Get knowledge." So I've been reading a lot.

I've been very politically active in the last couple of years. We did something last winter, *Poems Not Fit for the White House*. Three of us took over Avery Fisher Hall, and we got some of the greatest poets in America to come and read. It was one of the great evenings in New York cultural history, and the place was packed. The first night, people came through the snow. I was thinking, What was so great about that evening? I have a little button on my coat that says "Peacemaker," and I haven't been doing it very well. But evenings like that—just like evenings like this—are absolutely essential, because the best of America has gone to sleep, and we need to wake up. We need to take action. At events like that, there's a feeling of coming together. I went to a talk by Arundhati Roy. She ended by saying something wonderful. She said, "We can't afford the luxury of despair."

I've been feeling a lot of shame: shame for being asleep so long, shame for not being more active for many years. But you can't just waft up in shame. You have to admit that, in some way, every single one of us has made Bush possible. We get the leaders we deserve. But I think there's a trap in falling into too much shame and too much guilt, because that also leads to passivity, and what we need now are people who are active and alive.

I was at a bit of a loss, because I couldn't imagine what I would talk about beyond guilt, shame and the terror of fascism. Then I went to three nights of the Berlin Philharmonic, with probably the greatest conductor in the world, Simon Rattle—and it was clear as a bell: perfection, beauty, love and the way of the heart. When you hear one of the two greatest orchestras in the world, and when your soul opens, and when your heart melts, when you plummet into ecstatic joy with tears of bliss running down your face—for three nights! I'm exhausted! I thought, This is it. This is what we have to do. This is somehow what we have to bring into our work and into ourselves.

When *My Dinner with André* was the success that it was, we got thousands of letters! We got a letter form a Marine colonel who said, "You've changed my life. I'm leaving the Marines. I'm going to take up the cello." It was then—having had quite a big ego in my time—that I realized that *My Dinner with André* has nothing to do with André. It's the spirit coming through our organism so we can pick up messages to somehow give hope. I work on it any way I can: I work on it with my therapist, with my guru, by listening to music, by reading, by questioning—because this organism, this antenna, is covered in plaque. It accumulates plaque very quickly, and we have to scrub. We have to work on this antenna so the antenna is clean and clear, so that messages and visions of where to go can come from God (or whatever we want to call that) through this thing to give value to the world.

That's the most beautiful thing I've ever heard.

It's a life-long work, to work on one's self. Each one of us is an instrument. That's what is so odd, particularly being an actor: We are our own instrument. Do we want to be a banjo or a Stradivarius violin? It's our choice.

Let me tell you two stories: One is Ekkehard Schall, who was a great actor of the Berliner Ensemble, and his story is that he was in the Hitler Youth. He was sent to Stalingrad, and he threw a hand grenade in a tank. He saw two Soviet soldiers go up in flames, and he went into shock. He found himself in a prison in Berlin sentenced to death, and if the Soviets had not invaded, had not liberated Berlin, he would have been killed. And when Brecht hastily left the United States because of the House Un-American Activities and went to Berlin, he heard that this guy Schall, who I think was eighteen, was doing a cabaret in the ruins of the subway. He was a beautiful singer. Somebody said to Brecht, if you're looking for actors, you should go listen to this man. He went to listen and, after the performance, he went up to this man and said, "My name is Bertolt Brecht. I'm going to come back to Berlin, and when I come back, I hope to create a theater. I'd like you to be in the theater. You're very musical. I think you should develop yourself physically. And I'll see you in two or three or four years." And on that one little conversation, Schall became Germany's greatest high-wire aerialist without a net. He was so extraordinary physically that when he played Arturo Ui—the role is Hitler as Richard III as Charlie Chaplin as a killer in Cicero during Prohibition—he played it like a cowardly mad dog with rabies. I saw this thirty or forty times. He literally went into such fear that something in the inside created this black greenish foam that went down his chin. It was not a trick. It was something that came from the inside. In preparation for the role, he watched ten hours of news reels a day, of Hitler, for two-and-a-half years. He was Hitler. And Richard III. And Charlie Chaplin. And a mad dog with rabies. At one point, these other gangsters were moving in on him. He started recoiling like this mad dog. He was so terrified that from the standing position, from prone, he did a triple backward somersault into the air, landed on the back of chair with two six-guns shooting. That is a Stradivarius. That is work. Work is very important, because we're going to have to do a lot of work on ourselves, and a lot of work in this country to save it from becoming a fascist, Far Right, totalitarian system. Even if it becomes that, we're going to have to survive; we're going to have to live in it and still give out the light.

The other actor was Ryszard Cieslak, who was Grotowski's great actor. Cieslak was a hundred-and-five-pound alcoholic when Grotowski met him on a railroad station at night. He was drunk. They sat at the railroad station all night, and at the end of this night, Grotowski said to him, "You and I are going to make theater together." Cieslak could control forty-three muscles in the face alone. There was no gap—not a split-second gap between the emotional impulse and physical manifestation of the impulse, in all the different parts of the body. This is a miracle of work. He was so expressive that when he played the Christ figure in *Apocalypsis cum figuris,* there was a moment when all you could see was this one section of the leg. This section of the leg, I swear to God, was as beautiful and as expressive as that section of a leg in a Michelangelo statue. You didn't understand what it was expressing, but you were moved, the same way you're moved by a chord of music. He had tiny eyes and he was obsessed with making those eyes larger, because he felt that eyes are the windows of the soul. So whenever they went on tour somewhere, he'd go to plastic surgeons, seeing if somehow they could make his eyes bigger—and they can't do it. It's impossible. Then when he was in India, he met a guru who said to him, "It's simple. Every time there's a full moon, spend the whole night circling the moon with your eyes. Be sure to put butter on the lids or they'll crack." He said, "Do it for eight years, ten years, every time there's a full moon, and your eyes will be very large." He had eyes like a carp, these great big fish eyes. It was a Stradivarius.

I'll tell you one more story. There was a moment in *The Constant Prince*. Cieslak played a Polish nobleman who becomes a saint. The Inquisition beats him, they question him, they oppress him, they torture him and the last moment of the play he's standing, he falls to the ground, a little more slowly than we normally would. He takes his head by the hair, bangs it against the ground three times. All breath goes out of him. He's dead. The spirit is gone. Every time he fell, I felt as though a mule had kicked me in the stomach. Something about that fall—every time, and I saw it twenty or thirty times. Years later, I asked Grotowski, "Is there anything special about that fall, or is it just me?" And he said, "Oh, no, it's very special. We rehearsed that moment for nine years." Work. Work. It's very important. Grotowski said, "If you could stop action the way you can in a film, you would see there are twelve Stations of the Cross from where he's standing to where he's on the ground. At each station of the cross, he relives a confession that came out of those nine years of improvisation. The commitment of that gesture of the body has him relive that moment of confession, so that when the twelve Stations of the Cross are over, he's completely empty."

So the question is, do we want to do work like that? We can't all do work like that. We all have to do the work in our own way. But when I hear the members of the Berlin Philharmonic, when I see Twyla Tharp's dancers, when I see your actors, this takes an enormous amount of work. Why is this work important? When Leningrad (now St. Petersburg) was surrounded by the German army, they were surrounded for one hundred days. They had no light, no heat. It was forty degrees below zero. Cannibalism was starting on the black market. And Stalin wanted to do something to keep them going through that last winter so that in the spring he could liberate Leningrad. What did he do? He parachuted poets and musicians into Leningrad. Art was so important to the people in Leningrad that they literally walked across Leningrad so feeble and so fragile that they knew they could die walking from their homes to the concert hall, and in the concert hall, during the poetry readings and the concerts, musicians would just go to sleep and die. People in the audience would go to sleep and die. But they had to have art. They had to have beauty. They had to have poetry.

Our task is to keep the flame alive. Our task is to sit around the fire in these terrible, frightening, cold times, and nurture the flames. Our task is to give beauty, perfection, precision and hope.

Can you talk about your *Master Builder*? Maybe the context in which the work is done. And your thoughts about the tower.

Well, it's hard to talk about when you're in the middle of it. We've been rehearsing it on and off for seven years now. When Wally [Shawn] and I were first working on the play—Wally translated it—I said to him, "You know, the only thing I don't get is the tower. Everything makes sense except the tower." This was about seven or eight years ago. And he said, "The tower will make sense when they destroy the Trade Towers." I said, "What makes you think they'll destroy . . . who will destroy the Trade Towers?" He said, "The terrorists will destroy the Trade Towers." Now, the thing that's dangerous about Wally is that he is a prophet, and he sees with incredible clarity. We're not going to have the Trade Towers falling in the end. But we are doing *The Master Builder* as an indictment of male chauvinist, ego-power capitalism. And we're going to make a film.

Why are you doing a film, as opposed to a play?

Two of the actors live in Los Angeles, one lives in Chicago, one lives in Santa Barbara, four live in New York. There's no way to bring them all together and do it as a play. I wish we could.

What is that for you, the difference between stage and film?

I'm one of those people who can't put a light bulb in a socket. I can't operate a fax, I can't do email, I don't have a cell phone. I'm technologically a moron. So film has never really appealed to me, because it's so technical. But I have felt over the past years that we've been so affected by television and film that our eye has literally changed. I had the experience a few years ago of going to see an Ibsen play in a Broadway theater. I was sitting in the fourth row, and it already felt as if I were miles and miles away, because my eye was used to being close. So there is something about film that allows us to get very, very close. Also, I don't really like acting. I'm very interested in being, in actors being in the process of being. I don't really like to project, because then you get into acting. I haven't performed for more than forty people in thirty years. I always play for small—very small—audiences. Recently, about two at a time.

There is a paradox between doing theater that very few people can see and being outrageously political in your views. It's an interesting paradox.

You mean because it would seem logical for me to perform for a lot of people?

Maybe the issue of film solves that problem.

Well, the issue of the film certainly solves it. The theater is elitist no matter what. Even if it's twelve hundred seats at the Music Box or it's thirty seats at one of my theaters, it's still elitist. But I've always liked people who fight to get into something. I remember going to Paris to see Peter Brook's *King Lear*, and there were no tickets. So I said to the person at the box office, "That's terrible! Mr. Brook said he would leave tickets for me!" I think I was twenty-five. And I got put in a box, a beautiful box, and I got to meet Peter Brook.

When we did *Alice in Wonderland* in Paris, my stage manager said to me, "There's a young woman who knows she can't see the production, but she just wants to see the set." And I said, "Well, then you should show her the set." And she seemed very nice, so I gave her my seat. After the production, I said to her, "Where are you from?" She said, "Poland." I said, "Really? Do you know Grotowski?" She said, "Never heard of him." I said, "Can we walk up the Champs Élysées, and I'll just buy a book in the drugstore to send him as a gift?" She went to Poland, she delivered it to Grotowski, she became his dramaturg, and she worked for him for twenty-seven years.

I believe very much that anything you want—this is why I believe in prayer—ask, and you shall receive. You want something, and you'll get it. You just have to take an action. You just have to go out and do it.

How does that refer to prayer?

Well, I'll tell you a funny story. When Louis Malle said he would make a film of *Vanya*, he said, "If you can raise nine hundred thousand dollars in three weeks, I'll do it." And that was like climbing Everest, you know? It was a huge amount of money. I rehearse in my living room. I'd heard of a saint in Germany called Mother Meera, an Indian saint who gives *darshan*—she blesses people. There was a booklet she put out, and one thing really intrigued me: She said, "When you come to the Mother, don't ask for big things—spiritual enlightenment, spiritual surrender. Come to Mother the way you would come to your own mother on Christmas morning, and ask for what you want." So I went to Germany. And while she was blessing me—she had her hands on my head—I prayed for a therapist for my daughter, who is going through a hard time; nine hundred thousand dollars in cash; and a hot Saturday-night date, because my wife had died three years before. There had been no women in my life. On my way back to the States, I stopped in Paris for two nights, and I went to a café, and there was this very interesting woman who was writing. I thought, Oh my God, I would love to meet her. But, you know, it was France, people don't know my work there, I wouldn't quite know how to start a conversation in French. So I just kept reading my book. Suddenly, she touches my arm, and she said, "I'm writing a lot." I said, "What are you writing?" She said, "What do you think I'm writing? I'm translating Wally Shawn's last play into French." So I stayed in Paris for a week instead of two days. And so much money came out of the walls when I came back that I literally had to give money back. I think we raised one million two hundred thousand. So I was praying.

But also, I have a guru, and with her, I learned about what's called japa. If you see nuns with rosaries or Tibetan monks with beads, they're generally doing japa. They're doing a mantra, over and over again. I do a mantra all the time. One day I was standing on a street corner, and there was a Tibetan and he was doing beads, and I was doing beads. He said, "You know, the vowels of mantras are the name of God. Most of the time, we are doing bad japa. We are putting bad mantras into our bodies." He said, "You're a really bad father, aren't you?" I said, "What?!?" He said, "You see what happens to your body when I say that? All day, we are saying things to ourselves—I am a bad father, I am a bad actor, I am a bad director, I am not talented. It does something to the body. It diminishes us. It closes us. Instead of that, put the name of God into your body. See what it will do."

I found my guru through my daughter, and I went up to her ashram. I started getting what they call kriyas. *(He demonstrates seizures)* It went on for about seventy-two hours. I called my daughter on the telephone and she said, "Oh Daddy, you're very blessed! You're getting kriyas!" I was crying, I couldn't sleep. I was hysterical. So she took me to one of the monks, to explain to me what kriyas are, and he said, "It's as if we're driving through life with the windshield of the car covered with rain and dirt, so we can't see anything. We're driving blind. We're asleep. We're unconscious. We can't see where we're going. The guru takes a sponge, and wipes your window clean. All the bad karma of many lifetimes is coming out of your eyes, your nose, your ears, your asshole, and you're letting it go so you can be illuminated." So that's another form of prayer.

I found in my own life that whenever I knew what I wanted—and I think this is like a prayer—and asked for it, it was given to me. A story I have about that: I'd only directed one play, and I took a very famous director, Alan Schneider, out to lunch, and I said, "Mr. Schneider, I would like to direct. How do I go about that?" He said, "Well, if I were you, I'd start a theater out of New York." This was a time, there were only three or four regional theaters in America—San Francisco, Minneapolis, Houston. I said, "How do I do that?" He said, "That's your problem." So I got a big map of America, put it on my wall, and I started putting flags in cities.

There were black flags for cities that had a theater, red flags for cities that had no theater but they weren't really very nice cities, and then gold flags: No theater, nice city. One of them was Philadelphia. I went down to Philadelphia; I'd been given a letter of introduction to an interior designer. I started telling him my vision of the theater. I was twenty-eight. He got kind of excited. I said, "Could you get three friends who would have parties where I could go and talk about my vision. And he said, "Absolutely." So I went to these three parties, and I talked about my vision, and I said, "Is there anyone here with three friends who would have three parties? I would like to talk about my vision." I would go back and forth between New York and Philadelphia. My wife was just about to have a baby. I generally caught the last train back from Philadelphia, so I would see the coffins that were coming up from Vietnam. (They were hiding them then, just as they are hiding them now.) In two years, I talked to people, like a political campaign. And out of four hundred forty-three parties, I got eleven thousand subscribers and we got this little theater in an African-American neighborhood.

See? We can do anything. All we have to do is: "What do we want to do?" And do we really want to do it badly enough? Then we just do it.

Audience: You mentioned before the music you listen to for inspiration and for keeping that channel clean. What do you listen to?

Well, these three nights with the Berlin Philharmonic. I never understood symphonic music until I heard this conductor with the Vienna Philharmonic. I liked chamber music and soloists, and I used to listen to a lot of jazz. Now I love symphonic music. I've been discovering people like Bartók and Schoenberg. I heard an extraordinary piece at Carnegie Hall which Bartók wrote in 1936, just before he emigrated from Hungary and left a Europe that was becoming a Nazi Europe. It was an amazing work, filled with the terror of approaching fascism, the darkness descending, the terror descending. He worked through that darkness to find this extraordinary light, just at the end. The interesting task that we have is to face the darkness, and go to the light.

Audience: I'd like to play devil's advocate for a bit: We all know that the greatest Nazi criminals were fans of classical music and actually played music themselves. Art played a great role in the Resistance as well. But I think there is a certain danger in implying pure art is enough resistance against totalitarians.

Oh, no. No.

Audience: I know that's not what you meant. How directly political does the message on stage (or wherever) have to be, in order not to become also a kind of shield that's covering what's going on underneath? I am a not big fan of direct agitation on stage.

No, neither am I. I don't think I'm saying that art, in and of itself, is an answer in times like these. I'm saying that ever since Reagan, in this country and perhaps in Europe also, we have been brainwashed by capitalism and by the media to go to sleep. So the question is: How to wake up? How to help others to wake up? How to stay awake? How to have an art form that is an active art form, not a passive art form? Because the Broadway theater, which is now completely corporate, is putting everyone to sleep.

I find that every encounter I have now, whether it is on the subway, the taxi, the health food store—I always say to the person, "So what do you think about Bush? What do you think about the fact that there are no Weapons of Mass Destruction? Do you think he lied to us?" I do it on street corners, waiting for lights. Every little way that we can do it.

Audience: Even experimental theater (because that's what I do) takes so much preparation now—getting the grant, booking. Even at La MaMa, or places like that, it's like three years in advance. The immediacy is missing. From what I read, thirty years ago, somebody would be like, "Oh, I have a theater. Come here and do this next week."

I tried very unsuccessfully to get grants when we were working on *Vanya*. They said I wasn't a theater, I didn't have an organization, so I couldn't get a grant. I developed a very interesting structure which I've been using ever since, which is that I have sort of a gym for actors. Whenever they're not out making money, they come work with me. So they go make their money, because everyone has to make money. This is why it takes seven or eight years to get something finished. But it actually works: Year after year after year, they come into my living room, and we do it.

We have to, each one of us in our own way, find a guerilla tactic that allows us to do what we need to do, and allows us to render onto Caesar what is Caesar's and onto Christ what is Christ's, because we have to make a living. It's very important. Now, Wally has this peculiar career because he is a legend in Europe. He's been on the cover of *Der Spiegel*. Ingmar Bergman does his plays. He had seventeen productions in Germany alone last year. In America, almost nobody does his plays. He can't make a living as a playwright. So he plays goofy characters in movies—he sits in his trailer, and he writes his plays.

Audience: When you get out of bed in the morning, how do you find those "guerilla tactics" in yourself that allow you to take the action and to do everything you want to do?

I do it because I just love it. I can't live without it. It's never even seemed like a job. I don't feel like I've ever really worked. I love to be with colleagues that I love. I love to work on plays that I love. This is what I love to do. It's that simple. You know, it could be sex. That's fun, too.

Audience: Is it the love of doing it so much that allows you to get through the other things that you have to do in order to allow yourself to direct or to act?

Well, if you look at the beginning of *My Dinner with André*, the fun of it is that Wally looks like a completely beaten dog who is talking about all the things he has to do that get in the way of writing. But somehow he does it. There's a story I love about Tennessee Williams. When Elia Kazan did his production of *Camino Real*, it was the first play Williams had done after *Streetcar*. They were sure it was going to be a huge success, because Kazan directed it, it had wonderful actors in it. He'd really gone out on a limb to experiment. There was an opening night party, and these reviews came in—they were horrible and embarrassing, and they treated Williams as if he'd never written a play before, and he got more and more drunk, and he got up, and with tears coming down his cheek, he said, "This is too tough. I don't want to live this kind of life. The critics don't appreciate you. They're ignorant. They don't let you experiment. I put my heart into this. I am never going to write another word." And he went home to his hotel. A couple hours later, they all started getting really worried about him, because he had also taken pills, you know? So his agent and his producer went over to his hotel. They banged on the door, and he shouted, "Go away! Go away!" So they went downstairs and got a guy to give them the key. They went in, and Tennessee Williams had a big bottle of bourbon, and he was sitting at his typewriter writing his next play.

AB: You were talking about being interested in acting as states of being. I'm curious what kind of actors you're interested in working with, and what you think about acting now. I know you've gone on a journey from one end to the other: acting as states of being, as opposed to expression.

I suppose at its simplest, thirty years ago, when I did *Alice in Wonderland*, and I had this dream of an actor who could fly, and did Grotowski training, so the actors literally could fly. The times were very physical—One Million Man March on Washington; hippies were in the street; *Hair* was on Broadway. It was a very physical time. We were young, we were physical, we wanted to change the world. So our work reflected that.

Now I'm nearly seventy. I'm still physical. I work out, because I'm having such a good time, I want to stay alive as long as I can. I've also been on the spiritual journey as part of my development—so there's something more meditative about my work now. Something quieter. The two of us were talking about how much we loved our houses in the country, and how we hoped to work in our houses in the country. I've always been in the city, so the city holds no surprises for me anymore. But there's something about the sound of the trees. There's something about getting up at sunrise and watching the sun come up. There's something about sunset. There's something about the changing of the seasons. This has partly to do with getting older. I once met a woman who left America and bought a house in Ireland. I said, "Why did you decide to do that?" She said, "I have a house on the ocean. I'm eighty-two, and the ocean reminds me of eternity." So I guess you could say I'm quieter than I used to be. I'm more contemplative. My work is perhaps a little bit more philosophical, so I don't need to work with actors who are as physical.

When Mike Nichols came to see our open rehearsals of *Vanya*—they were open for twenty-eight people—somebody said to him afterward, "Did you like it?" He said, "Yeah, I liked it. It's going to be interesting to see what happens when they start moving."

AB: I have a theory about this. There was this period when you couldn't get into *Vanya on 42nd Street*. You had to be invited. I waited by my phone for two months. Finally, somebody called and said, "Do you want to see *Vanya* at the Old Victory?" I think that it's the most directed play I've ever seen. In other words, you go in, and it's a rehearsal. You put your coats on the seat. Everybody's wearing whatever it is they're wearing. "It's an open rehearsal," says André, lying through his teeth. Not true! I think it was the most directed play I've ever seen.

It's a nice trick.

AB: It had a secret underneath it.

I found with the two therapists that I've worked with (which is actually only one: they're mostly frauds), there's always this wonderful trick where it's all incredibly easy when you first get involved. The deeper you go, the denser it gets. So it's fun to work, and to make it seem easy.

Audience: What do you do when you get confused?

I think there are two very interesting stages in creative work. One is confusion and one is boredom. They generally both mean that there's a big fish swimming under the water. As Rilke said, "Live the questions." And not judge that there's something wrong about confusion, because the people who are working, say, on the cure for leprosy—they work for years and years in a state of confusion, and very often they don't find the cure. They find something completely different. But they keep living the question. Confusion is absolutely essential to the creative process. If there was no confusion, why do it? I always feel that all of us have questions we're asking all our lives, for our work, and if we ever found the answer, we'd stop working. We wouldn't need to work anymore.

Boredom—if you've ever been in therapy, you'd know that when you start getting bored, that's really important. The therapist sits up; there's something going on, because the wall that you come against—that's where the real gold is. It's really precious.

You know the director, Nemirovich-Danchenko, who was Stanislavski's sidekick. Somebody said to Vakhtangov, who was one of the great Russian directors, "Nemirovich-Danchenko was such a great director." And Vakhtangov said, "No, he's not a great director: He's never had a flop." So failure is very important in the creative process.

I did this production of *The Seagull* years ago. The first act was brilliant, the second act was boring, the third act was neurotic, and the fourth act was unfinished. Everybody hated it.

AB: I loved it.

Thank you. Very few people did. It was definitely unfinished. The thing that was great about it, for me, was that the first act showed me how to do *Vanya*, fifteen years later. If any of you have read [François] Truffaut on Hitchcock, there's one film that Truffaut says, "I guess that was a critical failure," and Hitchcock says, "Yes, the critics hated it." "Was it a financial failure?" "Oh yes, yes. We lost all our money." "Did any of the audience like it?" "No, the audience hated it." So Truffaut says, "So it really was a failure?" And Hitchcock says, "No, no. Do you remember that one shot of the glass? That showed me how to do my next movie." See, there's no such thing as failure.

Audience: When did your spiritual journey start, and how?

It started when my first wife developed cancer. I was quite terrified and very lost, and through my daughter I met my guru. And, being a sixties hippie, I made a trip to India, and something extraordinary happened to me in Western Tibet, where I was opened to the spiritual. I do some practices, though I'm a little sloppy.

My Dinner with André looks a lot like a man on a spiritual journey, but I wasn't really. I think there was just an intuition. I think if I didn't go into the theater I would have become a monk. Some way or another, I will always have a monk's personality. But it was relatively recently that I did start on the spiritual journey. Having been in the theater all my life, I don't think God, or whatever you want to call it, is up there. I think that it's literally in the body. It is in the blood cells, and with certain techniques, you can reach an ecstatic state where you feel one and at harmony with the whole world.

When we're in dark times, people really do need the light. They need hope—not easy hope; hard-earned hope. And whatever work we can do on ourselves.

Audience: Can you talk to us a bit about Chekhov, why you picked him? You've done him before. How do you pick the translation that you used in *Vanya*?

I like Chekhov partly because I'm a Russian. My parents, who are immigrants, sat in the kitchen till three o'clock in the morning talking about whether or not they should go back to Moscow. It was absolutely reality for me. But also I love Chekhov, and Beckett too—I think Chekhov is Beckett with furniture. (We don't use much furniture in our Chekhov productions.) I think Chekhov's plays are about the nature of what it feels like to be here, and to live this life. Not about themes or characters or plot. The reason I love the theater more than film: Because theater, for me, is an absolute metaphor for life. We're kicked onto the stage, we do our best for a few hours, and before we know it, it's finished. It's very moving.

I don't even remember how we chose the translation. But if I'd known we were going to work for four or five years, I would have asked Wally to do it.

Audience: Does he speak Russian?

No, but he doesn't speak Norwegian either, and he's done *The Master Builder*. We got a Norwegian scholar and we went over every single word of the text, and went over the associations and the connotations of the words, and then Wally wrote some version.

Audience: Are there any projects that are hanging in front of you, that you're chasing?

My house in the country. I know that seems odd, but I mean that quite profoundly. I found that in different periods of working in my life, that

I periodically come to an end—which used to scare the shit out of me. Now I just accept it. And I feel that these ten or fifteen years, whatever it's been, of working on classics in my little room, that that's drawing to a close, and something else is pulling me, and I know that it's close to nature, but I have no idea what.

Audience: Can you talk a little about what you know of the work of Grotowski?

Grotowski's searching for a modern idiom or technique of prayer. He was searching for new physical ways to bring up the spirit. Active prayer. And it was done for nobody except the people he worked with. A lot of work was done with the body. Had he lived, he might have come back to the theater in a way, I always felt, and done something like a sacred Mass.

Audience: Over the years, how did you find your collaborators? How did you find each other?

I never audition. I just have long conversations with people. And it's a question of falling in love. If I fall in love and they fall in love, if we fall in love, there's something interesting to pursue. It's so important to work in an atmosphere of trust. And trust is life. We don't know what it is about meeting the "right" person. You know, I'm married to this wonderful person. She's the "right" person. I don't know what it is about her. But she's who I enjoy being with, all the time. Wally, I work with, because I adore him. And Larry [Pine]. The play is not so important; it's Wally and Larry. The others who come in and out—Ben came in, will come in again. When we met, all we talked about was cooking. We didn't talk about art. We talked about cooking. We can't explain these things. It's very, very important to find your own people. I think it comes from the heart. And with them you can do anything.

Audience: What made you leave directing, and what made you come back?

That's a good question, one that I've never completely answered. On a personal level, I think I left because there was a strong part of me that always wanted my mother's love. When she was dying, she said to me, "You know, if I get through this alive, I'm going to leave him and the three of you and live in Germany." She was a tough one. And she loved artists. So there was some part of me that was working for her. When she died, I think, that was confusing. Also, I had my group for twelve years and had a project, and in general, ten years is really about as long as a group can stay together.

AB: Oh, I don't know about that. We're at twelve right now.

That's amazing. That's miraculous. Not many groups do stay beyond ten. But it doesn't have to be that. But my group fell apart. They fell apart for a very healthy reason. We'd all done such wonderful work together, we'd developed so much together, that none of us wanted to do the same thing anymore. So the group disbanded. And I'd also felt the theater was facing a crucial—something was wrong. This was '75, '76. I felt the era was ending. Something very serious was happening in the theater.

And probably most profoundly of all, *My Dinner with André*, which didn't exist, was pulling me. If I hadn't given up directing, I never would have been tearing around the Polish forest, learning to play the harp, going through the desert . . . so it was a new work that was demanding that I give up the thing that meant most to me.

Audience: And how did you come back?

I came back when my wife developed cancer. I was working with my daughter in an All-Out Holler Shakespeare Company. We were having a terrible time. I was playing an abominable Prospero. And my daughter was going crazy, and she came up and asked me if I could direct her and a friend of hers in a scene of Chekhov's—*Vanya*—and I hadn't read *Vanya* in twenty years. The minute I read *Vanya*, I thought of Wally, and that was how it began. That's what pulled me back.

Audience: What are your ingredients when you approach a scene, as well as a character? Do you have certain basic things that help you out to clarify what you're going to do to build a character?

No, not really. I just sit and wait. When I was younger, and I did a play in four or five weeks, then I had to have a stronger idea. If you work in a short period of time, then your task is to know what you want to say, and articulate it in the best way that you can. If you work for years, you're basically just fishing. You're just waiting for whatever unknown thing happens to pop up. Since we're all human, the very first thing we do in rehearsal is go for the stereotype. It's just natural. You can't not do it. The stereotype is not what you're looking for. You're looking for something much deeper. And in a long rehearsal process, you can let go. Isn't there a Hindu practice called "Not This, Not That"? Japanese. The way you search for God is you say, "It's not this. It's not that." You just know that you're looking, and when you see it, you'll know.

A good example of this was when we were doing *Vanya* for a small audience. Astroff and Vanya were doing the last scene in the last act, where Astroff demands the poison back—and it was filled with rage and hurt and beautifully done, and the audience was blown away. But we kept thinking, It's good, but it's not right. We didn't know what it was. Night after night, we'd do it and the audience applauded, and we'd say, "That's not it. That's not it." What we finally found was that it's a love scene— Vanya and Astroff love each other more than they love Elena. And once it was the hurt of a love scene, then we had it. We didn't know till we saw it. So if you work for a long time, you don't have to work with a prearranged idea. You can work with what comes up.

AB: Was that your experience, Lynn?

Lynn Cohen [actress who performed in *Vanya*]: Absolutely. I think I had more years of rehearsal than lines, actually. But I remember there was nothing that I couldn't do. I had the luxury of so much time. I remember one time I did the role totally in drag. I said, there's something in there; I don't know what it is. I ended up doing it in a vest and a little tie. You worked very strongly with the Russian. We found out things like, Maman, in every production I've ever seen, leaves the stage, so the first encounter with Elena and Vanya is alone. And it's not in the Russian. She's present. We worked with that, two years, never knowing what to do with it.

When I was working on the character of André, in *My Dinner with André*, we rehearsed it for fourteen months. We have so many different selves—I didn't know: Who was this André? I couldn't figure out who the hell was this André. On top of that, Wally did something that really screwed me up, which is that if, say, it was a story about being in the Polish forest, I would probably say, "We were in this big forest, and we lived in this tiny little castle, we ran around in the forest all day with all these women, we ate off of a great stone slab we used as a table." That's the way I would say it. Wally rewrote that, so that what it says in the text is, "We lived in a tiny little castle, and we ate around a great stone slab as a table." So I had to re-learn my stories, which was very hard.

But the big question was, who was the character? What kind of character am I? You've all had this experience. When I work out with my trainer at the gym, I turn into this loud, lewd, childlike jock. Other friends of mine have never seen that person. With each person that we're close to, they see another self. We have hundreds of them. I found four voices in the character—this came after eleven months of rehearsal. One was the Peter Brook guru voice. The other was the Spiritual Used-Car Salesman, who would do anything for enlightenment—let his family go, let his friends go. The third was the Off-the-Wall Upper-Middle-Class Rich Kid. And fourth is the Guy Who Tells the Truth. He appears very rarely. Once I had the four voices, I knew how to do the role, but it really did take me a long time, and I had all these preconceptions about who the character was, but they didn't work. They didn't come from a deep truth.

Audience: So when you have to work in a short time, say, a month and a half, you just see what happens?

Grotowski used to say there are two ideal rehearsal periods. One is two years and the other is two days. There's something about the two days, about the spontaneity, the danger. It's why being in front of a camera, it's quite dangerous, I find. Quite exciting. You go in, you've never met your wife. You don't get a rehearsal. They turn on the lights, there are eight hundred people on the set, and you just have to be there.

Audience: You mentioned you'd been working on *The Master Builder* for a number of years, and you'd worked on *Vanya* for a number of years before you committed it to film. When you have something that gestates for a long period, that picks up the ideology of several years or a great period of time, how do you know when it's ready to be launched?

I think you just feel that you've reached the end, that there's nothing else you have to say, until you have people watching it. Something special does happen in front of an audience.

I suppose you could say also that the theater that Wally and I do is political also in the sense that it's so completely anticapitalist. We don't get paid while we do it. We work for as long as we like. We have no producers. In general, we don't work for critics. We rarely sell tickets. And there really have been people who have gotten very, very annoyed, in a wonderful way. *The Designated Mourner* we did in the ruins of a Wall Street men's club. It was the club in which literally the big financiers had planned the armament business of the First World War. It had a great history. Nobody had been in it for forty years. It was, I think, the greatest space I've ever done anything in. But the problem was if we performed before April, it was too cold, and if we performed after July, it was too hot. So we could only play from April through July. And Wally, being a writer, wanted critics, and we got rave reviews. Nobody could get into it. A lot of particularly Broadway people said, "You should move it! You should move it!" I said, "No, I think that's it."

I have one last little story which I'd love to tell you. It's sort of at the heart of what I was saying at the beginning. I took out Erland Josephson—Ingmar Bergman's great actor—for lunch. And he said this amazing thing to me. He said, "You know, when I was young, I worked on everything the actor should work on: I worked on my body. I worked on my voice. I would go to museums to cultivate this instrument. I would listen to music, read books, did very arduous physical training. I did everything that the actor should do. But," he said, "you know? I don't know how I can do it, but now"—he was in his late seventies—"I would like to do that training, that other training, that would allow me to just walk on the stage and just be there, like a lighthouse, illuminating and giving hope."

Paula Vogel

I rony is an ongoing and vital force in Paula's life. I find it both remarkable and ironic that Paula, devastated in her youth by rejection from Yale when she applied to the graduate playwriting program, was recently appointed to run that very same program. Remarkable and ironic, too, that Paula wrote *The Baltimore Waltz*, a play about a brother and sister's trip through Europe before she had ever even left the U.S. But these ironies touch upon Paula's magical combination of perseverance and intellect, wit and belief in the human imagination.

Paula is a playwright and an educator. Lauded widely for her plays such as *How I Learned to Drive* (Pulitzer Prize, 1998), *The Baltimore Waltz*, *The Long Christmas Ride Home* and many, many others, she also understands that she can never stop teaching. From her first teaching experience as a graduate student at Cornell, Paula knew that this was something that she was meant to do in her life. At the age of thirty-three she was appointed by Brown University to start a graduate and undergraduate playwriting program. She single-handedly turned Brown into the most sought after MFA playwriting program in the world. I am not exaggerating.

Paula is also a political animal, an outspoken activist for causes, ideas and people she believes in. Her plays are considered feminist, but mostly she believes in the power of art. Like Tom Sawyer who pointed at a fence and suggested to his friends that the most wonderful thing to do would be to paint that fence, Paula inspires action and commitment from others via her own contagious enthusiasm and delight. When I think of Paula, I think of her as a conjurer and an enchantress. She makes everything she is interested in sound so exciting and luminous. In Rhode Island she initiated an ongoing program where theater artists work in women's prisons. The feat was the result of the combination of Paula's belief in action and art and her remarkable organizational skills.

Paula does not skirt controversy. Her plays look unflinchingly at disturbing and divisive issues such as domestic abuse, gender roles, stereotype, pedophilia, pornography and AIDS. I always find something always a little unsettling in her plays. "Why did you include that urine incident at the end of *The Baltimore Waltz*?" I asked Paula when I directed the play at Circle Rep in 1992. She explained that the last thing a body does before it dies is pee. The urine is necessary in the recipe that makes Paula's work what it is. What always liberates the work from the darkness and complexities of the issues she chooses is her humor and compassion.

December 15, 2003

AB: I saw *The Long Christmas Ride Home* at Vineyard Theatre and was once again struck by how absolutely in the moment you are in your writing and in your understanding of the theater. So often when I go to the theater, I feel like we're so behind the currents of our time. There's nothing quaint about what you're doing. You are extremely interested in the world and its inhabitants. You're interested in world theater, in memory, in the past and the present and the future and the present and the past—quantum ways of thinking. There's always something about your theater that brings the past into the present. I had the great fortune of directing *The Baltimore Waltz*, which was haunted by loss—the loss of your brother brought into the present event of theater. How does the past relate to your work? In every piece, you use the past in a very extraordinary way.

PV: I believe the theater is structure. I believe playwriting is structure. I think playwriting is not about the words. I think the words are the weakest element of the text—actually an almost fatally flawed part of the design. The purpose of theater is to undo the cognitive meaning of words. This is done through repetition and the actual structure of events, which is the way that we program memory and time. So I'm more interested when I start thinking about how I'm going to do the play, in thinking about the right structure. What kind of structure have I never done before? How can I create a different collision of sequence of events? I also think one of the things we're still grappling with in the twenty-first century is the notion of theater as the well-made play. The commercial theater continues to grapple with that, as does television, as does film. But to me, theater is really the unraveling of the play world. I think great plays in particular just unravel. They come apart. They simply will not hold. Whether it's *The Bacchae* or *Danton's Death*, it's all about falling apart. Yet we are told critically and in the commercial world that things are supposed to come together.

I start off thinking: How can I make us remember the beginning differently in the middle? How do we remember the beginning differently at the end? How do we remember the play differently the morning after? How do we remember the play differently ten years after? The Wooster Group's *Rumstick Road* has had a remarkably significant impact on me as I go through time. My initial response was to be sort of angry at it because when we first came into the Performing Garage we were all asked to take off our shoes. I thought, Oh, please, I hate theater games. I'll never find my shoes. But ten years later, I'm driving down the road and I suddenly think, Oh, you take off your shoes when you go to your mother's house. Now, anything that's going to stay with you for ten years so that you reverse its meaning—because my memory changes over time—is very exciting to me.

I've spent a long, long time thinking about the act of personal witness. It has to do with Tadeusz Kantor and how one remembers and continues to remember the play. The theatrical event has to wound our memory. The entire play world can't wound the memory, but ages can. This is why I keep saying that playwriting is about not writing. It's about structuring gaps. It's about creating a performance script. I've been very blessed because I've worked with you and other directors, and I've seen completely different play worlds for the same script. The script is created by the writer. The production is written by the director and the actors. But the play is written by a specific audience on a specific night. It's all of those different levels. So our memory of a play would be different if we saw it on Tuesday night and it was a silent night versus on a Saturday night and suddenly we're in the midst of comedy. They are absolutely different plays. That's another thing I adore about the theater.

That's a beautiful notion that the play is written by the audience. I know you've been working on film scripts and pilots.

I did pitch a pilot. I thought I was going to pitch it to HBO, which I adore. I fell into the trick of being told I had to do warm-up pitches—and in the warm-up pitch, for a network, it was sold. The president stopped and said—it's so corny—"Cancel my appointments for tomorrow." He said, "Where did you learn to pitch like that?" And I realized that a lot of people aren't used to theatrical imagery. Of course we're animated. Of course we're used to the audience writing the play, which I suppose is good pitching. So I was suddenly a contender for a producing contract with CBS—but nothing was ever made. I went on my own to see the woman who was in charge of television programming at HBO and she said, "Oh, we would have bought that." Here's what I love about television that I was hoping for: the notion of collective writing. Group writing, where you sit around and you collectively create the piece, is very exciting to me. But I'm an overweight, fifty-year-old lesbian with gray hair. Nobody at Warner Brothers is going to take me seriously. I know that going in. They sort of slotted me into a narrow box, fitting me into the franchise. That kept being said. "We've gotta think of the franchise, think of the franchise."

The thing that is possible—and I think that television writing is going to get there—is the notion of being able to have an open structure. That didn't happen with this studio apparatus. They wanted the structure to be closed, where everything was wrapped up, well-made play form. I had pitched something à la *Twin Peaks*, which then makes a different notion of time. In essence it's novelistic. It's what *The Sopranos* is doing. The woman at CBS who bought the pitch had wanted it to be open structure. She had been the managing director of Roundabout and said, "Oh, this is very theatrical. I love this." It's enormously appealing to a collection of writers. You can actually get some of the strangest minds together in a room and just giggle. But once you get into that box, you suddenly say, "This is very high-paid factory work." And I worked in factories. All my life, no matter how bad the money situation is in theater, I keep giggling. I'm not doing factory work anymore. I called my agent and said, "Please get me out of this." Of course, I'd signed a contract. He said, "You have to take every note that they give you, and you have to deliberately put everything they ask for in the script." I said, "What if they love it and I have to spend three years of my life doing this?" He said, "Trust me. If they suggested it, they'll hate it. You just have to take the notes." I spent three months writing—and he was right. They read it and they went, "Oh, you were right; we were wrong. Can you go back to your original conception?" And I went, "Oh, I've lost it. I think I have to spend a year walking on the beach." It was a useful exercise. I wanted to know if at age fifty I could get off a plane, go into a pitch session.

You're about to embark on, once again, a for-profit theater endeavor, and if you look at that and you look at the not-for-profit scene, and you look at audiences, and you look at your work—what do you see?

I feel like a twenty year old struggling to find a model I fit. I feel great frustration. I feel very akin to Aphra Behn, who said something like: "I would have been a poet / as good as any man / but the woman damns the poet." It seems to me that we're still in a very, very similar situation these many centuries later. Non-Aristotelian narrative does not fit within a commercial venue. I don't mean to be a cultural feminist here at all. I'm not saying that there is a woman's kind of writing. I do think, however, that Samuel Beckett made Irene Fornes possible, and made a way of telling stories that is about perspective, not action. Would it have ever been possible for Virginia Woolf to write theater? We're getting closer to that time. The novel was created by Aphra Behn out of a similar sense of frustration that she could not fit into the way plays were produced in London. She was more interested in a different sense of time and character than was permissible. I'm constantly struggling with this thinking. All right, time to start writing fiction. Time to start writing memoirs. I'm colliding against the apparatus of how plays get produced, whether it's Off-Broadway, not-for-profit or a commercial production. If you're trying to dismantle the apparatus through the playwriting itself, you don't have enough time to figure out how to interpret that in a production in four weeks. The machine just cranks on and on. This last play was sort of my big scare. I thought it was almost impossible to do. And we did it in five weeks and it was still impossible and it didn't come together, I think, until the last two weeks.

That was in Rhode Island or New York?

That was in New York.

The other thing that I think is frustrating, for example, is that you and I worked on *Hot 'N' Throbbing* for three weeks with a company, most of whom were doing other roles or were working in the MFA program. I could not figure out the structure. I want the structure to be bigger than I can accomplish mentally as the writer so that it gets worked out in the room with the director and the actors. That's a very time-intensive thing. It can't happen in a repertory system because the system is on to the next, on to the next. We've still not figured out how to underwrite art in this country. The only way now I can think of doing it is sequential productions. I spent a long time after *Hot 'N' Throbbing* talking with you about what would I do and how would I make that structure work. I tackled it literally ten years later with Molly Smith, and I still didn't get the ending right.

What's happening right now—particularly in New York and I'm extremely stressed about it—is that we are treating art as entertainment. Even if you look back ten years, we had more of a cultural conversation.

There's no chance for memory if we're not going to have cultural conversations, if we're only going to have trends, if we only have events, if we're only going to talk about backstage gossip as a way of selling tickets. There's no discussion at a commercial level about something like *Wicked*, which is saying, "Oh, by the way, we're in a fascist state right now." It's the most politically daring commercial production I've seen, whether it works or not. The way we're censoring now is by giving maybe a one-inch column or less in our newspapers. It's not even being discussed.

I figure there are only two ways I can proceed from here. One is to do very small workshops over time in regional theater, which I love. Perseverance Theatre in Alaska was very important to me as a model. I had fifty seats and a company that is trained, but is made up of people who worked as fishermen and lawyers and postal workers. They did, side by side, Chekhov, then my latest play. It was extraordinary, the kind of permission granted by that. To start something there and then work on it over a decade is really the only way to do that. I enjoy the conversation. I don't know whether or not I'm willing to finally face the isolation. I'm tired of my own voice. I want to hear the resistance or the response from other voices. That's the theatrical process.

In rehearsal? Or in the whole process?

Something that was really thrilling to me: We were doing *How I Learned to Drive* out at Berkeley Rep. I was really tired, so I was like, "I don't want to be in the talkback, but I would love to hear it." This guy got up and just ripped the play to shreds. He hated this play. It was completely invigorating. The actors were trying to shut him up and I was like, "Go for it!" I ran up to him afterward and pumped him a little bit more. There's something in me that loves the ability to have dissent. There's something in me that loves a theatrical event that causes best friends to fight, roll in each other's blood. That's what theater should be doing. We have lost the ability to have that conversation. We're not having it at a political level, and we're not having it at a level of theater—and I think the two are related.

I remember doing *Hot 'N' Throbbing* at a point in my career when I was doing too many shows at the same time. I remember Christine Jones, the set designer, coming in to have a meeting. Those were rehearsal marathon days, and I was exhausted, and I was like, "Yeah, whatever." I never went through the process of arguing with you or her or anybody. I actually met Christine ten years after we'd done it, and we looked at each other and said, "Oh, my God, I've been wanting to talk to you because

that design wasn't right." And part of it—I hope you will take this the right way—is that we did what you said.

Right.

I was too completely exhausted to fight. It was such a lesson. I never said this to you. I'm mystified.

I'm mystified, too. I wish we'd fought, too. I would have been happy to die after *Baltimore Waltz* because if you had this once in your lifetime, that's enough. I was so proud of that event, that we wrote the play in the room, that the audience was writing the play. It was my happiest moment in the theater. I wrote *Hot 'N' Throbbing* to continue that—in essence responding to what you were doing, thinking we would fight about it. I do remember when it was designed I went, "Oh, no." But I also remember that you were tired and that right after *Baltimore Waltz* you said, "You know, Vogel, you're kind of like a terrier on a pant's leg." It takes a lot of energy. But there's something about a great fight. It's not about my point of view or your point of view. It's about the play world actually having an independent voice. When we argue like that, suddenly the play world becomes focused and it's actually not us anymore. It's this phenomenon—almost a spirit. Theater is almost like the undead coming to life. There's this sense of this other identity, or this other entity, and it's not yours, and it's not mine as a playwright.

It's an animus that's created.

The energy to fight like this doesn't fit into four-week rehearsal periods and production cycles and doing your press. How can I do the press and talk about the play when I haven't written the play? When that animus starts collecting and spirit starts gathering and the play starts to take shape, I don't remember my intentions. I don't remember what it looked like in my head. I don't remember what the pre–Cherry Jones Anna looked like. I'd never been to Paris. I told you I went to Europe after your production of *Baltimore Waltz*. It was such a disappointment after Anne's Europe.

As a director you can make something, but you know it doesn't open until it's premiered six times, and gone to six different venues. In this country we don't ever have more than three or four weeks to rehearse. It's a process over a long time where you actually open a show, then you take it to another audience, and then another place. What is that for a writer?

It's not quite possible. In the marketplace right now, if you get reviews that are somewhat favorable, then the play has a future life and, if not, the play is essentially dead. So it's a one-shot deal for a writer. That's really grim. My favorite plays are done in the Perseverance Theatre model: fifty seats, production costs of maybe five hundred dollars. The difficulty right now is that writers don't really belong to companies. Usually we don't have that kind of access. So we're out there in essence—and this was useful to me in TV-land—selling our product. The only model that exists for new plays in this country is to sell it like a product.

One of the things I'm now thinking about is the narrative impulse versus the theatrical process. The narrative impulse of telling the story creates a direct, one-to-one relationship with the reader that slows down the perception of time. It makes one contemplate, makes one envision the scene, the characters—you have to read slowly, you can't read quickly—versus the theatrical process where time is whizzing by. There are no stage directions in my plays anymore. Instead I'm starting to write what I would call personal reflections that I am sharing just with the reader that will never be staged—shouldn't be staged. They're unstageable.

The reason this came to me is that I was reading *Cat on a Hot Tin Roof* and suddenly Tennessee Williams started talking about the mystery of character in the middle of the script. In the notes for *Cat on a Hot Tin Roof* he says something like, "I am reminded of the quality of light in a photograph I once saw of Robert Louis Stevenson's home on the Samoan Island." And I went, "Oh my God, he's talking to me." Now, there's no way you could stage that. That's a one-to-one. I mean, one of the great things about novels is that you can say, "I married him, dear reader." It's a personal, one-to-one relationship between the reader and the writer. The only presence of the playwright is in those in-between-the-lines things that are said to the beloved reader—which happens to be the actors, the director, but will never be put on stage. I never met Tennessee Williams, but I can pick his plays up and he is actually talking to me. I'm now getting more and more drawn to that.

Example: In *Long Christmas Ride*, I open with a poem. The whole play is a response to letters from my brother and his poem in which he writes about breath and the air. When I wanted the ghost of Stephen to be brought back to life, and I wanted to describe the dancer, I said, "Oh, let him be beautiful." You cannot stage, "Oh, let him be beautiful." But I wanted you to know how beautiful I think the male body is, and how beautiful I think the act of love is between two men. That is from me as a person. It is something I share with the readers.

Unfortunately, the first question in almost any press interview is, "Is this autobiographical?" The only way we can sell a product is to consume the personalities. We cannot reflect or contemplate our relationship to the material and project our own personal message, our own autobiography. We can no longer write the play. It's a capitalist model versus something else—and it is that something else that I am longing for. I want to see your Paris. I want to see your *Baltimore Waltz*. I want someone else to show my brother back to me. I want him to be your brother, not mine. Do you know what I mean?

It's big. The only way I can respond to you is by thinking about the word "space"— giving space both to the reader or the writer being the audience or the director. It seems like so much of what we see that feels old-fashioned is descriptive as opposed to creating an invitation to make up the thing. I've been dealing with some old plays lately—really ancient, like 1401. It's interesting because these plays seem to be more invitations to thought than descriptions of thought or descriptions of a result. When I'm thinking of your work, I think of the word "juggle." You put elements together, interests together, that don't have a resolution, and you say to the reader and to the director, "Take this. Start juggling it. See what the space in between these objects creates." One doesn't find that very often in writing for the stage. You find a description of a living room and then something that happens there—as opposed to an arena in which events occur.

I think that the reason that there's that space in the work is that I've worked with younger writers. I'd have never written *Baltimore Waltz* if I hadn't been teaching at Brown. That level of—the only word I can use is plasticity— in the younger writers kind of kicked my butt. *Long Day's Journey into Night* is not one of my favorite plays. Who was it who said that O'Neill was a genius without a talent? But it's a very interesting thing because you can feel the machinery of the three-act or whatever structure clunking. There's a way I can get back into that text even though it feels more Aristotelian or well-made to me, which is not to read it as stage directions but to read it as if I am the first reader. It's not O'Neill dictating the stage, but dictating his memory. Then I don't feel as much resistance to the text.

It's a strategy to open something up again.

It was your strategy when you did *The Women*. You put that little girl watching *The Women*. Suddenly the narrative act was resisting the theatrical act in your production of *The Women*.

What one can do is make the theater visible as opposed to invisible. A Danish woman I knew years ago—this was pre-*Lion King* and a few other things said, "I'm writing my PhD dissertation on the male bias on Broadway. Women can never be

done on Broadway. The feminist aesthetic is subversive." I really thought about that, and, well, it's true actually. It's difficult for me to put something out without also putting something that opposes it at the same time. It's hard for me just to say, "This is this." For me, the truth lies in the space between two oppositions. So, a young girl watching older women be bitchy creates the span of time between their lives. I think you do that. You put something forward and then you subvert it. I don't know that that's necessarily feminist.

I do think that Broadway is about reducing resistance, reducing conflict, reducing friction. There are exceptions—and the exceptions tend to be such that we can say, "Oh, we produced *Angels in America*. That lets us off the hook for the next decade." You can almost hear the sigh of relief. Now we don't have to worry again about having resistance for at least another ten years. I think the Broadway model wants events that can be entirely consumed in one sitting. So, what you're talking about in terms of the oppositions, which I find incredibly thrilling, there's no reason why there can't be a Broadway event like that. And there are. There are plays that I go to and think, Oh my God, how did they make that? Or occasionally this happens in terms of Hollywood studio films. Not very often, but occasionally it does. I think it's possible. I keep going back to *Threepenny Opera*. There's got to be a way you can have resistance and it's popular, something that incorporates popular culture as well as an intellectual feast. I think Kushner came extremely close to that. That's an extraordinary balancing act. I'm actually very interested in plays that are balancing acts. I've started a thesis (and abandoned it; this seems to be a habit with me) about *The London Cuckolds*, which was popular in 1679 with Tories and Whigs, and *The Octoroon* by Dion Boucicault, about an octoroon woman falling in love with the son of her owner. It was a huge hit with abolitionists as well as slave owners in New Orleans and New York in 1859. *Threepenny* in a way is in time with that balancing act.

I think that *Threepenny* was written by different audiences simultaneously. It was a popular commercial theater event at the same time that it parodied popular commercial theater events. I don't believe there's any possibility of having a homogenous audience. What's possible, though, is these extraordinary balancing acts that occur every now and then, when we're suddenly in a room enjoying our disagreement. If a play can do that, that is the theatrical form that was meant when *Medea* was written for Greek citizens or *The Trojan Women* was produced in a time of war. That's the actual theatrical intention at its highest level. It's extraordinarily hard to do. It's almost impossible to do commercially.

Because of money?

The texts that are created pre-judge the event in order to sell the event, produce the event, have money for the event. It has everything to do with the logo and—pardon the F word—franchise. It's done beautifully and brilliantly—puppet nudity. At a commercial level you have to create a response to the play before we even sit in our seats. We're no longer writing the play as an absolutely neutral audience coming in and informing it with our own intentions. It's been pre-intended. It's like cutting up our meat into bite-sized pieces so we can eat it quickly and digest it in one sitting. The only way that we can underwrite a production in a capitalist society is to sell it first, and once it starts getting sold, we're not writing it anymore; the logo is, the quotes from the paper are, the ads, the preview articles . . .

How much do you let in the outside world in your writing?

I don't know.

It's probably why you write successful plays. Because I think we start second-guessing.

I always am kind of insane when I write the play. It really is a form of insanity. I think that the reason I like working with writers is that morning after you just spewed out thirty pages, you think, Oh my God, this is total garbage. To live at that level of fear and know when I read it people will laugh at me—and then plunge ahead. That's something that we live with. I remember the first reading of *How I Learned to Drive*, and there were moments of silence and I just wanted to run on my sword. Nobody spoke. I thought, Oh, I finally did it. I finally went beyond the pale.

Somebody said once, growth is directly proportional to the amount of discomfort you can withstand. You were talking about your struggle with three different ideas of what to write next. Can you just let us in on it?

Well, you said, "Do you ever let in outside sources?" And to some extent, with the Signature Theatre Company, I am aware that I have reached this place in which the critics can write about me now: "Oh, we've figured out Vogel. We don't actually have to stay awake anymore." I'm pre-digested, so I am trying to figure out how to resist that in the formation of what comes out next.

I love history. So ideas that I've pitched before still remain with me. I want to do a music-theater adaptation. One idea: How would I do an adaptation of *The Country Wife*—that lovely, nasty little play? Four best friends in Los Angeles are celebrating Horner's (it's a family name) thirtieth birthday for the fourth year in a row, and they're all getting drunk. Their boyfriends are all in the industry and they're all leaving them for younger women. They're all competing for district attorney roles.

They're only thirty-four?

Yeah. It's a scary world out there. Horner says, "I am an intelligent woman. I have a mind. I have to force myself to get out of this field. It gets worse and worse and worse." She turns to all of her friends and says, "Goddamn it. I want a double cheeseburger and I want the margarita instead of this salad with dressing on the side." She says, "Tomorrow morning I'm going to go to all of the casting directors in town, everyone we know, all of our boyfriends, and tell them I'm a lesbian." Her friends say, "But you've never slept with women." She says, "I don't care. It's a role. Tell everyone in town I'm a lesbian. I have to force myself out of this business." Every man she ever slept with comes and says, "Was it me?"

For Molly Smith I want to write a kind of American *A Christmas Carol* called *Civil War Christmas*. It's a kind of Doctorow *Ragtime* approach, set on Christmas Eve in Washington, D.C., 1864, that incorporates Christmas songs and Civil War ballads and is a secular look. Why are we looking at Victorian poverty instead of looking at race? If we look at race and the relationship between the North and the South, and class, the Civil War is still going on. I thought this would be an interesting American Christmas tale to tell, where Mary Cassatt passes Mary Tyler on Christmas Eve in Washington, D.C. Walt Whitman is there attending to the soldiers. There are all these interesting collisions possible. To warm up to that I wrote *Long Christmas Ride* because I thought, All right, a Christmas play, the personal versus the political, I'll jump into this. It's so big and I can't write it at a small scale, I'm thinking of doing a short music-theater piece about women who are Civil War reenactors.

What are they?

There are men who starve themselves so they can look like Confederate soldiers—they call themselves "hard core" Civil War reenactors. This has become huge. And there are women who were Civil War soldiers. It's sort of like in *The Ballad of Little Jo*. And now there are women who are struggling to start doing reenactments because they have the historical right to be in the battles. There are also Civil War reenactors who are African

Americans who are reenacting Confederate soldiers. I mean, the issues on this are just extraordinary. Now, whether or not I actually go into that or if this is just encouraging me to write *Civil War Christmas*, I don't know.

Is there an audience for this?

No. There are people who do not talk about the Civil War as history at all. It is the "War Between the States." It hasn't been decided yet. They're still resisting. This is not their government. They've all become Republicans. It's very interesting. I haven't yet gone to a reenactment. I did spend sixteen hours with a [Colonel John Singleton] Mosby impersonator going over sacred ground in Warrington, Virginia. He was weeping as he talked: ". . . And on this spot Mosby dismantled his troops. And right over there is the block where slaves were sold." The hair went up on the back of my neck. I thought, What the heck is this? This is scary. There's something going on right now with reenactments. Now, probably it's not the sanest thing in the world to write. The more that I realize what reenactment is doing and where the reenactors are in this country, the more that I realize this is not a simple tale. It is deeply political. It's actually kind of dangerous.

Creepy. You have a fecund imagination.

I do these things called bake-offs, where I get writers together. For instance, when I was doing *How I Learned to Drive* I asked the writers working with me in a workshop to write a play that went backward in time, had a moon, and had a relationship between an older and younger person. While they were writing the bake-off in forty-eight hours, I cheated and I took two weeks and wrote *How I Learned to Drive*. When I started working on *The Country Wife*, I asked them to write a play with a cuckold, a eunuch and a plastic surgeon. Phenomenal plays. I'm thinking very much of my mother and of *Bosoms of Neglect* and *Man in the Moon Marigolds* and realizing that in American drama mothers are primarily defined by mother-son relationships. So I'm thinking of having a bake-off with women writers I know and love called "The Mother of All Bake-Offs," where we write mother plays.

And the last thing, I've been approached about writing a new book for *Lady in the Dark*—Kurt Weill score, Ira Gershwin lyrics, Moss Hart book—if they actually allow us to do this in a kind of *Cradle Will Rock* way, to look at what Broadway entertainment was in 1940, written by a Jewish immigrant exile who has lost his country, with a lyricist who has lost his brother and his collaborator, and an American man, who is deeply involved in Freudian analysis.

It's a great idea because people always want to do that musical, but it doesn't quite stand up, but it's got great music in it.

It's got extraordinary music. So that's where I am. Who knows?

Audience: What you were talking about, about finding the truth and drama in the space between opposition, I found that watching *The Long Christmas Ride Home*, in the space in between Basil's puppets and what happens after. A friend of mine who works at the Vineyard was telling me that you've done some work with prison theater. Could you talk a little about that, specifically in terms of the past and the present and the future, along the lines of incarceration and what these inmates were dealing with in a past life and how they can translate and use theater and drama as a place for future growth?

That's a great question. Unfortunately now it's been twelve years since I've done that work for women in maximum security. That program is continuing now at Brown University. Undergraduates and graduate students are going in and doing a variety of workshops, which is great. I have never seen such dramatic proof in my life of the necessity of theater on a daily basis. The ability to access memory, as painful as it may be, is still joyful compared with the entrapment of the space that they're in. It was an astonishing transformation. I would say that some of them got addicted. It's sort of like sharing your addiction. It was a very strange phenomenon for me to leave and go out at the end of the workshop. I knew there were women at the window watching me get into my car, and I couldn't bear to look back. And they watched as the car went past until it was out of sight. And that was beautiful.

AB: I've never thought of that before—the idea of constricted space, which is then gated by memory.

Yes. That's what memory is. When I did the program, I realized that actually the harshest punishment is aesthetic deprivation. They were not getting, for example, pajamas. Very ugly clothing. Smoke-filled rooms. And flakey green paint on the walls. That warden, fortunately, has since gone. While I was there, a reformed warden came, and she's a saint. She immediately painted the walls white and the ceilings blue. I remember coming in and one of the inmates grabbed me and said, "Look—the color of my sky has changed." I did a book drive because there were no books in the library for women. The argument for this was that when women get depressed they over-eat. When men get depressed they become violent and fights break out. So all the money for books and programming went to the men's maximum. They knew that women would just sort of sit there in a kind of stupor, and it was very cost-effective. So I said, "Well, sir, if you don't mind, I'm going to do a book drive with my faculty members in the English Department." He laughed. He said, "Are you kidding? These women haven't gone through high school. These women aren't going to read." I can't remember how many copies I got of *Hamlet* and the collected works of Shakespeare, etc., and so forth, everything I could, biology books. The next time I was there, a seventeen year old met me in the hall and, again, grabbed my sleeve and said, "Oh, that this too, too solid flesh would melt."

It really did demonstrate that memory dissolves space, dissolves the restraints of space. Another thing that was quite extraordinary was how the senses come alive. The writers that I worked with there were so aware. "Oh, I can tell by the way the keys are jangling which guard it is." It was like a Virginia Woolf landscape where no sensory perception could be shut out. Every sound permeated. They would hear the radiator. An extraordinary landscape of sound went into their work.

I went into this because of a theater company Olympia Dukakis, who is one of my favorite artists, founded with her brother and her husband. They wanted to be part of the community and they wanted to give back, so they started an after-school program in New Jersey. It only cost a simple three million dollars a year. First-time juvenile offenders would go in front of a judge and they could choose six months in a reformatory or six months in an after-school program at the Whole Theatre Company. They had an after-school apprentice program in acting, directing, production and writing, and the younger actors in the company ran it. The statistics were remarkable. The grade averages went up. Attendance went up. The rates of recidivism plunged. Then a certain Republican governor, who I think became involved in the environment under Bush, axed it after ten years. But when I met Olympia I was trying to talk my way into being director of education in that program. She said, "No, you don't have the credentials for it." I have worked with her since, and every time I tell her she was a cultural hero. She saved lives for ten years.

There are a couple of things I want to get back to when I quit my day job, and one is I want to work with the juvenile population. Where do we cut the arts? We're cutting it in elementary school. That's the point of crisis. I want to work with the senior population. I'll be of an age that I'll be one of them. I want to work with senior citizens on a production of *Romeo and Juliet* with eighty-year-old Romeos and eighty-year-old Juliets. I want people to interpolate the memory of the first boy or girl they loved. I've been working for the past three summers with elementary public school teachers on the Cape. I believe that all of us can write. I know that fourth graders can write. I know that first graders can write. I know that women who don't know how to write, who are actually illiterate, can write. They write from memory. They write orally. They write beautifully. I mean, the access of their memory and how they write is extraordinary. I've had colleagues who've said, "Oh, that's social work." The charge of cultural elitism is diminishing the art form and the function of theater. We have to think of a way in essence to replenish and propagate and make it accessible. And since we don't have any means in which tickets are free or are such a small amount, it's really about community centers. It's really about prison work. It's really about after-school work. It's really about everything I learned from Perseverance Theatre and Molly Smith, who went on rafts up the river to perform *The Importance of Being Earnest* in logging camps.

Audience: Why not just continue doing your work, which is so funny and strange and bizarre? I hear what you're saying about the box. It's stuff that we're all familiar with. Do you fight with yourself about what you said earlier?

Oh, I do. I'm in a period of postpartum, so take nothing I say seriously right now. I also feel that as a writer I have to stretch my muscles by doing what I've never done before. One gets entrapped by one's own voice. I know that I probably have a voice. I don't know what it is. I'm interested in writers who have a large spectrum possible, where no play is ever the same. I've never worked, really, with music. I've never worked, really, in terms of fiction or, as we'll call it now, creative nonfiction, in a way that might do something to my sense of time. There are a number of things that I haven't done that I'm terrified to do. I'm interested in seeing what happens when there's a writer's voice that's not between the lines. Part of it's the stretch. When I start talking about my approach to theater I say I'm a Russian formalist simply because over and over I thread the same damn two essays, translated by Victor Shklovsky, that say the function of art is to make one notice, to actually slow down perception. We only notice our watch when it's broken. That's when it has aesthetic function. In a play world it really is impeding or slowing down perception rather than the speeding up. This is a problem because we're no longer an audience that reads. We're an audience that processes cinematically. That is the way we think. Time is speeding up. There used to be six cuts in film in the sixties and now we're up to ninety cuts per minute. What is that doing to our perception of time? How do we respond with dramatic apparatus?

I am feeling the box right now. I'm feeling the box as a middle-aged writer. I feel a sense of frustration that next year I'm doing *The Oldest Profession*, which I wrote when I was twenty-nine years old. It's been done in Czechoslovakia. It's been done in Mexico City. It has been done in Russia. There's never been a professional production in this country. There've been university productions. There is a benign censorship, and over time the frustration grows.

Audience: Your censorship?

Not that I'm censoring myself. I hear directors in regional theaters and not-for-profit New York theaters talk about how the script doesn't work. I've read the scripts that they're rejecting. I read the scripts by extraordinary writers that get passed around, and I know that there's a great generation out there right now. That script works quite well, thank you very much. I can't get on a one-on-one with them right now, much less with my own work. So there's a point you start to think in an Aphra Behn way. Maybe there's a direct appeal in reader-to-reader. When I was younger, I think I started three theater companies on my own. But doing that on top of the day jobs, on top of writing, gets kind of prohibitive.

I'm not arguing that I won't write again, but I'm feeling a frustration with the apparatus. I believe in a very old-fashioned form of theater. I believe in playwriting. I believe in having a script. If you don't have a script, you can't have resistance to a script as directors and actors. Because of that kind of trifurcated modality, it is not a collaborative way of forging the work. It's a kind of call-and-response between participants that requires a production, that requires an apparatus of people in the seats. All of those things need friction. I am recognizing that I'm enjoying watching the work of my graduate writers and my undergraduate writers more than I am enjoying my own work right now. That's telling me something.

Audience: What are you enjoying about their work?

Voices I've never heard. It's a way of looking at theater I've never seen, that's never existed in the world before. I need to kick my butt in some serious way that it goes so far out on a limb that I don't hear the sound of my own voice anymore. I've been saying to myself I'm concentrating on the techniques. I'm saying to myself, and it's true, I enjoy the process and not the production. I do. I enjoy the process. What I don't enjoy, what gets very, very hard over time, which I should not be thinking about, but I do, is the money. I should not be thinking about the money. I think about the money. I know people tell me they don't read the reviews. I read every one. I want to see what's getting through and what's not. I'm very curious about how my future play is getting written by the response of critics. Maybe I shouldn't be doing that, but curiosity killed the cat.

So, it's not to say that I'm not writing again, but that I'm aware that I need to gather stock of different devices, different techniques. To stretch. I can't stretch myself if I know I only have four weeks and it's going to be produced like every other play on the planet in that regional or not-for-profit system.

AB: You're also burdened by your own reputation. You're burdened by a Pulitzer Prize.

It's the problem of voice over time. I often wonder how actors do two years—you suddenly get to the point where you go, "Oh, God, am I doing *The Count of Monte Cristo* again? I've been touring the country with *The Count of Monte Cristo* for so long." I think there's part of that also in the writing.

AB: When Robert Woodruff came and did Columbia's directing program, it was his first time to teach like that. I think his work with young directors took him out of the eighties and into the new century. I think he was totally stuck in the eighties. They kicked his ass into the twenty-first century. He knows it—and I think he's really grateful for it.

I saw the look on his face. He was working with these actors at A.R.T., and he doesn't want to leave town. I have a hard time coming to New York because if I stay in the room in Providence with these actors who have been gathered from around the country, I will see things that I will never see in New York. I'll see things five, ten years before other people see them. It's an addiction. It's a hook.

Audience: *The Long Christmas Ride Home* seemed to give me space to open to it. As you go through the black hole, they say time doesn't slow down, but it's suspended theoretically.

I think that space is also something I learned from Anne on *Baltimore Waltz*. The suspension of time is really whether or not there's a production text that does resist as well as speed up with the playwright's text. That's what interests me very, very deeply. Whose memory is it? There are personal moments of witnessing for every collaborator in every process.

Audience: If you write novels you're going to miss that.

I will. But I'll learn something that I think I need to learn.

AB: Robert Anton, who was one of the early victims of AIDS, was an extraordinary puppeteer. His finger puppets were so small—he could only seat eighteen people at a time. You sat around the stage and he built these mountains and castles out of ceramics, and on his fingertips he put puppets with incredible faces and beautiful headdresses. He would do these scenes with these puppets that were about huge things—huge romances and huge stories. And in the middle of the production I saw, he took the puppets off of his fingers and he created a scene between two fingers. That was the most emotional scene I've ever seen. If he'd done that in the beginning it wouldn't have worked. He brought us to a place where he had taken away all of the artifice. And what is happening in that moment is why you're right. The audience is writing the play. He's giving them the slightest signifiers to create a sign. That's the issue of space and slowness.

It takes me a while to process whatever I dared to do that didn't quite work. *The Long Christmas Ride* doesn't work, and I think I know why. I didn't quite counter the difference in language with inanimate objects. Language works with human bodies in a much different way in terms of text. I believe that we hear by what we see and we see by what we hear. The two senses cross. It's what Bert States says in *Great Reckonings in Little Rooms*: We hear through the eyes and we see through the ears. So the impact of how that language worked with puppets was something I failed at. What I was in it for was to see the contrast of the human body and the puppet. That's what was moving me. I talk about being in the throes of puppet love, but the truth of the matter is I was trying to find a way to slow down perception so I could see the human body again by colliding with puppets, and to see the contrast of that. I didn't quite realize how to make the text work with that. It would probably take me three or four years of just being quiet with it to figure out what that means.

I remember standing in the back of the room watching you and Cherry during *Baltimore Waltz* rehearsal. You would suddenly say, "Okay, Cherry, can you suddenly be an eighteenth-century lady with a fan and waltz to the end of the sofa?" And Cherry, of course, being trained by Anne Bogart, curtsied to an imaginary suitor, did a beautiful waltz, took her hand and there was a fan, and right at the end she got to the end of the sofa. My mouth dropped to the floor. I didn't know you could do that. It took me a while to write from that—four or five years. Four or five years for me is nothing— it's like no time at all. You know the questions that lead off most preview interviews? "Oh, you haven't been in New York since *How I Learned to Drive*. What have you been doing with yourself?" It's that slowing down of time. But in order to process that, it seems to me, we have to go to other art forms.

I'm still trying to think about why I failed with *Hot 'N' Throbbing*. I'm going to have to do that over next year. I'm still trying to grapple, and the things that are exciting are the failures. I think it should be impossible for a play to really work. I think plays ought to be some kind of messy, failed, flawed models that great directors make sense of in the future—in the way that you pick up a text written in 1401 and now it works. But it didn't work in 1401. It didn't work in its time. It has to be put together and rewritten in the room.

AB: That's a pretty radical idea—that a play should only work not in your time.

I also believe—this may sound kind of creepy—that theater is really a mediation between the dead and the living. When I write, I'm very aware that in every play I'm writing a tribute to other writers. I'm responding to the dead. Or people in my life who are dead. I'm thinking a lot about *Danton's Death*. I'm trying to respond. I think plays need to work to some extent in the time that they are written because we're writing the play. But I also think that JoAnne Akalaitis's response to *Endgame* was wonderful. I thought it made a play work beyond its time. It was set in a postapocalyptic subway station and, at that moment in time, it worked. It was a personal response from JoAnne Akalaitis to *Endgame* that completely electrified me—before it was closed by the Beckett Estate. I thought that the Wooster Group's handling of *The Crucible* was extremely true to the intent. We're in this delicate balance of wanting to be a participant in the room as writers, of wanting to have our voices coming through, but also wanting the resistance to the voice, and knowing that it has to be reinterpreted continually through time. And knowing that in many ways it's ephemeral. Theater is about mortality. It is us thinking that this is our brief hour on the stage. You're always thinking about that. What do I leave behind? Is there any way to leave anything behind? How do I get—in a good way—eradicated and reinterpreted over a generation?

I would like to see theater companies, major regional theater companies, have an evening that is produced by artists who are thirty or younger—designed, written, directed. What we've got here is this elaborate system where you quote-unquote "pay your dues," so that by the time they're finally producing you, you're working on three-martini nights and an ulcer rather than trying to send a message and respond to the world. We've got such a labyrinth to break through in the not-for-profit theater. I read plays by very young writers that I think do work in the moment and that I think will probably work better in fifty years—but they have to be done in the moment for us to have that reinterpretation. That's my greatest concern in this cultural moment. In the theater we have no way of listening. In art in general we're not listening—except to middle-age writers.

Audience: How do we fix that?

We need everyone to feel that they can write. We need to go back and open up the theatrical process in elementary school. We have people who are sports fanatics in this country because everyone is given a baseball, a basketball. We need to do that with theater and music and art so that we are not consumers. We are sports participants in this culture. We need to be arts participants. That's a longer-term fix.

Not only do we need that kind of participation very early on and all the way through, but we need more new producers. The Mnouchkine model is that we produce in a company: I'll be an artist on this show; I'll be an administrator on this show; I'll write the grant monies on this show; but then I'll act on this show. It's that collective model of producing that we need to know. One of the things that I regret about our notion of writing is that we put writers in isolation from knowing how theater companies work. We need to collectively be able to produce as writers.

AB: Ultimately what you're saying is that you don't do it by yourself. You are encouraged to do everything by yourself in this culture, and yet the resistance is to do it collaboratively.

I believe in the circle model—circles rise together quicker than individuals ever can.

Martha Clarke

Martha, to me, has always seemed preternaturally connected to an earlier, perhaps more colorful era. Her two homes in New York City and northwestern Connecticut were each previously inhabited by extraordinary, seminal artists who have stamped our culture profoundly. Martha's home in Manhattan was once that of Marcel DuChamp. Her Connecticut farmhouse belonged to the painter Arshile Gorky who committed suicide by hanging himself in her barn.

Martha, named by her parents in honor of Martha Graham, grew up in a family of musicians in Baltimore, Maryland. She studied at the Juilliard School with Antony Tudor and then danced for three years with the choreographer Anna Sokolow and the Dance Theater Workshop. She became a founding member of Pilobolus Dance Theatre in 1971. In 1978 she co-founded Crowsnest Dance Company. Soon afterward Martha launched a career as the creator of extraordinary full-length works of dance-theater. Her seminal work, created with the support and encouragement of the brilliant producer Lyn Austin and her Music Theatre Group was *The Garden of Earthly Delights* based upon the paintings of Hieronymus Bosch. What followed, also with Music Theatre Group, were *Vienna: Lusthaus*; *The Hunger Artist*; *Miracolo d'Amore* and *Endangered Species*, based upon fin de siècle Vienna, Kafka, Tiepolo and, literally, endangered animals, respectively.

With these radical works, it seemed that Martha had invented a new art form. Her passion for art history, especially painting, fused with a choreographic sensibility, musicality and theatricality made a meaningful imprint upon the field of performing arts. Following her work with Music Theatre Group, Martha moved into a global arena, directing opera, classic plays, song cycles and new adaptations from known literature. She has choreographed for the Nederlands Dans Theater, the Joffrey Ballet, American Ballet Theatre, Rambert Dance Company and the Martha Graham Dance Company, among others. She directed opera at Glimmerglass Opera, New York City Opera, the Canadian Opera Company, the Munich Biennale, the Hong Kong Festival and the English National Opera. She has collaborated with playwrights Charles L. Mee, Christopher Hampton, Richard Greenberg, Alfred Uhry, among many others. She is the recipient of a MacArthur Fellowship, two grants from the Guggenheim Foundation, two Obie Awards, the list goes on.

February 2, 2004

AB: Martha Clarke is engaged in many, many things. She and I both happen to have productions of *A Midsummer Night's Dream* open right now. Martha's is at American Repertory Theater. She's starting a Pirandello piece at New York Theatre Workshop in ten days. She's workshopping a piece at Lincoln Center Theater about Toulouse-Lautrec. She's also working on a new piece for the Martha Graham Dance Company. Martha and I first met because of the wonderful woman, Lyn Austin, who left us two years ago, who hired both of us at different times in our careers. She produced such Martha works as *Endangered Species*; *Vienna: Lusthaus*; the Kafka piece: *The Hunger Artist* and *The Garden of Earthly Delights*. She produced my work for twenty-seven years.

Rather than talking biographically at first, let's talk process. Martha comes from a dance background, and yet she makes theater—or dance-theater. What would you call it?

MC: Stuff.

Stuff. I think you work more intuitively than most people do.

I do work very intuitively, a lot through improvisation and instinct, and I research a lot. The first ideas I usually go with. Sometimes they don't work out.

Where do they come from?

The wind. I mean, the whole process of making things is incredibly mysterious, and I don't know where my ideas come from. They're like a cartoon with a little light bulb. When I was asked to do *A Midsummer Night's Dream*, I immediately thought of Chopin Nocturnes—first idea I had. I wanted the mechanicals to be on a wooden table. It was there. I've worked for many years with a wonderful designer named Robert Israel, and I work with a wonderful composer named Richard Peaslee. I've been very interested in flying. *Garden of Earthly Delights* was done in the early eighties, and *Midsummer* is my third piece working with [Peter] Foy and flight. It's not an aerial flight; it's flight that is connected to the ground. Somebody could take a step, then be out the door—just skim through. I think that when I do these various pieces, it's a continuation, it's my haystacks or cathedral or sunflowers. I consider everything I'm doing a draft of something. The look of *Midsummer* is from *Hunger Artist*. It keeps accumulating, whatever your taste for revision is.

Martha has a house in Connecticut and an apartment in New York. Both had previous inhabitants—and I think this is not coincidence. I think this is your kismet.

My New York apartment was Marcel Duchamp's, and my house in the country was Arshile Gorky's. I didn't look for it. I fell into both.

Are there ghosts?

Nice ghosts. To me.

Didn't Gorky, in the barn—he killed himself?

It was my neighbor's barn. But the house has a lot of presence.

Your sources are painters and composers. Where did that come from? Did you study it?

I went to Juilliard as a dancer and married a sculptor right after graduation. Now I live with a painter. So I guess I am very drawn to visual things. I think with my eyes, really. I think about space and the tension between points. I've worked at the National Theatre in England, and the actors want to analyze the text, and I say, "Just turn your shoulder away." Ultimately they got the same kind of information. I just worked with Gideon Lester during *Midsummer*—it's wonderful to have a really smart dramaturg to take care of the stuff that I really don't.

You said *Midsummer* was also your first play.

It's my first play of a dead playwright. I worked with Chuck Mee. We're doing *Lautrec*, and we did *Vienna: Lusthaus*. I worked with Richard Greenberg on the Kafka, with Sebastian Barry on a musical that flopped and with Christopher Hampton on *Alice*. They're major writers. Chuck and I have a very special working relationship.

Can you talk about how the text develops—the imagery—when you work with Chuck?

Chuck and I have a really bizarre way of working. We'll take a subject, and he'll just begin faxing me pages of writing—no character, no location and no progression. I take the pages into a room with a company of actors of dancers, and the actors speak, and the dancers move. My aim is to try to make the scene seamless. And we find an odd scene. Everybody's got copies of the pages, and I say, "Well, does anybody want to get up with this one?" With Toulouse-Lautrec at Lincoln Center Theater, we have four weeks with wonderful actors—Ruth Maleczech, Marian Seldes, Dennis O'Hare, Peter Dinklage, Michael Stuhlbarg. For the first month we had to find out what the piece was going to be about. Chuck's first writing was about Lautrec paintings. He wrote the paintings down into language in a way. I don't know what's going on with Joseph Cornell. Is that what you do?

No. He usually gives me a play, then we work on the play.

Well, ours is kind of a collage—like Joseph Cornell. I work in movement rehearsals. I do actor rehearsals. Then I work with musicians. Then I begin to interlock them and see at what points they fasten together. It's chaotic. It's fun. It fills me with despair because sometimes—a lot of the time—I don't know what I'm doing. You live with the stuff, and then finally it's like fastening beads on a necklace. It comes together. It's always very mysterious. I work a lot out in conversation. I don't have a company, but I have a small pickup group who are used to my process. By the end we save about fifty percent of what we have made.

I heard years ago someone describe your rehearsal. It's kind of a joke. This despair that you talk about—you say, "Oh, I'm so depressed. I don't know what to do." And then the actors and dancers will say, "Martha! We'll try something! Just sit down and have some tea." And you're holding your dogs, and they'll get up and they'll do something for you, and you say, "Um—could you try it again, but this time naked?" And then you say, "That's beautiful."

And then they'll say that I say, "Turn upstage and do it." They often laugh at me that I love backs. Backs and shoulders. Not good for directing opera.

You've done a bunch of operas. But you're kind of over opera.

A little bit. I think it's over me. I used to talk about fouling certain ponds of water. I'd leave a stage production and think, Oh, I'll go back to dance because it's fresh for me. Then I'd get tired of that, and I'd move on to opera. I just like the change.

What would you say are the differences between working with actors, dancers and singers?

Dancers are very instinctual. They feel their way into a physicality that doesn't need a lot of interpretation. The muscles, skin, bones talk to you, and then the language comes through the body. Actors need to break things down. Up at A.R.T. the company who played the mechanicals were used to working together. I just set them loose. This was like a sandbox for them. I went a few nights ago and they were still doing new things. I gave them a lot of space because they're so good together. There are places they have to get to and then they're free. They're like Monty Python. I pee in my pants, I laugh so hard. And they're wonderful actors. Actors approach things through words, so it's much more specific. Dancers' work is as specific, but the nuance of impulse and gesture gets more refined through repetition. Opera singers have more of a challenge. If they have stressed vocal chords or a cold there is no way for them to camouflage it. A dancer has an injury and in some way moves through it. A singer who has a bad vocal cord—it's over and out.

Which is why singers can be so neurotic.

They are more neurotic. There's a new generation of singers who are wonderful stage performers. I'm most at home with dancers and very physical actors.

I worked with an actor from Peter Brook's company, Robert Langdon Lloyd, who's a great actor. He came and did *Vienna: Lusthaus*. His part didn't need a lot of movement. He had a beautiful presence and a wonderful voice. So it's not just a movement that I like. But movement or stillness must be integral to what that creature, that character is. That gets sculpted.

Do you choreograph on the body?

Some. I have developed a vocabulary of lifts, partnering, that has come out of the work I did with Pilobolus. We do a lot of improvisation and if something catches my eye I begin to shape it like a sculptor with clay.

I think it is actually a big deal, your relationship with Pilobolus. Can you just describe how that began?

It began in the choreography class of Alison Chase in 1971. My husband was artist-in-residence at Dartmouth College, and we had a three-year-old son. I was in Anna Sokolow's company in the sixties; we were at the original Dance Theater Workshop. I quit because Anna's work stopped speaking to me. It was brilliant, but it was incredibly grim. I was terrified of her. She was brilliant—but she was mean. So when I met Pilobolus, it was just three really jocky, funny college guys. Alison and I just started improvising with them, and fooling around, and we kind of seduced our way into the company—it was four men and two women. It was really fun for a while. We were a big international success sort of overnight—particularly in Paris. We screamed a lot, and we adored each other, and we laughed together, and it was also a very fraught collaboration.

When I graduated from Juilliard I did my graduating piece with two dilettantes reading *A Winter's Tale*. Words were always important to me. I loved literature, and I loved biography. I've done work on Franz Kafka—two works on Kafka—one on Hans Christian Andersen, one on Lewis Carroll, now on Toulouse-Lautrec and next on Goya.

The Graham piece? Have you started rehearsing? What do you know?

Nothing.

What do you think you have to know before you go into it?

I used Goya for *Midsummer*. I don't know why I got drawn to that. It's not a family background. Egon Schiele inspired *Vienna*; Hieronymus Bosch inspired *Garden of Earthly Delights*. Do you use painters like that?

Absolutely, but not as much as you do.

I wanted to be a painter—but I was too good of a dancer. So I guess I paint with bodies.

With Lautrec, you've had four or five workshops. You say you throw out sixty percent. So where are you now?

The script is written. It's a process of cutting away to the essential. I've had great cast members I've let go because I didn't have enough for them to do. It's a financially hard time, so I've cut back to fourteen or fifteen now. We had eighteen or nineteen to start.

We as a company face three or four weeks of rehearsal and then we open. If we can workshop ideas at some point with the students, great—but the notion of five workshops before you even start a rehearsal is . . .

André Bishop [artistic director of Lincoln Center Theater] wants it finished so that we can have three weeks of rehearsal and then a tech. It's a contract, like Broadway. Each workshop he's been happy enough to go further, but he's not guaranteeing a performance. He wants to know that that audience in Midtown that goes to Lincoln Center Theater is going to go for a Charles Mee–Martha Clarke evening. He wants to be sure that it is not a downtown show.

For these workshops, are actors, dancers, musicians, designers all in the room together?

The designers haven't come yet. We're using Fauré, Debussy and Satie—and a great opera singer, Joyce Castle, whose playing Yvette Guilbert. You have to have musicians.

Joyce Castle is very tall.

Six feet one.

Standing next to Peter Dinklage.

And I have a French horn player—who's playing, actually, the Wagnerian tuba—who's as wide as she is tall. Then you have Peter, who is diminutive. Ruth Maleczech is playing La Goulue, who is kind of a floozy can-can dancer who died in the streets selling peanuts. It's a great story.

And Marian Seldes?

Marian is doing *The Royal Family*, so we're using Honora Fergusson Neumann in this workshop.

The idea of bringing Marian Seldes and Ruth Maleczech together in the same room is worth the price of entrance.

It truly is. And they're great together.

They're from such different worlds.

But they love each other. Then I have my beautiful dancers: Rob Besserer, playing Valentin, and Alexandra Beller, who is with Bill T. Jones, and is very voluptuous and big. I'm working with two wonderful new dancers named Gabby Malone and Andrew Robinson, who were with Twyla Tharp.

The dance vocabulary is created for each piece. I don't have a technique. I start all over again with each piece.

Audience: Have you been in a situation where you felt like your work didn't develop to the point you wanted it to while you had a deadline?

No, deadlines are good. I mean, *Midsummer* was my first Shakespeare. I had four weeks. And it's up. So, deadlines are okay. But there's a great play. When you're developing a whole new piece—I couldn't do it in four weeks, none of the text-choreography. Choreography takes me a lot longer than directing actors. That's why I'm very happy to be working with text. I just couldn't keep on choreographing. It's boring and it's hard and frustrating.

AB: Can you talk about the Pirandello piece? There was a little junket to Italy, I believe.

I went with Jim Nicola and Lynn Moffat [artistic and managing directors of New York Theatre Workshop, respectively] and the head of their board. We went to Sicily and we lived in a fourteenth-century fortress on the sea. It was pretty nice.

Jim has wanted to do Pirandello for ten years, and when *Vienna: Lusthaus (revisted)* was at New York Theatre Workshop two years ago, he said, "Let's talk about something else." I told him three or four ideas about things I wanted to do. We were walking home, over Greenwich Avenue, and he walked into World of Video and brought out a film called *Kaos*, made by the Taviani brothers based on Pirandello's short stories. He said to take it home and watch it, and I did. I called him and said, "I love it. Let's do it." We have an Italian-speaking cast. I have an Italian composer. The stories are like ancient Greek myths. They're about peasants in Sicily at the turn of the century. The first story is about tradition and those Sicilians and Italians who migrated to America. The second story is about insanity in a group. There's also the presence of Pirandello talking to his dead mother. We took the script of the film to Frank Pugliese who adapted the screenplay for the stage. We've intersected three short stories—it's a little bit like *A Midsummer Night's Dream*, which is three stories.

AB: So this is the workshop you're starting in ten days? Not the rehearsal?

Jim's not ready. It takes him a while to decide. The composer is writing amazing music. Do you know Sicilian songs? We're using the Lomax collection of music.

Audience: Since you both directed the same play, I'm interested in knowing what you learned, what you discovered about the play?

AB: Ours opened this past Friday at San Jose Repertory Theatre, which I'm here to report is the best regional theater—outside of A.R.T.—in the country. It's unbeliev-able—the way they take care of you, the theater itself. It's this big, blue modernist building. On the outside it looks kind of ugly and impressive, and inside it's this Renaissance jewel.

I learned this: I think we are very narrow as human beings in our culture, and I think we've been made very narrow in the rainbow spectrum of being. I find that the width of humanity inside of those characters in *Midsummer* puts us to shame. I was just blown away by the wide spectrum of humanity in the characters, in what they go through, their transformations. We had eight people playing twenty-six characters. Barney O'Hanlon plays Puck and is kind of the stage manager. Everybody else was an Athenian, a fairy and a mechanical, so they had to transform. It all comes together in the end, when they have to be everybody at the same time, which is really inter-esting. You realize that contained in one human being is the potential to be a fairy. I discovered for our production that being a fairy means where you go when you go to sleep. You lose your physical constraints and you go other places. And that's really, for me, the big realization.

For me it was just the writing—the emotionality of desire and transforma-tion. It's that huge pendulum swing. When I directed the Mozart opera—to sit in the presence of Mozart every day—I was awed by it, as I am awed by the language of Shakespeare. My favorite line is, "With leaden legs and batty wings doth creep." There are certain passages that were like painting. I am just in awe of the language—although Gideon and I cut about a fifth.

AB: For me the most important part of the play is when Theseus and Hippolyta wake the lovers up, and, after all the sturm und drang, after all the drugged dreaming, pas-sion, desire, Helena says, "I realized Demetrius is mine and not mine, like a jewel, that I know nothing." They come out of it saying, "I know absolutely nothing that I thought I knew before." That to me is such a moment of grace. Chuck Mee said the difference with Shakespeare and other writers, is that in most plays you start out not knowing the characters and by the end you feel like you know them. But with Shakes-peare, you start out thinking you know the characters, and by the end you don't know them. That's what I felt—that they just widened out. They became unknown.

Gideon Lester, the associate artistic director of A.R.T., saw Anne's production as well. He said they're so different, it's unbelievable. I even took that line away from Helena. Mine woke up to a Chopin Nocturne that kept over-lapping itself like the way sounds do when you're waking up from a dream.

Audience: How did you both handle act five of that play—after they come back into the world? Was that hard?

Well, Theseus and Hippolyta come into the wood, and it went pretty quickly with Pyramus and Thisbee. We just let the humor go. But there was nothing much made of the wedding—just the lovers. Theseus and Hippolyta were definitely a dysfunctional couple, as were Oberon and Titania (played by the same actors). Definitely sensual. Hippolyta was kind of an angry housewife. I had fairies flying. The fairies fell asleep, so that it becomes like a dream, and floated through the blackness asleep about fifteen feet in the air. We used the Mendelssohn. Those beautiful opening chords were the last thing you heard.

AB: I can't actually describe the fifth act without telling you how we got to where we went. As a company we've been touring for many years. All these arts centers, theaters and festivals, say to us, "We can't afford you anymore because you need a two- or three-day load-in, because you're so technical, and your lighting . . ." Rather than ignore this situation, I wanted to do a work that actually addressed that issue: Can I do *Midsummer* with eight people to begin with? Because it was in San Jose I started thinking about the dust bowl and Steinbeck, *The Grapes of Wrath*, and the thirties depression. I was also thinking about many indigenous villages in Alaska that have something called the talking stick. For hundreds of years, people would sit around at night and draw on the ground with the stick and start to tell a story. About fifteen years ago into all the villages came television, and for the first time in a number of years the sticks disappeared. This culture we're in is dominated by mediated experiences, really fast buzz, and that gets very confusing and disorienting. And yet this is also a culture where the poor are getting poorer and the rich and getting richer by the second. I wanted to bring this all together with a company no one can afford anymore. *Midsummer* is a play about the theater, disorientation and love, these three amazing things. I wanted to solve it without any technical things, and turn to the actors and say, "This play is about magic and theater and love. You have nothing. Please make the magic." I started talking to Neil Patel, the designer, about dirt. Neil came back with a mirror. Then a backdrop.

This is to get around to the question about the fifth act. The play is so much about the theater, and about making something from nothing. The fifth act, for me, has to break down all the rules of the theater—break down not only the fourth wall, but also it had to become these particular actors in a room with an audience. At the end of the play there is a blessing. I wanted to get to a point where the actors bless this house that we are all in together, so there was no barrier.

It's difficult doing Shakespeare. It's the same with Mozart operas. People come with expectations. We had an empty set. Bob Israel made these beautiful bright blue backdrops with oilcloth white stars. Robert Woodruff [artistic director of A.R.T.] said, "I don't think you need the backdrop. Why don't you just do it with a piece of black?" I think Robert was right—but some people say, "Oh, this is not summery." It's not frothy. Many people's expectations of *A Midsummer Night's Dream* is that it should be light. Ours looks like Goya and Ingmar Bergman. So it wasn't everybody's *Midsummer Night's Dream*.

AB: The issue with *Midsummer* is that there are scholars who look at it as a great, misogynist, negative work, and then there are others who say, "No, you can't do it that way."

Harold Bloom is coming to ours.

AB: Oh, you're in big trouble.

I know. Apparently the two *Midsummer*s he hates are Peter Brook's and Alvin Epstein's. He'll hate this.

AB: It's not bad to be hated by Harold Bloom.

No. It's not.

Audience: Martha, you said that the work you're doing now is often a draft for the work you'll be doing next. I wondered if that's something you realize in the moment, or is it only looking back that you see a thread that's run through your work? Are you conscious of it as it's happening?

I work a bit, leave it, come back, and clarity emerges in retrospect. Whales take twenty-four months to make a baby. You carry them around a long time. You have to work real hard and then you leave it alone. I used to be in despair all the time. I thought if I didn't suffer, I couldn't work. Now I know if I don't have a good time, I can't work. I have to like who I'm working with. I have to care passionately for it. But it's also just theater. It's not a disease; it's not rocket science.

AB: Rocket science maybe.

You think so?

Audience: What type of things intimidated you, and how did you reconcile what intimidated you and make it your own?

AB: I bet we're going to say the same thing—the text. It was our first Shakespeare. I don't speak the language.

Often when I go to Shakespeare I'm kind of bored. When I get to know it like this, I worship it. But when you just go to hear *Henry IV* or something, and you're not that familiar with the text, I fade. It could be wonderful performing, and I could know it's wonderful performing, but I just don't hear it. So I was worried about caring about every bit of language. For somebody who really likes the human body more than language, that was terrifying. But I had a great dramaturg.

AB: I actually stole her dramaturg for a day. I said, "Can you help me cut the text? I want to make it fast. It should be like an hour and a half." He's a Brit—and that's his language. We cut the shit out of it.

He said you put it all back.

AB: We put it all back. What I learned about is the monumental action of speaking that text. It is about embracing that. It is about not making it easy, but about making it unbelievably powerful and a mountain for both the audience and actors to jump on. It's a big gym.

You have to be literal and also throw it to the clouds. You have to harness it in the emotional reality completely so that it's completely understandable in our terms, then get completely poetic and musical.

AB: It's so odd because the Shakespeare wars among academics that have been going on for centuries—they're passionate about things that actually I think you shouldn't pay attention to at all. I empathize with the actors because it feels like you're jumping off a cliff, and carving as you're falling. If you're not doing that, you're not doing it right.

And I think many people in your average American audience want to hear a lot of the proper English elocution more than grounded emotional reality. Some people have trouble with the fact that they spoke the way we speak.

AB: Did you have a classical music background?

At Juilliard. My father was a lawyer, but also a jazz composer. Fats Waller recorded his music. My grandfather, other side, collected rare violins and chamber music of the eighteenth century. I don't read music. My son is a jazz pianist.

AB: Until I met Darron West, the sound designer for the SITI Company, I used to design all the music for the shows. I'd spend a lot of time with music. Music was everything, and music was under everything. I first worked with him about twelve years ago for *Eye of the Hurricane*. I'd brought in all of this music that was Cuban dance music, and I'd studied this music because I studied music for every project. We sat in his music studio and listened to the recordings, and then I just gave them to him. Most designers would come in at tech and then take my music and make it technical. Darron started coming in and being in rehearsal. That began what we've been doing for twelve years, which is that he's in every rehearsal. What he brings in is much more sophisticated. He's now always turning me on to music.

One of Mnouchkine's collaborators said once, "Music makes theater bearable."

Music makes life bearable.

AB: I find that, too.

It's transporting.

AB: I find that that can be a problem because it can be actually overpowering. We say in the SITI Company that we want the music to sound like it's coming from the body. So how do you do that as an actor to make it feel that way?

Audience: So many productions now essentially have created soundtracks for themselves, because they're playing to a film-educated audience. It's almost as if people are afraid of silence on stage now. There always has to be something telling you how to feel. The color is always having to be externally applied, rather than by the performers. When you're working with something like Shakespeare where the music is there—is it just like applying one color over another?

I didn't use it like a soundtrack. I used it to create a setting. And for the fairies. We had songs by Richard Peaslee, a cappella. I had one of my mechanicals play the clarinet. I had one little girl play little hand cymbals. She was a fairy. During Helena's monologue, Chopin came back, and we used it on a slide whistle. For the mechanicals: Will LeBow played old film music on an upright that was really out of tune. He played Chopin and kind of jazzed it up for Pyramus and Thisbe. It was very funky. And charming, but it didn't underscore anything. So there was just language. We used a lot of natural sounds. Birds. Every time Oberon spoke there was the sound of a crow. Tree frogs or loons. It was subliminal.

AB: We used underscoring at times, but it's really tricky. I think the point you're making is huge. I think if it's used properly, in a John Cage sense, something is as

silent as the sound on either side, or it's always as big. But the contrast actually makes you hear the silence in a more profound way, and the silence is an absolute thing. It's an object.

It tells you what to think. It gives you the tools to figure out how to smell it, how to see it, how to listen to it. In Lautrec I am using underscore for some of Chuck's text, it's alive with subtlety. We're using Debussy. It's wonderful with text over it because it's so spare. You can't take music away from Toulouse-Lautrec—except to make a statement, then you really dry it out. I use that expression: Dry it out.

Audience: Was that what brought you to this Shakespeare play, as opposed to any other Shakespeare play for your first one?

Robert Woodruff said, "What would you like to do at A.R.T.?" I said Chekhov. He said, "I'm doing too much Chekhov." I said, "Well, maybe *A Midsummer Night's Dream.*" And he called me in a few days later and said, "You're doing *A Midsummer Night's Dream.*" I said, "Well, I don't know if that's really what I wanted to do." But I thought of all the Shakespeare plays it was the best one for me. I was Puck when I was fourteen.

AB: It's amazing how many people were in *A Midsummer Night's Dream*. That's one of the reasons I chose it—people do come with built-in expectations. That's why I like things like *South Pacific* or plays that people have done a lot. They come with baggage.

Audience: What was your greatest obstacle with an actor, and how did you get through it?

In this production? I had to yell a little. I hate yelling. I had seventeen people in my cast, and fifteen I'd never worked with before. A.R.T. gets great directors. Anne's directed up there, and Andrei Serban and Peter Sellars. All these Eastern European dudes have directed up at A.R.T. You come into a company who has been together for twenty years, and the first few days I felt like they were waiting. I gave them a lot of freedom to improvise. I want to see what your instincts are, as an actor, and I kind of echo those instincts. They really all responded to the freedom. Some actors have to shoot themselves in the foot sometimes and get all bizarre and go through a kind of a meltdown, and it's part of their process. They have to get really upset before they find the role. Since I performed for many years, I know you just get paranoid that you're not good enough. We had very few *scènes de ménage*, and you just kind of stroke and talk and build up their confidence and they get through it. Performing is really hard. It's a really naked thing. I used to feel like a piece of meat going out sometimes. I have complete sympathy for having to sit through six hundred people per night for sixty shows in a well-known classic in a fucked-up production. You have to find the universe of the ensemble. It was as happy as I've ever been working—for one thing, because I didn't have to make it up. I always had a great play. We weren't dependent on our imagination to get through it. There were times when each performer was brilliant, and there were times when it wasn't very good. What you want to do is get them at least to a level of security where it at least can be pretty good and occasionally brilliant. No performer can turn in eight great shows a week. If they turn in one great show, two fairly good shows, three mediocre shows and one that stinks, that's a good average.

AB: That's depressing.

I mean, as a performer you don't love what you do every night. Some shows you just have a bad audience. You can't feel aggressive about it.

AB: I hate to quote David Mamet, always. He says good things—I just hate the way he says them. He said that audiences learn from one another. They give each other permission.

Audience: How do you approach the magical aspect of a show? There's a lot of magic in *A Midsummer Night's Dream*. Do you approach it differently?

I am developing a lovely new way of using flying. I knew my fairies were going to be earthbound but using the technique of flight. I'm not intimidated by magic. I lust for it. You know, it's the most exciting thing in our work. I'm like a child who finger paints. It's the inexplicable, the stuff that's not called for—that's stuff that I love. I never get scared by it, I am just challenged by it. Language is intimidating, but magic is something that is a delight to make. That aspect, to define the ineffable, is to me the most exciting.

AB: I think also what's so appealing about magic is that it is, at its heart, non-descriptive. And that's where it makes theater theatrical. It is poetry.

It's like saying, "Are you intimidated to have fun?" That's the reason we stay with it. I come back because I know there will be moments where the magic happens, and that has to sustain you through long dry spells.

Julie Taymor

I am in awe of Julie's presence in the world. I see her as an impressive persona striding across the globe, making huge demands on herself and others. And these demands pay off mightily with audiences and collaborators everywhere. Her high standards and hard work produce work with both artistic integrity and mass appeal.

While Julie's work in theater, puppetry, opera, design and film all feel to me like huge artistic adventures, I am most moved by the fact that she is foremost a *world* adventurer. Literally. She travels widely, always has, soaking in experience, studying native cultures and using her curiosity like an incisive knife. Her adventures become the material for her exuberant and brilliant work.

This travel began early. During the sixties, just a teenager, Julie lived in Sri Lanka and India as part of what was called the Experiment in International Living program. Later on, she studied with Jacques Lecoq in Paris. After graduating from Oberlin College in 1974, with a degree in folklore and mythology, she studied puppetry and Japanese theater in Japan. Then she spent five years in Indonesia where she began to make her own brand of art.

I remember when she first arrived in New York City, sometime in the beginning of the eighties. I first met her on the corner of Fourth Street and Bowery, where the director Larry Sacharow introduced us. Immediately I was impressed with her attitude, intellect and ambitions. In New York her influence quickly took root due to her innovative technique and indisputable originality. She began by working with the directors Andrei Serban and Liz Swados, bringing a visual dimension to their work that wowed audiences everywhere. Her collaboration with Andrei Serban yielded a production of *The King Stag* that toured the world for years.

Right now Julie is practically a household name due to her enormous success with Disney and *The Lion King*. But what many people do not realize is the broad spectrum of her oeuvre. Her opera direction and design include Stravinsky's *Oedipus Rex*, Mozart's *The Magic Flute*, Strauss's *Salome*, working with important conductors such as Zubin Mehta, Valeri Gergiev and Seiji Ozawa. She earned an Emmy Award for the *Oedipus Rex* that she directed in Japan and then filmed and edited for television.

Julie gives us unforgettable theatrical productions such as *Juan Darién*, *Titus Andronicus* and *The Green Bird*. And then there are the films. Who but Julie would have the courage to reimagine the work of the Beatles for *Across the Universe*. Her films *Frida* and *Titus Andronicus* made her a unique player in Hollywood. Julie is a visual genius. She designs masks, puppets, costumes and many of the sets for her productions.

Julie's impact upon our shared profession is profound. As a female director in the world, producing large-scale theatrical canvases with courage, intensity and expressive brilliance, she has no equal.

March 15, 2004

AB: For years Julie made other people's work look beautiful. Then she went on to show us all what aesthetics can be about in not only in an intimate theater, but in a large theater, in an opera house, on film, and in both the not-for-profit and the commercial worlds. What would have happened if you'd never traveled as a young thing? How does that affect you to this day in your choices, both in terms of what you're doing and how you're doing it?

JT: I wouldn't be me if I weren't a traveler so it's hard to say what I would be doing if I didn't travel. Even when I was going from Newton, Mass., to Boston Children's Theatre, from the suburbs to the city, even getting out of my own suburb, being with kids from South Boston, Dorchester, was already a thing that made me go outside of my own insular little world, my safe world. I went to Sri Lanka when I was thirteen or fourteen, went to Paris when I was sixteen and traveled all around. The major experience, of course, was the time I spent in Indonesia for four years at the age of twenty-one. I graduated high school early and went to Paris for a year and studied at Lecoq's.

Then I worked with Herbert Blau at Oberlin College. Where I thrive is being put into a circumstance where I lose my bearings. I like not knowing what is going to happen. The movie *Titus* was so difficult to pull off in Italy. The whole crew was Italian. We had these major movie stars. It was my first feature film. You do have to kind of wear blinders to keep you focused on your goal. It's not like you're floundering.

Your film projects have a certain—you didn't use this word, but I'll say it—perversity.

I don't think they're perverse. Everybody thinks their own thing is very commercial and everybody will love it. *The Transposed Heads*—I did that as a play in 1984. I did it as a musical Off-Broadway in 1986. I made a film script of it with Sidney Goldfarb, the playwright. We couldn't get enough money. It would be very hard to do this film for four million dollars. So every time I bring it for a larger budget, people just die when the heads get lopped off and put on other bodies. It just stops right there.

Is it not perverse?

Elliot [Goldenthal] and I have decided to do something even more difficult. We're going to make a movie musical, which will be even more expensive and weirder.

I say hold on and wait until that happens. Don't give in.

Oh, we're not waiting. I'm serious. We're doing it.

I loved what you said—everything you do is about going somewhere that disorients you. Could we just talk about your relationship to Elliot Goldenthal, who is not only your partner, but also your collaborator, which is an extraordinary and rare relationship to find. And it seems like it's really successful. Somehow your relationship has been a source of a lot of work.

Well, a lot of my things are very musically based. Music is a very important part. So, we are always looking to do things together. Except for *The Lion King*, I've only worked with Elliot—on *The Tempest* and Shakespeare and *The Green Bird*, two musicals. We're doing this opera, *Grendel* . . .

Twenty years in the making.

We started it in '86, and it's now scheduled for 2006. [In 2006, *Grendel* premiered at the Los Angeles Opera and was subsequently a finalist for a Pulitzer Prize.] I'm very excited about this opera because a composer in film is the last person on. They're really at the mercy of the director. It's amazing that we survived *Titus*. I learned what I would do the next time, which we did on *Frida* and it worked much better. But finally, with an opera, the composer is the top banana. I'm excited about that. I'm excited that if I don't like the music, tough shit. I'm hoping I'll like it, but there will be places where he gets to decide. Opera is a composer's medium.

Do you get different visuals with the music where you go through the music to come to the visuals?

Well, *Juan Darién* is a good example of that because we started with a six-page short story by Horacio Quiroga. It was our first real piece together. We started to work on it and just let it open up. We created a lot of it in Mexico. He did this music and I said, "It sounds like hundreds of butter-flies." So, in that case, the music inspired the imagery. I think with *Juan Darién* it was a lot like that because we were working simultaneously cre-ating it. It existed really just in scenario form.

What about in *Oedipus* the opera? That's a good overwhelming score.

Well, one of the things that I really do feel committed to is going to the original author's intent. So, in *Oedipus Rex*, Stravinsky and Cocteau wanted masks. My dilemma was putting a mask on Jessye Norman's face—or any opera singer. I understand the principle. The idea is that this opera is not about individuals, but icons. He wanted them larger than life, icono-graphic. You say the words "larger than life." I followed a lot of the ideas of Cocteau and Stravinsky for *Oedipus* and came up with the notion that—which I then stole for *The Lion King*, but it's different—if you put that larger-than-life mask on the head, then what the face is is really the emo-tion of the music. It's not about the individuality of Jocasta or Oedipus. It is really the emotion of the music coming through.

That's a fantastic notion.

So you have a duality there. The masks in *Oedipus* were inspired by Cycladic art. In Cycladic art there are these little sculptures, and they are the essence of humanity. There are no eyes. There's no mouth. There's just a shape. And they're so beautiful. It's the ideograph approach that's been a very big part of the way that I think.

Remind me of the ideograph.

Probably the word was introduced to me by Herbert Blau, but once I understood what it was, I went back to the mime school and I under-stood that's what we were doing. What an ideograph is—I'm going to try and make it very simple—you can tell the beginning and the middle and the end of anything, of an image, of a character, of a story, in three brush strokes. It's the abstract. It's the essence. It's the least you can do to tell the whole story. Japanese calligraphy is ideographic because they do a whole bamboo forest with just a *(Mimes brush strokes)*. I have used that as a director and as a designer my whole career.

You learned that from Herbert Blau?

I learned it probably in mime school without knowing what it was. I didn't really like mime. What I loved was that it really taught me how to use the body. One of the things that we did was to take elements and try to show with your body what fluidity of water was, or the burning of a candle. You're not trying to *look* like a candle. You're trying to get to the essence of what wax melting would be. Eventually that is what you can use for a character. You know how we use dogs. "She's a bulldog." In a way, when you say, "That woman is like a poodle," we all get an image of an Upper East Side white lady with a little . . .

So you can do an ideograph with a word?

You can. Let's use *The Lion King*, which many people have seen. I had the dilemma of the animated film. At the top of the second act, there is drought. In the movie, leaves fall off trees and trees burn—you have drought. You have all this detail. So I say, "Okay, if I were to show that in one motion, what would it be?" So you have a circle, which is the ideograph of *The Lion King* because of *The Circle of Life*. You have a circle of water, which is a piece of silk, which gets pulled into a hole. That's it. And that is drought.

How do you come to that? I mean, ideographs are a fantastic notion, but . . . how do you use ideographs? What's the process that gets you something as simple and as elegant as you emerge with?

Well, you say, "What would be the first word you'd think of for drought?" I suppose it's one of those games. You think of dryness and the lack of water. All through, if you pay attention, you hear they're going to the water hole, the water hole, the water hole. So the water hole is going to be the main thing. I don't need other details.

Are you sketching when you're thinking this?

Sometimes, but not always. I'll give you more really easy, simple examples. You have Mufasa and Scar. Even if you were to start like I used to, with a company, if I'm to make a mask of Scar, I'm responsible for the essence of the character. So if I were to say, "Who is Scar?" Start with the scar. Why does someone get a scar? It's like a puzzle. They get the scar because they were in a fight. And what else happened? Maybe they hurt their legs. Then they're lopsided. Say they're a snake because it's animals. Everything about Scar is serpentine. I looked at African tribal sculptures in performance, and whenever they had a mask with a head, for the legs, they'd just use sticks. They'll just walk around with two sticks. It's so elegant and beautiful. So I thought, "Wonderful. What if this stick is a cane?" So it's both his third leg—he doesn't have a fourth because he was in a fight. He's also very arch, so it's got that whole period style. I don't know if any of you saw Derek Smith do it. Derek had done the king in *The Green Bird*, and he's one of the greatest mask performers I've ever seen. So, he got the cat, the whole lion movement there.

And you go to Mufasa and you say he's all about balance and symmetry. The circle becomes very prominent. So what it does for actors is actually—I believe limitations are very liberating. Garth Fagan has a beautiful expression in the dance world: "Discipline is freedom." It goes back to this wonderful story that I heard of a Japanese Noh actor who was asked about the use of the kimono. And in Noh theater, if you raise your arm higher than parallel to the floor, the kimono will crease. *(She demonstrates, showing us the subtle distance)* So it's all how you go from here to here. I've often felt in dance, in modern dance or ballet, that we'd always see humans' limitations, but if you control it, and you bring it down, the artistry is how you do that within that structure. It's why period pieces are interesting for actors, because all of a sudden a woman can't sit like this. Or you have this collar, the corset, whatever. It informs so much of who you are. It makes you feel a certain way. It is definitely the outside-in approach. In my opinion you go both ways.

Then there's that thing that's really hard to talk about. The T word. Taste. You have taste. It's true. It's inescapable. Certainly there's an issue of influence, but you see it in—Frida the film is an unbelievable visual sensibility. Do you think that's DNA?

Yes. It's your aesthetic. When I started *The Lion King* I was very plain-spoken to the producers that it's just not my aesthetic—the airbrushed look. That doesn't mean I don't have a Timon that doesn't look like their Timon in the movie. But my Timon, if you really want to compare, he's completely lopsided. Even though they are familiar, they're not exactly in that Disney aesthetic style.

There's something a little bit off.

They're skewed.

Which, in a way, wakes up the image. I also don't want to miss talking about how you get by making sure you have control over your aesthetics in a piece like *The Lion King*.

Well, I think by the time I was asked to do that, I was an old lady. They weren't going to ask me, and then tell me that I had to—I wouldn't have done it. I felt with Tom [Thomas Schumacher] the producer, that he was very receptive to my style, how I wanted to do it.

That's interesting. It's not so much that you were making demands as finding the right producer.

Definitely. I've never had an issue in theater. Film is a navigation. I had huge fights on *Frida*—huge fights in post-production over taste. On the end-credit song, I got the suggestion that—I think she's a good singer, but that Christina Aguilera should sing it, not Caetano Veloso. You know what I'm saying? It's like, "Who's Caetano Veloso?" So we paid our own way and recorded him ourselves. I wouldn't shoot what I didn't want to shoot. There are games you play.

What is it that Hitchcock did? He would figure it out so that no matter what anybody did in the editing room, they had to do it his way because he would shoot it so scientifically.

If you don't have a lot of coverage, then people can't ruin it. But they can cut. It was a big fight about the cutting, about the editing. There was a six-month standoff. I took my name off the film.

Well, that's playing hardball.

Yeah.

Where do you get the balls?

From theater. And opera. And I said screw it. The film is two hours long and it's forty years of a woman's life and it's Frida Kahlo and it costs twelve million dollars and it's got all these movie stars, what's the problem? If I were doing *Lord of the Rings* or any big sixty-million-dollar movie I'd feel more concerned about the budget. You've got to do those test screenings. You've got to make the money back. But we made our money back. It was about power.

Can you describe what the process of rehearsal, creating ideographs, would be? Let's say for Titus. What would you do with actors?

Through improvisation, many images come up which that actor may or may not use. Anthony Hopkins is an ideograph kind of actor. His hands are always—I don't know if it was *Howards End*, but this hand would rise up and it was about him protecting, whatever it conjures is up to you. I was aware of how he would use gestures like that. And so for him, even when I was working on *Titus* the movie, we would work that way, which is pretty unusual for a movie. We had a three-week rehearsal.

Titus Andronicus the play version had much more of that kind of work because you're not under the gun. In *Titus* the movie, you had Harry Lennix, who did it in the play and who'd done a lot of Shakespeare, and Angus Macfadyen who had done Shakespeare, and Jessica Lange who had never done Shakespeare, and Jonathan Rhys Meyers who had never been in a play, or Laura Fraser who had never done theater. So you had a big, extremely diverse group of people, which normally we wouldn't have in the theater as much. I really believed in those actors because I saw them in auditions and I thought that they would be able to do it. But there probably wasn't as much improvisation with them. I can only remember there's an ideograph, I would call this an ideograph, when Titus's daughter Lavinia comes and she says, "Bless me." He puts his hand on her head and it's this gesture with some kind of transference of fatherhood, whatever it conjures up for you. *Titus Andronicus* is all about the hand, whether it's Lavinia's hand or the power of Titus himself. The imagery that Shakespeare gives you is there for you to try and support. That image of Lavinia on the broken stump where the blood comes out—when I did that in the theater with the actress, Miriam Healy-Louie, we tied her hands up in black and she held sticks. Because of course we don't need to blue screen her hands. The audience can make believe. She was on a broken column. In the play all we had were columns that were black-and-white photographic blowups on plastic that was deteriorating. So it already had the future and the past simultaneously because they were Roman columns, but they were on plastic that was able to move across the stage. If I were to say, "What is Lavinia?" how would you get to the essence of Lavinia? She's somewhere between the Degas ballerina—because we always think of the ballerinas as the most innocent and pure—and Marilyn Monroe, that image of the skirt going up, because it's sort of a vulnerable rape, in a way. It's a rape image, but it's sexy to everybody. And then, of course, Shakespeare kept talking about the doe, "My doe," so later she becomes, literally, a doe. But it's all the language. Marcus starts to move toward Lavinia and he says, "Speak, gentle niece—what stern, ungentle hands / Hath lopp'd, and hew'd, and made thy body bare / Of her two branches?" You're a dope if you can't pick up the appropriate imagery from Shakespeare because it's all there. Now, the trick is how to do it not dead-on. But I don't think people listen to language like they might have a couple hundred years ago, so when people hear something like that, they're not necessarily seeing it. So I think you can, as a director or a designer or an actor, support that language through heightened imagery.

You understand something that a lot of theater directors don't get—when you said, "Oh, this is the theater, we don't need to blue screen her hands." Audiences can see a woman holding a branch and understand that her hands are chopped off. That sophistication does exist. It's always shocking to me how few people understand the language of the theater as discreet from the language of film and television.

That it's real, plus that it's much more poetic and sophisticated, and yet the audiences get there. Look, with *The Lion King* with those white streamers—every kid knows those are tears.

But if you film that, it doesn't have the same effect at all.

It's very hard to find a balance—and *Titus* was a real exploration in the balance of stylization and what we call naturalism. The actors were extremely naturalistic in *Titus*. The language is very easy to comprehend.

Cicely Berry came and she worked one-on-one just to help people get over the fear of the language. It's natural language ultimately. When Anthony Hopkins is speaking, he's speaking. He's not orating. You would have a very hard time doing what he did in the theater. You couldn't. It's a real film performance. I was not looking for stylization in the actors, in the acting. The imagery, on the other hand, from time to time, is. So there was this incredible tension. Whenever people hear the word style, they think unemotional, sophisticated, intellectual, elitist, blah, blah, blah. They don't think of it as something that can really move you. Yet, there's not one person, if they talk to me about *Titus*, who doesn't say, "I had nightmares about that Lavinia image." Now, I did what Shakespeare did. I didn't show the rape. I didn't even show that much violence compared to half the films out there, but people will say it's the most violent film. And a lot of people say they couldn't watch it or it gave them nightmares because it's psychological violence as well.

It's tricky, and it goes back to ideographs as well. What is the least you can do so that when you say it's extremely disturbing imagery, it's not that extreme; it's very simple. But it's the juxtaposition that makes you have violent thoughts.

In the theater we did the whole thing within the revenge play gold frame. But you can't put a gold frame in a film because a film already has its frame. So I said, "Okay, what would be the ideograph of this piece?" It became the Coliseum because in real life, that's what the Coliseum was. It was a place where violence was enacted for entertainment. So I set the bookends in the Roman Coliseum.

At which point did you come up with the idea to have the Coliseum?

Right away. I was either going to do it in Las Vegas or in Rome. I really was. I was going to do it with Al Pacino. I was going to have the little boy be one of the people who lives in a trailer park outside of Vegas. Then you play it in Caesar's Palace. But then I had the opportunity to have the real thing, the real coliseums in Croatia and Hadrian's Villa. And I opted for that.

Can we go back to your comment about rehearsing with a company and looking closer at your work with Herbert Blau?

On *Transposed Heads* in 1984 Off-Off-Broadway, I hired the actors, we improvised for three weeks with the writer there, and they went away, and we wrote, he wrote, and then they came back. Now you can't do that in a commercial environment. That's really what hampers you. You're not allowed to do that with Equity. You couldn't afford to pay the actors the whole time. You end up having to think ahead of time. It's very hard to go and start in that nebulous, wonderful way where you just say, "Okay, here's the idea for this piece." There's no script. There's just an idea. I did that with Theatre Workshop of Boston back when I was thirteen, fourteen years old with Julie Portman.

That was a big influence on you.

That was the sixties and that was when a lot of people were developing theater and writers were not the first people involved. The original material was coming from a group of actors working together over a long period of time. With Blau we worked probably a year on *Seeds of Atreus*, and then on *The Donner Party*, the same. Bill Irwin hadn't done clowning or anything yet. He was more from Tai Chi and CalArts, where they did a lot of movement work. So we created *Donner Party*, for instance, from diaries and newspapers and stories and accounts of the events, and then breaking it up mythically into: What is the landscape? How does this hearken back to other stories? That kind of open-ended way of exploring the material is fantastic. But I would say about *The Donner Party* that I think the finished product wasn't as interesting as the process. I think people felt like they were looking through a keyhole onto some kind of unbelievable experience that these actors had gone through, but it wasn't completely comprehensible. I don't think that's the way it always is. When I was in Indonesia and I started my own theater company, I created the second piece, *Tirai*, completely from development of my company over a year.

What do you look for in an actor?

Well, it depends on the piece. If it's something that's going to have a *Green Bird* cast then the way that I audition is that I had about ten masks that had nothing to do with *Green Bird* because I hadn't made them yet. The actors would come in and they would read the part that they were brought in to read for the audition, but then I would give them four or five masks and tell them to go into the other room with a mirror and come back and improvise. You can tell right away, first of all, if someone is going to enjoy wearing a mask.

Pleasure.

Pleasure. And also that they're not going to feel that they're being hidden. If those could have been recorded, those were some of the best performances. So many actors don't even know that they have that ability and the mask is incredibly liberating. There's this skinny, nerdy white guy and he's got the big black man—they put the mask on and they're able to be that person. There's nobody questioning that. Or a woman can do a male role in this way. So I would let them improvise, work with them, and maybe go back to the material again. So, being versatile and game and having fun—but not everybody can improvise, so then you just see if they can express themselves through the movement.

Audience: I'm really curious about picking your work. In your earlier works, when you were working out how you wanted to approach things, did you only pick works that could become a really cool idea?

I only do things that have an emotional pull—I only do them because of the story—nothing to do with style. It doesn't mean I like everything in it. But if I don't connect—*Frida*'s probably the most regular of things I've done. Except for those moments with the paintings, it's just a biopic that's very colorful because Mexico is colorful.

AB: That's not true at all.

Okay. But it's not that I have to work that way, it's just that that's the way I think. If I can be moved by the story, then I'm interested to do it. There may be some cool or some wonderful idea that someone gives me when the story isn't completed yet, but if there's something in it that I can embrace both emotionally and intellectually, then I'll find the medium. The medium will be apparent. It's not the medium first. I cringe at the idea of puppets and masks because people just automatically think I'm going to do it. But I'm not if they're not appropriate.

What I saw about *Frida* when I received that script was an unbelievably passionate love story. It wasn't Frida Kahlo, it wasn't even the paintings. I didn't even like the paintings that much. I have learned to like the paintings more. But the connection of her paintings to her story is what moved me, that they were her autobiography. That moved me, that she was painting her life and this incredible long-term love story. I didn't think, Oh, let's see how we can make it a Julie Taymor project. But there's nothing about how she thinks as a painter. This is all objective. The entire script is a biography. That doesn't mean it's not emotional. But because her paintings are autobiographical, let's see if we can show how she comes to these paintings. That's the subjective experience. How does she think? Where did that painting come from with the hair that's cut off? Well, if you read her biography, it's very clear. So I could find a way to put seven or eight of these paintings into the biography—not lay them on top, but have them be organically in the storytelling. It came from the text. Or it came from the story, the needs. What's missing? What are we not telling here? And how are we going to tell it? Hopefully it's not an extraneous moment in the film, but it's organic to giving them a complete portrait of Frida.

Audience: I'd love to hear you speak about the opening scene in *Titus* of the boy at the table in a very Middle American kitchen.

The child was in the original play in the same scene at a 1950s chrome table, your everyman table. The everyman table that might be in Sarajevo, as well as Middle America or New York City. What is *Titus*? Well, ultimately it is about this unbelievably extraordinary family violence, and violence of tribe against tribe. What is the legacy? There's no child in *Titus Andronicus* except Young Lucius. He has two scenes. But the presence of a child in this drama reeked of needing to be thought through. He was the observer. He has no dialogue, but he's there watching the whole thing.

I don't believe that Shakespeare needs to be updated. I think he wrote exactly the periods and places that he meant. He set *Titus Andronicus* in a mythical Rome with a Greek mythology. But if you look at the etchings, you see the Elizabethan garb. So, I did exactly that. Remember I said earlier on that I'm trying to find what the original composers were trying to do. I don't feel that I that I'd played a trick by blending time. I didn't set it in contemporary America. I set it in its own time because I feel that's exactly what Shakespeare did. That myth of Lavinia's limbs and all of those myths are Greek myths. Or Ovid's *Metamorphosis* was also tremendous inspiration. Finally when you come to Chiron and Demetrius, they feel so contemporary. They feel like they'd be in music videos—those music videos where you can behead or flay or you get multiple choice on how you want the victims killed. And then you have Titus feeling much more old world. He comes in armor.

You need to set up a device to allow that to happen. The idea is that you're in this room, this kitchen. And it's just what children do. They play war games. They're all bombing each other and heads are being lopped off. But what I was thinking—and I don't expect anybody else to know what I was thinking—was that's God. There's this nasty-ass God there, playing around with the Goth soldier and the Roman soldier and this and that. But in that child's play it gets out of hand until what he has created is happening to him. A bomb comes through a window. The guy who grabs him is the Shakespearean Clown. He runs down the stairs and into the Coliseum. The Coliseum is empty because he's there at no particular time, he's there in "all time." He's there with the ghosts. They're all cheering, but there's nobody there because they're ghosts. Then the child turns around, and lo and behold these armies come in.

This was one of the blinder moments in shooting it because it was ten degrees below in Croatia. It's the only standing coliseum that exists. The Roman Coliseum was destroyed. This was right before the Croatian war. We were there one month before. The soldiers whom we used—Yugoslavians and Croatians—there were many without arms and legs. The boy looks down, and there are these soldiers coming. They're on motorcycles with wolf heads, and they're on chariots and everybody's covered in clay. That image comes from an idea I always loved of the Chinese armies that were dug up out of the earth. It was miserable to shoot this because it was freezing cold and it was snowing and people were with the wet clay. It's Christmas. Everybody wants to go home. It's miserable, and everybody's freezing and complaining. Poor old Harry Lennix is naked in a pit and it's snowing. It's awful. But if I can put all of them in a common denominator, which is clay, all those periods, then you're moving toward setting up the conceit, so that when you see that big Mussolini square coliseum, you understand it.

Audience: I'm curious about when you're thrown into a situation and you're disoriented—whether it's a location or a script—do you have a routine that enables you to get the most out of that disorientation? Do you come back to something comfortable like finding the beginning, middle and end?

Well, I'll tell you what I mean by that. Did I want to go to Mexico City to do *Frida* with all that kidnapping? The thing about it is, if you hire people to collaborate with you—for instance, I hired Mexicans, Mexican DP, Mexican set designer. It's very much about letting yourself respect the culture and using the best they have to offer. That's really important. So, in Italy, Dante Ferretti [Production Designer] and Milena Canonero [Costume Designer], Luciano Tovoli [Director of Photography] were my collaborators. There were other great people from outside Italy, but I feel that that's not a good way to go into a place. I first of all have to gather a group of people with whom I want to collaborate. You're not alone. I don't think there's anything other than just going for it.

I love when you have a difficult situation, you don't have enough money, perhaps, so you get to do a more creative solution. In *Frida*, the script called for a scene in New York City: "Frida and Diego in 1930 stroll down Fifth Avenue." We couldn't shoot in New York City or successfully re-create Fifth Avenue on a sound stage, so we created a collage from period photographs of New York City through which the couple walked. Much more unique, and more in the style of Frida herself.

AB: The big word that keeps coming up in my head listening to you is "courage." You have more courage than anybody I ever met. Where does your courage come from?

It's a nice thing to say. I think I've always been this way. I just think about, well, we'll just find a way, won't we? "Let's go make a play." What is that feeling? We'll figure it out. In *The Haggadah*, when Liz Swados came to me in 1980 and I'd just come back from Indonesia and I was twenty-five or twenty-six, I wasn't a designer. That was a fluke. I never studied design. And she asked me to do *The Haggadah*.

The fact is, if you look at the theater, a lot of it is epic or big theater that I have a good time putting into a walled space or proscenium space or a theater. It's fun. The idea of doing (even though I like the play) *Proof*, with a house and porch—I would rather have no set and do what Shakespeare has done, which is create it in the imagination. So, for me, the idea of taking some big story—it's not scary because it's the fun part. That's what theater can do really well. It's not about courage.

Audience: Was there any discussion whether or not to diminish Frida's mustache?

Oh, God, yes. You want to know something? If Salma had had a mustache, she would have won the Academy Award. That's the sad thing. There's always this discussion—if you look at the photographs of Frida, she never had as much of a mustache as she painted. She herself loved the masculine image. She loved to disturb people and to play with that. We put it on as she got older, justifying it. The eyebrows we were able to do. If she had had a mustache, that's all they would have talked about. People would have been obsessed because there would have been a certain amount of people who would be so grossed out. But I think it's better that it wasn't about the mustache, ultimately.

Audience: Can you talk about the theater company in Indonesia that you started?

Teatr Loh. I was in Indonesia probably a year, two years, before I started the company. I was going to go for three months and then spend a year with a Bunraku troupe on the island of Awaji in Japan. I was planning to spend a year with them, but I went to Indonesia first. And I stayed four years. I was twenty-one at the time, and I had done theater since I was eleven years old. I had ideas in my head of stories that I wanted to tell and ways that I wanted to work. I was so inspired by the traditional theater of Java and Bali that I thought about putting the traditional theater with the contemporary theater of Indonesia, and with contemporary ideas about theater that I had been gathering in Europe and in the United States. Because I was in a foreign country, trespassing was a very big part of what I was thinking about. And *Tirai* is just about that. It's about passing through the curtain, and the story reflects my own experience there. The work I did in Indonesia is probably the most personal work I've ever done. It was the time that I was coming off of working with Blau—using yourself and using what you thought about, what your experiences were.

I created Teatr Loh after two years with dancers and musicians and actors from Java and Bali and with one Frenchman, one German and myself. Ten of us all lived together in a place called Peti Tenget in Bali. There was no running water and no electricity. Every day for eight, nine, hours a day we trained each other, for eight months or so. I did all of the different techniques I'd learned from Blau and from Lecoq's and from Theatre Workshop of Boston, and the Javanese taught the Javanese dance, and the Balinese taught the Balinese dance. I taught mask performance. They did mask performance. So it was this big, incredible trading of techniques. You had really diverse people. It wasn't the Western-Eastern that was the biggest split. It was the Muslims and the Hindus. It was very tough because the Balinese Hindus eat pork and there were all these arguments about food.

I had done a piece earlier, *Way of Snow*, but that wasn't with the company yet. After I had done that, created an original piece, I decided to stay and I got a Ford Foundation Grant and created this company. We were to tour Sumatra, Java, Sulawesi and Bali. After a year of rehearsal, we took the ferry from Bali to Java and the night bus to Surabaya—and we crashed. Head on collision. The bus crashed with a truck. The truck driver died. I was completely embedded in glass, cut up, bones were broken. I was twenty-two years old, maybe twenty-three by that time, and had sixty year olds down to eighteen year olds in the company. I'm the one who brought these people out of their own villages and was doing this. It was devastating. I had a couple of operations, came back to the States, then went back to Indonesia. We had this ceremony and then divining event. We had a shaman divine the entire accident to figure out what happened. Apparently the Balinese in our company had prayed only for the Balinese at the three temples, mother temples, before our journey, and had not prayed sufficiently for the rest of the group. Well, that was one of the explanations.

Big projects have big risks. I hadn't even thought back to that connection. The shaman said, "You needed a strong force to crash against to make yourself stronger. So go back out on the road." We had to replace two people and we had to cut our tour in half because we didn't have any insurance. We had to pay for everybody's bills. We took holy water in a bottle of Coca-Cola with us. The oldest Balinese member of the group would do a ceremony on all of the masks before every performance. At this divining event—this is the most amazing thing—the priest took the Muslim mountain of rice and the pork for Bali and he mixed it all together and said, "Now everybody eat of this."

AB: This is a huge learning lesson for you.

It was amazing—because it was terribly frightening. I felt so horribly responsible, even though I was young.

Audience: When I saw *Titus*, I thought it was a fantastic combination of the theatrical and the cinematic. Earlier you were talking about how certain imagery would work in film or in theater and vice versa. Could you talk a little bit about your relationship to theater and film as mediums and how that has changed over the years as you've gotten more experience in the two?

Well, I haven't done feature films that long. *Titus* was my first. I guess my feeling about film is that I love the possibilities of film. I think some of the earliest filmmakers were much more expressive, the German expressionists, because they didn't have at their disposal the ability to go everywhere with a handheld camera and shoot what we call "reality." To me that's not reality. That's just a handheld camera jerking around and sometimes it works if it's the right moment to have you conscious of a moving camera. I've been a little sad that I feel a lot of young filmmakers don't use the medium or the camera to help tell the story.

As theater directors we have the discipline. We have to because the stage is there. The human beings are never going to get bigger or smaller. You can't come in with a close-up, so how do you do a close-up? Pull the lights down. You pull the sound out. We have to use different techniques and we don't have the luxury of editing. One of the things I love about theater is transitions. I love them in film, too—they're theatrical ideas, but I can use the technique of film, which is dissolve and edit, to pull it off. I love the possibilities of different mediums. I love opera, too. I love the ideas. What does each medium do best?

When I went to *The Lion King* from an animated film, I said we've got to show the strings and the rods. We've got to be exposing everything because film is the thing that hides everything. So let's make it ultra-theater. Let's be as abstract as we want. We're not going to make a real animal. So let's just use the textiles and do what theater can do. The audience goes with you. The expression is "suspend your disbelief." They all do that. They walk into the theater of a play and they'll do it. They won't do that in a movie anymore. What happened to those old filmmakers that were playing in a theatrical way?

AB: You describe working with the Blau company and how the audience felt like they were looking in on something they had nothing to do with. Your impulses are

completely opposite of that. It occurs to me that you think more about the audience than anyone I ever met.

I don't know about that. That's telling the story.

AB: It seems to me when I'm thinking through your work that it is all about the audience's journey—not to mitigate the actors journey, but it doesn't really matter. What matters is this symphonic experience that the audience has. You are really making this sensual, aural journey.

Well, I was interested in the double event. Many stories have been told. Even if you never saw *The Lion King*, you'd know that story. So isn't it *how* you tell the story? You have to balance the emotional throughline and the journey of the story with the sheer art of it. That's why I love theater because I think the audience can do two things at once. Broadway musicals are all about that, if they're at their best. I got that in Indonesia. They've been doing the *Mahabarata* and the *Ramayana* over and over and over again. So it's not the story, it's the interpretation. With the theater I feel like you've also got an obligation to say, "What is the form? What is it telling you?" The story will tell you what the form should be. It's a solution to telling the story.

Yes, I am interested in the audience. I'm in a public medium. I'm in theater, not sitting home and doing my own thing. I don't do it knowing that they might like it. We were in absolute shock all during *The Lion King*. We enjoyed it in rehearsal. But in that first preview in Minneapolis we were shocked by it.

Audience: How do you think the ritual and celebration in Indonesian performance still influences what your idea of what theater is and how theater functions in society?

Well, the word "ritual" always does get overused. With theater companies there's a sense of being together on some kind of journey. When you're just casting for a regular show it works, then it goes away. On *The Lion King*, you've got a seven-year-running show. Some people have actually been in it for seven years. Every once in a while I go back and I have to see it and I just die because I know when people are walking through something. It's a two-hour-forty-five-minute tough job. But they may not be fully expanding. This show is very hard, very difficult. But if you go in there and you really are there completely as a living meditation, your performance is different. When you're with that ensemble, that's the only thing you can do. Sometimes they all get together and they warm up together. Clearly with a theater company that's part of the tradition. That is part of your ritual. You can't force that on people. Everything we do pushes us against that in this culture. It's about the next job. Yet not everybody is like that. When you asked about my choices—I can't do anything where I don't feel fully that I could invest myself. That's what I think you need to do if you are an actor or a director or a writer or a designer. It's your religion. It's what makes you tick. It makes you breathe. And you love it. Half is torture, but half is why you do it. It's what you live for.

Bill T. Jones

Bill T. Jones is an irrepressible force. A well-known fact among those who have seen him speak or participate in panel discussions is that he cannot stay seated. Inevitably he stands up and begins to move, to sing, to evoke the muses. He is a big, beautiful man who has been scarred by life. He keeps returning to his art with astonishing courage. He locates what is meaningful in human existence. He finds form and shapes for the edges of what is unbearable. He shocks, appalls, delights, inspires and thrills an audience that returns to him again and again. He breaks rules and transgresses boundaries in the service of intense communion.

Born in rural upstate New York, the tenth of twelve children in a migrant worker's family, Bill enrolled in dance classes at the State University of New York at Binghamton where he was a theater major on an athletic scholarship. Dance stuck. In the early seventies he met his longtime partner and companion Arnie Zane. Together they formed the Bill T. Jones/Arnie Zane Dance Company and they developed solo, duet and ensemble choreography, including remarkable evening-length pieces. After seventeen years of collaboration, Arnie died tragically of AIDS. Bill continues, carrying the memory of Arnie with him. Bill's work expresses intense emotion. He explores ideas about memory, sexuality, race and mortality. He manages to find harmony and beauty in what we might perceive as chaos and despair.

Bill is now a fixture on the world's cultural radar. He is a tall, powerful dancer, a magnificent soloist, conceptualist and choreographer. He mixes dance with text and video—autobiographical material with historical and political content. What I find most inspiring and always surprising about his work is his ability to mix passionate intimacy with a wide and incisive perspective. He is not a stranger to controversy. His newest works are often debated widely.

Bill has received Tony Awards, many Bessies, and fellowships from all conceivable sources including a MacArthur "genius" Fellowship, and many honorary doctorates. With all this success, one would expect a certain complacency. Not true. Not with Bill. He soars. He continues to amaze and inspire us with his violent hopefulness.

Besides the prolific work with his own company, Bill has choreographed for the Alvin Ailey American Dance Theater, AXIS Dance Company, Boston Ballet, Lyon Opera Ballet, Berlin Opera Ballet and Diversions Dance Company, and others. He has directed opera at the New York City Opera, Houston Grand Opera, Boston Lyric Opera, and elsewhere. He has collaborated and crossed disciplines with extraordinary contemporary artists including Toni Morrison, Max Roach, Jessye Norman, Keith Haring, Robert Longo, Rhodessa Jones, the Orion String Quartet and his present partner, the visual artist Bjorn Amelan.

March 26, 2004

AB: Bill T. Jones is, I would say, a pioneer, unique, nobody-like-you, an inspiration . . . I think you're an inspiration to a couple of generations, wouldn't you say? You're that old now . . .

BTJ: It's true, painfully true.

From the first time I saw Bill's work, it has always given me a jolt of life. I think one of the most extraordinary things about your work is that it is both aesthetic and political. How did it get that way, or why did it get that way, or how did you get that way? I know that's a broad question, but you can handle it.

I think that I have not been consciously cultivating that. I started not knowing what the hell I was doing. *(He dances while speaking)* When I was a little boy, about twelve years old, I received a little white card in the mail. / two-seven-eight-one-five-nine-two-three-seven / When I was a little boy / one-five / about twelve years old, I went back to the place I was born Bunnell, Florida. I was sitting on the steps with my two old aunties: Aunt Mattie and Aunt Purity Roger. Aunt Mattie said to me, "Billy you ain't gonna do like your brother Avery did. He went up North and married a white girl. Because if you marry a white girl you can't come down here and visit us no more." I said, "Auntie, I love you." / one / "I love you." / three / "I love you."

Now that was the first solo I ever did in New York, in 1977, one part of it. I didn't know what I was doing. Anna Kisselgoff wrote in the *New York*

Times, "He's a brilliant young humanist," and wondered if anyone else could do my work because it's so much about my personality. For me, those were fighting words because black folks, black performers are all essentialists, it's just natural. In other words, you don't have this— *(Points at his head)* You have this— *(Motions to his body)* If you were a young male who could pass for a heterosexual, even if you're not, and you're beautiful and you take off your shirt and seduce people, you can get away with murder. But I wanted to prove I'm one of the big kids, I'm a real artist of the New York School. If you were a formal artist, the work was cool and distant, set back. So all this stuff about your auntie and your race and stuff— I felt people patronized it. I was maybe full of those judgments myself. So what was political in it, I thought, was just the stuff of poetry in my life. I'm sure—as for most people who identify themselves as a minority, and certainly women—if you talk about your lives, you are going to run up against something that is "political." That's what I thought I was doing.

It also sounds like it was a response to what's coming at you. That rather than accepting what's coming at you, you're rebelling against it.

Is that what it is? Talk back? Well, my mother and father were great storytellers and they were always bittersweet. My mother told cautionary tales. My father's tales were outlandish—but they were always talking to us, trying to tell us about the world in that way. What I meant to say was that, yes, the angry young man played very well.

And then there was Arnie Zane, a five-foot-four, Jewish, obviously gay man, and I'm a six-foot-one, African-American man, and suddenly we discovered these partnering possibilities. The two of us partnering was already enough to make some people very uncomfortable. Ah, the dawn of identity politics. So when you use the word "politics," for me it's been through various permutations. We were still doing strongly structured work—except that I insisted on a stream-of-consciousness, sotto voce reporting of everything that was going on between me and Arnie at that moment, dancing this abstract work, and then stopping and saying, "This man's sitting with his twelve-year-old daughter there. What would you think if your daughter was to marry me?" First of all, it's his twelve-year-old daughter and I am there sweating. White man, and you come over to them, you put your arms around them—already it's charged. If you just tweak it a little bit, it becomes political.

When Arnie Zane and I founded the company we thought, To hell with high white art. In 1983 we were at BAM for the first time. We did a piece called *Secret Pastures* with Keith Haring doing the décor and Peter

Gordon doing the super-hip, downtown art-rock music. Warhol is in the audience, Madonna is in the audience, and it's because of Keith, of course. The idea was that we were going to get rid of the barriers between high art and low art. That was what we thought was the big thing that had to be done at that time. Was that a political act? Whatever it was, some people condemned us and said we were careerists, trendy and fashionable. Someone said it was the first modern dance influenced by MTV, which we took to be a real compliment at that time. I don't know if I would take it as a compliment anymore. In other words, to hell with the boundaries. We are now in a brave new world.

Then Arnie Zane died. Even while he was sick, the press was looking for a real, live, jumping person with AIDS who would actually come forward and say, "I have AIDS," and talk about it. We went on *MacNeil/Lehrer* and talked about it at a time when there was almost nobody else in the art world, in the dance world, who was talking about it. Arnie suddenly was that person. Was that political?

So Arnie dies, I'm on the phone with a writer from the *Advocate*. Be careful of who you think your brothers are. I was talking a little too freely, and I mention that I'm HIV-positive, and next thing you know that's the leading line. I called him up and said, "You never checked with me." And he said, "Well, you did say it." So I had to own it. Is that political?

Now you're not only a choreographer, you're a real, live time bomb. We're waiting for you to drop over dead. So you don't. You don't drop over dead. You keep going, and you try to talk about anger, all of these personal things. But now you are *that*, a black man who is gay and HIV-positive, so everything you say is now political.

There was *Last Supper at Uncle Tom's Cabin/The Promised Land*, which ended with fifty-two people drawn from every community we performed in, naked on the stage. People of every different shade and color. In the section called *The Table*, I engaged a local person of faith asking questions such as, "Is AIDS a punishment from God, a sin?" My mother was first. All those things in the middle of a dance concert. I was doing a spiritual investigation, but there were a lot of people hurt, there were a lot of angry people out there who wanted somebody to speak for them. What's more, I had Larry Goldhuber in the company, who was three hundred and fifty, almost four hundred, pounds at that moment. "What are you getting at with that big guy there? What are you getting at?" Fat people can dance! That's a political statement, right?

No, I'm saying it was an aesthetic statement, I think. I grew up where most women around me had asses like that and bosoms, but on Saturday night people got down. People danced. What are you talking about, that's not a dancer's body? You ever seen Nell Carter on Broadway? Have you ever seen what Bessie Smith looked like? Do you know what the shimmy is? Do you know what the dirty shimmy is? But then, once again, now you're talking as a black person—that's an anthropological observation.

Then there is *Still/Here*. With *Last Supper* I thought, This is where art ended and became an act of faith. It turned off a lot of people in the art world. It's getting kind of soft-headed, because you're going into issues of faith, but if you survived a great tragedy you know about faith—I think a lot of people need a little bit more tragedy to focus on how they feel about body and spirit in their art. For *Still/Here* I decided the work would have a very special demographic; it's going to be for people who were or have been dealing with a life-threatening illness. So I did these workshops, made this big rambling work with Gretchen Bender. That piece was very, very powerful and caused a huge stir. It was denounced as victim art. It was considered the latest insult to the discourse, because all of these angry minorities were demanding that everyone feel sorry for them.

Who said that, Arlene Croce?

Her position was, "I cannot review a person I feel sorry for. It's unfair for me to have to look at this. I say to all of my readers if you feel that this is the case in a work of art, just don't go." She never saw the work. Now we can all scoff, but you know what a firestorm that started. Well-meaning— well, I guess they're well-meaning—intellectuals who should know better would come up to me and say, "I read that article about you, and maybe she had a point there." Is the work of Sylvia Plath weakened by the fact that we know that she committed suicide in the end? She was imbalanced. It suggests that we shouldn't have to deal with her poetry as poetry because it's the rantings of an imbalanced person. It is to say: There's too much of this complaining now—women are complaining, gay people are complaining, Indian people are complaining. Robert Hughes said this is the culture of complaint.

So the person who was telling you about his old aunties was suddenly now faced with being accused of being manipulative and cheap—when it was in fact about a life issue. What did I do? I think I went into a kind of shock, and I said, okay, I am not going to share my heart like that anymore. I'm sick of my feelings. There's got to be another way to make art. I listened to Beethoven. I would make movement not about anything. Trisha Brown. Classic modernist strategies. Free it from politics. Free it from identity. I'm still struggling with that. Somehow or other, in those moments where I least expect it, suddenly I am speaking my mother's voice. What she was doing was an outrageous thing, standing in front of a room full of people, many of whom were disbelievers, but she was actually communicating with her god, as if everyone was on the same page. I've never seen anything stronger than that, more powerful, more direct. I have no god to call out to like that, but I feel the Southern Baptist inside of me. That betrays me, because then the emotions come back and the engine that drives the work kicks in. It has to do with something about history, pain, slavery, outsider-ness, confusion about male-female, mediocrity of the world, all of those things are in those old songs.

The last work I made was called *Reading, Mercy and the Artificial Nigger*, based on a short story by Flannery O'Connor. Two old crackers— I don't mean to offend you. Am I allowed to call people crackers?

Audience: I don't know what a cracker is.

A cracker is an ignorant white person. That is what black people call— well, actually that's what you call all white people. It's an old-fashioned term.

Audience: It comes from slave days, when they used to crack the whip.

Oh, interesting. I thought it was like saltine crackers, pale, flat white bread.

The Artificial Nigger is a perfect, beautiful story, but what's it about? I say it's about racial and religious reasoning, and how it stops us from getting at the stuff that really divides us. So in other words, it's looped back to what you were saying. It's political. But for me it was a challenge to bring pure formal dancing and that story together, so that the story could do what it had to do and our dancing could do what it had to do. I think that is the future for my work right now.

AB: It's interesting, because your aunties piece is formal already. Where did that come from? What are your influences?

That's a good question. I bet it came from sign language. At that time we were working a lot with deaf people. Arnie Zane's gesture work in *At the Crux Of* made a big impression on me.

AB: I'm really interested in something you said: We need to get closer to tragedy in order to get more focused.

It can sound like a very un-generous thing to say.

AB: Not at all, it's immense. It's actually quite radical.

Well, if you accept that I don't sound like a creep saying that. There are colleagues of mine that I've seen with great facility, formal facility, and then when you look at their work, you wonder, So what? We celebrate tragedy, and that's a terrible thing, but what I'm getting at is that you die or ratchet up. There's more at stake.

AB: I wish you great tragedy . . .

It's a terrible thing to say, though, isn't it? Because when Arnie died, literally, he breathed his last breath, and I'm holding his hand, and I don't know if it's imagined or not, but you feel a breeze and you say, "He's gone!" That is a moment that is life altering. After that, anytime I looked at anyone in love I felt fearful for them. Anytime I saw a mother with a child I felt fear for them. You have to get over that and recommit, and that's when things change.

AB: I remember once, years ago at a TCG conference, and I was supposed to interview you and your sister, Rhodessa Jones, at Smith College. I felt blown off the stage by your and Rhodessa's energy. It was completely thrilling. The two of you are dynamos, and that's only two of your family. So that's my entry point: After great tragedy, what is it that makes you explode in an expressive form called dance?

Dance saved me. I felt luckier than a lot of people who felt lost in the world. Arnie died March 30, 1988. We had one of the biggest seasons of our company's life scheduled at City Center four weeks later. We jumped back into rehearsing. We were grieving on our feet. I didn't have the luxury of not showing up. The company needed me. We started another work called *D-Man in the Water*. That work, I realized, was a way of kind of organizing our grief, because I didn't really have that break. I think it made me a little bolder. Plus, I expected that I was going to die. Everything was a grand summation, and grand summations always get you into trouble: "This is going to answer all of the questions." And then it's over and you're going to have twice as many questions. There was lots of really good energy.

AB: You do have an extreme amount of courage.

Sometimes I confuse courage with a type of fear. I try to talk in my book about what it was like. I grew up in upstate New York in a German-Italian fruit-, potato-, corn-growing community. We were there because we had been migrant workers who had come to harvest those things. I grew up always being the only black kid in the class. Big family. My mother and father did not join the PTA, but we were expected to act like everybody else. Sports. My mother and father didn't go to the local church, but we kids were expected to go. All the immigrants in the room know what I'm talking about. Parents: "No, not for me, but you have to do it." But I say this, because when trouble started at school, or when we thought we had done wrong, oh my Lord, you come home, you tell Estella. She was a big woman and she would get herself dressed in her leopard print dress, with big shoes, a hat this big, the purse and, "Come on!" Everything was a political statement. You'd go over there into the principal's office, and you know, they didn't have too many two-hundred-fifty-pound-black women coming in there who understood that such and such struck her child. And she would go, "Just because my face is black!" That's the first thing she would say. They would calm her down, but it's a feeling. It's complicated. I'd rather my dad had gone to the principal's office. Someone rather dismissively said to me one night in Germany that as an African-American man I couldn't know about patriarchy, only matriarchy. Sometimes when I feel myself do very aggressive things, I think it is a way of dealing with fear. I think that was what she was feeling when she would get that head of steam up like that—I think she felt fear, but the way it had to be dealt with was, "Don't mess with me!" They used to say, "If a fight starts, you gotta be ready to die." Where does that wildness, that craziness come from? There was an unspoken, "They do not want you in this country. You have to be careful, because as soon as they can, they're going to cut your dick off and throw you in jail." This is what was taught to us without being taught, and I hate to go into this racial place, we're trying to talk about things like courage and politics and all that. Yeah, was it courage or was it fear?

AB: Great point.

And I don't know. I find that as I get older it's harder to access them in a way that is pure. There's just lack of focus somehow. I truly have to believe my own critics: that when I get angry, I'm losing it. Anger is no longer a useful emotion. Now you should be able to access other ways of dealing with problems.

AB: Can you describe the genesis of *The Table Project*? I think it's not unrelated to your question of what to access.

I had already begun to think that I had lost myself with how far I had gotten from the time when we had people of a broader physical description in the company. I had gone into this research around style. I was working with people who had dance training, and it was making it small. I felt that I needed to find a way that I could make a work that brought real people and put them into our world again instead of putting our world aside and going out there. So I was with my companion, Bjorn Amelan, at a breakfast place in Berkeley, sitting and watching three or four guys of a certain age, I'd say about fifty. You know, sitting at the counter with their big asses spilling over the backs of their pants. They were so relaxed you know, they didn't even care what they looked like. They were having a good time with one another, and they were guys. I said, "Imagine those people on stage doing something where they would be looked at, scrutinized." Then I thought, We don't know the answer to that, but what if we found men like this of a certain age—but they had to be important men. Find the men that had the most at stake and have them on stage being lyrical or vulnerable. We were going to do counters, a diner counter, but Bjorn designed a table, a ziggurat that had little steps, but on the top was a table, stools around the side. We took a heartbreakingly beautiful romantic piece by Schubert. I made this ritual, simple thing.

The curtain raised and everyone raised their hands, they're sleeping, they have these different characters, someone is pushing someone around, some of the people get pushed around, they rebel, they climb up the table—very, very simple. The big thing about it was how to recruit the guys. How do you tell them about who I am? How do you talk about what I want them to do—and why I wanted it to be somebody important? The thing that got them, I would quote José Limón, the great choreographer. His model of a male dancer was King David in ancient Israel, who every year would open the gates and lead the dance. Can you imagine? The most powerful man in the country is the one who has to start dancing. They liked that but, of course, it was very pretty, very moving music. I conceptualized a circle of types. If this is the old bulls' neighborhood, then what would be its opposite? I thought it should be the least powerful—little girls. And at the end we would have ladies, like from the 1950s, opposite little boys. And you can imagine the permutations. We did it in Minneapolis with all four groups. That first six minutes would be done by the men, they would leave and then immediately it would be done by the little girls. They'd do exactly the same movement. I told people that it was an exercise in watching oneself watch. It was amazing when women did it—people were beamed into it. The men, people are laughing at them—there's Joe the mayor. Little girls, you know, their hearts are charmed, but the ones that people liked the most were the little boys. Maybe it was just that cast, but little girls are already aware they're being looked at, but the little boys had something very disarming and charming about them.

AB: Last year, I watched Bill teach a workshop at Emory, and there were these young dancers, undergraduate dancers, but a very professional program, and they had poles up their asses. I watched over the course of an hour, and Bill started teaching them something he had just made, and it was not easy. They were used to learning moves. Then he ripped into them, "Okay, make it your own." Watching them was transformative, because they had never been asked to make something their own before.

I talked to them like adults.

AB: It was amazing to see them actually sweat. I mean, actually sweat as people sweat. Human sweat. Maybe people who have danced with Bill could explain what you're asking for. It's deceptive, because on one hand there's an ease, and on the other hand there's not an ease at all.

Bill T. Jones/Arnie Zane Dance Company Member: It's amazing how one sentence changes the whole perspective of the dance for us. We'll learn it from the video, and we'll learn the music, the positions, the movement, everything, but then it's that little thing that all makes sense when Bill comes in and gives it to us. Maybe it's history, maybe it's where that movement is coming from, maybe it's what he was thinking that day when he was making it. Something that opens the gate for us.

Bill T. Jones/Arnie Zane Dance Company Member: Also, it's a simple term, but you talk about the "task," I think it's the action. And you get very impatient when we forget what the task is—like if the task is to move the arm, and we drop it. There is an alive interaction in the moment of what I am supposed to be doing right now and why I am supposed to be doing that. It's a pain in the ass to remember what the task is, but it keeps a level of engagement with the work.

You know this raises the question about coming from a postmodern dance tradition, as opposed to a theater tradition. What I think is great about the postmodern dance tradition is that it said no to characters, no to audience manipulation, no to illusion—and what is theater if it's not illusion, right? So these people, like [Yvonne] Rainer, were laying down the laws. These were the new rules. I think a lot of us heard that, first of all, there is the action of what you're doing, and then there is somebody doing that action, and that somebody is trying to do, almost, what I'm doing here, but without the words. There's something behind the gestures. I think that they have to know what the task is, and then suddenly they own it, suddenly this is no longer their choreography, but I'm speaking my heart. I say we're doing church now.

Audience: One of the most amazing things about watching you move is that there is an infinite number of questions being asked at every moment. Questions that you're asking of yourself, being vulnerable, questions you're asking of other people, who are asking political, sociological, anthropological, dance, critical questions of you at every moment and you're still willing to ask questions of yourself in front of them. And I feel the most poignant sentences that you have ever said were always asking questions of us. And the idea of the task is basically: What are you trying to do? And so the point, when you would say one of those sentences is always to get us back to a place where you think you have an answer for this, you have an answer, but this is a question and you're not asking it. So you have to go back and answer that question.

AB: That's fantastic. And I think that's something that—

Not very scientific, but . . .

AB: Maybe it is. And it seems to me that it joins the best of theater and dance, that each gesture is a question as opposed to an answer. That notion of waking up inside of somebody. And I say maybe it is scientific in that it's more of a quantum notion of the universe as opposed to a classical notion of the universe. It also brings up the issue of choreographer or director, and what you're doing is you're always trying to ask the bigger questions, whatever anybody's doing, you try to ask the larger one at the same time. There's always a striving toward something, just when you think you've got it, a bigger question is asked.

I think I envy the director. You know I am a big fan of yours and some of the things you've done, both *bobrauschenbergamerica* and the thing that you directed, *Alice's Adventures*, and I don't think I saw them enough. The reason I went to Beethoven and things like that, I thought these are great works, they have all the stuff in them, all I have to do is just serve it. I was going to ask you about Shakespeare. These works are great plays, just do the language well, just stage it halfway interesting and you'll be able to do the work. Isn't that the opinion of classical art? That's the attraction to it. That's the masterpiece, and now, serve it.

The tradition I come from, we're often making things up and you have to be the medium, you have to demonstrate everything, the intellectual and the physical meeting in that gesture, and that is the beauty of it. You know what I'm getting at, the classical theater?

AB: I know exactly what you're getting at, with Shakespeare, for a director it's just getting out of the actor's way. But that makes me wonder that when choreographers decide to direct they become really bad directors. I always wish choreographers would take their choreography into the theater, but every time I see a choreographer say they're going to direct, they suddenly become so removed from all of their tools. And you say no, you want that.

Well, this thing you're talking about right now, I don't know how you feel about actors, but my dancers, I say they are sublime materials. In other words, sublime means consciously chosen, it's immune, transcendental vibration. And if you give them the right movement and you allow them to own everything that's going on inside of them, then you are going to get blazing performances. The simple movement of the arm suddenly is going to be questions. If you can just get them to: "Where's the tragedy in life? In this moment, where is the revelation of the tragedy?" All of that has got to be in the individual. This is my notion about individuals anyway. Everybody has those great stories inside of them. Now dance is that. Now, you have a text. You don't want too much of them, and I'm not speaking for you, but isn't that the difference? Directing as a choreographer becomes about the text, and thinking, I have to honor this text because the work has been done there.

AB: You know what makes great acting is an actor who is listening to the text as they're speaking it, as opposed to delivering their position on the text. They are actually experiencing it in the moment of speaking. And I think it's a wide open thing, it's not like you want to hide yourself. You actually have to open yourself so that the audience is watching the power of speaking and experiencing it as it's happening. But to me, speaking is many things. Speaking is text, but speaking is gesture, it's the same thing as the experience of that gesture.

I try to tape myself in my own performances. I spend more time now watching my folks perform, but sometimes my best performances, well, very powerful performances, there was something that I felt where the world slows down and what you're doing, and what you're feeling, and what you're seeing yourself feeling and doing . . . you can almost feel the people witnessing it. Those moments are rare, but they do happen. But other times, what you're doing is to demand such awareness, but you don't have any time to go to that place.

AB: Your job is to slow down time inside, right?

Yes, that's a good one. Remind me of that one please. Leah! Slow down time! Well, Peter Martin once described virtuosity—he said true virtuosity, particularly in a male dancer, as the material gets faster, it never loses clarity. So, in other words, that demands a great facility, but inside of you, you are still, even as it gets faster and faster.

AB: What obstacles are there for you right now?

Obstacles? Self-consciousness. These lefties I used to do social therapy with said that success is a conservatizing factor on us. It's true; there's more at stake. The more you've done, the more self-conscious you are about what you're able to do. And you've already heard all these things inside your head, and from the outside, about who you are and what you do, and it's really hard to be like: *(He shouts)* "That's what I'm saying. Start a new work. I want to do something, I want to do something."

AB: Maybe you just need more bad reviews?

Another tragedy, you're saying? Well, that's true, but some of us are thin-skinned. Believe me, I am.

AB: It's painful.

It's true, but for some people it works, for some of us it's so expensive.

AB: I just know that so much of my years in the theater was riddled with bad reviews, that at some point I just didn't care anymore. And I'm actually deeply grateful for that.

I can take them better now. I was always criticized, but I was always praised. Something about your body, maybe actors know what I'm talking about, but for dancers, I am this. *(Points at his body)* You criticize this, what I'm doing, you are invalidating me. And you deal with that. Perhaps what I do is not me, or does it really matter what you think about what I do? Unfortunately, it matters more than I would like. My strategy has been to close down, so they can't hurt. Give more to fewer people. And to just protect, don't go there. I can't help it, if I'm there, no matter what, somehow I'm going to crack and I'm going to be confessing, or you're going to be able to see who I am, so don't go there. You know, if you do that, you are going to let it out, you are going to embarrass and hate yourself tomorrow.

AB: I think what keeps people from full expression is the inability to say the words.

I'm capable of standing up and bearing witness. I suffer later. You know what I'm getting at? I remember once being at the zoo in San Diego, before it was a cool zoo. I had never been to a zoo before, but it was filled with kids and there were these boys, teenage boys who started throwing things at the tigers. And here I am with my friend, Arnie Zane, hair down to here, white streak, you know, it's very obvious who we are. And when they did that, I remember outrage and yelling, "Hey! Stop that!" Watch them come over and kick my ass, right? But at that moment you have to be willing to go there, you've got to be willing. Let's go. You want to spill blood? Let's spill blood. I can do that.

AB: Your mother taught you well.

You learned. You're fierce that way. I don't know about you, but I said to Billy Forsythe, a very wild ballet choreographer, he tries outrageous things, he's a really great artist. And when I heard him say that he is related to Eileen Ford at Ford Models, that's his aunt or something, he comes from the bluebloods out on Long Island and now makes contemporary art in Germany, and I said, "I thought you were working-class because you seem to have so much to prove." This is my class bias—that only people who have a lot of hurt have a lot to prove—they are the ones who are going to get up and be hit again and again. I am sure that's not true, is it? What I'm getting at is that because of this hurt you have a lot to prove. I would suspect that if you had to, you'd "take the bullet." Do you know people like that? Those are the ones that I want to storm the barricades with.

Ladies and gentlemen, I've got news for you: I think we've got something coming. Just remember this moment, ten years from now, think back on it and look at what we will have been through. Oh, we have it coming. I told a group of young dancers in Rotterdam a few years ago, in another twenty years at least a third of this group will have died of ghastly violence. It's true, we've got it coming. Are you ready? I don't know if I'm ready, but we've got it coming, and who do you want to be there when it happens? And are you ready? Are you going to be the one? When you think about the World Trade Center and what people were doing, who was doing the saving, who was being saved, and at that moment nobody knew they had it in them. At one moment to take somebody's hand and say, "Let's go." It happens, you know. *(Singing)* "I want to be ready, I need to be ready, I want to be ready, ready." Now that's the song, that's what we're talking about, right? And when your actors or dancers are up there, you want to be like, yeah we're doing modern dance but what we're actually talking to the world about is, we are soldiers. We are the soldiers of the imagination. We are the ones who are not normal, we believe in abstraction and beauty and all of those things. We are ready to fight the good fight. We are expendable, they burn us for breakfast. Literally, they will burn you for their breakfast. You will run through the machine, and you say I'm not scared. I am beautiful, I am bad, I can be vulnerable, that's why I am a performer. I am not normal. There's something about this courage and being ready. Are you ready?

AB: In the theater world if you treat the stage as this sort of extraordinary space, then you can train to be ready. But if you treat it as a quotidian space or a place that you can step onto easily—

But we need to be comfortable on stage, don't we?

AB: Well, you know as well as I do that that is a paradox. There's relaxation and there's tension.

We've been doing these things lately, because we tour and we do repertory, the curtain goes up, we do a dance, curtain goes down. Curtain goes up, we do a dance, curtain goes down. Intermission, curtain goes up, we do a dance, curtain goes down. Lately, we've been trying this experiment: We don't close the curtain and—what's more—I have miked the stage manager so you hear everything. I want to hear, "Lights to half, curtain going up, sound cue one go." And they go, "Oh—her mike is on!" But then they hear it again, the piece is over, the dancers take their bows, leave, and then the crew comes out on stage, they start changing the sets and all. I've been really doing that lately, in other words, it's demystifying the stage, but here's what happens—they suddenly see the energy drop on stage, but a moment later people go into performance mode and in the middle of the piece you realize the stage has been changed. And then it's over. We take our bows and then right in front of you it goes back into a stage again. There's something in that that I'm interested in.

AB: Well, it seems like at times there are conventions that are entirely asleep. In the theater world it's not the same because there are no curtains in most theater. It's house to half, house out, stage to half, stage out, people creep on and by that time it's— *(She snores)* So the issue is to play with that expectation, so what you're doing is you're looking at art centers around the country and the world and what the expectations are.

People are a little confused, because when the intermission happens the lights come up, and suddenly there is a dancer doing whatever they want to do on stage, whether it's a phrase from class or whatever. The lights are up, the program says intermission, but because this one person is up there in their sweats moving, the audience feels that they don't have permission to leave. So you tell them, it's intermission. And I've heard that theaters are now—word got back today—concerned about this, it wasn't clear where intermission was, no one was told it was intermission.

AB: Did I say "pioneer"? I actually meant "anarchist." Any questions?

Audience: You spoke about masters, and you were speaking of Beethoven versus Shakespeare, and my question was if you did Shakespeare, he wrote for actors, but Beethoven didn't necessarily write his pieces to be performed by dancers.

Oh, he probably would have hated it.

Audience: So, those are very different concepts then, they're both great artists, so when you approach a master like that, do you even think about that in terms of what was the intention, I mean you're taking a piece of art that had a certain intention and you are making it your own. And what is that process?

Well, that is subversive. I can't be concerned with what he would have thought, but do I think that I have a viable chance to have a dialogue with his work that would be useful? That is, to make something that would move people. I'd rather err on that side. What else can I do? I've got to do my homework and understand the music, I've got to try to meet it as honestly as I can.

Audience: How do you meet something—you take a piece of Beethoven that is essentially finished. He's finished that piece of art. So how do you finish that? You are adding on to that, so how does that process work?

You know, someone was saying poems are never finished, they're abandoned. I don't think I have a perfect answer. One thing that I love to do when I work with Beethoven is to put on the music as I would put on James Brown or what have you and just improvise to it and record my responses in the moment. And you see oneself thinking. You also see oneself responding to things you couldn't even think. And then Janet [Wong, associate artistic director] actually analyzes those improvisations. She actually learns them. And then she teaches them, then they become vocabulary. So a lot of that material did not come from a place that was conscious, it came from a place that was somewhere else. Then the work is over months and weeks, it has to be cultivated until you say, okay, it's ready to be shown. And even then it can still change. It continues, if I don't like this or I want to take that away. We've been doing works sometimes that are almost two years old and I will still be changing them.

Audience: You said very early on you wanted to bring formal dance and story together—that this work, you thought, was the future.

You mean the text and the movement together? There was something that I could feel in my gut that I was interested in, a way of working—that there was this world of stories out there. So there could be a whole body of work of which this was only the beginning. That doesn't often happen. Sometimes I feel like I'm repeating myself, sometimes I feel like there's a dead end. But you do something and you think that effort was successful and now I think I should try it again. Usually I'm scared to try it again, I think I cannot repeat that. I have a piece in the repertory which is called *D-Man in the Water*, which is very popular with audiences and I've never been able to repeat that again. It would be so useful to have an audience pleaser like that but I can't do it. So that's what I mean.

Audience: I was wondering what you thought the difference is between using music and text and the creative side. I know a lot about your process with music, but I never really worked with you with text as your musical source.

What do you think, Janet? The difference between music and text? I'm freer with text?

Janet Wong: No, it's very different because music is so abstract, you can bring anything from your memory, your life history to it; but text is specific. So I think the approach is very different.

I like text because I feel the boundaries are clearer. And there is something about a narrative. I know where this is going. I trust that this train is going to stop. I'm hearing it stop. I'm insecure, so I think I felt more relaxed working with text. With the music, some of the music that I have been working with is big music, tough ideas. And text, somehow, you know a short story, I felt secure and supported by it. Now I'm trying to find the next one. I'm thinking about Yukio Mishima's *Patriotism*. Anyone know it? If you want to read one of those tough stories of the world, tough—did you read it yet, Janet? Oh my God, if you want the most detailed account of ritual suicide, complete with the guts spilling out and the vomiting, everything which is described in the most luminous language, this is the story. It's not a little parable—it's big time—and it's dangerous because it's about a right-wing young officer, a Japanese man in the army, who rather than attack his friend and to try a coup, he has decided that there is only one solution which is to open his stomach. And his young wife, married for six months, agrees to go with him. So it's very formal in that way, the woman, the man, there is honor, the knife. And she can't be in the next room, he needs a witness. So she has to watch the whole thing and then she has permission to kill herself after he does. Which is a show of his trust for her, because if a man didn't trust his wife he would kill her first, but he gives her the privilege of killing herself after. So, you know there's this story and that story, this relationship and that one, so is this the one?

Audience: You were talking about insecurities and self-consciousness earlier, if you had to put on a five-second dance right now in this room, what would be your inspiration? The things that you would look at inside of yourself or inside of the room to do that?

You. That's where I would start. Then I would take five places, it would be you here, you here, then here, that's three, four, then I've got to get back to the front, and I wouldn't sit down because I have to take this and make it something else.

Audience: That was fifteen seconds.

But I was talking the whole time, did you ask me to make a piece or perform a piece? I could have improvised it, it would be very fast, but that's what it takes. Now why five seconds, why the time?

Audience: I didn't want to trouble you too much. Just enough time to actually accomplish it.

But five seconds is a hard thing to—

Audience: It's a long time.

No it's not a long time. In terms of dance, no it's not. In silence, yes, it is, but in terms of doing anything in space, like that, it's gone, and what's more, how much time did you have to apprehend it?

Audience: Well it's given me a year's worth of education

Five seconds. Well, I think that's a great idea. Little tiny short things. You'd have to do a lot of them. *(To Anne)* Have you done that?

AB: We've talked about doing these things. To actually say, in each play that we've done as a company, what do you need to cultivate as an actor to accomplish this piece, and what is something you need to do it, really? It's too good of an idea,

which is to find this small piece that represents the lessons we learned in learning to do this particular piece.

Wow. An existing play?

AB: **Yeah, from all the productions we've done in our twelve years, to say in order to perform** *bobrauschenbergamerica*, **what would Bondo [Will Bond] need to do to make other people learn what it took for him to learn how to do that.**

That's very smart.

AB: **Well, I didn't come up with that idea. But I think we should do it.**

I have a friend, Lois Welk, who has a scientific mind. At the American Dance Asylum, she encouraged us to try. Our classes would start with improvisation. First thing in the morning, you'd have to dance, you'd stretch and you'd dance some more, and it was always structured. It was a method—a training. And then I realized one day as she was talking, that she had a box with cards and all those structures, those exercises that were generated, she would write down, and she could refer back to them—that calls for a scientific mind. I have an improviser's mind and I can make it today, tomorrow, I won't remember where it came from. That's a frustration that I have.

AB: **I have to ask you a question, then. When you were asked that question just now, the instant before you actually started to do something, can you describe it?**

I'm not proud of that one.

AB: **Is that a "Fuck you for asking"?**

No, no, that's such an easy one, I could have— *(He jumps up and starts dancing)* What is that? That's called "Go." There is no moment before. He was asking me something I thought I would really have to shape, so at that moment I wanted to challenge him. I was calculating when I did that, because I was being put on the spot. But when you "just go," there is no time, it's between you and God. Go! Who wants to go? You want to go? Come on, let's go— *(He dances with an audience member, Christine)* Go is easy. It's easy. Now, how to repeat it, how to make it not just something Christine and I did, how to develop it, how to capture it, that is my problem. I want to be a good craftsman.

Audience: Have you ever been tempted to leave this country for any length of time? Would you think about it?

Well, my friend over there is smirking because it's an ongoing conversation. I think that it's too late now. The blush is off the rose. There was a time, maybe fifteen years ago, when the French would have been all too happy to take another disaffected African-American artist, and I could've done that, but I didn't. You know, with all I've said about "we've got it coming" and all, I still think I am an American artist. It's weird to say, I'm a world human being, but I'm an American artist. Every place else feels like a place I visit, I couldn't live there. Because living there, I couldn't—my brother's ashes are buried in the rosebush, Arnie's ashes are in the tree, this is the house we got together, this is where Bjorn and I are building now, the company, the dancers, there's Shaneeka, there's Ayo, there's Malcolm, Chicago, there's all those things, there's Anne, this is what is real to me. My friend thinks I'm limiting myself, that it could become real somewhere else, but I don't think so. *(To the audience)* What about you?

Audience: I used to. I don't anymore.

I want to be loved here and I want to be able to grow old here. And I wonder about that—who'll catch me if I fall? There's no safety nets, and that's scary. I'm here.

Audience: What are you working on right now?

That's what I was talking about with the *Patriotism* story.

Audience: That's a piece?

I don't know yet. It's between that or Schnitzler's *La Ronde*.

AB: Would you do the play or . . . ?

That's just it, what would it be? Would it be two actors reading the parts and then my company dancing as some sort of counterpart to it?

AB: No.

My company learning the text and dancing to it as they did the text?

AB: Better.

So you see where I'm at. Or do something like we did in *Mercy*. Have a story read in some way, and then there's another activity that goes parallel to it. That's why I was saying this is a very, very difficult story. That's where I'm taking it right now. I'm thinking about that—how to continue with text. Then I heard professor Peter Wapnewski, an eighty-year-old German philologist delivering the opening address at a concert hall in Dortmund, Germany. Bjorn translated the lecture for me. At one point in his speech about value, worth, meaning and language, Professor Wapnewski said, "We believe in equality and individuality, and yet these ideals, individuality and equality, are opposite and unreconcilable." In his speech, this philosopher of language wondered if modern society could ever achieve true democracy. And here, as I looked at this German intellectual from central casting, an older man, hair out like this, glasses down his nose, I tried to reconcile his identity and ideas with my own and the body I live in.

How do I cope with these ideas? Do I let the speech happen and then we sort of demonstrate what we are? Is my company representing the energy of the future, confronting—to use Secretary of Defense Donald Rumsfeld's term—"old Europe"? I love old Europe. I'm a fan of early romantic music, honor, value, language, worth, all of these things. And yet we practice this esoteric art form, which has to do with the body and what Christine and I just did. What was that brazen display? As a Romanian critic once said to Arnie Zane and me after a performance of early duets at the library of the American Embassy in Bucarest, "I noticed in the piece that you just performed, you stood on your head, and that's not dancing. That's not touched by the hand of God." Think about the value system behind what she was saying. Such value systems are behind many of the enduring masterpieces we have. How do I use Mishima's text as a kind of foil to interrogate, to critique? The piece is going to be called *Blind Date*.

AB: That's great. Was that your idea?

That's mine. These elements, these questions meeting, unannounced, unmitigated, on a date. That's what I'm working on.

AB: I just want to take this opportunity to thank you on behalf of everybody in this room.

Thank you thank you thank you.

Zelda Fichandler

Many years ago, Zelda had a big idea. She wanted to move the axis of power of theater away from Broadway and into the regions. She united idea with action and, in 1950, together with her husband and Edward Magnum, she co-founded the Arena Stage in Washington D.C. She remained its artistic director until 1991. Zelda did a lot more than found a major regional theater. She became a spokeswoman, a writer, an educator, a speaker and an activist. Her big idea exerted a tremendous influence in the culture of the American theater. Even those who do not know about her or do not realize what an effect she has upon their lives have been profoundly influenced by her action in the world.

For me, the name Zelda Fichandler has always carried a lot of weight. "Zelda!" I always thought. How appropriate that a woman with such immense ideas would be named "Zelda." For my generation she was considered the mother of the regional theater movement. She was a model in the world of a woman who made things happen and she brought people together. She is, to this day, universally known by that first name: Zelda. Zelda!

The arts world we know today is the product of the not-for-profit arts revolution led by Zelda and her colleagues. Zelda called it the "long revolution," describing the slow, continual development of institutions and funding sources that radically changed how the arts were produced in this country. This revolution created the rich diversity of dance, theater, music and visual art that we benefit from today.

At Arena Stage, Zelda embraced a vast sweep of dramatic literature, making a home for important European playwrights such as Brecht, Frisch, Ionesco and Mrozek, alongside significant American revivals of works by Albee, Miller, Williams, O'Neill, Wilder, Kaufman and Hart, and classics by Shakespeare, Shaw, Molière, Ibsen and others. Broadway, too, has felt the impact of Zelda's work, especially with the development of new plays. *The Great White Hope, Indians, Moonchildren, Pueblo, A History of the American Film, Zalmen or the Madness of God, Raisin* and *K2* all started at Arena Stage.

From 1991–1994, Zelda was artistic director of the Acting Company, and from 1984 until very recently, Zelda was chair of the graduate acting program and Master Teacher of Acting and Directing at the Tisch School of the Arts at New York University. Her commitment to young people coming into the field is undeniable. Both at the Acting Company and NYU, she exerted a powerful hand in making sure that the training of actors was considered and executed seriously.

The list of honors that Zelda has received illustrates the immense admiration the field has for her: the National Medal of Arts, awarded by President Clinton; the Common Wealth Award for distinguished service to the dramatic arts; the Brandeis University Creative Arts Award; the Acting Company's John Houseman Award for her commitment to the development of young American actors; the Margo Jones Award for the production of new plays; the Washingtonian of the Year Award; the Ortho 21st Century Women Trailblazer Award; and the Society for Stage Directors and Choreographers' George Abbott Award. The New York commercial theater world awarded Zelda and Arena Stage the Antoinette Perry (Tony) Award in 1976, the first to be given to a company outside New York. In 1999 she was inducted into the Theatre Hall of Fame, making her the first artistic leader outside of New York to receive this honor. In 2007, she was recognized at NYU with the Distinguished Teaching Award.

In 2009, for its fiftieth anniversary, The Stage Directors and Choreographers Society established their Zelda Fichandler Award to honor a director and choreographer each year for accomplishment and future promise in the regions outside of New York.

October 4, 2004

AB: Zelda Fichandler really is one of the founders of the American regional theater. Zelda has been, I think, a stateswoman for the theater throughout her career and continues to be so, in terms of the art on the stage, in terms of training. She runs the acting program at NYU, which is, I think, the best acting training in the country. She was awarded the National Medal of Arts by President Clinton. She's a part of the Theatre Hall of Fame. When Maureen [Towey, former SITI administrative staff member] was looking for a catchy phrase for the email, I said, "Zelda's like the doyenne of the American theater." In the book *The Tipping Point* there's a thing called the maven, which is the person you don't know is actually the cause of everything. I think sitting next to me is a maven. I hope we get into substantive issues about the times we're living in, the role of theater in these times, because I can't think of anybody better to speak with about this issue. You in the fifties, sixties, starting from scratch—can we start with this story?

ZF: Well it's a long story and it starts, really, way back when. The word theater in Greek, "teatron," a place for seeing—seeing into—tells us that our art began with a deep connection to life, as a way to understand and connect to that life. It had nothing to do with acquiring whatever the exchange unit was at the time, with treasure, with money. One imagines that some tribal leader or maybe the best hunter, got up and said, "Gather around and let me tell you what happened on the hunt today." And he started to talk and then maybe someone got up and acted out the hunter, and someone else acted out the bear, and it went on from there. And that's how we imagine that the theater was born. And if you look through history, this idea of theater never died. People were always examining their own lives except when a culture was in decline. And then theater would disappear and something like circuses—entertainment—would take its place.

In the years after World War II, I don't know why it happened then, a few people looked at the theater we had and thought it wasn't good enough. Ten blocks of Broadway was what we considered to be the American theater. It wasn't enough because it was only in one place in this vast country and it wasn't enough because the aim was essentially to make money rather than to illuminate living experience. We wanted to change the way it was and bring back theater to its age-old connections to the living process. So we tried to do that, and to over-simplify the struggle, it has worked. It's an astounding story really—I can hardly believe it. There are around a thousand theaters now in the United States—can you believe it?! Where artists can work and people can participate in the telling of stories. We don't know yet how far this development will go in terms of artistic achievement.

As for starting from scratch, so did I, in a way. In 1950 with my husband and my teacher and a small group of Washingtonians, we began a theater—a place for seeing—with the financial help of our neighbors and friends. I had no idea how to make or lead such a thing, but I thought we could figure that out as we went along. When I was eleven years old I entered a contest sponsored by the *Washington Star,* a local newspaper, for the best essay on "What I Want to Be When I Grow Up." I won the contest and my first dollar. I said I wanted to be an actress, not for the fame or money, but to show people how people behaved and why they behaved the way they did. I didn't become an actress but the notion of theater as a life's work remained.

In my late teens I stumbled on a program at Cornell University called Contemporary Soviet Civilization. I was the youngest of some four hundred to five hundred people who signed up for it: journalists, politicians, some doctors, teachers—all grown-ups—I learned Russian, read Chekhov and, later, Stanislavski in the original language, but, more than that, I got a new grasp on political and social history. It was my gateway to the world and I became a social activist. After I graduated and was working for military intelligence at the Pentagon, writing the manual on the Red Army from captured Russian documents, on the side I organized workers to join the Public Workers Union, a left-wing union. For this I was fired, or as they put it, "reduced-in-force." Actually I felt increased in force and happy to leave that terrible building.

All this fed what I was to do with my professional life, and I guess since I didn't know much about theater, what was important was my ability to use logic to get from this point to that, something I think I learned from my scientist father. To get what I want by charting a path from A to B. It was a kind of "wiliness," what in Yiddish is called "saykhel," which means, I guess, good, common horse-sense.

Horse-sense?

Yes, an ability to use to our advantage whatever it was we found around us. And an indomitable will—which, thank God, I still have, because I still need it. Everything in society stands against the attempt to create an institutional life that persists and develops, that grows from within the lives of the people who are creating it and isn't pasted on from the outside, and at the same time has some orientation that is beyond the artist, so that there is a genuine intersection between the creative center of the community and the creative center of the art. And so it was helpful that I knew the community. I was really one of them. And in a certain way, the audience built itself on what we gave them by way of repertory and evolving artistic values.

I want to mention here the large contribution made by Alan Schneider, the American director who directed the original production of Albee's *Who's Afraid of Virginia Woolf?* and introduced Samuel Beckett to this country. His artistry was a significant factor in the success of our early years. And I consider him my most influential teacher of the stage as a space of the imagination. While I eventually found my own way of working as a director, he pointed the way, and encouraged me. His influence was strong in Arena's taking-off. Later, in 1961, he opened the newly built Arena with the American premiere of Bertolt Brecht's *Caucasian Chalk Circle.* And, in 1973, he and I took the acting company in *Our Town* and *Inherit the Wind* to Moscow and Leningrad under the auspices of the State Department, the first American company to play there.

What was it like at the beginning?

Well, at the beginning, would you believe this? In the first year we did seventeen productions. I slept on the floor many times, then I became pregnant and couldn't sleep on the floor anymore. The audience was small, so it was two- and three-week runs. We couldn't close because we had to pay the rent. The repertory was wild. It was a series of offbeat, well-chosen plays that interested me and my radical political background.

We went around and we collected fifteen thousand dollars by calling people up from the phonebook, small businessmen mostly, and by getting groups of people together. We opened with about two thousand dollars left in the kitty. We were not Equity until the end of the year, when Equity came down and unionized us. Actors took turns being the stage manager. With a carpenter, I built some of the sets in the back alley. It grew upon itself. This is the story of every young organization. It's nothing really elaborate or interesting, deeply, except that it grew upon itself, whereas everybody predicted failure. We had four newspapers then. Everybody predicted that it would not be successful as other attempts had failed. Then at the end of five years and fifty-five productions—by then I had two children—we found, despite the filled seats, that with two hundred forty-seven seats we couldn't pay for what we needed. I wrote a paper for the board—"The Economics of the Too-Small Theatre." We closed for a year and a half, reopened at an abandoned brewery.

Where were you first?

Ninth and New York Avenue. In the slum area of D.C., strangely enough, directly across from the main public library.

What kind of building was it?

It was an abandoned porn movie house, actually. And the landlord's name was Sidney Lust.

That's too perfect.

But we had to pay whatever the rent was year-round, so we had to operate year-round. So that's how it got to be fifty-five productions in five years. Sometimes nobody came. We did a play called *Mr. Arcularis* by Conrad Aiken, and I remember one of the headlines was, "*Mr. Arcularis*, What Cold Feet You Have." It was about this guy being transported dead in a coffin. Not designated to sell tickets. So we'd have six people in the audience at the matinee. But then it grew.

What did you do for that year and a half that you closed down?

We disbanded and we looked for something else. My husband was supporting us and the children. Later on, he gave up his prestigious job as an economist with the Twentieth Century Fund and joined in full-time. There was no discussion. I said, "You're needed here." And he said, "Okay." Instant poverty for one family.

When you started the theater, what words did you use to describe it?

I wrote this—it's now become sort of a signature paragraph. It's far from profound. It just said that the ten blocks of Broadway had become the American theater, and it was now time to make theater part of a community as were its schools, its libraries, its churches, and that we wanted to engage in an ongoing dialogue about matters of importance to all of us, and that people who were coming on were making Washington their home for the first time and that many of the artists were making Washington their permanent community. I might have said something about a home—not a hotel—for artists.

Those are eloquent words.

They are? They seem to me to lack aesthetic content, although I believe I spoke about an acting company. It was an arena. My teacher, Edward Magnum, who only recently died, and who left in the second or third year for health reasons, came from Dallas, which had an arena. He was very hot on the arena form as it allowed for viewers to see the same story from different perspectives, and at the same time it was democratic. Everybody had a good view to the stage. I came to have different feelings about it. I liked it because if the pitch was steep it became like a choreographic space, and you could actually see the kinetics of thought and feeling. I liked it because you could explode the life within the text, because there's a front on any place on the stage. It's not a directional stage. It's a nondirectional stage—like a stage for a choreographer—something like the way Merce Cunningham uses the space. Then we moved to the Old Vat Room, which we named because the costume designer decided that since it wouldn't be the Old Vic—because it was a brewery—it would be the Old Vat. It was at Twenty-Sixth and D, on the waterfront, which was where the highway to the Roosevelt Bridge moved. And there we stayed for five years.

Can I take a look at the context of theater in the United States? When did Nina Vance start Alley?

Around the same time. Margo Jones started first. Margo, Nina and I started within two or three years of each other. Margo was first, in the late forties.

In Dallas? And that was the arena that you were talking about?

Yes, a one hundred ninety-eight-seat theater in a fan factory on the Dallas State Fair grounds.

Which of the two of them dumped out her wallet and said, "With whatever change I have we'll begin a theater."

That was the Alley. And I think it was two dollars and fourteen cents and one hundred people showed up.

That was Nina Vance?

Yes. We actually raised money—about fifteen thousand dollars. There were seven or eight of us, we put in one thousand dollars and others put in less. That's an act of faith in 1950. Tom and I had two thousand dollars in the bank; one thousand went to the down payment on our house and the other thousand went to this remote enterprise. Then we called on members of the community: a White House policeman; a tennis champion; Bess Davis Schreiner, who ran the Theatre Guild at the National Theatre; Burke Knapp, the vice president of the World Bank, whose wife was an actress.

So you just went to these people.

We knew no fear. I drew the blueprints myself for the theater design—as well as I could draw them. I remember calling up Kay Jewelers and saying, "We're members of the same community and my friends and I have an idea for a resident theater company in the district. Would you let me come and talk to you?" He thought, Well, this kid, let her come over. And he gave us a thousand dollars. It bolstered our sense of possibility.

You have to ask.

Yes.

You have to have the words, and you have to ask.

You have to have the words, and you have to have the enthusiasm. You have to believe it. If you don't believe it, body and soul, don't let on. There are very few people you can ever share doubt with, and you need to be posessed, for sure.

It occurs to me that, unless we find other people, the first three theaters were started by *women*.

There was one more—Dorothy Chernik in Rochester, New York. Hers folded. It was fifty-three years ago. Fifty-four?

And the Guthrie was the sixties, right?

The Guthrie was 1963.

And A.C.T. was later—the mid-sixties. The boys came later, right?

An early one was the Actor's Workshop, Jules Irving and Herbert Blau in San Francisco.

But the very first one was Margo Jones, and people forget her. Her repertory was classics—and she defined that as a play fifty years old or older that has lasted—and new scripts. She's the one who launched Tennessee Williams on his career. She had a company of eight professional actors and a small staff, and that was the beginning, really. I remember ANTA arranged for me to see her one hot summer. I bought a hat. In those days, a lady wore a hat. I came prepared to meet, you know, the doyenne. And she was there in her sandals and no stockings and sitting on the desk and swinging her legs. Unfortunately, she died at forty-two, which was a great loss. She wrote a book called *Theatre-in-the-Round* in which she predicted that there would some day be forty theaters in the United States! I sorely regret that she couldn't see what she launched. Her book is still important to read. It's inspiring and at the same time chatty.

I love chatty books.

Chatty and even gossipy. Gossip's good. Without gossip, the need for gossip, the enjoyment of gossip, there wouldn't be theater. You have to be interested in what other people are up to. Gossip is not trivial. People who are interested in the human species tend to be interested in gossip—even if it's not true. It's a story. It's a story about somebody's involvement with other people—or with money. Or with land. Or with the need to get ahead. Or with pain and suffering. It's not trivial. The only thing I like about the plays of the Restoration is their love of gossip and how they use that to make their way.

Anthropologists say that for human beings, gossiping is the equivalent of animals nit-picking.

That's interesting. That's true. You see a woman straighten the collar of a man's jacket or something like that, brush dandruff off the shoulders— that's like animal behavior.

I wanted to share a story with you—something that Bob Brustein said. After he left Yale and went to Harvard to start American Repertory Theater, he had this idea to continue what he'd done at Yale and start a school for actor, playwright, dramaturg, director training. So he went to the president when he got to Harvard and said, "You know, it's all fine and good to have a theater, we have the A.R.T., but we actually need a school for advanced training in acting, directing, playwriting and dramaturgy." And the president said, "At Harvard we do not do art schools." So he went away and about a month later he sees the president again. He says, "It's all fine and good to have a theater, but we actually need a conservatory." And the president said, "We don't do conservatories here at Harvard for the arts." So he left, and he came back about a month later, and said, "Mr. President, it's all fine and good to have a theater, but I want to start an institute." And the president of Harvard said, "Ah, yes, we do do institutes here at Harvard." And thus began the Institute for Advanced Theater Training.

Oh, that's amazing.

I think it's a profound story.

The profound power of words.

Because if you can find the words to describe your thing they're like keys. They unlock doors, but they have to fit.

And they have to appeal to something—an image, the imagination of whoever you're talking to—so they feel they're putting their faith and their money into something that matters to them or that brings them prestige or that connects them to a spiritual, functional endeavor. Words are very, very important in building an institution—because, as you know, you also have to invigorate the troupes with language. You have to find words to inspire, to inspirit. To keep alive the creative impulse.

I think in this culture we give up too easily on language.

I think that's true. Not enough people believe in the cracks in the universe that you have to wiggle into to get anything new established. There are cracks—places that are not filled in that need to be filled in, so the edifice doesn't crumble. And if you believe in the arts passionately, they fit into those cracks, because without those connective tissues of understanding all we are are people who go to war every so often.

That is such a stunning thought—to look for the cracks. We work a lot with a music group called Rachel's, and Christian, one of the musicians, plays with the View-

points—they watch the actors on the stage and they play music. I said once, "How do you do it? You make this music and it's so supportive of what's going on." He said, "I listen for what's missing." Usually we feel like we have to make something happen—we have to create out of stone or whatever, but actually the notion of looking for the cracks is stunning.

And that is the reason that this regional theater movement now exists in every state, in Alaska. Small, large—the largest is the Guthrie right now. But the reason is that there were those cracks. Touring companies were not enough. They were facsimiles of something that came out of New York. Our new theaters were a community enterprise. They grew out of the community and engaged the community. We attracted people who wanted to see what we wanted to do, even though it took years—decades, even— to establish that linkage in a larger way. The linkage is made over time, chiefly through the repertory. "Repertory is destiny," is my thought.

But isn't that destiny often shaped by the administrators rather than the artists?

Yes. It's often the marketing director who wants to do the season. The marketing director is pressing for what will sell. In the spring you do something for group sales, for the tourists—particularly in Washington. I chose to do *Three Sisters* at a time when the classics were not "in." There was a period in the fifties and sixties where the rubric was "No More Masterpieces." I think Artaud's slogan. It was astounding how this story of how time wears away life and burns up dreams appealed to the Washington public. That was a great experience for me and emboldened me.

But now, not because of marketing directors per se, but survival becomes very important in a theater, especially in a second or third generation, where you don't want it to go down on your watch. You don't want to be the one to kill a theater. Theaters are precious and many of them by now have a long history and long tradition and even a specific style, an aesthetic style. A new artistic director, who comes in after the founder or after the second artistic director, wants to keep that theater alive. Nothing is really settled; there's a new state of dis-equilibrium, and you hope that things will get better. So that's what they're holding on to. I feel for them. I understand their predicament totally. I think they have a great deal of courage. I think some of the artistic directors are compromising what they would really like to do. But it's not over till it's over. And if the regional theater seems to be resting right now—not on its laurels, but just resting. It's treading water. It's like somebody that's waiting for the tide to shift it. What will shift it? Good question. It needs an infusion of funds perhaps. It needs an infusion of artistic leadership, I don't really know.

I want to tell you about the hierarchical structure. When the Ford Foundation came into the arts, into theater and into dance—that was Mac Lowry, who was the vice president in charge of humanities and the arts. He tried to help us organize a structure in the interest of the good health of the institution. What was there to copy at the time? The business model. So you have a board of trustees who are responsible for the fiscal health of the institution, for contact with the community, for raising funds. You have an artistic director—actually, I wanted the title producing director— and the managing director, who were, supposedly, hired by the board. Then under that you had administration and artistic staff members. That's sort of a business model. The idea of there not being artists on the board was really ridiculous. Artists are terribly smart about their own destiny, and they know very well the power of promotion and publicity. They know how to economize. They know what matters. They know that wages for artists mean more than costumes. Artists should be, I think, at least a third of the board and can educate as they go, can educate the board to the values, to the culture of that particular institution.

Was the Arena board like that from the beginning?

The first Arena board was a regular for-profit board and was invited by Ed Mangum and me, with assurances about artistic freedom through something called a Voting Trust. Our thinking was not advanced enough to include other artists. We became not-for-profit later in the fifties and the original board selected new members as they replaced themselves or added additional people.

And so it went over time, by habit. Artists were always invited to board meetings to talk with the board or present examples of their work, but were never in a decision-making position, and I take responsibility for that failure. It just never occurred to me. After '91, when I left, things continued as they were.

When it came time to talk about a new building, I woke up. The artists and I wanted it to stay in the old location, near the Potomac River and the sky, and made our opinions known. But the board wanted to move downtown where some other smaller theaters were moving, to create a kind of D.C. Broadway. Only cost considerations prohibited that. There was a lot of contention about this—I would come down from New York City for meetings, and write contesting memos to the board. It was then that I realized how important the voices of the artists could be.

I think board members, being largely businesspeople, see artists as whimsical, capricious, temperamental people who can't understand numbers or make grown-up decisions. Maybe artists don't belong on the Investment Committee; nor do I.

Audience: Is there a model other than the business model you could see?

I don't know enough about what's going on at the moment. I imagine a company like Bill Rauch's Cornerstone Theater Company must operate differently. I think that their artists participate in decision-making. I remember the Joint Stock Theatre Group that Mark Wing-Davey works with, with Caryl Churchill. It's difficult because like all positions it contains the possibilities of its opposite, so the danger is that there'll be divisiveness in decision-making, but that has to be worked through, I think. I'm beginning to believe in smaller companies—smaller spaces, less real estate, smaller budgets. The Guthrie's budget is going to be, I think, nineteen million dollars a year. That's got to affect repertory. Arena's budget is about fourteen million, but if they build a new building it's going to go up. It's got to affect repertory. How could it not affect repertory?

AB: You were talking about doubt.

Everybody who's ever led anything—whether it's a family or a camp or whatever—lives with a lot of doubt because you make a lot of decisions, and they're either right or they're wrong. And some of them are going to be wrong because we're imperfect creatures. So you live with doubt if you have any sense. If you have any wisdom, doubt is appropriate to leadership. That's why I think Bush is such a fool. I don't think he's aware of doubt in himself. But you can't go around saying, "I don't know why I picked this play. I'm not sure it's a good play. I don't think this is going to work." You can't do that because there are too many people who are going to be affected by doubt. You can say, "I want to think this over. How can we do this better? Who's got an idea of how we can expand this particular aspect of our work?" That doesn't mean you close off input. But your face and the tone of voice and the way you walk down the hall shouldn't be the way you feel on the inside. That's what you do at night. Or early in the morning, when you might gag a little bit. I used to gag in the morning. My children even remember that. I used to have the dry heaves. My husband would help me with that: "Of course you can do it." He might have had doubt, but he never let me know. I think it's doubt that exhausts one. And then you have to sort of get it up again and keep going. Doubt: Do I do this weird East European play simply because I like it? Or is it socially useful to the community? Will they find something in it that's generative? Or interesting? Or resonant to their own thoughts and feelings at this time? Do I? So, you do.

AB: I've been playing with a theory: The end product of certainty is always violence. Patriotism leads to violence. Certainty kills art, too. There's the paradox of having to move with certainty or act with certainty as an actor, a director or whatever—but the inside opposition of doubt. Strahler said what he learned from Bertolt Brecht is to doubt everything, and the importance of doubt. Even for fundraising, I don't think you can ask people for something without the feeling of doubt. And they will accept it.

But need moves you away from doubt. Need generates belief—because you want to rescue something. You have to be on fire with belief, actually, when you're trying to lead. And in the privacy of one or two relationships you can say, "It's not working." And you may even have to lock doubt away within you, at least for a time.

AB: Jack O'Brien, who has run the Old Globe for a billion years, is one of the most enthusiastic human beings on the planet, in the sense of enthusiasm meaning filled with God. When I was going to be artistic director of Trinity Repertory Company, he said, "Anne, you have to go in the building, and you have to touch the fabric. Your mood affects everybody. If you're in a bad mood, everybody will be in a bad mood. It's really important how you walk in that building."

I wasn't always good about this. Somebody was doing a story about me, and they talked to my colleagues. One woman said, "Well, she's very moody." I read that and I thought, "Hmm. I'm not very good at this." And I tried to change and not be so moody, and not let my moods affect other people.

AB: Was that a good thing to do—that adjustment?

I think it helped.

Audience: What brought you over to NYU? And what was your impetus when you got there? It seems that you created a school that made the perfect actor to go straight back into Arena. It seems like the most natural jump.

Well, that's what I did. I was coming to the end of my imaginative power for an institution. I didn't know where to take it further than it was. I ended with a three-million-dollar multicultural grant, the spillover from which is still going on—an apprentice program that trains people from various ethnic groups in all the different arts in the theater; we had an integrated acting company; we introduced various playwrights of different colors. I wanted to create a young company. I wanted to create a school attached to the theater. I wanted to tour in the area and bring the theater to people who couldn't get to us. The economy was dipping so that we were actually cutting back rather than moving forward. We were always able to finance our work up until the end of the eighties. Since the early nineties, the budget has been cut back. The budget now at Arena is about the same as it was when I left twelve years ago. They have to count how many actors they can have in a season. That changes the repertory. My desire was to show the interaction of social forces, either contemporary or of a time, with individuals. So we did big plays. I had some reasonable need to know that I couldn't use thirty-two people in half the plays, because I'd have to bring in too many actors outside the company. But I didn't have to count the way people have to count now.

So I had reached the end, but I had been teaching, always. I taught at Boston University, University of Texas at Austin and NYU. I was asked to be on a committee to pick a new chair for the acting department at NYU. And then one day I heard a voice—this is the truth—say, "You know, I'd like to throw my hat in the ring for this job." Our company was getting older. And the young actors I was bringing in were not able to do as diverse a repertory as we were doing. I felt that we needed young actors of a different kind. I'd always been interested in training. So I took that job, and I didn't know how to construct a curriculum, how to integrate a faculty, how to pick students. But I knew the end product, and I had to work back through process and construct it. I picked actors who, if trained, could create out of nothing, who could work on new plays, who could do Shaw, Shakespeare, who were able to reach their emotions and thoughts and act in a more realistic manner. Theater is not a place that is real by nature. People are looking at it, and other people are making believe that they believe. The belief comes from nature but is not real-real but real-theatrical. There is nothing real. Anybody that talks about realism is not understanding the paradoxical nature of the stage, I think. Nobody really dies at the matinee performance. The show must go on.

AB: There was a test that was done on actors and Olympic jumpers where they tested the vital signs of both, and apparently an actor in front of an audience speaking a monologue is under more stress than an Olympic jumper. So, you realize: No, it's not natural or real.

It's amazing. I did a little bit of acting. I hate to admit it because, when I look back, it was pretty bad. But I lost weight every time I did something. I used to lose weight because of the stress. If you don't believe in the fiction, then the audience doesn't believe it, then contact isn't made and nothing occurs in that room, where you both live in the same space at the same time.

So, the training is built up around that idea. It's a good training program. They're able to work because they can sing, they can move, they can improvise, they can talk, they can scan a line, they can be funny, they know the clown in them, they're unselfconscious. The actor has learned that they're the only one of the kind in the world. Each actor is unique to him or herself. And your biggest competitor as an actor is you. I found I enjoyed teaching as much as directing.

AB: When you looked around originally you looked for the cracks. When you look around now, what do you see?

That is so hard. I think, maybe, what my students want to do: get rid of their loans so they can make choices; create material; work in a simple way, rather than an ornate way, in an operatic way, in an over-expensive way; work in collectives. They're trained as an ensemble. Each class is trained as an ensemble, and they are able to work with each other no matter what year they graduated. There are maybe a dozen companies that could be formed out of the people who have come out in the last twenty years. I think they want a place to work. They want a home—the same thing actors wanted at the beginning. They also want to be able to act in the other media, which is different than when I started out because the other media were not so compelling. Even the commercials now, I think, are quite respectable. They want to get away and do film, but they want a home base where they can create work. I notice our graduates want to continue studying with the teachers that they studied with in school. We send faculty out to the West Coast, where we have a lot of people. I think the crack is—really, it's not an institutional crack. It's an artist crack. It's about where the artists go to be artists. There are no companies anymore to speak of. San Diego has a company. The Alley has a small company. The promise of our theater—the generation that I come from—was that there would be artistic homes. There aren't artistic homes. And actors aren't paid enough. And they're not going to be. So they need to make money on TV and film.

AB: There is another practical creative crack—because I think when young people come into the field they come in and they see a regional theater that is resting, as you said. I find that arts centers right now are more interesting in terms of the audiences. The audiences are more diverse. They're more ready for an unusual experience. I find it to be a really wide crack that's just screaming for more work.

Do they pay well?

AB: They do. They commission work or else there are consortiums of arts centers that get together to bring plays around—and what you hear over and over again is that there's not enough theater to go around. There's the Acting Company—which you ran for three years—which is . . .

Underfunded.

AB: There's the Wooster Group. There's my company. There's Cornerstone. But there's just not enough to go around. I heard recently from the directors of these performance venues that audiences are asking for less dance and more theater. Go figure. It's the dance companies who have been filling these houses. So it's a big, wide crack.

In the third year at NYU we set aside close to a month for something we call Freeplay. And the actors can do whatever they want. They can cast themselves much better than they think we do. They can direct a piece. They can create a piece. And more and more they want to create their own work. One of them has created a really big thing this year. It played at the UN. It went to some kind of festival. It played in D.C. If you had a company that managed to produce recognizable classics and self-generated work, there might be a place for several of these. That's how the Acting Company was born. It was born out of the Juilliard School.

AB: It was Houseman who started it, right? Who said, "When you graduate, you need a place to go." It was made originally to be a touring company to begin with. So, be on the road for two years you might learn something—which is true, in front of all these different audiences. That's the best actor training: to be in front of the audience and change the audience every night.

The audience is your partner, and until you've gotten in front of them you're doing things in the void.

Audience: As someone who lives as an artist and as an administrator, I always feel that living that fire is as important to the artist as it is to the administrator. To be an administrator you have to have as much belief in the work as the artist. I wonder what your experiences are having a truckload of administrators at Arena and what has been effective and what hasn't been effective in terms of bringing people in now.

Well, I have to say, I haven't been at Arena since 1991, but our administrators stayed forever and were treated as artistic human beings because it's creative work being an administrator if it's done sensitively and well and effectively. I had the nicest thing said to me recently by this woman who doesn't work at the theater anymore, but she said, "There was never a day I came to work that I didn't realize I was working for some higher purpose." I really felt good about it.

AB: That's it. That's really it.

And what that does is having information. They know what's going on. They know what the thought process is. They know what the goals are. They're part of the five-year plan. They have to like the work on the stage. They have opinions. They're invited to rehearsal, they know what the approach is, the artistic approach to a production. There's not the Berlin Wall between the administrators and the artists. They have to believe in what they're doing.

Audience: It rings true with me for administrators to be able to work in a creative way. That's something I always try to do here. There's such an amazing collaboration that goes on in this room and we try to have our own collaboration going on in that room and figure out creative solutions.

You know, process is process, and—whether you're an administrator or an artist—you move from the unknown to the known—to what you would like to know. You move back to the unknown. You move deeper into the known. It's the same process. Everybody in an institution has to buy into the vision. The vision can be generated from someone—but a vision can be shared by many.

Audience: Compared to Europe, is it really romantic for us to think about our government helping us with money for the arts, or should we abandon that thought and maybe go on a different route? And as an educator, as well as the great artist that you are, you must have seen your share of mediocre theater. What would be your advice to guard against mediocrity in theater and what do you do with it when you confront it in your world?

You blow it up. I have no idea what you do with it. You don't come back. You leave at intermission. I don't know.

Government funding is a little bit of use. It funds projects. It doesn't fund the individual artist anymore, so it's safe. It gets a little bit of a raise this year. But the dean of Tisch School of the Arts is a woman I admire enormously, Mary Schmidt Campbell. She stopped with the government. She stopped applying for money. She has a dean's council of rather well-known artists who have money and other people in the New York community who have money, and she raises privately. She even has given up on foundations because they've switched to social programs. The great thing that happened in my generation was that we could get money. Our development department just followed whatever I wanted to do, through the sixties, seventies and eighties. Then, starting with the nineties, it wasn't there anymore. Then the foundations started pulling back .

AB: You mentioned McNeil Lowry earlier. It's never foundations or corporations— it's always individuals anyway. It's somebody who has a vision and can describe it. He was a great pioneer, and he was singularly, with the Ford Foundation, this one man who made it possible for so many theaters to be formed and founded in so many different cities.

He paid off the mortgage of our building. More than the NEA, and before it, he made the regional theater possible, not only with funds but with an understanding of its artistic mission.

AB: It isn't the Ford Foundation. It's McNeil Lowry.

It's true.

AB: And right now there are not those McNeil Lowrys around.

And corporations? What are they doing now?

Audience: Corporations give money to their artistic equivalents. Corporations give money to huge artistic corporations.

And to work they can bring their friends. So, individual giving has become very strong.

As to mediocrity, let me just read you a poem. The poem is entitled, "Let Us Be Great," by Yevgeny Yevtushenko, a favorite Russian poet of mine. "I ask of doctors and of dock workers and of whoever stitches up my coat, things should be done with magnificence. No matter what a thing is, nothing should be mediocre. Down from buildings to pairs of rubber boots. The mediocre is unnatural. What is false is not natural. Command yourself. Be famous. The lack of greatness is a matter of shame. They shall every one be great."

Audience: When I was teaching, I read something that kind of staggered me, which is that in Japan eighty percent of the budget goes to teachers and twenty percent

goes to administrators, and in the U.S. sixty-five percent of the budget goes to administrators and thirty-five percent goes to teachers. Now, to hear you talk about the regional theater being administrator heavy—is that just the way we do business in this country?

I don't know the figures anymore. But the marketing and selling of culture in America costs a hell of a lot. You know what an ad in a newspaper costs—the cost of advertising has gone way up. The cost of paper has gone way up. And artists unfortunately will work for less money because they want to do their thing. They want to do their work. The development director can earn his or her salary by bringing in more money. The better the development director's efforts are, the more money comes in. Forgetting that the audience comes to see the artists. It's the artists who are making the money. But we don't revere teachers and we don't revere artists unless they are box-office names. Isn't this a star culture? Who is more important, a rap artist or a first-grade teacher? If you have kids, and there's a first-grade teacher that can't help them unlock the code of reading, then that kid is permanently behind the eight ball. I don't want to put down rap artists. I kind of like rap, but I can't compare it to the contribution of a teacher, who can define the future of a human being—particularly in the lower grades.

AB: They're like different countries.

I don't think teachers should make what rap artists make because the commercial opening isn't there for them, but I do think they should be respected and paid accordingly.

AB: Maybe the way we talk about ourselves, the words we choose to describe ourselves are more important. You think of a boxer who says I am the greatest. Perhaps we have to use those words to describe ourselves

Audience: There's that schism: You go out there, you audition, you audition, you audition, you get told: "No, no, no, no, no." "I'm the greatest!" "No, you aren't." "I'm the greatest!" "No, you suck. Get out of here."

AB: You know, that's the incredible paradox about auditions. From being on one side of the table, the way the person walks in the room, how they own the room, how they interrelate, is so important. But if you walk in like a pauper, it won't work. So it's the tightrope that we walk. It goes back to the issue of doubt—to be full of doubt, but to be strident and particular. And I think attitude is my favorite word right now—the

attitude that you have to your work, to each other. Attitude is different than feeling. You can choose an attitude. It's really the big issue.

It's actually—you know, there's a branch of psychiatry now that teaches attitude to deal with neurotic adjustments. It's like, "Whenever I feel afraid, I whistle a happy tune." It's the backward part of acting. You act a certain way and then the feeling comes out of the way you're behaving. It's evidently proven itself out. Liviu Ciulei, the brilliant Romanian director and architect, works with actors primarily from form to feeling and if the actors come to accept the validity of that, their work is superb.

AB: It's back to Rousseau, which is: Do you feel fear when you see the bear, or do you run when you see the bear, and the running makes you feel fear?

Audience: Aren't we as artists supposed to be humble?

Well, humble—you can be humble and self-assured at the same time. Those are not contradictory. There's a wonderful book that Joanna Merlin wrote about auditioning. She's on our faculty, by the way. "What a wonderful opportunity I have to do some acting." You can go in with that attitude. "I can figure out what this is about and what kind of person this is. I get to act. And, you know, those people are looking to fill this role. They're probably a little bit anxious, too, that I be good." Because that's the truth of it. You sit on that other side and you think, Who's coming in? Maybe this is it? I don't think you should walk in like Bush and pull guns out of your pocket. It's just that you have some sense that you know what you're doing and you can share that knowledge with people.

AB: I think we tend toward the inferiority complex as artists and there are historical reasons for it. It comes out of actions that have made this country what it is. I just think we have to question our inferiority complex and not use it as an excuse.

It's difficult because acting is based on a sense of self—a strong sense of self. Because you have to will to imagine, you have to will to take an action, to deal with an obstacle, to engage with your partner. And when you get rejected, which you're going to be, that ego tends to crumble. So it's important that you have other outlets besides these ones of being judged. That's why artists should have a home to go to, to work out and work, so that the center of their ability doesn't crumble in the marketplace. Because you can lose the sense of self. I can be away from work for four days and begin to think I don't know what I'm doing. I mean that quite honestly.

AB: Didn't having kids and family help?

Very much.

AB: That's an issue for a lot of our field: How to do that? You seem to have success-fully done that.

And having grandchildren now *really* helps. I learn from them. I didn't know enough to learn from my children. But now I know enough to watch what the human animal does as it learns and negotiates reality. I feed it back into the school—the use of the body, body before language. This has got nothing to do with the business side, but my six-year-old grand-daughter is getting to keep the class pig for a period of time. She gave me this book about taking care of pigs—not that I'm to take care of one. But I'm a great believer in our animal nature, which means that action comes before words. Words are the result of wanting and needing. There's lan-guage for this baby pig: touching each other's noses is a greeting and acknowledgment. Murmurs, gurgles and grunts are contentment, com-fort, shared feelings. Stretching is relaxed comfort. Jumping is happiness, exuberance, delight. Squeaking is pain, fear, loneliness. Cooing is a calm-ing sound, reassurance. Sitting or standing up is begging for food. Standing straight up on all fours: making an impressive statement of power. Standing straight up, tilting the head back at an angle: signaling strength. Lowering the head, growling: fear. Rattling, hissing, teeth chat-tering: aggression, warning the enemy, trying to impress. Growling, grunt-ing, rattling: male mating sounds. Mouth wide open, showing teeth: female rejects male's advances. Isn't that wonderful? And then in a few million years, that's us. Many millions of years.

Audience: If you were going to start all over again, go somewhere and start a the-ater, where would you go and what would you do differently?

I can't even imagine what I would do. I would take a group of people that have trained with me—not just with me, but the group of faculty—and find a space and raise some money and get some of the people who have money to be continuing supporters of the group through other media. I would start with a group of younger people—because I don't care if younger people play older parts if they can do it. And then I would have guests, who are established in the profession and who could help support it as artists on a continuing basis, take part. I'd try to get sponsorship by the school where these kids had been trained. Actually, I'm trying to do that right now. We're trying to set up a connection between our graduates with actors-in-training. I've never thought of working without a company.

AB: Why is that?

A company is the language for making theater. Plays are about webs of relationships and if you start with a company, just picked out for that one thing, you don't have a vocabulary. You don't know the person who is under the costume. And somebody's going to say, "Is he really going to do that while I have this monologue?" I mean, it has to be a community—a company is a creative unit that would not be the same without you and you wouldn't be the same without it. It's a natural instrument for transformation, growth and change. The theaters we know as great all had companies—Shakespeare's, Molière's, the Group Theatre, the Berliner Ensemble. The company affected the playwriting as well as the acting.

Audience: What do you think is the importance in a graduate education in the arts and about meshing that graduate training with undergraduate training?

A lot of the people who have come to our program have not majored in theater at all. They've dabbled. They've done it as an extracurricular activity. Last year I had a most talented woman who was a physicist. She left a job that paid her sixty-five thousand dollars a year to come to graduate school. She'd only acted in extracurricular stuff. She is extremely gifted. Others majored in psychology, literature, economics, pre-law. And some have majored in theater. But majoring in theater in many schools means nothing. Forgive me for saying that.

I think it's important not because you get an MFA and therefore can teach or whatever, but I think it's important to make the transition to being an artist who can create new value in the world as well as knowing how to act—to be really an artist. And to concentrate on it. It's like pre-med. It's like your internship as a doctor. It takes that much concentration. You have to put on hold your personal life. You have to put on hold free time. You have to really believe in yourself as an artist to do that.

Audience: You talked today about the importance of words, and you said you wanted to be called the producing director, not the artistic director.

Producing comes from the Latin "producere"—to bring forth. And I wanted to know everything about what was going on. I didn't want to say, "I'm just going to take care of the stage." I think an institution is an artwork—the whole of it is an artwork. How the parts fit together, how the whole connects to the community, how the people feel about themselves. So I wanted to be responsible for the people in the box office knowing what the production was about and the program copy, the brochure copy and images, all the words, the words that went out. I think it's very smart to know if you're going to be an artistic director or invest in the whole of it—you can delegate, but delegating doesn't mean you give it away. Delegating means, "You do that, and let me know about it. Keep each other up to date." All aspects of the theater interest the producing director, for each of them is creating the form that is a theater.

Of course the stage is the nucleus of the circle—absolutely every aspect of the institution exists for the stage. All the arrows point there. I gave seventy-five percent of my time and energy to the work on stage and felt responsible for every production not just my own. Responsible for the season, to serve the company as well as the audience, for understanding each text, for the company being creatively cast, for helping new designers understand the Arena space, to be present at run-throughs, previews, to resolve any problems during rehearsals. Each play was the first and the last and I loved that sense of concentration. Artists said they felt bolder, looser, freer by my interest and involvement, and that satisfied me.

Maybe we should be called producing artistic directors—and a few of us have taken that title. To bring it all together and put it out there, time and time again, hopefully over the long run in some kind of imaginatively ascending pattern, surprising the audience with something unexpected each season—it's a wonderful job!

People say I run the school as if it's a theater and I think that's true. Each student gets eight to ten roles over their three years, most of them produced in conjunction with Susan Hilferty's design department, in styles that range over the world's repertory. In addition, of course, to all their class work. When they graduate they're ready to make a contribution to the art form and they do so not only as stage actors but also in film and TV, as playwrights, several as media producers as well. And they keep coming back to the school as to a home, and take part in graduate projects. My culminating goal is to form a company of some of these talented actors, some of them already in their forties. It would be quite possible to replace an actor for a period of time if necessary as they have all been trained to work the same way.

JoAnne Akalaitis

From the first time I saw JoAnne's work, the effect was catalytic. *Dressed Like an Egg*, 1977, based upon the life and literature of the French writer Collette, initiated my adventure with her direction. I loved the theatricality and poetic nature of the experience. JoAnne became a beacon for me but her persona intimidated me. Much later when I got to know her I realized that her abrasive veneer hid a great deal of vulnerability, a fierce and funny sense of humor and a warmth and potential for deep loyalty and friendship. Cooking and directing are closely related in the world of JoAnne Akalaitis. She is simply a wonderful cook and I am sure that the skill is connected to the brilliance of her creative work in the theater.

I have seen much of JoAnne's work over the years since *Dressed Like an Egg*, ranging from original creations to classical to contemporary playwrights and composers: *Cascando, Endgame, Beckett Shorts* (Beckett); *Southern Exposure* (Crump); *Dead End Kids: A History of Nuclear Power* (original); *Request Concert, Through the Leaves* (Kroetz); *The Photographer* (Glass); *The Balcony, Prisoner of Love* (Genet); *Cymbeline, Henry IV, Parts I and II* (Shakespeare); *In the Summer House* (Bowles); *The Rover* (Behn); *Tis a Pity She's A Whore* (Ford); *Suddenly Last Summer* (Williams); *T-Jean Blues* (Kerouac); *A Dream Play* (Strindberg); and there are probably more.

To my great disappointment I have missed quite a lot, too. She is prolific: *Red and Blue* (Hurson); *Green Card* (original); *Help Wanted* (Kroetz); *Leonce and Lena, Woyzeck* (Büchner); *Dance of Death* (Strindberg); *Arts & Leisure* (Tesich); *The Iphigenia Cycle, Iphigenia in Aulis* (Euripides); *The*

Birthday Party (Pinter); *The Screens* (Genet); *Life Is a Dream* (Calderón de la Barca); *A Penal Colony* (Glass); and *Phèdre* (Racine).

Oh yes, and of course there is opera: *Osud* and *Kata Kabanova* (Janáček), *The Visit of the Old Lady* (von Einem).

JoAnne grew up in Chicago in a Lithuanian Catholic atmosphere. She received an undergraduate degree from the University of Chicago and studied philosophy at Stanford toward a PhD but became more interested in the theater and quit studying. She moved to New York and later Paris where she joined up with Lee Breuer and Ruth Malaczech with whom she co-founded Mabou Mines in 1970. She married Philip Glass, also then a member of Mabou Mines, and had two children. She continued working with Mabou Mines in New York City for twenty years where she not only directed productions but also acted in seminal company productions such as *Come and Go* and *The B-Beaver Animation, Shaggy Dog Animation*. She left Mabou Mines in the early eighties to continue a career as a freelance director. But JoAnne is not a person to remain unaffiliated for long. Hand-picked by founder Joe Papp, in 1991 she became the second ever artistic director of The New York Shakespeare Festival. She also ran the directing program at Juilliard before accepting the leadership position at the theater program at Bard College, a roll she continues today. She is the recipient of countless Obie Awards including one for Sustained Achievement.

November 18, 2004

AB: People say, "Oh, JoAnne Akalaitis, she's so strident and difficult." But you're actually the most generous person I know—and a fabulous cook. Your work really has had a huge impact on both the national culture and the international culture. You have developed a very particular aesthetic. When I look at a show you've directed, it has a sort of visual boldness. It's politically engaged. It's aesthetically strong. Could we start by talking about where that aesthetic, those qualities, developed? Who are your influences? What happened during the course of your life that fashioned this kind of approach to the theater, which is highly theatrical, and something that an audience has to deal with.

JA: I actually don't think I have an aesthetic. I don't have any philosophy. I have very few ideas, really. I know that it sounds disingenuous, but it's not. I suppose that one realizes that one has an aesthetic by seeing when you repeat things. And I feel it's kind of dangerous for artists to repeat. I'm trying to figure out whether repetition is a personal style, and whether it's dangerous or not to one's work as an artist. I do know that there are certain things I'm very interested in, so perhaps those things that one is interested in form a kind of fabric that could be called an aesthetic. For example, I'm interested in music almost like film. I'm interested in certain kinds of gestures, which I call *mudras*. I'm now becoming interested in the possibility of the inclusion of an original language in a production.

I'm working on Heiner Müller's play *Quartet* right now. I had a meeting with the designer, Kaye Voyce, today, which was very stimulating. Wouldn't it be interesting if Karen Kandel, who's playing the woman, exited instead of the guy. It's so boring for him to exit. We actually use the act curtain, and she came out and gave a short lecture in German about Schopenhauer, who was kind of an influence on Müller. First of all, I don't ever want to read Schopenhauer again in my life. I thought this would be something that my dramaturg would be interested in. But she didn't know who Schopenhauer was. I said, "Well, find someone who does." She wanted me to provide the content. I guess I'll just peruse through Schopenhauer.

So I try to avoid aesthetic as much as possible. And one can't because the theater is an aesthetical medium. As for a philosophy, I don't really have any. As for politics—I think that I am politically sane, in that I do not believe in the current government. I hate Republicans. I abhor racism, anti-Semitism, sexism. I'm just a politically sane person.

I learned not so long ago that the definition of aesthetics, which I always thought was some highfalutin idea or theory, just essentially means sensation. It's as simple as a sensation that you receive from what you're watching, which basically means that everybody has aesthetics.

Except in the academic world. Aesthetics is systematized in a way that is very inaccessible and basically is as dry and arid as metaphysics, which should be interesting.

Since you said the word "academic"—you're running the theater at Bard. I have the same issue, too, of working in an academic organization that is antithetical to sensation. How do you manage to keep the juices going in terms of artistry? What is that like for you?

Well, I think it's hard. What the academic institution does is create a system of redundancy. Also it has created its own language. If you read academic theses, it's crazy. It's as foreign a language to me as Polish or Greek. I went to this talk about Gertrude Stein. A professor there was talking about what was paraphrasical. What did he mean by that? He meant you can tell it. You can tell the story, which you can't always tell in Gertrude Stein because it's fragmented and abstract. Why couldn't he speak English? Because they can't. It is ingrained in them, sometimes in undergraduate, but especially in graduate school. And I am now in the process of reading two hundred fifty documents—applications—for a tenure-track position at Bard College. The way people try to impress you is sometimes very pathetic. They don't know how to be sincere. Also, the academic world has created in this system of redundancy a love of email and a devotion to stupid email and memos and committees. When I was evaluated—and I didn't know I would ever be evaluated—I said, "What am I supposed to do?" "You have to draft a teaching statement." "What's a teaching statement?" I spent so much time writing that teaching statement in a state of paranoia that I wouldn't write a good enough teaching statement instead of doing what I should be doing, which is preparing to teach my students. What it does—besides the redundancy, the opaque language, an atmosphere of fear, hysteria and paranoia—it makes it very hard to really have what one wants to have, and what I think I do have, which is a wonderful relationship with my students, who are extremely brilliant. I have to work really hard to keep up with some of my students. They're smarter than I am.

I'm teaching the Greeks now, and being involved with the Greeks is such a workshop in everything—relationships, love, war, human sacrifice—a form of drama that has not ever been really repeated and is unique, the beginning of Western theater, the responsibility of theater in the polis or the society, the whole idea of Dionysia where these playwrights would do three tragedies and a satyr play over the period of a few days for the entire population, all men, Athens, fifteen thousand people. It would be the equivalent of Sam Shepard, Arthur Miller and Tony Kushner having to write three plays, present them to fifteen thousand people, and having those plays actually criticize and theoretically inform the behavior of the audience. That's what plays were doing then. I find that extremely moving and absolutely astonishing. I think if you teach Shakespeare you don't have to know anything about Elizabethan society. But in order to teach the Greeks you really do have to know something about society. I'm behind. I'm not a classicist. I'm not a historian. I'm just a theater person who means to study the plays. But you can't just talk about the plays without knowing the context, at least that the plays that Euripides wrote were written during the great war years of the Peloponnesian War, which led to the eventual decay, decline and end of classical Greece. So basically I'm like a graduate student. I'm sitting around reading the *Cambridge Guide to Greek Drama.*

Do you find you wouldn't actually do that if you weren't teaching? Is that a bonus of academia?

Yeah, but don't you do dramaturgical research?

Absolutely, but as you say, staying ahead of your students is almost impossible to do. You have to study sometimes harder.

That's true. But do you find that it hurts your work to teach?

No, I can't direct without teaching. We have such a short rehearsal process, four weeks. How the hell are you supposed to do all of your research in those four weeks plus direct a play? In order to hit the road running I need six months of work on a project that's going to take four weeks to direct. I do it in the context of a university setting. That's the way it worked out, not living in a subsidized culture. In that first rehearsal, I have a lot of stuff in my hands, which I thank my students for because I put them through that research. They get something out of it as well.

I don't do that. I try to separate them. I consider myself poseur, really. You know, we sit around and say, "Okay, survey of drama. Who wants to teach what?" I raise my hand and say, "Oh, I'll teach German theater." As if I know anything about German theater. And very cleverly avoid Goethe and Brecht. I felt I just couldn't handle that. Then: "You teach O'Neill because I hate O'Neill." It actually works out that way. We sit around and say, "Oh, how about post-colonial American theater? Or seventeenth-century women playwrights?" It is remarkably unsystematized. When I taught at Juilliard, which was the only other real teaching experience I've had, the directors wanted us to deal with George Bernard Shaw and Ibsen. My colleague, Garland Wright, and I both hated both of those playwrights. We just said, "No. We're never going to do that. Go someplace else or do it on your own. It's never going to happen here at Juilliard."

Talk a little bit about where you come from, Chicago. You spent time in San Francisco, you spent time in France. That trajectory has created an approach to theater that I think is unique.

I consider myself fundamentally a Midwestern person, and admire what I think is a kind of naivety of living in snow. I also consider myself an ethnic person. I am Lithuanian. I don't think I integrated. I know I'm a Lithuanian American, but I am a Lithuanian. I went to a Lithuanian Catholic school. I went to Lithuanian high school. I had a fantastic education, and I was not abused by crazy lesbian nuns. I am the product of wonderful role models who were women.

When I was fourteen years old, and I was kind of rebellious, Sister Edith said to me, "I think you're an artist. I think you have the personality of an artist." She did something really great for me. She gave me an entire wall of Providence High School to paint with another rebellious girl. We made—we drew, we sketched it out, then we graphed it out—this fantastic mural called "Providence Girls at Work and Prayer." It showed all these girls playing volleyball and basketball and debating. I was captain of the debate team, and I was voted the most versatile in my high school graduating class—because I was also the editor of the newspaper, I played all these sports, and I was very involved in visual arts. I thought I was going to be a painter. And I was in plays. I won prizes in plays. It was a deliriously happy time in my life. I got to go in a streetcar away from my family, who I didn't particularly relate to, although they were fine people. The real relationships that I forged were with my girlfriends and certain teachers, certain nuns. I think it is the case for probably a lot of you that you kind of developed through a high school teacher or a drama teacher. I remember the drama teacher—her lipstick was always sort of crooked and she always had mascara on her cheekbones; somehow she couldn't get her makeup right. But she was so inspiring to me and to many other girls. Because I was tall—it was a girls' school—I played boys. I played men. That was very empowering and liberating also.

But I don't think there's any path. I went to San Francisco, and I met some of the people who would later be my colleagues, and the Mimes [members of the San Francisco Mime Troupe]. Then I decided to quit theater when I came back to New York because I felt there was no place for me in it. I felt strongly that there was no place in theater for someone who was a mother. There was a particular event which turned me off. I went to a rehearsal of a play I was in at La MaMa, and I had to bring my daughter, who was ten months old. They told me I couldn't. I just said, "Well, fuck you. I don't want to be involved in any kind of institution or form that does not include or welcome families." That was one of the things that I found admirable, and still do, about Mabou Mines—that children were always a part of the picture. Because there were children. Babysitting was budgeted into production budget. For the purposes of the NEA budget they were called rehearsal assistants—which they were.

You caused revolutions in various regional theaters. Even when your kids were grown up, you'd say, "Where's childcare?" They'd say, "There is none in regional theaters." You'd say, "How is this possible?" And suddenly all these women who'd worked there for years would go, "We've been thinking that for years, but nobody ever said it!" There were revolutions in the regional theater about childcare.

But are things better? I don't know if they are. I remember having a very big fight with [Liviu] Ciulei in the lobby of the Guthrie Theater because he was misdirecting some Greek play and he was forbidding a woman to come in with a child. I performed an intercession there. I just said, "You can't do that. I'm going to go to the artistic director and file a civilian arrest or something." I said, "If the baby cries, she'll leave the theater because she's not an idiot. I mean, she's not going to sit there with a crying baby and disrupt your performance."

At which point did you go to Paris?

It was in the sixties. There was no reason to go. I went because I was involved with someone who had a Fulbright scholarship. I was following someone, frankly. I thought it was important to live in Europe and travel around Europe, and also to travel around Asia.

Why? What did you learn?

Well, I think it's life-enhancing to live in another culture. I think it's even more life-enhancing to travel in Asia, or in an Islamic country where there is no theater as we know it. Of course it's simply great to go to the theater in France and Germany and England and to see all that—because it's different. But then to go to a country like Pakistan where there's not theater. It's different. You and I went to East Jerusalem to visit Occupied Territories, and it was very thrilling.

We were in the Gaza Strip. It was against the rules for more than ten people to gather together at the same time—but all these theater companies from all over the Gaza Strip showed up at the YMCA, in the basement, and showed us their work. It was unbelievable. And they all could have been arrested. You feel a different relationship to the art form.

Well, Robert [Woodruff] and Joe [Haj] and I did get arrested while you were—

With Michael Greif in the other car. I'm so sorry. You and Woodruff refused to stay in the car because you were sick of sitting in the car, and all of a sudden all these military cars surrounded us. Our car took off into the back streets of the Gaza Strip. We were terrified for you.

I was terrified because the guys jumped out with machine guns and surrounded us. Fifteen Israeli policemen ripped the film out of Robert's camera, then took our passports away. They took the Palestinian's papers away, and then they said, "Follow us in the car." My first instinct was—I said, "We have to come up with a story about why we're here. Let's say we're Quakers." Quakers visit every place, right? And Robert and Joe thought that was bullshit. They were very militant. They took us to Rafah, which is right on the Egyptian border. I was really, really sacred. They took the Palestinian into some other place, and we were left to talk our way out of that. We succeeded in doing that. Succeeded in getting our passports back. And they were going to keep the Palestinian. That was not acceptable. Then they said that he had a violation on his card, and that they needed four hundred American dollars. We managed to get four hundred dollars somehow. I felt so shook up by that.

And we got out of Gaza and had a fantastic dinner in East Jerusalem that night—I mean, the best falafel I think I've ever had in my life.

The first work I ever saw you do knocked me out. To this day I remember both of them really well—*Cascando*, a radio play by Beckett, and *Dressed Like an Egg*, based on the work of Collette. I'd never seen anything like it. Where did that work come from in those days?

Well, the Beckett script—it didn't seem to me like a radio play. I saw something. I saw a group of people in Nova Scotia. That's what I saw. And that was what I staged.

You know what I learned from it? It was a really small stage, and it was jammed with stuff. It was the most cluttered stage I've ever seen, a set with so much stuff on it. I remember at one point, the table floated. I couldn't believe it. What I learned from that is what the Germans say, "Wenn Sie es tun, tun Sie es." If you can do it, do it. If you can have a lot of stuff, have a lot of stuff—or have no stuff at all. And it was hallucinogenic, that setting.

I know that Beckett didn't like it, and he was too polite to say. He saw it in Germany, and I could tell it upset him. I think that Beckett was just too shy to say, "You can't do this." That came later.

And then the Collette. I don't know. I thought this kind of female icon—again it came as an image, which was Collette leaning against those bars with her French bulldog. It just came from a picture. I think that pretty much everything I do comes from some picture or some dream. I did have a dream about a dress printed with eggs on it. That all somehow ended up being the piece.

It was immense. *The Photographer*, which was at BAM, a billion-and-a-half years ago [1982], was centered in a little, tiny pool moving really fast. This was based on Muybridge, the photographer. How did that happen? That was an extraordinary thing.

Well, it happened because Philip Glass asked me to do it. BAM was interested in doing it. That came from one of Muybridge's photographs, but I don't think any of the photographs have water. Or maybe they do. Somehow, I thought of fabric and water and the occasion of that. When you move fast the fabric gets wet and the water kind of bounces around through the air, and you get light. Jennifer Tipton did the lights. I like water on stage a lot.

We both ended up in a panel discussion called "Authors Versus Directors." They brought in the Grove Press Beckett people because of what you had done at American Repertory Theater with *Endgame*, setting it in a subway. I was there and the Rodgers and Hammerstein people were there because of a production I'd done of *South Pacific*. All of this to bring up the issue of Beckett a little bit more. I long to do a *Waiting for Godot* with two women—Kelly Maurer and Ellen Lauren as those two guy characters. How do you even approach doing that when the rules are so stringent?

Well, I've heard that the Beckett estate is even more watchful. But I actually think it should not be done with women. I think that *Godot* is the ultimate man-play.

Really?

Yes.

All the more reason.

I love *Godot* because I think it's about intimate men who are impotent, who have a prostate problem.

I don't know what's going on with these estates. Now I'm in trouble with the Genet estate. I'm not allowed to direct any Genet play ever. I don't know what I did wrong. Some incredible misunderstanding came about. I was going to do *The Blacks* at A.R.T. I had all kinds of intercessions, like Edmund White, who was Genet's biographer. They said no. It has something to do with Philip Glass and music, which I don't understand. I said, "Philip Glass is definitely not involved in this project." Then I was going to do *The Maids* in Chicago, and I had this funny little feeling. I went to [A.R.T. executive director] Rob Orchard and said, "What's your advice?" He said if the theater has the rights, do not say who is directing it. They don't have to say who's directing it. But the managing director in Chicago chickened out. She got scared. She called the agent in London and asked, "Are there any restrictions about directors on *The Maids*?" They said, "Anyone but JoAnne Akalaitis." I always thought of myself as Mrs. Genet.

You did a production of *The Screens* that is legendary in Minneapolis.

I can't do it again.

Is it the family?

Genet's heir, who is the son of one of his dead lovers, somehow got involved in all of this. He lives in Morocco or Greece or some place like that. He doesn't know the theater. He doesn't know anything about it. I think it had to do with this: Philip Glass wrote a wonderful score for *The Screens*, and he owns the music. He made a CD of it. He performs it all over the world. They believe, mistakenly, that he made a musical of *The Screens* and made a lot of money. They want some of the money or something like that. There was no way of convincing them that this was not the case, including the producers of this concert going to the agent's office. It's just a hideous mistake.

After *The Screens* I did an adaptation with Chiori Miyagawa and Ruth Maleczech of Genet's last book called *Prisoner of Love*. Philip Glass wrote the music for it. I think it's really unfortunate that I'm eighty-sixed from the two greatest dramatists of the twentieth-century, Beckett and Genet. I'll never in my life be able to do their work. But also think it's unfortunate that they are stubborn and stupid in a way. The production we did at the Guthrie was an incredible production, and Paul Schmidt's translation was brilliant. A publisher wanted to publish a book—a picture book with Paul's translation and a CD. It was a very nice idea. And the estate only wants the Grove Press translation. He's a bad translator.

I want to ask a difficult question. What is the role of theater now? How has it changed in the past few years? What do you see as the role of theater in this particular moment?

Well, I wish it were important. Sophocles wrote *Philoctetes* because he was mad at the government. Philoctetes, who's got a foot that smells, is exiled to this island because nobody wants to smell him. It's basically a protest against Greek government. Euripides wrote *The Trojan Women* after the Greeks invaded the island of Milos and killed all the men and infant boys and took all the women and girls as sexual savages.

I went with my students to see that Albee/Beckett program. We went on an evening when Albee was doing an audience discussion. One of my students asked him if he had any response to 9/11 or the state of the world or the war in Iraq. He was very defensive about it. I think he's a defensive guy anyway. It's not that I'm saying that we should not believe in art for art's sake, because we do. We have to. But what I'm struck by is the utter irrelevance of theater in our culture. Especially now. I'm also struck by these artistic directors who have no money, because their theaters have no money, who want to do plays that have two characters and no set and nobody comes from New York, and stuff like that. I feel sorry for them because they're not being supported by audiences. I think that people actually are turning away from theater.

One of my best friends is the editor of *Tricycle*, the Buddhist review. She said that after 9/11 they received more contributions than in the whole history of *Tricycle*. I said, "Oh, I get it. Buddhists will figure everything out, not us theater artists." All these theaters are saying the same thing: "We're going to cut back. We're going to do one less play this season." In a funny way, it doesn't affect me. I don't really have a big career. I'm not an important person. I'm not Tony Kushner, who is unbelievably, articulately, close to politics and theory. He's a thrilling political essayist. Tony maybe has some influence. I don't think I do. I feel lucky to direct a play every once in a while. But I don't know what it means for so-called emerging directors and actors.

Audience: Do you find that part of the thing that's important to you as a theater educator is to instill or excite that in your students so we can move some place else from this sad place we are in our country right now, in the arts? How do you go about doing that?

Well, we talk about that. We talk about politics in the classroom. You're not supposed to. You get in trouble for doing it. But I don't care. I brought that article in that was in the *New York Times Magazine* about George Bush's faith-driven thing, because we were talking about *Antigone*. Creon says, "You're either with me or against me." Then I realized—and I asked them, "Are there any born-again Christians in this group?" Maybe I could offend someone. But then I thought it's the same as in post–Hitler Germany. I'm sure there were occasions where there was discussion of anti-Semitism. It is the ethical duty of an educator to discuss unethical situations. One of my colleagues said, "Well, you could get in trouble." I said, "Well, go report me. I don't care."

AB: For me, that's very important to instill in students going through training not to expect, when they get out, the corporate ride. You actually have to make it yourself. It is important what you do. It's important what you say. It's important what you make. Because if you don't say those words, then it isn't. The articulation of the role that the arts—and theater in particular—play in our lives starts with the words trying to describe it. That's a big deal. I find the arts—and theater in particular—are more important, now more than ever. It begins with how you approach it.

Audience: Do you think there's anything specifically from an Asian cultural point of view that has seeped into your work?

I actually didn't see much Asian theater. I'm very interested in kathakali theater, which is seen not a lot, and Balinese theater. A lot of people are.

Asia is very in right now. We have to be very careful not to appropriate it, not to be that equivalent of orientalists. I think everything you do is important to your life as a theater artist. I think cooking is important to my life as a theater artist. I have a course that I teach sometimes called Theatre Salon, in which I invite a guest to come, an artistic director or a playwright or somebody. And I cook dinner for twenty students. It's really a lot of fun. I mean, it's a lot of work, but it's a lot of fun. Everything you do in life informs your work. You walk around thinking about it all the time, dreaming about it. It's just there. At a certain point it simply doesn't go away. So the reason to go to Asia isn't to go see theater. The reason to go to Asia is to go to Asia. The most incredible curry.

Audience: Once you decide to direct a play, is there a specific way you approach it? Is there an Akalaitis way, or does each play tell you what to do with it?

Well, I kind of do a lot of exercises in the beginning, and those exercises could change from play to play. I don't have an approach. I don't block plays anymore.

AB: What do you do?

They do it better. I do less as I get older because I trust everyone more. And also I'm kind of lazy. I don't want to be there late at night. I want to go home and watch *Survivor* or the Food Network.

Audience: Does *Survivor* influence your work?

Yes, because it amuses me. That means when I go into the rehearsal room— and I mean this—I have had a very nice evening watching stupid TV.

Audience: What exercises did you do in the last play you directed?

It's not interesting, actually.

Audience: Just a little bit?

Well, one of my new favorite exercises is called Choreographer. It's hooked to Aretha Franklin's song "Respect." It's very simple. There's a choreographer. Everyone in the company gets to be the choreographer. Everyone follows the choreographer. With these young actors who have this incredible physical energy, it's really fun. What they do and what they can do is outrageous. That's an example. I always do this exercise called Stopping and Starting. It's movement. I'm interested in impressions. I do this exercise where everyone internalizes blood, all their organs, their muscles, their skin with an acting image. I do an exercise, which I call Pathology. I ask the actors to think about what disease they have, if they have cancer or migraine headaches or if they're alcoholics or drug addicts. They don't tell me. There are certain things I think the actors should own that I don't—that I should not know. In fact, most things I don't think I should know. I'm not interested in talking about their characters; that's their job. I have an exercise with a group where everyone writes their story—especially relevant in a Greek play because the chorus doesn't have names. I ask the chorus to name themselves and to tell their story. The stage manager collects all the stories and xeroxes, and then the entire company has everyone's story. But I don't. So it's theirs. I encourage them to make a tribe that is not connected to me or dependent on me.

Audience: That's a *Survivor* term.

It is. But I don't learn anything as a director from television. Or that's minor compared to sitting around reading Foucault, which I sometimes do. That's really important. Or Nietzsche. I'm trying to read philosophy again because I think my brain kind of got shrunk.

AB: How did your brain get shrunk?

If you don't use it, it does.

AB: That's actually physiologically proven.

Now at Bard I require the entire program to read five books. One of the books is *The Birth of Tragedy* by Nietzsche, though I disagree with everything in it. Have you read it?

AB: A while back.

I read it a while back. And I was astonished how hard it was for me to read it now at my age. I bribed my son-in-law, who's very smart, with a bottle of Irish whiskey, to give me a tutorial. The same thing with Foucault—tough going. Very, very tough going. I used to sit around when I was in my twenties—I don't know why; I must have been insane—and read Kant, who I despise now. But that's one of the things we did last semester in Theatre Salon. We read philosophy. It was good for the theater students to do it because I think they don't read enough. They don't read enough plays. They don't think enough. They don't write good enough. They don't talk good enough. I want them to be more intellectually rigorous. It only helps.

I thought it would be interesting to have a department-wide—like a book club. These are the obvious books: Artaud's *Theatre and Its Double*, Grotowski's *Poor Theatre*, Peter Brook's *The Empty Space* and *The Birth of Tragedy* and Elinor Fuchs's *The Death of Character*. Of course it's not working out because I wanted them to discuss with each other and they want to come to me or their advisor and have us explain the book. There's so much wrong with every one of those books, except Ellie's. I think these books, as far as I'm concerned, are the ABC books. If you're in the theater, you're really out of it if you don't read these books.

Audience: I was at a panel on the legacy of Joe Papp at Columbia. Greg Mosher was moderating. Eduardo Machado, who is the artistic director of INTAR and head of playwriting at Columbia, was there; Kevin Kline; Woody King, Jr., who first produced *colored girls*; Diane Paulus, who did *The Donkey Show*. I came off thinking how pessimistic it was. They're saying, "The state of theater is this. The state of theater is this."

AB: I don't think you can afford the luxury of pessimism right now. I think it's against the rules. The obstacles in front of us are the biggest they've ever been in our lifetimes—for anybody who hasn't lived through the second world war. I just don't think we can afford that attitude. That attitude predetermines the success of everything. I think it's so easy to complain. It's so easy to let yourself off the hook.

Let's not complain anymore about Bush and what happened. But let's pick our battles. It's boring to complain about him. He's the president. There's nothing we can do about that. But let's wait and pick our battles—because there will be battles.

Joe Papp was my mentor. He was the greatest genius in American theater after David Belasco. There are so many things to learn from Joe. But one of the things to learn from Joe is to choose your optimism. This was the guy who had the nuttiest ideas—but those ideas were based in a fundamental belief in the power of theater. I actually spent the day thinking about Joe and thinking about his apartment and his last days and how he sort of summoned everyone to his apartment. He had some idea that David Greenspan was gong to direct *Richard II*. Some idea. And the reason Joe could get away with all this is because he believed in it. This is a guy who, when he was a stage manager for television, refused to testify for the House Un-American Activities Committee. From the very beginning he was a fighter, to the very end. That's what he's taught us. So if there's any panel about Joseph Papp, the tone of that panel should be utterly uplifting and optimistic.

AB: What keeps you going?

I'm really interested in theater. It's an interesting form, you know?

Audience: It strikes me as so appropriate that amidst all the complaints about losing funding that some theaters, some artistic directors' response to that—such as Molly Smith at Arena Stage, who just did a huge capital campaign—is to say, "Oh, we'll just be bigger." I find that to be an intensely political response. It reminds me that sometimes as a theater artist I can fall into being reactive to the society of which I am a part. Certainly that's part of what we do—we react; we respond to. But we do this other piece, too. There's a great interview that Tony Kushner did in *Heat* magazine right before the election. He was talking about people working for the Democratic party and the Kissinger real politic thing. It wasn't about wearing black bandanas and bombing Starbucks. He said at the end, "If we fuck it up, it's our fault." I found that so inspirational. I can get kind of victimy as a theater artist. That's anti-creation, I think.

AB: I think that relates also to directing in the sense that, whatever situation you're in, there are always little problems. I think the director's job is to think past the problems and put a big globe around it. That is exactly, I think, what you mean by saying, "There are problems here, so let's build a new theater." The point is to really contain all of the problems inside of a bigger—I don't like to use the word "vision."

People get into mental institutions—

AB: With visions. I know.

Audience: They also become Jesus.

Or Joan of Arc. I feel the capital campaign in certain major urban sites is exciting. Washington is a really exciting town and has a very cooking audience, on every level. I went to see this production in a church by T. S. Eliot, and I thought I hated T. S. Eliot, but it was brilliant. It was cold. There were only like twelve people there. And that was great. At the same time, I love walking in the door of the big, old, rich Shakespeare Theatre, which has the greatest props, greatest shops, greatest everything. When you arrive there to direct a play, they have these volunteers who open the door of your very beautiful apartment. When we did *The Trojan Women*, there was a basket of Greek food, a bottle of wine with my picture on it. This is a theater that works! So I think there's room for that cocktail party, and there's room for big, old Molly Smith and Michael Kahn in the same town.

Audience: One thing I thought from this election or the current state of affairs is that middle America is very hungry for teaching, for morals, for community, however you want to perceive that. You were talking about the role of Greek theater in their society. Do you have any advice for us as young theater artists for how we could reach out and make theater have a more important role in our society? Reach out also toward middle America and the values that they perceive, to stimulate that intellectual side?

AB: As Americans we have a tradition that's based on populism. I learned this by going away from this country and confronting people who weren't from a populist background. When we work in the theater we aim low. We say, "Is Joe Schmo going to get this? Is Peoria going to get this?" There are historical reasons why we do that. An actor can sense this. An actor senses if I'm watching for his or her absolute best work. An audience also feels the same thing. I think the answer is to aim really high because the reason that the theater doesn't have a lot of impact right now, doesn't feel very exciting on a lot of stages, is because so little is asked of the audience. Theater at its best is like a great gym. You grapple with it.

What is middle America? Are they somehow inferior to us? They're not. I come from middle America. I've never questioned the art. I have only had positive experiences with audiences—except in Philadelphia. There's something wrong with Philadelphia. I don't know what.

The example is those places where they bus those high school kids in, and you see them outside. The most thrilling audiences to me are those kids who are standing outside saying, "Fuck, fuck, fuck, fuck." Then go in the theater and they're enthralled. They're absolutely enthralled. You can't lower standards. It's all high. And it is the case that audiences love great theater. They always do because they're human beings.

AB: And Philadelphia?

We were booed at the Annenberg Center. *Dead End Kids* was booed.

AB: Maybe it was all those bad jokes.

That's what they booed.

AB: There's a whole section of that play with David Brisbane telling one foul joke after another—and they were graphic, kind of gross jokes. It was a great show.

Audience: What are some of the most interesting responses you've gotten to your work?

In Chicago when they did *The Iphigenia Cycle*—in the preview discussion, every night the audience asked the same question: "Why are Agamemnon and Menelaus smoking?" My response was, "Well, they're not wearing fur." Politically incorrect. That was the most interesting response.

Audience: What were the moments that validated your path? When did you feel like you were really on the right path to becoming a major director in the American theater?

I still don't feel that I'm on the right path. I've never felt that I was on the right path. I think I'm an extremely lucky person. I'm a really lucky person in that I get to do what I want to do. I mean, I could be selling metro cards or something. I look around at the world—and I do look around at the world—and so much of the world is not doing what they want to do—not just people selling metro cards or people who are corporate lawyers. I am a lucky person. I have a family. I have children. I have grandchildren. I have friends. I just can't get over it.

AB: I'm going to try to answer for you. As long as I've known you, you always say, "Oh, I'm going to give it up and cook in a restaurant." You're always on the verge of giving up. Richard Jones did *Titanic* on Broadway. He's such a philosopher. He told me this story about being in auditions with all of these producers and their poodles and lunches and saying, "Why don't you cast that person?" It was this big, Broadway, commercial production—and every time somebody would try to get him to do something he didn't think was right, he'd say, "Oh, you've got the wrong director," and he'd get on the Concorde and go back to London—because it's Broadway—and then wait for the phone to ring. They'd say, "Please come back, Mr. Jones. Please, we need you." And he'd say, "Well, all right," and he'd go back, but he was completely philosophical about it. It had no attachment to his career success—it was just, "Well, this is really *interesting*."

I find the same thing with you. You don't say, "This is good for my career." If anything it's your absolute honesty and interest in the art. I remember going with you down in the basement of the church in Jerusalem where Jesus was. We were going into the space and you're looking at this light bulb or some lighting fixture that was kind of greenish in the basement of this church, and you said, "That's the most beautiful thing I've ever seen." I was so touched when you said that because you were so just there with it. You are just interested.

I think it's important not to care. Caryl Churchill's in town. She's a friend of mine. She happens to be, I think, our greatest playwright. She says, "I don't know if I'm going to write another play." She's interested in her grandchildren. She is absolutely the least driven theater artist in the world. Sometimes she says, "Well, I have writer's block. I probably won't write another play." And that's fine with her. She's not seeing a therapist about it. She's fine. "I've written a lot of things. Fine."

Audience: I've been meaning to ask you this for a while: What do you like about umbrellas so much?

I don't use them in every play. Two plays. One was a piece called *Frank Gehry Had a Dream*. After the entire Dutchess County objected to where he wanted to build his building, he had a dream about where he really wanted to build it. So we did a piece there with a whole bunch of students—*Frank Gehry Had a Dream*. I don't know. I thought those umbrellas would look nice—fifty red umbrellas. And then it started to rain and the audience attacked the field and took the umbrellas.

Audience: Is that a kind of validation for you? That just came off the top of your head—let's have fifty red umbrellas.

They came in handy, didn't they?

AB: They're poetical, aren't they? Umbrellas.

Audience: Do you work with new plays by living playwrights?

I haven't for quite a while. I think the last living playwright I worked with was Steve Tesich. The experience, according to his sister, caused his death of a heart attack. I love Steve. But it was really traumatic for him and for me—and he did die of a heart attack soon after that. I would very much like to direct a play by Caryl—especially because she doesn't like to travel and she likes to stay in her house in London and not bug you. I have some students whose work I'd like to direct. I don't know why . . . working with living playwrights just kind of went away.

Audience: Did you write?

I used to sort of compose stuff. I am in the midst of a seven-year collaboration about Louis Armstrong's wife, called *Lil*, with Jerry Armstrong, a jazz pianist. I think writing is lonely, and it's hard.

AB: You worked on Kerouac, a piece you put together.

I did. I think I'm more like an editor. That was the Collette also. I think I have stopped.

Audience: Did you collaborate on the new translation of *The Screens*, or was it presented to you?

We had an intense collaboration. A great collaboration. Genet is a very juvenile, adolescent and messy writer. We rewrote the entire end of the play, Paul Schmidt and I. It had to be redone. We changed a lot—with permission from the agents. We kept calling and saying, "We're doing this. We're doing this. We're doing this." We added the French language. They were speaking Racine—Paul's translation of Racine's *Phèdre*. When I read the Racine I couldn't get over how fantastic it was. What a great playwright. What a great artist. I said, "The audience has to hear some of this French."

Audience: In the theater, what are you interested in right now?

I think I go to too much theater. I'm interested in not going to a play right now. I'm serious about that. I feel brain dead.

Audience: What do you like about directing?

I like the interaction with actors. I love actors. I love the heady intellectual climate of collaborating with designers. The help and support I get from dramaturgs. I would say that fundamentally it is the communal aspect of creating a work of art that thrills me.

Audience: You mentioned that there was a point earlier on where you didn't consider yourself a theater person. How did you come back?

I didn't want to be part of a system where I was judged by directors. I didn't want to have a photo and a résumé. I didn't want to go to auditions. It was because of Mabou Mines—a group of us decided to start our own theater company in which we were all equal. We were all the artistic directors. We all received a salary whether we worked or not—whatever that salary was, because sometimes it was zero because there was no money. It was—and I assume still is—so collaborative. That interested me.

AB: I remember somebody once sat in on a Mabou Mines rehearsal and said, "It was really strange." This was a long time ago. "They sit around and drink coffee and nothing's happening—and then all of a sudden this amazing thing happens. And I totally missed how that happened."

Endless rehearsals. I'm not part of Mabou Mines now. I haven't been for a long time. A lot of that has to do with my not wanting to be involved with a company, and wanting to meet new people in new situations.

Joseph V. Melillo

Joe is an enthusiast. The word enthusiasm etymologically means "to be filled with God." Joe is filled with a love and appreciation for the art of performance and he takes significant action based on this enthusiasm. He is the executive producer of the Brooklyn Academy of Music where he supports and presents what he believes in. The seasons at BAM offer without doubt the most consistently exhilarating theater, dance, music and film to be found in New York City and the boroughs.

What I find most remarkable about Joe, besides his outstanding achievements at BAM, is the way he relates to time. Joe's time is constantly in demand. Everyone wants to meet and woo him. Nearly every week he is on a plane to a different part of the world to see new works of theater, dance and music. And yet with Joe one never feels hurried or affected by the pressure that he must be under. He makes time for young artists. He meets with them to discuss their work seriously and makes suggestions about people they should meet. And then he remembers and makes a point of making introductions for them, too. Joe is what Malcom Gladwell calls in his book *The Tipping Point*, "a maven": someone who accumulates knowledge, collects information and puts people together. Joe is the axis around which a lot of events turn.

After earning a BA in English and theater at Sacred Heart University in Fairfield, Connecticut, Joe received an MFA in Speech and Drama at Catholic University of America in Washington, D.C. His pre-BAM career covered a wide range of activity. He was general manager of the 1982 New

World Festival of the Arts in Miami; theater program director of Foundation for the Extension and Development of the American Professional Theater (FEDAPT); marketing director for the Walnut Street Theatre in Philadelphia; thematic specialist in contemporary American theater for the Institute of International Education, Department of State, USIA; and producing director of the Chelsea Theater Center of New York. Prior to his current role as the executive producer at BAM, that began when Harvey Lichtenstein retired, Joe served as BAM's producing director, following a six-year tenure as founding director of the Next Wave Festival, during which time he produced the premiere productions of *The Photographer: Far from the Truth* and *The Gospel at Colonus*. He worked closely with Philip Glass and Robert Wilson on the first revival of *Einstein on the Beach* in 1984. His hand can be seen in the broad-ranging Next Wave productions such as *The Mahabharata* and *Nixon in China*.

In the years since taking responsibility for the institutional artistic direction, BAM has enjoyed increases in both programming and attendance. He was named a Chevalier (1999) and an Officier (2004) of the French Legion of Honor. Also in 2003, Joe was awarded an honorary Obie for his outstanding commitment to British performing arts in America. In 2007, he was appointed Knight of the Royal Order of the Polar Star, in recognition of his role in solidifying ties between the performing arts communities of Sweden and the United States.

Joe currently serves on the faculty of the Brooklyn College graduate program in arts management and he has served on innumerable boards of directors, panels and councils.

November 29, 2004

AB: Joe is executive producer of Brooklyn Academy of Music and is curating for New York the most interesting seasons that there are. There's really an appetite for this work. What brought you into the world of performance?

JVM: I am an Italian American from New Haven, Connecticut. I went to undergraduate school in Bridgeport/Fairfield county. And I was a reader. I was not very active as a student. I just liked to read. I went to college and my major was English literature. In my sophomore year, taking a Shakespeare course in which I was studying Shakespeare as literature, I was in the cafeteria and I recognized there was a group of kids across the cafeteria who were having a great time. I found out that they were the theater students. I thought, Gee, they're having so much fun. I want to be a part of that. So I found my way into their social unit, and I learned that there was a kind of disconnect in my brain in understanding that Shakespeare is to be produced, interpreted and created as an active theater experience. I learned that through the interaction with these students, and took theater as my minor along with philosophy.

I graduated, and began to teach in an intercity school system in New Haven while I was taking post-graduate courses in the theater. I knew I couldn't be competitive getting a masters in theater. Then I matriculated to get my MFA, concentration in directing, from Catholic University of America, in Washington, D.C. That's when the clouds parted and it was revealed to me what the professional theater could possibly be. There was a great relationship with what was going on in New York City and what was happening on campus in Washington, D.C.

I graduated and I was in a relationship with an actress at the time. She got accepted to be in the acting company at the Guthrie Theater. I was stage managing and I followed her to the Guthrie. I had the great joy of being in the rehearsal hall with Michael Langham, who was in his first year of being the artistic director of the Guthrie Theater. He was rehearsing *Cyrano* [*de Bergerac*] and *Taming of the Shrew*. I was in the room as he was directing Paul Hecht as Cyrano, Roberta Maxwell as Roxanne and Glen Carrio as Christian. And I was watching what he was doing with these actors and I thought, Oh my God. I don't have that ability. What he was doing was not only working on their characterizations, but he was working on the subtext of the character, while dealing with the text, the literature. There were multiple levels on which he was working—that was not my training at all. I saw how brilliant he was.

You have that self knowledge: What I really want to do is become a producer. I can make theater by creating the environment for someone like him to do his work. That began my path.

When you said, "I could be a producer," at that moment in time, what did that mean to you?

In that time, being a producer was finding the script, finding the director, working with the director to find his or her collaborators, designers, casting the play with actors, and making the rehearsal process possible. Today it's a completely different point of view. Today, my understanding of what a producer is has everything to do with life experience in the theater and what it is to interact with creator-people. You find a way to activate or— the word I think is really good—"animate" their creativity.

I want to deal with history a little bit. You started the Next Wave Festival?

Harvey [Lichtenstein] created the idea. He gave me the privilege of producing the first Next Wave Festival.

In 1982 I produced America's largest performing arts festival, the New World Festival of Arts, in Miami and Miami Beach. My title was general manager. Robert Herman, who was the general director of Greater Miami Opera Company, had created this idea that in June of 1982 there would be this festival. He was thinking that he was going to create the next Spoleto.

He came to New York City and landed on my doorstep. I agreed to do it. I had eight months to produce it. I delivered twenty-two world premieres in three weeks, and then in August of 1982, came back to New York. So I had this reputation then of being able to stand up after twenty-two world premieres and talk in simple sentences and have intelligent conversation. Harvey Lichtenstein had conceptualized the Next Wave Festival and he too was looking for someone to produce. I was summoned to his doorstep. We talked and eventually he offered me the job. When I walked into the Brooklyn Academy of Music in 1983 to produce the first Next Wave Festival, Harvey Lichtenstein handed me a piece of paper. My biggest mistake to date is that I didn't hold on to that piece of paper. I've learned a lot about archives because BAM has an active archive that goes back to 1861. I have a full-time archivist on my staff. I've learned something, but I don't have that piece of paper. On that piece of paper was a list of names of artists and productions. He said, "This should happen." My first decision as a producer of the Next Wave Festival was to take a manila file folder and put a name of an artist or a production on each one. If it doesn't exist, I've got to make it real. I've got to make it exist. So it existed in names of productions and artists.

What were some of those names?

Robert Wilson, *Einstein on the Beach*; Lee Breuer, Bob Telson, *The Gospel of Colonus*; a woman named JoAnne Akalaitis; a woman named Lucinda Childs; Robert Rauschenberg, Laurie Anderson and Trisha Brown, *Set and Reset*.

And that was the mandate, this list of people?

The mandate—and this is probably the most important thing about the Next Wave Festival—is that it could be quantified. That New York City would have, in the autumn of each year, very much like Paris has the Festival d'Automne, a festival for these artists to do large-scale interdisciplinary work. Today this is still the motivating force in my curatorial judgment—trying to provide large-scale, interdisciplinary work by American artists, as well as international artists or global artists, and to provide those opportunities within our spaces. BAM has large venues: an opera house with two thousand seats; and the Harvey theater with nine hundred seats in a very specifically architecturally designed format. In any way, shape or form, that's large-scale-ness.

Back to that first beginning, I hate to be speaking in absolutes, but no one in New York City, no one had seen performance art or multimedia, interdisciplinary work on a large scale at all. Ever. It was not happening at City Center. It was not happening at the New York State Theatre. It wasn't happening at Avery Fisher Hall. The only time it happened was in 1976, when for two performances at the Metropolitan Opera House, *Einstein on the Beach* was presented. Think of that.

The opening production of the Next Wave Festival was directed by JoAnne Akalaitis with music by Philip Glass. It was called *The Photographer: Far from the Truth*. It was a triptych, and the first part was a play that JoAnne commissioned from Robert Coe on the life of Eadweard Muybridge. The second part was multimedia projections of Muybridge's work imaged by Wendall Harrington, who is on Broadway mostly these days. The third part was a movement-theater-dance work by David Gordon and the Pickup Company, in which the entire company was involved in this imagistic, physicalized storytelling of Eadweard Muybridge's life. It was ninety minutes in length. And people were shocked by it. Shocked. It overwhelmed some people. Angered some people. I remember people throwing their programs on the stage. And some people just went, "At last. We have it."

I was one of those "at last" people coming from the downtown world. What I remember about that show—I mean, I remember all of the imagery—is Valda Setterfield sitting in this tiny pool doing, at top speed, the Muybridge positions, but with an inner stillness that was uncanny. I learned about speed and stillness from her doing that in the middle of this big stage. I feel it would be irresponsible not to pick up on something that you said, which was "1861." What was BAM before Harvey?

In 1859, in the city of Brooklyn, a group of decision-makers determined that the city of Brooklyn should have a citadel, a temple—a cultural center in our terms. In their terms they were using the words "temple" and "citadel" because in Latin that's what the word "academy" means. Our forefathers were emulating Europe. What they did was build, on Montague Street in Brooklyn Heights, a wooden opera house—a pure, simple wooden opera house, which opened in 1861. Not only did they create music, they were doing great discussions and they would do speeches there. You trace American history with the Brooklyn Academy of Music. It's Abraham Lincoln, Washington and Carver. They would give elocutions, they were reciting poetry and they were then doing music. They brought the Metropolitan Opera to the city of Brooklyn. On horse and buggy they would take the sets and costumes, travel them down Broadway to the New York Harbor and on barges they would transport the sets and costumes across. This was pre–Brooklyn Bridge.

Regretfully, in 1903 there was a fire, and that wooden Brooklyn Academy of Music burnt down. The founding fathers, the decision-makers of the borough of Brooklyn, a committee of one hundred, made a fundraising commitment—think of it, a fundraising commitment—on the demise of that building that they were going to build a new Brooklyn

Academy of Music. They set out to raise the money and, in 1907, the cornerstone was laid in the location that BAM is today. They determined that that was going to be the new center of Brooklyn because all the roads were built all around where BAM is today. Of course that didn't happen. The current building opened in November of 1908 and has been operating continually since. Whoever has the job of being artistic director or executive producer feels stewardship, trusteeship, feels the legacy of it. All you have to do is go to the archive and you go, "This is the most extraordinary thing." In doing your job, you're making a contribution to the continuity of the Brooklyn Academy of Music in American society.

Harvey batted out a lot of ideas for BAM.

When I entered BAM to produce the Next Wave Festival there was a lot of tension about this. Was this another "Harvey folly"? I thought it was just a gig. I thought I was just going to do it once. I told Karen Hopkins, who was the fundraiser, the development director at BAM, that I was going to go off and look for another job. She said, "Oh no. I raised the money for three years." I said, "Oh great! I have a job for three years.

So it was becoming very, very clear that they had no idea what the festival was going to be or what it was about. I had produced a festival. So there was a lot of translating about definitions of processes and languages and procedures and how it was going to happen. It was the first time I was working with "nontraditional artists." It wasn't like working with someone who was just going to do a play in the most traditional way possible and articulate the text. I would have a creative meeting with JoAnne Akalaitis and say, "Santo Loquasto is doing the set and Jennifer Tipton is doing the lighting and I envision this red set." Then the next day JoAnne would come in to rehearsal, "The set's going to be blue." "Blue?" "Blue." I was learning how to really listen to them in a different way than I would listen to any other artist.

This is a difficult question, but what formed your taste? I mean, clearly you went in and there was a list of artists. But you also had your own taste and it continues to grow. Is there any way to describe the sources of that aesthetic?

I was a sponge at Catholic University of America. I was stunned. At that time, from 1960 to 1971, the training was all about the Greeks, Molière, the importance of the word, the structure. I can't escape that as something that I'm attracted to see performed. And yet I am a creature of the twentieth century and the twenty-first century, so I am interested in speaking to my time, but I believe in structure and form. I'm so much a man of craft. I know there is something called virtuosity. I can't describe it, but I know when I'm in the presence of it. I know the different between efficiency and proficiency.

That's actually very clear. Form, structure, virtuosity.

Just once in your life being in the presence of Yo Yo Ma playing the cello— it astounds you as to what is possible with a human being, this instrument called the cello. It doesn't diminish what another cellist does. This person, who happens to be walking and talking on this earth, happens to have this gift. I have learned from artists. I've lived a blessed life. I've seen George Balanchine choreograph in this studio when I worked at City Center. John Cage was my next door neighbor. I have been profoundly influenced by individuals who are creative. Who are creators.

You left BAM for a year, is that correct? Was that about ten years into it?

No, it was actually seven. When I completed my seventh Next Wave Festival I knew that I needed a sabbatical. BAM could never afford to give me a sabbatical. So the moral decision was to resign my position. A strange thing happened. Someone named Martin Segal had created the New York International Festival of the Arts, and he asked me to be artistic director. Basically what Martin Segal provided me was an eight-month sabbatical to travel all over the world. He had a limitless checkbook. That was like getting a PhD in cultural anthropology and global aesthetics. But I had a particular methodology in how to make this festival happen. It was not what Martin wanted, so I left.

I had worked with several artists in the Next Wave Festival who had some ideas about changing their performance work into new media, and that happened to be television and film. I had a professional colleague who was the executive producer of Alive from Off-Center at KCTV in St. Paul, Minnesota, so I took those projects to her and I participated in the pro-ducing of those two projects. One was a David Rusev project, and the other was by Susan Marshall, both choreographers who had ideas about dance-theater.

I started to do some other projects, then Harvey Lichtenstein called and said, "Let's have lunch." Then, "How'd you like to come back to BAM?" The woman who had replaced me was not happy doing the job.

Why not?

Harvey Lichtenstein was twenty years older than me. I knew I was there to service his vision. And in the process of making the Next Wave Festival a reality for BAM, I had kind of crossed an arc in our relationship, and there was a certain kind of understanding between us. I didn't want Harvey's job at that time in my life. The woman who replaced me, Liz Thompson, took the job, but what she wanted was to control the Next Wave Festival. You couldn't control the Next Wave Festival because it was Harvey's vision. What you really had to do was facilitate his vision, complement his vision by new ideas.

Because I was hanging out at P.S. 122, the Kitchen, studio spaces, traveling, I was giving him new information. I was servicing him: "This is what this artist is. You really should see this production. You really should see this artist do this work." She didn't want to do that job. She wanted to say, "I'm the artistic director of the Next Wave Festival and this is what it's going to be." And that was not going to fly with Harvey. And they loved one another. They had known each other for much longer than I had known Harvey. It was just a clash of ideology. I said, "Harvey, I'm not interested in coming back to be the producer of the Next Wave Festival. Been there, done that. What I would be interested in doing is coming back to BAM and working with you on the complete artistic season. So through a series of lunches and dinners and riding in his car with him, we finally agreed that I would return to BAM as the producing director of BAM. I was Harvey's right hand for art and Karen Hopkins was his left hand for fundraising, institution, board of trustees. That was in January 1992. Around 1995 he started to talk about the R word: retirement. Through a series of misadventures and really fascinating conversations that terrorized both Karen and myself, he finally made the decision that he was going to retire in June of 1999 and he was going to walk out the door and not look back. And that's exactly what he did.

Now that you're without him, do you feel responsible to BAM audiences? Do you feel responsible to BAM tradition? When you choose a season for the Next Wave or the whole year, what are you listening to?

When I program the Next Wave Festival, I am a festival director. When I'm programming the spring season I am an individual curator. It's defined by one specific artistic choice that would say to New York City: Pay attention to this art. You have to come to the Brooklyn Academy of Music to have this singular theatrical experience. That's what I mean by being a curator, versus the Next Wave Festival, which is a series of experiences in the performing arts that I think are important to bring to New York City. I also know that there's a certain legacy that I want to respond to. Pina Bausch considers BAM her artistic home in New York City. But there are other artists with whom Harvey worked, that don't need BAM's theaters because other colleagues of mine are stepping up to the plate. It's a combination in the Next Wave Festival today of honoring a legacy, looking at that large-scale interdisciplinary work that is the tradition of the Next Wave Festival and finding the discoveries within the theater, dance, music and music-theater genres that I think we should discover collectively.

But you're the astronaut.

I'm always interested in having audiences, but I don't program for the audience. I program for the individual artist who is making art and I believe New York City as a community should have this experience. I'm servicing BAM as a New York City cultural institution. I want New York City to be the cultural capital of the United States of America, and if these artists don't get to our stages, they're not coming to New York. If we're going to grow as creative people, we have to be exposed to those new ideas, new techniques. How are they telling their stories? They're galloping away. They're galloping away in a wonderful way—because they have the money. Their cultures provide a financial underpinning to their experimentation, their production. They have a network throughout the European Union. They're growing because they have resources and American artists don't.

You get on more airplanes than probably anybody. You go to Berlin and you see Thomas Ostermeier doing something, then you go to the Volksbühne. And you make a choice. Talk about that choice.

The choice is a difficult thing to quantify because it would be wonderful to make it all happen. I like to say I have a healthy appetite for art, but I have to ultimately come to the reality that there are financial implications to everything that I do. There are financial limitations. I cannot do everything that I want to do. It's really difficult to quantify—saying Ostermeier has a value that I think is greater to the form of theater in New York City now than Kristof Martal does or that Frank Castorf does.

But I also think next year when Michael Thalheimer comes with a production from the Deutsches Theater, something other will be articulated. He is working on re-imaging or deconstructing or contemporizing a classic in the theater. It's a European tradition—Ivo van Hove doing

Hedda Gabler for Jim Nicola's theater, New York Theatre Workshop. It's part of that European fabric of approaches to classicism that I think we should be conversant with. It's very important that I put this in a context for you because I think I'm having a conversation by my artistic choices. I think I'm having a conversation with you. Who are you? You're curious New Yorkers. You're interested in the performing arts. As an artistic director, I think I'm having a conversation. Look at the customers. Look at what Jan Lauwers is going to do with this amazing production of *Isabella's Room*. Even I, in all my enthusiasm, find I'm incapable of describing to you how brilliant it is, and what it is. There is something inherently life-affirming in what he's crafted in that piece, which uses music, song, text and dance to tell this one story about this fictive character, Isabella, who's living a life like we are. And that's the beauty of the piece.

You just sold it.

There are limitations of language. But that's what I think I'm doing.

The thing that knocked me out that you just said is that New Yorkers should be conversant with this kind of work. That's very moving as a motivation for me, and I think it's true that New Yorkers are better for it, for being more conversant, for having a relationship with that kind of art.

I saw you a little bit after Iraq had first been bombed or laid siege to or whatever words you use. And I said, "Joe, is it different now, traveling around?" Can you talk a little bit about being an American in the position you're in and going to Europe, in particular, Asia, the Middle East, wherever you go. What's changed? How you think your responsibility has changed?

Well, it's very important to say that there is a tremendous amount of generosity because I'm a New Yorker. Even today, post the election, we still have tremendous generosity, if you can believe it. The most difficult thing to answer is when they ask you why George W. Bush—why did you initially elect him? I had lunch with Peter Brook on Saturday. I've grown up with Peter. I produced the *Mahabarata* in the Next Wave Festival in 1987. Peter wanted to know why. I said, "Peter, look at the structure of the United States of America. We're a blue state. We now know as New Yorkers the majority of people in the United States, who are the red states, they don't like us. We know it pure and simple. I don't want to live in any one of those red states. And guess what, those red people don't want to live in any of these blue states." I use that as a microcosm to say that's what conversations I have. This country is so big in comparison geographically to their own cultures. The great diversity that is American society is so dramatically clear to us. You're not interacting with the people of the Great Plains. Or the people of the Deep South. We perceive reality differently.

I had coffee with Tony Kushner two days after the election. He said, "The best that we can hope for is that after George W. Bush we'll have a moderate Republican in the White House." And I said, "What?" He said, "There is not a single Democratic candidate currently who can speak to those red states in a way that they understand." It's about perception. I can't change it and they're certainly not going to change me.

The other part of this, which is on the professional side, the institutional side: I am doing this great project in the spring called *Songs of the Sufi Brotherhoods* with Hamza El Din, Hassan Hakmoun and Rizwan-Muazzam Qawwali. And guess where they're from? Pakistan. The agent for them says, "I can't get them into the country." We had to decide to partner with a commercial agent and BAM, in order to protect its engagement, had to take on the responsibility of doing the visas for the entire project. So my staff not only has to worry about their own work, now here they are having to work with a commercial agent. The artists need birth certificates. "Well, my father told me I was born when there was a full moon. The crops were this . . . ." They don't have birth certificates there. So having to do all the processes and procedures, getting the musicians to go to Islamabad. I'm certainly interested in all of our safety, but the rigidity that exists in this process now is isolating us from the globe. That is pernicious.

It makes it a more remarkable thing to have a group from Pakistan perform. It raises the stakes for you, but also is a richer thing. So what you're doing is magnified.

BAM is a fantastic institution with fundraising, a lot to do with Karen as we mentioned, and the relationship with then-called Philip Morris, now called Altria.

That's the only corporation, actually. We get two hundred and fifty thousand dollars. This is Fundraising 101: People give to people. If you go to the *Chronicle of Philanthropy*, every year they do an analysis of where is the money coming from in the not-for-profit sector. Remember, the not-for-profit sector is colleges and universities, hospitals, social agencies and us: arts and culture. The highest amount is always given by individuals. Don't look to corporations. Corporations are into marketing pure and simple. It's not philanthropic. Of course that's a gross generalization. There's always an exception to the rule. But marketing is really their mantra.

Private foundations—Ford, Rockefeller, Pew, Mellon—are absolutely interested in solving social and cultural problems. The age of growing an institution within our culture is over and done with. They have said pure and simple, "We are not interested. We have done our job. So, now we recognize that we need to invest in individual careers."

What made that shift?

It started several years ago with many of the usual suspects sitting around. There was a convening with presenting organizations and producing companies—symphonic music, ASOL, Theatre Communications Group, Opera America—talking about how there's no money. We all exist because of an individual artist in our community. And the structures that the foundations had put together had moved away from the individual artists, putting all the money with institutions—with them there was a safety valve. They believed that the institutions were being responsive to individuals. That was not the case. You could demonstrate that the National Endowment for the Arts had walked away from the individual artist completely. The New York Foundation for the Arts, by example, was structured by the state arts council to give money to the individual, but those contributions are modest in comparison to what is given to institutions. Something needed to be done. Susan Berresford, who is the president of the Ford Foundation—so intelligently said, "This problem needs to be researched and examined," and she engaged a woman named Holly Sidford, who used to run the Wallace Foundation, and Holly did a year, eighteen-month, study, involving a lot of colleagues, including myself. Every day an individual artist is telling me, "I don't have enough money to create." There's no avenue for that. Susan Berresford then had concrete evidence to go to the board of trustees and say, "The Ford Foundation should vanguard this." She then went to her colleagues in the foundation community, and they are creating this fund. That's just one example. The same thing is going to happen at Rockefeller Foundation in a totally different way.

But you wanted to talk about fundraising. So, corporate giving is only interested in marketing: how many people, how many hits, demographics, all that stuff. Private foundations: solving a problem well (lay out the problem, lay out a potential solution, investigate). Then, the majority of the money is raised through private individuals. In terms of fundraising, anyone who is interested in doing a project, who has an organization, who is looking for a way of capitalizing their creative vision, their art: spend your time with individuals.

Do you spend a lot of time doing fundraising?

I am Karen Brooks Hopkins's professional partner. The institution is held in joint tenure. The institution—we use this as a generality—is a twenty-five-million-dollar corporation. There are one hundred fifty full-time people, one hundred twenty part-time people who depend on their salaries. The twenty-five-million dollars breaks down to eight million dollars earned revenue. The earned revenue is box office, the parking lots at BAM, the licensing of the restaurant and bar and the interest on the endowment. On the other side of the equation, you have seventeen million dollars. Two million of the seventeen million dollars comes from the City of New York. BAM is owned by the City of New York. The private corporation of the Brooklyn Academy of Music, Inc. licenses the usage of the building as an arts center for one dollar a year. The city gives us two million dollars a year to operate the building—we have to hire union security, union maintenance. It pays for electricity. So that's where the two million dollars is going. The fundraising department at BAM raises fifteen million dollars every year. Each year it's the individuals that grow even bigger.

Audience: Will you talk about how you met Pina Bausch and brought her to BAM?

In 1984 there was an extraordinary event in Los Angeles called Cultural Olympiad. Whenever there is an Olympics anywhere in the world, both winter and summer, it's in the charter of the Olympics that the host city has to do a Cultural Olympiad. It can be whatever structure. Los Angeles had the Olympics in 1984 and Robert Fitzpatrick, who was the president of CalArts, was given the opportunity to be the artistic director. He put together the legendary Cultural Olympiad—and that made it possible for Harvey Lichtenstein to make a commitment to Pina. He had been desperately trying to meet her. He had only heard about her work. Harvey was able to make a commitment to Pina to present her work for the first time in June of 1984.

   She is one of those artists with whom I have a personal relationship. I've grown up with her. I've seen her work all over the world. Pina Bausch has a system of accepting commissions from a culture. It's a joint partnership. She takes the full company and they're in residence there for four weeks. They live a life during the day. Nothing's regimented during the day. There is a time, usually late afternoon, where they come together and share their experiences of living in the culture. They may do an improvisation. Some may relate a story and enact the story. It starts creating this universe. And then Pina starts working with the company. She goes back to Wuppertal and they continue to rehearse. She showcases the work in Wuppertal first, then she goes back to the culture to premiere the work because they commissioned it. Then she tours it.

Audience: I've been hearing the phrase "international theater" tossed around a lot, and it seems that for a lot of people international theater is simply not American theater. I'd like to know what your definition is.

I use the word "global" in my vocabulary. I'm interested in global theater, which is non-USA theater, in relation to American theater. I'm interested in theater from Asia, South America, Mexico, Central America, Canada, the United States. I guess it's all on one landscape for me. It's definitely not Eurocentric theater. And that's the important thing. In the Harvey years he would use the phrase "international theater," and it would be exclusively the European community. European work. My tenure is really much more about the Mideast, Africa, the Americas plural and other parts of the globe.

Audience: When you go out and you're looking at theater from other countries, do you find yourself looking for work that is going to represent that culture, or things that are really talking about the dynamics of global nature from a non-American perspective?

You train yourself to be subjectively objective. I am looking for storytelling. I'm interested in how this individual artist is telling his or her story. Do I believe that story is communicated to me? If it's communicating to me—because I am subjectively objective—then I believe we would all understand it.

AB: That is so gorgeous. Beautifully spoken.

But I live that. That's not just hot air or words or academic speak or whatever. I really do live that. I think it doesn't matter—I'm really not trying to be a cultural anthropologist. It really is: Is this artist successful on his or her terms at telling the story?

Audience: How do you see the future of the American theater with regard to the fact that we don't have that network that there seems to be in Europe? There seems to be less communication and less support especially for companies that are trying to make group theater. What shall we do?

The positive side of this is that I believe in you. I believe in your passion. That you being an artist collaborating with other artists—you're going to find a way to make your art. What I do think is problematic is when you want to try to distribute that art to other communities. I'll go back to the geography of our country. Trying to find communities with like values who would be engaged by what you are communicating in your storytelling is a profound issue. I think I am very critical of the presenting community, which I am a part of, because it doesn't travel enough. Here, throughout the United States, I'm hopeful, as I said, that these private foundations are on the verge of making financial resources available to individual creators.

I do think that the American artist in the theater is continually blocked out of the global marketplace because there don't seem to be any mechanisms for communicating. I can only see a finite amount of work. It's a bit troubling to me as to what the future will be.

The other community, which is the resident theater, is where I think American artists who are working in new forms don't have access to resources. I'm really mystified as to what people think they're doing with these jobs.

AB: In the institutional theaters?

If Ben Cameron of TCG were here, he would be highly insulted. He would say, "You're just grossly generalizing about the resident theater." And I know that I am. But I read *American Theatre*. I see what they're doing and what they're talking about and what kind of discourse there is. I recognize that those audiences are aging. And I don't see a younger audience member. This is a no-brainer for me. Invite a younger art-maker to come in and get that young artist out into your community. Go to the clubs. Hang out at the bars—where everyone young would want to be—and is. Where they're not is in the theater!

AB: I was in a circle with about sixteen graduate directors at Columbia and I asked them all where they were going to be in the future. Only one said "regional theater." Only one mentioned it. Because it's not sexy. It's not interesting.

But the problem is, that's where the financial resources are.

AB: I said that to them: What do you do with all these palaces around the country that are made to generate work? They have the shops, the crew. They have everything. They weren't interested.

I think it's a constituency that hasn't made an entrée to these young creators. I don't want to give you a mixed message here. I want to say I'm encouraged, truthfully, because I think there still is an interest to create theater. If you're dedicated, if you have a vision, I know you'll achieve that. I'm not sure about the methodology. It's like cottage industries. An individual will find an individual way to make something. I believe in the creative imagination. I believe the form. Our form—in this case we're talking about theater—will exist. But it's not going to be something that can be quantified in ways in which I can do the quantification.

Audience: We put on plays, and we have audiences and they are mostly our peers. They're other theater people and they're young and we don't charge very much for the ticket so that they can come. But those aren't necessarily the people that we want to be coming. I don't know how to even reach those other people. How do we let them know we exist?

Since we've had our website, the number of tickets that we have sold has doubled. It is the belief of our marketing department that it will continue because all of the indicators are—with our audience, which is a much younger audience—that this comfortableness of using the computer to purchase is part of our society and will become more so. In terms of communicating to the audience that you want for your theater, for your art, you start thinking about how we use this mechanism of a website and what you can do to start linking to other websites.

I was a marketing director at one point in my life. I'm intimately involved in the creation of our communications mechanisms because marketing is messages. You're creating messages. My lifeline of making my art complete is the marketing department because they deliver the audience. So I am sensitive to the creation of the message through our brochures—and then the image that goes on the website. Your message, framed on your website, linked to other websites of like value where you think your audience could be—that's my suggestion to you. It's not brochures. And let me tell you right here: Don't use postcards. Do you know how many postcards are being used by young theater companies? You're proliferating them and people are not paying attention to you.

AB: I'm really fascinated with what you said about when you're going out and finding pieces to bring back to BAM, you're not catering to set audiences at BAM. Every single time I walk into BAM, it's packed. So clearly, something right is going on. I'm curious about the relationship to the audience. I'll go see anything if it's at BAM because I trust that—

You see, that word that you just used. That's a great compliment to me. Thank you very much. "Trust" was the word. There is, at the foundation, at the primal spine, a trust (not for everything I do, but enough), so that curiosity is raised when the Next Wave Festival brochure arrives in the mail. The majority of that audience, who has already purchased a ticket, knows that there's a limited shelf life to the art on my stage. It's not like we're doing a four-week, six-week run. If you open on a Tuesday, you close on a Saturday or Sunday. The audience who gets that Next Wave Festival brochure over the years knows that. If they want it, they have to immediately respond in order to have access to the art. And what they will do is, building on that trust, select who they absolutely have to—"Oh, I've got to see what Declan Donnellan's doing with *Othello*." And then find out, "What is this thing called *Lost Objects*?" You live in New York City, and whether you're here as a taxpayer, as a home owner, renting an apartment, employed here, working in any way, shape or form, academically, going to school here, you're here because you're innately curious. Bottom line. And my job is to perk and pique your curiosity. And that trust, for us, is the aesthetic spine to making sure we have an audience.

Audience: Have you had the experience of seeing art in small spaces that you want to bring to BAM, but you have to kind of coax the work into big spaces?

I consistently do, when I travel, see work that is at much smaller venues. The aesthetic judgment, of looking at the work and saying, "This will not work in my theater," I can be wrong—and I have been proven wrong. I am completely reliant on trust that the directors who I have invited to come into the space, once they see the space will know how to take the work. In the case of Anne Bogart's work *bobrauschenbergamerica*, I categorically said, "My theater is not right for this." And I was wrong. I'm constantly learning. But sometimes I think that I am absolutely correct in my judgment that no, you can't transfer. Or, in some cases, that it would be too expensive to transfer and make happen.

Sometimes I will send my director of production to go see this production and to meet with the designer. Then when he comes back, he has a meeting with me and says, "It can happen. We can resolve it." Or, "This is production issue a, b and c and it's going to cost you this amount of money if we take a or b or c." I also invite artists to come into the Harvey when there's no set, when it's completely empty, and just say, "Can you see your work here?" That's another way of trying to give the opportunity to an artist to conceptually allow their imagination to fill the architectural space with their artistic space.

Audience: I've been able to get into disabled choreography. I've found it in New York very difficult. I'm just wondering as a presenter and in your global travels, do

you have a point of view as to where professional artists might fit in the mainstream on stage?

The biggest challenge today is getting to the art-making, the theater that you're crafting, and concentrating on finding the art, and not marginalizing you even more. In dance there are disabled artists working in the art form of dance who are put into the educational category and not on the main stage of these presenting organizations' seasons. What I think needs to happen is that artists who are disabled need a voice within the presenting community.

There are two organizations that exist. One is called the Association of Performing Arts Presenters, which is based in Washington, D.C., which is like the TCG for the presenting organizations. And the second one is called ISPA, International Society for the Performing Arts, which is based here in New York State. Both convene in New York City in January. That is where the platform needs to be. The presenting industry of the United States of America is currently the largest purchaser of art and culture in North America. When you have an underserved artistic community, then that issue needs to be put before that constituency: "Deal. Let's discuss. Let's examine." And that is where change occurs.

I think the same thing is true with Theatre Communications Group. Your issue needs to get to Theatre Communications Group, which governs more than four hundred not-for-profit theaters in this country. We need to frame this issue. We need to create a way in which we can talk about art-making from a very specific community. That's how I think it needs to happen. I really believe—going back to what I said—the age of institution-building is over. We're entering the era of the individual artist—and finding resources for the individual artist to make work.

Lee Breuer

As a young director during the 1970s I secretly followed artists I admired on the streets of New York City. Curious to know more about them, I stayed at a distance but kept close watch on their actions. I hope that they were unaware of my stalking. I wanted to suss out what made these people tick. I wanted to know what they might look at and how they paid attention.

Lee Breuer was one of the people I followed on the streets of the East Village. I followed him because I loved his work and I wanted to know more about him. I noticed that he would stop and gaze intently for a long time at advertising—posters, signs and announcements. He seemed to be curious about how messages, whether commercial or community-oriented, were written and laid out. I liked the audacity of his interest and I wanted to adapt his intense brand of curiosity and make it my own. In those days, this is one way I learned.

What drew me to follow Lee Breuer on the streets was his remarkable artistry as director and writer. The theatrical worlds that he constructed in his plays were unlike anything I had ever experienced. The powerful originality of his productions were both wildly idiosyncratic and at the same time, accessible. Over the many years that he has been making theater, at least since the early seventies when I was first introduced to his work, Lee seems as edgy and innovative now as he was back then.

Lee grew up first in Virginia and then in Southern California where he entered UCLA in 1973 when he was only sixteen years old. His mother hoped that he would study pre-law but when his father died he decided that he wanted to be an artist instead. From Los Angeles, Lee headed to Big Sur where he found himself in the company of Henry Miller. A few peyote and LSD trips helped him to understand and experience art. Later, in San Francisco, where he met Michael McClure, Jack Kerouac and Allen Ginsberg and mounted Lawrence Ferlinghetti's *The Alligation*, he began to direct at the legendary San Francisco Actor's Workshop. In addition to staging plays by Genet, Lorca, Beckett and Ferlinghetti, he began to write and devise his own creations at San Francisco venues such as the San Francisco Mime Troupe, the Tape Music Center and A.C.T.

Having worked with future Mabou Mines co-founders Ruth Maleczech, JoAnne Akalaitis and Bill Raymond in San Francisco, it was while living in Paris in the late 1960s that Lee met the other Mabou Mines cofounders Philip Glass, David Warrilow and Fred Neumann. In Europe he directed works by Brecht and Beckett as well as his own compositions. He and his friends headed to New York and Mabou Mines, named after a place in Nova Scotia, became an entity in 1970. Lee is still engaged with the collective as playwright, director and lyricist, realizing many seminal productions, including *The Red Horse Animation, Come and Go, Play, The B. Beaver Animation, The Saint and the Football Player, Shaggy Dog Animation, A Prelude to a Death in Venice, Hajj, The Gospel at Colonus, Lear, Peter and Wendy, Ecco Porco* and *Dollhouse*.

Lee also works outside Mabou Mines in film, on Broadway and on a variety of theatrical projects in Europe, Africa, Asia and North and South America. Over the years he has collected a staggering number of awards and fellowships, including ten Obie Awards, a MacArthur Fellowship, a Pulitzer nomination, several Rockefeller fellowships and Guggenheim, Bunting, and Fulbright fellowships.

February 28, 2005

AB: I think of Lee Breuer as a wizard—a wizard not only in American theater, but theater around the world. He's an iconoclast in every way, busting icons left and right. But I was so surprised to find out, when we were teaching a class together at NYU a couple of years ago, that his background is with the Method. I want to get to political, aesthetic and acting issues. Could we start with what initially drew you to the theater and what keeps you there now. Has that changed?

LB: I'm doing a workshop at the Flea [Theatre in New York City] for a piece of mine that I think is the most baroque, contorted, unbelievably complicated series of jokes I've ever put together, called *Summa Dramatica*. It pretends to be pataphysical. [Alfred] Jarry's theory of pataphysics is a theory of imaginary solutions. So we're comparing that with the pragmatism of different works.

I grew up in L.A., and I went to UCLA in the fifties, and like everyone in L.A., I wanted to get into film. UCLA had the only film department cooking at the time, and I was hankering to hang out there. I didn't like anybody in my other classes. It was around 1958, and there was no independent film. There wasn't Stan Brakhage and experimental film. In those days they didn't even have tape recorders. The idea was that the only way to get into film was to go in the mailroom and see who noticed you. And that didn't seem to be the way I wanted to go. So my imaginary solution for not getting into film was to conceive of a theater that was filmic, which is what I proceeded to do. In terms of cuts and dissolves and whatever technology existed at the time, I tried to create theater as a live film experience. This all worked pretty interestingly as we were moving into a more conceptual view of art.

Some ten years later, the major turn in the world happened. Around the seventies, we went from Jackson Pollock to Jasper Johns, from abstract expressionism with consummate emotionalist abstractionism into cool, conceptual, withdrawn, let's-organize-it-all-and-look-at-it-from-a-distance stuff. And, lo and behold, I found out that all of my ideas about doing live film were highly conceptual. In other words, what was being represented on stage was a concept that was filmic, however it was live and theatrical. This was very clear when Mabou Mines did our first piece, *The Red Horse Animation*, in 1970. This was a piece in which everybody laid flat on the floor and you looked at it down very steeply so that the space was switched ninety degrees. Everyone was playing with a lot of space themes at that point, so we had a piece that really appealed to the art world. It was done at every gallery in New York.

What was interesting is that this idea—my fantasy solution for not getting into film—became a conceptual idea, and a lot of my life has gone on that way. These kind of fantasy solutions move into a zeitgeist that seems to have some intellectual validity for a while, like the concept ideas in the seventies. These fantasy solutions achieve a certain amount of intellectual reality for a while and then they vanish into blue and no one cares anymore. In other words, I did get into theater with an idea of following imaginary solutions, and I kind of still do.

Pataphysics is the notion that if there isn't a solution, you imagine it?

Yes. Jarry was just amazing. *Ubu Roi* is the simplest he ever wrote. If you get into the real pataphysical text, it's a complete send-up spin on metaphysics. He'll give you a mathematical equation that the sun is square. There's this wonderful voyage when he and an ape roll through the skies above Paris and stop off in different islands. One is covered in shit, for example, and each island represents a poet that he hates. They're all personal send-ups of these different intellectual figures and political figures. My little take on this is to compare it to the William James stuff. If you look at things with a sense of humor, reality is so unreal. So a solution to reality is to perceive it as unreal, and then you are very at home with him. And by reality, I also mean realism. We experienced that in a fascinating way when we did *Dollhouse*. Supposedly Ibsen was the master of bourgeois tragedy and supposedly the inventor of realism on stage. Well, Ibsen didn't write realism. Ibsen wrote melodrama, which we found by putting melody under the drama. As soon as we put melody under the drama, and made it melodrama, it made tons of sense.

What else is real? West Coast reality is different from East Coast reality. East Coast has a little bit of Italian in it; West Coast is about haircuts. You just find that there is no definition whatsoever, that reality itself is an imaginary solution to the idea that you have a base. There's a critic at Duke, Toril Moi, who makes the case that Ibsen, far from being a realist, is a modernist, which makes a lot of sense—for only a modernist can be post-modernized.

In *Summa Dramatica* we have the actress play a cow. We decided we were not going to look at the cows having any character center. Basically the imaginary solution to the text was that whatever seemed to work for that paragraph, we would use it. So for one paragraph, we have a Peter Sellers German accent, for the next one, an Indian accent, for the next one we're using an emotional Hollywood movie—no semblance whatsoever to the character. And yet, in going completely around in a circle, we'd try to touch every clichéd reality that we could, except formalism, and then we started attacking emotional realities. There's one scene where the cow, for absolutely no reason whatsoever, becomes emotional and cries; and with no validity to it whatsoever, she completely cracks up in another scene. In other words, what would be really nice is to take every little emotional reality that you see in every feature film and put it back to back and then run it backward or something like that.

I consider myself a formalist, but basically other formalists appear to see form as physical entity, as something you can draw, something you can stand up. I see *emotional blocks* as formal tools. If you look at your classic Hollywood denouement, where the emotional structure leads to someone dropping a tear out of his or her left eye, that's a formal structure. That's just as formal as a Robert Wilson position. That's just as formal and slowing up and walking backward at a half pace. If these emotional clichés were put in some abstract form we should see them as just as formalistic as the materialist formalism that you get out of a Robert Wilson or a Richard Foreman. I think that the difference between what I'm interested in is that I do see that Method is so great. Just check out a Method movie. You have to go very deep to see an emotional structure that you haven't seen some place before, read some place before, felt some place before, that isn't a formal emotional base. Sometimes great coups happen and you get some sort of genius actor or actress who finds a way through these emotional clichés and into something completely original and completely brilliant. These are the absolute best actors. But once they've found their way through it, within a year, it's become an emotional cliché. For example, I'm sure Marlon [Brando] found his way into some beats that no one had tried before. He had done these kind of androgynous, wonderful numbers where he had all these muscles, but he was emotional and vulnerable like an ingénue should be. It was great to see this, and then a couple of years later, this became the key to how to be a rock star. This brand of discovery of the formalism of androgynous emotional excess coupled with a macho presentation is now a dialectal cliché, but when Brando invented it, it was mind-bogglingly original. Where it began to be pasted up was with Elvis. When we got to Elvis, we saw how far this could go, and every major rock icon since then has this androgynous vulnerability connected with a macho presentation. So, what I want to bring to the table, to the discussion, is that it's not just a physical formality; it's emotional blocks that can be seen as a formal structure.

Do you actually have a background in Method yourself?

Yes, I love motivational acting. I read Stanislavski backward and forward. Some of my collaborators studied with Grotowski when he was really interested in motivational work from an abstract point of view and considered that he was picking up where Stanislavski left off, which he did. He was moving the Stanislavski system into a level of abstraction, and simultaneously the tradition of Meyerhold was turning toward formality. The thing that was really interesting about Grotowski in the early days— the seventies, around the time that JoAnne Akalaitis, Ruth Maleczech and I hung around with him—was that he felt that there were ways of accessing the emotional below the level of realism. Most of the time, Stanislavski was caught inside a "realism," limiting how deep you could go to a psychologically realistic situation. What Grotowski was trying to do was find what the emotions of the subconscious were. So you have this really freaked-out junkie spinning in the middle of the street, like you used to always see all the time in the late sixties and seventies, never leaving, in traffic, wandering around, completely out of her mind. You start to think, What the hell is she doing? Where's it coming from? What level of her subconscious is this? How do you understand the motivation of crazy people? How do you understand the motivation of people who dabble in drugs? What he was trying to get to was the subconscious. Realism is an agreement between us that behavior is real because we've agreed that those significations are real. But could you be standing there and take one finger and knock your eyeball out? Would that be real? No, that would be insane. But I'm sure that if a hundred people knocked their eyeballs out [in front of us], we would all agree that that was pretty real. Our reality is an agreement. Anything outside of that we can label as surrealism, as expressionism, as crazy, or whatever we want to tag it.

The key here that Grotowski was onto was how do you motivate an expressionistic move? How do you motivate a surrealist cross across the stage? When I was working with R. G. Davis at the San Francisco Mime Troupe, they were excitedly, desperately looking for how to motivate pantomime. How do you make French pantomime real? Supposedly, they had some answers: You go into different parts of your brain, you contact different emotional realities. We've also found that Brecht had a little bit of an answer, too, which was his idea of dialectical presentation of opposites. Like with Brando, the many different dichotomies that Brecht set up—like doing a horrendous, bloody battle scene and playing toy music over it—are now cliché, but at that time were very hot, intricate, cerebral and fantastic. We have seen this as a key to what is ironic on stage. Everybody does it. I do it, Richard [Foreman] does it, Liz [LeCompte] does it.

How do you work with actors to find moments of irony and juxtaposition? I think that the rehearsal process is a kind of intercourse—and it's hard to ask about sex.

Everybody's work of art is basically a description of how they have sex. If I hear someone's song being sung, or watch somebody's play being directed, you'll know exactly how the director makes love. I think that's right, too—that the really special work that takes place between actor and director is a constant psychic intercourse between the two. It's a constant give and take. In desexualized theater, you go to sleep. The tension that live theater lives off of, the idea that it presents an extraordinary emanation from the stage itself, that the energy is double, triple, quadruple what normal energy and conversation is all about, is the fact that we are dealing with a heightened sexuality, and that sexuality is transferred from the play to the audience. The intercourse between director and actor is transferred to become intercourse between actor and audience.

Which is why I say it's hard to ask that question—because what I'm asking is: How do you work with actors?

I really love those moments where they don't know what they're feeling—when you don't know whether something is laughable or serious. Shall we get into the sexual metaphor here? It's got a little bit to do with a vulnerability that comes from a deconstructed metaphor. By deconstructing a moment, by actors deconstructing each other, deconstructing the script, basically you produce a level of vulnerability that's really sexy. That kind of vulnerability is what turns me on, what I try to put out there. I find it and get to it through this technique of doubling, this you-me business, the oppositions—that I can be very emotional and cracking myself up at the same time, or be very aggressive, etc. I think that these combinations are what keep things hot—almost a formula for what keeps things hot. If you're looking to make a *very* sexy show, you *always* want to use the element of surprise, so that nobody ever knows what's coming.

In rehearsals? In the product?

In rehearsals it can be very subtle. It can be intellectual. It doesn't have to be, you know, we're in the middle of having tea and you jump across and attack someone. We can have a general aura of respect in our action and a sociability; it doesn't have to be crazy. But if you embed it in its core with a nut of craziness, that nut will radiate right through the audience and will basically create a very special event.

When I think of your productions over the years and now, that core of craziness is conceptual—doing a show in a football field with a choreographer and famous football players; the whole approach of *The Gospel at Colonus*, to crash history and society together; the way you approached Beckett, which was one of the best productions I've ever seen in the United States; and what you did with *Dollhouse*. It seems like something that you do has to do with context. You place dissimilar notions together in one context which creates another context.

Right. And it doesn't always work.

Which is probably why it sometimes does work. If it were guaranteed to work—with the right formula—then it never would.

I remember when I was getting over-confident, in my earlier days like 1972 or 1973, I did something called *The Arc Welding Piece*. Wow, that didn't work. We took that to Amsterdam. It was a sculpture with an arc welder cutting apart this piece of metal, with sparks flying, and with three or four actors behind, enlarged, in masks. They were basically an emotional chorus, which I had picked up from something I had done in San Francisco with a play called *Acting without Words*. It was an idea about how can you get four or five people, a chorus of people, to have the same and simultaneous emotion in one moment. Can you get seven people to all sit in chairs and all start to cry simultaneously? Can you get the same seven people to do something else simultaneously? So the idea was to do this behind the enlarged faces and have it relate in an oppositional way to the shapes being made in steel. It didn't work.

That just means that in order for it to work sometimes, you commit fully.

I've just had better ideas. Later on I realized that I usually use a rule of thumb about having a literary tie to these oppositions, balances. *Dollhouse* is a prototypical idea—the idea of Torvald being called small by Nora, and to take that literally and make all the male actors really small—that was crazy, but it was right in the text.

I was a kind of part of the art world from 1970 to 1980. I made money moving art from one gallery to another in the truck. I knew a lot of artists, basically got the language, used to be able to sneak into parties. During that time, particularly with Bruce Nauman's work, the artists weren't very good writers, but they tried to use titles differently than surrealists used printing. Bruce invited me once to his studio. He was working on a piece called "Flower Arrangements." There's a story about Bruce. A friend of mine told me he saw him lying on the floor in his studio with hands full of white flour. He had piles of white flour every place. The visual pun was the kind of thing that always made Bruce's stuff so funny and so great. A lot of people try to take these little verbal jokes and puns literally. It was a purely conceptual idea, but of course, the conceptual bus ran out of gas after about eight or nine years of punning, and they weren't very good writers and the puns weren't that good, and so it didn't quite succeed. You could feel the conceptual movement getting thinner, going to more and more remote galleries. It was a moment, just like Cubism was a moment, and Dadaism was a moment, so was this idea of conceptual art. But it taught me a great deal. It taught me to look at a script differently. It taught me to look for things that could work literally.

Sometimes it isn't a word. With *Gospel at Colonus*, *Black Athena* had just come out, and I was very interested in the African connection to European culture. There was this idea that Africa, particularly Nubia because it was Egypt at that particular time, had a tremendous amount to do with European religion, theater and music. So, having been hanging around a lot of gospel singers and really getting into it, I started to think, "Where did this come from? What are these six beats going on? What are these five beats?" And then it suddenly dawned on me—another imaginary solution—that they were where the percussion track went. Going along with that came the idea that maybe we could reevoke an African contribution by moving it into a contemporary metaphor like soul music. Out of this came an idea of: What about the exotic, beautiful black gospel singers? It brought me back to when Plato spoke of music and the study of music as being critical of the Republic, and he meant the study of literature. Music was a metaphor for all of literature—everything rhythmic, everything lyric, the whole deal. Then I started thinking that the only way to understand literature is with music. From then on, I couldn't do a piece without music. *Dollhouse* couldn't be done without Eve Beglarian. And it kept going on that way, one musical idea after another. It's still going on.

What is the imagining, pataphysical approach? It's not some highfalutin imagination—you don't close your eyes and come up with some wacky idea. It comes from a very literal examination of text.

I think it's about wanting to define the secret. You're looking at this text and you're looking at the play and you're trying to think of the secret of how to make everything come together. One of the keys is the surtext/subtext. Arbitrarily, what about deciding to reverse them, putting the subtext above and the surtext below? This is an effort to play the subtext and to subtextualize the surtext.

Define the surtext.

The words, what they say, the text itself. The subtext is: What did he mean? What is the essence? What is the poetic, metaphorical meaning?

We tried to do that when we did *Mabou Mines Lear*, which was a big experiment. *Mabou Mines Lear*, which I hope to be able to bring back some day, staged *Lear* in a genuine reproduction, I think our first genuine reproduction, though there have been some since. But the important part was that we put it in West Virginia and we used redneck accents. That came from a study of Shakespearean language that advised me that there were two Englishes that made the jump to the U.S.: One was Shakespearean English and one was Anglican English, which became the Bible and jumped to Boston. Shakespearean English jumped to Jamestown, then found its way west to Tennessee, and sits today in Appalachia. So the best place to hear great Shakespearean English is a Johnny Cash recording. You can't believe how fantastic Shakespeare sounds that way. All the stuff makes sense. When they say "snuff," it's amazing how it rings. And it's completely historical. There was a BBC series on Shakespearean English in which they showed the Shakespearean dialect moving on to Cornwall, and they had a recording of Cornwallian speech, and it does sound kind of like North Texas. The damn problem I had [with *Lear*] is I didn't ask actors to go far enough. They had *light* redneck accents. And what I really needed was for them to go too far.

Why didn't you ask the actors to go further?

I was chicken.

Why is it we get chicken about Shakespeare?

I was chicken. And also I had some really good actors and they, of course, wanted to be very Shakespearean.

That's what I mean.

But I had some really great people. There were four Obies in there—Ruth Maleczech as Lear, Karen Evans-Kandel as Edmund, Isabell Monk as Gloucester, and the fool was gay, a drag queen, which was right on. A middle-aged West Virginia patriarch might very, very probably have a best friend be a drag queen and they would be together forever. Greg Mehrten played the drag queen and got his first Obie. The coxcomb became a dildo. We wrote a few songs to make that work. We had two electric cars—a 1937 Plymouth and a pickup. I had a brilliant cast, and it was really hard. Of course, we got trashed in that production. People were saying that I was doing a John Waters tribute. A part of me was, but *it* wasn't. I am in absolute awe of the legacy of Charles Ludlum and the playhouse of the Ridiculous. It was an inspiration for *Dollhouse*. It was an inspiration for parts of *Lear*. Charles was a very good friend of mine, and the legacy he left when he died will go on and on. But the point is, this wasn't all send-up. This was a very serious idea about the time warp in Shakespearean English. I hear there's a time warp for Spanish, that there are Spanish enclaves in South America that speak nineteenth-century Spanish. Canadian French is a time warp for French; Louisiana French is a time warp. I think that we caught it and I would like to really go further with it. It was a hot idea and it had that balance. Whether an idea works or not—for example, *Dollhouse* worked and *The Arc Welder Piece* didn't—all I can say is when I teach this idea, it's like having two balances and a scale. You have to get both sides of the scale off the ground. If your opposition is too heavy, it's not going to work, and if your opposition is too light, it's not going to work. You have to be able to get this balance completely suspended. That's the key.

So what was not oppositional about *The Arc Welder Piece*?

It was too conceptual. I didn't have enough surtext. It was ninety-five percent subtext. I should have had something written, something clear and straight.

I'm so loath to drop the notion of putting the subtext on the surface and the surtext underneath. It feels somehow true.

Also it's dangerous, it's emotional. To get back to the Method, I love to work with people who were trained motivationally. In the seventies and the eighties a whole slew of performers developed, many of whom came by conceptual art and the idea of performance art. They were cooler than thou. They were either not that interested in feeling a thing or they couldn't. I think a lot of this kind of theater is happening today—a lot of high-tech, video, computerized imagery—and to many of a younger generation it is one hundred percent satisfying. You can look at a magnificent, formalist trick, idea, sound, sound score, dance sequence, whatever it is, and be thrilled and not need anything else. Somehow, that didn't become my thing. I really want to be deeply moved—like a great Method actor can greatly move you—and yet be able to distance myself enough to catch up. Withdraw, and then get sucked back.

It's the old story of Brecht. Brecht was so interested in alienating and distancing from the emotional vomit of the tradition he came out of, that everything was directed to cooling down, anti-feeling, technical commentary. To have the true emotional distancing, it often helped to have some emotion to distance from. I feel that what has happened is that people are distancing like crazy, because we have nowhere to go. We don't feel shit. Nobody can feel shit, nobody wants to feel shit, and nobody enjoys watching other people feel shit. It's uncool or we're afraid to get sucked in by the dirty word "empathy" and overemotionalize. If you're going to parody soap opera, it would be nice to have a really great baroque emotional moment that you can distance from.

So, I became interested in wanting to have something to distance from. I turned to people who had the ability to feel and the brains to make commentary about their feelings. I miss it when I see people with incredible brains and formal knowledge completely willing to let the seed of feeling vanish

I keep going back to three Beckett plays you did. Beckett is so hard to do because if done wrong, it's just painful. I was so knocked out by the acting. It was crystalline.

That was the first time we had any national notice. And I think David [Warrilow] got an Obie. It was our breakthrough.

What made you do Beckett at that moment, and how did you approach it?

When I was a student in the fifties at UCLA, Beckett was just published in Evergreen Press for the first time. The first production of *Godot* was given by the Actors Workshop of San Francisco with Herb Blau, and I remember hitchhiking up to see it, and I remember being really disappointed. But then I saw Herb's *Endgame*, which was the formal idea of how to do Beckett, and that was in my head for the next twenty years. I was a Beckett nut by the time I was twenty. I was also a Genet nut because that was also the first time Genet was published. I'm sixty-eight, and I come from a generation where the only way out was art. That was the fifties. There was no other way out. In the sixties you had politics, drugs, pills—lots of ways out. That's why artists who are exactly my age—like Phil Glass and Richard Foreman—are obsessed with art. Because, Jesus Christ, this was the key to our lives. You went there, you had an imaginary solution, and you better stick with that thing and be careful you don't stop imagining or you just die, instantly. Before the sixties, all you could do was imitate, pretend you were in Paris drinking cappuccinos wearing a turtleneck. This was pre–rock 'n' roll. That's why I smoked: Camus looked so hip with a cigarette to his lips. What was very sexy then was Artaud, Beckett, Genet. I remember nothing about my education. It was one big empty parking lot except for one course taught by some little guy named Giacometti, who tried to pose like Camus and wore Italian suits and kept saying, "Theater does not exist," and in one semester introduced me to Artaud, Beckett, Genet, Sartre and about five others. I had nothing else I wanted to think about for the rest of the time I was in school. I left shortly after that. Nobody graduated back then; you left because you had too many parking tickets.

The idea here was that Beckett was the great awakening to formalism, the great awakening to absurdist thinking, the great awakening to a philosophical play. Everybody wanted to emulate this particular lifestyle. Later, when I was living in Paris, I bumped into Beckett three or four times. Fred [Neumann] knew Beckett very well. Beckett actually wrote a play for David [Warrilow] called *A Piece of Monologue*. David was one of his favorite actors. So it was funny, this idol of mine since I was sixteen, I would pass on the street and I'd ask him about good restaurants. About ten years later, he did come to see *The Lost Ones*. He doesn't go see his performances because people would want him to comment on it and he would never let on.

Did he comment on it?

He said he really liked it, but don't tell anybody. But the point is, I love Genet more than Beckett. But after I did *The Maids*, which was the very first professional play I ever did, I couldn't do any more Genet because I couldn't afford to. Genet was too damn big. The thing about Beckett is he's cheap. One box set, one character, a wheel, this and that. You can do it with nothing. Genet, my God, you need "son et lumière." You need a producer.

You did something with one of the Beckett plays that was so sophisticated. You had a mirror hanging at an angle.

That was *Come and Go.* The performers sat behind us and we could look at them in the mirror, and that was wonderful because they looked completely lost in space and about half normal size. The voice came from back and the image came from the front.

That was really radical.

It was radical theater, but it wasn't radical to the bunch of conceptual artists we were hanging out with. That was the stuff they dealt with every day. We just happened to be the only group doing theater with it. In other words, we helped to invent what was later called performance art. There was no performance art at that time. Quite frankly, Phil Glass led us into performance art. He was working for all these painters. He was the entrée to all of these guys with these great and rather esoteric ideas. The painters didn't believe in theater. Theirs was an art reality. Ours was a theater reality. What was interesting was that the reality was so clear and so strong it forced us to perform in a certain way. We really realized the incredible difference between the art and theater worlds and why none of these artists could really truly embrace theater. Performance art stayed art—even Laurie Anderson, who probably has the most theater sense of any of the true art people. After Laurie, it wasn't performance art anymore, it was stand-up comedy passing as performance art because people wanted to get cheaper and cheaper, and hand-held microphones were cheaper. We were totally unusual in that we were experimenting with emotional formalisms in the art world that were only used to pictorial formalisms. In the theater world, we were able to bring pictorial formalisms in a sophisticated way. We're not cutting edge about pictorial formalisms now; there are many companies much further out. The Wooster Group is doing some brilliant sound stuff; Richard [Foreman] is doing some great images. But at that particular time, I think we were probably—with Richard—both introducing the idea and making the idea of art stick. But we dealt much more with internal work than Richard. Richard stayed at the "look at the outside." This is why he and Yvonne Rainer got along so well. She was interested in the dance perspective—of staying to the outside and looking at things objectively.

Then you moved from the gallery scene.

We never performed in a theater from 1970, when we started, to the end of 1974.

And that was Joe Papp?

Joe Papp picked up *The Lost Ones* and moved us.

Was that a choice? Did you guys say, "We want to perform in galleries. These are our people"?

No. Galleries accepted us and thought we were great, and no theater was interested. We still have very, very close friends in the art world who come to see us. But still, they understand the intellectual. They just won't feel. The art world tends to be smarter, and the theater world tends to be more connected to the work. You just don't get high off an art world response. But sometimes you get some great ideas off it. You pick and choose.

I have one more question, which is about the world we live in now and how it's changing. How are you adjusting to that?

Badly. It's really becoming a little bit more ironic and more cynical. I got really interested in the classic idea of cynicism.

What's the "classic idea of cynicism"?

I think cynics were the first performance artists. Remember that guy—Diojoues—who lived in a pot of his own shit. He thought it was ridiculous to do anything in private. Then he masturbated in public and people didn't like it. This was the first performance art. I think that cynics are incredibly romantic, great romantics, who are so petrified that they've covered themselves in every possible layer of protection so they won't permit any kind of penetration whatsoever.

I don't like either side. Curiously enough, I'm so inured to the idiocy of the Bush conservative that I almost forget about him. But being a cynic I'm also bugged by the liberals. I hate the *New York Times*. It's like a friend who has done you false. The liberal academic community is the reason I don't like to teach anymore. I used to think I could talk to that side. But I am much more pained by the blues because I trusted them once. They're just a bunch of greedy fucks, too, but they're not quite as deteriorated as the reds. They still have some pretense of a cerebrum. I do not really feel that there is a social structure that will honor me. I go through wonderful imaginary solutions. I have a real, romantic nostalgia for good things, nice people, a pure point of view. At one time we would have said "a Christian point of view," but we don't say this now. When I see these fools critiquing other fools, the anti-Bushes critiquing the Bushes, and the *Times* mumbling about positivism and morality, I just think at two hundred thousand dollars a year, go ahead and critique and harangue all you want at the *Times*. Greed culture is a really interesting thing to study. I think we're Rome in their last sixty years. And in sixty years, the barbarians will come down from the Alps and come to the gates, and there we are, welcoming a new dark age. I think the key here, is humor. If I can turn something into a joke I'm happy. So what I feel about the world today is that it's completely full of shit, but half of the shit hurts me more than the other half.

I really love to look at society as a biological metaphor, to see analogies between viruses and multinationals. But this is old sixties stuff—Burroughs's *Naked Lunch*—but it's still a lot fun.

When I moved to New York in 1974, fresh out of college, I used to secretly follow my favorite directors down the street. I was curious about what they would look at. And you were one of them.

What would I look at?

You looked at advertisements. It was late at night, and you would stop and read the advertisements. I found that fascinating, that perverse fascination. I don't mean just reading the text, but really reading the advertisement—which seems consistent with what you just described.

Audience: I want to bring you back to the point about how you work in rehearsal. I think everyone is very curious about the nuts and bolts of the process. Lee is the most collaborative director that I've worked with. He really actually solicits more information from both directors and designers. I think the reason you've directed a lot of award-winning performances is that no one else specifically builds parts around particular actors like you do.

I really love intimacy in directing. Many of the people I work with, I've worked with for some thirty years. I think that when I work well what I find myself doing is negotiating. The actor has an idea about the part and how they want to perform it, how they want to personalize it. This is Stanislavski, jumped to Grotowski, jumped to us, the modern idea—we really, really use personalization.

AB: It's called Affective Memory, right?

Yes, that's probably what it's called. But when the actor finds a certain behavior or emotion that they want to deal with, you have to look at that like a little circle. It might be totally outside my idea. But if it's real, I want to pay attention to it. It's so seldom that you get something real. What I try to do is make a second circle—my concept—and then the negotiation is bringing the circles together. What I want to be able to do is place the performance circle inside the conceptual circle so that the performance validity and reality will enhance my conceptual circle by always exploding. For those of you who are directors, this is what we need to know about each other.

Audience: I'm a painter, so I work with form. But I actually don't work with form. I let form find me. I think that's what you're talking about. If you go into the work with an idea, that idea will never happen. From a sense of formlessness manifests the form by itself.

The big key is to be able to step back and see a form that's just manifested. A lot of times it will surround and blow you around so deeply, you won't see the form. There's always this moment when you don't have the vaguest idea what you're doing, and it's a gift. It shows you what you're doing.

AB: I think the director's job is always to think on the other side of everyone else, or encircle everyone. The actor should have a full and solid circle of ideas and approaches, a take on it. It's not my job to interfere with it; it's my job to put them in a context that is larger than that. And however large they get, my job is to get wider.

In a way, as a director, I think we secretly have to work like actors. I think we have to get an original, emotional idea about what we want to do. There has to be a motivational core to our directorial concept. That is the reason I can parallel the actors circle with the directors circle. It starts out just as emotional as the actor's circle, and then we [directors] can blow it up, make it bigger by intellectualizing it, pushing the limits back, allowing it to encompass that. The key in the beginning is that we have to feel it. I'll use *Dollhouse* as an example. I know that when I was in Oslo with *Dollhouse*, I had to do a panel and I was absolutely amazed by the fact that all the directors of five or six different productions of *A Doll's House* in Oslo were men. I said, "Do you *really* think that you can validly feel enough to understand how to direct Nora?" And they all said yes. I may be a man directing *A Doll's House*, but I know I could never direct it from Nora's point of view. I have to use Torvald's point of view. I know about being walked out on and left with a kid. I understand that. It was a really deep, mind-boggling experience that tested my sanity, my confidence, on and on. I had just read an essay by Strindberg in which he said he thought it was Torvald's play, and the fact is, it's both, but it's a complex interaction. I had a real emotional experience, which was: I knew Torvald's side. But I didn't know Nora's side and I didn't pretend that I did, and I felt proud of myself that I was the first to admit that I didn't have the faintest fucking idea what was going on inside of her except by a secondary bounce, like through a mirror.

I left Nora's point of view up to Maude Mitchell who played Nora and was also the production's dramaturg.

Working on *Dollhouse* while touring I was able to refine the motivational/formalist balancing act. *Dollhouse* itself was a balancing act between my partner Maude and myself. Even the Obies were balanced—she took one for performance and I one for direction.

Maude was Meisner-trained, and I was a writer who liked to stage stuff like I saw it in my head, which was somewhat conceptual and somewhat like a movie. We acted out each other's creative agendas. I wanted my forms filled with feelings—I was not a post-modernist of the minimal-structural blueprint school—and she wanted her feeling shaped by form.

We developed an acting dialectic, half Stanislavski, half Meyerhold. A Jarry-esque, imaginary neuro-theory could speculate that emotions and commentary like humor take different paths to the muscles—one chemical and one electrical. It could actually even be true—but the imaginary paradigm would work just as well. Tears for example are cued by a chemical brew that takes fractions of seconds to travel from the brain to the tear ducts. Comic energy is electric and travels much faster. Thus an actor could weep and instantly make a joke, and then continue to weep as the comic electrical energy penetrated the chemistry and, as quickly departed, leaving the slow-moving tear stimulus intact.

Audience: Could you talk about when you and Ruth went to Berlin and it changed your idea about directing?

When we were living in Paris in 1968, we hitchhiked to Berlin. The wall was still up. We stayed in a little hotel and walked through the checkpoints. At that time, Helena Weigel was still alive and she welcomed us with open arms—these American kids come over into East Berlin to check out the theater. She said we could attend any rehearsals we wanted. We started attending rehearsals for *Mann ist Mann*, and I couldn't believe what I saw—a chorus of eight people on stage, but six directors! One director was watching one actor, one director was watching two actors. There was a general overview from one director who organized all the other directors. They were all directing together. Well, you cannot believe the thrill I experienced watching group directing. I have tried to continue with that. In Mabou Mines, four or five of us will work with one actor on a particular scene, and if it's my show, I will be the arbitrator if people have counter-feelings. I have to be politic about that—moving their circles inside my circles and working with all these director circles. Sometimes it's very labor intensive, and sometimes you do lose your way. But this level of collaboration is really exciting, and I did learn that at the Berliner Ensemble.

AB: I think of a production like a pie, if you take one little slice of pie, that's my area. It's got to be really thought-out, I've got to really get involved, it's really dense, so I fill in that section. Everybody else has to do the rest of the pie. If I try to get involved in the rest of the pie, it would not be very tasty pie.

I think that's a great way to share a pie. Everybody gets a slice.

AB: Would you talk about the show you're doing at the Flea?

It's an attempt to imitate an academic, nineteenth-century language, and it's delivered by a cow who's a yoga instructor named Sri Moo, and she gives a long lecture and harangue about methodology, this and that, post-modernism. The gimmick is that after a hiatus of a hundred years she's picking up the William James lectures, *Varieties of the Religious Experience*, and of course James forgot to include theater as a variety of religious experience. I just love my daughter and her mother Ruth [Maleczech], who is the co-artistic director of Mabou Mines, for doing it. I think they are really brilliant. Very few people could make language like that work. I'm very happy with the way the workshop is going. It's only forty minutes long. Eventually it will become the prologue of a full-length play that will continue.

AB: Is there something else coming up?

We may be able to get up four performances of *Red Beads* next fall, which we did at Mass MOCA two or three years ago. It's a make-or-break let's-get-it-up thing, and I think it could be really exciting if we can put it all together. It's my collaboration with Basil Twist. He was also the master puppeteer for *Peter and Wendy*. We put some pretty wild ideas in this. First of all, the puppetry is environmental puppetry. There are not individual puppets. We used nothing but Chinese silk, and it's all in mid-air, blown up by fans. It's exactly the way the water worked in Basil's *Symphonie Fantastique*, but we're now using wind. The actors and dancers are all in mid-air also because they're all flown in. So you can see everything under everything. You'll see someone crawl over a mountain, and then behind them you can see the back of the stage. It's an opera with a score by Ushio Torikai. It takes ten to fifteen students just to hold the cloth, while three or four blow the wind into it—just to give you an idea of how out-of-sight the logistics are. It's a glorious extravagance. It's like Bob [Wilson] at his best. I think Wilson is an icon of how to do the impossible and make it work. He's had the support of the art world and it's worked for him.

Pretty much everything I do is different from the thing I've done before. *Gospel at Colonus* has nothing to do with *Peter and Wendy*. One's a yang show, the other's a ying show. Neither of those have anything to do with *Dollhouse* or *Summa Dramatica*, the cow piece. So either I have no center or I really believe in this idea that you can re-form yourself for the moment and the work.

Elizabeth Streb

One can see Streb from a distance because she stands out in a crowd. She is a visible icon on the New York landscape. And Streb is what you call her. The name fits: a brief punchy word that encompasses the impact of her presence. The risks that she takes in her work are nothing less than outrageous, exciting and inspirational. Her company of athletic dancers is challenged to transcend their physical and psychic boundaries and test the unknown on a daily basis.

Streb has created her unique signature work in New York City since 1975, and she has toured extensively to venues as expected as Lincoln Center and the Spoleto Festival and as unexpected as Grand Central Station, a mall in front of the Smithsonian in Washington, D.C. and the boardwalk at Coney Island. She is a recipient of a 1997 MacArthur Fellowship as well as two Bessie Awards and many grants. She has received honorary doctorates from SUNY as well as Rhode Island College. Her work has been seen on the *David Letterman Show*, *CBS Sunday Morning*, *CNN Showbiz Today*, Nickolodeon, NBC's *Weekend Today*, MTV, *ABC Nightly News with Peter Jennings* and *Larry King Live*.

Once called the Evel Knievel of dance, Streb grew up in Rochester, New York, attended Catholic schools, bought a motorcycle and participated in a variety of extreme sports. After receiving an undergraduate degree in modern dance from SUNY Brockport, she performed extensively with choreographers Molissa Fenley and Margaret Jenkins. She moved permanently to New York in 1975. In order to develop her own brand of what she calls "PopAction," she scavenged from the disciplines of athletics, circus, boxing, rodeo, daredevil stunts and dance. In 1979 she created her company STREB/Ringside. In 2003 Streb established S.L.A.M. (STREB Lab for Action Mechanics) in Brooklyn.

Streb seems to be on a constant search for new information about what a body can do. The work of her company is extremely demanding and necessitates endurance, dexterity, great physical strength and the ability to be daring. The dancers are trained by Streb to follow a movement's natural force to the edge of real danger. She plays with the limitations of the human body. In recent years she has begun to incorporate text, video and projections into her work. In order to understand the effects of movement on matter she studied math, physics and philosophy as a Dean's Special Scholar at New York University.

I think that the special appeal of Streb's work is that the audience vicariously experiences the risk and real daring that is happening unmediated before them. The audience receives a powerful physical charge from the activity that they are witnessing. The sensations arise from being direct witnesses. And the experience can affect their lives in very real, direct and physical ways.

March 28, 2005

AB: Elizabeth Streb is a phenomenon on feet. Her work defies the boundaries of what we think the human body and soul can accomplish. I accuse her of being a theater person more than a dance person, and she accused me of being more of a dance person than a theater person.

How did you get into doing what you're doing—not just logistically, but also why? I don't think anybody is an artist unless they're curious about something, so what is that realm for you?

ES: I think the first time you felt your consciousness pricked with something other. That's what I would point to. I was wandering around East Rochester in upstate New York when I was about ten. If you lived in Penfield, you weren't supposed to go in East Rochester because that's where all the bad people were. It only took fifteen minutes to walk there, so we would all trundle over there all the time. One day this whole gaggle of people walked into the diner. My whole world changed. If you think that you need a fuller experience than a couple of seconds in life to make a transformative change, I don't think so. I thought, Who the hell are they? And it was this culture shift, in my whole being. They were a theater group from New York and they were performing there. They were like beatniks. It was pre-hippie. I still think beatniks were the coolest. That was what started everything. I thought, That's the wild side. I'd never seen anything like that—you could dress that way, you could be in a state of mind, your life could be based on ideas, and not what your hairdo was going to be when you're seventeen, which was a big worry of mine at the time. It represented freedom to me—also the idea of motorcycles. My sister's boy-friends had motorcycles, and I thought that was the sound of freedom. I put those two things together: theater company and bikes.

I don't want to drop that notion of freedom—what that means in that moment when you're ten years old, and now.

There are certain things you have to be willing to embrace, and I think that's one—leaving home, leaving your turf. Those people represented to me that you're going to have to leave here, and never come back. For me that was true. I knew I had to get the hell out of dodge. I knew that was something that freedom represented—leaving everyone behind. Not having an identity that was attached to people who know you is a big thing to take on.

The other issue is danger. Movement was the thing I noticed most in the world, so I knew from early on that movement was going to be my stock and trade—and the danger would have to be a part of that. Those are metamorphoses that I knew would gather together in what I would make choices about.

I knew my job was cut out for me: leather clothes, not a good material to wear up there. Plus, I was dark. It was nothing but blonds as far as you could see, so I was different, if you can imagine the levels of difference. I got a part-time job, because I knew I was going to save money to get a motorcy-cle. I became a counter girl at Woolworth's in Rochester. My parents were very rough-tough, German stock. They said, "You can have anything you want, but you have to pay for it." I saved five hundred dollars. I got an ad out of the *Times Union*, and it was for a Honda 350. I took the money and the ad to my father. He just looked at it, bereft. And he let me buy it. That was the begin-ning of having my own mobility, and that was the biggest thing for a kid.

Were you doing sports then?

I did downhill skiing and baseball, basketball.

That explains everything!

Yeah, velocity and impact. I went to an all-girls school, so we had a serious team.

Was it a Catholic school?

In those days I think it was always Catholic if it was all-girls. I am gay. I'm queer. I don't think I knew it then. I didn't like the way if boys were in the class you never got any attention. I was really looking forward to going to an all-girls school where the nuns just paid attention to you. They had these very serious varsity sports teams where you could really get rough. I played a very rough game of basketball.

You were the kind of girl I was scared of.

You would have been scared of me. But I knew I wasn't as big as some of the girls we played in Rochester, so I would—what would be called cheating, but they could never catch me. The other team would get the ball, you see who's going to get the ball, so you waft around behind them, and you mold yourself one millimeter from their body, totally out of their peripheral vision, they have no idea you're there, then they turn and you pretend they hit you really, really hard and throw yourself across the court: "Foul! Foul!" And I, of course, practiced my foul shots constantly. So I would get hundreds of foul shots.

In a way what you do now doesn't involve fiction. But that seems like a huge amount of fiction.

But they really did hit me.

You got in their way—you came up as close as you could.

When I got there I wasn't in their way. They were in such a position that there was only one way they could go. I knew that, and I put myself in that spot. It was actually very complicated technically.

The seeds, I think, of a career.

But fiction is interesting. You say that in your work you tell true stories. But how would you define a true story?

I think you create reality by the way you describe it. For example, I ask you to tell us the story of your life, and it's not the way you experienced it: "I was twelve, then I went to high school." You lived in a series of existential moments, but you turn it into a story, and that story becomes a truth that other people measure themselves by. Everything you do in the theater, you choose the person you want to be and you decide what the story of your life is. One of the directing students at Columbia was saying James Joyce had to create a person who could write that way. You became the kind of person who could make this work, which deals with velocity, impact,

danger and freedom. But in your work it seems as though fiction is not something considered. You're interested in the real thing.

It boils down to what highlights you are choosing to remember about yourself, and not extenuate.

Or what's necessary to remember.

Sufficient and necessary. Just enough, and what part. I grew up with a sister, though we were not related by blood. Apparently she remembers everything verbatim that happened—really what happened. Our notes don't jibe with each other. I forget a lot of things, and I probably make up a few stories.

I think that impulse of making up stories is what draws people to the theater—telling stories in time and space. But I do want to pursue this story of your life.

I went to college and majored in modern dance, State University of New York in Rockport, between Rochester and Buffalo. It was the first dance class I took. It was 1968. I thought dance was a fairly arduous set of activities. I was constantly waiting to move. I thought in the next class they'd do something really fancy and really challenging.

So you were not challenged?

Well, obviously I was with stretching and the line and all those fancy moves. I was definitely challenged. I stuck with it into my forties, taking technique classes. But no, I wasn't very thrilled about the experience of doing those moves. I spent a lot of time thinking about what it means to be upright, and the ballet stance. I believe that anyone who had a straight back were people who didn't work—who didn't have to. I found that there were a lot of privileges of technique that took twenty years to gain—and those were the people who had twenty years to devote to an exercise and technique. I thought the demonstration of the form, therefore, was mean-spirited in a certain way. I have struggled with trying to glean a content out of right-side-up dancing, transferring weight from foot to foot. I did spend those four years doing that. Then I hopped on my motorcycle and headed west.

What techniques did you study?

Ballet for modern dance. In college, the Limón technique and the Humphrey-Weidman technique, and once I got out of college it was

Margaret Jenkins in San Francisco, which was Cunningham technique. I came to New York to study with Viola Farber, who was one of Cunningham's first dancers.

What happened in San Francisco?

I went to lots of gay bars. Learned about Folsom Street. I had my motorcycle. It was completely my identity at that time. San Francisco was a town I was in for the first time away from home. People said, "What's your name?" And I said "Elizabeth" for the first time. People called me other versions of it in the past. San Francisco was learning how to pay bills—or not. I lived in Haight-Ashbury. Janis Joplin had just passed away a few years before. I felt her spirit in the donut shop. I had a steep learning curve, being on my own.

You went to college, didn't you?

I went to four colleges, undergrad. When I was in high school I decided I wanted to be a director, and I directed *The Bald Soprano* as my first play. I'd grown up always being the assistant—doing *Oklahoma!* and *Charlie's Aunt* and *Brigadoon*. But then I swear to God, my French teacher, in 1957, decided to do *The Bald Soprano* in Middletown, Rhode Island. Before the opening she called me and said she was sick and I had to take over directing. All the right things happened. Jimmy Cammeto, was playing Mr. Smith. We had a crush on each other, so love was there, chasing each other around. To this day, sometimes I think the way I direct, the rhythm, the way a play moves, the sense of humor, is exactly the same as what I did when I was fifteen. I study so hard to grow, and yet . . .

I really wanted to be a director, so I applied to Vassar (where my mother had gone), to Sarah Lawrence (where I wanted to go more than life itself), to Bennington, Sweet Briar—you know, all those girl's schools. I wanted to go to a girl's school. I got turned down from all of them, I think because it was a lousy high school—and I think I had drugs on my record, too.

I was so devastated. So I went to a school where they would take you if you could pay the check to go. It was a terrible school, and I directed all the shows there that year—and decided I *really* wanted to be a director. So I applied to all the conservatories, the then forming CalArts, Carnegie Mellon, every serious school. They all turned me down. So I ended up going to four undergraduate schools. By sophomore year, I was in Athens, Greece, where I studied archaeology and Greek language and history.

I probably didn't know about applying to fancy colleges or a similar thing would have happened. I remember at an awards ceremony, one of the teachers at one of the fancy colleges which, had I known about them, I would have gone to, said, "All of my students . . ." and listed me. Maybe I looked like someone else she taught there. I was very flattered, but also a little bummed because I didn't get to go to that school.

My mother was so devastated that I was turned down from Vassar, because she went there and was so proud. Years later, before she died, I got a letter from Vassar asking if I would be interested in running their theater program. I phoned my mother. I've never heard her so happy. She said, "You have to call them! You have to call and tell them they turned you down!"

Did you do that?

No. I've said this before, but I think my whole career is based on revenge. It's a very useful energy. Either you're mad and it eats you alive and you drink and get sick and die, or, if you take the energy of revenge, it's very useful.

I take another approach to that. I think dance is different than theater.

Is it?

Theater is so respected. In text alone it has accreditations that dance doesn't have. With dance, a lot of time it's musical issues that attach themselves to the dance, and that becomes its legacy, rather than, "Did you see that eight moves in a row?" Who remembers fifteen moves in a row? Not even four moves in a row. It's never the thing where people attach to what just happened. It's more like a blur, and song. It's more phenomenological.

But in a way, you force that in your work. You force them to look at that chain of movement.

I try to, but it's still invisible, and there's very little I can do to quantify an invisible idea. The thing that happened before, and the thing that will happen just after—right in the middle there's a body that is enormously distracting a person's attention. That's one of the reasons we go fast and hard, so you don't have time to go, "Oh, she changed her hairdo." My job is mostly to give the audience the physical experience. We're actually going to start advertising the asymmetric exercise that you get automatically just by watching the show: You do not have to make one move at all, and you come out a healthier, stronger person after a day and a half. Why didn't I think of that years ago? If I can make enough unpredictable moments in a row—and what's nonpredictability is a very complicated thing. You're looking at somebody doing something, and everyone has an expectation about what the very next thing can be. We know about our physical world, and we exist in it, and we have bodies. You have to figure out what you can do that would be true to the world of movement rules but that no one would expect. That's my constant effort, to find out what that nonassumable next move might be.

Music is the same way, anything that moves through time. Your job is to set up expectations, then either fulfill them or break them. There's no other choice. It's amazing to have an expectation fulfilled really consciously, or to break the expectation or the truth of that.

If you fulfill expectations, in my world that would be entertainment. People like to go to things they expect and it makes them happy. If I do what they expect me to do, then I would be entertaining them a little bit. I think it's entertaining what we do—Streb PopAction—but I think we try to defy expectations, not fulfill them.

I heard there were plans of taking your company to Vegas, right?

I still have plans to do that.

The entertainment capital of the world.

I feel that's my destiny. Isn't that weird? I think it's because it's the land of the exceptionally odd and maybe banal in some ways—but also the eccentric, the extraordinary, both in terms of the persona of the people who live there and the shows that go on there. The eccentricity of the audience, which mostly doesn't pay attention. I think they really want to go and get hit in every direction with everything they didn't go there for—plus they want to gamble, they want to drink, maybe they want to see *the* most outrageous show in the world. I guess I also want to compete with the most outrageous show in the world. The market may not quite be ready, but I'd wait.

About fifteen years ago an article came out in *Time* about Las Vegas. Las Vegas had to be reinvented. The rest of America had caught up to it. All of America had become that extraordinary thing called Las Vegas, what with the malls and McMansions. The attempt to bring Cirque du Soleil and Blue Man Group and Streb and company—

I'm all for it—is, in a way, to jumpstart Las Vegas. Disney's trying to do that, too, hiring Annie Hamburger, En Garde Arts. It's interesting in terms of what an audience's expectations are, what that means in terms of performance.

Also in terms of fiction: the Bellagio, making Venice be Venice in Las Vegas, which is so American, all these weird, fictionalized, but unbelievably wild places that are not here.

I've talked to some people who've seen the *De La Guarda* show. They said it's like going to a rave, but you don't have to stay all night.

Do you think it's about being told a story versus having a new experience? My conceit is about action. You decide that you're theater; I've decided I'm action. You ask of your discipline what can it do best. My idea is it has to be extreme, it has to be dangerous, if people are going to sit and not move and not talk for a long time and just witness. I have to make them feel as if they are doing it and it becomes an experience for them. It's kind of like how Marshall McLuhan described the difference between your experience watching television and how active you have to be to associate all those dots together into a picture, versus film, which is completely resolved. And even though you're not physically aware of having to do more work with television than you do with film, your experience is completely different. So maybe film is theater and TV is dance.

No. I don't want to miss something you said: I do theater, you do action. At some point you had to say no to the word dance, correct?

Well, I try not to say no because—Rena [Shagan], my agent, would say I'm definitely in the dance world. No?

Rena: Somewhere between theater and circus and dance and spectacular and spectacle. I think you're not definable.

It depends on how people define dance. My reputation is, I think, in the dance world, so it's hard for me to say it's not dance. I like to say that modern dance—given sports, gymnastics—has a lot of work to do if they're the art of movement. They've got to get the heck off their feet. They've got to stop adhering their timing systems to another discipline. Oral issues, physical timing issues, are not the same. I have a lot of quibbles with the dance world. I think they're formally being extremely naive and not investigative or rigorous enough.

AB: Were you influenced by the Judson Church movement?

Definitely. I came to New York in '74. I remember seeing them at the Kitchen. I remember seeing Lucinda Childs and Yvonne Rainer. I went to the Grand Union. I got here a little after the Judson showed some of their work. I remember thinking, Wow, these are some of the most brilliant people I ever saw. You could tell that it was absolutely brimming with a very deep idea about either time, space or body. It was outlined clearly enough that you understand what their confines were. They were disciplined enough to put it on in live time, isolating a moment. You isolate— Okay, I'm only going to be in this spot in space, foot on the ground. Then you started to see how infinite the potential was of that spot in space. You started to develop the richness of your language. That's what Development Vocabulary was about. I think I was incredibly attracted to that genre. I was also pretty ignorant because I slept through my eight A.M. dance history class. So when I was doing a lot of my early wall and harness work, I got this hate letter from some anonymous person. It said I was ripping off Trisha Brown. I did this big piece on a wall called *Look Up*. Now I realize looking back that if I was going to pick one of the Judson people, it would be Trisha. Her early work was everything. I did a piece in '81 on a hill. Simone Forti did one in '61 called *Slant Board*, but I only know that because they reconstructed the Judson pieces at St. Mark's in the early eighties—and I found all new reasons why some of them maybe hate me. I wanted to go up and say, "I didn't know." But then I thought, That's worse. Then they'll hate me for two reasons separately.

But I felt that my niche in the dance world was interest in the expansion of vocabulary, not ignoring space, questioning grace, really. What is in action format versus sound, and hundreds of questions that I felt maybe weren't answered by the dance world, or maybe weren't asked. I think that if your concerns and interests lie in this formal set of ideas, then you mathematically go about seeing if they bring forth any fruit. That's been, and continues to be my process.

AB: At a certain point, though, you decided you needed to have your own company and your own situation, right?

I did solos for probably the first five years, then I brought one friend in, Michael Schwartz, for the hill piece. He passed away in '94 from AIDS, a great video artist, and just a beautiful dancer. That's the only person I worked with who I didn't pay. We did duets together for a few years. Then I brought on Diane Sitchell, Paula Gifford, Henry Beer. My thing was for one hour a day and pay them ten dollars an hour, and that's how I did it.

I was so terrified of telling people what to do. I'd work on it for hours, and then they'd come in and I'd go, "Do this, do this, do this, do this. Okay, good-bye. Here's your ten dollars." I did it for a long time, until I had too many people, so I did it for two hours, and I was spending hundreds and hundreds of dollars. I had to drop it to seven dollars an hour. This was the early eighties.

AB: Most people complain about not having the hours and hours and hours to fuck around. You're saying you'd do it in an hour.

Well, I did the fucking around for hours and hours. But I didn't want anyone there.

AB: I heard a rumor that you're a really good fundraiser. Is that true?

I really, really like to raise money. I feel that that's true of anybody who really loves what they do. I'm really good with foundations because I think it's their job to give me money, and they have to give it to someone, and they have this much to give each year and that's that. Individuals I'm less good with. I don't like to raise money from individuals that much. I've been successful with a few, and I only do it when I'm comfortable with them. A lot of them are professional philanthropists as well as individuals. That comes from, you get raised, and your mother says, "Don't ask strangers for money." If you're a good daughter and you learned well, you just never, ever do that. But otherwise I think I'm really, really good.

AB: That is rare, don't you think?

I don't think so. Do you?

AB: I'm coming around to the notion, but it's taken me a while to get there, to think of fundraising as part of the art—the idea that every time you describe what you're doing to ten people, the idea grows. If they react to it and you adjust it because you need to, it grows even bigger. That little act is part of the creative process. It doesn't come so easily as it does for you. I like your attitude. It's an attitude that you bring to your own work. You say, "This is worth something. You should pay attention to what I'm doing."

I started by having to make all the calls myself to the funders, and now there are some funders who I've been calling for twenty-five years. I have deep respect for them. A lot of times they don't have any money to give me. But I'm just chatting, telling them what I'm doing, asking them to come. I have now development directors who write the grants and strategize and educate me. I was in L.A. a couple of years ago, and someone was telling me that it's really unprofessional that I call the funders, that I shouldn't call funders. It's, "What's the matter, don't you have enough money to hire a development director?" I said it's not really like that. It's more just carrying on a relationship that's ongoing. I almost feel like I could become your fundraiser. Sometimes I think that would be a better model for the arts: Anne Bogart calls for Elizabeth Streb, I call for Anne Bogart. Because you know what? I'd ask for way more than you would probably.

AB: Matt Bregman, who's on our board, is a development person. He has an idea, which I think we should do, which is to get a consortium of companies and go to corporations—because corporations are too big to give money to one little company. Say, "You should buy into this whole consortium." And it's sexy for them to have this group of cutting edge artists.

What right now interests you artistically? What makes you the most curious?

I was thinking that in the first twenty years I asked a lot of Newtonian questions, which were hard enough to figure out. We have one hundred forty kids come through the S.L.A.M. Lab. We have a space in Williamsburg called Streb Lab for Action Mechanics. We teach kids action. I house three kinds of action—PopAction, that's what we do; Kids Action, well, if you've ever seen kids on the playground; and Circus Arts, where they just come in and do, and we just watch. Newton said you can't be in the same space at the same time. But Newton also says if you go fast enough you can pass through things. That's sort of a quantum idea. These two kids—I saw it coming, I watch them a lot—were running like bats out of hell across the room. I thought maybe it's my angle of view, but it really looks like they're running on the same path. If I were a nice person, I could have said, "Look out!" But I didn't. And sure enough, whammo. I was just like, okay, it's true. You cannot occupy the same space at the same time. Kids have less thought about the future than we do. We tried it at Streb for a long time, but we've been unsuccessful.

AB: Can you describe what you were trying in terms of occupying the same space at the same time?

Well, just pick something that you know can't happen physically. One of the things for me was you can't be in the same space at the same time.

I built this eight-foot square, and have eight people around it, going through the center spot in space and time. The crashes kept happening. The dancers are incredibly great in my company, but they do look askance at certain times: "How many more times do we have to crash before you understand that this is not going to happen?" So then I back off a little. We did this thing where we cheated time and space, just a millimeter, half a second. But you still had to go, having the experience of crashing, you still as a body had to go, and you were positive that you were going to crash. That became the psychological revamping. And then, lo and behold, man, they really did miss each other. It just didn't look like they were going to. Or somebody does a gymnastic flip, and there's enough space in there some of the time for someone else to dive through. If you go at the wrong time, you crack someone's head open.

AB: Danger.

The practical side is the willingness to spend an inordinate amount of time on just a few seconds of theatrical moment.

AB: That's the whole deal.

It's expensive.

AB: You can't do it in an hour for ten bucks.

So how does that work for you?

AB: I think what you're talking about is magic—or alchemy or transformation. It's a group of people committed to working on something in which something might occur, but none of us has any idea what it is or when it will happen. That hole that you're talking about is metaphorical, perhaps. It's not a literal hole you pass through, but that body has to go through that hole in rehearsal. It feels just as dangerous. That's the magic. There's no way people can meet, there's no way you can have this alchemical switch where you turn metal to gold, quality of human relationship, and yet you try. All you do is you place yourself over and over and over in proximity to one another, and then something does happen. If you're not present in the moment, then you miss it. So all of the work of training and thinking and research and table work and study all brings you to something that has nothing to do with any of those things, but has to do with co-presence. It's hard. It takes a lifetime of training. But to me it is about what you're describing.

So this place isn't a place that you recognize before it happens, then you recognize it. You don't map it.

AB: What we try to do in rehearsal is have a series of actions that require that organization of energy that would re-create the possibility of something you found in rehearsal, that is not repeated emotionally. What kills most American theater is we get an emotional moment and we repeat that. It's not about repeating the emotion you found in rehearsal. It's about repeating something, it might be the way the bodies are lined up, the task, or how you're breathing that's very physical that allows the emotions to be different every time but poignant in a different way.

That's interesting because we do this exercise where we show the audience this much of the body, fifteen degrees, thirty degrees, forty-five. It really matters—how much of your body are you going to show and when? As a subject it's as poignant. The eight positions of the body in ballet are really referring to a rectangular room, just because they happen to be in a rectangular room. Not a good enough reason. But just choosing what you're facing to the absolute degree could elicit meaning. When we take a horizontal plane, when your shoulder goes too far, you pile into the ground and rip your shoulder out. Or if your shoulder doesn't go too far, the person landing an inch next to you crashes into you. So the specificity of space does elicit emotional things. And I really believe that out of that comes all the rest of the stuff. It's not, I'm making a dance about love. I've been in love once, and I know about it.

AB: It's that old theory of Rousseau's, which is: Do you see the bear and feel fear and run because you feel fear? Or do you see the bear and run and feel fear because you're running?

Let's think about that for a while. Oh, I've thought about this so many hundreds of times. "Fear Factor" asks what would you do? Same for the grizzly bear. I was told that if you're ever in the woods and you run into a grizzly, face to face, you're supposed to stare at it and not move, because they can run faster, they can climb trees, there's no way you can get away. It will charge you, and it will stop a foot away from your face, but you can't lose eye contact. Just stand there. I'm thinking, Wow, would I do that? This ranger was telling us this story that the bear charged eleven times, and then the bear walked away.

But the wild animal thing, like eight seconds on a bucking bronco: Synoptically my next investigation, quantum questions, is creating a turbulent, uncontrollable event in the middle of the space—some structure that creates an insurmountable place to be. It's there one second and gone the next. We're doing a lot of rotational, angular momentum experiments. In a circle, you can create a huge amount of force, and it stays put because it's a circle. The question would be creating something that will, without hydraulics or a lot of gizmos, create a turbulent condition on stage. You go there and mount it and it explodes on some level in different ways, but it doesn't want you there. The job is to figure out how to survive as long as possible and do certain things. We have a truck strap, simple thing. It's attached to the two trusses about this high, really tight. So I ask the dancers to just run, pretend you're running across the stage, and just step over that. You have to really hike up because it's really high. It really will do eighty million different things besides just step up on it. It'll splat you down, it'll turn—just like on the back of a bull, it will do different things every time.

AB: I want to ask a little bit about the company and the space. At a certain point you got concrete. Supporting a company and a structure, an administrative structure, there's a cost to that, a personal cost.

There is.

AB: But you decided to do it. Are you happy that you did it? Is this the right thing?

For me it is. I've done it for twenty years, and it's totally the right thing for me. There are moments sometimes of feeling like you're an employment agency, and there's a lot of time figuring out the insurance or worker's comp or rent, and it's a very intense amount of money that goes out. But I can't have a pickup company. There's no way. We're working now at S.L.A.M. at creating a more feasible economic, sustainable structure—making it so that we have a lot of other income streams. One of them is just about to bud. I spent a couple of years building it, but it's a flying trapeze. We just have to get the insurance. That's a little complicated. Nobody wants to insure a flying trapeze.

AB: Is your insurance situation and worker's comp out the wazoo? They come and look and see what you're doing and they say—What? What can you imagine?

"Doesn't look like a dance company to me . . . ." They saw us on a television show a couple of years ago and our status switched from modern dance faster than—they first called and said, "Congratulations. You were on *The Today Show*. You're circus artists." We have a lot of liability. In this new space my landlord demanded that I have a huge amount of liability, five million dollars. I had to get a life insurance policy. It's New York, right? The landlord says, "If you die, I want fifty thousand dollars to empty this place out." "Could I give the other fifty thousand to my girlfriend?" There's a lot of crazy things you have to do. But I'm extremely inspired by the adventure of having a company that does action. This is a field where we're all cottage industries, and we all join arms and walk into the wind. I can't imagine asking for a better life than that.

AB: You don't seem to be moving away from the danger at all. You seem to be moving more deeply into it. Do you find yourself getting more physically rigorous with your company than you were before, or are you backing off with sympathy and empathy for aging of bodies?

I think I'm getting much more intense with what I'm asking them to do, and a lot of it, unfortunately, is because I don't know what it feels like. There's good news and bad news in that. I'm trying to make this little piece. A little magnet will come down, there's a square metal thing at the very bottom. So you watch this magnet descend. I was thinking of using Mozart or something. And the magnet comes down, and it clicks to this thing. I had climbed up way high to put these little screws, way high where my dancers fall from the truss at S.L.A.M. I was like, "Hmm, I wonder why my legs are shaking." It's very intense. I'm fifty-five now, so I was forty-eight when I stopped. I had planned to stop when I felt that my performance was becoming about how old I was and how great that was. I immediately stopped. Also I didn't want to spend four hours a day working out anymore. It was really way too time-consuming. Fighting gravity beyond—I mean, there's just so much.

In answer to your question, I think the work's gotten more intricate, more difficult, more up in the air, harder. Not as hard—my version of my work from '80 to '95 was all about impact and ground work mostly. I got my first trampoline in 1995. I wasn't really a flyer; I was a ground animal. It was grizzlier because of the impact in a certain way. But this is scarier and much more high-pitched in terms of danger because you're upside down and you're hurling through the air. The ante is upped for them. But isn't that good? A director is not about being a practitioner.

AB: It never has for me. I'm a terrible actor. I've always been amazed at people who can do things I can't do.

I was laughing because a lot of times my dancers will do different things, and a lot of times we're putting more rigorous play into my rehearsal process. A lot of the invention in my early years came from just recklessly flopping around in there with an idea. They do that now more. I hear them go, "Don't do that! She'll make you do it again!" That's really great. There's a new piece called *Roof*, and we have a thirty-foot-high ceiling, and one of my dancers wants to jump off the roof onto the street. I mean, onto a mat, of course. But it's way higher than we've gone unassisted. But since they mentioned it, I walk into my space every day, "Yeah. Hmm." Just even looking up gives me the heebie-jeebies. That might be going too far.

AB: They're pushing you now? The dancers?

Oh, completely.

Audience: What propels you toward danger? Has that been something that has been with you your entire life?

In movement terms, if it's not that, then it's comfort zone. It has to be dangerous, usually, to get out of your comfort zone. Danger is a good colloquial way to describe this idea—but it's mostly unfamiliar territory that because it's in movement terms ends up being dangerous at first, until you figure out how to move that fast or have reactions. A lot of our stuff is about having reactions that happen snappily enough to get the head out of the way.

Audience: Does that translate to other parts of your life?

When I'm crossing the street, and I'm jaywalking, I really like to come as close to the car as I can without the car's wheel going over my toe. This is not very good, but, I want them to think I'm going to walk in front of the car. I kind of play like that. I also want to feel the force. I see a car coming, I sense what its velocity is, and I want see if I cannot change mine. I can but come really, really close, so close that that car thinks it's hitting me, but there's no thud. That's the pedestrian practice of how I work.

AB: This has got to be DNA.

I guess it's just in my nature—just always curious. Motorcycle is driving along, you're going fifty, and you think it's on the ground. I wonder how fast you'd have to go for the wheels to lift off the ground. Those questions just come into my mind, and I guess I don't know exactly why. I'm not mean to people usually, so it doesn't transfer into my emotional life.

Audience: When I'm watching movement or dance, as opposed to theater, often I start to physically feel it. Often in theater it's head/heart. In movement, it's heart/ physical; it has less to do with my head and my heart connecting, which makes a lot of sense when you talk about that thing of getting close to a car, that moment.

To become something besides flesh and blood. To become that action track. To see if you could blend yourself with it a little bit. I'm curious about things like, could an elephant stand on me? Or could it stand on four bodies, one paw for each body? An elephant trainer told me, yes, but the hardest thing would be to train them to step on a human, because they learn their whole lives not to do that. Someone was telling me Penn and Teller have a semi drive on them, but they use plywood. How much weight could you hold? Questions like that. I'd like to know what it's like to get shot. I would just like to know that, because I don't know. That would increase my physical range, because I think people's ability to do whatever has to do with what they've gone through.

I really believe it's a class thing—the poorer you are, the more physical difficulty you've had. If you have a little bit of privilege, you can keep all the bodies away. If you have a little less than that privilege, you have scars all over you.

Audience: Michael Ventura is writing about how safe we try to keep our children. He was talking about growing up in the Bronx, and he has a great phrase, which is: "Danger makes for grace." Part of the danger and part of the grace in both of your work is that you demand from the audience a kind of precision that you give to the work. For me the exhilaration of theater is the precision that is hidden from me but is in the work clearly, and that makes me understand that meaning is at the base of something.

AB: I think there is a price or a cost for precision, so if something is exceedingly rigorous, whether it's sunken or visible, then the actor is actually paying a certain price for the exactitude, so you're actually watching someone at emotional and physical cost, and that communicates somehow.

I'm thinking of war. I remember in Vietnam, people would go back, sign up for more tours of duty. They'd go back and I used to be plagued by it. How could they go back? We were in Virginia, and I'm thinking, Who's going to understand the narrative of extreme action work? Do you have any responsibility for who's going to end up in the audience? A maintenance guy was watching the dance I used to do in the box, and he said one of the most flattering things anybody's ever said about the work: "The last time I saw movement like that, someone yelled, 'grenade.'" I thought,

Okay. How wide is your physical spectrum, experientially? And who recognizes it? I know when we go into certain places nobody has any trouble with what we're doing. They face it every single day.

Audience: Where do you find your dancers? They are like superheroes. How do you keep them?

When we hire new people, we have auditions, but also we do classes and we know people all around the world who are movers. They find us. But the audition process is pretty grueling and weeds out people who are—

Audience: Afraid.

No. We are afraid, believe me, every single day. Your fear shifts around, and we learn to respect fear. I can usually tell, once I know a dancer, when they're scared, and I intervene. We don't tell people to leave in the auditions, so it's a completely populist, friendly, getting to know you. It's all self-selected exiting. By the third day, if you walk in the room, we have a lot of respect for you, and you obviously want to be there. How long they stay ranges—I insist they stay two years. If they come in the room, they're willing and ready to do it. They're really action-engineers. They're method-inventors. It really takes a certain headset to be curious. I don't tell them how to do the moves. I just inscribe the moves and they have to figure out how. We're jumping from thirty feet. We're doing this one dance now, which is like diving, but it's falling. And I want them to not just tip and fall, but do a bunch of moves, and then you have to land. You have to be in the right position so that when you land from that height—you have to land on your back probably. Even your stomach is too vulnerable at that point. It takes a certain anima to do that. I have so much regard for them.

Audience: Have you been able to perform for the troops?

I've never been invited to do that. It would be a great enterprise. The closest we've ever gotten was Wolftrap, celebrating an anniversary of flight, and a lot of the people were veterans of the war, pilots, the Tuskegee Airmen, and I even used one of the anthems, "Off We Go, into the Wild Blue Yonder," to end the trampoline dance. One of the comments was, apropos to your question, "Wow, that was outrageous, that's worse than basic training times five." They really related to the physicality of it.

Audience: Where does your circus arts thing come from? What made you interested in that?

It was the only show I went to when I was young. My parents took me to the circus. It's just an affinity. I love the gypsies. I love the wandering people. I just have so much respect for their lifestyle. They do these death-defying moves. I try not to incorporate literal circus acts into my show because we couldn't compete. They spend their whole lives on one move. We're generalists on that level. We occupy lots of spaces but in a more generalist sort of way. However, we did something for Cirque du Soleil in July. They invited us to help celebrate their twentieth anniversary. I realized, Wow, they never hit, ever. Hitting is anathema to the circus. It means death to them. I realized a lot of distinctions between us because of that. We're pretty heavy-duty in terms of content. Let's say they have sentences, but we have long paragraphs, in terms of choreography. The audience didn't seem to mind.

Audience: In your work with movement are you finding that there's something that defines American movement as opposed to movement in other cultures?

Well, I think we invented modern dance. I get into a lot of arguments with Europeans about that, but I really do take them on. I think the great thing about the United States is that there's jazz, there's tap, there's modern dance, there's hip-hop, rock and roll. We are phenomenal. In answer to your question, Europe doesn't love us. I've had some of the most rugged reviews in Europe, England, France. Asia seems to like us a lot. But I think I am quintessentially American. Take ballet, which was invented in France in the sixteenth century. I call it European folk dancing. I think all dancers believe in flight. Their idea, with ballet, I'll make the short distinction, is some shoes that are hard on the end, going up three whole inches. As a result the base of their support got way smaller. Their balance had to be better. They're still dealing with vertical places in space. They're still dealing with a base of support that's still at the bottom of where you are—not a whole lot of organizing in my world, to go onto your toes. The whole notion of the baroque idea of manipulating your limbs and calling that movement—I'll admit it's meta-movement, but it's not movement. I feel that the angles of the body, the skeleton is made to increase the angles from which you can explode your entire body, many-factor force, and hurl. They don't figure anything out. They just do what they can do. I have so little respect, and as the years go on, so much less respect, for forms of movement that are so decorative as ballet.

Audience: In Europe today we have something called New Circus, and New Circus has a consistently large audience. And what we see is a rather a degraded form of several steps. They're trying to combine narrative with some form of gymnastics. It strikes me as odd that there should be so little receptivity of your work in view of the enormous influence that you've had. It's really a question about influence. You're the original—or maybe Trisha Brown. You're passing something along. Why is it that there's an audience for this degraded form and not for you?

I think timing is interesting now. If we're full-on frontal, then it's a little less than that. It might be more palatable to an audience that needs to work its way up to something more full-on frontal. But osmosis, movement is an oral form. It passes itself on by what's happening in the air. Someone saw someone who saw someone. People used to say that Madonna did this video and she copied my box dance. Good. We are in fact like water. That's the beauty of movement. I went to the circus yesterday. There's all these ladies lying down, and I saw the elephant coming toward the ladies, and I thought, Oh my piece! They must have heard me say it once. Stole my idea. But what the elephant did, is step one foot at a time. It was really nerve-racking. That was almost more dramatic than my idea, I thought. I don't know if it's possible to track influence when it's not text-based.

AB: I'm convinced that *A Chorus Line* is only possible because of Joe Chaikin's work with the Open Theater, that kind of performance, and it's always to me revolutions in small rooms. In these small rooms in weird cities spread the virus everywhere. So the question is where you line up in that virus chain.

It's just like John Cage is responsible—and you have to admit it's true—for MTV. Whoever would have been able to handle nonsequitur moments on mass television if it weren't for John Cage?

Elizabeth LeCompte

Over the past several decades Elizabeth LeCompte and her posse have made consistently groundbreaking and adventurous creations based upon outlandish ideas, cult films and classic plays, all smashed together, in dialogue, in disagreement, always a dizzying and exhilarating journey. A sampling of the fare: *L.S.D. (. . . Just the High Points . . .)*, *North Atlantic*, *Route 1 & 9*, *Frank Dell's The Temptation of St. Antony*, *Brace Up!*, *The Emperor Jones*, *Hamlet*, *The Hairy Ape*, *House/Lights*, *To You the Birdie!*, *Poor Theater*, *Hamlet* and the opera *La Didone*.

I remember Elizabeth LeCompte in the role of the prostitute Yvette in Richard Schechner's production of Brecht's *Mother Courage and Her Children* with the Performance Group, the precursor of the Wooster Group. I am embarrassed to reveal how many times I returned to see *Mother Courage and Her Children*, but suffice it to say that I was usually waved past the box office, probably dismissed as an overzealous fan of the Performance Group. What a radical vision of the play, what fun, what a deep sense of physicality, theatricality and reality all at once. Then all of a sudden Elizabeth was making her own creations with co–Performance Group member Spalding Gray. She constructed a quartet of plays entitled *Three Places in Rhode Island* that began by dissecting the tragedies and ironies of the Gray family history and moved on to interweave personal histories from other members of the company. Idiosyncratic, personal, poetic and profound, I had never seen anything quite like these little plays. And this was just the start. This early work was the beginning of the Wooster

Group, and in 1980 they took over the space once inhabited by the Performance Group.

Elizabeth grew up in New Jersey, graduated from Skidmore College, moved to New York City where she worked as an extra in B-movies, sold postcards both at the Metropolitan Museum of Art and the Guggenheim, modeled for art classes and worked as a welfare caseworker. She also founded and ran a bookstore with friends in upstate New York. Since then she has received a MacArthur Fellowship, numerous Obie Awards, an NEA Distinguished Artists Fellowship for Lifetime Achievement in American Theater, a USA Rockefeller Foundation Fellowship and France's arts award, the Chevalier des Arts et Lettres.

The Wooster Group has thrived in New York City as well as arts centers and festivals nationally and around the world, producing plays, opera, dances, radio, film and video. The members are fiercely loyal. The use of technology in design will probably change the face of what theater is, and can do, forever. Young artists who have interned with the company have gone on to form countless new companies inspired by the Wooster Group.

Elizabeth still attends every performance so that she can overhear audiences' responses and constantly work and rework the event. I admire that.

April 25, 2005

AB: One of the things that distinguishes you from others is the permission you give yourself and your company to do what you do—to create something very unlike what you see in most theater. Where does that permission come from?

EL: It comes from a lot of places. First of all, it comes from having a space that's mine, that's ours, our very own. So when I start work, there's not anything that's saying to me that you have to do this for somebody else. If it doesn't work, then I don't owe anybody anything. For many years, we never took money up front for a new project. We would make the project and then, if people liked it, they would book it. No one came to us and said, "Oh, we'll give you money to do . . ." Now, looking back, I think that was a good thing. There was no reason not to play, not to do whatever you wanted to do. It's different now because sometimes people do say, "Oh, if you'll do this, we'll give you some money." But I think it's a habit that you learn when you're young to just follow whatever and not to put another voice out there except your own or another artist's.

That's something that is becoming truer and truer in the way I understand it—which is that if you don't do that when you're young, you don't do it when you're older. You think, Once I get to this place, I'll actually do the thing I want to do. You actually never get there.

The other thing is that I didn't study theater, and I didn't plan to go into theater, so I think I come at the practice from a very different place. I'm interested in ideas, and then I've got the space and these people. I try to work out ideas that are not necessarily ideas that should be worked out in the theater—in fact, plenty of people will tell you that they shouldn't be. But in a collision of my vision of what I want to do and what I have at hand—performers, technical artists, a space and an idea—I have to reorganize my thoughts around that. A lot of times I start out thinking, Oh, it's not even going to be a theater piece. I'm going to make a video. Or, We're just fooling around. I don't even ever say when we begin that it's going to be a theater piece. I think that helps, too, coming from that.

Can we talk about performative influences? You studied visual arts in college. What is it that altered your DNA to look at the world in the way you do?

Television was huge. I grew up watching television. I saw theater on television. I saw painting on television. I saw cartoons on television. I saw everything. That's all I had, was television. My family had the first television set in our neighborhood, and that was in 1949 or 1950. So I think that was huge. Also, music. I liked sound. Maybe that comes from television. I don't know.

You did take the bus from New Jersey to New York to see Broadway shows.

Yes, but that's later. In those days New York was—I guess it still is—a big draw for young people. So I skipped a lot of school and just went to New York. In those days, films just weren't that important. The "Arts and Leisure" section of the *New York Times* was called "Theater." Theater was the happening art form. Film was for fun. TV was for more fun. I think I went to see theater because I was trying to jump class. I was trying to be a serious person in a nonserious world.

Jump class not like school—you wanted to jump class?

I wanted to see the ballet and whatnot. I was from a middle-class family, and I wanted to be an artist. Why I wanted to be an artist, I don't know. That's a good question.

I'm really envious because I was brought up with no TV. When I was in high school my family finally got a television, and I was only allowed to watch *Perry Mason* and the news.

Perry Mason's good.

And then I got through college and finally got a TV set in New York in the East Village and I was cram-coursing. Now I'm understanding why my work looks really different from yours.

Television was very different then, too. In the fifties there was a lot of live TV. That was exciting in a way that theater was exciting because you knew that people were making mistakes all the time. You knew it was rough, watching Ernie Kovacs. That was forming for me. That was playing around with the medium. People were discovering television the way I'm discovering theater still. I'm still going, "Oh God. People have to enter and exit. How can I do that? What's a new way to do that?" And with television, that's what Ernie Kovacs and people like that were doing. They were trying to figure out ways to turn the camera. If they wanted something to slip off the table, they'd turn the camera sideways, and we'd all laugh. They were doing stupid kids' stuff. Kukla, Fran and Ollie were stupid puppets. If you watch them now, it's really boring stuff. They didn't understand what television was compared to live performance. There were all kinds of odd timing things. It was a rough medium. I think I enjoyed watching them figure it out. Watching the McCarthy hearings on television was amazing—because they didn't edit then. It was better than C-Span. The camera was just fixed there all the time. It didn't do anything else. That was a huge influence on me—watching those hearings every day with my mother ironing, staying home from school.

How did you get to painting and visual arts?

I read a book called *Benjamin West and His Cat Grimalkin*. It was a children's book. He was a painter, Benjamin West, a really good American painter. I don't remember the cat. But I do remember that he made all his colors himself out of earth. It just seemed like a really good way to do something. So I started saying, "Okay. I'm going to be a painter." But then it was downhill from there. I took one of those painting courses in Morristown, New Jersey, for the local PTA—you know, women painters, and they had this one guy and all of them were having an affair with him. We'd go to the school late at night, and there'd be fifty-year-old women—they were probably only twenty, but I thought they were fifty—and a couple of gay men who were there painting still lifes. At the time they were trying to model it after Cubism. I would have to try to make these still lifes look like Cubist art. I wasn't good at it. This teacher would come over, and he didn't know what to say. First of all, he didn't know how to talk to a child. So then I forgot about that for a while. I started taking a mechanical drawing class in high school. I loved it. But then I had to apply for school.

Elizabeth and I were just talking. We were both turned down from everywhere we applied.

Well, I did get in—I think I got on a waiting list at Goucher [College]. But it had no painting department at all. I don't know what I was doing. To get into school, I sent in mechanical drawings. And then at one they wanted a painting of something. And I didn't have a painting. I hadn't drawn in years. But I had this album of Harry Belafonte that had this watercolor picture of him on it. I loved Harry Belafonte. So, I copied.

It's all coming together.

I copied the picture of Harry Belafonte. I mean, I did some embellishments on it. But I got in—so, of course, that was the successful way from then on.

When I first moved to New York in 1974, I saw *Mother Courage and Her Children* at the Performing Garage, directed by Richard Schechner, something like twenty-five times. And you played Yvette. How did you get from visual arts to Yvette in *Mother Courage*?

Well, I couldn't make a living painting, needless to say. So I taught myself photography, and Richard hired me as his assistant director and as his photographer for the company. I began helping him out, taking notes, watching performances. He would go away a lot and I would fill in. I found it very congenial. I really liked telling them what to do. I enjoyed making the stage pictures—three-dimensions. I'd done a lot of architectural drawing, so I already had that feel for space. I think I got into performing because Richard used anybody who was there and it was cheaper to have me do three jobs.

You were good. There was something called *The Marilyn Project*. Because Richard had too many actors in it he decided to do it simultaneously twice. There were two casts, all playing the same roles, doing the same moves. You played one of the Marilyns and Joan MacIntosh played the other. It was supposedly Marilyn Monroe's last day of work on a film before she died, so she was really out of it, drugged up and stuff. You were unbelievable in that. You had to do all the same moves as Joan MacIntosh.

It was a mirror image. It started out as a naturalistic play, but Richard couldn't make it work. I have that fabulous story—I got a bad review from Lee Strasberg. I didn't really want to be a performer, so it wasn't a huge deal.

The Actors Studio showed up. Lee Strasberg. Elia Kazan was there.

I didn't really know who they were.

Robert Penn Warren was there.

No. Come on.

They were all there.

I knew Richard was sweating. I knew it was Actors Studio. I'd heard of the Actors Studio. And I'd heard of Lee Strasberg. But I didn't know. I just knew that Richard was really nervous about it. And afterward they all stayed around. What I remember is that they turned to Lee, who had all his acolytes around him, and Richard said, "Could you speak about it?" And Lee started to talk about the side that was Joan's side. Joan's this wonderful performer who could really act. And he started to talk about Joan's back, how it had gotten mottled with emotion at the high emotional moments, and I'd been working on something else on the other side, and it wasn't about mottling my back. And then he turned, and all the gazes, I just remember, all the men looked over on my side, and I'm sitting there. And he said, "And over here I felt nothing." I either had to take that as a call to arms and go on and make work about nothing—as Seinfeld did so successfully. Or I had to kill myself. You know which one I did.

Rumstick Road was the first thing you did?

No, I did _Sakonnet Point_ first.

Was that the first time you'd directed?

Yes. But I have to say, I'd been technically directing because Richard was away so much. I'd done a lot of work with performers. I just hadn't been able to design the sets.

Can you talk about that process of _Sakonnet Point_—how you put the elements together?

I didn't. Spalding [Gray] did. Spalding really kind of teased me into it. I wanted to get back to painting. I wasn't committed to this theater life. We were both interested in dance. We were going to see Robert Wilson down the street. We were seeing a lot of different dance. He just said, "I want to dance." So we picked some friends and they would just improvise on the floor and I would sit above and say what I liked, what worked, and then edit: "Keep that, do this." But there were no words. It was very musical.

There were no words in *Sakonnet Point*?

No. There was music. There were no words. There were some people talking in the tent, but it wasn't to be heard. We enjoyed that, liked it. From there, when he got really sick, when he had the nervous breakdown, he started recording his father and his family, and we just brought a bunch of people in and listened to the tapes for hours. People just started moving around it. People took roles the same way we do now, in a weird way. We just started playing around with the tapes. I started simultaneously thinking about it, a visual structure. Then we started taping it out on the floor. Again, the nice thing about how we work is that it was really sort of about getting Spalding better at the time. So there wasn't this great thing about we had to make something that worked. I mean, I wanted to, because I like to make things that work. But I didn't have any ambition beyond making something beautiful that would sustain Spalding.

How exactly did the Performing Garage transfer to you from Richard?

Well, Spalding and I both weren't interested in acting—for two very different reasons. Spalding just wanted to talk about himself. Always. Even in the early days. He's the only one in [the Performance Group's] *Commune* that didn't take another name. He kept his own name. He didn't join in the action. He did do a couple of roles, but he was never really very happy doing that. He kind of led me into it saying, "Let's do something else." I was perfectly happy assistant directing, taking pictures. I wasn't ambitious at all. It gradually became a company. We didn't make it a company. We just started making pieces in the crevices of the Performance Group. And so if Joan had an accident so we couldn't perform for a month, then we worked during that month. We worked at night. We worked around the major company. People in [the Wooster Group] now do the same thing. They work at night. We give them the Garage.

Marianne Weems did that, and John Collins.

It wasn't so great for Richard, but it's good for me because I'm a different personality. I like knowing these people are working around in the cracks. It's just very comforting to me that it's not dependent on me, that there are other people there. But for Richard I think it was hard. I say this standard thing whenever I'm asked about this time: "Richard just dissolved the company and we went on." And that's true in a way. But I think Richard lost interest. I think that the losing interest started around the end of *Commune*. *Commune* wasn't successful. He started to feel he had to make these big plays. And I think that bored him. I think he's more interested in ideas. I think he was better when there was a different perspective.

Was there a point where he just said, "I don't want it anymore. You take it over."?

Yes. What we would do is share the money. By that time Ron was doing so many weird things with the books.

Ron Vawter, who came in as a bookkeeper, and then became one of the greatest actors ever.

Yes. He was even then. He was just very quiet about it. But we'd share. Richard would be doing a show and some of the performers, some of us, would be in that show. And then we'd be working on our own show. And then when his show was finished, ours would go up. We would share the space. Then we got a second space, which was next door, and then we got overextended in many ways. It was almost impossible to keep two companies. We had a couple of failures, big box-office failures, with Richard. It was too expensive to keep up the second space, but Richard wanted to be able to keep it up—it was great, a lot of people performing with us. It was a good time. But we were way overextended—another thing that we don't do anymore. That was deadly. Then we ended up owing two hundred thousand dollars, and nobody had paid taxes through the years, and Richard just said, "I can't. I want to leave for a while. I want to stop." So he left us the Garage.

Did he say to you personally, "You take it over."?

Yes. I think it was a meeting. We were all sitting around in our usual circle. I remember he said, "You take it." And we were nervous about it because we had a two-hundred-thousand-dollar debt and no taxes had been paid. We didn't know how to do that. I remember talking to Mabou Mines and them telling us, "Don't do it. You can go to the Public. The Public will pay for you. Look at us." But we were addicted to having our own schedule and not having anyone else tell us what to do. So we decided to do it. We dropped the Performance Group name and kept the Wooster Group name and applied to the NEA under the Wooster Group and wrote in our proposals, didn't mention Richard, and got grants. The grants kept coming, and we took them. We all worked part-time in order to pay off the debt. And that took us about four years. Then the New York State Council on the Arts dropped us after *Route 1 & 9* and then we had to work side jobs another four years. It was a hard time financially.

Was there a managing director? Who did that work?

A bunch of people. Jeff Jones [the playwright] came in. What happened was that people just came around. We didn't ever choose a company. In *Rumstick Road*, Spalding said, "I want to work with Libby Howes." And I said, "I want to work with Ron Vawter." So, we had those two. Then there was a technical guy, Bruce Porter who was having an affair with Joan at the time, so he wanted to get out of the Performance Group. He was our sound guy and technical guy. Jim Clayburgh, who I had a good relationship with, kind of came in and out. He stayed in both companies. He was the only one who stayed in both companies. So it just happened that that's who we were. We taught a class in the late seventies at NYU while we were making *Rumstick Road*. Kate Valk joined us. She came in and said, "I can sew," because she was working at night as a seamstress in sweatshops. She basically washed, scrubbed the floors, did everything that we do, but even more so. Then when Libby had a nervous breakdown—there were a lot of nervous breakdowns in the company—she had to take over Libby's roles. She went right into the company that way. Peyton Smith, who was with us for many years, and who is still a member of the company, came to see *Nayatt School* and she spoke to me and said she wanted to work with us. So, we said, "Yeah. Come on along." I never said, "I'm going to make a company." I just kept thinking, Oh, I'll make this piece, and then I'll quit. And that did go on for quite a long time.

There's two things—besides imitation, which we'll get to—that seem remarkable to me. One, thinking that it might not be a theater piece. It might be something else. And secondly, thinking, I'll quit after this—how that changes the way you work in the room. They probably don't feel unusual when you live with them.

No, that doesn't seem unusual, but probably because I thought I was going to be a painter, and you can quit painting any time. It's different when you have a bunch of people. Another thing that this has come out of is that the people who stay with us aren't people who need to say, "I have this role. This is going to make my career, and I'm going to go on to something else."

It's people who come in with the overall view that they get on board for something else besides, "I want this part." Sometimes after we've worked on the nugget of an idea, and I have a core of people who are making that idea, then we say, "Oh, we need someone to play this role," and then someone will come in specifically for that. But when I start a project, I like to start it with people who, if they don't end up on the stage, it's okay with them. On one side sits: I want to see them doing something fantastic and see them happy. And then on the other side is: I don't need to. Both are there, present. If it was only: I don't need to, I wouldn't make any work. I would have long ago retired.

There's a story that I'm sure is not true, but I find it so entertaining that I'm going to tell it. It's something that you did—maybe you never did. Was it working on *The Crucible* that everybody took acid—except for Peyton, who drank instead?

Yes. Peyton was afraid of acid.

You videotaped a reading of *The Crucible*, and the way I like to hear this is that then the rest of the rehearsal process was to re-create what happened that day or night, and that was the play.

That was a section. It was a play that had four sections, and that was one section. It was the high point of *The Crucible*, the court scene. I had a whole bunch of people from the neighborhood. Everybody was in it because it's got a big cast. And it was boring, watching them trying to do it. My usual way is to try to entertain myself—which is really important— I think I have to be entertained all the time.

It's television!

People get so angry because I don't have this idea that if you work on it, it's going to get better. It's got to be good the moment they do it or else I just can't stay with it—but I have a wide latitude of what's good, because I like to watch people fumbling around, too. So this was just where I thought, Well, if I loosen them up with something . . . So, they had memorized the parts—they knew the parts. Or they thought they did. It wasn't a reading. They had memorized the parts. So, they took the acid and then they tried to do it. And they so didn't do it . . . they were looping. In the beginning they were pretty clear, and then it started to deteriorate. And for some reason I videotaped it—which was odd.

That wasn't the idea in the beginning?

No. I just wanted to see if they would be better on acid. And they were. But once I saw the videotape and saw them just looping and looping and trying to find their way through—you know, all those things about watching someone else who's on acid. I did the taping, so I saw it all through the camera, and I didn't realize we were going to be reproducing it. I was having a contact high.

Were you taking acid?

No. Not while I was working. But I had a contact high watching them in the camera, you know, these old cameras, all very black and white. It was wonderful. I would scan across, so I would never get the whole table. So when I decided, "Oh, we should try to reproduce this," we put a timing thing on it—which is all the stuff I'm doing now, just more technological. It was all right there. Then they had to learn what they'd done on acid and watch themselves by quarter seconds. They had to time it exactly with everybody else. It was incredible work, sitting in front of this television, writing up how they did it. I was trying to find this way: The first part was them doing it as a play, performing it, like actors. The second part was this change—what happened to the play, same play. What I discovered happened when they learned it off the tape is some people really loved doing that—finding that gesture that most actors wouldn't even call a gesture. Most actors would just call it a mistake. Other people couldn't do it, so they would generalize when they got to the performance, and they would start to make it too much like the first part. I would have to constantly say, "You have to go back and look at the tape again and see that you went like this here."

Although what you're doing is extremely unusual, on another level it's not. A director's job in a way is to remove nuance. You keep removing it until the actor has brought much more, but not so much on the outside.

I was coming around to the backdoor to find what most people do more directly. I still enjoy coming around the backdoor.

While we're on *The Crucible*, you had a huge obstacle thrown at you when Arthur Miller said you can't use his words.

What was more of an obstacle was: You can't do this piece. He said, "You can't do *L.S.D.*" We'd already named it. At that point we hadn't even done the acid trip. He'd just seen a twenty-minute re-creation. So, I changed the name to *Just the High Points*. We didn't advertise. So we got away with it.

But there is the issue of the words.

Yes. We had this wonderful and incredible and greatly influential person working with us, Michael Kirby. I said, "We'll do it in gibberish"—because I wanted to keep the meter. Everything was scored around the meter of the words. I didn't care what they meant, by this time, I just wanted to hear them. Well, I cared what they meant, but not that way. So we bought all the Samuel French versions and marked the section and put them on the back of the chairs and asked everyone in the audience to read along as we gibberished. But, of course, then they found out about that and said, "No. You can't do that." Michael said, "I can just take all the words from the transcripts of the trials." So he got the transcripts of the trials, and all I asked him to do was make sure what he wrote was in exactly the same meter. It had to scan exactly so I didn't have to change any gestural language. I didn't want to have to reblock it. That was important. So, he went back to the transcripts, and a lot of Arthur Miller's words are directly from the transcript. He went to the original Salem Witch Trials, then he went to the House Un-American Activities Committee and mixed the two. Sometimes it didn't scan or I did have something I wanted to get across. We would be able to say seven or eight words. What is it? Before you're illegal? So we would be able to get that in, if we needed the line or it was something I liked. And at that point, somebody would buzz out and then we'd have to go back to the other script. So we could get Miller in when we needed him just enough to keep the story going. We had a lot of lawyers advising us. Some said seven words. Some said seven sentences. Some said seven minutes. We just tried to stay just under the line of something that would make it an Arthur Miller play. We heard later we could have gotten the rights under parody, the way we did it.

I do want to pursue this notion of beginning. It occurs to me that we should either talk about *Poor Theater* or *Hamlet*, since you're just beginning *Hamlet*.

I'll talk about *Poor Theater* because *Hamlet*'s so new. This is going to be all one piece, eventually—two pieces next to each other, *Poor Theater* and *Hamlet*. Poor *Hamlet*? It's a really intuitive process for me. I do remember having a hard time around *To You, the Birdie*. A lot of times it's a conversation with my last piece—what didn't go into it, what got me angry. *L.S.D.* was in reaction to *Route 1 & 9* because I thought, Oh, this big white male had written a black woman's part, let's see how they take this. Then it takes me someplace else. So, people said *To You, the Birdie* was cold, that it was hard to warm up to it. I would feel that in the audience. I would feel their respect for it. For me, it was so emotional. It was weird. I thought, Oh, wow. I've just gone to a place that is not where my audience is. They admire this piece, but they don't love it. And, you know, you go into theater because you want them to love it. You really do. I would have long ago left it—but I want to be loved. So, I thought, What's wrong? I think I'm just not a theater person, and I have to leave the theater. So, that made me go back to thinking about what I first loved in theater, that piece I saw. Richard Schechner had brought Grotowski to New York, and I was lucky enough to get a ticket to see *The Constant Prince*. I saw that and I also saw *Akropolis*. Something in me just thought, well, maybe for my final piece I should just do a videotape.

As your final piece for your career?

I thought, I'll show them. They want to see cold? I'll show them cold. So, I had this idea that there'd be two visual images, something to do with Grotowski on one and something to do with the sky on the other. We applied for a grant to discover—we made up language—what happened to Polish theater. But the truth was that I think I just wanted to hear that piece in the Garage done by live actors as a kind of homage, you know, just as a way of saying, "Here's my connection." People loved that piece. I thought maybe I could find in me what was in that—if I just rubbed up against it, I would find my bearings again. And either go out with that, saying, "I can't do this. That's the end," or it would give me a new way, another avenue to go. There's a tape of an *Akropolis* rehearsal, a 16-millimeter film that was made of it. We watched that a lot, and I tried to put in the in-ear receivers. I would tell them, "Get up and do it. Make the piece for me here." And of course it was just horrendous.

So at a certain point, you said to each actor, "You're playing Ryszard Cieslak."

No. I just said, "Do it," and they decided. Things seem to flow down to whatever they did. We began reading things on Grotowski. When I have nothing to do and I don't know what I'm doing, a lot of times I'll watch TV. So we watched every piece of television we could find on Grotowski. In fact, we made a faux documentary that kind of follows the documentary of early Grotowski.

Produced by Margaret Croyden, right?

We interviewed Margaret Croyden. I knew her because Richard Schechner was wooing her to review *Commune* back in 1970, and we had a residency in New Paltz at the time. On our days off we'd all go up to High Falls and we'd all take our clothes off and swim in this beautiful place—just hippies, everyone with no clothes on. And Richard decided to bring Margaret Croyden with him and be interviewed by her sitting on that high rock—him naked, and her fully dressed. And if you know Margaret Croyden—hairdo, makeup, everything there. So I remembered her when she called us and said, "I know a lot about Grotowski." She, of course, was very upset with the piece, that we put her in it. But I took her out. I learned. She's not in it anymore. I only needed that as a transition—because she asked the question: "Why would you do something like this? What is the point?" And I didn't know the point when she asked that. It was about making work. It was about whether or not I was going to continue working. So I felt like I had to have that question there. She asks it in such a fabulous way. "Why would you want to do that?" And it's true. Why would you want to copy that piece? I didn't know why. And so I needed that question, not from me. I needed it from somebody else. I didn't need it once I realized why. Once I found Max Ernst I realized why. I put a section on Max Ernst in.

At the end of *Akropolis*, all of the actors crawl into this tiny little hole in the ground and then they shut the door.

Yes. Grotowski used the metaphor. The writer, Wyspianski, was actually just talking about All Saints' Day or All Saints' Eve, when all the spirits of the past come back from the dead. They reenact scenes, in this case, from some Greek history, from some European history, and there are these tapestries in Poland and a story about how these tapestries come alive on All Saints' Eve. Grotowski took that and put it in a concentration camp. And we took his concentration camp and put it in William Forsythe's dance. We just relocated the way he relocated. So, at the end, they go down into what for Grotowski was an oven. For us, I don't know what it is. It's a hole. But a hole has a lot of meanings.

How did William Forsythe find its way in?

At the same time as I was thinking about how I was going to leave theater, I heard that all of Billy Forsythe's funding had been withdrawn, and I realized that it was the end of a certain time. It was the end of postmodernism, in a way. And I'm a child of postmodernism.

The end of postmodernism is marked by what?

By people not coming to see his work. People were going to see more narrative stuff and more individual people telling their stories. Spalding was a huge influence on that. I felt like I work like Forsythe, in a way. I identify with him. So I thought, Oh, wow. Times are changing a lot. I wanted to chronicle that in some way.

So you invited him to come into the Garage?

Well, I just said to the actors, "Dance like William Forsythe—at least you can try to dance like William Forsythe." And they did. You should see the tapes. Horrifying. They didn't have the form, but the timing was there. So I thought, Well, this is a place to start. But then we ended up just wanting to know more about him, so we asked him to come, and he did a workshop with us, then we went to see stuff, we got every tape we could. We worked with four or five of his dancers. Each one would come in with a different idea of what Billy Forsythe was about, and we'd take that in. But at the same time, we'd always go back to the televisions, improvising off them. The biggest thing was that you're not Billy Forsythe. You're just copying— or not even copying.

This is a really difficult thing because the way we work off the television sounds like copying, but it's not quite like that. Television can be a way to channel energy. It takes you outside yourself. We don't see you making up what you're going to tell us. Film does it all the time because they can take a cut where the actor didn't realize he was on—or if the actor is particularly good at fooling himself or herself into one time, one take. But the big, beautiful thing about the theater is that you can see the actor controlling the situation. It's what Grotowski talked about. You see the actor controlling the situation, knowing what he's going to tell you, and then telling you. And that's both its beauty and its limitation, because we now know the real thing. What are we watching now all the time? We're watching people really live all the time. Nobody even wants to watch the soaps anymore. They're watching people really perform live on all the reality shows. That's been a huge change for theater. It's decimating it, in a way. I wanted to find the same thing I love about television and film to some degree. I wanted to find the way to get that experience out of a performer where you lessen that gap between when they get the impulse to say or do something and when they do it. And if you take it off of something that's out there, then you're channeling it. You don't make the same kind of decisions.

It's a technique. We use all kinds of things with it. If you're watching the television, if the camera moves this way, you have a choice. You can move your head that way. You can move your arm that way. You can move that way. So it doesn't take away the creativity of the performer. It actually enhances it because they make up their own blocking. Or if they see a person who scrunches their head, they can do that literally. Or if the person disappears off the screen, they can follow that to the next TV that has another image on it and pick that up and continue. There was a lot of channeling, of course, in *House/Lights*. We used it in a different way in *To You, the Birdie*, where we took a lot of Martha Graham's and Merce Cunningham's pieces. They're randomly supplied, so each night in *To You, the Birdie* they had a certain score. They had to get from one side of the stage to the other. But they could take off of and make the psychology using these impulses from these other dance works.

So there's something live happening at every moment that is unrehearsed.

Yes. Now, mind you, performers are interested in routine. Some people would take that and find that same place every night. But the trick was that you can't think about it. I think everybody does this—any good acting training. Again, it's coming around the backdoor—to try not to think of what you did in the past and what you're going to do in the future, to be able to give over to that moment. It's the most incredible thing in the world and very difficult to do. So, even with the television, if there's a certain image that comes up, they have to not plan when they're going to see it. They have to do the same thing every actor has to do with the words. They have to do that with the images. It's the same technique.

I'm always drawn to see the work your company does. There's something attractive in that approach to acting—in the sense of a magnet.

Audience: Isn't it the element of suspense? Just the total unpredictability, like reality TV or an animal moving on stage.

Yes. It's like an animal on stage.

AB: Although you always sense that there's something very organized there. There's an organizing principle that's very, very compelling.

Audience: If I'm going to do a piece and I feel I may need a reminder about doing only what I'm going to do and not what other people are going to do, then I'll always go to see a Wooster Group show, because it's a touchstone for integrity in the form.

In every other show I've seen where people use microphones, the body is relaxed and the microphone is exactly where it should be, right in front of the mouth. And I was watching a Wooster Group show where they would be speaking into the microphone, but they would be contorted in these weird positions where they would physically be working really, really hard with an object that's actually supposed to make it easy to speak. There's an intensity there.

Audience: When you look at the performers, there's a kind of oscillation that happens. Somebody can be making fun of something and paying homage to it at the same time. It can be cold and hot at the same time. It can be very removed and very emotional at the same time. Is that sort of a byproduct of this process?

It's probably more my personality.

Audience: It looks like they're having fun. They're not trying to work.

That's interesting, though, because this woman just said it looks like such hard work. Both things exist at the same time. I used to say that I like you to laugh and cry both at the same time. To me that's the greatest theater, if you can laugh and cry at the same time.

Audience: What I experienced in *Poor Theater* was a virtuosity that I get very rarely in the theater, but I do get in dance, depending on the choreographer, when the dancers are asked to do things that I can't do. I think from the copying I get this sense of virtuosity that you get from a great athlete or pianist.

We started performing it when they couldn't speak really good Polish. Because it was about the attempt. It was about how you make work, how we live our lives in the same way. So it's not about whether they're good at Polish or not. They'd like to get good because they enjoy doing that. But the truth is they're not that good at Polish. If Polish people came, they'd say, "Ooh. Ari could be a Polish Czech. But the rest of them are just not so good." People are coming and saying, "Oh, you're such good dancers." And then the Billy Forsythe company would come and say, "Oh. That was just horrible. But the Polish was really good." Billy says it the best. He says, "We don't go to the theater to see what's done right. We go for some kind of transcendence." And it's hard to come by.

AB: Why do you have audiences so soon in your rehearsal process?

I'm always dealing with these things about hot and cold, and sad and happy, crying and not crying. There's a balance in that when you're dealing with those two very different impulses. You need an audience to let you know how far you've gone with one or the other. It's a balancing effect. If I just went on my own, I would be lost. It could be that I'd made the whole thing and then everyone laughed instead of laughing and crying. And that would be wrong. I'd have to go back in and figure out where I went wrong.

AB: You listen? Or you just feel the audience?

Oh, yeah. I can tell.

AB: That must be painful sometimes.

But I obviously have a compulsion to do it. Believe me, it's not fun all the time. But in *Poor Theater* it was really a joy, because we can't lose. If we're really bad, that's what the piece is about. I made it failsafe in that way. So, that was a pleasure to do. The way I got around it in *To You, the Birdie* was I finally had to go on the in-ears myself and speak in a microphone to the performers so I could be part of them because it was so painful being outside of that piece.

AB: That's like a director's dream, being on in-ear: "Don't do that!"

But it's a funny thing—that's when I know I've got something else going on. I can be pretty down to earth in a rehearsal, "Oh, that's boring. That's horrible." But when the performers were coming out on the stage, I found myself going, "Oh, you look great. You're looking like a million bucks." Why? I don't know. I'd say that every night. Then I'd go on to say, "No. Stop!" I wanted to tell them how great they looked. And they would look up at me and smile, but it was to the audience. It was wonderful. I needed that connection. Of course, I used that as an organizing principle as well. Because there was so much chaos in the beginning, and they were working from so many different tapes. The only organizing principle I had was to say, "Turn left" or "turn right."

Audience: The sound in *To You, the Birdie* was so incredible. The whole thing was like an opera. I'm assuming that the sound starts from day one.

Something like *To You, the Birdie* is a little more complex because we did two outside things that we don't normally do. Suzzy [Roche] and Koosil-ja and Katie [Valk] wrote music, then Katie took Paul Schmidt's text and made songs. So they worked outside on the songs and I integrated them in. And we worked with David Linton, who made loops of material, then he brought them in. So during the process of working we would just experiment with different things. I have this great team of technical people who like to do that kind of thing—build it in the same way as the performers build the performance. So many of our pieces are the combination of the sound that comes off the videotape that we're using mixed with peripheral sounds that we found, or taping things that actually happen in the room and then putting them onto the soundtrack. John Cage was a huge, huge influence.

AB: You keep a healthy balance of low-tech with high-tech.

We don't have enough money for it.

AB: But it actually seems really wise—like if you just went high digital, I think something would be lost.

Well, I wouldn't be doing theater. With high digital I'd be making something else. I mean, the thing about theater is you have a performance every night, and it's all about mistakes. The great thing about technology is that there are mistakes all the time. The performers are always dead on. The technology has mistakes, so there's always this room for accidents that the performers have to deal with. And you know, if you're a performer, how fabulous that is to deal with. If you're comfortable and know who you are on stage, to deal with a mistake is this fantastic opening.

Audience: I read somewhere you said, "Theater is entrances and exits." Can you talk about that?

Oh, that was one of those cute things that I said. I think I was just trying to say that the thing about theater is the expectation of coming onto the stage. That's what's exciting. If you go to see a film, you know what's going to happen. When you go to the theater, when somebody comes on stage, it's big, it's in real time. Whereas with a cut, you don't have that. That's something that's so unique to the theater. That, and the curtain goes up and the curtain comes down—even if there isn't a curtain. There's a certain beginning and a certain end in the theater. If you have a film, you know it's going to go on again, and the tape is a loop and it could go any time.

Audience: You're both sort of unusual in that you both have these companies that have survived and grown and stayed together over quite a long period of time, at least by American standards. How does a company continue?

We've probably dealt with this really differently. For me, it's about the space—that everyone comes to the space every day to work. In America it's so much about personality. There aren't institutions that are built for great directors to come in and out—great young directors—like in Europe. Somebody has a successful piece in Europe that is twenty-five years old, that person could be running the Schaubühne in two years. That doesn't happen here. There isn't that access. For us, the space itself gives a certain kind of bottom line. So, we can have all kinds of things go on, we can have fights, it can be awful, but finally everybody comes back to that space. They don't only come back to me. They don't only come back to the work, so to speak. They come back to the space, with the possibility that there's something there that they can make. Then it happens naturally. I think that's one of the reasons for the longevity of this company and a really important one.

AB: It's different, I think, not having a space. Ours is shorter, fourteen years. We've lost two people in fourteen years, which is remarkable. One, Jefferson Mays, I refuse to accept that he's left, but he's got this career. With KJ Sanchez, it was a horrible fight. And she came back last year and did another show with us. We call it dating. We're dating again. It's ownership, I think. In other words, it's not my effort to keep the company going. It's the fact that everybody involved in it feels terribly personal about their relationship to it. It's not a space, but it's a thing or an idea or an agreement. It's alchemical, I would say—kismet and timing and the right personalities, who are willing to make certain sacrifices. But also, early on I said—although I couldn't always follow through on it—that you get paid. A lot of theaters in New York say two hundred and fifty dollars a week is enough to live on. Equity will say okay about that. And we said, although we can't always do it, actually you need at least eight hundred dollars a week. So I think the actors in the company really feel that that is a commitment to them, even if it isn't always successful.

We always had that too. We committed very early to have insurance, which is incredible. We can't pay as much as you pay, but we do try to pay. We pay a full-time salary, but basically it averages twenty-eight thousand dollars a year.

AB: You pay more regularly. We pay per show.

Oh, that's it. We pay the whole year. And that's incredibly difficult to do.

AB: You're not Equity? You don't deal with that.

No.

AB: We deal with union issues. The union just told us we needed to do EPAs—Equity Principle Auditions. I wrote a letter to Equity saying this is ridiculous. People come into the company through the training program. We do long-term workshops. The response was that I was being snooty.

Oh, we've been through that. When we performed uptown in different theaters, we had monstrous fights, where we had to hire and pay people to sit—wardrobe people when we didn't have a wardrobe. Thousands and thousands of dollars to sit there all night. But it's one of those things where that system just doesn't work, doesn't mesh up. But that's why we stayed downtown.

A big portion of our money that we take in is box office. So that means a lot of performing. You ask why we do performances before we're ready. That's another reason. We get money in. It is good in the sense that it does force you to do a lot of performances. Everyone thinks of us as this company, "Oh, they only do one piece a year." We perform so much. That's really great for performers. That's another reason, I think, why people stay around, is because where else can you have that kind of performing? Where else can you perform so many roles? The old repertory theater is kind of gone. Companies like ours, you get to do something you wouldn't normally.

I also work around everybody who wants to do any commercial work. If they get a job, I make the piece around that in some way. I mean, there's a certain amount of—if Kate went out and got a job, I don't know if I could go on. But it has never been a deep artistic problem. Sometimes it's annoying because the scheduling is really difficult and you might be working on a scene and that person's not going to be there, but that always sends you into a place, and you find another way around that. It's just a problem. And a problem's a chance for new solutions.

Audience: You mentioned the love from the audience. Do you have an expectation for the audience going in?

Yes. But it's not articulate-able. It doesn't mean, at the end, that I want the audience to clap or whatever. I have a sense when I'm with the audience that I want to rivet them, that I want them to be interested, that I want them to listen. Or, if I don't want them to listen, I want to be in control of that. If they're bored, I want that to be because I've decided that they're supposed to be bored at this time. So I have an expectation, but I can only sense that when I'm with them, whether it's working. You know when people sit back and they're not there. And if they're not there, I have to go back and say, "Do I want that?" And if I do, why? And what does that mean in terms of this section of the piece? Do I need them to leave that there even though the audience is bored? I have to make all kinds of decisions that way, which are really important why I'm making the work. A reality check.

Audience: I'd like to hear you speak a little bit more about the role of emotion in postmodern theater.

Well, I can't speak about it in postmodern theater, but I suppose I could in my work. I think that I relate to two things happening at once. Paradox. I think that I'm an incredibly sentimental and emotional person. My natural balance for that is to check it with form—some kind of form to hold it. Because if I didn't hold it, it would just be gush. I spend a lot of time making a form to hold this incredible amount of junky emotion. And sometimes it seeps through and seeps out, and when it does I'm like, "Oh, is that too much of it? Is this too much?" And sometimes I feel like I've hidden too much. I love the two things in balance—form and content. If it's too formal, I feel bored and lost. If it's too emotional, I feel too exposed. So those things always work together. But I think that's a modern thing. I'm working on *Hamlet* now. He's always in at least two places at the same time, too.

AB: But you're also dealing with Richard Burton playing Hamlet in 1964 on Broadway, which is what's so fascinating.

Yes. There's another example of someone who's a totally emotional performer. And John Gielgud [who directed it] is totally into the meter and the sound of the words. The two things together are fantastic. Why they worked together, I don't know—why Richard Burton said, "I need you, John."

AB: Right now, the company is working on copying Richard Burton's *Hamlet*.

We haven't quite gotten to the copying stage yet. We have this record of it, like we had for *Akropolis*. That, again, was a changing point in the theater, just as *Akropolis* was. After *Akropolis* the people who were interested in that incredible gripping thing about theater ended up in a cult in California and left theater altogether or killed themselves or died of drugs. After this production, nobody did a play, especially *Hamlet*, without a movie star in it. This was the first play that they recorded with seventeen cameras, and they called it Electronovision. It was going to open in movie theaters across the United States, and somehow that was going to save theater. It was going to be "epoch-making," as Richard Burton says in the trailer promo. So, in two ways these things are crucibles or something. In the sixties, there were a lot of changes in the way we—the way I—saw theater. So these two pieces will be about that, among other things. That's the form outside. The emotional part is always about loss.

Meredith Monk

Meredith Monk exerts more influence on all of us than we are conscious of and more than she probably would admit to. Robert Wilson would not be who he is if he had not seen the early work of Meredith. Bruce Nauman, Björk, John Zorn and others are marked. Me, too. Meredith's work transcends definitions because it crosses so many disciplinary boundaries. She is a composer, a playwright, a choreographer, a filmmaker, a singer and a dancer. She pioneered the use of multimedia in her work. She continues to experiment with new technologies.

In the mid-seventies I saw a seminal work of Meredith's entitled *Quarry*. I returned to the La MaMa Annex almost every night to be wrapped again in that vision, in that extraordinary and rarified atmosphere. The production combined intense intimacy with a wide political and historical canvas. What this play/opera/dance did for me, is it granted me permission. And permission is the most precious commodity for an artist. Emboldened by Meredith's example, I went on to produce and direct big dance-theater works and stopped worrying about how to define what it was supposed to be.

Meredith graduated from Sarah Lawrence in 1964. A few years later she founded The House, dedicated to an interdisciplinary approach to performance. In 1978 she formed Meredith Monk & Vocal Ensemble. She continues to this day to tour extensively with her music and dance-theater work. A sample of her performance pieces include *Vessel, Education of the Girlchild, Recent Ruins, Specimen Days, Turtle Dreams, The Games, Facing North, ATLAS* and *impermanence*. She has performed several times at

Carnegie Hall, BAM and Lincoln Center and international venues everywhere. She has been commissioned by the Kronos Quartet and Michael Tilson Thomas and the New World Symphony, she collaborates with the visual artist Ann Hamilton, and she has performed for the Dalai Lama. Her music can be heard in films by Jean Luc Godard and the Coen Brothers. Her albums include *Dolmen Music, Turtle Dreams, Book of Days, Facing North, ATLAS, Volcano Songs* and *mercy*. She has also made film and television: *Ellis Island, Book of Days* and *Quarry*.

Meredith's work is informed by a deep connection to the bardic traditions of the world. Inspired by cultures where performance is considered to be a spiritual discipline with healing and transformative power, she manages to reestablish the unity that underlies music, theater and dance. Her forms are definitely contemporary but her themes are redolent with the authority of myth and legend.

Meredith has received numerous awards including a MacArthur Fellowship, two Guggenheim fellowships, a Brandeis Creative Arts Award, three Obies (including one for Sustained Achievement), two Villager Awards, two Bessie Awards for Sustained Creative Achievement, the 1986 National Music Theatre Award, the 1992 Dance Magazine Award, and a 2005 ASCAP Concert Music Award. In 2006 she was inducted into the American Academy of Arts and Sciences and named a United States Artists Fellow. She holds an honorary Doctor of Arts degree from Bard College, the University of the Arts, The Juilliard School, the San Francisco Art Institute and the Boston Conservatory.

May 16, 2005

AB: Meredith Monk had a huge influence on me. I moved to New York in the seventies and I think the first work that truly blew my mind—was it 1976?—was *Quarry*, which was this immense work in the Annex at La MaMa. It is uncategorizable, because it's not theater, it's not dance, it's not music. Maybe it's opera, I don't know. Funding is difficult with Meredith because people never know where to put her. Where does she belong? I'd love to start by talking about what made you who you are.

MM: My mother.

So we'll start with your mother, who's ninety-four and lives in Southern California. Maybe it does start with your mother, but what was your training? How did you get into that container that you created?

I said my mother because I'm actually a fourth-generation singer. My great-grandfather was a cantor in Russia. My grandfather was a Russian bass baritone. He came to the United States in the late 1800s. He didn't do the Ellis Island route, but traveled second-class, which was unusual for a Russian Jew at that time. He opened a conservatory up in Washington Heights and also concertized all over New York, Brooklyn Academy, Carnegie Hall, with a contralto, which was an unusual combination. You don't see that anymore. My mother was a commercial singer. She sang the original Muriel Cigar commercial, DUZ Does Everything, Blue Bonnet Margarine . . . So my whole childhood was spent in NBC and CBS control rooms during soap operas.

So you grew up in New York?

In Queens. My childhood was a lot like *Radio Days* because every single day at one o'clock she would sing the DUZ Soap commercial live with an organist. I was usually in the control booth with a script. I'd draw pictures on it, trying to be quiet, watching those actors with the microphones. Music was a very early language for me. I was sung to a lot and there was a lot of music in the house. The way that I comforted myself was singing. Apparently I sang melodies before I spoke, and I could read music before I read words, so music was like a primal and primary kind of language for me.

I have an eye challenge where I can't fuse two images. I see one image at a time out of each eye. I was right-left uncoordinated. My mother heard about Dalcroze Eurhythmics, and every Saturday we would go from Queens into Manhattan to Steinway Hall where I would take my Dalcroze lessons. Eurhythmics was developed by a Swiss composer, Emile Jacques-Dalcroze in the late nineteenth century, as a way to teach children music through the body. I remember catching balls and balloons in time. We learned solfege, which is the do-re-mi-fa-sol-la-ti-do system, but it was also always in relation to the body. I think I remember musical staffs and seeing the notes on a blackboard. I knew music already and I was very rhythmically gifted as a child—but my body didn't know some basic skills. I didn't know how to skip or anything. I was learning my body through music; the other kids were learning music through the body. That early background of having a kind of kinesthetic idea of perception, and then also no separation between music and the body really influenced my life.

What age was that?

I was three to seven. I never realized how important that Dalcroze training was until I made my piece *ATLAS* in 1990 for Houston Grand Opera. It was like a real opera in an opera house with an orchestra and everything. I auditioned hundreds of people to get eighteen because I wanted them to be good actors. They had to be open to do different things with their voices, and they had to be at least game physically and have a generous spirit. I needed people that weren't afraid to improvise sometimes. Improvisation was also a part of Dalcroze training. I never realized how engrained that Dalcroze was until I tried to teach my rhythmic kinds of phrases that can be quite complicated. In Western European, classical tradition, the rhythmic articulation is not as complex. That's not what that tradition is really about; it's much more about line and sustained breath. The classically trained singers couldn't hear what I was doing if I would go off into a long cycle of rhythm and then come back around. Or they'd go, "Well, how did you find beat one?" And I'd go, "I don't know. I just feel it. I feel that I can come back there." And they said, "It's that Dalcroze thing." Then I realized, "Wow, that's probably what it is." I never thought of how important that was to me.

Did you also have a background in visual arts?

I think that, because of my strange eye situation, I compensated. When I was at Sarah Lawrence I designed and combined a performing arts program. I was in the voice department, the dance department and the theater department. In my senior year I realized all I hadn't done, because at Sarah Lawrence you can only take three courses and you study them in depth. You can invent the wildest projects with your teachers, but I realized I never had visual arts in the time I was at Sarah Lawrence. This is sort of the kind of person I was at that age. I was so intense. I just went in and took all these art books out of the library and I gave myself a course on the history of art. Then, when I came to New York, my earliest performances and my earliest interest was going to galleries. I performed in a lot of galleries at the beginning.

Would you consider yourself part of the Judson Church movement?

No. Well, it was going on when I was in school, and I was definitely aware of what they were doing. The spirit of it felt very harmonious with what I was exploring. I was making pieces already in school that combined different modes of perception. This idea of combining forms was something that I needed to do probably because of my fragmented sense of self. It was more like a kind of psychic necessity of identity or something like that. When I came to New York, which was in 1964, the Judson Dance Theatre had disintegrated as an entity, but Judson Church was still available for performances. I did a few performances over the years there, but I was never part of that group. In a way, I was in a dialectic relationship with that group.

Can you describe that dialectic?

Well, first of all, let me tell you what I felt close to. There was a wonderful community of people that were coming from all different arts. They were the downtown world, you could say. There were painters and sculptors, and they were doing theater pieces and they were doing wonderful dance pieces, and there were dancers that were writing plays, and there were playwrights that were writing music, and there were poets that were making sculpture. It was an exploration of the "anything is possible" kind of spirit, which I still try to maintain to this day. It had a sense of expansion. What we're working with now is a world that's very compressed. I still feel that this sense of expansion is what we as artists have to give to this poor world. I felt very close to that aspect of it, the exploration of, who says that dance is this, and who says that music is this, and who says that a play is this, and who says that a poem is this? To me that's very exciting.

But the dialectic was that I always was very interested in theatricality, and I was very interested in magic. In a way, the beauty of what the Judson Dance Theatre did was that they were very iconoclastic because they were reacting to choreographers like Martha Graham and this kind of precious, expressionist and very rarified idea of art in the fifties. They broke through. "Yes, I can just walk across the stage and that's a dance." That was very, very—

Anti-theater and anti-magic.

Anti-theatricality and anti-illusion and anti-magic—that kind of honesty. What you see is what you get. If you saw Yvonne Rainer's work, *The Mind Is a Muscle*, it has its own magic because it's going into the most truthful idea of the body and the most truthful idea of art with everything stripped away except what's necessary. To me that has a different kind of magic but it didn't include a lot of the aspects that I was interested in. You could say my work was mythic in terms of making contemporary myths, and more mystical. I hate to say that word, but it was. It was much more ephemeral, more dealing with not necessarily what was actually there but what wasn't there.

That notion of the compulsion, in a sense, to put disparate parts of yourself together— I don't want to let that go.

I think I always knew that I was going to be performing somehow. When I was fourteen I sensed—and this is just very intuitive—that I wanted to make things myself, my way. I don't exactly think about it as compulsion. There was an internal necessity to weave things together, to find these forms that were woven together. Also early on—I don't know if it was in school or after I left school—I realized that there was a very spiritual and social aspect to this. One can say that the Western European tradition is the only one that separates these forms, actually. I was very aware that by putting together these forms it was also a way of affirming the human possibilities of all our perceptions. That was also a kind of counter impulse to the society that *does* want to continue fragmenting. There was a social aspect to it—a healing aspect, holistic.

Could you describe the piece that you did at Sarah Lawrence?

I did a piece called *Arm's Length*. I think it had five garbage pails in it. There were crinolines. There was movement, and then there were little bits of text and little bits of voice, of singing. There was a main character, and then there was a group of about five or six people that were in counter pattern. I was very interested in the relationship between the performers and objects. After I finished school the first piece I presented in New York was called *Break*. It was also a kind of break with what I'd learned—both in music and in dance. There were these certain compositional principles— like you bring things back. You use a little bit of material, theme and variations, then you bring things back. So I decided, "I want to do absolutely the opposite." So I did *Break*.

Great idea! Take all the rules you learned and break them in one piece.

Do the opposite. Also my parents had been in a car accident, so I think that was in my mind, that moment of impact. This is in retrospect. I was thinking much more about form when I made the piece. I was extremely interested in cinema, which I still am, and I was thinking about how would you make a solo piece where you have constant sharp cuts as if it were a film. The solo figure can shift instantaneously from one energy or emotion or character into another. In those days I was quite fast. My movement was very sharp and very fast. In the Washington Square Galleries where I first presented *Break,* there was a white wall, and I was dressed completely in black. There would be times when I would literally disappear; at one point I stood behind the audience and so there was an empty space. Then I ran in and flung myself against the wall so it was like something splattered against the wall. The soundtrack was—I had made these collages of car crash sounds. At that time there were no multi-track tape recorders so I worked with two tape recorders and built up tracks. There was a little bit of text. *Break* had a very Beckett-like quality to it; a very Buster Keaton kind of deadpan, seemingly nonemotional but actually heightening emotion. I was trying for the space between laughter and tears.

The Beckett thing—where did that come from?

I hadn't read Beckett by that time, and I knew Buster Keaton when I was a kid, but I think it was this idea of dealing with emotion in a new way. A lot of people were thinking in those terms. I was very interested in phenomenology. It was more like, how do you actually take the emotion away but somehow by doing that get more emotion? That was a real style. A lot of my early work was like that.

That's also in the generation of Judson Church, getting rid of nuance.

I think *Break* was pretty nuanced, but it just was not expressing emotion directly. It was implying emotion by flattening it out, which actually created more emotion.

Was your vocal work in conjunction with the theater work, or was there a separate track?

I was in the voice department, and I was earning my way through Sarah Lawrence partially by singing with my guitar and doing folk songs for children's birthday parties, which sometimes turned into glorified babysitting. I came from a folk tradition. Then I was doing lieder at Sarah Lawrence.

So you were classically trained?

I was classically trained. I was in the Opera Workshop but I knew I would never do that. I was trying to keep the singing going as much as I could. My first season in New York I did a lot of stuff. I did my own work, I performed in some of the last "happenings." That was 1964–1965.

How was that? You look now at the New York community and it's very different.

When I was working on *Break*, I met a friend of mine, Kenneth King, who's a wonderful dancer, choreographer and writer. You know how you just bump into people, and we liked each other and so we shared that first concert and then that created an audience. Toward the end of the year I did a concert at Judson, and that situation already had a built-in audience. People saw me perform. I think one of the hardest things was saying no. People wanted me as a performer, but I knew that I had to concentrate on my own work.

What did you think when you thought, My own work? Vocal pieces?

Vocal, physical and image pieces. I remember some of the happenings, which were much more improvisational kind of pieces. They were not all free-for-alls, although some of them were. Painters and sculptors were really trying to think about how to put their work into a time-art structure. To be totally honest, a lot of the time-art aspect of them wasn't necessarily the strongest part. So there were pieces where the images were incredible. I mean, you would have to wait like half an hour for the next image to come, but usually if the work was good it was worth the wait. I sang in those a lot. [Allan] Kaprow was still doing work outdoors. A lot of people, like [Robert] Rauschenberg, Jim Dine, Ken Jacobs, [Claes] Oldenburg, did pieces. Unfortunately, I never saw Kaprow's work, but I certainly knew about it.

The visual artists were smashing up.

Dick Higgins was a person that I also worked with, and he founded the Something Else Press, which published all kinds of happenings' scores. He had studied with John Cage and was a member of Fluxus. That generation was very kind to me. I think they saw that my work was very different than what they did, but they were very welcoming. There was a piece called *Celestials* that Dick did in a boxing arena out in Queens. I loved performing that piece.

But I actually started missing out-and-out singing—missing the intensity of singing. I started going back to the piano and vocalizing. Then one day I had a kind of revelation that changed my life. I realized in a flash that my voice could be an instrument—that I could basically build a vocabulary on my voice just in the way that I'd built movement on my body. Within the voice could be gender, male-female, within my voice. It could be any age. It could be animal, vegetable, mineral. It could be different ways of producing the breath, different ways of producing sound. It could be landscape. I sensed that it had this incredible, primal power— that it was the earliest human instrument. I sensed the power of it. The other part of that moment was that I felt that I was coming home to my family lineage, but in my own way. The movement and the theater had given me a little bit of my own place in a family of singers, but that day when I had my revelation, it was also like coming home.

It's also remarkable because it's actually very novel. I mean, people weren't thinking that way.

No they weren't. I was very alone, which I think was a blessing, actually. I had no precedent at all. But you know, I'm a Scorpio and I have Aries rising and I am a pioneer kind of person. If someone's done it before, I don't want to do it. That's kind of my nature. I don't know if it's ego. It's really more curiosity.

But belief in your path.

In the deepest sense, but believe me—I've got a lot of doubt. All the time.

Stubbornness, then?

There is a kind of stubbornness. Movement was always really challenging for me, so I had to find my own way. I did find a kind of style that was built on limitations.

Did you take classes in New York after college?

I did, for the first few years. I went to Judith Dunn, who'd been a teacher of mine at Sarah Lawrence. And then I went to Mia Slavenska every day for about a year or two. That was to keep my physical strength going. I didn't begin voice lessons until many years later and took them just to maintain my voice. Because of my family background I had a virtuosic instrument even though the virtuosic aspect never did interest me particularly. After a year or two, I stopped taking class because I wanted to start working more intently on my own vocabulary.

There was a generational change happening in music. There's John Cage, who was a generation before. There's Steve Reich and Phil Glass. Did you feel yourself a part of that?

I didn't really know their work in the early days. Steve and Phil are a bit older than I am. They and other composers of that generation, like Terry Riley and La Monte Young, came through music conservatories. There were two different models they were very consciously breaking away from. They were breaking away from the nineteenth-century European model, which is the climax-denouement narrative structure of music. And they were breaking away from the European music of the fifties, which was serial, tone-row music. Rock and roll was coming in, and I think that they were all basically instrumental composers and they found this niche in very different ways. I don't like to put them into a school at all. Each person found their own way of, in a way, going back to the body and in another way going into a much more circular form of music. I was coming from a song background, so even my earliest pieces have some kind of inherent song form. It was like taking a song form and then making it more abstract because I was not using words. That day of revelation in the mid-sixties I realized that the voice itself was a very, very deep language and that it could uncover energies and feelings for which we don't have words.

You hear it in your work. It's emotional and sometimes ancient.

I sense that ancient thing. And maybe it's because I came from a movement background, that the nonverbal form didn't scare me. It felt natural to me.

When did you start recording?

My first record was with my old friend Don Preston, who was the Mothers of Invention keyboard player. We made a record called *Candy Bullets and Moon*. I was playing bass and singing, and he was playing organ and drums. That was 1967. A few copies of that still exist. My first album was in 1970. It was called *Key*. And actually my partner, Mieke, met me through that album before she met me. Lucas Hoving, who was a very famous dancer and choreographer who had originally been in the José Limón company, was teaching in Holland while she was teaching there, and she was kind of unhappy being in Holland. It was feeling too claustrophobic for her. He would always talk about, "There's this woman, and she does pieces with horses and motorcycles and a hundred people in four different places. And I have a surprise for you," and Lucas put her in this room that was all silver and he put on *Key*. And she said that she heard it and it was like the most familiar thing in the world to her. It was like she knew this person.

That's amazing. When did you meet her?

The end of the seventies. Her hearing *Key* would have been the early seventies.

In *Quarry* there was a piece that you did that was on a bed. What was that choreography?

My character was a child sitting up in bed. I did a complicated rhythmic song with my breath while I performed simple arm gestures. At the end I slowly rolled down my back to a lying position as I was singing. I had to have very strong stomach muscles. It was almost like doing sit-ups. She was a sick child and her sickness was a metaphor of this world. There are many ways of thinking about the piece. Her nightmare or her illness becomes a kind of metaphor of the world illness, World War II. So, little by little, the piece goes on and it gets more and more dark. But there was a little whimsical dance that I did with the maid character, where we danced around and around the bed. My character was mischievous and wouldn't go back to bed, and the maid kept trying to make her go back to bed.

You were in the middle of this huge space and it really all could happen on that blank—on that bed—and yet there was film.

There were four different corners. I thought of that piece as a mandala. I love that visual configuration very much, but it's harder to get that form on a stage. La MaMa Annex was always my perfect space. You could have the audience looking down, and they were on two sides. There was no front and back. I thought of that audience set up as an aerial view of the piece, and yet you could touch the people. They were so close. It was sort of epic and miniature simultaneously. I thought of the four corners as the four corners of the world. In the first corner, you had one couple who was elderly, both with white hair. They were obviously European. The man was probably a European professor. An intellectual who ends up getting taken away. In the second corner you have three young women at a table with linoleum on the floor and they're American young women who just came back from the factory. Then in the third you have an urban and sophisticated woman who's an actress and she's rehearsing her lines. And last you have a biblical Jewish couple, and then as the piece goes on and there's a rally and a dictator and things start getting bad, they turn into a Jewish couple from World War II, and within them you get that ancient root. That corner is a kind of time warp, which is something that I've always been interested in. This time travel thing.

I felt as a young director that what that piece gave me was permission. It basically said, "You can do anything. Whatever you want." The lesson is: Be very specific, have a heart in the middle of it, a heartbeat, something vulnerable, something personal. You can be as extreme as you want, so long as that heartbeat is there. For me that permission was important. What gave you the permission to do that?

I'm not sure how to answer that, but part of the process each time is to give myself permission to walk through my fear into my curiosity and not get in the way of the world of the piece. Sometimes I'm able to not get in my own way. For some reason, *Quarry* came through me, and I wasn't in its way. But between works like that, which seem to come naturally and organically—you might have a few of them in your lifetime—you have to be a good shoemaker, and you have to keep your chops up and keep your craft going and you pray that another one's going to come like that.

One of my strategies is to keep on putting myself into risky situations where I'm doing something I don't know. I always think that every piece brings up certain questions, and that that's actually what the piece is about. I've done a few really risky things in the last years. Where I'm starting to understand myself a little bit better is I see that I'm really scared, but working with that is part of the process. I made my first orchestral work two years ago. A number of years ago the great conductor Michael Tilson Thomas came and said to me, "Meredith, why don't you do an orchestral piece?" First I said, "No, Michael. I don't know anything about an orchestra." But he kept on asking for years, and I finally thought, Well, maybe it would be interesting to try it because it's so weird. I'll learn something about the orchestra. There were times in the five years I worked on it that I was in the fetal position in terror, thinking, What would Igor Stravinsky do in this situation? This was way over my head! And then something happened where I started getting into it, and then interest took over and I wasn't really fearful after that. I always say I start from zero. It's really not comfortable, but I think that a part of being an artist is that you tolerate the discomfort of hanging out in the unknown.

That's big. That you can tolerate hanging out in the unknown.

That's a spiritual practice, also. My Buddhism has helped me a lot in that.

You and I both took part in something three years ago called *Show People* at Exit Art. They chose certain theater artists who'd been around the block and said, "Here, take this space and do whatever you want for people who might not know your work because they're too young." How did you put that together? Obviously you were thinking of the past and the present at the same time. What was the process?

I had done a huge installation at the Walker [Arts Center in Minneapolis], which was a room one hundred feet long and fifty feet wide, and people walked through this whole thing. It was gigantic retrospective and took a number of years to make. So for *Show People*, I had already explored some of that. There were a lot of great things I could work with within the Walker because I built rooms and I had music in each room. It was music from different pieces, but I transposed each composition into the key of A, so that when you were in a certain spot in the room you heard all of them at the same time, but in the same key. I had these different layers so there were some things in these rooms that you could walk into, microcosmic aspects, but then the macrocosmic aspects were like timeline principles that went through all the work. So, for example, there was a history of shoes called the Shoe Timeline. There was a long glass case containing shoes that I had used in my pieces from the sixties to now. I also had a piece called the *Life Backpack*, and it was a giant backpack hanging upside down. Projected out of the backpack onto the floor were slides of all the different pieces, not in any particular order, dissolving from image to image.

I still am very interested in the shrine idea as part of a piece. In *Volcano Songs* at P.S. 122 I made a shrine that had video images and objects. The installation was open an hour before the performance and you could sit in front of that shrine and just quiet down. Then you went upstairs to the theater. Some of the images in the piece had a little bit of resonance from what you'd seen in the shrine. There was another shrine for *Politics of Quiet* of this beekeeper figure with a video of bees in what would have been his face. There were everyday objects covered in wax in front of him and you could smell them. In the piece itself, the performers dipped objects in wax.

The *Show People* exhibit was much smaller than the Walker. I had two main pieces as installations and then some other elements. On one end of the room I had a screen with the rock film from *Quarry*, which was an actual film that was in the piece. Then on the other end of the room I had elements from *16 Millimeter Earrings*, which was a very important piece for me from the mid-sixties. That installation included a projection on the wall of a doll in a miniature room burning, and a dome that I had put over my head with my face projected on it, as if it were a mask that was alive. *16 Millimeter Earrings* was very much about scale. It had a giant table I would sit on top of like this tiny, little person on this giant table with this big head on my head.

In the *Show People* exhibit I also had on the wall little, teeny monitors with earphones so you could see two films from both of those pieces. The exhibition also included the Shoe Timeline on one long side of the room, and in the middle of the space was a tree that was made out of these singing suitcases. That was like an installation piece that stood by itself. You could open each suitcase and hear my voice coming out of it, and then, when you closed it, it stopped. Three of them together were like a little composition.

You had something to do with Naropa from the beginning. I always heard these wild stories about summers in Boulder, Colorado, with these wacky artists who would get together. Is that true?

Well, I was there in 1975 but I heard that the first summer in 1974 might've been wilder than 1975. I taught a workshop, and I sang *Our Lady of Late*, and I did another piece called *Anthology*. I didn't have all the wild experiences, but I sense it's why I started getting interested and curious [about a spiritual practice]. It took me years until I became a practitioner— years because I was very skeptical. But I sensed this incredible trust in silence and space, which is what I always try to do in my work. I felt that the audience was completely in tune with that, that I didn't feel like I had to entertain or speed up anything. My work always had that kind of existential space and silence within it. I felt very close to that, to those people. I felt a basic affinity to that way of thinking about things. I do remember parties and people do say that they took off their clothes, but we all took off our clothes at the drop of a hat in those days, you know?

But it did lead to a spiritual practice.

Eventually, after a lot of resistance. I would say it has saved my life. You know those Chinese toys where you put your fingers in and the more you pull out the worse it is? There was a certain time in my life that was like that. I'd gotten myself into situations that no matter what I did I just couldn't find my way out, and I was making other people's lives rather miserable, and so I was kind of at my wit's end. I was in my punky period at that time, so I was very skeptical. But a friend of mine said I should read *Shambhala: Sacred Path of the Warrior* by Chögyam Trungpa Rinpoche. When I was at Naropa I had gone to his lectures, and I had liked them very, very much. But I think I was scared of what you had to give up or something like that. There was this kind of fear as an artist: "No one can take my art away from me," as if it's one or the other. I remember crying tears of relief reading the book, and so I went to the Shambhala center and started doing the Shambhala practice. It's like Buddhism, but it's for laypeople. It's quite close to Zen. It's basically sitting and watching your mind reel itself off and trying to come back to your breath. It's very simple, very down to earth, but a very disciplined thing. Everything starts softening up, and I think particularly as a person getting older I feel like I've learned so much from that. I'm so grateful to those teachings.

I think as I go along what I've been finding is that my practice isn't over here and my art is over there. It's really one in the same. I feel as a young artist I was more evolved than I was as a person. There was definitely a split between me as a person and me as an artist, but as I get older and do this practice I do feel that they become more and more the same. We do at a certain point try to figure out how much time we have on earth and, having had a death close to me, I see that nobody knows. The only thing we all do know is that we will die and we don't know when—so you start thinking what are you really giving and what are you really doing and what is your life about at all. I've been feeling that all along my work was dealing with these timeless sort of things, but I guess that now I'm more aware. I'm contemplating something at the same time as I'm making the art piece. Doing a piece called *mercy* was contemplating mercy. You're not going to be able to make a statement about mercy, but just contemplating the notion of mercy and making the piece become the same process.

Now I'm working on a piece called *The Impermanence Project*, which was begun with a group of people about two months after my partner died, so I was thinking about nothing but impermanence. They're a group called Rosetta Life, and they go to hospices all over England and help people who are dying make art pieces. One person might want to write a play; one person might want to do a musical; some woman wanted to do choreography. They facilitate them doing their own artwork about the dying process. We did it as a work-in-progress last July, but it's not a piece about impermanence. How can you make a piece about "about"? It's really more exploring what that is exactly.

Giorgio Strehler, the Italian director, said that when he does a play he feels like he's making an essay about a play, which is a kind of contemplation. Can you talk about your work with your company?

My first group was Monica Mosley, Signe Hammer, Blondell Cummings, Dick Higgins and Daniel Ira Sverdlik. I would bring the six of us to a place, like Chicago, and then I'd get one hundred people from the community and work on these large mass kinds of things. Sometimes the six people would help the other people, but sometimes they would be making other images. I was pretty much the only singer. I did lots of music scores with me and the organ. At that time, the late sixties, I was working with big pieces where the architecture informed the structure and I was trying to subvert our ideas of time and space in performance. For *Juice* you got one ticket and the first part was at the Guggenheim Museum, using the whole building. I had about eighty-five people in the cast. Then you got a ticket a month later at the Minor Latham Playhouse, and it was nine performers. Then the third part was in a gallery, and there was just a videotape of the four main characters and all the clothes, the eighty-five pairs of combat boots, all the objects from the other two parts, were arranged in the space so you could touch them and smell them, but there were no people.

Ping Chong was a student of mine at NYU in the spring of 1970. I took one look at him and went, "Wow this guy's amazing." He always had his own sensibility and he knew a lot about film and he came from a visual arts background. The first piece of mine that he was in was *Needle-Brain Lloyd and the Systems Kid* at Connecticut College. That was the one with the motorcycles and the horses. I thought of it as a live movie. I was thinking a lot about cinematic ideas of long shots, close-ups, cutting, dissolving. The audience would move from one outdoor space to another. The piece began at four o'clock and ended at ten o'clock at night with a one-hour dinner break. That company was Ping, Lanny Harrison, Blondell, Signe, Danny. I think of my companies as family. After a few years of Ping being in my company it just felt right to make a piece together, so we made *Paris*. Conceptually we started out together quite aware that if we were going to come out with a third thing each of us had to give up something that was very recognizable as ours. That's the thing about collaboration—you have to know what to give up. So I didn't do that much singing. He didn't do any audio-visual stuff. It was a very different piece for both of us. We did that whole *Travelogue Series* collaboration, which was three different pieces based on place. Then there was a long period of time where I think he really needed to do his own work away from my work, away from my group, which at the time was mostly actors and some dancers.

Then, with *Quarry*, something else happened. I started wanting to work with more complex forms, instrumentally and vocally. There was a big chorus of twenty-eight young people, very good singers and very good dancers. I'd never had very good singers to work with, and I got really excited about that. I made a piece called *Tablet* that had equally complex vocal parts for women. That was the beginning of the Vocal Ensemble, and that became the next group. I was doing some theater things, but I also wanted to work strongly vocally.

I was in Berlin but never at the right time when you did *Vessel* at the Anhalter Bahnhof, the train station.

In 1980, just one wall of the old railroad station remained because the station had been bombed by the Russians at the end of the war. This was a revival performed by the Schaubühne Ensemble of *Vessel*, which had originally been done in 1971 in New York. The first part was in my loft at 9 Great Jones Street. The poor audience had to walk up five flights of stairs. I think we could get about a hundred people into my loft. It was pitch black, so people were led in groups. I had a long, long skinny loft. It had a low ceiling, and then the whole piece was looking down this black alley to these images that would come out of the dark. Then the audience would come back down the flights of stairs, and I had rented a bus for them and they were taken down to the Performing Garage. I had this big mountain that was made out of muslin. I used the Performing Garage as if it was a vertical, almost like it was a medieval tapestry. The audience was sitting down at the bottom looking up—a lot of people performing in that little space. It had the density of a crowded kind of tapestry. The first part of *Vessel* was black and white. The part in the Performing Garage was very colorful. I was working like a painter in those days. All the audience members that had come from Monday to Friday for those two parts—one hundred people each night—had a ticket to come to an outdoor parking lot where the Soho Grand Hotel is now. There was a church there at that time. That was the third part, a sort of Joan of Arc thing of her being killed publicly. It was the first time that I used any kind of reference to a character at all. It was still very abstract, but it was the closest to working with narrative that I'd come.

Did you replicate those three stages in Berlin?

Yes. The first part in Berlin was at the S.O. 36, which was a punk club from the period. Then they rented a double-decker bus and brought the audience to the Schaubühne and set up a fancy version of our funky little muslin mountain that we'd put up ourselves in the Performing Garage.

They bought New York culture, didn't they?

Yes but they fixed it up. My first meeting with my costume designer, Yoshio Yabara, who I ended up working with for many years—he had this book and he started going through the two hundred fifty characters that were in this piece: "What does this one look like? What does that one look like?" He drew them all, and I said, "Yoshi, we just got these costumes in thrift shops." He said, "There are no thrift shops in Berlin." He basically built those costumes. I was in complete shock. Then for the Anhalter Bahnhof— this is how far they would go. In New York those motorcycle riders were some Hell's Angels and some friends who had bikes. In Berlin the motorcycle riders didn't want to get their bikes dirty. It was raining, so there was too much mud. They were all dressed from head to toe in leather like you could not believe, and they didn't want to get anything dirty. So Peter Stein went and got trucks to dump clean dirt on the site and pack it down.

I do have to ask you about your work with Ann Hamilton, who I think is such an extraordinary artist and installation-maker. You did a piece together at the Wexner [in Columbus, Ohio], and now you're doing something new.

That was very risky. It was the beginning of the risky period. Both of us are very strong. We're both used to making our complete and total worlds. Julian Beck said something one time. He said, "The subject of Meredith's work is perception." So when I'm making a piece, the way that these different things weave together—it's very important to me. And the same with Ann. She's dealing with sound, she's dealing with video, she's dealing with space, everything. We liked each other a lot. That was number one.

The second thing we did was cook together in Columbus, Ohio. We felt that if we could cook together we could work together. Some of the challenges were who is going to do what and what are you going to give up. I gave up the video aspect of it, for example. Obviously I was going to do the music. I was going to do the more live kinds of stuff. We worked together on the overall spatial thing. The second part of the risky thing was our vocabulary. We realized at a certain point that she meant same words differently than I meant the words. For example, for me, "structure" is time. I'm a musician. I think of structure in time. She thinks of structure as space. I think "space" but I don't call it "structure." It was about trust, about building trust as the year went on. I think what was really beautiful about *mercy* was that first image of us sitting across from each other at a table. Sitting together is, in a sense, the most fundamental and elemental idea about mercy. The process was contained in that image and you could sense that we'd gone through quite an intense journey to get to that place. Now I consider Ann one of my dearest friends. Just knowing that she's alive makes me feel better, just knowing that there's an artist like that.

Now I just finished my first string quartet for the Kronos Quartet which was another one of those risky things.

Do you write for strings from the voice?

I did. I also wrote some of it with keyboard, but I think that what is most successful is what I did vocally. Kronos performed *Stringsongs* at Carnegie Hall in February and they're doing it on Thursday night in Paris. I need to revise it a little bit and that's a whole other story about scores, music on paper, which is very difficult and challenging for me. I don't really work that way. I usually score after I finish.

Audience: I'm hoping that you will expand on what you touched on briefly earlier in the conversation about expansion. The world needs more space, air.

In my moments when I try not to get too depressed about the political reality that we're living in, I think of it as larger movements. There do seem to be these periods where things do expand and then they seem to have to contract in order to expand again. So growing up as a child in the fifties was like the ultimate compression. Girdles is a good metaphor. Everything's so tight—rules, fear, politeness. When the sixties came—even though I was very young, it was such a relief. Girdles off! We weren't totally aware of it, but there was a sense of relief, a sense of exhalation, and there was a kind of illusion that we could change the world. I think that what happens is that it does get wider and wider, and then the fear starts again, and the backlash starts happening. That's what we're in now.

I'm struggling a lot financially, struggling a lot to keep my group going, struggling to keep going in every way, but I feel like I try so hard because I think that every time I'm able to go to a college or to be with young people that they need to know that there is this "anything is possible" idea. They need to at least see that. I intend to continue nevertheless. Somehow that seems very important right now. It isn't that you go to school just to find out everything you need to get a job or something. We never thought of what we did as a job. We thought of it as our work, our life. Then there was a certain point, I think, in the eighties where people thought of their identity as this and then what you did was a job. There was a separation between the two things.

I pray that now there will be some loosening and we'll feel this sense of, just as you said so beautifully, space and breath. No one's breathing. That's why I feel that doing art is so important. It makes you dig in your heels even more. It's a life-and-death kind of thing. What is the other alternative? The other alternative is that you're living in a culture that's basically trying to distract you from the moment. It's trying to distract you from your life. It's trying to distract you from who you are, and it's trying to numb you, and it's trying to make you buy things. Now, I don't really think that that's what life is about. I'm excited because now I have this real sense that there's this counterculture, you could say, or counter-impulse. It's not for-and-against, but there is a kind of dialectic where there's a kind of resistance you can actually hit against, or at least address in one way or the other.

AB: I feel that the culture we're living in is more and more fundamentalist. Not just religious. I find that in audiences these days there's this sense that: "I bought this

show, it's mine, if I don't like it I'm going to leave. It's not what I expected it to be."
There's a kind of ownership of the work as opposed to being part of the process of
the work. I'm not sure what to do about it.

This is part of what we were talking about before, of not wanting to be part
of the discomfort of the unknown. Starbucks is Starbucks. You know what
you're going to get when you go there. To me, when I go and see something, I'm most excited if I don't know what it's going to be. If I know what
it is, then why would I go to it? If I know what my piece is going to be and
make a grant application three years in advance, why would I make the
piece? If I could verbalize it already, what am I working on? I think that
what we're working on in art is the unnameable.

AB: Then how does an audience relate to that? I find that in a really recent time that
the quality of the audience, not just in my shows but in shows in general, has
changed. Their attitude, what they bring into the room is different—an intolerance,
a sense of fundamentalism and a sense of ownership, as opposed to being part of
the process. I don't want to just complain about it. I want to actually contemplate it
in a sense of making work about it.

What do you think is threatening for them? You have to think, What is
threatening?

Audience: I moved to the States about three years ago from Germany. That struck
me when I would go to theater—and also to opera or to dance performances. But
then I thought: People here go to theater, Broadway mostly, but all the way down the
line, and they conceive it as entertainment. There's this "give me, feed me" attitude. As a theater-maker myself, I depend upon an interaction between the stage
and the audience. I noticed people with petulant tones: "I didn't understand that."
I would say, "Well, what did you see? What did you hear? If you didn't understand
it, did it make you think of something?" Sometimes they would play along with that,
but sometimes they would look at me like, "Well, they should tell me!"

In the kind of work you are talking about the audience actually hasn't been
given anything. The experience is just so empty that you basically go home
and forget about it one minute after you've walked out of the theater.
When you ask how do you adjust to it, the ultimate of that is Broadway,
where everybody is trying to second-guess. There's so much money
involved. Everyone is trying to second-guess a group of people who are
actually a group of individuals. On a certain level, you can never second-
guess an audience. I know what you're saying. You're saying, "How do you
open the door so they can come through the door?"

AB: I think that audiences are detectives. What you do is leave behind clues. If you leave too many clues you lose their interest, and if you leave too few clues you lose them. So is the solution to leave a few more clues?

This is something we think about all the time. It's hard to figure that out. It's not like you're doing it in the closet for yourself. We are working as communicators. We're working to get this figure-eight of energy going back and forth in one way or another. So how do you do that and keep the complete and utter integrity of what you're doing? If you don't do that then nothing's left there. You might as well not do it.

Audience: You've just done what you wanted to do. Whether it's today or twenty years ago, the fear of the audience and the fear of how they're going to take it is something you've dealt with, and I'd like to know what you've done when you knew something wasn't good? How do you keep yourself moving ahead?

It's about communication. At the same time you're working you're trying to be very clear, and I don't think the first thought is necessarily the best thought. I don't think the first solution, the easiest solution, is necessarily the solution you're going to keep. There's this kind of strange thing when I'm working that it's like, first the material is coming from the inside out. Then there's a part of me that steps back when I make my structure. I step back, trying to see, "Is this clear so that human beings can actually see what this is or experience this?"

Audience: Do you reach a point where you can't see it clearly?

Oh, all the time.

Audience: What do you do?

Cry. Get on my hands and knees. Ask for help. Maybe sometimes let something go for a while and come back to it. People don't talk about how hard it is to be an artist, actually—I'm not complaining, but it is. I feel I deal with doubt and self-doubt all the time. That ends up being a quite rich source ultimately. Maybe it's a female thing. The boys don't seem to do that as much, I notice.

Audience: Yes. Some of us do.

Oh, I'm so glad to hear that. I was thinking maybe men are brought up differently, to think that they're supposed to be on the planet and they're going to do really great stuff. I think that then the next level is, "Why am I doubting, and why do I always have to do this?" As time goes by you realize that doubt is okay. Doubt is good, actually. You're also asking, "What am I missing? What is missing?"

AB: I think it's an ingredient. I think if there's not doubt in your work you look like an asshole.

You have a smug quality. The times in between things are always very hard for me, and there have been times when I felt that I'd never have an idea again, or that I've explored everything that I possibly can because as the years go on you have the backpack of your history. How do I find something new to work with? I read a beautiful book by Mable Dodge Luhan, who lived in New Mexico and started Ghost Ranch in the 1920s. She married a Native American, Tony Luhan, who lived in the Taos pueblo. She said that she noticed in the pueblo that in the winter everybody had very soft moccasins and they tiptoed around. They hardly talked at all and it was very, very quiet. She asked why they did that, and they said, "Mother Earth needs to rest. We are making it so that Mother Earth can rest so that in spring she can come forth." I felt that that was so comforting; to actually nurture those times where it seems so empty, to have faith that something will happen if you savor those times, not try to push against them or fight them.

AB: That's just gorgeous.

Audience: You were saying earlier about finding your best work when you were able to get out of your own way. Are there any symptoms that you can see when you're starting to notice that you are getting in your way or feel that you are not on the right path?

It's deceiving because I can say, "Well, the ones where you're not in your own way feel easier, as if everything is flowing," but that's kind of a lazy man's approach, you know? In fact it might be that you do have to work really hard and then you find what it wants to say. It's hard to figure that out. It seems like the ones that are coming through you are coming easily, but then there are pieces that I worked very, very hard on, and then somehow there's been a kind of release at a certain point. Maybe when you get in your own way it's when you're thinking too much, expecting something, or when habitual patterns start showing up.

AB: It seems like habit is the biggest enemy.

You know, if Anne were working on something and she goes, "What would Anne do here?" That's not a good thought. That's like Anne having to have Anne 's fixed idea of Anne. That's dangerous. "What is a Meredith piece?" That's so dangerous because you are going to make the same thing over and over again.

AB: In a way I'm very lazy, and if I didn't work with a company of people who really bust me, I could just do the same habitual things over and over again because it makes everybody happy. It's the colleagues that keep me awake, and my students as well.

If you have people that really hold up the mirror, you are really lucky.

Eduardo Machado

Eduardo stirs the pot. Whatever pot is around he is sure to stir it. And the world is a better place for that stirring. He is a great playwright and a master teacher of playwriting. He is very articulate about his influences and he is, in turn, an influence to a vast array of young playwrights and theater people. Eduardo was the artistic director of INTAR in Manhattan and is currently a professor of playwriting at New York University.

Many of Eduardo's plays are biographical, and for good reason. His life story is traumatic and the imbalance has had a dramatic effect upon his writing. Born in 1953 in Havana, Cuba, Eduardo immigrated to the U.S. at age eight, sent by his parents to flee Castro's revolution. He arrived in the U.S. speaking no English. He lived with relatives in Hialeah, Florida, and moved to California when his parents arrived a year later. Eduardo began to write plays when a therapist suggested that he compose an imaginary letter of forgiveness to his mother for sending him away. In 1977 he met playwright Maria Irene Fornes who proved to be a powerful inspiration in his life and work. In 1980 he moved to New York City. Since then he has been busy stirring many pots. But mostly Eduardo has been writing.

Eduardo is indeed prolific. His plays include *The Modern Ladies of Guanabacoa, Once Removed, Broken Eggs, Fabiola, A Burning Beach, Stevie Wants to Play the Blues, In the Eye of the Hurricane, Kissing Fidel, Cuba and the Night, Crocodile Eyes, Havana Is Waiting, The Cook* and *That Night in Hialeah*. And this is just a small sampling.

Eduardo also directs, acts and makes films. When he is unhappy about something, he does something about it. If he feels, for example, that a particular playwright is being ignored, he will produce and direct a play of their's. He makes sure that it gets into the world.

I had the great fortune to direct Eduardo's play *In the Eye of the Hurricane* at Actor's Theatre of Louisville during the Humana Festival of 1991. Besides the play being big, beautiful, personal, poetic and political, I have to say that Eduardo and I had an awful lot of fun together. We laughed a lot, we gossiped a lot, and we thoroughly enjoyed the process of rehearsal, talking and eating. Sometimes we cooked. One night we cooked a Cuban shrimp and rice for the entire cast and crew. It was fantastic.

But there are more sides to Eduardo than the fun one. He can be passionate and angry about the status quo; frustrated by the way things are politically, artistically, economically; impatient for change; ready to slash out verbally and call things the way he sees them. He is infamous for his fiery speeches and his loyalty to people that he believes in.

September 26, 2005

AB: Eduardo Machado is now the artistic director of INTAR. He has a show there right now called *Kissing Fidel*, which is controversial as hell, right?

EM: Yes.

He's a writer I've admired for many years. I had the great pleasure of directing his play *In the Eye of the Hurricane* years ago. Eduardo really writes for theater, as opposed to film or television. I'd like to talk a little bit about where this really unique vision of a theater comes from in your deep, dark past. And I'd also like to talk about process and also just about the field we're in today, what it's like—your thoughts and ideas. What was it that drew you to theater in the first place?

I never wasn't in the theater—since I was a very little kid. The house I grew up in in Cuba had a round tank of water that looked like a stage to me, so I started acting out plays when I was like two. I never ever thought of doing anything else.

You started as an actor?

I started as an actor because I couldn't spell, so I thought I would never get to be a writer because of the language difference. And because I love becoming other people. I found that very comforting. Then, at a certain age, I found it extremely frightening to become other people. I came to realize that I couldn't shake it off. I would realize two months later that the part that I was playing was not me. I got in a very harsh place in a play by a writer named John Steppling. So I wrote a play, and then Ensemble Studio Theatre in L.A. did a reading of it. It was a half-hour play. They talked about the play for like two hours, and I knew them well enough that I knew if they were talking about it for two hours, it meant something happened. A friend told me we were getting NEA money so I could apply for a grant. I did, and I got a grant for my first play. My friends who are playwrights tell me that that's not fair. I locked myself up in a room to write and stopped acting, which is something that I regret. I thought you could only do one thing—and I became a writer.

How old were you when you left Cuba?

I was eight.

Can you describe that circumstance? I think it has a huge effect on who you are.

I left right after the Bay of Pigs. We left because our businesses were taken over by the government. I left on one of the Peter Pan Flights for kids. I didn't end up at an orphanage like other kids did. I ended up with my aunt.

So your family sent you?

My family sent my brother and me.

Why?

To . . . not become communists. And to, I think in a certain way, protect us. They thought we were going to go to Russia. It was actually a CIA scam as it turns out.

In the Eye of the Hurricane **is a beautiful play about that time. When you and I first met to talk about the play, you said, "You know, Anne, you have to understand"— we were talking about the design—"people think that Cuba's like any other Latino country. My family wanted to be the Kennedys. The way we dressed—we were really not what people imagined." Of course, the first design we got back from the designer was full of—**

Like Taco Bell.

It was like Taco Bell. Exactly what it shouldn't be—the worst cliché. I think that the family you came out of is very particular, and I know some of your family members through your plays. There you are in this cauldron, in this huge political moment. Your family stays. You leave.

It's very dramatic and it makes great stuff for fiction. My family never did anything quietly. They liked the newspapers, they liked the tabloids, so whatever power they had, they used it to be in the paper—especially my dad's father. If he was dating a showgirl, it was in the paper. When I went back to Cuba to the town where I'm from, which is near Havana, I saw this huge house amongst the very little houses, and it all became very evident to me why they could want so much attention and get it. That colors my work. My work is about very egomaniacal people who only know what they want—and get it.

You grandfather was Oscar in *Hurricane*?

I have two grandfathers. The grandfather I would like it to be is named Fernando. My other grandfather started off selling fruit on the street when he was eleven and then owned a bus company. So both were pretty driven people.

And they stayed behind?

They stayed behind and then came in '66.

And where did you go first?

I went to Hialeah, next to Miami. Then we moved to Los Angeles, which is where I grew up.

And that's where you started acting.

I got my union card when I was seventeen years old. I played extras on *Maude* and *All in the Family*. Then I joined Ensemble Studio Theatre where I did more serious theater. Then I was part of Padua Hills Playwrights Festival.

This is where Maria Irene Fornes comes in?

That's where I met Irene. She mistakenly one day told me to write something. And I did. Because I walked into her class.

Irene had a huge influence on you.

When I look at my writing I think I'm very lucky because I had Irene, and I had the people at the Ensemble Studio Theatre. James Hammerstein taught me something else, which was how to rewrite, how to be tough, how to have standards.

Can you describe Irene's workshop?

Irene's workshop was upstairs at the INTAR building that was just torn down. It had an oriental rug. Irene had these eight tables built. We had a coat hanger that had brass elephants. All the coffee and demitasse cups were paper cups. She didn't want writers to have real cups. And we'd do kung fu for forty-five minutes. Then we would sit down and all write together. I lived across the street from Irene at the time, and Irene and I wrote every day together for two or three years. We would read stuff to each other after we wrote it. It was all long-hand. We'd go home and type it. There'd be piles of scripts. In her workshop, I wrote *Broken Eggs, Rosario and the Gypsies, The Modern Ladies of Guanabacoa.*

And what was it that Irene released in you?

Passion. She taught me that anything can happen and anything goes. Irene gave me the right to express myself, which no one had ever given me. She gave me freedom. Irene's a very interesting person. Being around Irene is like being around the Pied Piper. You can drown if you follow her all the way, but if you follow her just enough it can give you a tremendous amount of liberty to express yourself.

You are in the process right now of rescuing Irene's work from oblivion. Irene is dis-integrating—I think that's no secret—and her apartment is full of plays that nobody knows what to do with.

She really influenced my life for ten years, until I was around thirty. We had a falling out. And now that I'm fifty-two I'm back to being completely surrounded by her. It's really fascinating. She forgot we had a fight, though, so it was good.

You know I'm going to ask you about the fight.

I think the fight is an important thing. I was writing *The Modern Ladies of Guanabacoa.* The Ensemble Studio Theatre was going to do it, and Irene hated the play. She said it was the worst play I'd ever written.

Did she say why?

No, but one day she invited me over for dinner and she said, "I haven't read the rewrite, so we're going to read it together." Carmen, her mother, was sitting right there. She started reading the play. She went, "'Short hair, short hair, the answer to all my prayers.' Bad line." And she crossed it out. Three hours later she had crossed out the first twenty-two pages of the play. It took that long to read twenty-two pages. I went home and I woke up the next morning and I thought there was blood all over my walls. I called the guy who ran the apartment and I said, "Did somebody die in this apartment before I rented it?" He looked and then he said, "We'll repaint tomorrow." I was walking to EST, and I said to myself, That's not blood, that's ink. I went back to the apartment and I had taken every pen in the house and thrown it against the wall—unconsciously broken them and thrown them against the wall. That's the biggest lesson Irene ever taught me.

Which is?

Do what you want to do. It doesn't really matter if people who you admire like it. And so we had our big fight. At that point I thought it was either her or me, and that I needed to survive. Irene used to tell me stuff like, "You're as bad a writer as Eugene O'Neill." And I went, "Oh, thank you." We had a very turbulent relationship. The person who is making a documentary about Irene called one day and said that Irene could be sitting anywhere and say, "Oh, is that Eduardo?" So it was a very deep thing for both of us, but sometimes you need to get away.

You killed your mother, right? But in a way, that's a great gift, as you say. Her crossing out your lines is—

A fuck you.

You need a huge "fuck you" to get on in your life. Reviews are hard and we have muscles we can build.

When I get a good review I get really happy for a day. Then I throw it out. When I get a bad review, I get really depressed for a day, then I throw it out. I go on with my life and I judge my work by my own standards. Being a playwright is a funny thing. You have to be strong and you have to have an open ear at the same time, or you get nowhere. I try to listen to what people say, then I make my own decision.

That notion of being really strong and having an ear is beautiful. If you just have an ear, you have no way to edit, right? You have no take or something. But if you're just your vision—

You can't see the world. And a play's about the world, and a play is about everybody who's in it. The play is about the stage managers and the ushers. The play is about the designers. The play is about the relatives it was based on. The play's a big thing that you can't control yourself. I always tell my students: "If you think actors are assholes, go to a play on a Tuesday night after the opening night and see how hard actors work. You don't know what it's like to be in a play with a hostile audience because that's one of the things playwrights don't have to do."

So you're also talking about compassion.

Well, yes. Theater is about being compassionate for the people trying to create your image. It is not about yourself. I have no idea how to write these plays really.

I want to go back to Los Angeles: We're in Los Angeles, you're writing . . .

No, I'm acting. And I have dyed hair and a mustache. I want to be Freddy Prinze more than anything else. I figured since he got praise, it's my turn next. I think I was a very funny actor. I just wanted to be in L.A. I didn't know anything about the theater very much until I met the people at the Ensemble and at Padua. I by chance did this Brecht play, a showcase, called *The Beggar or The Dead Dog*. Florence Eldridge waited for me after the show. She was the original actress in *Long Day's Journey into Night*. She said, "You know what? You have what it takes." Those words—hearing them from her—I left the world of sitcom. I think it was also doing a Brecht play. I was twenty-one years old, and I really didn't know what the play was about, except that it really upset my dad that I was playing in a Brecht play. But something in saying those lines on stage changed me completely. That play got me to meet the people at the Ensemble, which got me to the people at Padua.

So, when did you stop acting?

I stopped acting when I moved to New York. I came to New York because Dolores Sutton told me, "You've got to come to New York to act." I came to New York and I acted a little bit, then I started writing all these plays. I felt like I was telling my story and I didn't have to try not to be Cuban. I didn't have to worry about getting hired. I didn't have to be worried about what I looked like. I was able to gain weight, which was a big thing for me. I didn't have to live on zucchini and string beans. I read this play called *The Cuban Thing* by Jack Gelber when I was a young kid—it was just so off what happened in Cuba. That was the only play about Cuba that I ever read. I wanted to say something about Cuba. I was lucky. Frank Rich liked my first plays, so that gave me a career.

Where were your first three plays?

At the Ensemble Studio Theatre.

That was related to the same EST in Los Angeles? They were sister companies?

Same one. I had a very lucky couple of years. I once had four productions in New York and three in L.A. I thought that was normal.

Would you mind talking about the L.A. experience at the Mark Taper Forum with *The Floating Island Plays*?

I grew up around the Taper. The Taper was the only thing I ever wanted in my life. I said, "Some day they're going to do my plays." So I went on this tirade of getting this to happen. Gordon [Davidson, artistic director at the Taper] didn't think one play was enough.

This was after they did *Angels in America*, so they wanted another cycle.

They wanted to do *Floating Islands* as a four-play cycle. I could have said, "Do the plays in rep." But I just wanted it so bad. I just wanted it because I was from L.A. Unfortunately they figured out too late that the plays were eight hours long. So we had to edit them and screwed them up. I understand that people can't do eight-hour plays. There are teamsters to worry about. I understand the financial implications of bringing down a theater. So I did the best I could with it. It was not the best for the play. I've never seen so much money spent on sets. I could do plays for the rest of my life for the amount of money that we spent there. But, even though it was disastrous, everybody knew who I was after that. So, actually, it was the right risk.

The other part that I think about a lot is that you're only supposed to get so much. If you get a little more than you're supposed to get, then they're going to come after you. That was the first time that I was really confronted by it. I didn't ask for all that attention. I just really wanted to sell tickets because the theater expected me to do it. I still have to explain my plays in the same way that I had to explain them years ago. They still want the set to look like a taco stand. They still say, when they're doing *Broken Eggs*, well, let's get the clothes on 14th Street [in Manhattan]. I still can't believe it. In many ways at the Taper I got the whole pie—all I could want. I couldn't resist it. So I made compromises that I don't think I will ever make again.

What were the compromises?

I edited my plays. I didn't believe what was going on on stage and I let it happen. I didn't fight to make them in rep. I just cowered myself away because I wanted the big bang.

When they do that much press buildup on something, one of two things happens: They either kill it completely or they praise it to the skies. There's nothing in between.

You know what I did after this? I was in bed and I couldn't get out of bed for three months. So I decided to do a play set in an office. And I wrote this play, called *Three Ways to Go Blind*, and I asked my friends to be in it. I ran the lights and I directed it. I could only have thirty people in the room at a time. I told the critics they'd have to write me letters so that they could review it. I had the best time of my life, and I understood why I was a playwright. It was the beginning of my new life as a playwright. I stopped being in bed because I had to go to rehearsal.

If the basement of the work isn't something that is in a little room—like in some ways kids playing in a basement—if you start working in a way that ignores that root, you die. If you lose it you have to go back to it again.

You have to play the strange line between being a commodity and being an artist because no one's allowed to be just an artist, unfortunately.

What do you look for in a director?

Someone who likes my plays. *(Laughter)* That's the first thing. Someone who's not going to do exactly what I had in my head. Someone who believes in my political beliefs. That's very important to me. Someone I could have fun having drinks with. Someone who challenges me. Directors are a tough thing for a playwright. You're handing over something that is you for someone to turn into something that isn't you. I like to go to rehearsals.

I like to give notes and shape things. I like to listen to stuff so I can rewrite because I love rewriting more than anything on earth.

I can talk to you about a bad experience with a director. We will not name names. I was writing this piece. A year ago, for the first time in a long time, someone said, "Hey, we have a job for you." I tried to write this piece. After we'd done two workshops, my friend Estelle Parsons wrote me a very good letter about what was wrong with it. She said, "You're the real talent here. Why don't you start using it?" I kept the letter for a while. Then I hid the letter. The director was someone who didn't want to understand what the subject they were doing was about. They didn't read a book about it. Everything's a formula. You just start going crazy. They changed all my lines to make it easier for the actors. It was a nightmare. It continues to be a nightmare, except that I decided Sunday morning I was just going to give them all the material—for a price. I said I wanted to be called Oscar Hernandez in the program. Now they can do whatever they want with it. That was completely freeing.

So, that's the worst, someone not respecting you. I guess what you want from a director is someone who wants to get into your head and challenge your head—someone who will go in there and not say everything's great, but also know what it is you're saying. The terrible thing in this country is that you're not supposed to fail. Well, to be a great artist, you're supposed to fail. But you're supposed to try not to fail. You're supposed to try to say what you want to say. Sometimes you fail. And it's not a big crime.

A conductor was talking to directing students at Columbia, and I asked her, "Describe a nightmare director." She said, "It's very simple. It's a director who arrives at the first rehearsal and opens the score, and as it opens it goes creak." I always admire directors who have the ability to say to a playwright, "You know, you've got to work on that second act, and here's why." I've never been able to do that. I always think the play is written by God and it's perfect. If I'm working hard enough on it, and I'm deeply engaged in it, then the playwright will see whatever it is that needs to be rewritten.

That's true, too. But most playwrights only want to hear the play the way they hear it in their head—which is so boring. Most directors want to start talking to the playwright before they've really gotten into their head. You have to really get into the play's head or the playwright's head before you start talking to them about the play because they'll eat you. The playwright will devour you. The easiest thing for a playwright to do is take control of rehearsal. They're saying your lines. All you have to do is nudge the director and then you have chaos. It's all over. It's the last thing I ever want to do to a director. I think it's a mutual study of each other for a play to really work. The actors, by the end of rehearsal, know the play better than the playwright or the director because they've been learning the lines and they've been doing it. The playwright can really rewrite the play when an actor really understands it. He's giving them the play—and giving them the silences, which are the lines that you should cut because they know how to play it. Then, miraculously, after that happens, every other actor who plays it will know, even though you took that line out, what that moment is. That is the magic.

You're an outrageous director. When I saw your directing of your play *Crocodile Eyes*—it was a reaction to *The House of Bernarda Alba*—I thought that it was some of the best directing I've seen. It was sort of balls to the wall—is that the phrase? Balls to the wall? Balls to the wall acting? Really out there and physical and it was a spectacle. How did that happen?

That's the kind of theater I want to see.

Why don't you direct all the time?

Because there are plays you don't want to direct because they're too personal. When I choose to direct one of my plays it's because I feel like there's something I want to finish and something else I want to say. I haven't directed very many of my plays.

The trick about directing is that you have to give actors the play and then you have to pretend that there's this big picture in your head. The hard thing about playwriting is to shut up because the actors are going to find something better than you thought it was.

What do you look for in an actor? I mean, you have big, voracious actors.

I love truthfulness. I love actors who can speak and have real voices rather than fake voices. I love actors that don't overact, but can fill the room with emotion.

I'll tell you what my two favorite performances in my whole life have been: Maggie Smith in *Private Lives* and Núria Espert in *Yerma*. They still play in my head. Núria Espert was doing *Yerma* on a trampoline—everything was downhill with Lorca after that. I saw it when I was twenty. What I always remember about Maggie Smith in *Private Lives* is that when she saw her husband on the other side she started to vomit. She stopped herself from vomiting and then she said hello. I've never been able to forget that. I remember it at least once a week. I think, Oh, that's great acting.

Compression. Expression.

Yeah.

How do you write? What is that process for you?

I think about a story for a long time. But I don't think about anything that's going to happen in the story. I think about characters. I think about how I feel about things. I think about how I feel about the characters.

When you say "think," what do you mean?

I talk to them in my head. They tell me things, and I tell them things back. Then they start telling things to each other. I don't write when they start telling things to each other. I wait to see what else they have to say to each other. And then when that's been happening for a while in my head, I start writing a play. I usually write plays in four or five days, then I rewrite them for three years.

I've seen you in moments when you've just finished writing, and it's usually very fast, and you look like you've just had the best sex in the world.

It's a pleasant experience. It's voices. It's very Joan of Arc schizophrenia playwriting. I write very fast. I wrote a musical this weekend because we're having a fundraiser and we needed a musical. I knew who I was writing for. I had been wanting to write about J. M. Barrie. I had seen a play of his, *Dear Brutus*, that was the greatest play I've seen in about ten years. *Dear Brutus* is like *Peter Pan* for adults. It's about having a second chance—about late middle-age. They did it at Joanne Woodward's theater, Westport Country Playhouse, this spring. I saw it, and I started reading about him. It just fit into this musical. I didn't go outside all weekend.

I don't want to drop this issue of characters talking to you and in particular of you knowing the moment to not write, listening to them, and then all of a sudden writing.

There are fake lines in your head. I'm going to see if I see a play now. There's a woman in this big dress. There's a guy with candles. The fake line is, "Oh, why are you here?" He goes, "To light your way." But actually, that's the real line. So, "To light your way," is the real line. And she says, "But I don't need to see." Those are the real lines. If I'd gone through the fake lines, it would have been a scene about what's happening rather than a scene about what they're feeling.

But in watching you just now, you were listening.

Writing is all about listening. Writing initially is about listening, and then after that it's about producing. Writing is initially about listening to the characters, and then after that it's about editing the characters and setting up a world for the characters and setting goals for the characters and setting goals for yourself as a writer—like, I want this play to only have one blackout. That leads you to a certain kind of work past the initial inspiration. You find different restrictions for each play—like, the band always has to be on stage. All of sudden you have a world that these characters can inhabit.

I think that's something that can be forgotten—the notion that there's freedom. You say you learned freedom from Irene. Then from Hammerstein you learned—

He taught that we're going to pretend we're on the road—because on the road everybody rewrote everything.

People wanted my plays to be very surreal when I started writing. My plays were surreal. I think I've only written one naturalistic play—*The Cook*. I write plays that are surreal, but I think they need to be based on something. The set that we ended up having in *Eye of the Hurricane*, which was fabulous, was just a wall of wallpaper, a table and two big tires that came in as the bus.

Ten-foot-high tires.

They were rather big. When they did *Hurricane* at the Taper they got two buses that cost two hundred thousand dollars. I kept on telling them, "These buses are not going to work. This play can't be this real." It ended up that they could only fit one bus onto the Taper stage. Everybody was freaking out, going, "How the hell are we going to do this scene?" And I looked at the back fence and I saw all these bus lights. I said, "Can't you just light two of those and two of those?" They went, "Yeah." I said, "Okay. That'll work." And it worked.

That's the difference between theater and film or television. Something fascinating in your writing is a deep sense of the real. Then at the same time there's the poetic. As a director, when I read your plays, I want the language to lead, the spoken language.

I want to get rid of most of the crap on the stage. That then demands that you speak a theatrical, poetic language that is not descriptive of a place but expressive of it.

That's all I want from my plays. Except *The Cook*, which is very naturalistic. All I want is to for you to say, "All I need is a tile floor and some lights." I want my plays to be characters in action without any of the bullshit. I don't want the cuteness. I think it demeans the art form. I don't want anything else but the characters' struggle and whatever you need to bring the characters' struggle across.

Your plays are like Chekhov in the sense that they're not—or rarely—about one person. Your plays are about society. I remember somebody came in to our rehearsal for *Eye of the Hurricane* and you said, "That person looks immediately Young Man because most plays are about the Young Man. But he's going to be confused because he's going to find out that it's not about that young guy at all. It's about this family and this old man and this old woman and they are as important as this young man." Usually audiences go, "Oh, who's the pretty young man or pretty young woman who it's about?"

Not great plays. Great plays are about everybody.

It's about family—and insanity.

It is about insanity. In many ways my plays are.

We were talking before about the difference between, say, an academic situation like Columbia, where you have meetings that go on forever that aren't really about anything, and when you have a meeting about a real theater or theater company. Everything you're talking about really has real meat-and-potatoes meaning—which way you put out the garbage can. It all evolves from a vision, a hope, a belief, so that you're dealing with real issues—getting butts in seats, getting shows up. These are all real, real-world issues. You like being an artistic director, don't you?

I do. I don't just want to speak for myself. When you're heading a group, you're allowed to say a lot of things that I've kept inside of me. When I was in my twenties I saw great theater. I know the difference between great theater and mediocre theater. That's always been my downfall because even in my own work I can see what's not good enough.

What did you see?

I saw *Follies*. I saw *Yerma*. I saw *Private Lives*. I saw *Moon for the Misbegotten* directed by José Quintero, which was something. Also, his *Long Day's Journey*, his *Doll's House* were so amazing. His *Miss Julie*. The thing I believe in most—maybe because I didn't spend my life doing it—is acting. I believe in actors. I don't think they get enough credit in the theater anymore. I think the big relationship is just between the playwright and the actor. It's easy to write a play in a weekend if you know who you're writing for. I don't think actors get enough freedom to contribute. They used to get a say at rehearsals. Great theater acting is really special, and it's really transporting. It isn't just the lines. And if actors are difficult people? Well, they should be. They have to put it out there every night. The rest of us are protected. Nobody's going, "That's filthy," to me. They're going, "That's filthy," to the actors. I can say, "He takes out his cock," but I don't have to take out my cock. I think the problem in the theater is thinking that actors are dumb, thinking that actors are difficult. Most of my friends are not writers—they're actors. And that's mostly because I trust what they have to say more than I do writers.

I think that's probably one of the reasons that your production of *Crocodile Eyes* was so strong. You feel like the actors were listened to.

I really listened to them. But also I am a complete dictator when I direct.

What do you think about audiences these days? And what about INTAR audiences?

Well, INTAR needs to find an audience. And we're working very hard at it.

I had a great experience with the audience at Hartford Stage. That's where I did *The Cook*. It's been the greatest experience of my life anywhere I've done it because people fall in love with that actress. Then, secondly, they fall in love with the part, but first they fall in love with Zabryna [Guevara]. The first day I thought, What are all these people here in Connecticut going to think about this? And they stood up every show, every night, the whole run. An audience can't fake it—because it's happening. When I see my movie, sometimes I think the movie was really slow and the performances were off, depending on the audience. Sometimes I would see it and think it was really great and really funny. One day I thought, But it's the same movie. And that taught me something about what people think about theater—that it's off and stuff. But it isn't. It's the same play most of the time. It's just that the audience is different.

I remember I worked with Christine Estabrook on *Once in a Lifetime*. She's a fantastic, big actress. I came back at the end of the run, and I said, "So, Christine, how's

it been going?" She said, "Oh, there's good audiences and there's bad audiences." I said, "What do you mean?" She said, "Well, there's audiences who know how long to laugh. There's some who laugh too long." She said, "There's some that have good timing and some that have bad timing." For comedy, which is what *Once in a Lifetime* is, there's a rhythm. You watch actors play an audience. It's all about breath. An actor who can get an audience to breathe at the same time—that's the thing.

But it's not in the moment. It's perceived as in the moment. I'm telling you. Do a movie. It's really just the energy that's coming from the audience. The moment can be the same.

What would you say about audiences at INTAR? How would you describe them?

I think they're, ah . . . a mixed group. Everybody comes. It's Americans mostly. Latinos aren't that interested in Latino theater. That's what we have to change. But it's not like an audience at Manhattan Theatre Club or anything like that. It's like an audience downtown. Our zip codes are the Upper East Side and the East Village—that gives you some idea. And Connecticut.

What zip codes do you want?

All of them.

How are you going to change?

Begging. No. Going out to schools. It depends on the show. A show like *The Cook*, you don't have to do anything. Everybody shows up.

That's part of your job, proselytizing for the art.

Yes. I really believe in it. I really believe in the theater. I really believe that people who don't get a voice should get a voice. I read this thing from TCG that said how many plays have been done in regional theaters since 1980 by playwrights who are Latino. I started looking at it and I had like sixty percent. Nilo Cruz had forty (just because I started earlier). That leaves nothing. It was like two percent. That's not fair. We're both Cuban. That leaves that whole other continent on the side. And that's one of the reasons that I have to run INTAR. I think the problem is that the people who are building these theaters like INTAR and other Latino theaters—when they got a lot of money they didn't use it to develop new work.

They used it for what?

For Lorca. It should have been balanced. It should have been about Lorca and people in Latin America and new work. I couldn't get myself arrested at INTAR. It took twenty years for them to put on my plays.

Then they took you as artistic director. So you have now a lab, right?

Yes, I started Irene's lab again. INTAR is now only doing plays written by Latinos who live in the United States. In English. And a little bit in Spanish. We changed our mission. The board actually changed the mission before I ever came.

Audience: Once I'd written about five hundred pages of a play, and you said to me, "Throw it away and go home tomorrow and start it again." Do you think that as we change as humans we write a better play? Do we take whatever it is that exists, the story, and are able to write something better with time?

Here's what I think. I think if you write five hundred pages you're out of control with the play, so you have to take that and bring it back to life, and figure out how to write the play so that it is two hours long. It doesn't mean you don't use the material that you have. You have to put it aside and say, "How do I limit myself so that this story can happen in two hours?" That's why I told you to throw it away.

Audience: Do you think that if, as we change as people, we revisit the same material something better will come?

No. The material should be left alone. I wouldn't want to write *Broken Eggs* again. I think after five years you should stick with it. I don't think you should have a play produced unless it sat in your closet for a year so you can look at it again and rewrite it. The key to writing is rewriting. The first time you write a play it's just a personal gripe. The second time you write a play you pay attention to the characters. The third time you write a play you're in control. It doesn't mean you changed everything in the play, it just means you learned how to control the personal angst you put on the page.

AB: I love that the first version of the play is a gripe.

It really, really is. Because it's always from your point of view no matter how gifted you are. It's the reason why you're writing a play. If you're gifted, then the other characters will come to make more sense. If you're not gifted, then it's just completely a gripe and you have a lot of hard work to do. But you always have work to do.

Audience: Could you talk about teaching a little bit?

Teaching is the most frustrating thing on earth. I've been thinking a lot about teaching because I'm on sabbatical. I've been teaching for a really long time now. I've been doing this since 1990. You have to be very strict and very giving at the same time. It's a really hard balancing act. You can't teach people how to be talented. That's impossible. You can teach people how to find their talent. You can't even teach people how to write a play. You can guide them so they're not falling off a cliff. But it's frustrating because you want to help and you want to slap at the same time. I tell you it's the most goddamned frustrating thing I've ever done in my entire life. It also taught me a lot about writing and I'm very grateful that it did. But I know why Irene cut out all my lines. I understand that now.

AB: Why did she cut out all your lines?

To have me really question myself. Teaching is not just students and the teacher. A lot of students treat you like you're a machine and you're supposed to immediately have all the answers that you don't have, so you manufacture answers. It's also very creative and very fulfilling. But it's not an easy ride. It's harder than writing. The hardest thing about teaching is to keep a perspective—to have your students keep a perspective and to have you keep a perspective. Every day I think I'm doing it all wrong.

Audience: You once said that plot is your enemy. How do you balance plot being the enemy and still havie structure?

When you start writing, plot is your enemy because all your scenes are about plot. Once you learn how to write, plot's your best friend—because then your scenes don't become about plot.

Audience: When you're building the play in your head, do you start with the images? And when you're laying the lines over it, do you think of gesture and movement?

I just listen and look. I don't think when I start writing the play. I write a play because I have to, not because I think I should. I write a play because I think I have something that I have to say, that I need to say, that if I don't say I'm going to die. So I start listening to the voice inside of me that wants to say this. Then I start listening to the other voice telling me what I want to ask for. Somehow those two voices become characters. I started writing because I was losing my mind. I had had a nervous breakdown and I'd been in bed for four months. I went to a therapist and he told me I had to write a letter to my mother to forgive her. I couldn't write it. I spent three days writing this letter and tearing it up and throwing it out. And then one night I wrote that first play that I got the NEA grant for. I wrote it in one night. I knew enough about writing because I was an actor and actors know how plays work, but I wrote because I was losing my mind. I only write what I'm losing my mind about.

AB: It sounds like it's an act of survival.

And it's an act of definition at this point. I've survived. At this point it's an act of defining for myself what's in my head.

I had this great experience. I worked with Joe Chaikin right before he died. They were doing this improvisation at the Actors Studio that somebody was supposed to turn into a play about 9/11. And the guy who was supposed to write the play from the improvisation couldn't write a word. So Joe called me and said, "Please save us." I wrote like twenty pages a night, and we had a full-on play with five songs in two weeks. It was just about getting into what they were saying: "Why are these actors wanting to improv that? What does Joe Chaikin think he should spend the last three months of his life doing?" It's about looking at what's going on inside of them and becoming aware of their soul. Then you can write it. Was it my best play? No. Did it have something to say? Yes. It had something to say about people as a group, not just me. When I'm writing a play I don't just think it's me writing it. My ancestors are writing it. It's not what they would like to say. It's what they think they can say. That's what the play is about. A play is a very serious subject. It's not like a screenplay. A screenplay is a series of images that then becomes a very serious subject underneath the counter. But a play is all about language and the struggle of language and these characters

I think you have to live to be a writer. You can't just be in show business or see your world like this. You have to live. I think to write you have to like people. And hate them. And you have to look at them. And you have to have something to say. If you don't have anything to say and you want to be a writer, make a lot of money and write for television—because that's just about technique and not having to say anything. I'm not being mean—it's a great profession. You become so rich. Then you can give back to the theater. It's a big job. Make sure you want it.

Audience: I was interested in what you were saying about the difference between the playwright and actor. Where does your understanding of the character and my understanding of the character, as an actor, overlap?

My understanding of the character is linear because I created it. Your understanding of the character—that has nothing to do with lines. It has to do with behavior and emotions. Your understanding of the character is multifaceted.

Audience: Have you ever changed lines based on something an actor did on stage?

Never. I would never let them have that much. I've changed scenes. For *Modern Ladies*, we had a reading and Irene came—to the play that she scratched out. This actress named Diane Venora is there. She's holding her kid because the kid's sick. She starts reading this play and she's just phenomenal. It's about this woman who is pregnant in the second act. At the end of it I had coffee with Irene and she goes, "So I suppose you know the actor is a hundred times better than your fucking play. That's the only reason it worked." So I became friends with the actress and I studied her all the time and the play became much better. She didn't tell me the lines. But she happened to be the right actress because she was a repressed Catholic like all the characters in my first four plays. She inhabits those first four plays. She was never in them, but she did readings of all of them and she dictated what those characters were about. She really helped me create these characters because I didn't know enough.

I wrote this play called *Stevie Wants to Play the Blues* for Amy Madigan. That play sounds a certain way because I know how Amy Madigan sounds so I know how to write for her. It's not any different than using your relatives or somebody you met. It's not just you.

AB: There's something you said that I don't want to let drop because I've been thinking along similar lines about giving voice to people who are dead and didn't have a way to say it.

Giving voice to what they think they can say. Not what they actually said. You look into yourself and you look into the characters and you go, "What do these characters actually mean?" This is how I actually work. It's very Stanislavksi. I go: "What do these characters actually mean? What do they need? Where is that need in me? What got in my way; what got in their way; and what did that person need that got in their way?" That's how I really start writing a play. It's about being very personal and very outside of myself at the same time. Then they start saying things they didn't say. Then somebody has to stop them. Drama is between the two lines. It's not the line. The line is superfluous. Nobody remembers the line. They only remember that little area, the seconds in between the lines. This is really hard to puzzle out.

My aunt called me because *Kissing Fidel* is about her and she said, "I'm coming to New York." I said, "What?" She said, "I'm coming to New York. What's the play about? Anti-Fidel or pro-Fidel?" I said, "Both." She goes, "So what's it about?" I said, "You. But you will know that it's fiction because I didn't fuck you." In the play the characters have sex with each other. She went, "Can we watch *Hairspray*?" That character is everything that my aunt hasn't said. I know that because I know my aunt well enough. The character is funny because my aunt is so funny. Not because I'm funny. It's her humor that's in the play. It's her saying things she's kept to herself.

I bet if my aunt actually saw it she'd have a good time. She'd want to kill me afterward with a knife, but she'd have a good time. We talked her out of coming. My sisters did. We told her it was also about homosexuality and that crossed the line for her.

Audience: What does the rest of your family say about your work?

You don't write plays for your family. They're never going to be your audience. My sisters like *Kissing Fidel*. You can't write plays for your family because that's not the job of a playwright. The job of the playwright is to have people having fistfights on stage. You cannot be middle-class and be a playwright. It doesn't work.

AB: What's middle-class?

Middle-class is wanting to have a nice family and having your parents to like you.

The actor David Warrilow once handed me this little piece of paper, and it said, "Being a playwright is going up to your best friend, sucking all his blood out and spitting it on the page." I really think that that's what it is. It's not nice. And the person whose blood you really spit out is yours. It's not comfortable. It's not fun. Any playwright who can sit through their entire play is faking. It should be unbearable. Even if it's a comedy. You should have a moment like that about all your plays. "This is crap. I don't want to listen to it anymore." And you should walk out. That's being a playwright. I've never seen a whole play of mine ever. It's too personal and uncomfortable. You want to vomit and you can't stand the thought of looking at it for another fucking minute. People want to tell you, "Oh that was nice." And you just want to say, "Fuck off." That's really what I feel when I'm in the audience of one of my plays.

Ben Cameron

Ben Cameron is an amazing public speaker. He galvanizes and inspires vast numbers of people who come into direct contact with his special brand of passion, warmth and powers of communication. Ben is also a workhorse. He is constantly on the move, all in the service of the health and effectiveness of the American theater. Most recently he was appointed program director for the arts at the Doris Duke Charitable Foundation in New York City. Before that Ben was the executive director of Theatre Communications Group for eight years. And before that he was active in corporate philanthropy at the Dayton Hudson Foundation and Target. From 1990 through 1992 Ben was director of the theater program at the National Endowment for the Arts.

Ben also worked in the proverbial theater trenches. For three years he was the associate artistic director at Indiana Repertory Theatre after a stint as literary manager for PlayMakers Repertory Company in Chapel Hill, North Carolina, as well as freelance work at Baltimore's CENTERSTAGE and Yale Repertory Theatre. He is also an educator. He taught at Yale School of Drama, the University of North Carolina, Virginia Tech and Columbia University.

A Southerner to his bones, Ben grew up in North Carolina, and he claims that the South is part of who he is. But he also claims that New York is a part of who he is and that gay culture is part of who he is. Ben belongs to the many cultural pockets that he inhabits. But he does more than belong. He takes responsibility for the many constituencies. He stands up

344 CONVERSATIONS WITH ANNE

for art and artists and boards and cultural organizations, he harangues and cajoles and entreats everyone to do their best and to be smart and to make progress in a humane and expressive way.

After receiving a BA from the University of North Carolina, Ben studied dramaturgy at the Yale School of Drama and received his MFA in 1981. Since then, he was awarded an honorary doctorate in Humane Letters from DePaul University in Chicago and an honorary MFA in Acting from American Conservatory Theater.

Ben currently serves as the secretary of the American Arts Alliance and the vice president of the national Arts and Business Council. He serves on the boards of Grantmakers in the Arts and Theatre Development Fund. He has appeared as a panelist on the Metropolitan Opera Quiz each season since 1996, and he is a member of the Tony Awards Nominating Committee.

October 24, 2005

AB: Ben Cameron is the person who knows more about what's happening in theater in this county than anyone else in the world. He came through working at the NEA for four years. He was at the now Target Foundation, which was then called the Dayton-Hudson Foundation. He taught at Virginia Tech and University of North Carolina–Chapel Hill. Before that he was a director.

He's been around the block. But I also think that he is particularly suited to his current job, which is executive director of Theatre Communications Group. What prepared you for this? What tools do you need as the executive director of TCG to actually function? Where did you figure out how to do that?

BC: That's an interesting question. I don't know. Next question? I would say it's a good fit in terms of the moment in time for TCG. That's not necessarily the same as saying I'm the ideal leader for the long-term or even the next ten years. But one thing that probably led to a right fit was my experience as a director. I'm certainly not a great director. The field did not lose a great director when I decided no longer to ply my craft in that area. But the way I directed was by listening and by orchestrating. I really valued that kind of depth of listening. Do you want to get really Freudian about these things?

Oh, absolutely.

I think three things have suited me for TCG. My father was profoundly hard of hearing. He and I were never really able to have a significant conversation with any depth. So I learned to put a premium on listening at a really early age. A lot of what I thought TCG needed at the time I was invited to join it was listening to conflicting and sometimes difficult and fractious opinions about where our field might want to go. That was what I thought I could bring to that moment in TCG's history.

The second is the diversity of experience that I had in both the for-profit and the not-for-profit worlds. What I appreciated when I went to Target was that my fantasy from a not-for-profit side of the table of what corporate life was, was totally misplaced. I had large assumptions about how the corporate world worked. Target was the least hierarchical place I have ever worked to this day, TCG included. It dismantled every perception I had. I learned so much at Target and I thought this could resonate on the not-for-profit side of the table.

The third thing is that I was an English major in college. As an English major you learn to think analytically, you learn to think in large systems, and you learn to be curious and look ahead. A lot of what I really love about my job at TCG is that a lot of what I get to do is ask interesting questions.

Could you talk a little bit about the inception of TCG—what it was meant to do and what it's turned into?

TCG was called into being in 1961 by a man named Mac Lowry, the head of the Ford Foundation's Arts division at that point, who had the very simple premise that if you assembled all of the not-for-profit theaters in the country in one room at one time, they would know more collectively than any one theater knew individually. So they issued the invitation, and all twenty-three theaters showed up. I say that quite deliberately because it's a reminder about how young our field is. I mean, there were literally twenty-three professional not-for-profit theaters.

A lot of the theaters we take for granted now, like the Guthrie, did not exist yet. American Conservatory Theater did not exist yet. Yale Rep as we know it did not exist yet. TCG's initial purpose was just to say to a burgeoning industry, "If you want to be a professional not-for-profit theater, this is what that means. This is how you structure an organization, this is what a board does, this is what you should pay attention to." Over time that's changed. We've grown. We currently have forty-two discreet programs, all of which fit into one of five big "bowls." Bowl number one is publication: *American Theatre* magazine; we're the largest publisher of drama texts and trade editions; we publish *ARTSearch*, the employment bulletin for the field. The second bowl is advocacy. With dance, presenting and opera we lobby for federal legislation favorable to the arts. Bowl number three: international. There's a ninety-country network founded by UNESCO for the exchange of artists and theater companies across international lines. Each of the ninety countries has a designated international center. We are the center of that network for the United States. Bowl number four is management services. We do the only fiscal assessment of the health of the national field; we have a program for trustee leaders; we hold what is now an annual national conference for eight hundred or more people; we do manager training. Fifth and, finally, are our artistic programs. We give away about three and a half or four million dollars every year in grants to individual artists: to directors, designers, sound designers, playwrights, etc. In about three months we will announce our newest grant program, which is for actors, completing our individual artist portfolio in a more comprehensive way. Additionally, we give money to theaters to expand the rehearsal process, to premiere new work and, through the New Generations program, sixty-five-thousand-dollar grants over two years for one of two reasons. Reason number one: developing a new generation of theater audiences. The other is New Generation: Future Leaders— sixty-five thousand dollars over two years to mentor a future leader of the field. What I love about that program in particular is that in addition to fellowship money, if the leader has outstanding student loans, we'll cancel out fifteen thousand dollars of student loans on top of the grant. People say, "I'd love to stay in the theater, but I'm coming out with fifty thousand dollars on my back in student-loan debt. You expect me to work for three hundred and seventy-five dollars a week at a regional theater? I've got to go do soaps." And even though we can't pull that whole student loan balance away, we try to mitigate it.

In addition to expanding what we do, I would say that we've changed in another twofold way. If you take the Peter Zeisler [executive director of TCG from 1972 through 1995] era where we really said, "This is how you think about being a theater"—a lot of that early model was like king of the mountain. There were the amateurs at the bottom of the pyramid, then the semi-pros, then summer stocks, then small LORTs [League of Resident Theatres]. And the idea was, sort of, the more money you had, the fewer of you there were, so therefore the more important you were. What nobody expected was that there would be an African-American professional theater community. Nobody foresaw gay and lesbian theaters or Asian-American theaters or feminist theaters or theaters for young audiences as a field. With that diversity, we've reframed the field as an interdependent ecosystem. You'd better believe the LORT theater needs the African-American theater and the African-American theater needs the gay and lesbian theater. It loops back. We can't be talking at each other vertically. If it's an ecosystem, we're going to talk horizontally. That's really changed, I think, the dynamic of the conversation.

The other thing we've recognized is that the institutional models, which are great for some theaters, don't apply to everyone. One thing that really stuck with me: Keryl McCord at African Grove Institute said that the reason African-American theaters are so fragile is because they've patterned themselves on white mainstream theaters, and white mainstream theaters depend heavily on individual contributions. She said, "I give back to my parents and my grandparents who took every nickel and dime and quarter to get me through school and have nothing to retire on. My children are going to give back to me a little bit and they're going to secure their own future. It's their children who are going to give to the arts because giving to the arts is a third-generation, middle-class activity and we are the first generation of African Americans in America with our own playhouse. Therefore, the model you've posited doesn't apply." That need for diverse models changes fundamentally the originally prescriptive role we were designed to do. So we're a gathering place now rather than a prescriptive place.

I don't want to jump over what actually happened to those theaters. When you started with—what was the number?

Twenty-three. And now fourteen hundred.

Going from twenty-three theaters to fourteen hundred. Could you talk a little bit about the chaos theory of explosion. I know it wasn't a gradual build. There were explosions.

There were. I think there was a thing in the environment and then I think three things happened. The thing in the environment that we rode the wave of, even if we didn't articulate it at the time, was when GIs came back from World War II there was an awareness of world culture and a curiosity about world culture that had not been present. It's hard for us to imagine because we're so hooked into the internet and TV and to film that the idea that we didn't all grow up knowing those images seems impossible to us. And then, the GI bill said if you were a GI you could go to college. The whole liberal arts thing exploded. The GI bill also said we'll help you buy a house. So there was a perception of affluence and there was a perception of cultural curiosity. Now, more particularly, three things happened. Mac Lowry, God love him, and the Ford Foundation said, "It's important and critical that no matter where you live in this country you should have access to the work of the professional artist on an ongoing basis." And in the fifties the Ford Foundation spent millions of dollars—*millions of dollars*—starting theater companies and operas and ballets all over the country on that premise, that it's going to be good for the audience. Mac also said, if you do that, artists will have more jobs and a better standard of living, so it's going to be good for the artist. And you're going to be able to take chances and stretch the art outside of the commercial spotlight in New York. So it's going to be good for the art form. It's almost inconceivable how much they spent. They gave the Guthrie in the Guthrie's first five years of existence, I think, millions of dollars. When you factor inflation that's like a foundation giving roughly tens of millions of dollars to a start-up company in today's math.

Now, the other two things that happened: One was that *Look* magazine ran an article that said, if you want your city to be a world-class city, you have to have a resident theater in your midst. The reason a lot of theaters are where they are is that the city fathers sat up and said, "If you will come, we will build it."

The great story about the Guthrie is that Tyrone Guthrie was given a full page in the *New York Times* and said, "I want to start a theater company and here's what I want to do with it." And multiple cities around the country called him and said, "Come to us. We'll build you the building and make it happen." They chose Minneapolis for two reasons. Minneapolis had the highest per capita readership of *Harper's* magazine anywhere outside of New York City. So they knew there was a literate public interested in the kind of work they had to offer. And the biggest thing, which I think is fantastic, is that they went to all the cities and in ten of the cities the mayor and the city council were all men in their fifties or early sixties. They went to Minneapolis and everybody around the table was thirty to thirty-five. And they said if we go anywhere else those men will write a check and be gone. If we come to Minneapolis, we've got them with us for the next thirty years.

Finally Kennedy and Jackie, when they were in the White House, made a home for arts and culture to an unprecedented degree. When Kennedy died there was all sorts of sentiment that led to legislation, and one of those pieces that was passed was the creation of the National Endowment for the Arts in 1965. When that happened state arts councils were started in every state that didn't have them. Local arts agencies were started in so many municipalities. The government kick-started or really threw into hyper-drive what Ford had seeded. You put those three things together and, zoom, the thing goes. You look at any of the biggest theaters in the country, with the exception of really two or three, virtually all of them had been started by 1972 or 1973.

The thing that's also moving about that story is that it's individuals—a Mac Lowry who says to Ford, "This is where to put your money." Or a Tyrone Guthrie who writes in the newspaper. These are big steps by big courageous people, and I think we need to take courage from that, especially in a time when we have basically nothing to lose.

I agree. There are two things I'd add to that. One is that Mac as a grant-maker responded to vision. Mac invested in the Arena because he had Zelda [Fichandler] in the room and he said, "I believe in what you're trying to do. I don't need fifty pages of documentation. I believe in you and here's a big check." The other thing I love about the Guthrie is that they had a volunteer network of women who sold twenty-one thousand subscriptions to the first season before the first actor had ever set foot on the stage. So they opened to twenty-one thousand subscribers because a community came around and said, "We share that vision and we'll work to make it happen." Some of the work I do now with theaters in trouble is say, "Look, every theater started with a dream, but it only happened when people rallied around their dream and sacrificed a lot of hard work and a lot of money."

There are problems that go with inheriting those institutions. I remember being in a room with Gordon Davidson, who was then the artistic director of the Taper, and I think Bob Falls was there. There were some big, major artistic directors of these big, huge institutions. I think it was Gordon who started by saying, "I think the only thing to do is blow 'em up." What? "It's not working." Going back to that top-down thing. These other major artistic directors were saying, it's just not working. This hierarchical system we have doesn't work. And so I said, "Well, what should it be?" I can't remember who said it, but someone said, "Cells." I said, "What do you mean?" "Like groups of people coming in and taking over parts of the theater." Like communist cells. I wonder if we could go into this area, these huge institutions. Now you have the Guthrie building this huge new building. What about them? Do you see them in trouble? Do you see them flourishing? Is that too general a question?

Yeah, we could talk for about twenty hours on this. But I love this idea of the cells. Did you read the *New Yorker* article about Rick Warren about a month ago? Rick Warren is this guy who is a pastor in a church in Southern California. He's written a book called *The Purpose-Driven Life.* This story is about how he started his church. He didn't have a congregation so he had gone and knocked on every door and said, "Hello. Do you go to church? Why don't you go to church? Okay, thank you very much." And he just took notes. And he started a church based on why everybody told him they didn't go. And right now they are training little group leaders because the congregation doesn't come just because they believe in

God. They come because they're part of a group of ten people and they have book club together and volunteer together, etc. It's a culmination of their social infrastructure. I'm interested in the cell idea.

In terms of the resident theater, there are a couple of things I'd say—and this is my own personal bias. I think of "institution" as less about size than about history. It seems to me that when an organization comes together around a particular artistic energy, there's a vibrancy and responsiveness. At a given moment, that person says, "I'm done." Or that group of people says, "We're old and stopping." At that moment, do we stop and say, "Weren't we all lucky to be there for that, but we're done"—which is a great option? Or do we say, "No, we've got to keep going"? The second we say, "No, we've got to keep going," then we start to answer questions for different reasons—now it's not because we are continuing to support that artist; it's because we have a staff we have to keep employed, or we have a building, or we have an audience. Suddenly the rationale that keeps us going shifts. In my mind, the second you say, "No, we're not going to stop, we're going to keep going," that's the moment you become an institution. And so, for me, there are a lot of very small groups out there that I would call institutions, and a lot of big groups that are only now having to confront what true institutionalization is going to mean. For example, David Emmes and Martin Benson, who started South Coast Rep together in 1963, are still there. They don't know what that's going to mean to how that place thinks when those guys say, "The end."

Part of what's exciting to me right now about institutional leadership, which doesn't feel to me incidental to some of these worries, is that two of the biggest institutions have now trusted leadership to scrappy, far-left individuals who started small ensemble theater companies years ago. Arena Stage is now run by Molly Smith, who started Perseverance Theatre in Alaska to be a feminist alternative to the movement in that landscape. And the Public Theater here is now run by Oskar Eustis who started the Eureka Theatre in San Francisco. I mean, Oskar still calls you comrade. So, while we worry that institutions are going to the middle—I think this is an interesting moment about whom we are going to trust them to.

I think any organization worth its salt wants a new building because of what it will afford the artist. I don't think any organization worth its salt wants a new building because it's going to seat more people. When you talk to Joe Dowling at the Guthrie, he says, "I want a new space because I have a thirteen-hundred-seat house and that's all I've got. I want to develop new work and you can't put a new play straight out of the gate in a thirteen-hundred-seat house. I want an intimate space where I can do that." That's what's driving that sucker up the hill. All the other things come with it that are going to please a lot of people, but a lot of that is an artist saying, "For this work to come alive, I need a different space."

Or, in Molly's case, the Arena has predicated a massive reconfiguration of that building based on what it's going to offer as the event-ness of the theater. Arena is three different spaces each of which has its own entrance. It was built in the fifties. As Molly says, part of the excitement when you go to the theater—when you go to the Public—no matter which space you're going to, we're all in the same lobby. You feel the buzz. The heart of her renovation is a common lobby because if we're going to be a social form, we need the space where we can take advantage of that social dynamic.

Now, there are a lot of empty, badly conceived spaces I think going up right now for a lot of other reasons where people haven't even conceived of the programming. I see it in the creation of community arts centers or civic arts centers, where civic leaders come together and say, "Let's just build a big complex, and then we'll bring in all this stuff"—without engaging artists in the conversation. We saw this confusion in Yerba Buena [Center for the Arts] in San Francisco a few years ago. This was going to be a great gathering space for all these small, poor companies to perform in. Then they put the whole facility under union contract, so none of the companies who were positioned to run the space could afford to perform there. There's a lot of that—out of very good intentions. Those city fathers sometimes love the arts, they love what the arts can bring. But it's not coming from an artistic place, necessarily. And that then invites all sorts of misconstruing around what the space can be.

I selfishly want to talk about audiences because I'm a little obsessed with them right now. I find the kinds of audiences going to the Arena, for example, very frustrating as an artist because they are so old. I don't mean in years. I mean old in spirit. There's a tiredness. I know that's something Molly is struggling with. I find that audiences at arts centers are very different than audiences in regional theaters. I find people who go to international festivals, or festivals in general, different. I find myself frustrated with regional theater audiences and I want change. The New Generations Grant is something that is fantastically trying to do that, but what else? Do you have any words of wisdom?

You know, it's the single biggest thing that I think worries me and us more than anything else. I had an epiphany at Barnes and Noble. I came tearing around this corner, and I almost tripped over this kid who was sitting on the floor with his back up against a bookshelf reading. And part of what struck me in that moment—after apologizing for spilling his coffee almost—was that when I was growing up, if you wanted to read in public, you went to the library. And the library was about big, leather armchairs. It was about total quiet. You washed your hands. You were not allowed to carry food or beverage in. Often the book you wanted was kept away from you and the library would have to bring it. It was a sort of sacred space. Churchlike, almost. Now, for a lot of people, if you want to read in public, you go to the Barnes and Noble. You sit in the café. You sit on the floor. The big leather armchairs are gone. Not only is it not quiet, there's big, loud music over the speakers. You carry your coffee with you, you don't have to wash your hands, you get the book yourself. And I thought, Okay, is this the answer for regional theaters? We pipe the music in, we tell people to bring their coffee in, and we tell them to sit on the floor or whatever those adjustments may be? But I guarantee you if you said, "Let's revive the libraries. Let's bring loud music in, allow people to bring coffee," the people who gave their lives building those libraries, the people for whom those libraries are deeply meaningful, who still value those things—they would be out the door so fast you should stand back because the suction would drag you down the highway. There's a real generational gap in what we expect a meaningful social experience to be. I don't know how we reconcile those things very easily.

The two biggest predictors if you will go to the theater are your income level and your level of education. If you've got a post-graduate degree and you're at least middle-class, boy are you low-hanging fruit for us. And if you didn't get out of high school and you're in a lower economic class, we've got to struggle to get you in the door. I used to think that was about how, in the theater, we love ideas and the higher up you get in the system, the more open you are to the discussion to ideas. Then I started thinking, self-critically, if that's what we do, what happens when you go to most theaters? You walk in an area. It's somewhat quiet. There are often muted colors, often carpeted. If there's music it tends to be quiet. It's a place to sort of mute your energy. We hand you something, we say, "Here, read this. Go sit in that chair. No, you're not allowed to sit there. You have to sit right there. You're not allowed to talk to those actors. We'll tell you when you can go to the bathroom. If you get there late or try to go to the bathroom we're not going to let you back in. And at the end of the thing we're going to stand somebody up in front of you and tell you why you were too stupid to appreciate what you just saw." I'm being hyperbolic. But on an odd level, we've re-created 1950s school. Maybe we with the education degrees go because we flourished in the education system and we feel absolutely at home there. But for people who didn't come through that educational system there's not that connection, and it's a deadly thing rather than a vibrant thing.

I think part of this requires examining our own rhetoric about ourselves. We all say in the business, "No two performances are alike." I think that's sort of technical for those of us who are in the business, and I think that's highly suspect if you're not used to coming. But if no two performances are alike, how come every time I come in the lobby it's the same lighting? Are we really serious about that? Let's pay the set designer another two hundred and fifty dollars and extend the set into the lobby. I mean, if we're promising that, how do we promise that?

When you talk about audiences, really you're talking about one of three things. You've got to make a strategic choice: Do I like the people who are coming? I just want more of the same kinds of people. Or, do I like the people who are coming, I just want them to come more and deepen their investment with us? Or, no matter what I think of the people that I've got, who I like, presumably, I want to attract people who are different. Each one of those decisions is confronted by different obstacles and different issues. And around issues of age and race especially, we have said we want people who are different than the ones who come. But we have used cosmetic solutions that don't really address the core problems that keep other people away.

Where is that happening? Where do you get a sense that theater is not like the 1950s environment, but there's a sense of fluidity and change?

I think a lot of smaller, young companies, as they form, begin to address that different dynamic as part of who they are. That often manifests itself in the work. I see a lot of work where I'm really engaged by the way the audience is engaged by this work—because I'm too old to quite get the work itself.

There's a lot of those groups, also, who are being aggressive about how they think about organization. A group called Sledgehammer Theatre in San Diego was seeing a decline in their subscription audience. They looked around at some of their colleagues. Orchestra subscriptions are holding and opera subscriptions are holding. What's that about? Maybe part of that answer is, if you're an opera fan, in certain cities, and Renée Fleming is going to come to town to sing *La Traviata*, she's probably going to sing two or three performances and if you don't subscribe, you don't see Renée Fleming. And if you're an opera fan, you're going to see Renée Fleming. Or if Martha Argerich is going to play Tchaikovsky once, you don't subscribe to the orchestra, you don't see Martha Argerich. What does that mean for theater? We play forty performances. We don't play one hundred percent. Why would you subscribe? If the number of performances is a liability, how do you make that your asset? So they said, "Let's not have subscribers anymore. Let's have repeat offenders." And what that means is that you pay actually a higher premium and you can sign up to see any show as many times as you want. So if you go to *Streetcar* on Friday and you love it, you can stop by the box office on the way out and say, "I love that. I'm coming back on Monday." And assuming there's still a Monday seat, you get to come back on Monday for free. Everyone knows that a full house plays better than an empty house. If they have an empty seat, it's being filled by somebody, and it's being filled by somebody who likes the show. So the quality of performance ratchets up. They're coming back for free, but ninety-nine times out of a hundred they've picked up the phone and they've called somebody. They're doing a targeted audience development, reaching people whose names and addresses we don't even know how to get. It's about really tossing out the assumptions and saying, "What are the liabilities that we have and how do we make them a strength?"

The few times I've been to HERE Arts Center—it's such a happening place. You go in and there's three theaters there and you never know who's going into which theater and you feel actually at home there. I think that Molly Smith is really right that you need a space where people hang together.

You know, on one level we think about reinventing the work. On the other level we think about reinventing the totality of the experience. I've heard you talk about this—about what it means to an audience to let them witness the rehearsal process. It's a real question on the table—are we willing to open the halls? What would that mean? You've had great success with that. Streb's had great success with that. Miami Ballet had huge success when they put their rehearsal studio on the pedestrian mall. People would watch during lunch. Now that they've moved their facility, their numbers have gone down. People love to be part of the process in a different way. People are hungry for social experience.

I asked Chuck Mee [the playwright] about this. He's recently spent a lot of time going to European festivals. Chuck said he thought it was because in this country we've gotten to a place where we think in terms of ownership. The audience thinks they own what they bought with their money. There is a kind of fundamentalist intolerance, which he didn't find in the theater festivals he was going to. He said he'd felt like what those European artists and theaters were saying was, "You are participating in our process." As an American I feel I'm making a product: Here it is.

I hope you like it. That attitude, in a sense, perpetuates the problem. It's a completely different attitude toward making and presenting work.

Part of what I've been having my own bugaboo about—you say, "Now we're going to have audience participation, we're going to pull somebody from the audience." And I think, Oh, dear God, please don't choose me. No matter what I do, you're going to spend all of your energy trying to get me to do what you've predetermined I should do, rather than responding to what I actually do. And in a lot of subtle ways, we have trained our audiences that way. Now we're reaping the rewards of it. One of the few really good talkback sessions I ever really saw—and I was a dramaturg, so I say this with all due respect to my fellow dramaturgs—was for *How I Learned to Drive* in San Diego. The night of the talkback the staff and the actors sat down on the front lip of the stage, and basically said, "We're here if you need us. Go." And that was about the last word they said. That audience went at each other for about an hour. They got about to the exact realization the dramaturg would have explained in the first three minutes, but they got there in a way in which they felt heard. They felt recognized, they made the journey of discovery themselves. If you go back to the root of education, it was a leading out, rather than a cramming in. But that was about genuinely being willing to surrender to what the audience wanted to tell them or not, rather than predetermining what the audience's appropriate role should be. And we haven't done that as a field.

That makes me think of Grotowski and the terminology "active culture." We live in the most passive culture in the history of humankind, I think, in the sense of being fed and expected to accept that regurgitated knowledge. I think we have developed an inferiority complex about participation. It goes back to your intentions as an institution or as an artist: Is it to deliver, or is it to activate culture? It's a completely different process.

One of the few places we've seen large social growth is in book clubs. When you buy a lot of novels now it's not critical notes in the back but questions for discussion. Have you noticed that in books? Nobody's giving them the answer. I think there's something really fantastic there. A lot of the theaters in the country have a pre-fixe deal where you go to a restaurant around six and they give you a piece of beef and a glass of red wine and you go to the theater at eight where you struggle to stay awake with the beef and red wine. And at ten-thirty, you look at that other couple you came with and you say, "Okay, curtain's down. Boy, wasn't that lovely. Good night." But there is a theater now doing a six o'clock curtain with the pre-fixes at eight-thirty and when you arrive at the table there's a jar of questions. The play is becoming a springboard for the social encounter rather than the terminus point. Now, maybe nobody will succeed in this. But it's at least an interesting question about how do we activate rather than deaden.

More Stately Mansions is the longest O'Neill play that nobody ever does except for Ivo van Hove at New York Theatre Workshop. It was a lesson to me as a director. These three actors come out. Joan MacIntosh was in the middle. They kind of bow to each other. Two of them sit on folding chairs on the side of the stage. Joan MacIntosh inhales—and then starts to speak, at top speed, O'Neill's first twelve pages of monologue. I have never seen anybody ever speak that fast. And then you start to hear *flip, flip, flip, flip.* The seats are flipping. People are leaving in droves in the first ten minutes. I would say, I don't know, forty percent of the audience left. And the rest of us, for five hours, were completely transfixed. What I learned from that is, again, the American proclivity—Ivo van Hove is Dutch—to say to everybody at the beginning, "It's going to be okay. After a while you'll sort of have to kick in and participate." But he said, "No! Right now!" I don't have the arrogance to do that as a director. But what a lesson, you know?

I'm really interested in buildings in terms of how they subliminally affect our response to the work. My favorite building for theater in New York is by far the Harvey at BAM. Because of the lack of finish in the building, the way the walls are sort of sandblasted out, the building signals to you the minute you walk in the door something unexpected and unfinished and exciting is going to happen. I don't respond the same way when I go to the Opera House because of the polished marble, the chandeliers—it's telling me a different thing about the finished level of the work.

When you read audience focus groups, and I've read a lot of them, there are two things at the theater that upset people time and time again. One is language—when people say "fuck." The other thing is "betrayal"— and the focus groups didn't use that word—because the show wasn't what they were expecting. I wonder how we're, in a positive kind of way, going to counter that. When you leave from a fifteen-second movie trailer you know so much about style, about period, about emotional tone, you know if it's going to be comic or tragic, you know if it's going to be violent, you know if you want your kids to come, etc. You see *"More Stately Mansions* at New York Theatre Workshop," in print, you know nothing about what that is. We know we can stream video on websites. We're going to have the ability to do that. So that might be a good thing. In some way it's about expectation.

The piece about walkouts that worries me right now is what I worry about as a nation—our inability to listen to anybody's ideas that don't conform to what we believe. At the Alliance Theatre apparently, they did a Pete Gurney [a.k.a. A. R. Gurney] play—and Pete's a great playwright in his style, but not exactly what you'd call a social provocateur. There's a character who says, in effect, "If I had time with W I'd tell him to play nice with others and share his toys." And people did not wait for intermission. They climbed over each other to get out of there—loudly. They were so angry they wouldn't sit through a play where somebody had insulted the president. That's symptomatic of a larger collapse in the frame of social discourse that if we don't solve, we are down the tubes as a country, I think.

Audience: I want to go back to what you said about cultural curiosity coming out of the fifties and sixties. Certain people seem to go to the theater because they want to see something they recognize, that's familiar. Other people—I'm not sure it's generational—want to see something new.

We recently had a meeting in Portland. In our meetings we tend to engage somebody we call the fly on the wall, which is somebody who observes the meeting who is not from our field, who then reflects on that meeting. This person said, "It's really interesting that all of you in the theater"— this was a meeting of theaters and presenters—"are really taken with this idea of how hard it is to sell new work. From where I sit in advertising, new is the asset. That's the single biggest thing you have working for you. Every single consumer wants it."

We reap rewards in retrospect of what we have done badly. I think we train a lot of theater audiences badly, through school programs and well-meaning education programs, to be passive observers. We've inculcated a whole generation of passivity to the theater experience. I always contrast that with sports. If gym class had been, "We're going to watch Michael Jordan play on the videotape. We're going to draw diagrams of the plays. But we're never going to put the basketball in your hands," who would care about sports? We love sports because we had to do what Michael Jordan does and therefore we get how hard it is. So much of our arts education was, "Watch. Don't touch." I'm hopeful, now that arts education is putting kids in the position of being creators as well as observers, that that may reverse the dynamic a little bit.

I think there's a group of people from about the ages of twenty-eight to forty that may behave differently than people older or younger. When the internet first exploded and when *Sesame Street* first exploded there was such a pendulum swing. Kathleen Hall Jamieson calls it the "visual associative framework of perception" as opposed to the linear narrative. I grew up on linear narrative, but suddenly there was this visual associative. On

Sesame Street, letter A, number ten, Afghanistan, as opposed to an hour of history, an hour of math, an hour of science. What we're seeing now is a more moderate place where people are both. Small kids now are linear narrative *and* visual associative. After *Sesame Street*, the next generation of TV shows was not hyper-*Sesame Street*, but *Blue's Clues*, which is a dog that solves mysteries for the linear narrative thinking. There's a responsiveness to linear narrative, but I think we lost a group. The people that made those theaters received information differently than the people between the ages of about twenty-five and forty.

There is some question about the degree to which we should be concerned about the twenty to forty year olds not coming to the theater. The question's being raised for two reasons. When you look at national demographics, the general population is skewing old. With life expectancy, the real people we need to engage in the theater are the forty-five year olds because that's where the demographic growth is going to be.

The other question somebody raised that was really interesting is what if going to theater was like going to church. What we tend to know about religious attendance is, for many people, you go until you're eighteen because your parents took you or made you go. You go to college. Sunday mornings are about brunch, racketball, recovering from Saturday night or whatever. You stop going. Around the time you are thirty-five or forty, if you were raised going, you start looking for deeper meaning in your life, you have children of your own, they need to go. You start going back when you are thirty-five, but there's a big hole in the religious community of twenty to thirty-five where people in many cases just disappear. But they come back. A lot of people ask, could that be the same in the theater. Should we be worried about getting the pre-eighteen year olds and the forty-five year olds and let the thirty year olds go?

AB: I think you're right. I think we have hit the end of a pendulum. I think it's the end of postmodernism. It's the end of deconstruction. We've deconstructed to the point where nothing needs to be anymore. And the associative visual is unsatisfying spiritually. I think there's a rediscovery of story. I find that we're at a birth of that place. I think it behooves us to name this new place because in the naming of it we create it.

Audience: As a young artist, I wonder how I will pay for my rent when I haven't been working for a corporation that's matched my 401(k) and I haven't retired with full benefits. Where do you see the artist community responding to that? How do you see that shifting in this generation where art seems to be thrown away even more than it ever has before?

What's just really interesting to me is that I didn't even think about retirement until I was probably forty-five. It's interesting to me that you're cognizant of that arc. I didn't even own a bed until I was thirty-six or thirty-seven. Wherever I moved to town, I'd just go to the foam-rubber store and just buy a big piece of foam rubber, and when I moved, I'd throw it away.

I think the real work for me has been less about—and this is a personal thing—being able to move through the morass about what is going to constitute my life having been worth living and the life I was meant to live. Put in another way, what will you do even if you are punished for doing it? If you're clear about what those things are, your life's journey sort of reveals itself to you in a way. What I really try to convey to people is: "Does that give your life the substance that's going to give you the other things and benefits in a way that's appropriate and proportional to what's really important?" Power and material things are great. They are fantastic. If you want them, absolutely go into politics. Go to Hollywood. Don't work in the small, resident theater, because those things aren't offered to you there. If those things are important to you, you'll find a way to pursue them. And if they're not important to you, you're allowed to make other choices.

I really believe in the bottom of my heart that physical exhaustion is something we all have to be protective against, but burnout is something else. Burnout for me is not about the hours on the clock—because if you spend eighteen hours a day doing something that feeds your soul, you say, "Keep it coming, keep it coming." Burnout is really when you disconnect from you core values. If we're not clear about what those things are, how can you possibly reconnect with a life that would be fulfilling? That's sort of a circuitous way to say, basically, I think what we've got to be really clear on as a nation, which we're not, is our core values. That starts with us being clear individually and going out and fighting for them tooth and nail. I think one of the ways to galvanize communities around that is through art. Art has a power to achieve that end, which we have not begun to tap.

Audience: I am a Latina, who happens to be black, too. When I think of my family, they are people who came to this country and a lot of them work very hard and do very well. They don't go to the theater. I go to the theater and there's no one who looks like me. There's no one who looks like me on stage. The productions that cater to a young, urban audience, if you want to call it that, tend to be really dumbed down. Why can't we find some middle ground? I'm frustrated by that.

I do think that every theater experience, or every meaningful connection, starts with seeing yourself on stage on some level—or seeing yourself in the story. I think we've wrongly assumed about changing the audience that people aren't coming because it's too expensive or they don't know about it, so if we just eliminate those two logistical barriers they'll come. If we're serious about transforming organizations, it's not about marketing events *at* groups, it's about making relationships *with* groups. That's a very different dynamic than we've historically employed.

The only qualifier I have about this is—I assume that what you're saying is that most large, mainstream theaters have that dynamic. There are a lot of very vibrant Latino, Chicano theaters out there that are doing work where absolutely people are going to recognize themselves and see themselves. Part of what I love about this field is that I am able to say I can't imagine an American who can't see themselves on stage. You may not be able to see it in your city. You may not be able to see it in this theater. But as a field, boy, there's so much great work. One of the things I found really interesting this year is—we do a survey about the ten most frequently produced plays in the not-for-profit American theater. And this year, six of the top seven plays were written by women. Choices one and two were written by women of color: *Crowns* by Regina Taylor and *Intimate Apparel* by Lynn Nottage.

If you want to see a young audience, go to Universes in the Bronx. If you're twenty-eight you'll probably be the oldest person in the room—and what's going to happen in that space is *kaboom*. The fact that you don't see young people in old theater organizations doesn't mean you don't see a lot of young people in theater. You just don't see them in that theater. You may see them in other theaters.

One of the things I was really taken with was Indiana Rep—a big theater—beating their head against the wall about not being able to break through to the African-American audience in Indianapolis. They were making all sorts of pejorative assumptions about why that was. One of the people from the town said, "You're all white people who haven't been here long enough to know this. That building was built in the 1920s and until about the 1960s it had a colored-only entrance. We're not going in that building." They didn't know. You can't have a conversation or a relationship if you don't know what's keeping people out. You can make the assumption that it's the wrong play, but that may not be the issue at all. That's a transformation of how we think about that.

E'Vonne Coleman, an African-American woman who was at the NEA when I was, in expansion arts, moved to head the Durham Arts Council and, in Durham, North Carolina, she basically formed a breakfast group of ministers. She spent about a year with them having breakfast with them and saying, "What do we want for the community? What do we dream for this community?" A year or so later when she decided to bring Tim Miller in, who was one of the NEA Four, very controversial at the time, the ministers rallied to her defense because they were part of the same vision for the community.

Audience: We want to feel that safety when we go to the theater. We want to be guided through and not be forced to feel, and that's what theater is. When you go, when you're really at the theater and the audience is active, you're forced to work.

Anne gave me what is still one of my favorite images, which I think about all the time. You said that, "I don't want a theater where people sit with their arms folded. I want a theater where people sit forward." It's about being engaged. I think a lot of people feel deadened and not engaged. I don't necessarily want to work. But I also don't want—this is me—to be where my imagination is not engaged and all my work's done for me. I can get that on TV. So the idea about how is my curiosity, how is my imagination, engaged, is a very vibrant piece of it for me, whether it's engaged intellectually or engaged visually. If what you mean is, "I've got to engage with," if you're equating that with work, then I disagree with you. But I get the point about *work*, even though I think there are some people who are hungry for it.

AB: The theater, from my experience, is a gym for the soul. And I think when you get off work and you go to the gym for your body, you actually feel better. You generate more energy. To say, "Come here. You actually have to change your clothes. You're going to have to shower afterward"—that invigoration is actually contagious.

Maybe that's the asset that we've been trying to deny that we should sell. Nike is about how hard the work's going to be. It's not going to be easy. All those "Just Do It" commercials—it's people pouring in sweat. Maybe what we should be saying to people is, "Hey, are you ready for the theater? Are you ready for this? Step up to theater." Maybe we should be the Nikes of the spirit.

Audience: I have to talk about ticket price. We just spent a couple of months traveling through the former Yugoslavia. The packaging is very much the same. Theaters look the same, the advertising—but the ticket prices are unbelievably affordable. You can see any show in any country for the same that you'll pay for one or two beers in a local bar. Yes, I can use my expired student ID and get a discounted ticket, or get a discount ticket through my church group, but the message I'm getting is, "You can't afford a real ticket." I just think in this country, if ticket prices keep going like they are, we can forget about ever breaking that income barrier.

This goes back to that political question. There are two reasons that difference exists. One is that their government subsidy dwarfs what we do. When I was at the NEA—and these are old numbers—we paid sixty-three cents per tax payer for the arts in this country. That was when the budget was twice what it is. Now we pay thirty-three cents. In France, they are paying thirty-seven dollars per tax payer. There's the difference, from thirty-three cents to thirty-seven dollars—and that thirty-seven dollars is largely about keeping the tickets affordable so that everybody can go.

Pat Graney, a choreographer from Seattle, once said that part of the battle we all have to fight around the subsidy issue is we're a Puritan nation and we ultimately believe that if what you're doing doesn't cause you intense pain and suffering, it's not worth giving money to. Everybody looks at arts and says, "They're having such a good time. Why should we give them money?" There's a degree of truth in that. It's compounded by, in certain countries like England, geography. Maggie Smith can walk out on stage and get paid a buck ninety-five, and you keep your ticket prices low, because London is the theater capital and the film capital of Britain. So at night, when she's on stage, she's been shooting movies that afternoon. There's a permeability of the sectors that financially reinforce each other. In our country you work anywhere other than in L.A., which is not a theater town, you don't have that option. That affects ticket prices.

In our research we're seeing that right now ticket prices are tending to segregate. People are really bumping up the top end, while trying to keep the low end as low as they can. What they're finding is that people who can afford the top, don't mind if you say, "You paid fifty dollars last year, you pay seventy dollars this year." That allows us to keep the bottom end at fifteen dollars or whatever.

The other thing that's interesting in our research is that typically it's the perception of price more than the reality of price that tends to act as a barrier. Most people, when you ask, "How much does a ticket cost?" They'll say seventy-five dollars, because Broadway is now one hundred dollars a seat. And when you say, "Actually, the top price here is thirty-seven dollars and fifty cents and you can get in any night, as long as you're willing to sit toward the back, for as little as twelve dollars or fifteen dollars," people are astounded. I agree with you about the perception.

Audience: Where do you feel the kind of vitality is that could take us to a new place?

I feel it in a couple places. I'm really interested in young artists who are coming up the ranks right now. Peter DuBois, who is now at the Public Theater, who followed Molly Smith at Perseverance, is part of a younger generation. He wanted money to travel around and interview Gordon and Zelda and those people. He says, "I want to talk to Gordon because it's like having conversations with your grandparents. Gordon and I can have a conversation that Gordon can't have with the person who follows him." It's easier for us to be honest with our grandparents than it is with our parents—or maybe you have more functional families than I do and that's not true. The reason that we all want to talk to Gordon and Zelda right now is that they made a path where there wasn't a path. Instinctively I think artists know, "I'm going into a moment where there's not a path out there for me."

I'm really excited by the number of unsolicited manuscripts a typical dramaturg gets. It's through the ceiling—eight hundred fifty, nine hundred manuscripts a year. That's a lot of writers.

Somebody said we graduate four hundred thousand MFAs in this country every year—in all arts disciplines, not just theater. As much as we denigrate ourselves, we've convinced enough people that this is a life worth investing in. What's more exciting to me is if we lose three hundred ninety thousand a year—that means people running the political system, people running the school systems—they'll be people trained in the arts, and boy is that an exciting notion for this country.

Tina Landau

The muscularity, intelligence and theatricality of a Tina Landau production are undeniable trademarks. I, like many others, am drawn to her
work because it is always full of life, ideas and a certain irrepressible joy.
And yet she is so seldom satisfied. She tortures herself with doubt while
audiences gush and rave. She reads the critics' reviews of her own shows
searching for clues and useful analysis. She is a glorious and uncompro-
mising theater artist.

Tina grew up in New York City and Beverly Hills, the daughter of film
producers Ely and Edie Landau. She likes to joke that the pinnacle of her
career transpired in high school when a professional producer picked up a
play that she wrote (composed and directed at Beverly Hills High School),
then transferred it intact to a commercial venue in Los Angeles. In fact,
Tina went on to undergraduate studies at Yale where her productions are
still legendary. It seems that the graduate students at the Yale School of
Drama preferred to work under her direction than with their own School of
Drama contemporaries. I first met Tina at the American Repertory Theater
where she was studying directing at the Institute for Advanced Training at
Harvard. I quickly learned where to find her after the opening night curtain
call of any play she directed: hiding under a wood saw in the scene shop.

In those early days Tina claimed that she hoped to reinvent the American musical. And to a large extent she has done exactly that. Her ongoing
works with composers Adam Guettel and Ricky Ian Gordon have born
rich fruit: *Floyd Collins, Dream True, States of Independence* (all of which

she also co-authored) and *Saturn Returns*. She brought a bright new perspective to the classic *Bells Are Ringing* on Broadway and is currently working with composer Regina Spektor on their new Broadway musical, *Beauty*. She writes plays too: *Beauty* (on which the musical is based), *Space*, *1969*, *Theatrical Essays* and *Stonewall*. She adapted Daphne Du-Maurier's *Rebecca*, Dickens's *A Christmas Carol* and the epic *Gilgamesh*. She stages classics, Shakespeare, Chekhov and the Greeks. She works with contemporary playwrights who adore her—Charles L. Mee, Jr., Tracy Letts, Tarell Alvin McCraney, José Rivera. Tina is an ensemble company member of Steppenwolf Theatre Company where she directed *Hot L Baltimore*, *The Brother/Sister Plays*, *The Tempest*, *Superior Donuts*, *The Time of Your Life*, *The Diary of Anne Frank*, *The Cherry Orchard*, *Time to Burn*, *Berlin Circle* and *The Ballad of Little Jo*. In New York, she directed Mee's *Iphigenia 2.0*, *The Trojan Women* and *Orestes*, and McCraney's *Wig Out!* and *In the Red and Brown Water*, as well as various other plays at the Vineyard Theatre, the Public Theater and Playwrights Horizons. The lists go on. Tina is prolific. People love to work with her because she is at heart a great collaborator. She is incredibly intelligent and always listens intently to what is happening around her. She is self-depreciating and brilliant.

Tina and I worked together on several plays and our book *The Viewpoints Book*. I never cease to wonder at and admire her thoroughness in thought and consideration for detail. At the moment when I think that we must be finished, when I am ready to move on to other things, this is usually the very moment when Tina begins to seriously question, penetrate and find better ways of accomplishing whatever we are attempting to do.

Tina is the recipient of numerous honors, including the Richard Rodgers Award, the Lucille Lortel Award and numerous Drama Desk nominations. She also received support from the Princess Grace Foundation, the NEA/TCG Directing Fellowship and Rockefeller and Pew grants. She was named a 2007 United States Artists Fellow.

November 14, 2005

AB: I'm a little bit prejudiced in introducing Tina, because I would say that she's one of the finest directors in the theater world right now. She is a member of the Steppenwolf ensemble in Chicago. And we have collaborated together over many years and also collaborated on a book. Although Tina and I share a lot of beliefs and ways of working, the result is very, very different. When I first met Tina one of the first things she said to me was, "I want to reinvent the American musical." Where did that come from?

TL: I grew up here in New York. Both my parents were film producers. Way back they did a series, *Play of the Week*, that was on the original Channel Thirteen, then did *The American Film Theatre*, which were plays on film. They've recently been re-released on Kino International. My family was an odd hybrid of film and theater. As a kid we frequently went to see Broadway musicals. When I was young, my biggest influences were Hal Prince and Michael Bennett, especially *A Chorus Line* and *Dreamgirls*. I grew up loving musicals. I went to a theater camp called Stagedoor Manor, which some of you might know from the now-released film called *Camp* by Todd Graff. I played piano as a kid, and, when I first moved to New York after college, I actually played show tunes as a living. I played cocktail piano for a while.

So half of me was firmly entrenched in the American musical. When I went to college, at Yale, I went into the closet a little and developed this sort of schizophrenic artistic personality. I'm a Gemini also. One half of me was this would-be experimentalist. I probably would have said then that I wanted to usher along the next wave of the avant-garde. And the other half of me was running off in the summers to direct *Music Man* and *Guys and Dolls* and *Brigadoon* in summer stock. I feel like, as an adult, a lot of my journey has been attempting some kind of synthesis, trying to figure out where those two people meet and live and make art happily together.

I have a theory that every director is either a good beginner, a good middler or a good ender. I, for example, flourish in the beginning. I love bringing in research. I love uploading every idea. I could begin forever. But when it gets to the ending, I walk into tech rehearsals—SITI members know this—going, "Wow! There's this book about Orson Welles." They're going, "Anne. We have to finish the piece we're doing now." I'm a terrible ender. I get bored in the ending—which is why I work with actors and designers who are great enders. Tina is a magnificent ender. When previews come, she will work until the cows come in. And as much as she seems to be a great beginner to other people, she hates it. She gets panicky.

I have had major anxiety and problems with first days of rehearsals. About ten years ago I had a series of really intense panic/anxiety attacks that kept me from finishing jobs. So if anyone wants to talk about that kind of neuroses of being a director, I have much to say about it. But the good news is that for years and years I've worked hard to contend with it and have made much progress. I hate speaking in public, to the extent that I've decided at times I'm going to follow Woody Allen's footsteps and just not do it, period. In the last years I've gotten better and better, and then, just a few weeks ago, I started having these anxiety attacks again.

First days of rehearsal are, to me, so sacred and so much set the tone for everything that's going to happen. Right when I graduated from college, my first professional job was at the Yale Cabaret. I was twenty-one or twenty-two, and the artistic director came in and said, "We're now going to do our meet-and-greet." I said, "What are you talking about? What's a meet-and-greet?" And he said, "Oh, it's where we all come in with the staff. We all sit around and introduce ourselves. And you'll talk and explain about the process, and everyone will get to know each other." I said, "Oh, no, I don't do that. I would like to sit in a room alone with the actors and talk to them about why this project now." And he said, "No, we don't do that." We got in a big old fight, and I stormed out on the first day of rehearsal. I went back the second day. He had cooled down and said it was okay if I started with just the actors in a room. But it took me a long time to get used to the institutional brou-ha-ha around making art, and I had a really hard time with it.

There was a Macedonian director, Slobodon Unkovski, at American Repertory Theater when Anne and I were both there. He said that, as a director, you prepare alone, and you sit in the fire and fever of what you're doing for a long time. Then your job at the beginning of rehearsal is to spread the contagion—to pass the disease. But he said *dis*-ease—to pass the dis-ease on. I've always felt that the state I enter when beginning a project is so full and intense that I very often hit this kind of—what Anne, à la Marshall McLuhan, calls "information overload." But sometimes it didn't equal pattern recognition, as McLuhan suggested it would. It just equaled brain shutdown. It's that feeling you get when you have so much you want to say so quickly, and you're so impassioned about it, and words suddenly seem highly inadequate, and your senses start shutting down.

The director Les Waters said something that I found amazing, which was that directors have to function with a million things happening, but when all of that stuff's happening, he gets very calm and can do one thing at a time.

The breakdown moments started when I was at Actors Theatre of Louisville. I had been invited to create a new piece with five actors, and we decided to work on Freud. In retrospect, I'm sure that was part of it, because I was so immersed in and overwhelmed by the material. I ended up leaving that job. My next job thereafter was a musical called *Doll*, in Houston. It was the first day of rehearsal, and I was sitting in a room like this, talking about the piece and why it mattered to me, and I zoned in on a guy's foot right next to me, which was shaking. I'm thinking of this because of what you said about Les. It was exactly that feeling of there was so much going on for me, and all I could see or concentrate or focus on was that one foot. I stopped talking and said, "Excuse me, I have to leave now," and I got up and I left the room. And Stuart Ostrow, who was the producer, came out into the hall and said, "Come on, kiddo. Jerry [Jerome] Robbins used to throw up before every first rehearsal. Just buck up and get back in there." I did—but I let the authors do the talking. And that was the second job I left. That was over ten years ago, and of course a lot has changed for me since then.

Is it the same level of anxiety in the commercial world as it is in the not-for-profit, would you say?

I have to say that the anxiety has nothing to do with anything rational. It doesn't have to do with high pressure around a show. It has to do with some sense of the enormity of what's at hand and a sense of my own inadequacy in the moment to convey it. It has to do with the ways that, as directors, we perform. The challenging part of being a director isn't just knowing the work or being in the moment, it's also knowing the responsibility you have for a group of people. My growth as a director has been about learning to trust myself to freefall. To surrender for and in the presence of others.

A student who went through the directing program at Columbia said to me the most obvious thing I'd ever heard and never thought of. He said that a director, in rehearsal, has to do everything that the actor has to do in front of an audience. You have to be spontaneous, ready to laugh, ready to change.

I ask most of my ensemble in the beginning to work with an open heart. If I had any mantra to kick us off it's the idea that there's a sense of generosity in the room. We can go anywhere, and I am so committed to the notion that I have to practice what I preach and that it does trickle down from the top, and therefore my practice is all about being in the room with an open heart.

How does that relate to people who are not actors? In other words, if you're in a situation with producers . . . I'm interested in that issue of the difference between the commercial and noncommercial.

I've only really had one commercial experience, which was *Bells Are Ringing* on Broadway. I mean, I would love to direct again on Broadway. This is not answering your question, but I would say the big lesson I learned personally is that I am ready and willing to go through the backdoor, but not through the front door if it's on someone else's terms. It was one of my childhood dreams. And it's very odd to achieve at age thirty a goal you decided when you were four. But although I was strong and smart and clear about what I wanted that experience to be, I was really surprised at the end of the day about how much it diffused in ways I didn't even see happening in the moment. It was a watered-down version of where we began. I can't even place to this day when and how that happened exactly.

I remember coming into the rehearsal, and I was so thrilled at the end of it. You had so much freedom and these Broadway singers, dancers, they were having the time of their life. I thought, This is extraordinary. I felt you were born to do this.

There's a little part of me that's still ashamed to say this, because we associate so much of the Broadway commercial world with something that is crass or sellout or about making money. For me, it's about the power to communicate with a lot of people. It's the place in the world where something can run the longest and speak across the world, potentially. And that interests me. It is true that when I was working on Broadway, I used to walk out of the theater every day and feel completely in my element. It was so strange. But it was the same season *Metamorphoses* opened on Broadway—Mary Zimmerman's piece. That to me was that kind of odd mirror image reflection of yourself that you both hate and wish you were at the same time. I remember thinking, Yeah, I want to be here. I want a show that can run, that can have audiences. But I hope I can do that in the future with work that I'm really clear about why and what it is. Mary went about doing her work at Northwestern, and it had a very natural life.

You also have that Gemini thing in that you'll do *Theatrical Essays* in the Garage space at Steppenwolf, which is the opposite impulse of a commercial Broadway musical. What is it, this Gemini issue?

It really does feel like a war inside myself. Steppenwolf asked me about a year ago what project I want to do next on the mainstage. I said, "You know, I don't want to do another slick, ambitious somewhat-successful show that opens and closes and who cares and what's the point of theater anyway?"

When we were talking in Chicago the other day, someone said, "How do you deal with burnout?" You said, "I don't know. I just love what I'm doing." That's one way we're opposite. I go through, "I'm going to quit," at least every six weeks. It comes from this incessant questioning.

The other commercial piece I did do was a piece with Disney that I worked on for about three years. It was called *When You Wish*. It subsequently became something completely different called *On the Record*. But I was originally given the catalogue of Disney music to make a new piece out of. This was pre–jukebox musicals. We developed this thing over three years, did workshops that I am positive cost more than a full production at Steppenwolf. And ultimately, because of all sorts of corporate thorniness around that time and some displeasure at the top, that project never happened. That was 2001. It was the same year I turned forty, and the year of 9/11, obviously. Most people I know went through something extraordinary that year. But those kinds of events were really a wakeup call to me in terms of asking that question of why we do this—*really*. I was running around Chicago, and at U of C they were doing a series, "What Matters to You and Why?" Seeing that plastered all over campus—"What Matters to You and Why"—everywhere I turned I felt the universe was asking me that. And I kept adding the word "really." Thankfully that year I found William Saroyan's play *The Time of Your Life*, which I did at Steppenwolf.

And it toured.

It went to a number of theaters. The paragraph that Saroyan wrote at the beginning, that we actually painted on the theaters, begins with "In the time of your life, live."

You also wrote an amazing piece that you emailed me that you read on the first day of rehearsal. It was one of the most beautiful things I've ever heard.

Well, that's related to my first-day anxiety. The way I've gotten through this is my therapist helped me figure out that it was okay to write everything down. If I got stuck on the first day, I could read it. I woke up that morning of the first day of *The Time of Your Life* and my girlfriend at the time, who was also the dramaturg, came into the room and said, "So, do you have your speech? Are you ready to go?" I said, "Well, I know I'm supposed to be talking about 'Why Saroyan?' And how 1939 parallels today and why it's important. And that's not coming out. Let me read to you what I wrote." And I did that, and she said, "Yes. Read that. It's from the heart." And what I basically said to the cast was that in looking around the room on the first day—instead of feeling like the cheerleader that could answer all its questions as to why and why this now, I was mostly filled with dread. I was tired already at the mere thought of starting this process. Getting older—it's not getting easier for me. It's not like I can just slough it off and I know my bag of tricks. It gets harder with every show because I know what it takes to really go there in making a piece of theater. I said to them, through what I read, that I knew we had to make something actually happen in the theater—that I was really tired of this feeling of going to see plays where nothing actually occurs in the room, on that night, with that audience watching. We always pretend something happened, and it never does. I didn't know how to do it, but if we couldn't all commit to doing that in some fashion, making an event in *The Time of Your Life* live, and being in the room in a present, live moment where something extraordinary occurred, I'd rather stop on the first day. I'd rather go open a shoe store. That's a feeling of being at the end, of burnout. In a way it was the least anything ever mattered to me, because I wasn't thinking about critics and how the show was going to go. And in a way it was the most anything ever mattered to me, because I had no stakes other than knowing that something had to happen.

It's a huge production—a huge ensemble piece and a great American play about issues that we should think about every morning when we wake up: Why are we liv-

ing? But I felt in that piece that the ensemble's brain, led by your brain, met Saroyan's brain. The biggest collisions are the most beautiful pieces of work that you do. The collaboration comes from a kind of collision, and therefore you're not called on to make things happen. You had a careless attitude when you were doing that.

I did. A sense of abandon. But it also matched Saroyan's, in a way. When I read the play for the first time my impression of it was that it reminded me of Chuck Mee. Saroyan wrote a beautiful description of the play where he said, "Let this be like a circus, an opera, a melodrama, a tragedy, a courtroom drama"—and he goes through this list of like thirty kinds of genres. "Anything you wish, anything you can imagine." To be given that kind of blessing—to have the author say to you, "Go anywhere," was such a gift at that time.

One of the moments in that piece that people talked to me a lot about was at the very end of Act One. There's a guy, Joe, the main character, who sits at a table the entire first act. He never stands up. He finally stands up at the end of Act One, and as he was walking out he turned and looked back. All of a sudden for about eight seconds the entire cast that was on stage at the time broke out into a little bit of soft-shoe to "Sunny Side of the Street," and did it in perfect unison on this set that was broken out into the theater, so it was sprawled like one of those murals from the thirties. They tap-danced for a second, and then we went to black. A lot of people said to me, "What was that? That was so amazing." What it came out of was, in rehearsal, I was talking to Jeff Perry, who was playing Joe, and I turned around and Guy Adkins, who was playing one of the characters, said, "Tina, look what just happened." The cast had asked him to teach them how to do this little soft-shoe moment. They said, "We just want to show it to you. Surprise!" And without thinking, I said, "It's in." Honestly it was probably the first time in my life where not a cell in my body thought, Why? What does that mean? Is that dramaturgically correct? Like I had never actually been free until that moment to say, "Because because." It was pure intuition. And that was the kind of abandon that I was working with.

It's interesting that you mention that you compare Saroyan to Chuck Mee, because something that I learned, and that the SITI Company learned, from Chuck Mee and working with him, was that we're so disciplined. We start on time. We work really hard. And if we're not suffering, it's not good. But we started working with Chuck on *bobrauschenbergamerica*, and I'd say, "Chuck, should it be this or this?" And he'd say, "Well, which feels better?" I'd go, "Feel better? I don't know. What do you like?" He'd say, "Well, this one feels good to me. It feels delightful." And it was a contagion that spread in the company. And now we just want to work that way. We just want to be completely happy and do things not because they dramaturgically line up but because they feel good—and to trust that the audience is delighted, just as the audience was delighted with that tap-dance soft-shoe.

As soon as I say this, however, I think: Yes/and. I think: Everything and its opposite. I think: That works *sometimes*—but not necessarily *every* time.

One of the things I've never been so clear about is how Viewpoints has really functioned well for me as part of the "Everything and Its Opposite" philosophy. The SITI Company trains physically but is classically trained and does text work. I was thinking about that with the Saroyan, too—that you work truly with both your head and your heart. It's my Gemini leaning again. I remember Chuck said that once, and I took it as the biggest compliment. He said he thought I was able to work from both my heart and my head equally. Sometimes it does feel like war. But it was a good lesson on the Saroyan to let my heart truly win out.

Audience: I know you, Anne, said you got Viewpoints from Mary Overlie and Tina got Viewpoints from you. Could you talk about differences in approach that you feel Mary Overlie has and that you feel you have?

AB: First of all, and it's important to say: I think there are real inventors and then there are scavengers. Mary Overlie is a real inventor. I'm a scavenger. I look around the room and say, "That's great. That's great. Let's put 'em together." And Mary very deliberately looked around—she was influenced by the Judson Church movement of the late sixties, early seventies—and literally went into a kind of hibernation, asking herself, "What is performance? What is space? What is time?" She came up with what she called the six View Points—two different words in those days. Two of those, story and emotion, we mention in the book as hers, but we don't even use.

She and I got to know each other at NYU where I was teaching in 1979 and 1980. We co-directed a show, and she started showing me what she was doing with the six View Points, and it really knocked my socks off. I found it incredibly, immediately useful to actors and to directors in a way that I didn't see any equivalent in the theater scene. The majority of the theater scene felt really old-fashioned to me. The work that Mary was doing seemed to me to be far more related to breakthroughs in quantum physics, for example.

Now, theater is known to be, throughout its history of its existence, the slowest art form. It always comes last—maybe because it carries so much baggage. It's all of the art forms in one, so it goes slowest. So I was thrilled by the speed of Mary's thinking. Much to her continued simultaneous chagrin and delight, I really took what she was doing and started playing with it and changing it and forgetting what she did and moving in another direction. To this day, that sometimes annoys her and some-

times delights her. I think it's very, very hard for her at times. She said she was in Chicago, I think, and somebody said, "Oh, did you study with Anne?" So this has always been an uncomfortable issue.

I met Anne in 1987 at A.R.T., where I was going to assist someone else and sat in on Anne's first rehearsal for a Kleist play. I barged up to Bob Brustein and said, "I have to be in the room with that woman"—and I was for the next eight years. Watching the training of the SITI Company, I used to bug Anne a lot about things like duration. When we started talking about duration, it really came from watching the company, so adept at so much, and yet there were things that we felt that we could point to and discuss about what was going on in the training that we couldn't quite name yet or talk about. Out of those years and us talking about it, eventually came three additional Viewpoints that we both use now.

Then, after that, we started doing work on what's called vocal Viewpoints. That came out of an interest not so much in text, although it is text-related, but more in the voice as an extension of the body.

One of the differences, I think, in the way we work with the application of Viewpoints has to do, for me, with working with folks like those at Steppenwolf, where sometimes the notion of what you set or at least discuss is the acting beats, the internal life. You do your emotional-relationship-objective homework, but what keeps the work fresh and spontaneous every night is that whether I throw the chair at you or the bottle at you—it's going to change. Perhaps a slight exaggeration, but the point being: You better be on your feet, because something different is going to happen every night. So, while there's an agreement about what needs to go on in the meat of it, the physical behavior is really up for grabs. That creates the danger of the spontaneity.

At the other extreme—sometimes Anne works this way and other people do—is the notion that what you set is the physical life. It's exactly the opposite. You set a physical score whereby that cross happens on that word. That light cue happens on that hand gesture. What remains open is how it's filled every night. It's how you might think of a piece of music or a score, if you were playing the piano. The notes and the meter are the same, but how you fill it and the attack change on a nightly basis. I sort of negotiate on every piece, depending on the material, this very tricky question of what is set and what is left open. I've only recently started incorporating into my work sections that are purposefully designed to be open Viewpoints sections, even if they only last for thirty seconds or a minute. On *Time of Your Life* I did a thing where there was a mural that was being painted on the back wall that started on the first performance and wouldn't be finished until the last performance. I was really trying to open up questions of what can remain authentically open in performance to address this issue of allowing something to actually occur.

AB: I think it's true that whatever your process is, you need to make certain agreements that are like signposts, and there need to be certain things that are free. Because if everything is set—if the emotional life is set, if the physical life is set—it's lifeless. But if nothing is set, then you can't see anything. It's all improvised. Depending on the project, you decide the agreements. The agreements are basically the foundation of any production. They can change per production. It doesn't always have to be the same kinds of agreements. But you come up with a set of agreements, then you bring the chaos of living into that.

Another huge difference in the way Anne and I work with Viewpoints comes simply from the fact that she's working with an ensemble that does the training consistently, if not daily. She's creating material with people who don't need to be trained, but are practicing. It's sort of second nature forming what gets made on stage. For me, Viewpoints is something else because I'm almost always working with some people who have not done the training, and I use the work a lot as an ensemble-building technique.

AB: For the SITI Company it's a way of practicing creating fiction and using time and space on a daily basis. You have to practice, like scales, in a sense. Although what will happen is that we do fifteen minutes of Suzuki training and fifteen minutes of Viewpoints improvisation before any rehearsal and any performance. But sometimes, if we're about to rehearse a scene that is, say, dealing with Restoration comedy, I'll say, "Restoration comedy" for the Viewpoints, and stuff will come up in the Viewpoints training or the Viewpoints improvisation. Somehow the play gets filtered into the improvisation. The mistake I think people make about our work is that they think that we actually improvise to make a play, which we do not. We do not do improvisations. I would go so crazy. I would get so bored. It's essentially a training technique. It informs how people work together.

Also, in response to your question, I really hope there are more people in that line—Mary, Anne, me. I think part of why we wanted to do this book was really as an invitation to say, "Think about it as seriously and long and deeply as we have, and then chuck all this out and find the next four Viewpoints."

AB: I think one of the great innovators in Viewpoints right now is Barney O'Hanlon, a SITI Company member. He's really extended the Viewpoints more than anyone else I know in that direction of constantly reevaluating it.

Audience: Can you talk about your relationship with text and where it lies in the series of agreements? For instance, when you write *Theatrical Essays*, the text doesn't come first necessarily, but when somebody hands you a script and says, "Direct this play," or you pitch a play or you have Chuck's play—where does the text come in in the setting of agreements?

AB: It's a big deal. You know the playwright Romulus Linney? Great playwright. He used to teach at Columbia a long time ago. His second-year playwrights and the second-year directors would do a project together, and at the end of that Romulus and myself and the playwright and the director would sit in a room and talk about how it went. And at one point we were talking about how a piece had gone with this playwright and director. And Romulus said, "After all, the first rule of theater is never move while you're speaking." I said, "Romulus, I've dedicated my life to the relationship of moving and speaking." But actually, he's right. What he means is: "When you're moving I can't hear the lines." He's absolutely right. But what I want to say to Romulus is that if the gesture ends at the end of this word or begins before the word, you can actually use movement as punctuation, as periods, commas, exclamation marks, and actually create the grammar of stage language. Using the Viewpoints can, I think, help do that.

One of the things that really struck me about Viewpoints as I learned about it was this notion of nonhierarchical elements in the theater. The Western theater in particular has been so language-driven and text-based, and the notion Anne and Mary were playing with, as were many people in all the art forms, was: What if we took all the elements that we know make up a performance event—text, language, lights, sound, movement, time, audience, whatever—and instead of lining them up vertically, with text being the most important at the top, we're going to line them up horizontally, or on a circle. I like to think of it as a multiple track recording studio or something. You can say, "We're turning this knob down to point five for this show and this one up to eight." That the hierarchy of what reigns in performance can really be juggled around and switched.

AB: So the knobs are like text, music, emotion.

Well, yeah. You might break up language; and then sound, which is related to music, but it would be separate; light; movement, which can be broken up into a million different elements. You can put anything on there. You can put costumes on there. You can put the seating arrangement of audience—how important is that? The time the show starts. There was a book I read once that listed the key elements as theme, character, spectacle, plot, mood, I think. It was talking about playwrights, and it said, if you look at

Chekhov, what's dominant? You might say mood and character and maybe secondarily theme, but you wouldn't necessarily say plot. But if you're looking at *The Mousetrap*, you'd say plot, maybe. Or if you were looking at Beckett—it's interesting to me.

But, anyway, the point is that, the way I look at it, it's really project-specific. Where the text is in that configuration is really based on what it is and what the project at hand is. I also want to say in regard to *Theatrical Essays*: When they came to me and said, "Do something on the mainstage," I said, "I don't want to direct in a big space. I want to go into the Garage with nothing. Give me six lights and one boom box." We are really, in making composition work, writing on our feet and creating meaning and telling stories and creating events, characters, through light and sound and movement and time and space. In that case, that became the text. The text was an über-three-dimensional text.

Audience: I've seen three SITI shows, and I saw *Time of Your Life* at A.C.T. What struck me about all of those was the actual use of stage and how it's completely open. I saw the wings. I haven't seen that with a lot of other directors. And I'm wondering if you can talk about what you're experimenting with there.

AB: Well, the question is whether you want to represent places or describe places, or create an arena. For example, if a play is written in a living room, you can say, "Do I want to create a living room in which this happens?"—in which case you build a set that looks like somebody's living room. The other way, which leads to sets that you're describing, is where you say, "This is the arena of a living room. What are the most essential aspects of a living room?" You aren't actually representing a space, but you are expressing a space, which is very different. The spacial relationships between objects can change because of the subjective nature of reality. You know, if you walk into a living room in a certain mood, it's spinning around you. So you could create that kind of reality on stage, if that's the expression of the moment—as opposed to locking it into a repetition of something we see in daily life. We want to use a more cubist approach. I like the word "arena" because it makes you think, even though family comes into the arena of the living room, they are gladiators.

My answer is, in a way, much more practical. I've also developed work in spaces that are made of elements that I can use in rehearsal. I cannot bear rehearsing in one place with certain things, then moving into a theater and having all new things. It's that simple. In terms of the "practice what you preach" mode, architecture is one of the Viewpoints. Designers I work with will come in, scour my rehearsal room, and take away anything they don't want to appear in the production. I tend not to have sets that are built elsewhere while we rehearse here. Now, part of this came from early lessons I had with En Garde Arts. That was a site-specific theater company here in New York, where I learned more about the Viewpoint of architecture than I could have possibly dreamed. But when I go into a theater, for me, it's really become about the question of an event that actually occurs. It's like an honesty issue. I've grown fond of the notion of acknowledging where we are—not in a Brechtian way that reminds you every moment. A lot of theater spaces are amazing and architecture is amazing. I always go into a space, and I can start dreaming the piece in that space, and I have really taken to heart the notion that architecture can talk to you and give you stagings and notions and a way of experiencing something that you can't dream alone with a set designer looking at a little box.

AB: In that spirit, for the SITI Company there is the issue of touring, because our bread and butter is touring, nationally and internationally. You don't want to go into a space and say, "This space doesn't exist. I'm going to put my set inside of it." You want to create a design that can adjust to whatever space you go into, in the sense that Tina's talking about, and saying, "It really feels different in here, what the audience's relationship is to the actors is very different. So how do we adjust the elements that we have and keep the spirit of the piece?"

It's really the heart of Viewpoints, which is how to work with what's actually there rather than what you wish would be there or impose on being there.

Audience: Since the space seems to be such a big component of your performance work—have you ever been invited to direct a work in a space that you didn't feel was going to work? And then what do you do about that?

Gosh. Have you? I don't know that I have.

AB: But I think that's against the spirit of Viewpoints.

Well, I'll tell you a little story. It's not a production. But it's a Viewpoints story. I went to teach the first day of Viewpoints one summer at the Steppenwolf school. I walked in and I was in a really bad mood because *Bells Are Ringing* had closed the night before on Broadway, and I was foul, and it was eight o'clock in the morning and I didn't want to be there. I walked in, and they had put me in this room that was the lobby of the Garage Theatre at Steppenwolf where they had put up velours with paintings hanging on the velours that they were showing as part of an art exhibit. I said to the guy who was running the program, "You have got to be kidding me. I cannot work this way. Viewpoints cannot occur in here." It was like walking into a theater and saying, "I cannot do my show here." I said, "You have to leave right now and find me an alternate space." And he scampered out. And I sat down and looked at the students and said, "All right. What do you guys want to do?" They were like, "Well, it's only our second day here, and we talked a lot yesterday, and we're really looking forward to getting on our feet and moving today and it's a little cold this morning." They were all kind of looking at me. And I thought, I cannot sit here for the next six weeks and talk about working with what you have and what you are given and say, "But I can't work in this space." And so I said, "All right. Let's get up on our feet." And we did an extraordinary Viewpoints session in the twenty-foot space with the velours and the art, and we made something of it. I can't think of a parallel situation in the theater. I think the reason I probably can't is because—

AB: It's against the philosophy of Viewpoints.

If it's wrong and small and bad and unheated and uncomfortable, then we'll make something of that.

AB: Last week, somebody asked me, "What do you do if you're working with a group of actors and they don't want to do this Viewpoints thing?" I found myself telling this story: When I was in my twenties I had a job in a halfway house. It was for people who had schizophrenic breakouts, who were not well enough to be out on the streets, but were also not sick enough to be in the hospital. They were on a lot of drugs, and my job was to give theater workshops. When I got the job I was really excited. I was like, "I'm going to go in and do a lot of physical stuff. Run in circles. Chase around. Really physical stuff." And I was excited. So I went in and there were about eight people in the room, and I started with this physical stuff. And they hated it. They really were not into it. So the next week I went back to teach, and there were like three people there. And I tried again. Physical stuff. And they hated it. Next time I came back there were two people. I thought, This is not working. So I said to the two people who were there, "Well, what do you want to do?" And they said, "Musical comedy." I said, "You know, I don't really know much about musical comedy. Can you show me?" So they said, "Yeah," and they got up. The next week I came back and there was like seven people there. We did this musical comedy stuff. The next week I came back there was like twenty. And the next week, forty, I swear to God. They had to change us and put us in a huge room, and there were mats on the floor. This one guy was way puffy because of too many drugs. He came every week and just slept. One day he stood up in the middle of an improvisation

and just entered it. Unbelievably creative people. It was amazing. I had to follow it. I had to follow what was happening. I learned so much.

Now I think that's Viewpoints. It's not making people do spacial relationship or run in circles or anything like that. I think it's in what Tina's saying about your space question. To me, the heart is when you ask, and always ask, "What is it? What is it really?" And now I find myself having to say, "What is Viewpoints really?" It's about working with what you have, being present and listening.

It's so interesting because I definitely started doing Viewpoints as a technique for helping me make theater. These days Viewpoints are really teaching me how I want to live. It's amazing. Who knew that would happen? Thanks, Anne.

AB: Thanks, Mary.

Thanks, God. Or whatever you understand That to be.

Audience: I sometimes feel like small artistic disagreements can seem like huge chasms between people. How do you deal with that over the long term—you know, when you're working with people for, like fifteen years? When do you put in your feet? When do you compromise?

AB: Well, it's a way of thinking. In other words, if I had an idea and I presented it, if the actors or the designers said, "Okay," and did that, nothing would happen to it. Everything I put out, the other person's job is to disagree a little bit. It sounds like you're talking about a disagreement to the point where things shut down. Many of you probably know Morgan Jenness. She was a dramaturg. She is now a literary agent. She was Joe Papp's assistant for years. She's somehow at the heart of everything that happens in the theater. Since I've known her—I've known her twenty-five years—she's always walking around with a stack of plays. She's reading everybody's plays. She's always going to meet her playwrights. I asked her once, "How do you read so many plays? I can't read one." It's so hard to read a play. It's an investment of imagination unlike any other literature. It's hard. She said, "Well, what I do is I read very quickly, and when I feel that the play stops moving, I turn over the page, the corner of the page, and I keep reading." And then when she meets with the playwright, she'll sit down and open the play up to the pages that are turned over and discuss why the play stopped moving.

I think it addresses your question. If things stop, then you've really got to work differently—if the disagreement stops the process. You actually have to become incredibly sensitive in your sinews to the moments when things stop moving in rehearsal. So, what I would suggest is whenever that happens, give up your idea for the other one. Always. Ideas are cheap. They're the cheapest things we have. We tend to think that ideas are the reason that we're in the room. But you know, as Picasso said, you paint the first stroke on the canvas and all the rest of your work is to correct that mistake. That stroke is going to be a mistake anyway. So it doesn't really matter which idea you choose. It's how you handle it and develop it. I would say get very sensitive to the moment it stops, then go somewhere else. And if somebody has an idea that they feel strongly about—God bless 'em! That means they have ownership, which is a commodity much more precious than an idea.

In terms of the Viewpoints and in terms of the notion of the first stroke—and this seems so simple and stupid, but it's very radical—many directors think that their job is to make the first stroke on the canvas. What if you say, "No." What if the actor makes the first stroke? And I think that's the heart of the Viewpoints. They're responsible for making a choice. And then the director responds to that. You adjust, you adjust, you adjust. So who starts first? Why should it not be an actor? I think the result has more ownership ultimately, and it's not about who has a better idea anyway. That's, I think, something Viewpoints is about, which is saying: The person on stage makes the choice.

Audience: I'm curious about your anxiety and your research—like what you're actually bringing to that first rehearsal. Are you the kind of person who will cram your brain full of research? Does that make you more nervous? Does that shut you down? Does that help you?

The thing I've found that has really worked for me is a notion of being prepared, in order to forget—to fill up to an extent that you feel comfortable and not like you're a fake or unprepared, and then really trust it enough to let it go. In a way, it's the same thing we ask actors to do—to come in with something, and then be open to what changes. That actually requires a kind of confidence.

I will admit that I no longer do classic, old-fashioned, read-the-play research. I just don't. I don't want to say I don't read the play—because it's not quite that extreme—but sometimes it's close. I'm about to do *A Midsummer Night's Dream* at McCarter and Papermill with this rock band, GrooveLily, and what I have been doing in the past several weeks is reading about every other production of *Midsummer* that has ever been done on the planet, and I have to tell you, it is really inspiring me. I'm understanding context in a way that I never thought about before—what it means to be in dialogue over time with other artists that might not even be alive.

I tend to do a lot of visual things. In the last several years I've started painting and making collages like crazy. I bring those in and I plaster them all over the walls. I'd say, mostly, collage and music are where I go—so what I'm coming in with is not the details of the staging or the blocking or how the scene is broken down, but a pile of toys and mud for people to play and swim around in.

Audience: Where do you begin when you have basically just the embryo of a project that doesn't yet have a script? Do you start with the ensemble? That seems like one of those tasks that there's so much, it becomes very daunting.

A number of pieces I've done—a musical called *States of Independence*, the musical *Floyd Collins*, the play *Space*, *Dream True*—all started by walking into a room with a group of people and saying, "I know one word." In the case of *Space* it was "space." Fortunately I have found, in this country at this time, even without a company, there are a lot of opportunities. My mother used to say to me, "Work begets work. Just work." I never really bought it. What I bought instead was: "Do the kind of work you want to get hired for next. Only do what you want to do a year from now." There's no such thing as, "I'm doing this now, but really later . . . ." I found as soon as I started doing that kind of work, I discovered a million opportunities. I've done a lot of projects where I've gotten a group of people, started with a word, done composition work, research, Viewpoints, other things, let it go for a little while, come back and done the next step with another group of people, often through universities—and ultimately developed full-length projects. That's my way of saying: "Do it."

AB: I do it very differently. I spend a huge amount of time doing research and I'll usually come in with about one hundred fifty pages of possible text that I've sampled, and I'll talk for about two days about every idea I've possibly had. I talk a lot. I upload everything, every thought, every notion, every stupid idea, so then it's in the common culture. Some of the things I say on the first day come back in tech to surprise us all. They've somehow gone into the unconscious and they come up at a very fruitful moment. I find it really important to spend a couple of years researching a project if it's an original piece—really living with it. Not that it's the only thing I'm working on, but collecting, so I feel like my image is: I come in with everything, I dump it on the table and say, "It's yours. Now we'll make it come together." I also feel that my job is to describe the world in which the play takes place, whether it's an original piece, devised piece or a classical play. That's basically what I do. I describe it as much as I can, then we see what happens to that. But I have to imagine a world that the actors feel they can inhabit as actors and as characters. Sometimes it's really crazy. With *La Dispute* I said, "I think everybody's a bird."

Audience: I was surprised to hear you say that you felt like quitting every six weeks. I'm an actor, not a director. I feel like quitting every second day. I've always assumed

that you get to a certain point and you don't do that anymore. You just think, I'm getting what I want to do consistently.

I love it so much that it hurts sometimes. Making something, having it judged, having it evaporate. I can't go see theater. I hate going. Someone really got on me about that the other day. And I said, "Well, I'll go see *great* things." I can't go because there's so much that is upsetting to me. I often feel that I live on another planet—"This is what people are responding to?" So feeling like quitting really comes out of this. It has nothing to do with, "Can I make a living at it?" or "I'm discouraged career-wise." It's about longing for connection. Whether or not you're being true and brave, and then whether or not you're being heard and understood. I think of it like Kierkegaard—in *Fear and Trembling* what he describes as "the leap of faith." In that book he uses Abraham having to kill his own son as an example. But when he talks about the leap of faith, he also references dancers, actually, and what it feels like to be in the air and to be in that moment where you know you're going up and you don't know what's under your feet or where you're going to land or how you're going to land. In this lifetime I want to somehow feel like I was a citizen of the world, so I sometimes question what it means to do things in little black boxes for all my little friends who come to all my same plays. I go through that a lot. I go to a place of just questioning what theater is in this day and age and how we're speaking to people. I feel like the monks who did the illuminated manuscripts—the monks, trying to keep a thing alive.

I was thinking about *Midsummer*. Part of me wants to embrace the elements—water and earth and do it all by candlelight, only people on stage. Another part of me wants to do the music video, cyber, hyperlink version. One slows the world down, the other *is* the world. You were talking the other day about tempo in the theater, and how important it is to work with a certain extended time in the theater while the world goes fast like this. And as you were talking, I was thinking, No. The world is going fast like *this*. So why aren't we going fast like this to express it and riff with it? No wonder no one's coming. I'm just being devil's advocate. I go back and forth between the two frequently. It's these kinds of questions that keepe me wondering. And these questions never go away: Why do I do this? For whom? To what end? As long as these questions remain, you remain in midair like that dancer of Kierkegaard's—having taken a leap but not knowing if or how you'll land.

Oskar Eustis

first met Oskar when he was still a teenager. I was already in my mid-twenties. We participated in a workshop conducted by the Iowa Theater Lab in a small space above Playwrights Horizons led by the visionary director Ric Zank. Already an outstanding intellect and person-in-the-world, Oskar had, by the mid-seventies, moved to New York City from Minneapolis and founded a theater company, Red Wing, with his friend the remarkable Swiss dramaturg Stephan Müller. A couple of years later, he and Stephan left New York to take their act to Switzerland. They opened an experimental wing at the Zurich Schauspielhaus and conducted highly successful workshops throughout the German-speaking world. I missed Oskar mightily when he left. He did not return full-time to New York City until almost thirty years later when he became the artistic director of the Public Theater/New York Shakespeare Festival. But in my mind he had been circling the building on Lafayette Street the entire time he was away.

Recently I was standing in front of City Hall in downtown Manhattan. I looked up and saw a vision: Oskar riding a bicycle down Centre Street in my direction, a cigar firmly between his lips. When he saw me he pulled to a stop and explained that he was on his way home across the Brooklyn Bridge. Of course he was. What a perfect expression of his physicality, bravado and practical sense.

I have always been in awe of Oskar. How did he become so erudite without ever attending university? How does he instill such confidence and ease in everyone he commiserates with? How does he function so emphatically and intelligently and with such infinite humanity in the world? He is a brilliant public speaker, a socialist, a political animal, tremendously empathetic and humane. He has big plans for the Shakespeare Festival, and I hope with all my heart that he can achieve them. If anyone can, it would be Oskar.

During Oskar's return visits to the States from Switzerland, he headed to San Francisco and began a long-term relationship with the Eureka Theatre Company, eventually becoming its artistic director from 1986 until 1989, when he moved on to the Mark Taper Forum as associate artistic director. In 1994 he became the artistic director of Trinity Repertory Company in Providence, Rhode Island, and finally, ten years later, he landed at the Public Theater/New York Shakespeare Festival to take the reins of an institution with a substantial reputation and history. Oskar is in the habit of filling very big shoes.

Perhaps the most remarkable achievement of Oskar's is his support and encouragement of playwrights. He contributed and continues to contribute to the trajectories of Tony Kushner, Emily Mann, Susan-Lori Parks, David Henry Hwang, Craig Lucas, Anna Deavere Smith, Paula Vogel, and the list goes on.

December 7, 2005

AB: Oskar Eustis has an extraordinary life story. He's been an institution-builder from New York to San Francisco, Zurich, kind of a builder in Los Angeles, Providence and now back in New York. I want to discuss where he's going right now with the Public Theater. Oskar's work with playwrights, with Tony Kushner and many, many others, is amazing. His family is communist. Oskar does not have a bachelor's degree. He has a high school diploma. Is that true now? You have honorary degrees.

OE: I claim to have a high school diploma, but my high school shut down the year after I left it, so maybe I should prove it.

He's also the most well-read person I know. We've known each other for thirty years. Could we start with your background—Minnesota, New York.

My stepfather and mother are members of the Communist Party, my stepfather for three generations. My folks divorced in the sixties and as part of the ferment around everything that was happening in the late sixties—including the antiwar movement, which was really central in my life, and the civil rights movement—was the peculiar way that artistic radicalism, lifestyle radicalism and political radicalism all had these incredibly blurry boundaries and seemed to flow into one another. We had a belief that—the collective we, those of us who felt ourselves progressive in that time, living in that community—there was no distinction between being in an avant-garde theater event and being against the war and living in a commune and building socialism. It was all the sense that the world was transforming massively and we were part of it. It was an incredibly exciting time—and an incredibly silly time. It was very interesting for me coming from essentially the most puritanical, rigid wing of that. My mother joined the party, a very distinct part of that movement, and the party became central to her life and the family's life. I embraced it and rebelled against it by running away and joining the avant-garde. Thirty years ago, I followed the Performance Group into town and lived at the Performing Garage in New York. It was a heady, extraordinary and, again, profoundly silly time.

You started a theater company called Red Wing. You were how old when you started it?
Sixteen.

When I met him, he was sixteen.
A very old sixteen.

In New York. Living in a theater.
And getting scabies. It took about two months to get rid of them. But what happened during that time is that everyone sort of bought into the idea of the avant-garde. The avant-garde is very broad and there was a lot of fighting within it at the time, but the spectrum ranged from Charlie Ludlum to Robert Wilson, from the Performance Group to Richard Foreman, from Mabou Mines to the San Francisco Mime Troupe. It was all sort of in the realm of experimental, ensemble, avant-garde theater that I found myself right in the middle of and bought hook, line and sinker. I founded the Red Wing company with my friend and colleague Stephan Müller, who's a Swiss director who I'm still close to. After working in New York for a while, we went out to San Francisco, where the company was in residence at the Eureka Theatre. Robert Woodruff ran the Eureka at that time and brought us in. This was the fall of 1977. And then Stephan brought in some people he knew from the German–speaking theater landscape who hired us to come to Schauspielhaus in Zurich and found an experimental second stage.

So, at the age of nineteen, I was suddenly in Zurich, running this experimental second stage for the largest of the state theaters and really sort of running out the string on something I had been doing since I left home. I had a huge crisis of conscience because what finally caught up to me in my time in Zurich was the contradiction between what I was doing aesthetically and what I believed politically. That contradiction really hit me like a ton of bricks. We were actually very successful in Zurich. It was all going very well—and yet, it felt terrible to me. The audience was appreciating us, I think. They were coming. The critics were writing nice things about us. And the Schauspielhaus seemed to love us. And I didn't believe for a second that we were actually communicating anything of value to that audience. I didn't know who that audience was. The analogy that I used is: At the Basel Zoo in Switzerland, there is, in the middle of the African veld exhibit, a little grass hut. Until 1959, they had Africans living in the hut. This is true. This is a country where women didn't get to vote until 1971. Underneath its pacifism there is a river of conservatism in the Swiss psyche that is so deep. What I realized is that in a certain way this audience was viewing us—and I'm exaggerating to make the analogy, but not entirely—as anthropological. We were an exciting, exotic thing that had been bought from America—because we were paid an obscene amount of money to do these exciting, exotic things. And I realized this is the definition of decadence. I was doing something that pretended to be a work of art, pretended to be a communicative device between an audience and an artist, but really was a consumer experience. We were creating a commodity that pretended to challenge the identity of the audience, but its actual function was to totally reinforce the identity of the audience.

There's a wonderful essay I read at the time by Roland Barthes called "Whose Theater? Whose Avant-garde?" that he'd written in the fifties. His point is that there's a very specific kind of avant-garde that seems to challenge bourgeois conventions, but whose actual function is to utterly support those conventions by supporting the high art mantle and therefore reifying the entire social structure. We all know this experience because we participate in it in certain ways. We like being part of the in-crowd. We like feeling like we understand what is going on in performance to the exclusion of others, the sense that understanding something that other people don't understand is a way of reaffirming our specialness. We get it. They don't. That makes us special. We may be poor, but we're special because we get it and they don't. Some of us may be very rich, but we get it and they don't—and that makes us *very* special. And then what happens is that the art form becomes not just a commodity experience—it becomes a socializing experience in the worst possible way. It is a form of exclusionary club membership, and it becomes a badge that you can wear to differentiate yourself from the others—the general public. You can call them the bourgeoisie, but what you really mean is you're defining yourself as the elite in some way. And as this idea became clearer to me, it was morally repugnant.

I remember there was a terribly specific event. I had a subscription to what was then called *yale/theatre* magazine. I spent the Christmas of 1978 in Berlin, East Berlin, and I had a copy of this and I read an article by Joan Holden, who was the lead writer of the San Francisco Mime Troupe. The opening sentence of that article is, "We are a theater that does not despise its audience." And I burst into tears. Because I realized that action and that anger—despising and defensiveness toward my audience—was actually at the root of what was fueling my work here and that was wrong.

You know, that really explains something to me, which I've been puzzling about for many, many years. I've always been impressed by something you said years and years ago. You came here at the age of sixteen—and we were part of something together where every Sunday we did workshops at 123 Prince Street, which somehow you and Stephan got into for free. The theater community, friends of ours, would come and go and we would do workshops and then talk and eat. When you left and went to Europe and really had a lot of success there, at a certain point the question became about whether you would come back to New York. You said to me that if you came back—you didn't say it would be too soon, but you said you would be too accepted. I think it's actually a little profound. You needed to go to a place where you would not be considered too good too soon. It's why I celebrated when you were appointed at the Public. I thought, This is destiny. This is what's supposed to happen. And I feel like, as your friend and someone who has been watching you over the years, that you have circled this position at the Public, waited for a time that was ripe, waited to come back to New York and make a big splash. It has to do with what you just said—that you can have an effect without actually having a real relationship with the audience. You can be accepted without creating a link. And I think you have come to the Public Theater at the exact right moment.

After Zurich you went to San Francisco. You created quite a body of work there, at the Eureka.

I appreciate your mining that. The way I put it, sort of stupidly, was that I tore up my passport to the avant-garde, and I didn't know how to be in New York without being part of that. I needed to change. I needed to be different. I went to San Francisco partly because it was beautiful and partly because we'd had a really successful time there at the Eureka. I thought I might actually be able to make a second home there. At this point it was no longer being run by Woodruff. Tony Taccone and Richard White were running it. I walked in and said, "You guys don't know me, but I was here a few years back. I'm going to work here." I had enough money saved up from my Swiss francs that I could do that for a couple of years. Then, as now, when you show up as free labor at a theater company, it's a very powerful thing. They start to think you're a lot smarter than you are. Your goal is to make yourself indispensable so by the time your money runs out they have to pay you something because they can't afford to not have you.

The interesting part of it for me was that I knew I couldn't do what I was doing, but I didn't know what to do instead. Almost by chance I was able to start reinventing myself as a dramaturg at the Eureka. There were sort of two different traditions that I was combining. One was what I experienced in the German-speaking world, from what I was seeing and learning of what the great dramaturgs did—what Hermann Beil did with Claus Peymann, what Dieter Sturm did with Peter Stein. The great dramaturgs of European theater provided not only the research and academic and literary basis for work, but a theoretical basis for the work. They were responsible for helping you carve out the idea of their respective theaters—why that theater deserved to exist.

When I was over there I got to see the last performance that Peymann did at Stuttgart. Claus Peymann is one of the great directors of the German-speaking landscape, and he had formed a company in Stuttgart that was one of the premier companies in the world. Their sort of signature production was a *Faust* in which they used only German popular theater forms—everything from public plays to the mystery plays to carnival to take this masterpiece of the German enlightenment and create this brilliant, wonderful show. But what he'd also done—this was 1976—was put a note up on the green-room board trying to raise money for Ulrike Meinhof's dental work. Ulrike Meinhof was one of the leaders of the Red Army, the Baader-Meinhof gang, and was locked up in a windowless cell somewhere for being a terrorist, and her teeth were rotting out, and somehow Peymann heard about this and was trying to raise money and get her dental work done. Well, this gets out, there's a fiery debate and Peymann is fired. Whereupon everybody in the theater—these German state-theater companies are big, so it was an acting company of seventy-five and an administrative and production crew of about four hundred fifty—all quit en masse. The entire company resigned. Then the city of Bochum hired all of them (Bochum already had a resident company, and they all got fired, but that's . . . there's always bloodletting in a revolution). And this night that I got to go see *Faust* was the last night that Peymann performed in Stuttgart. It was eight hours, and of course there's a huge standing ovation at the end. They came out and bowed, and the standing ovation kept going, and they came back. Fifteen minutes in, it started to get kind of chaotic because nobody knew what to do. The standing ovation showed no signs of diminishing. The staff of the theater started piling up on stage. Peymann got up on stage. Everybody who worked at the theater came out. The standing ovation kept going—thirty minutes. There was no stopping. At this point, everybody standing on stage has collapsed, bawling. I felt like I was present for a city thanking the artists for what they had done for that city. It was the most moving thing I've ever seen ever. It was astonishing. That's the aliveness that's possible. It's not easy, but it's possible to make a theater that's that indispensable to people.

So that's one tradition. The other tradition that was shared by almost all the avant-garde, from Mabou Mines to the Performance Group to Richard Foreman, Robert Wilson, was the certainty that, whatever their aesthetic differences were, the era of the playwright was over. The playwright might be over because it was the era of the director or the era of media or it was an era of collective creation—but what everybody was sure of was that the playwright was a literary dinosaur left over from the pre-interesting days of the theater. In this brave, new world the playwright, if they existed at all, would be a minor and secondary figure to the other auteurs of the theater. My realization—it's abstruse—was that that can't be true. At this point I was heavily influenced by the English playwrights of the early-mid-seventies: David Hare, Caryl Churchill, Howard Barker, David Edgar—the second wave of political British playwrights. However different, however devised, only when the playwright was somehow present did I feel that you could get the combination of ideas and feelings and thoughts and experience that could actually reach an audience with ideas that were sharp enough to actually affect their minds and change them. It could be wrong, but that's what I felt.

Part of that was also saying narrative is actually fundamental to the theater because stories are the great equalizer. Stories are the thing that you don't need an education to understand; you don't need an avant-garde passport; you don't need an aesthetic license to understand what happened next and "once upon a time." That is the astonishing achievement of Shakespeare. With Shakespeare, what's different is that he wrote for the most educationally diverse audience that had been in existence in the Western world since the Greeks. That was the last time you got everybody in the city sitting there at the same moment—from the illiterate groundlings to the aristocracy watching the play at the same time, all demanding to be entertained at the same moment. It's not Shakespeare that created that audience. It's that audience that created Shakespeare. That audience demanded writing that would speak to all of them at once. You could go another step and say it was also because he had a resident company of actors to write for, but that's a different story.

All of this is a way of saying that I became convinced that I had to return to the playwright, which was something that had not been central to my work for years, in order to achieve politically and socially what I felt I needed to achieve.

You were really affected by Heiner Müller, weren't you?

Well, you know, I admired him. I got to know him a bit. He was an unbelievably interesting and powerful man, but I didn't do any Müller until

I came back. And then I found there was not a great love for Heiner Müller in the United States. It was hard to figure out how to make Müller communicate in America. When I did finally produce the American premiere of a play of his called *The Horation* in San Francisco, I went back to Europe, and, in one of his famous late-night drinking sessions, two bottles of vodka vanished. At this point I was an old man of twenty-one or twenty-two, and I was patiently explaining to Heiner that we were going to produce his play in America and, of course, being an American I didn't have the cynical worldview that he had. I said, "Here's what's going to happen with my production." I wrote on the back of an envelope. "This line is the line of your play."—Big Arrow—"My production will parallel your play, but then at the end it's going to lift away from it and create a distance from it, because I don't believe in your cynical, dark, depressing thing, but in hope and change." He's actually an unbelievably sweet man. He said, "But you left one thing out of your line." I said, "What's that?" And he took my pen—and at this point, you can imagine, we had the straight line and the curved line going up—and he drew a series of wavy lines from the top to the bottom. He said, "That needs to be in your drawing, too." I said, "What's that?" He said, "That's your blood dripping across the page." Suddenly I felt like a very young man from Minnesota.

So I came back and announced to San Francisco that I was a dramaturg and nobody ever asked where I got my degree from, so I started working with playwrights, which I do to this day.

How long were you in San Francisco before you became the artistic director of the Eureka? You went, and then you were free labor for a while, then suddenly you were the boss.

No, I wasn't the boss. I was part of a group. They eventually called me the artistic director, probably after about five years, but it was always a very egalitarian—painfully so—group of directors and actors: Tony Taccone, Richard Seyd, Susan Marsden, Jeff King, Lorri Holt, Abigail van Alyn and Sigrid Wurschmidt, who has since died. It was really that collective group.

During the time there you commissioned *Angels in America*. You had a lot to do with its development. What other plays you did you do at Eureka?

There were six to ten shows a year, so there were an awful lot of things we did that were already written. We did all of Caryl Churchill's work on the West Coast for the first time. We developed a very close relationship with her; with David Edgar, a wonderful and still underestimated writer; Trevor Griffiths. We translated a bunch of Franz Kroetz's plays. We did a number of Dario Fo's later works. Those were the writers who were mainstays—the European writers. I worked with Emily Mann for several years on a play called *Execution of Justice*, which we also commissioned, about the murders of George Moscone and Harvey Milk.

Why did you leave San Francisco? I mean, here was this theater that people were passionate about. It was very different than when you came. It was a stridently political and yet artistic home for a lot of writers and actors and artists of all kinds. And yet you left. And I think in your leaving, it fell apart. Am I being too brutal to say that, do you think?

Yes. I think it would have fallen apart if I'd stayed. I think two things happened. The first was completely personal. I expect most people in the room have experiences like this. That particular group of people had been together for a decade—an incredibly productive decade. It was coming to an end. It was shaking up. The sort of crucial moment was when Sigrid Wurschmidt, an actress in the company to whom the *Angels* antimigratory epistle is dedicated, was diagnosed with breast cancer. It was the day we were performing [Tony's] *A Bright Room Called Day*. It was the only show we canceled. Sigrid went through three years of struggle before she died. But one of the things that was revealed is that she was the only person that everybody in the company liked. You know how it is with groups. There's somebody who's the glue, somebody who is the emotional center of it. It's not that we all hated each other. It's just that Sigrid was the one we all believed in and who made the connections between us and who softened all of the conflict. And when she got sick, she withdrew. Then our managing director died of breast cancer. To be in San Francisco in the middle of the eighties and to be sort of in the center of the plague and suddenly to have two women in your company die of breast cancer, it felt like God was laughing, and it was awful.

The second thing was an analytical thing. I made a choice, which I still stand behind, which was that at the Eureka basically, in addition to what we were doing artistically, institutionally we were part of a movement which I would now characterize as trying to institutionalize the counterculture. There was a wave of theaters, there was Wisdom Bridge and Victory Gardens in Chicago; Empty Space in Seattle; LATC down in Los Angeles. There were a bunch of theaters all founded essentially in opposition to the dominant not-for-profit regional theaters in the community. Usually we were leftier than they were; usually we were more avant-garde; usually we wanted younger audiences. What we were trying to do was say, "All right. There's room in the American theater landscape for another LORT theater in San Francisco that is the countercultural theater as opposed to Berkeley

Rep and American Conservatory Theater." I think that failed, and I moved on. It was absolutely an intellectual decision in 1989 for me to say, "That isn't going to work. There isn't enough mandate in this culture to form permanent institutions that are analogous to those other institutions, that exist in opposition to them." There is in some European countries. There isn't here, at least outside of New York. So, the job is to take over those institutions. The job isn't to form new ones. The job is to move our agenda and our bodies into the motherships. So, I went to the Taper [the Mark Taper Forum in Los Angeles]. Tony Taccone went to Berkeley Rep, and then I went to Trinity with exactly the same impulse. What I said at the time was, "It's time to go to theaters with fountains in front of them." It just felt to me that for the particular agenda that we had, this was the route to success. I still actually believe that, and it's obviously true for me personally. One of the things that is interesting to me in watching the younger generation form theater companies is that I feel that there's not that same institutionalizing impulse. We were all trying to get subscription bases and find audiences, and now the younger theater companies that are forming are much more entrepreneurial, much more project-to-project, much more fluid. That organizational model feels to me like a much smarter and realer organizational model than trying to become the dinosaurs that we were at the Eureka.

A couple of months ago you wrote an article in the *Village Voice*. I wept. One of the things that made me so emotional in reading it is that you have the balls to actually say the words that need to be said, that people aren't saying. Like: Free theater for everyone. I mean, this is insane, right? I wonder if you could talk about the impulse behind that article and describe a little bit about what you're doing.

It seems to me that one of the things that we obviously have to look at is audience. If you look across the country, one of the trends that's happening at the institutional theaters—and I think most of the institutions would admit this—is that essentially the number of audiences have been on a slight decrease for a number of years now. Theaters are sustaining themselves by getting more dollars per audience member. Essentially what is happening is the beginning of a process that I think is really terrifying if you follow it through to the end, which is to say, "It's all right if fewer people come as long as those who come give us more money." And that of course is not utterly alien to the Public Theater downtown, having top ticket prices that are pushing fifty bucks and an average ticket price of around thirty bucks. This was called the Public Theater partially because it's in a public library building and partially because Joe taught himself English—apocryphally, but sort of true—in the public libraries from reading Shakespeare. Part of the idea behind that theater was always that theater should be provided to the citizenry by the public the same way it provides books. Go in and check it out. That's what Joe did in the park for free, obviously, famously. I was here for the fiftieth anniversary and yanked up this speech that George C. Scott gave to the city council in 1968 in which he says, I'm sure somewhat to Joe's surprise, that it's the goal of the Public Theater to give away all of its seats free all of the time, downtown as well as in the park. I just said, "Well, why not?" Look at what happens in the park. In the summer I get completely romanticized about it. The lines that line up at the park, and then you sit in the theater and the audience is younger than any audience for Shakespeare anywhere in the country. It's more economically diverse. It's more racially diverse than any audience for Shakespeare—practically for any theater. And eighteen hundred seats a night and there isn't an empty seat all summer. And that audience is also unbelievably excited to be there because, of course, they've waited in line to get those seats. The one bad performance night all summer was the big benefit gala—the night nobody had to wait in line.

What is that?

It's the desire to be there. It's the desire to get in. Everyone in theater has heard some marketing person or consultant say that people don't value what they don't pay for, so you have to charge them for it or they won't value it. Bullshit! Fifty years in the park! Bullshit! No, I'm serious. These people are valuing this event *way* more than the people who are paying for it—way more than the audiences at some of my sister theaters around town, whom I adore and love. Young people don't go to the theater. It's not about economic barriers? Oh yeah? You remove the economic barriers, they all show up!

Well, okay, then you start to think and, you know, again, this is me speaking. This is not the policy of the Public Theater. We are engaged in a long-range planning process and we'll see what comes out of it. One of the things that you can do economically is bemoan the fact that we have all these spaces that are so tiny. The biggest theater at the Public is smaller than our smallest theater in Rhode Island. It's two hundred ninety-nine seats. How the heck can you ever make an economically profitable transaction? You have to transfer things commercially to make money off them. *A Chorus Line* becomes not this rare, isolated gift that endows the theater. It becomes a business plan. But wait a minute. This is a lousy business plan for a not-for-profit, just like it's a lousy business plan for most commercial theater producers. We all know that commercial theater producing is not a sensible business. And certainly not what you've got in a not-for-profit mission.

And so, okay, what are you going to do? A thought that was floated at one point is that you redesign the Public so you get a five hundred-seat theater.

Audience: Joe wasn't crazy when he went to Lincoln Center. It may not have worked the way he envisioned, but he knew what he was going to do with that.

But nor was he crazy when he turned his back on it and gave it up. And he gave it up specifically because when *A Chorus Line* hit he said, "The money we're making on *A Chorus Line* shouldn't be used to subsidize the kind of work that I have to do at Lincoln Center. It should be used to subsidize the kind of work I do at the Public." So the size of those theaters is not necessarily something to aim for. Maybe the small size is an advantage. We don't make any money at the Public. We can't make any money. We sell out all the tickets and we don't make any money. We're losing bucketloads of money. So what if instead of trying to transfer shows—which everyone else is doing—we said: "No, we're going to hold down the not-for-profit fort with intensity and say, 'Not only are we not-for-profit, we're like majorly not-for-profit.' We're going to give up the idea of earned revenue." The Guthrie Theater in Minneapolis right now has an endowment of about sixty million dollars. We have an endowment of about eighteen million dollars left over after various problems. It would require an additional thirty-million-dollar endowment to entirely replace the earned revenue of the Public's earned box-office last season. One good campaign for an endowment and you've replaced funds annually—not once, but for every year in perpetuity. Suddenly the amount of those campaign dollars seems kind of small. What are they going to spend on renovating Lincoln Center? Seven hundred and fifty million dollars?

Audience: Or building a performing arts center at the World Trade Center site.

Right. It's tiny. It's a drop in the bucket. And you don't actually have to replace all the earned income because: "I'm sorry, I can't wait in line. My life does not allow me to wait in line." And we shouldn't actually prohibit people whose lives for various reasons don't allow them to wait in line, but who do have some money, from seeing the show. So, okay, do a membership. Somebody pays two hundred fifty bucks. They're a member. We reserve twenty-five percent of the seats of the theater and they can call up and get them. That still means that we've given away seventy-five percent. And of course this is what we do in the park. We took some flak in the press for this about eighteen months ago, but in reality this is what has always been done since the Delacorte was built. There's been no change. The only thing is that we made the programs public, so that people can actually call up and join them, as opposed to them being private deals. Always about twenty-five percent of the seats in the park have gone to donors. And, you know what? I don't care. That's good. Because those donors are who let us give it free to everybody else. So on any given night in the park we'll have three hundred seats that may have had money attached to them at some point. But you have fifteen hundred people who stood in line to get in for free. That's a pretty good ratio.

So, you apply that. You don't even need to replace all that earned revenue. But would people wait in line for a new play they've never heard of in the middle of the winter? I don't know. But it would be really fun to try and do that as opposed to try and figure out how to afford ads in the *New York Times* to fight what Charles Isherwood said about your show, which is really boring. The other thing about the park is that it's review proof. It's not word-of-mouth proof. But it's review proof. Nobody cares what the *Times* said about it. What they care about is that they heard the show is worth seeing. And that's what propels them. Isn't that what we want? A world where that's what matters?

AB: That notion of lines, people actually having to undergo something to get in, is big. But there was also something in the article about how there might be a playwright-in-residence as well, which was interesting.

It's a whole other subject. There's an actual, logical connection between doing Shakespeare and giving it to the people and then doing new work. Putting those two things side by side was a fantastic, brilliant insight. They don't look on the surface like they have a lot to do with each other, but it turns out they have everything to do with each other. The New York Shakespeare Festival turned out to be the perfect place to create *Hair*, to create *The Basic Training of Pavlo Hummel*, *A Chorus Line*—which, of course, in the middle of the seventies is a musical about trying to get a job. It was completely responding to the moment. That's why it landed—not because it was an in-theater joke, but because it was a city winding up trying to get back to work.

AB: Going back to your avant-garde passport—I always think that *A Chorus Line* only happened because Joe Chaikin's work at the Open Theater made that approach to the human being—actor—playing character in relationship to a story like that happen.

I used to walk in the Public lobby not knowing what I was going to go see. It had that big board up there with the five different theaters, and they almost always had five things. If you couldn't get into one thing, you could get into something else. It was not just new playwrights and Shakespeare rubbing shoulders. Mabou Mines was in residence. Why? Because Joe liked them. JoAnne Akalaitis doesn't become JoAnne Akalaitis if Mabou Mines isn't in residence at the New York Shakespeare Festival. So the people who are doing what Mabou was doing then and the people who were doing Shakespeare and the people who are doing new plays are not in separate niches. They're all mixing up and rubbing shoulders in the lobby and seeing themselves and thinking, Oh, I wonder if I could do that? And "What can I learn from . . . ?" That's what makes a great theatrical culture.

For writers—as for actors, which is an even more complicated issue—one of our huge problems right now is that the entire American theater is taking this passive approach to allowing its artists to create a life in the field. We're moving in this direction as a field where we're sort of saying to writers, as to actors and to directors, "You know, we actually can't support you. You actually can't make a living in the theater. We're not even going to say it out loud, but the way we pay you and the way we treat you is basically telling you you're going to have to make your living in film and television. And you work out how you can make your living, then we hope you have time left for us and that you'll come and see us occasionally." The long-term consequences of that are so bad for the survival of the American theater. How are we going to handle that with actors? This is not just the not-for-profit. The commercial theater does this to actors. But with playwrights, I feel like we should do what universities do and have chairs of playwriting—endowed chairs. Again, it takes a tiny amount of money in the big picture of things to endow a chair of playwriting. If somebody gave the Public two million dollars to endow a chair, and put their name on it for the rest of eternity, that kicks off a hundred thousand dollars a year. With that, on an annual basis, say you pay a playwright a sixty thousand dollar salary. You pay all of their retirement, pension, health, cover all those matters, and there's enough left over for a workshop every year. And you appoint senior folks to those chairs in five-year terms—or, I don't know, maybe ten-year terms. And it's exactly like a chair at a great research university. You don't get one of those chairs in order to perform. It's the university saying, "We want you to be present here. Occasionally see a student." In playwriting terms: Interact with the theater a little bit. We'd like to look at what you write. But fundamentally, you get this chair to do your work because your work is of value to society. Not because we're going to make a profit off of it. Not because we'll get you to teach eighty hours a week at the same time. But because your philological research is of social value that is not compensated by the marketplace, so we in the academic community will step up to the plate and make sure that we can keep the life of the mind alive. The reverberatory effects of that are not just whoever gets those chairs. If the Public maybe establishes five chairs, ten million dollars, five playwrights at any given moment are having a living wage, pension. What you're also saying to the people who don't have those chairs is, "Look, here's a model. You can look down the line and not feel like an idiot because you didn't take that TV series." I bet you if we establish five of them, Todd Haimes would have to look me in the face and do two of them. Every theater worth its salt should have this. How the hell else are we going to support a culture? We all work off these playwrights' work. If the great playwrights stop producing great work, what are we going to do?

So that's just one. There are other things we should do for younger playwrights, too.

AB: What?

Money, money, money. Groups and commissions and I've got a whole manifesto that I'll publish.

AB: Don't you feel happy that not only is Oskar thinking these things, but also speaking them out loud?

But the real point is now succeeding in doing them, which is a lot harder than talking.

AB: I don't think it's necessarily harder to do than to say. I think the first step is to think and connect the words. And I think the actions follow. I think the people follow. I think there is a need in our field for that sort of articulation—because basically it's logical. It's not like what you're saying is pie-in-the-sky. It's based on ethics and philosophy and it's practical.

Audience: Is part of the plan for actors to work on things for a long time?

I wouldn't say plan yet. We're starting in a very slow way trying to do some readings, a few days, sitting around the table with *Three Sisters* and *King Lear*. We're trying to start a process with actors sitting around the table with some of the great works so that that becomes part of the normal presence without saying, "And it's going into rehearsal next March." Saying, "Let's take a little while to look." In every one of these conversations somebody says "*Vanya on 42nd Street*" within fifteen minutes, so it's also the influence of André [Gregory] and that methodology. Again, we're trying to figure out how we can be sufficiently creative, about how you keep actors involved in the life of the theater over a long span. I knew how to do it when I was at my previous home in Rhode Island, where we had an acting company. That was a model that was simpler and that I understood. In New York it's more complicated, because it doesn't feel like it's the right thing for the Public to have an acting company. What feels right is to think about how is it possible to get actors engaged over a longer arc, to find ways to work on material that's outside the four-week rehearsal period.

Angels is a perfect example: We sort of created a company around the development of *Angels in America* that went on for six years. It had lots of firings, including my own, and that was part of it. But it, nonetheless, was a continuous process of work among a group of artists for six years, and that is absolutely at the heart of why it's a great play. Tony had three women in *Angels* who would not have been in that play. I can't tell you how many times Tony would whine to me, "Why do I have to have these women in this show? This is a play about gay men. I don't know what to do with them. Abigail, this mother. Okay, we'll make her Joe Pitt's mother, but I don't know what the mother's going to do in this play." Well, he had to have these three women in the play because we had these three women in the company. If those three female characters hadn't been written in the play, I don't think we could be sitting here talking about *Angels in America*. It's absolutely part of what stretched that play to have the reach that it ended up having.

So, we have lots of informal ways of figuring out how to keep the work going over an extended period of time. The only thing I'm sure of is that we have to produce more work. There's no way one Shakespeare in the Park in the summer provides enough employment for enough actors to keep those chops alive. So we have to do at least two.

Audience: The theater scene in Minneapolis seems so vital and much more sophisticated. Do you have any idea why?

I attribute it to a couple of things. The first is that there is a prairie socialist system that is epitomized by the Farmer Labor Party, that merged with the Democratic Party, that runs very deep in Minnesota. There is in its tradition community and equality and a kind of Scandinavian generosity on a social plane that underlies the city in a very real way. I think that has had a real influence on its approach to the arts. You couple that with the fact that when you're in Minneapolis, you're a long, long way from anyplace else, and the winters are very cold, and therefore indoor entertainment is a very good thing. You have many months in which it's important to be indoors. You also had—until recently—a pretty cohesive corporate community. The senior senator, Mark Dayton, is from the Dayton-Hudson family of the department stores, and is sort of the perfect example. You have this man who was raised in absolutely the height of, for Minnesota, old money corporate privilege, who goes into politics and is elected as a quite liberal Democrat. That comes from the tradition of corporate responsibility, which is certainly not without blemish—Honeywell made napalm—but is nonetheless real. So you have a group of corporations, from Dayton-Hudson to Target to Northwest, who have a corporate culture that's seriously interested in investigating community—and gets punished by the community if they don't. And then the fact that the Guthrie has been the most financially successful regional theater—and at times the most artistically successful.

Here's an interesting thing that has nothing to do with money. The Guthrie mastered the art of artistic director transition better and faster than any other theater in the country. It was founded by Tyrone Guthrie. Five years later, he was gone. Michael Langham replaced him. Seven years later, he was gone. So the Guthrie, from the beginning, though it was named after Tyrone Guthrie, built itself as a stable institution separate from any individual running it. That tradition stood them in brilliant stead when it came time to do their big endowment campaign, because it wasn't who was the artistic director. The Guthrie Theater had it's identity. That's a lesson we can really all learn from in these big institutions. It's really important that the institution plays its role in the community, not simply the charismatic individual.

Audience: I read in the *Times*, I think it was before you came, that the Public was thinking of reviving the mobile theater, which—I'm not exactly sure what it is, but I imagine some kind of truck going from borough to borough.

That was just as I arrived. There are nights that I've cursed myself for saying that because it's going to be really hard—and important. We've got the plans in the works. The idea is that regardless of any other lack of economic barrier, there are cultural barriers to people going to the Delacorte in Central Park that we are never going to completely overcome. There are just people who will not wait in line in the middle of Manhattan to go to Shakespeare that night no matter what we do. So for those people we've got to go back out to the boroughs and perform there. We've obviously been working off the ideas of a lot of our compatriots, including Cornerstone. Rather than put on a production in the park and put it on the truck and bring it out and show it to folks, what we're trying to do is get teams of artists who we will send into communities to form relationships in those communities and try to create productions there that are somehow grounded and specific to each of the five boroughs. Now that doesn't mean adhering to the Cornerstone model—amateurs performing along-side professionals—but it does mean trying to not simply take culture to the people, but actually derive culture from the people. I think we've matured enough as a field to be a little more sophisticated about how culture impacts people and how much they have to be present within what you've created in order for it to actually create a vivid event. It's turning out to be a colossally expensive experiment, which is what's giving me the headaches, but I think it's an idea that has to happen.

Audience: How's the Public's relationship with the city government? What do you need from them?

We're compiling a big list of needs, but fundamentally the support is spectacular. I have to say that, regardless of what one thinks about the politics of the Bloomberg administration, Kate Levin, commissioner of culture, has been amazing—not just in terms of providing support, which she does, but she's been a really interesting, valuable, dive-in partner in terms of trying to figure out what we should be doing. A lot of the job right now is trying to figure out specifically what the Public has to offer that is not being covered elsewhere. I was here in the seventies, went away, and I look at the Public again, and so many things that used to be exclusively the Public's domain, now other people do. Everybody's trying to bring shows to Broadway. P.S. 122 has taken on a lot of being the housing for avant-garde performance. The Shakespeare franchise is no longer exclusive to the Public. We have Theatre for a New Audience, Lincoln Center, BAM. So the landscape's changed, for better or worse, mostly for better. So now, you have to redefine the question of what the Public adds to this mix. The worst feeling in the world—and this has happened a few times—is when you're competing with your compatriot theaters for getting a show. The reason it's such a terrible feeling is that if we're competing for doing a show, we're actually not providing something that somebody else isn't going to provide anyway. If Manhattan Theatre Club wants to do this show—let 'em! If New York Theatre Workshop wants to do it, let 'em do the play because the play will get done. And isn't our job to get the play done? That's why we're a not-for-profit. If we were a profit-making enterprise we might want it because we could get something. We're supposed to be filling the need that other people won't fill.

AB: Do you have any idea what that is?

I hope I've provided a few thoughts. I am a second- or third-generation of artistic director in the not-for-profit theater in this country, and I'm really following in the footsteps of giants. I am here at the Public because in their ways Joe and JoAnne and George were each a giant. I feel like my job is to—and reading between the lines in what I was saying about the Guthrie—not to be a giant. We've had giants. My job is to try to get the institution stabilized, focusing on its mission, focusing on what it's supposed to be doing and making sure that it is doing it as well as possible and it has the support to continue to do it in the long haul. If you look at the other major not-for-profits—Lincoln Center and Manhattan Theatre Club and Roundabout here in town—they don't have the boom-and-bust history that the Public has. The Public has economic crisis, boom-and-bust history, and that's scary, because at a certain point, you have enough of those boom-and-busts and that *Chorus Line* money is all gone and somebody else is doing Shakespeare and, you know what? We don't own the Delacorte. Maybe Lincoln Center should be programming. Christopher Plummer should do *Lear* there. Suddenly the whole mission could go away. That's what I feel my job is—to make sure that doesn't happen. That's an institution-building job.

Audience: I didn't read the *Voice* article, but I'm about to cry just hearing what you have to say. It's sort of amazing and incredible. But I was wondering about the tension between the two things you were saying, which is that doing it isn't as easy as saying it. What's getting in the way? Why is it so hard? I sense that it is.

I think it's hard because it's hard. If it were easy, it would have been done before—somebody giving away all your tickets for free or endowing chairs for playwrights. They're not simple. However, I really agree with what Anne said. I think they're logical. I think they are arguments that follow not from fiery personality and Blake-ian vision. I think they're arguments that follow from the mission of the theater. And what I'm hopeful for— and this is where I think we have a little bit of a track record in Rhode Island—is that if an idea is good enough, if it really benefits what we believe about the theater, it attracts support. It takes time and it takes persistence to attract that support. I have no question that the resources are there—but we have to make it clear enough and make it a compelling enough vision to attract the support.

Audience: I guess my question is more specific then. Who do you have to convince?

AB: What is that theory of memes? It's really kind of bullshit, but the theory is that we're put on earth to spread DNA or memes, which are ideas, and there's a kind of

influenza of ideas or influence of ideas that gets spread from one person to another. I think Oskar's doing it. His work is happening right now in this room.

That's absolutely right—but the major thing in my head is my wife's horror that she's going to have to listen to me do this how many millions of times. Don't leave me, honey.

AB: No—it's a great thing that Laurie does because you have to keep it fresh because she's hearing it again.

At the end of the day we're talking about fundraising, right? It's a huge part of this. But really who you have to convince is everybody. You have to convince the audience who you expect to show up. You have to convince the staff who are working themselves to the bone to try and make all this happen. You have to convince the board, who are the fundamental fiscal guardians. You have to convince everybody you've set up to raise money from. You have to convince the artists who come and do work here. You have to convince everybody, and everybody is convinced by a different slight angle of the story, but it has to be fundamentally the same story. It's why I don't mind fundraising. It's not really any different than what I do in the rehearsal room. You have a text, you have people sitting around the table working from the text. Essentially what you're trying to do is figure out how everybody in the room can feel ownership over this text and care passionately about it—so passionately that they're willing to throw their resources into that. It's exactly what you're doing when you fundraise. You're trying to get somebody to care enough about your theater that they believe they own it and they're willing to throw their resources into it. Their resources are financial. Your resources are emotional or artistic. If your theater is actually doing what I said it's supposed to be doing, which is filling a role in a community, it's not different. It's not just for the artists. It's for the city. If Joe Papp made anything, he made a theater that was supposed to be for the city.

Molly Smith

Molly Smith is one of the most courageous women I know. She once described how to handle a kayak in dangerous currents. "Paddle directly into the roughest water," she said. Our natural inclination is to avoid the trouble spot but that is an unwise and unsafe thing to do. Paddle toward the problem.

Molly is presently the artistic director of Arena Stage in Washington, D.C. When she assumed the position at Arena she made a massive decision. The work at Arena would celebrate the American voice. She has made good on her commitment. The theater has commissioned countless indigenous writers, it has uncovered the works of neglected American playwrights, and it has produced beloved American classics right alongside.

Then Molly made yet another courageous and groundbreaking decision. She proposed changing the existing Arena Stage building and constructing a much-enhanced, expanded and renovated complex to be named the Mead Center for American Theater, a three-theater facility dedicated to the development and production of American theater. She, Stephen Richard and her board and staff have raised well over one hundred million dollars based upon her enthusiasm for and belief in the plan. Molly was able to articulate her excitement and vision, and people wanted to be part of this new idea and endeavor.

Molly grew up in Juneau, Alaska, transferred to Catholic University as an undergraduate and received her master's degree from American University. All during her studies in the "lower forty-eight," Molly harbored a dream to return to Alaska and found a theater in the city of her youth where there was none. And she did exactly that. She and her then husband hauled fifty used theater seats to Juneau and spread the contagious excitement of her mission. The result of what she calls her "fire in the belly" is Perseverance Theatre, which she founded in 1979. She remained its artistic director for nineteen years. The theater continues to prosper as the flagship professional theater in Alaska.

While still an undergraduate at Catholic University, Molly began a creative relationship with the playwright Paula Vogel that continues to this day. She has commissioned and directed premieres of Paula's plays, including *The Baltimore Waltz*, *How I Learned to Drive* and *The Mineola Twins*. At Arena Stage Molly also commissioned and directed work by Sarah Ruhl, Moisés Kaufman and Tim Acito. Playwrights benefit from Molly's belief in them in the form of her support and through her friendship and warmth.

In addition to receiving honorary doctorates from both Towson University and her alma mater, American University, Molly serves on the boards of both Theatre Communications Group and the Center for International Theatre Development. She has directed two feature films: *Raven's Blood* and *Making Contact*.

December 19, 2005

AB: Molly has one of the most extraordinary stories in the American theater. Molly is the artistic director of Arena Stage in Washington, D.C., which has itself had an extraordinary history and an amazing woman who started that. We were on a panel a couple of years ago in Baltimore with Tina Packer and Ellen Lauren, and I suddenly realized that all the women on the panel had actually gone through the backdoor to get to the front, including myself. Molly said, "I'm going to Alaska." I had said, "I'm going downtown." Tina left England and started a company in Western Massachusetts. And through that we came out into the major mainstream American theater. I might be overgeneralizing—but the boys kind of crash in the front gate. I thought that all of us went around to the backdoor.

I would like to start with the past. You went to high school in Alaska, is that right?

MS: Yes. I was born in Yakima, Washington, which is apple country. I always felt that I was there by mistake and needed to be in a city. From the time I was a kid I was very interested in the theater. My family moved to Alaska when I was sixteen. I went in some ways kicking and screaming, although, after about six months, I fell completely in love with it and in love with the people. I think because of the mountains there I had a sense of place that I hadn't had when I was in Washington State, which was more of an irrigated desert. When I was nineteen I had just finished my first year of school at the University of Alaska in Fairbanks, where it gets to sixty below and much more than that with wind chill factor. It's the kind of place where you have to plug your car in. The most hip thing to do was to live in a cabin and have an outdoor toilet. Imagine the level of ice on those outdoor toilets. After my first year, in which I pursued a pre-law degree, I traveled for three months with a friend over to Europe. During that time it just hit me: I should stop following my head, which was saying, "Be a lawyer. You can make money," and really listen to what I wanted to do, which was theater. So I decided, at the ripe old age of nineteen, that I wanted to start a theater in Alaska. I came back and told my university professors. They patted me on the shoulder and said, "That's very nice, dear." And with that I took off. It had always been a family thing to finish school in the east. So I was a transfer student at Catholic University, and went on to get my master's degree at American University. At Catholic University, my best friend was Paula Vogel. We met each other as transfer students, and we'd sit in the dark corners plotting the downfall of the American theater. And then at American University I met Joy Zinoman. She was one of my best mentors and she eventually started the Studio Theatre, which is one of the best-known small theaters in Washington, D.C. By small, I don't mean small—they have four theaters that are all two hundred seats. She's really revitalized a whole area of Washington, D.C., in the Logan Circle area.

I stayed on in Washington, D.C., for several more years because my former husband was in the Naval Academy. During that time I worked with a lot of small professional theaters like New Playwrights Theatre, ASTA, Back Alley. But from the time I was nineteen I wanted to start a theater in Alaska. I was like a homing pigeon. I wanted to go back. Billy kept saying, "Shouldn't we go to San Francisco?" "No, I've got to go to Alaska." "Shouldn't we go to Seattle?" "No, no, no. I have to go to Alaska." I studied everything I could in Washington, D.C., because I figured when I would go back to Alaska I would need to teach people.

Alaska's huge. It's the fifth of the size of the United States. It used to be five time zones. That gives you an idea of how vast it is. You go all the way down the Aleutian chain, to the panhandle, up into Nome. It's truly, truly enormous. There was a professional theater in Alaska, Alaska Repertory Theatre in Anchorage, but it closed in the nineties. Well, that's over six hundred miles away from Juneau. Juneau is in southeast Alaska. It's on the panhandle, quite close to Canada. In many ways it probably should have been part of Canada because it's just this little angle that comes down. But it's the state capital. There are no roads in or out. So you have to take a plane or a boat in order to get there. It has a population of thirty thousand.

So when we headed back to Alaska, Billy was still whispering in my ear as we drove across the country, "If you want to stop someplace else, we can." And I said, "No, we can't."

Is this when you had gotten the seats?

This was right at that time. About a month before we left, a friend of mine who had another theater that she was renovating, an old porno house, called and said, "I have fifty used—probably very used—theater seats. Do you want them?" And I said, "Yes, yes, I want them." Billy and a couple of his friends hauled them over to the house and stuffed them into the back shed. Then a month or two later the military was moving us back to Alaska, and the poor guy who came in to move us opened the shed and was faced with fifty heavy theater seats. He immediately ran inside to call the office. God bless the United States Military and Navy. The guy looked it up and pulled the papers and said, "It says right here that used theaters seats are household items. You gotta take them." So it's the story of how the military started a theater company. For me, it was an icon. It was this symbol of this thing that I kept wanting to do. My friends in Washington, D.C., thought I was crazy. "Why are you going back there? Why don't you stay here? Theater's much more interesting here." It was kind of an odd trajectory to eventually come back to Washington, D.C.

Then, I thought it would take five years to start a theater in Alaska, but in six months the theater was born. The first play that we did was called *Pure Gold*. We went out and interviewed fifty senior citizens who were anywhere from seventy to ninety—people from the Chilkoot Trail, all the pioneers, natives, Native Americans who had been there for centuries, the Filipinos who came up in the mines—and did a readers theater piece. That launched the theater. Eventually it toured ninety times both around Alaska, to all those little strange places like Kotzebue and Nome where the sun never sets or rises, and all the way around the world with a couple of productions.

You transported those actors by plane, right?

Yes. We would transport actors by Beaver Plane, which I think is one of the best planes in the world because it's a World War II plane. It's very, very sturdy. It has maybe about twenty seats in it. We would go out to logging camps on boats and ferries. We would go to native fishing villages. We traveled up north to places like Toksook Bay, which feels like it's on the edge of the moon, right on the Bering Sea, where the hunters are subsistence hunters. They are whalers; they are seal hunters; they are walrus hunters. And we would take productions like *Taming of the Shrew*. We would take productions like *The Importance of Being Earnest*. We would make a theater in each one of these communities. We would go in and rebuild the inside of a Quonset hut or go into a church social hall. We were a traveling theater troupe that would come to this place in the middle of nowhere and bring a piece of magic to people who didn't have one. Life was pretty rough in some of those villages. We would teach workshops.

I remember one thing that I don't want to forget. When you went to Juneau there was no theater. My image of the story is you wandering down the street saying, "Who wants to be in a play?" What I find remarkable is that you did *Pure Gold*, which was about people's experiences, and the people who went to see it said, "Oh, theater's about us." And the only other professional theater in Alaska at this point was Alaska Rep, which was about bringing in professionals from the Lower 48, and it closed because it didn't mean anything to the community. But Perseverance Theatre persevered, and to this day perseveres because of its relationship to the community, even though it's a professional theater company. The other thing—and maybe you don't want to toot your own horn—but I went there in 1984 and was knocked out. Alaskans are strong people. It was impressive. It changes you to be in that atmosphere among that kind of landscape. But what is also remarkable is not only did you do theater that was about the community, you also trained not only actors, but directors and playwrights.

STAR Program (Summer Theatre Arts Rendezvous).

Which was also amazing to see, again, that kind of ownership by the community that was transformed into professionalism.

It was a very interesting time. It is twenty-seven years old now. In those early days, coming to the National Endowment for the Arts to argue about a theater that had a relationship to a community was a shocking notion. People did not believe it. They did not understand that oftentimes theater gets made by the amateur coming together with the professional. That's where a lot of times you can have that spark. I used to have long, rabid arguments with them. "What are you trying to do? Is this just social work?" This whole idea that a theater is a reflection of a community was such a rare idea at that time. Now it's become a part of our vernacular. We think, of course, that's exactly what it's part of. I think it was at that time that the theater was really starting to stop from being so inward looking and start looking around. For many, many, many, many years it was art for art's sake. And then there was this whole other piece.

I think Anne is absolutely right. In the early years of the theater I would go into bars and I would drag people off barstools, and I would say, "Come. Audition for this play." Some of those actors have continued to be actors with Perseverance Theatre even now—which is so odd and wonderful to me. It was really about how you find the creativity within each human being. It's also true that most people who live in Alaska don't think of themselves as a single thing. In cities, people tend to specialize. In Alaska, the first thing you would ask somebody is, "What do you know how to do?" "Well, I know how to fix an engine. I know how to make blueberry pie. I know how to fix a snowblower." You find out what people are able to do because there's always a little piece of survival. It's cold weather. It's difficult getting in and out. You could always end up in trouble. That ended up making people really wonderful storytellers. If you were a good storyteller, you would probably be good on stage as well.

One of the most interesting projects we did was called *Yup'ik Antigone*, a retelling of the *Antigone* story from a Yup'ik point of view. The Yup'ik Eskimos live way, way, way up north. They are subsistence fishermen and hunters. Dave Hunsaker had this idea. What would happen if we married a really ancient tradition in Alaska, which had to do with the Eskimo people, with the *Antigone* story? Eventually we had eight Eskimo actors in it. It was all done in the Yup'ik language with Yup'ik dance, Yup'ik movement. There was very little storytelling in it. It was the first time there had been on stage an entirely Eskimo cast telling stories about who they were in the Yup'ik language. It had a combustible effect throughout the whole state. Eventually, three different native theaters came about because people wanted to tell their own stories. That traveled pretty much around the world because people were so fascinated by it. It also came here to New York, to La MaMa. It opened, got fantastic reviews and sold out the run within about two days. Then, two days later, the Eskimos found out that an elder in their own community had died, and they said, "We go home."

So *New York Times* reviews don't mean anything to them?

Exactly. It became the story of the show that didn't go on. Ellen Stewart was fantastic when I talked to her about it. She said, "Well, they've got to go home." I said, "Well, you won't stop a Yup'ik Eskimo."

I remember also that there was a discovery that the Yup'iks have a similar story to *Antigone*. They said, "We have this story." So it was not a new story.

In talking to the village elders, because Dave Hunsaker worked through the elders the whole time in translation, they said, "Antigone was right. She needed to bury her brother." During the time we were there making this piece, there were two people in the Eskimo village of Toksook Bay who were lost. One was "lost" in Anchorage, and one was lost out on the ice.

Every night we would see about maybe thirty snow machines out tracing the ice for hours and hours looking for this body of this man. They knew he was gone. It didn't matter. They did that for about a month. They also sent another man to Anchorage to try and find this guy who was lost. He went down to all the restaurants and bars and finally found him cooking in a restaurant. Eventually he brought him home. It's kind of a fantastic story. They really look after their own, whether it's their dead or ones they feel should come home.

So Molly talked Juneau into starting a theater in a bar on Douglas Island. And then at a certain point you said, "That's not good enough," because you'd sold out all the fifty porno seats. You built another theater. You made a company. You made a success. And at a certain point you also took a sabbatical, I think. Then you decided to move on. What was your thought process in terms of leaving—in creating a successful theater and then leaving?

I knew that there was something inside of me that was changing. I was more and more drawn to film. I started to make films. I really tried to move Perseverance Theatre in the direction of making more films. People were very uncomfortable with that. It was too hard for them to make the shift. But I knew, as an artist, that I had begun to move on. I felt as if I kept hitting the same problems within the organization over and over again. I thought, "It's time for me to leave."

I thought leaving meant that my partner Suzanne and I would go down to Seattle where I would make more films. Then a phone call came. It was Arena Stage. They said, "We're interested in throwing your hat in the ring." I said, "Are you crazy?" I had always loved the work of Arena Stage. I was a young artistic director in training watching Zelda Fichandler in the seventies. As you said, Anne, I completely came in the backdoor. I was a dark horse at Arena Stage. I'll never forget at one point as I was talking to the search committee, the board president came out, and he was a little bit rumpled looking. We'd just been in there for four or five hours and we'd done lots of hard questions. He said, "Don't you realize, Molly, you're a dark horse?" I said, "Yeah, but I'm running fast."

You probably don't know this, but you've had a big influence on me at various key moments in my life. At one very key moment, at a very difficult time, you said, "When you're kayaking and you come across rough waters, your instinct is to want to move away from the rough waters. A good kayaker knows that you have to go right into the middle of it." I'm still working on that. But you seem to have done that with Arena Stage. You don't have a small opinion of yourself, and I don't mean that

in any way in a derogatory sense. You actually have a strong sense of you in the world. Does that come from being in Alaska?

I think as women leaders we have to. If you don't, someone else will take it away from you. I think we're conditioned in society to be givers and let go and support other people, and as leaders, a lot of times, you need to lean into whatever the conflict is.

You've had a major affect on me as well, both in your work and in life. When you came to teach in '84 it was pretty spellbinding for me because of the way in which you were working—improvisation with the actors—and the ideas you had. You would just set people on fire. I would see these people who I had been working with for five or six or seven or eight years, and suddenly they were spinning with ideas that they hadn't had before. It was incredible. You've always been brave that way.

I think as artistic director of Arena Stage it's part of your duty to talk about Zelda. Zelda Fichandler, who started Arena Stage in 1950, is another person, a woman, who started something from nothing. She started with a brain.

She did. She was twenty-three years old. As a matter of fact, today, she started rehearsals for *Awake and Sing!* at Arena Stage. It's very exciting. People are really jazzed about it. She, in true Zelda Fichandler fashion, spoke for about twenty-five minutes on the play. She's a great scholar and thinker. Anyway, she was really the beginning of the resident not-for-profit theater movement. She felt that you could do fantastic work outside of New York, so she and her husband and a man by the name of Edward Mangum started Arena Stage. They started it with a theater in the round. She wanted the theater to be world literature. Eventually Arena Stage was the first theater to travel to Russia. It was the first theater to travel into China. First to have an integrated theater in D.C. First to create Accessibility Programs. It had an acting company with actors like Dianne Wiest, Bob Crosby, Jane Alexander, James Earl Jones—really great luminaries of the theater. They did fantastic productions like *The Great White Hope.* They did huge American cycles of plays. There are two theaters spaces, one a large theater in the round that seats eight hundred and fifty and one a beautiful thrust that seats about five hundred twenty-five. She really built Arena on the idea of company. She was a groundbreaker. She is also consistently one of those human beings who teaches and pulls others forward. It was always her idea to start more theaters all over the country. People have always come to her for more sustenance. Now she's the head of the NYU graduate acting program. I think it's one of the best programs in the country.

She has such energy. You can package it. When you came to Arena, you came very wisely with an agenda about what you wanted to do. Can you talk about that process, what led you to make that proposal?

When I came to Arena to speak to the search committee, what they talked to me about was that Arena had somehow lost its way. More and more theaters grew up in the Washington, D.C., area. There are now eighty theaters in Washington. When I had been there in the seventies there were maybe five or six, so it's just been this tremendous explosion of theaters. Arena Stage was the major flagship, the mother ship that had started all of this, but it had kind of lost its essential juice. We all know theaters have to be constantly reinvented. If they aren't reinvented, they die. They have to be reinvented on a yearly basis, on a monthly basis, on a daily basis. But there are large arcs of time where theaters need to be changed radically. Doug Wager was the artistic director after Zelda Fichandler. Doug had a real interest in American musicals and producing and directing pieces like *Coconuts* and *Animal Crackers* and fantastic productions like that. He had been her artistic associate for many years. Eventually he left. As they were talking about this, between one session and another, I went out to a bookstore and really began thinking about, "What's Washington, D.C., to me?" Having lived there for a number of years, I realized it was a major crossroads for America. And so, by the evening session, I came in completely on fire with the idea of focusing the repertory of the organization—as opposed to an eclectic repertory—on American plays and American voices. What would happen if we really focused? What would happen if we looked for lost American plays? The great American musical? Contemporary plays, premieres of plays?

That was something that they were very interested in. We are now the largest theater in America that is focusing on American work. That has been a very exciting process because of projects like working with you and SITI on Sophie Treadwell's *Intimations for a Saxophone*. Projects like Zora Neale Hurston's *Polk County* that had never had a production before, that then went on to several other theaters. Plays like *Passion Play, a cycle*, Sarah Ruhl's great epic, which just premiered this year. Or *Cutting Up*, about African-American men in barbershops, which is on stage right now, another premiere. That also includes American classics like *South Pacific*. I started directing musicals about four years ago. I just finished *Damn Yankees* because Washington, D.C., has baseball fever now that our Nationals are back. We also work with writers on adaptations of novels and things like that.

That idea, to really change the repertory, was compelling to this board and to the staff. Zelda said repertory is destiny. I think that's true. You will get the audience that you want within five years of doing certain kinds of work. One of the things that was very important to me was to reflect the Washington, D.C., area with the work. At least a couple shows a season are African-American. Almost thirty percent of our single-ticket holders are African-American now. That's probably a better percentage than just about anybody in the country. And it is because of doing consistent repertory and because of opening our doors to a cross-cultural community.

Do you think that the search committee decided to go with you because of your idea about repertory or because you were on fire when you came back from the bookstore?

I think it was probably because I was on fire. I think that search committees fall in love with people in the same way that people fall in love with them. The guy who ran the search said, "We want you to come take a look at this position," and I said, "Why?" And he said, "You share similar values." That's a deep thought—and that made me start questioning: What are my values? What do I value in the theater? Well, it's pretty clear that there's often a social/political context. It's often about reflecting a place. They were interested in what happens when you dig underneath the skin of Washington, D.C.

You're an institution builder. I want to talk about the positive sides and the challenging and difficult sides of running an institution and being an artist in an institution devoted to making art. How have you changed? You said you had to start thinking of deep thoughts. What's the cost—both in positive and negative ways?

Moving from Perseverance—it's a small organization. It's always been a million dollars or less. To move from that to a thirteen-million-dollar organization, from a staff of nine to a staff of one hundred fifty with three hundred artists a year coming in, is quite a radical shift. I think the good cost of that is that I had to stretch and open myself as an artist and as a thinker. I've always been really fascinated with structures and structures work within organizations in terms of relationships. There are flattening structures and hierarchical structures. I've always been interested in flattening structures. So that was a lot fun for me to work with at Arena Stage.

A flattening or circular structure is a conversation around a table. You think more in terms of equality. There's always a leader, but everybody around the table is encouraged to lead. Hierarchical structure is, "I report to you, I report to you, I report to you." It's more of a ladder, which is what you often see in corporate America so that things can be done quickly. At

Perseverance, since it was small, we were able to do much more of this flat structure around my grandmother's table. I got to Arena Stage, and it was large charts and ideas. I kept trying to flatten things because as an artist, I like that. Different people have to lead in different ways. They have to think in different ways. It uses more of the creative being.

The cost for me in being in a large organization like this—I think there's a cost to my health. There's a lot of stress in these big organizations. I went through breast cancer ten years ago. When I came into this position I said, "If it's too much stress for me, I'm going to get out." I have to really monitor that. There is a cost for me in my family life. I'm obsessed. It's not possible as an artistic director to completely, always put it away when my family needs me or when my partner needs me. I think there has also been a difficult cost for me as an artist—both wonderful and also difficult. If I were a freelance artist I would have the difficulty of, "How do I find the next job? How do I find the right work? How do I find relationships with people that I want to work with that there's a certain amount of freedom in the work?" For me, when I am directing something like *Damn Yankees*, I'm also doing administrative things later in the day or in the morning or on my breaks. I'm always quite tethered to the organization and look on the directing work as real freedom. The good cost is that I think I've gotten much better as a director because I have a broad canvas to work from. I have an ability to work with very strong artists at Arena, and I have the ability to set the tune at different points, to have an extra two weeks of rehearsal on something like Sarah Ruhl's play. But I don't have the ability to do things like I did at Perseverance Theatre, where I'd say, "I want to spend two months just working on *Alaskan Odyssey*, just thinking about it, before we even go to rehearsal." But, in Alaska, I really felt that I needed to go to a larger stage. I wanted to talk to more people. I think as artists, for periods of time we're quite happy talking to small groups of people. And then there's a certain point in our career where we want to talk to more and more people. We want to have more and more conversations. We want them to have conversations with us. I had hit a point in Alaska where it wasn't possible for me to do that. Washington, D.C., provides that in a very, very broad way.

I've learned so much. We're in the middle of a building campaign right now. I would have never guessed five or ten years ago that I would be raising over a hundred million dollars. What has that called on me as an artist or an administrator? Those conversations about fundraising and talking to people about the needs and the desires and the hopes and visions and wishes of the organization are intense. But that's all growth. I'll keep at it until or if I reach the point where I just say, "It ain't worth it." In some ways, that's the beauty of being an artist. At a certain point, we do say, "It's not worth it. It's time for me to move on."

Now, with this big new venture, redoing the old theater and raising a huge amount of money, is it hard for you to make the ask? Are you straightforward about it? Do you get nervous before you ask for a huge amount of money? Do you feel sick to your stomach?

For days. For days before I do it.

So it's hard for you.

It is as difficult to ask somebody for ten thousand dollars as it is to ask for twenty million. It's the same story because it depends on the person that you're talking to. For one person, ten thousand dollars is as much as asking somebody else for a million. The difficult point is when you get into really large numbers like twenty million. My fear is, "Is this going to frighten them so much that they're going to have a heart attack if I ask my question?" They know that you're coming in to talk to them about money. They probably rarely know that you're going to ask them for as much as you're going to ask them. So everybody is bracing for the moment of the ask. So, you say, "I would like for you to consider—and please don't answer me now, but I think because of your love for actors, I would like to ask you for a million dollars to pay for rehearsal halls." Then you shut up. You don't want to shut up. You want to start talking. You shut up. And then they sit back, think about it, or immediately blurt things out like, "No way." I got that at one point. That kind of threw me off. He eventually ended up giving about half of that, so it was fine. You let them talk. Then, at the end of them talking, you say, "I would love to leave this information with you. You've been a great friend of the organization and I really appreciate that you're even thinking about this, and let's talk within a couple of weeks." And then you talk in a couple of weeks.

Now, who taught you this whole business about how you shut up?

Steven Richard, who is the executive director of Arena. We also work with fundraising people. They coach you. You have to be coached. It's not natural. But this is something that can work with even small amounts of money. You ask the question. Let them start talking, rather than you talking because what will happen is that you'll try to talk it down because you just get nervous.

Do people usually give you half of what you ask, or sometimes as much as you ask? Is there a pattern?

Sometimes as much. Oftentimes less—which is why they say to you, always ask for more than what you think you want. You also want to know something about how wealthy they are because you don't want to insult someone by asking them for too little.

Can you talk about the Sarah Ruhl project—your relationship with her and also with Paula Vogel and with other living writers, particularly women writers and American writers?

I first came in contact with Sarah Ruhl when she was a student of Paula Vogel's at Brown University. I read a version the first part of *Passion Play* eight years ago. Paula whispered in my ear, "She's the real thing." So we started to track Sarah and we brought her to the theater. We did a reading of her play *Eurydice*, and, fairly soon after that, commissioned her for a play. We asked her, "What do you want to write about?" We said, "We'd love it if you'd write something about America. Whatever you want to write about America. Are you interested in politics? What are you interested in?" And she said, "Well, actually, I have this *Passion Play* that I have now written two parts to, and I would like to write a third part to it." And we said, "Great. Do it." So within a year, year and a half, she had completed the third part. *Passion Play*'s Act One takes place in 1575 in Northern England. Act Two is 1934 in Oberamagau, Germany. And Act Three is in the seventies and eighties in Spearfish, South Dakota. In each one of these acts there is a group of artists who are performing in a Passion Play. The person who plays Pontius Pilate plays him all three times. The person who plays Jesus, plays him all three times. But it is also about the political, social, but mostly the political life of each of these communities. I think Sarah is getting to something quite deep about religious and political icons and about our relationship to the stage and reality.

Paula and I became fast friends at Catholic University. A number of her plays were first produced or workshopped at Perseverance, like *How I Learned to Drive*, *The Baltimore Waltz* and *Mineola Twins*. We had a very long, creative relationship, which continues to this day.

I remember first hearing Sarah Ruhl's work in the basement of Actors Theatre of Louisville. It's almost like you get a shock in your body. "This is a writer!" Did you feel that? She's totally extraordinary.

Even with her very first play, it was clear that she is a poet who can drive a plot—because a lot of poets can't. She's original. I think ten years from now people will say, "Oh, this is a very Sarah Ruhl–like play." I think she will become part of the common vernacular.

Mac Wellman once said to me, "All of the great playwrights in the history of playwriting were also poets." And I realized that that's true. Even Brecht. You think back, they all are poets—and that poetic impulse and its connection to writing for the stage is remarkably palpable. I guess the language emanates from the right hemisphere of the brain as opposed to the left. What other playwrights are you excited about?

I'm very excited about—well, let me tell you about a person who I am thinking about right now. You were talking about women writers. I don't know if you all know what's going on with Wendy Wasserstein right now. She's very ill, gravely ill, in a New York hospital. She has been sick for a number of years with Bell's palsy and now with what looks like a brain tumor. I'm very sad about that because I've always felt that she is a very interesting writer. I think she went through some difficult times with some of her writing. I think that people have a tendency to think that writers who are able to allow audiences to laugh are lesser writers. Wendy is one of those writers who really elicits that type of sympathy in an audience, and for that I've always been grateful for her writing. She strikes me as a whole theater person. Any person who I consider whole is also an educator. She has always been someone who has helped young artists. She is someone who has always gone out and tried to garner young audiences in the theater. She had a program where she would take groups of ten or fifteen kids out to see Broadway shows, then have pizza afterward and talk about the plays. And what a gift, as a twelve-year-old kid, to be able to sit down and talk to Wendy Wasserstein about the play you just saw.

You've commissioned a new work by her?

We have. We did *An American Daughter* several years ago.

I love that play. It didn't really get very well received on Broadway, but it was a great impulse. How did it do in Washington?

The *Washington Post* didn't like it, but women critics did. What can I say?

You said it. But you have a new commission with her?

We do. She was writing a play about her mother, who was a great dancer, I believe in ballroom dancing or something like that. She was in the midst of doing that. We have also been working with Nilo Cruz on a new play. Robert Schenkkan recently finished a play for us. We're working with David Henry Hwang and Tazewell Thompson.

He's usually a director, right?

He's usually a director, but he's written two or three plays now. He's a very interesting writer. He has this big love for women. You notice, maybe, there's a pattern here for me. I have to say there's an underground thing I'm doing, which has to do with getting some great roles for women. I seem to be attracted to people—whether they are male or female writers—who do that. I try and balance seasons, so even if there are a lot of male writers, there are a lot of women directors, or vice versa, to balance it. I'm very interested in Tazewell because he's writing a play about Elizabeth Keckley, who was a force during the days of Abraham Lincoln.

Who is Elizabeth Keckley?

She was a seamstress who had a friendship with Mary Todd Lincoln. It's the story of their relationship.

I have a big question as my last question: How do you see the American theater right now, where do you see it going, and what do you hope for it? Not only for your own theater and work—but where do you see the movement?

I'm really concerned about shrinking audiences and the fact that more and more people want to honeycomb. They want to go home. They've got their TiVo. They don't want to go out. They want to stay in—for whatever reason. They're frightened or they feel that whatever they're doing at home with their television sets is superior to going out and being with real people. I think that's scary. I think we've become less and less a country that meditates on anything. More and more it's just about information. I think theater is a place of meditation. I have a concern that we're becoming an uneducated country, and it's not possible to have a democracy without an educated country. It is not possible. If people are not reading, if they are not thinking, if they are not looking at the newspaper, it is not possible. So, I'm worried about a lot of things.

Where is your hope? Do you have hope?

Yeah, I think I do have hope. I have hope about young people—young people coming to the theater and young people working in the theater. I think that's where all the work gets infused. I have hope for young people coming in and changing the world. Change it. It always needs to be changed. I guess I have hope that has to do with different forms being created in the theater. I'm always interested in that. I don't know what the next barrier is. For a while I thought it was sound, and I think that that really has become something quite impressive in the theater. I have hope that theaters will stop producing just two- and three-person plays. That there will be theaters who have imagination so that you see plays with fifteen and twenty-five people on stage. I think we're hungry for that. We're hungry for those big, extravagant stories. I long for poets in the theater. I really do. I long for poets that can teach us about worlds and places that we can't imagine.

Audience: I'm curious about the balance of doing more than two- or three-character shows with the declining audience participation. How do you see being able to take the leap to do a big production with maybe fourteen or fifteen actors with the funding as it is and the participation as it is?

Perhaps, save up for it. Perhaps do it as a reading series so it could be something that you're building up to it. Find an angel. Find somebody who's interested in large-scale work and encourage them to fund it for you, to become a sponsor for that single production. Frame a whole season around it so that people get really excited about it as you go into it. It's always the great conundrum in the theater. We never have enough money to do what we want to do. It doesn't matter if you're big theater like Arena or if you're a small theater. It doesn't matter. You never have enough to do all the things you want to do. So then what happens, and this is the tough part, you have to get selective. It's horrible. You have to make choices about things that you want to do. And then you have focus, focus, focus like crazy. Or else it doesn't happen, and nobody really knows what you are. You have to get very specific. It's a very noisy market out there. There are things that are competing for everybody's minds, thoughts, cash, time. Time is the thing people are most frightened of giving up. We have people who will say, "I'll give you money; just don't ask me to come and see the play. I don't have the time. I barely have time to spend with my family." Get people who are loyal to the theater and to the organization and bring them on board. It's very old-fashioned, but I think that's the way you get people interested. Those are also the kind of grants that big-thinking grant makers are interested in. They'll see a theater company going beyond what they normally do. They want to see something that's larger or something that's more intensive, something that's more unusual—and you can get them with your imagination.

AB: It's a great thing to keep in mind: No matter what your budget is, you never have enough money. I mean, that's true of anybody living in life.

Your ideas always should be larger—and your ambition should always be larger—than whatever your cash is. And it should always be a push with whoever you're working with.

Audience: What do you think about regional theater's place in the global conversation? It seems to be so interesting that regional theaters have really been developing new voices in American writers, but also European countries that can't play in New York are starting to play in regional theaters.

I think that that's absolutely true, and I think that there are people who have been working to bring international theater to this country for a long time. Philip Arnoult has been working to bring the Romanians in. Now he's into Russia. Before that he was into Hungary.

I think it's extremely exciting because you bring this whole fresh energy to thinking here in the United States and audiences are either really pissed off about it or are really going along for the ride. I think we're seeing it more and more and more. The borders have to be permeable. Although, I must say, it's becoming more and more difficult to bring in any foreign artists—more and more difficult to get the paperwork passed. But it is happening at a lot of the resident theaters around the country. They're providing that welcoming hand.

Audience: Thinking about what you did in Alaska in a community that is the size that it is, where it's not hyperbole to say that everybody knew who you were and what you were trying to do, and then thinking about now being in D.C. Obviously there's a scale difference in what you're doing. Does that translate into an essential difference?

I think it does in lots of ways. I think that because Arena has been there for fifty-five years and has such a glittering history, expectations of the organization are at a very high level. Any time it does not hit that mark, it's a whipping boy. That makes the work very complicated in a way. You always see these things that people say in their mission statements. "Excellence." It's actually alive and well at Arena. I've never seen an organization before that knocks itself around as much as it does if it doesn't hit that bar. It has to hit it on every single level. Those are the standards that have been built into the organization and, in a sense, the myth of what the organization is. From that point of view it's very difficult. There's another point of view, which is that Arena has been very well known in Washington, D.C., because of this history, and in some ways because of the present. But we are sitting in a forgotten quadrant of the city, in Southwest Washington. It is the smallest quadrant in the city. It's cut off by the freeways. The best part about it is it's got a fish market down there. It is very rich and very poor, right next to each other. So it's a really complex place to do theater. The city has moved more and more to the center of the city—the downtown area that used to be dead. Right now there are thirty-nine cranes in the air. The amount of reworking infrastructure in the area is incredible. Arena has to keep pulling focus, pulling audiences. Distinctive work has to be able to pull people over into that area of the city. People will say, "Oh, yeah, I know Arena. I was there ten years ago." "Oh, yeah, I know Arena. My parents were season ticket holders. But, hey, I go downtown to see this theater." That scale question is something that we've been working on a lot. It's the same idea as we had at Perseverance Theatre in Juneau, Alaska: You don't just reach out to a community. You reach out to many different little communities. That's how you bring those communities back into the center of the organization.

Audience: You really changed my perspective around what we as artists do in the context of the cities that we work in regionally. When I was working at Arena, Ronald Reagan died. We're all way to the left in the company, and had our feelings about that. I remember the moment when my perspective changed. We were standing backstage having a moment of silence to honor this man. In that moment what I realized was it's not about my ego. It's not about my personal agenda. It's about understanding the community that I'm in, meeting it, and still being—somehow my vision meets that place. There was a profound respect for the environment we were in. I was just amazed by this, because I could see that there was no sacrifice of the integrity of the vision of the theater, or of your vision as the artistic director in doing that. And that seemed to me to be a great place to be as a regional theater—an important place to me, not just as a theater, but as a presence in the community.

It was interesting to me when I came to Washington and to Arena Stage and I realized it's the official Washington theater. People from the Hill come to see theater there. Mrs. Bush will come and see a play there. It's official in that way—which also means that we can do provocative work and that the Supreme Court justice, who maybe you will influence, will come and watch that production. It is a very interesting place to do theater. It is possible to talk to people about the given moment within what you are doing. I think that that makes it a very powerful place to do theater. It's one of those cities where I think the two favorite kinds of theater there are Shakespeare or musicals—because they are all such left-brained people that they need something for their right brains sometimes, just to let go. There are things which have to do with abeyance to an office. It can have to do with abeyance to the image of a person as well, but to recognize that that person has been a part of that town that many people are grieving, even if it's not my personal grief.

Audience: When you're choosing a season, are you thinking about the Supreme Court justices?

You know what I'm thinking about? I'm thinking about the Metro section in the newspaper. I go around to the churches and I hear what they're obsessed with, and that goes in the season. I walk around the city and get a sense of what the people are interested in. Like, this year, doing *Damn Yankees*. People go, "*Damn Yankees*, why are you doing that?" But there's a thematic idea which I think is really important. I mean, it's the Faustian story. What would you sell your soul for? It's got great musical theater in it—and hey, by they way, baseball is back in Washington after being gone for thirty-five years and it's a non-booster town and it's lovely to see it boost itself. Plus, we have twenty-three different children's choirs from the different metropolitan area who come in every night and are part of a rally at the end of Act One, singing "You've Got to Have Heart." You've got to give it up to them. So it's become a community celebration. Now, that's like an idea straight out of Perseverance Theatre. Are people uncomfortable with it in Washington, D.C.? Some people are. Do other people absolutely adore it and feel as if it makes the theater permeable? Absolutely.

Robert Woodruff

Robert cultivates a dressed-in-black-just-climbed-off-a-motorcycle appearance that is part of his charm and also part of his mystique. But underneath the facade Robert is one of the most vulnerable and accessible people I know. His artistry as a director is a constant source of astonishment to me. His productions are bold, theatrical, and contagious with energy, wild imagery and a deep penetration of the text.

Despite his anarchistic persona, Robert is also a great institution builder. His tenure as the artistic director of the American Repertory Theater (2002–2007) produced five years of groundbreaking national and international theater works. Earlier in his career he founded not only the Eureka Theatre in San Francisco but the still-thriving Bay Area Playwrights Festival.

Brought up in Brooklyn and Long Island, Robert received a BA in political science from the University of Buffalo. He began graduate studies at the City College of New York, but, in 1971, disappointed with the intransigent New York theater establishment, he moved to San Francisco. It was the following year that he co-founded the Eureka Theatre where he remained artistic director until 1978. And at the Bay Area Playwrights Festival he began a five-year creative relationship with the young playwright Sam Shepard. The collaboration signified a turning point in the careers for both men. Robert, as the sole director of Shepard's work during those years, staged the premieres of *Buried Child*, *True West* and *Savage/Love*.

Since those early years of working with Shepard, Robert has contin-
ued to forge strong relationships with living playwrights including Edward
Bond and Charles L. Mee. He is a natural collaborator, working intensively
with the Brothers Karamazov on a celebrated production of *The Comedy of
Errors*. His investigations of the classics include *The Tempest*, *Julius Caesar*,
The Duchess of Malfi, *In the Jungle of Cities*, *Medea* and *The Changeling*. His
long-term collaborations with designers include Douglas Stein, Susan
Hilferty and George Tsypin. Robert is not so interested in agreement, pre-
ferring creative disagreement in the process of making theater.

In addition to directing large-scale productions at home institutions,
regional theaters and abroad (significantly in Israel and Holland), Robert
is committed to mentoring young artists. During his five years with me at
Columbia overseeing the graduate directing program, he deeply affected
the lives and careers of many young directors. He continues to be part of
their lives and careers today.

Robert's life shifts between his commitment to a home base and travel to
far-flung lands and cultures. Upon completion of a production, he typically heads for an airport, buys a ticket to a remote destination and flies off
with few plans. Adventures ensue until he must return to direct another
show. Whatever experience he gathers on those travels clearly feeds his
rich theatrical visions.

September 14, 2006
Lobby of A.R.T.
Boston, MA

AB: The older I get, the more I realize we are who we are because of the people we hung out with earlier in our lives, who gave us goose bumps and formed the DNA of who we are as artists. What are those major influences that you still feel in touch with today and still inform you when you are working as a director?

RW: I was very fortunate. I was out in San Francisco. I met Sam Shepard over a pool table, which is the best place to meet a writer, and we started talking about performance, theater and its value. Storytelling. A love of actors. A kind of simplicity of design. And then he introduced me to Joseph Chaikin, who introduced me to a spirituality and a sacredness about the event of theater, combined with an unbelievable idea of physical rigor of performance—almost a physiological approach to evoking emotion in a room—to the idea of that being the performer's job: to evoke thought, to evoke emotion in a room. The combination of Sam's idea of storytelling, and how important that was to him, and Joe's idea of sacredness and the idea of performance being so alive and evocative—I think that combination of people, those ideas, got carried around for three decades. It was pretty seminal for me.

Since then, are there visual artists or musicians that you're able to translate into your work, that make your pulse run faster?

I've seen Godard's films since the late sixties, actually followed all the steps in what he's been making, from very political films, frontal in their approach to subject matter, all the way to his work now, which is really extraordinary in terms of independence: He's one of the few philosopher-filmmakers that we have in the world. His journey—which included his idea of filmic gesture, the idea of density, the vocabulary that he introduced in film—that was readily available to theatrical exploration. I think his work has always been something that has been feeding me—and also his independence in the system—that he's working in a system that he has almost no right to survive in, and he's been able to do it and make his own statement, which has been amazingly personal and political at the same time.

Musically, the idea of the rhythms of jazz—difficult jazz, where sonically I've found it difficult—how do you reach that idea on the stage? I've always found that a challenge. Bob [Brustein] gave me the opportunity to do that with *In Jungle of Cities*, somehow combining Brecht and free jazz. When Arliss [Howard] was doing his monologues, we actually had free jazz underscoring that text. So you have this great poet—Brecht was just writing feverish poetry in the 1920s, and this play came out of that—wedded with Coltrane at his most evocative. Putting these two elements on stage at the same time was one of the great joys I've had in creating theater.

Can I pursue the jazz part for a bit? Personally, I can't stand unstructured jazz. It makes me mad. I get this feeling in my stomach. I was in a martini club with [sound designer] Darron West, and there was a jazz ensemble doing that noodling thing, and I said, "I can't stand unstructured jazz!" Darron said, "Follow the baseline. Just listen to the baseline." I found that helpful. I still have trouble. I'm curious: I love your theater—and when I think of it, yeah, I see the relationship between jazz—really free-wheeling jazz—and what you're doing. I get that in the theater. Can you just say a little bit more about jazz?

What's great is, you know, with jazz, like blues, you have a great sense of form—you have a pattern. The band starts with a pattern, and then they get to go where they want to go. But they've given you a pattern, so psychically everybody's holding onto an idea—a musical idea. And hopefully, the tangent that you take is not too long, so when you come back to the music, to the theme, to the thing that's holding them in the room, they'll still be with you. If you're dealing with a play—if you're dealing with a classic—then how far away can you go so you're still telling the story? How far can you go in between the gestures? Then you have to come back and hit the note of the story. How much can you extend the gesture before you come back, so you won't lose them?

So it's not unstructured jazz—which reminds me of a scene you did in *Baal*, at Trinity Rep. It was the most extraordinary production. I've never seen a successful production of *Baal* before. There was a scene that Annie Scurria was in, and she comes up and has sex with Baal. The character Annie Scurria was playing was going to leave, and Baal was in an attic room. I had to see this scene ten times; I didn't believe it was possible. Annie Scurria, obviously in love with Baal, who's sort of lying there lethargically on the bed, not really caring about her—and the stage is a floor Doug Stein designed with a trap in it, as if she would go downstairs, out of this attic room, by going down the trap. She left. She came back. She looked at him. She swore. She left. She came back. She left, she came back, I don't know how many times. Every one of us in this room has probably had that feeling about somebody, where we leave, we come back, we leave, we come back. Your description about jazz of going out, coming back—I completely see that now, that that is a jazz notion. You can go away from the structure: The play never says, "She goes out, comes back, goes out, comes back." It's like the play stopped, but it didn't stop, because the play kept moving like gangbusters. And yet this relationship opened up into this thing that we all associate with, in our own way. That's jazz, isn't it? Okay, I'll listen more. I'll listen to Coltrane. I'll try.

We did a jazz piece with Sam [Shepard], *Suicide in B Flat*. That was when Sam would do three world premieres at the same time. We did it in San Francisco. That was literally a jazz improvisation. The music was improvised every night, and Sam would sit in on drums during the production. That's where the frustration would actually happen. Danny Glover was actually in that production; he played Niles. They would create this amazing improvisation where the text would meet the music in some just stunning moment. I'd go to the piano player, Harry Mann, and say, "That was great! Can you keep that?" And he'd go, "Heeey. Some nights; some nights, something else . . ." The movement of that piece was so alive. I think the basis of improvisation is that if it's structured enough, it's not about failure—but it's how far you can push it and keep the train on the rails. We were off the rails in that production often, actually.

Is it possible to say, as a director—you're in the room, and it's really going somewhere: Annie Scurria has left five times. How do you keep it on the rails?

I'm actually not sure all of those were scored. On a different night she might have done it more or less. I know we also threw Robert down the stairs seven times. "Get out! Get out! Get out!" And Robert would keep coming up the stairs. I think there was a negotiation in how many times he could do it. And I think it was probably about listening to the room and feeling that night how many times they could do it: It was Robert's choice about how many times he would go back.

Great for a stage manager, huh?

There was a moment in *Orpheus X* where there's a silence at the end of the production that lasted six-and-a-half minutes. And it wasn't about: How long is that silence going to be? Suzan Hanson as Eurydice works with Rinde [Eckert] in the moment. I said to Rinde, "The length of time in that event is just extraordinary. The audience is breathing with you. Everyone is just waiting for the next moment." And he said, "It's all Suzan. She really controls this whole event." There's a performer who really has a sense of space and time, and she knows that she can take the audience with her; she's leading the event. She's really a shaman, in the best sense of the word, in terms of running a road and leading a journey. She can extend that moment, bring them with her—and they'll stay with the story.

I'm obsessed right now with the function of theater in our times. And we're living in difficult times. And one of the most profound things you can do in the theater is change the time signature in the room. We live in a really bad time. We went from MTV time to internet time to FOX News time to a time of manufactured paranoia: The time signature is really inhuman. And to be able to be in a room and actually be able to change the time signature, and to be able to invite an audience into that alternate time signature, is a radical and political act in our times. Doing bobrauschenbergamerica—the audience isn't used to using those muscles to change the time signature with you, and it's awkward and strange. It occurs to me that maybe I should listen to more jazz, because what you're describing also is an actor having control over time—not really the director, not the audience.

I've noticed a lot of directors of late are starting slower. I think it's harder to get people into the room. I've noticed a lot of pieces that are starting with a longer sense of stillness and allowing the movement, allowing the heart-rate, allowing the breathing of an audience coming in from a world in which they've been bombarded to begin to breathe in this space. I love Krystian [Lupa]'s beginning of *Three Sisters*—just that note of music when Molly [Ward] walked into that room and a long extended stillness. A character connection. That beautiful note of music. No text yet. Nothing. It really eased us into the room.

The opposite of that: When we did *Orpheus*, I didn't want the audience even to have sat down. I wanted them to have been behind. So Rinde just walked out on stage, and I said, "Can we go to one hundred immediately?" The band was full blast, and they were rocked back in their seats, and they were way behind: They were lost, they were "What? Whoa?" and information is coming at them—very sonically, very dense—and that is another way of shocking the system and making them get here. "Hurry up, come on, you've got to get here, you've got to get here!" It's the opposite idea of, "Okay, let's bring them in, let's change together. Let's breathe."

Also, composers in new classical are doing that in time signatures, too. They're writing in more extreme—music that changes every three measures. I think there's more and more interest in differentiating of time, how one moment is different than the other.

Evan Ziporyn, when he wrote the *Oedipus* score, his time signature—he drove the singers nuts. He'd switch on a dime. It was incredibly difficult.

Speaking of difficult: You said something to me before you ever became an artistic director or were even thinking of it. You said that the health of an institution is reflected in how it's falling apart. I wonder, now that you're running an institution, what do you think about that?

Okay. I need context.

I'll tell you where you said it: I was running Trinity Rep for one glorious and horrible year, before I was fired. And you were coming to do Baal, and at some point you were arguing with me on the phone, and you said, "What is this, summer stock? Four weeks of rehearsal? What are you doing?" And out of this argument this phrase came, and it came from the point of view of an artist who wanted to make his work, and wanted to make it really good. And I was working from a point of view of having an institution, balancing a budget, dealing with the board—so there was this odd straddling going on.

Boy, I want to be really smart here. Maybe it's in the struggle. The institution is really a reflection of the artist working there. The artists are trying to create the work, and to create the work there's a difficulty—and you see, on the stage, the difficulty of creation. You see the grist of something being made, and I don't know that the institution should be immune to also feeling that heat and difficulty. The falling apart—maybe it's just in terms of the struggle—that parallels the artist's struggle to create.

Audience: Can you talk about the different struggles that are happening here at A.R.T.?

Ultimately, it's how to maximize a real commitment to creation and to freshness, and there are so many things pulling at that. The building is an oasis, I think. What happens on that stage is truly—it's almost sacred space in the sense that it's a community that's functioning; it has its own politics, its own personality, and its goal is to put something on the planet which is a statement about strength and beauty and idea and struggle. Everything is committed to that, ultimately. But we're not in a vacuum, and it's a difficult culture: I have a friend, an Israeli, who in the darkest of times, I said, "How do you make things now? How can you possibly keep making things?" And he said, "Well, I have to make something so when this all ends we have something to point to and say, 'There. That has value.'" So when the smoke clears, that's what we want to invest in, that's what we've been fighting for. This is really the light through that haze of this war and this insanity. If we have nothing to point to when it ends, we'll go, "Why are we doing this?"

AB: That's gorgeous.

It's an amazing metaphor, and when it gets dark there, it gets really dark. It is hard to figure out why you're going out and creating something.

AB: In that spirit—and I'm not talking about choosing a season, but for you, in this time right now—how do you choose plays? How do you decide what the content is going to be?

I think it's a reflection of that: "What do you want to leave behind? What is the imprint you want to leave in the chaos?" This season, this is it: It doesn't get any better than this. These are amazing artists who are going places we've never been. There's a great sense of experiment, imagination, tackling big subjects. It's political; it's personal.

AB: So the way you choose a play for yourself is actually the same way you choose a season.

At some point, curating becomes about what excites you. And that personal-political thing tends to be at the center of that.

AB: I'd like to go back into the rehearsal room with you. I mean that literally and figuratively. A couple of times, sitting in on your rehearsals, I've had fun contagiously because you're having fun.

And you're the only artistic director I've dragged into rehearsal and said, "Look at this. What do you think? I have a problem with this scene. What do you think?" Everybody else, you just hope they don't show up.

AB: I've never told you this or said this out loud, but going into one of those rehearsals once, back in the time of Trinity—I was really in despair, not only running a theater, but also artistically I was having a hard time. I was in some difficult collaborations at that moment, and they were good, but I wasn't having fun. I walked

into your rehearsal and you were hopping all over the place. You were hopping. I was so jealous, because I realized for the last two years (so it wasn't just Trinity; it was this situation I was in artistically), I'd been sitting like this and worried that the collaborators didn't like it. I was just dead inside. That's when I really changed. It was because of being in the rehearsal with you. I just said, "Fuck it. I'd rather do less good work and work with people I have fun with and have freedom with and I can jump around myself, or I don't want to do it at all."

Is there a way to talk about the rehearsal process? First of all the way you work with actors is The Deal. The way you work with actors is unlike anybody else, and it creates an active culture in the room rather than a passive one, where the actors are doing what the director says.

Somebody said something last night, describing another director, and it was exactly what I do in the room: "It looks like you're looking for an answer to a question that you don't know." That's exactly right: I'm looking for an answer to the question and I don't know the question. That's ultimately why it's so open. I have so much respect for people who go in and they know the exact question that they're researching. "This is what we're working on. This is what we're trying to understand." That's a gift, because then the work gets very focused. I find however that I'm more instinctive. I don't know what the question is. So it keeps moving. It's true there's some answer. It's never found, maybe. Maybe there's a sense of movement that's constant.

You said you don't direct actors, you direct a play. That's a mantra of yours that you've shared with students. There's something about—if you put an actor in a great position and give him the physical landscape and give him or her enough of an obstacle to create something—they'll do it. You've given them the challenge. It's about both—freedom and obstacle. If you can create both for them, they can paint it. It's putting them in that position, and if you haven't done that, then you're failing. You're failing them.

AB: The notion of the director directing the play came from a Russian actress who visited us once from the military theater of Moscow. She said the actor's job is to direct the role. It's the most radical thing ever! Because it's so obvious! But I think most directors in this country think it's their job to direct the actor's role. Or most actors in this country think it's the director's job to direct their role. But actually the actor's job is to direct the role, and the director's job is to direct the play, and it's very different. I think you can feel in a room, in a rehearsal, whether the play or the role is being directed by the director. And I think one of the reasons your room is very exciting is because every actor is directing their role.

Could any actor in this room who's worked with Woodruff describe what he's like as a director?

Audience: As an instructor in our class, when we see him in then hallway, he's got such a mellow personality. He seems very laid back. But when he gets into a rehearsal, or the class space, it's very frenetic and, like you said, jumping up and down. And it gets into everyone else in the room.

AB: It's contagious.

Audience: It's kind of like good cop, bad cop, where he'll tell you to do an exercise, and he'll lay it out all nice, and you'll start to do it, and he's up in your face, yelling at you and trying to get you to lose concentration, and just when you're about to give up, he'll get in your face: "Do it! Do it!" And afterward, you'll go up to him and ask him questions about something you might have a problem with—and he'll let you answer it yourself. "What do I do about this?" "I don't know. You figure it out." So you get a bit of drill sergeant with a twist of caring fatherly type.

AB: So it sounds like what you're saying is, he does make an obstacle: He's the obstacle.

Audience: I feel when I'm working with Woodruff entirely safe and completely terrified, constantly. Safe in the sense that he won't let me do bad work. But at the same time the emotion level in the room with him is unbelievable, and it's something I haven't experienced with other directors.

Audience: I want to piggyback on the safety idea. My experience with this class and other situations is that you're simultaneously being stripped of anything that's miscellaneous and really getting down to a specific grounded yet frantic core. And the safety is so important to that. I've exposed sides of myself I didn't know were there.

AB: I always think that, as a director, our job is the atmosphere in the room, the philosophy—and that our respect is contagious, our interest is contagious.

Chuck [Mee], when he sees productions, says, "I know how many times a director's been fucked over, how many bad love affairs he's had." There's something about all that that you leave behind.

AB: Somebody once told me a theory I think is very funny: He said you can always see the director's body on stage. You go to see a Richard Foreman play and it's like, "My foot hurts!" You see Robert Wilson and everything is very tall and angular. You go to see Peter Brook and everyone is so round and healthy, I remember one of the first times I met you, we were walking down the stairwell in the back of Playwrights Horizons's old building, and—I swear to God—you were wearing cowboy boots, walking down the steps, and, without stopping, you took off your watch, threw it down, stepped on it, and kept going. That's just like your plays! I didn't know you well enough to be like, "What did you just do?"

Robert Brustein (Founding Director, American Repertory Theater): I'm interested in this idea of the relationship between the individual and the institution. It seems to me very similar to the relationship between the individual citizen and the society. And it seems to me when people make an artistic institution, they're trying to make an alternative to a bad society.

And you think that's wrong?

RB: No, I think that's right. In other words, they're trying to create a place in which people can work together affirmatively, well, positively, in loving terms—which society does not allow them to do. And that means some sort of a communal organization. And that comes into conflict with an individual ego. And the question is: How does that individual ego adapt itself to that communal effort? That's a continual tension. I don't think it should ever be resolved. If it's resolved this way you destroy the institution; if it's resolved this way, you make the ego conform to an impossible situation.

AB: Which is a kind of fascism, really.

RB: Yes, it is. So it's ultimately a political idea, and that is how you try to create that more perfect society and whether what is being produced there is reinforcing this idea, or at odds with it, or combating it, or supporting it . . .

In its greatest sense, though, the community doesn't diminish the integrity of each individual. It's still built on the uniqueness of each individual, and their strength and their brightness, without being subservient, and it's really the collection of all that individuality and all that brightness. Maybe you can also look at the institution as the individual and its relationship to the larger society. How much does it have to sacrifice to its relationship to the outside? I think where we have to grow as an institution—it can't just be an alternative, because then you get like this. It has to have an exchange. With fluids. With the larger community.

RB: That's known as the audience.

Yes. The audience, and not just the audience—groups and interests and ideas and people who represent ideas. An extended audience.

AB: What you're saying is so beautifully put—you can't actually swing in either direction. You can't make it an organization about individuals, and you can't make it the opposite.

RB: The collective.

AB: If it's only about the collective, then it turns into some communist nightmare. But we hear that so rarely: to understand that there's no answer, no solution—that it's a constant struggle, between the individual running the company. I'm looking at my gang back there. If any one of us becomes "The Thing," then it's gone. Yet we can't be a complete democracy. We can't vote about everything. It's not collective.

It's such an interesting issue—that will never be solved. Actually, the responsibility is to keep that dissonance and that irritation. I support that. I would love to look at that in relation to the social system we're in: What does that mean in relation to what we're actually experiencing?

RB: What we're experiencing now is the transformation of the country into some sort of corpulent beast. I mean that physically as well as spiritually: Everyone's getting much huger, and their souls are getting fatter. It's all thumbs and people's eyes. That's why I think an artistic alternative is so important, and that alternative must establish an alternative way of being that reminds us that we're human and compassionate and full of sin and full of problems and full of difficulties, and nevertheless that we're moving forward rather than backward with the beasts.

AB: Leon Ingulsrud said to me last summer that actually it wasn't acting techniques that blew people away when the Moscow Art Theatre came in 1923 to visit the United States and changed the culture of our theater. It was actually the way that people were, on stage—that it wasn't a technique of affected memory or anything. It was that they'd never seen a culture behave together in that particular way. And then I think about the bit of revolution that the Viewpoints causes. It's not necessarily a technique, but it's the way people are behaving together on stage, which is in essence non-hierarchical and involves a tremendous amount of listening, so that what we do—certainly with *bobrauschenbergamerica*—is create a society or a tribe that is functioning in a certain way.

Which brings up mirror neurons, which is this new discovery in science that everyone is up in arms about, discovered by some scientists in Southern California. It's a neuron which we share with other primates, with certain monkeys. The development of the species came about because certain species had these mirror neurons which muscularly imitate what we see. Like a child, we teach them to eat: "Open your mouth." And they muscularly learn. We have grown as a species because we can learn; we can see, and our muscles actually make movements—which means when you watch something, it doesn't look like it, but your muscles are repeating what you're watching.

What that means in terms of theater is an extraordinary thing. An audience is actually having a muscular workout in what they're experiencing. I always Google it, every two minutes, to see what the newest thinking in mirror neurons is. And the latest thing, in England, some scientists hooked up some Royal National Ballet dancers and some capoeira dancers to fMRI (functional Magnetic Resonance Imaging) machines and had them watch another dancer perform. What they learned is, the more you've trained in something, the more your muscles do the same thing as the person you're watching.

So in theater, because we actually reflect behavior—we do the closest to how we actually live—you are watching and practicing, because you are the audience, a certain kind of societal behavior, which you are presented on the stage.

It's amazing. The more you know, the more your muscles participate. Someone who hasn't studied ballet—their muscles will not be twitching as much as a ballet dancer, watching another ballet dancer.

Are you saying they're less engaged?

AB: Yes, someone with less training will be less engaged. The old problem in theater is that people think they can act because they can walk and talk. But actually walking and talking on stage is very complicated. But I think that might work in our benefit in terms of mirror neurons.

I think we're very engaged by things that are distant from us, *because* they're distant from us. We don't know, we don't recognize, the behavior. We're in a foreign culture. Maybe we don't have those neurons firing, but, still, it's so alerting. As opposed to something that's so familiar—those neurons are static. If you present something very foreign—when you look at something beyond your normal range of perception, you can be stunned by it, because it's so foreign.

AB: Well, actually neurologically—I've been studying neurology since you got me interested in it when we were planning the brain project—what activates it is difference. The reason we don't remember things we do every day is because we do the same things. But as soon as we do something different, we remember that: It impresses itself on us. So anything that is more foreign, it makes an impression, whereas things that are regular become a blur.

Audience: We've had a couple of conversations over the years about the audience and the relationship of the artist to the audience, and I wonder if there's a difference, say, between the relationship of the director to the audience than the artistic

director to the audience, or if being an artistic director has at all influenced or changed your thinking about the audience.

You want to present work you're challenged by. I think we're programming for ourselves, in the best sense—if we're challenged by it, and think we can lead the audience to it. So, I think my work has been fairly aggressive in the past. Krystian's voice is aggressive in another way. To put that on the stage, I think, is remarkable for this audience. It's so distant from theater, from the sense of time of what they've seen before. People have strong voices, personal voices. I want to bring those voices to the audience. The connection to the material is very strong. For every artist that comes here, it's different: There's something about that person, their relationship to their work, their relationship to a given piece of material, that combination—it leads an audience to a place they've never been. There's a freshness to that thinking that we're trying to keep up.

The hard thing is—I find it so hard to make anything, in general. I find it frightening. It's just scary. And then to profess to put seven or eight things on the stage over the course of the year is so daring. It takes such chutzpah. Yiddish is so good. It's just arrogant to say, "I want you to come here seven times. I'm going to take you where you've never been." Really, that's the only thing the theater wants to be—and can be. So it's a monumental task.

So, going from the micro—your own self, and the making of something once a year—to the macro—the vision of an institution, doing it seven or eight times a year—that's a ride.

AB: Dovetailing on that, what's your relationship to audience development? Getting more people through the doors?

You know, I don't do it. People who are in charge of that in this institution, they do it. It's their gig. They have a question, I'll feed it. But my job is very big, and everybody in this institution has expertise, and they have to do it. I really have to trust it's going to be done. If someone calls on me and says "Can you help?" I'm going to commit whatever I can. But this is about everyone in pulling their weight, and making their portion of the institution successful in that way. I don't know anything about audience development.

AB: I think that's one of the great things about you being an artistic director. I've known you for a long time. I've found you've become bigger— in a good way. Easier. Wider. And your art hasn't suffered. It's actually better. It's more in the present moment. Because you have so many things to deal with, you've had to go—

Well, there are also so many great people here.

Audience: Anne first asked you about influences, and you talked about Shepard, Chaikin, Godard. Music and jazz. But I wondered about other theater influences— other directors. I remember seeing In the *Jungle of Cities*, and it didn't look like anything I had seen in this country before. In a way, parts of your work belong to theater aesthetics of other cultures. When did that contact with other theater cultures happen for you, and who was it you saw?

I made the hajj to Berlin twenty-five years ago.

Audience: What did you see?

I saw [Peter] Stein's work there, Heiner Müller, Peter Zadek. I was captivated by the aesthetic. But in the end, it was about space. The anthropomorphisms of space. I've always liked the idea of air and space. It's never been about density. It's been about sparsity. When you work and start your institutions and you're working with nothing, you learn the value of a dollar, and there's something about the sparseness you maintain in your aesthetic.

AB: Sparse is expensive.

I know. It can be really costly. The openness of a room—the breadth of that landscape is really nice. The audience imagination in a room that has space is bigger. They have a place to roam. It's not dictated. There's more room. They can wander.

I work with great designers. George Tsypin is truly a magnificent man and an incredible collaborator, and he delivers—he essentially gives you an obstacle. He dares you to create the work in this space. He gives you physical obstacles to creating the event, rather than giving you a path. So you already have something you're banging into. And, boy, do I love that. There is something just extraordinary about that.

Working with Doug Stein was the opposite. He really gave you room. He didn't give you enough places to land. He would give you too much air. So you'd fly around, looking for that obstacle. That's great, too. Great colleagues. And now David Zinn and Riccardo Hernandez have become great partners.

Audience: How about "revelation space"?

That's Anne's word. What's great about Anne is she's given nomenclature to ideas that we use though we don't know we use them. It's a great tool, so you think about it.

Audience: The most beautiful things I've ever heard you say are not necessarily about students but are in situations where you were asked to speak to students, beginning some number of years ago, before you were artistic director here at American Repertory Theater, when you gave the commencement address here at the A.R.T. Institute. It was unbelievable.

We have an institution of about eighty or ninety people, plus we have fifty students. So more than a third of the population of this place is students. That's really extraordinary. There's an artistic innocence, in a way, which needs to be honored. I think it really creates a tone in the building. You can't put anything on that stage that could diss them. That's it: You burn in hell. So, you can't speak to them untruthfully. It sets the bar so high. Plus, they have to kill you, because you're the parent and they're the child. So you have to give them the tools to kill you. You have to give them everything you know, so then they can just run amuck and destroy everything you believe in—which is kind of the nature of, the evolution of, art. That's a big responsibility. All you can do is give them that, and then . . . watch the blood flow.

But, you know, when we were at Columbia University, the great thing that we noticed right off the bat was that I think one person, out of the thirty-five wonderful directors that passed through our program, who actually had the word "career" existing in his head. Everybody else was like, "I want to make things." It wasn't about, I want to work at this institution. You really had a sense it wasn't going to be about culture palaces. It was going to be reflections of society—individual reflections of society. I think it's still going to happen. They'll find a way to make it happen. And whether the institution responds, well, they're at their peril if they don't.

AB: It's also a paradox: The one person you're thinking of, who was obsessed with a career, has had the least of a career. And the people who were least obsessed with a career, getting their muscles and working and craning—they're the ones who end up working.

Good thing.

Audience: What do you want from your students, with your time?

I don't know a short answer. I think getting bigger. Everybody gets a little bigger—their sense of themselves on the planet. They get more of a sense of what that role is, and they want to take on more. That'd be great.

AB: That's the hardest thing. It's easier to say, "Get this technique." But "Get bigger"—it's huge. Nikos Psacharopoulos, the once (now-deceased) artistic director of Williamstown Theatre Fest used to say to actors: "Today you must kill for love. Go!"

Audience: Doesn't what you were saying about neurons mean basically that Aristotle was right, and it is about mimesis? It's what we're familiar with that creates the pity and what we're not familiar with that creates the fear. Along those lines, can you talk about why *Britannicus*? Neoclassicism?

The short answer: We're giving to the audience so they're seeing themselves on the stage, and really the theater should be about seeing the other. I don't know where that fits in with what you're saying but somewhere in there it's really important. It's a great thought. Why *Britannicus*? God, that's hard. I think it's a great story. You'd slit your wrists for a great story. The challenge is, how can you tell that great story? It's such a difficult story to tell. The personal part of that play is so raw, and yet there's a political frame. There's a meeting of those two worlds again. Exciting.

Mary Zimmerman

I first got to know Mary Zimmerman during the interview for this book. Perhaps our lack of acquaintance is an expression of a certain disconnect between New York and Chicago artists. But her reputation certainly preceded her. We met for the conversation on the campus of the University of Chicago in front of a full house of Mary Zimmerman devotees who offered penetrating questions at the end of our chat.

Mary's life and work in the theater express the depth and sophistication of her choice of subjects, stories and themes. She creates completely new works of theater by turning her attention and craft toward such great myths as *Metamorphoses*, *The Arabian Nights* and *The Odyssey*, finding successful theatrical shapes that excite audiences everywhere. She fashions fantastic brand-new productions based upon the lives of Proust, DaVinci and Galileo. She directs opera. She directs classic plays including a great deal of Shakespeare. She has won countless Joseph Jefferson Awards, and in 2002 she received a Tony Award for *Metamorphoses*. In 1998 she was awarded a MacArthur Fellowship. She is a member of Chicago's Lookingglass Theatre Company as well an artistic associate at the Goodman Theatre. She is a professor of performance studies at Northwestern University.

Brought up in Lincoln, Nebraska, the daughter of two university professors, Mary grew up wanting to become an actress. She began her studies as an undergraduate at Northwestern University as a comparative and literature major but swiftly changed to the theater department. She later returned to Northwestern as a graduate in the department of performance studies where she discovered that, for her, creating and directing theater were synonymous. She received her BA, MA and PhD all at Northwestern, and she is now a revered and beloved professor there.

Mary's incontrovertible success is matched by her demonstrated commitment to innovation in the art of theater. She manages to focus her successes back into the projects with which she is involved. She is ambitious but not egotistical. Her enthusiasm for theater as an art form is contagious not only to enthusiastic audiences nationally and internationally but to the countless students who study with her. It is rare to find such a genuine combination of scholar, artist, innovator, inventor and teacher.

November 7, 2006

AB: I thought I'd start with the hardest possible question. Today is a very particular day—election day. It's a very important election, and we live in exceedingly difficult times. Some people might call it war time. I might call it junta time. Things have changed. It is difficult to be an artist in this time. Or maybe not. I'm curious as to your thoughts about how to be working in the climate we are in now. Has it changed for you?

MZ: Do you mean a sense of irrelevancy, or do you mean a sense of hostility in terms of funding, or do you mean . . . ?

Keep going. Yes.

I feel like I should know what the answer to that is, but I don't have a very good one. My own feeling is that I have been doing what I do as a citizen of my own community. It's the baker's job to make good bread. And it's my job to do whatever I can do with my own skill in whatever way I find most interesting. But I will say that because of the way I work—I generally do adaptations, but I have no script going into rehearsal—the final product is always very contingent on and in relation to events of the world and what we come into the rehearsal room talking about. Lots of my shows have ended up bent toward political means or expression without my really intending that.

I'll give two examples. I was slated to do *The Notebooks of Leonardo Da Vinci* for the third time at the Goodman in the spring of '03, and as things sort of heated up in the fall of '02 I said, "I don't want to do *The Notebooks of Leonardo Da Vinci* anymore. I want to do Seneca's *Trojan Women*." And the Goodman, for all its being a gigantic tanker of an institution, was able to make this wide turn in its season though tickets had already been sold and it was already out in the brochures and so forth. That was a scary experience to tell the truth, because our first preview, maybe tech, was the actual day of the first crossing the border from Kuwait, and every day that play felt as if it had been written that morning. It was sort of unbelievable. In David Slavitt's translation—I've used his translations now for three things—the very first speech by Hecuba talks about the ruins of smoking towers and how we gag when we think of what the particles in the air are made of. The demand for the son of Andromache, who's just this little boy, is a kind of preemptive strike, because he will grow up and avenge. All of that felt so absolutely contemporary. We did it in contemporary dress and the set was as though the theater itself had sort of collapsed in on itself. We had trusses fallen in the middle of the stage. We littered the stage with that kind of 9/11 crap that was on the ground—that gray, papery stuff. That was a really conscious and deliberate choice, and it was a bit of a scandal. I don't actually read my reviews, but I know that one of them ended with the phrase, "This play does not make you feel good about being an American." It was the last sentence in a very negative review, apparently.

But more subtly, in a way, less agit-proppy, I'm doing *Jason and the Argonauts* right now. The reason I *thought* I chose that text, was because I really like episodic, really old stories that involve sea voyages. It's just a thing with me—really difficult things to stage, sea monsters and people flying, dark, strange tales that feel symbolic, but you can't really get to the end of their symbolism. You can't pin down exactly what you think they're about, yet they *feel* like they're about something in a really strong way. So I thought I chose the text because it was that kind of story I've done several times before. And then I started reading it—because I often pitch into these things without having actually read the text since I was a child, and then usually only a children's version of it. The second half of that book is about Medea, this teenage girl who is shot with an arrow of love by the gods because they want to use her to help Jason get the Golden Fleece. And she suffers and suffers and struggles and struggles to not have to help him and not betray her family and her father, but in the end she does. We all know how that ends—although in *The Argonautika* it doesn't go that far. It stops where Euripides starts, with his abandonment of her. So then I thought, oh I see, it's all very personal. It's about betrayal and love, and now I understand why I really picked this. But then very late in rehearsal, this third thing started to emerge—the story as a kind of antiheroic epic. It's an anti-go-to-the-foreign-country-and-accomplish-something epic. They go—it is very much to the Middle East, to the Black Sea, where no Greek's ever been before—to retrieve this Golden Fleece, which is believed by the person who owns it to have magical properties, but in fact it doesn't. It's just actually a sheepskin. They achieve their mission. But so much is lost in that attainment that the victory absolutely empties out. And so, toward the end, I took a phrase from the original text and expanded it into a speech for the chorus that begins, "Oh these glorious missions of men—they start out so well, so full of noble intent." Something like, "Go off and punish the foreigner, defeat the tyrant, defend the nation and hip hip hurrah hurrah, become a man. Seize that Golden Fleece and utopia will descend. Seize that Golden Fleece and the world itself will change. Seize that Golden Fleece and there will be an end to evil. Whatever. They all turn out the same in the end." It changes this whole evening that you've seen, that's very adventurous and a lot of fun initially—their energy to go is so infectious. yet, when I was initially staging the show, I did not have an ironic thought in my head about it. I think this is why the play ends up being effective. I wasn't really thinking about where this is going to go. This is the result of having no script when I start. I'm in the moment. But then the piece comes to this barren conclusion—this wiped-out, bloody, empty betrayal and scene of destruction. I don't think the play would have ended that way if I'd done it—I can't say ten years ago anymore, but fifteen years ago.

That makes me think of something that Leonard Bernstein said once: "If somebody asked me to write a symphony, I could do it overnight. I have the technique. But it wouldn't be very good. It hasn't had the time to pass through my subconscious." That makes sense to me in terms of what you're saying. How do you deal with the political reality? Well, you make your work, you bake your bread, but at the same time you allow your subconscious to work on it in ways that you can't control.

I think that's exactly right. I actually work out of the unconscious. I believe in it really strongly. People think that because I go in with no script that I develop these shows and work on them for two years in workshop. I've never had a workshop. I have four to six weeks of rehearsal, then I go into tech like everyone else and then I open the show. But I start with no script. I do that for a variety of possibly neurotic reasons, but one of the effects is that the pressure is so intense that I can't censor and I can't be polite. I have to go with the first fucking thing I think of. Then, in tech previews, that other half of the brain comes into operation. I usually don't change a lot during previews, but with *Argonautika* I cut twenty minutes out of the first act and rearranged a story. I actually did it on opening night.

I'm not making these things up whole cloth. They're books or stories or myths that exist already. My feeling is that I'm always trying to get out of the way. It's the way musicians talk all the time, that they're the vehicle or the antenna of the music, that they're just catching it, but its own sort of spirit is coming through. That's always how I feel in rehearsal. That kind of pressure of four weeks and all the tickets are being sold and you don't have two words of it written—that cracks me open in a way.

That's a really big deal. We think utopia is having tons and tons of time, but—

That would be hell.

You put pressure on yourself, intensely, but at the same time—and I know this is true, so you can't lie and say it's not true—you have to slow down under that pressure. You have to slow your blood pressure down, because if you get rushed, you're sunk.

My metaphor is that creating works—devising theater—is an act of archeology: You are an archeologist who is rubbing away the sand from an object that's been buried some time ago. If you rush, you will damage that object that is trying to emerge. If you are not disciplined and on time, you will arrive on opening night with dirt still obscuring the form. All of this implies that the object already exists. In a way, it's inevitable because of the personalities—I have my cast, I have my design, I have my opening night. And yet, it's unpredictable and unknowable. It's utterly absolute, and it's also contingent. It's a really paradoxical thing. It's an object that we've already made, but we've forgotten how we made it. We have to sort of reconstitute it through the act of performance.

I have a bunch of conflicting metaphors for how I work because it's not really describable. It's a sort of mystery to me.

Let's try to figure out how you got that way. We're going to go back a little bit. So, you're this kid from Nebraska. I'm interested in your influences. What happened to you that forged who you are?

My parents were both university professors, and I was in a really academic environment. When I was five, my dad was on a Rhodes scholarship in Cambridge, England, and my mom took me to all sorts of plays. And I had a primal scene of theater. We lived in Hampton Gardens suburb on the outskirts of London, and there was a woods behind our house called the Little Woods, which is a very English type of name. Down the street was the Big Woods. I would play in the Little Woods all day long. Unbeknownst to me, every year in the Little Woods, there was, in a clearing, a perfor-mance of *A Midsummer Night's Dream*. I came upon a rehearsal—"Ill met by moonlight, proud Titania." They weren't really in costume. They said their words to each other, then Oberon took off and this music came on, I think, a victrola. He had these streaming fabric things on his arm. And he ran around a few times and the music was playing and suddenly he started laughing and everyone started laughing and they all kind of fell on the ground. And he said, "How many times? How many times do I run?" I had no confusion that I was seeing actual fairies. It was nothing remotely like that. The really striking thing for me was to see adults playing like that and to see adults laughing like that. I'd never seen anything like that in my life. I was just so attracted to it. I went and got my sister and we would watch. And to this day I can't believe this, but the director kicked us out from watching—as though we were some sort of a threat to the process.

It became forbidden to you.

I guess you're right. But then we went and saw the show. I think we went and saw it every night. That was just thrilling.

But the method I have as a director . . . I went back to Northwestern as a graduate in performance studies, which at one time was the department of oral interpretation, which concentrated on literature in performance and so forth. I had this very strong narrative impulse, but then also I took this performance art class. My performances started getting more and more elaborate and longer and longer, and eventually it was easier for me to not be in them—and that's actually how I became a director. I kind of discovered directing. I'd loved theater since I was five and had done plays, community theater and in my backyard and in my basement and had written plays as a child, but I never thought for a moment that I could be an actress because I knew I wasn't pretty enough, and I was told that as well, quite explicitly or implicitly, whenever I spoke of my desire.

So I had initially come to Northwestern as an undergraduate major in comparative literature, but two weeks in I transferred over to theater. I never for a second thought I'd have a career in the theater. I just couldn't *not* do it. I remember just horrific guilt: "I'm wasting my parents' money . . ." As a graduate student I started doing these performance pieces and started directing that way, and it was like a door opening up. I understood that this was how to be in the theater for me. I'm everywhere in it, and I'm nowhere. I'm visible in it, and I'm invisible. To tell the truth, all my life in theater, I loved rehearsal, but I didn't really like performing that much. I didn't like getting dressed up. I didn't like putting on the makeup. I didn't like uncomfortable costumes. But I loved rehearsal. So, that's now the part of it that I have.

And what would you say were the big influences aesthetically and otherwise?

A lot. Frank Galati was a teacher of mine, but also, when I was in my early twenties in Paris, I saw *The Mahabharata* by Peter Brook at the Bouffes du Nord. Also in my twenties, I saw Pina Bausch's *Arien* at the Brooklyn Academy of Music. Those two things are extremely important for me.

What was it about *The Mahabharata* and the Pina Bausch?

I guess it's their scale. *Mahabharata* was three evenings long and over three hours in each evening, and it was done on basically on an empty stage in this old theater. It was also done outdoors in Avignon, through the night and the sun would come up with it. It's very international in its cast. Its story was so rich and large and deep and big. I remember that they had bows and arrows—huge bows. They would take the arrow and go "fwump" with their hand, and that equaled shooting. That kind of slightly symbolic vocabulary, presentational vocabulary, was so huge to me.

And then *Arien* was done in water, which stuck with me for a very long time. It's this dance piece, but people talk. I think what it might have taught me—and lots of things at school taught me this too—was that, in spite of all the evidence to the contrary, things can be profoundly emotional that are not narrative and do not contain story. You pour yourself into these visions. Pina Bausch's pieces, they go on without an intermission and they're kind of a scene and another scene and they sort of overlap and there's a lot of quiet in them sometimes and there's a lot of music and running around. The dancers are trained dancers. Again, very international. But their vocabulary of dance is often related to everyday movement: sitting around and talking, brushing your hair or at a dinner party or just walking or sitting in a café. It's very ordinary.

I think both of those things were influential—the vocabulary they both employed, how stunningly emotional and beautiful I found both pieces, one very narrative-based, including having a narrator, and the other without narrative, but equally somehow complete.

And both with a company. I'm curious about your relationship to Lookingglass and your relationship to people you work with over a long period of time.

I'm not actually a founding member of Lookingglass, and they were very hesitant to take me on. They'd been in operation at least five, six, seven years before I became a member, but I had directed them three times during that period. They were started as an actors' company, as many companies are, and I wasn't really an actor. I think they feared I would sort of take over—I had no desire to take over—and it would become my company. That very clearly hasn't happened. The thing about working with a company—it has advantages and disadvantages, which are all kind of the same. Like, you've worked with them twenty years—and you've worked with them twenty years. I always say that the first day of rehearsal at Lookingglass is actually the twentieth year of rehearsal. There's just such a shared vocabulary and such an immediacy and such an efficiency. The disadvantage, in a certain way, is that the company was formed twenty years ago next year. It was formed by a set of people some of which are now different people and have different feelings about things, and their differences have become more apparent rather than more integrated. There isn't always room for every company member in every show. And I'd like to point out that, unlike Steppenwolf, our company members—like ninety-eight percent of them—live in Chicago and are in all our plays. We didn't move away.

What do you feel like your responsibility to that company is?

I go to the monthly meetings. I direct there when I feel like something I feel like directing is right for the company or right for the space. In terms of *Argonautika*, I think our new space, our Water Tower space, is fantastic. I know that citizens go in it and they don't realize they've been in it before because when it's a proscenium, it's like it was built as a proscenium. When it's alley, it's like it was built as though it was alley. Whatever way you do it, it kind of mathematically works. It's just a great, intimate space. It also has the problems of an intimate space, which is that its maximum seating capacity is like two hundred and twenty, and we traditionally do really large-cast shows. And financially that's—

The mathematics doesn't work.

It's ruinous, and there's no way around it. It's just a sort of insoluble problem.

Let's shift to the relationship with actors, designers, writers that function over time. You have a reputation. When anybody's in tech rehearsals with you, the rest of their lives go down the toilet. *(Laughter)*

Meaning I'm so exacting?

Meaning it's so all-encompassing nobody has a life outside of these tech rehearsals.

But that's brief. I have no life outside of anything anyway. I actually would say, Anne, my designers are much more OCD than I am, and I just sit back. I'm doing the *Times* crossword puzzle sometimes. I mean, they are so, so obsessive compulsive about the shows and about minutiae of design and timing. I've managed to find the people who will do it for me.

That explains it. I won't blame you for it.

Working with designers is my very most favorite thing. And I've worked with them enough now that we have, again, a huge vocabulary. The things that are really hard to talk about, which I think are lights and sound, now I can say, "Well, sort of like the waltz in *Proust*, but don't do it on piano." We have this vast reference library of our past works.

But also, I was teasing my set designer about *Argonautika*. I went out on the first day of tech with him for dinner break and I said, "It's really good, right?" And he went, "Yeah . . . it's good . . ." He doesn't see it yet. And I felt bemused. It's all kind of in my head and a lot of my stuff in the rehearsal room looks like nothing—because it's flat and it's nothing. There's a paucity to it. It's missing its elements. I know there will be this exquisite music and these ten hundred things scenically will happen and then, you know, this costume isn't in yet. I'm not saying I'm in control of any of that or know it exactly, but I know that it's going to come together. But in a couple of days he was running up to me in the house, and I could see that he sees it because the elements were there. But I was bemused because we've been working together twelve years. Unlike for a lot of plays, the script is only an equal element to those scenic and gestural elements. It's not the dominant element.

That's a big, important deal. Non-Aristotelian.

It is extremely non-Aristotelian. I wish I were, but I'm not.

One of my students at Columbia made me understand that the Aristotelian notion of catharsis is essentially a male orgasm as opposed to—

A female one? Couldn't it be?

Not from my experience. The sort of non-Aristotelian structure of many orgasms.

Well, I do think, without a doubt, the narrative structure as described and graphed by all of our professors is absolutely male. But I don't think arousal and release is necessarily just male. I think it's sexual without a doubt, and it has to do with suspense and anticipation and approaching and retreating and then you're kind of ready for it to shut down after the big moments.

I was yelled at once by a really great opera singer, Lauren Flanagan. At one point I said to her, "Oh, you know, the lights will fix that." And she screamed, "The lights never fix anything!" She's absolutely right, and it was a great lesson—you can't say that the dramaturgical issues of a play are going to be solved scenically.

I agree. But in the sort of theater I do, image sometimes carries the story, carries the meaning. I rely on all of the elements of theater to generate meaning, not just dialogue. The story itself is at the center of all, but how that story is conveyed relies on certain images that are not complete until all the scenic and technical elements are there. Light not only reveals the image, but creates it.

Though I say there's nothing in the rehearsal room, I need them to have the rehearsal props. I need the space to be right. We need to do this like we're actually doing it. I always tackle the transitions in the rehearsal room. I never leave them till tech. I love transitions. I always do them *a vista*. I always try to make them part of the thing. It's choreographed. I like to do sort of cross fades of scenes. I think I've had two go-to-darks in my life during the course of a play—and they were not for transitional purposes. That's what I love about theater—it's half the illusion and the ephemeral beauty and all of that, and then, on the other hand, it's so heavy and materialistic and practical. As a director, and as a great actor too, you have one foot in each of those. You have to be really practical about, "Can this be carried on? Is it worth it to be carried on at this point?" It's not film, which can magically transpose things. It has to embrace its clunkiness and the laws of physics and the weight of it. You have to play into that and remember that it's there.

How about working with actors over a long period of time? You start with no script. Can you just describe the process with actors?

I used to begin with group auditions. They are very physical, very ensemble-oriented. Actors came in groups of like eight to twelve for forty-five minutes. I always have a musician. I always have a drummer. We do a lot of different things: everyone goes to one side of the room and someone leads the others dancing across the room, just whatever that means to them. I have a thing where they're in pairs and one closes their eyes and the other has their eyes open. I go through a series of movements, and the person with their eyes open has to make the person with their eyes closed do what I'm doing without talking. All of this tells me a lot about a bunch of stuff, not always the obvious thing that it seems to be about. It tells me how able they are to throw themselves into the other person and even forget that they're auditioning. It shows me how they are in their body. There are other things I do that show me a little bit if they're show-offy or if they're selfish, where I ask them to compose themselves in scenes. Then, I've generally made up a few scenes of the play—that may or may not make it into the final show—for the sake of auditions and the callback was a more traditional scene reading. In recent years, I've reversed the order and the initial audition is a read and the callback is the group thing—which shows a shift in my own values, I think. They have to get past the qualifications of strong ability with text before we go on.

Then in rehearsal, on the first day, we show the set, because that all has to be designed, same as on any other schedule as if there were a script. Same with costume for the most part, although lots of roles are not assigned when I cast. I'll cast the ensemble. I'll know who's playing the leads. If I'm doing Ovid's *Metamorphoses* or *Arabian Nights*, I don't even know what stories are necessarily going to make it into the show. I have ideas, but I'm not certain. On the first day, we take the book and we'll read a section I'm thinking of doing, and we'll pass it around. We'll read it paragraph by paragraph. Then we'll talk about it. Then I talk about why I like this story and the cool parts of it that I think will go in and things I don't know how to approach and problems there seem to be in the original story that are hard. Then I start staging generally, I'm not kidding, the first day. I'll say, "Let's do six ways to do a boat. Let's do five ways of how to fly. Can we have a camel? I have this idea. Let's see if we can do it."

Every single day it's more. I usually write between two and six in the morning, then I bring that in.

When do you sleep?

I go to bed early. Like at nine. Then I wake up at two. This is how *Argonautika* went. Went back to bed at six. Slept until nine again, then went to rehearsal.

So there will be a little bit more every day. When it is something I am adapting, I don't actually read a lot of secondary criticism. I'm susceptible to smarty-pants commentary; and I want to have my own strong, intimate dialogue with the text itself and not beging from a point of received or standardized interpretation. I need to be experiential. I often have an opening image and a closing image that I'm working toward. With something like *The Odyssey*, the structure is one of the great literary structures ever. It's so good. So you follow that structure and really what you're doing is just editing episodes. But with something like *Arabian Nights*, which in every edition the 384 stories are in a completely different order, what you're doing is searching out the structure. Or Ovid's *Metamorphoses*; there are hundreds of myths in there. I'm pulling from the capabilities of my actors and what the set is pushing us toward.

The single hardest part of working this way is that every night I'm casting it. I'm terrified of making a mistake—either a mistake involving the actor's aptitude for that part, which I'm sort of just guessing at, or a logical mistake. If I use them here—I'm thinking about doing this other story and would I then use them there? Or what if I reverse this order of stories like I'm thinking about, then someone is the lead in two stories in a row? That haunts me. Sometimes I'll change my mind about assignments walking into the room. I start with the caveat on the first day that I may end up reassigning, but I've only ever done it on the most minor, tiny things. I've never actually wrenched a part away from someone after they'd been practicing for a week.

When you say, "Six ways of staging a boat," how do you start staging?

Well, you might go, okay, we can make a boat physically by doing this move, which we've made up in Lookingglass, called the prow of the boat, someone standing on someone's thighs while they're holding their arms. What if we have rowers behind that? No, that looks like shit. All right, let's try fragmenting the boat. You do the sail over there and oarsmen be here.

How much of it do you come up with and how much do the actors come up with?

I generally come in with an idea, but that idea can just go instantly. In one second, you go, "Oh, that doesn't actually work with real people." The actors tend to exceed those ideas and improve upon them.

I always find that if you don't have that idea, you haven't earned the right to walk in that room. But if you hold onto it after you get in the room, then you're in trouble.

Actually, Anne, I'm pretty sure this is a story about you, which I tell all the time and which I love. Someone up on stage asks, "How do we do this?" And I've heard that Anne Bogart says, "I have it," and stands up and starts walking toward the stage when she does *not* have it. But by the time she arrives on stage, she has something.

That's a miniaturized version of what you described as your four weeks of rehearsal. If you give yourself a minute you can do the same thing.

That is you, right?

It is.

I've told that story a lot. And I recognize it very much. You know, you fall, and you grow wings on the way down. You just have to let go.

I think that's what an actor does as well. They dive off of a cliff and they start speaking and they have to carve it on the way down. Otherwise, they're constantly stopping. But I think the same thing in terms of directing. You have to just go.

I think my actors are way, way braver than I. I mean, it's brave, I guess, for me to step off that cliff, but I'm in the driver's seat. They are handing that over to someone else. They are definitely contributing hugely to that process, but when they go home at night, they're not responsible for making up the next day's work. They just surrender—it's an incredible act of trust. There's a perpetual thing that's said about my shows: "Oh God, it was so good. If only you had really great, famous actors in it." No great, famous actor would agree to this process in a thousand years. They just wouldn't. A rare few might. But most people, if they're famous and lauded, it's because they've looked out for their own spotlight. They know how to do that, and they're charismatic. They're not very interested in entering something where they don't know the scope and size of their role and where it's not really about any one actor. The story usually in my work is so much more important. The longest role in *Metamorphoses* is seventeen minutes. That's the longest anyone is a single character. And yet I find it remarkable that the audience is weeping and weeping for a character they met eleven minutes ago.

What do you think that is?

I don't know. Even Shakespeare: "What is Hecuba to I or I to Hecuba that I should weep for her?" I love that it's a mythic reference, because I feel the same way. I do these little pieces and they're very episodic sometimes and you meet a man and wife and they part and the man is killed. And the audience is practically keening. They're so broken up. I honestly think it's because that person has not had time to become particularized to them, and so he stands in for the beloved in one's own life. He is the one I loved and lost. And he has not had time to prove that in fact he's a very different character than your father, your boyfriend, your son or whatever. He's just the man or the woman or the child, and you pour into it. But people who are really, really interested in acting, in representing a character and taking him through the arc of a three-and-a-half hour play—they're not interested in that.

In my conversation with Julie Taymor she brought up ideograms—making ideograms rather than making characters or moments.

That's a really great way to put it.

I'd never heard that, and I found that very useful—that you make a gesture that the audience reads into.

It's a sign and symbol and it resembles the thing that it stands for.

It's not the whole thing, so a resonant one can be very powerful.

Less is more sometimes. And that, again, goes against the ideas of Method acting or maybe even ideas of Aristotelian investment in the tragic heroes. It goes against a lot of theories about how catharsis and identification work—to dare to say, actually, the more general the characters are—wait, that sounds wrong: I don't believe in general acting. Everything must still be very specific in your body and detailed in gesture and voice, you don't approach the text generally—but nonetheless, I've seen these huge effects on the audience's part given almost no time and no acquaintance with the character at all.

How do you choose material, and what attracts you in particular in terms of myth?

Very tiny, little moments attract me. All of my choices have been very peripatetic or random-feeling or could seem that way. Two examples: *Journey to the West*, I loved the title. My boyfriend at the time was reading it, and he read me a scene aloud about a man crossing a river to enlightenment at the western heaven. As he crosses the river in a little boat, he sees a figure in the water floating by. He says, "Who is that?" And his companions say, "It's you, master, it's you. Congratulations." And we know he has transcended. And on stage, you know, to have this actor holding an actor clothed like him, as himself, and then . . . letting him go into the water quietly. I went to Bob Falls and I said, "I want to do this thing called *Journey to the West*. I've never read it. It's two thousand pages long." I knew the general outline of it. And I loved the title.

So that's one. Another, Paul Giamatti is a friend of mine. He's now a famous actor. But I ran into him outside of Coliseum Books. He is a huge reader, like no one I've ever met—and that's saying something because my mom and I, we're huge readers. But he's got us beat. He's compulsive. He had a stack of books and one of them was called *Haft Paykar*. It was a Persian twelfth-century story, and I read the back cover and it said, a king has seven brides, and they live in a castle with seven domes, and each dome is of a different color, and each princess is from a different county. Every night for one week he goes and hears a different story from each princess. They are stories of alternating fulfilled and unfulfilled love. And the objects in the stories usually have the color of the dome. So if it's the green dome it has trees in it or whatever. And that was all I needed to hear. What a visual opportunity. I love old poems. I started to read it. And that's *Mirror of the Invisible World*, which I'm remounting at the Goodman this spring.

I always say that I don't choose what text to do any more than you choose who to fall in love with. It's just happened before you know it, and you're utterly compulsive about it, and you can't stop yourself. And as soon as I get some idea to stage something, I'm convinced that everyone in the world has the same idea—because it's so obvious that you must stage this—that I have to hurry to do it because so many other people are going to be doing it, because how could you not?

So, you run across something. You get a whiff of it. And then you become possessed with it, and it ruins your life for the next year.

But you've got to have your antenna out.

I don't really because I'm really lazy. I'm a full-time professor, and that's actually a great thing. I don't need to direct to support myself. I don't need to hitch my little creative pony to the plow. So anything I've ever done has always been because I've just had a huge bee in my bonnet about it. I've just had to do it. But I've never lived the freelance life where you're actually earning your living solely from that.

I wonder what kind of different director you'd be if that were true.

I don't know. I'm not actually paid for *Argonautika*. And it almost killed me.

Why?

Because we don't have enough money. I actually got paid, but then I write a little check back because otherwise my costume budget is four thousand dollars. I don't want a costume budget that's four thousand dollars, so I write a little check and I put it back. This isn't really altruistic because the show has to look good for me. I do have a portion of the backend, as they say. But I'm compulsive about how I want it to look. The company doesn't have much money. No company does. But I have this really good living. I'm a professor at Northwestern University.

What do you actually teach there?

I'm in the department of performance studies. I teach performance art because of the brilliance of someone who came way before me who snatched that class into our department, so at Northwestern it's not in the art department. I teach courses called, literally, the Solo Performance of Poetry, Solo Performance of Drama.

So, practical classes.

Yeah. I teach graduate students, too, and some theoretical classes. I don't teach directing. I never took a directing class.

Audience: Earlier in the conversation you said that the object exists, we've already made it, but we've forgotten how we made it, and it has to be reconstituted for performance. I really like the metaphor of reconstitution. I'm wondering if, within the metaphor, you see that actors as ingredients. Are they part of the reconstitution?

I think they're partly the archaeologist that's scraping away, but they are part of the object. I think who you cast in a play is destiny. You have signed, sealed and delivered your fate. They say it's ninety percent of the director's job, and it is. It is everything—everything to do with your personal plea-sure in rehearsing or not. And everything to do with the whole gestalt of the play, just by virtue of who they are and the ten thousand choices they are going to make specifically that are different than the ten thousand someone else would make in a paragraph. You can direct as much as you want, but direction's just that. It's kind of a blunt—you know, I'll shove you in that direction, but it's a big stream. You're not in control of some-one up on stage at all. So, I guess they are part of the object but the mak-ers of the object as well.

For years upon years upon years I wouldn't remount any of my shows with anyone other than the peple I had originally made them with. I did that for over a decade. Then I discovered that my shows have some kind of portability to them. They could be imported or exported onto other bodies. I didn't think they could. Part of that is because, for example, if some-one in my cast can sing, then suddenly there's a song for that character. Someone in my cast can play drums, suddenly that happens. Trying to recast that in a different city, to find that exact skill set in another person adds a whole other dimension to the casting that makes it even more dif-ficult. Some of the acting in my older plays was more general than one would like. It wasn't masterful—because they had so many other skills, like the ability to lift two people at the same time. We were specialists; my shows got made around those specialist qualities.

I have three plays in print. They're now done all the time in high schools and colleges. I love seeing the photos that they send. You can sort of shift those skill sets, and the tracks of the particular actor could be dif-ferent that the track that I assigned, which is something I didn't under-stand for a long, long time.

AB: I remember seeing the Martha Graham company for the first time after Martha Graham was dead. I was so knocked out because there were dancers who weren't born when the original dance was created. They somehow brought from the past something extraordinary, and I think it changed them as human beings to step into those roles. It's moving, the idea of a piece that's made on the body.

I have to say, as much as it has an air of virtue to it, preserving all the orig-inals, there's something a little narcissistic about it, about me. I had a deep feeling these shows would fail if I had replaced the casts. When I did *Arabian Nights* at Manhattan Theatre Club in New York, the set was better, the acting was better, costumes were better, lights were better—show was not as good. There was a little spirit thing that was not right, that did not quite carry over.

Audience: Ira Glass talks about writing for radio, and he has a formula. The formu-la doesn't make or break your story, but, he says, on *This American Life*, we need to change pace every forty-five seconds. I would never suggest you use a formula for anything, but I wonder if you have a theory about this.

I think the way Ira and I work is very similar. He starts the week not quite knowing what the show's going to be. He knows the outlines of it. He knows some of the elements. Then it all has to come together over the course of the week. I'm not at all ashamed or think it's a bad thing to have what you called a formula. What I still find interesting about doing plays is trying to understand the deep structure of aesthetic pleasure. It exists and you feel it. You're always looking for the feeling of rightness. That's what it's all about. It snaps into focus. It eludes you, then it's there and it's so obvious and everyone feels it. Learning more and more about that structure just makes me feel better and better, even though it is not the wild, crazy left-brained side. It's the logical side. It's the more boring, work hard, disciplined, unglamorous—and yet I think that's what remains the perpetual mystery for me, the thing that you're perpetually chasing.

In *Argonautika* I made this huge change three nights before opening. The next morning I woke up and I knew it was wrong. I've never had this experience before. I had to sit through it again that night because we didn't have rehearsal that day. Then I woke up the next morning, opening day, and we put back in the cut that I'd made and took out a different twelve-minute scene. So the first time I saw it run in context was opening night in front of one hundred press. I've never done anything like that. In school I always got my homework done on time. I never pulled an all-nighter. I'm not one of those people in previews who just cuts and pastes madly. I actually think those little flaws, if you just wait long enough, the actors will sort of fix them. Those little irritants are like the grain of sand in the oyster—they will become pearls, they will become inevitable, they will become the right thing.

We had received a standing ovation the night before opening. Everyone was like, "Phew. She probably won't want to make those changes." And I said, "We just have to." It was totally structural. The first act was too long. Not one of those scenes was bad, but this one scene was tonally wrong, and it was in the wrong place. It was fantastic. But we just had to cut it. And the actors were all so brave and glorious about it. I was so proud of everyone. Everyone was so studiously calm. Everyone was joking like we always do. There was no sense of urgency or panic. We decided to make the play that we wanted to run for eight weeks and that press night was not the important night. I went home after opening night, and it was one of my happiest nights in the theater. It was just two weeks ago. I drove home down Lakeshore Drive, and I knew it was right. We came so close to not making that change because—how can we? Opening night? But we did. And we didn't do it in panic. If it had been like a panicky thing, then I don't know that it would have been the right thing.

Audience: I have a lot of friends who are classically trained ballerinas, and when they try to switch dance genres it's very hard to get that out of the body. Do you find that with classically trained actors?

Sometimes in our cast we have people who went to Juilliard and people who went to NYU and it's a very funny debate. I honestly think a good actor is a good actor, and they're really flexible in terms of style and they have great taste in their choices. With a dancer, maybe the body just automatically goes to the place. In acting, they don't do those exercises every day that dancers do, the barre. They just kind of hang out all day at the coffee shop, then do the play. I think they have more flexibility.

AB: It's that T word, which is not talent, but taste. It's the hardest thing to talk about.

It's all about taste. I always feel like what being a director means is your taste wins. You get to be in charge of the taste of the show. Physically, in the set, your taste in actors, your taste in stories.

Audience: I'd like to know how you watch theater, and the kind of theater you like to watch that's not your own.

You know, I don't go to as much theater as big theater-lovers do. I'm in it too much—going to the theater is a sort of busman's holiday. I would always go see something by Anne, something by an interesting director. I don't want this to sound snobby, but if an international troupe comes to town, that's always more exciting. There's so much that I have to go see because I know the director, the writer, the actor, the designer. You have so much obligation theater—students, for God's sake. Although, some student theater is just fantastic, and some is, "Kill me now."

I think you might be asking, can I forget I'm in the theater while I watch? I can absolutely get swept up in something. And yet, here's another thing that I think is against conventional wisdom. Conventional wisdom is that you see an actor in a play and you forget you're in the theater and you're in the story and you're utterly subsumed by it, and that's what makes it good. I don't think so. I always point to John Malkovich or certain virtuoso actors on stage whose virtuosity you are aware of at all times. And I liken it to that optical illusion where there's two halves of the face or a vase and sometimes you see the face and sometimes you see the vase. It's that transition between the two that's physically pleasurable. You think, "Look at Al Pacino go!" It doesn't mean that you aren't caught up in the character or the story, but you're caught up in his virtuosity as well. And you're going back and forth. Whereas, in Method acting and the kind of conventional way of talking about theater is that you forget it was theater. That's a retroactive pleasure—and I've had that. You leave a movie and you're talking about the movie and about twenty minutes later you say, "Wait, that person was an actor." It didn't provide the pleasure in the moment of, "Look at the actor go." "Look at the designer go." "Hear the composer go." But in my opinion it's often the rub between being inside the story and simultaneously seeing the manufacture of the story, being inside the character and seeing his manufacture, seeing the real and the unreal right on top of each other and feeling the friction between the two that causes such pleasure.

AB: A theater audience is actually part of the artistic creative act. And in the artistic creative act you have to have ecstasis, ecstasy, stepping back and closeness, intimacy. The audience has to have both, too, and gives you, I think, what Artaud called the double—in it and out of it at the same time. In film you let it wash over you.

Film is utterly concerned with the erasure of its own production. If you see the shadow of the mic, if you see a mistake, that's a weak, bad film. It has "ruined the illusion" In the theater the essence of the theatrical is metaphor. When someone dies they may not necessarily die "realistically" but instead pull from themselves a length of red silk. You know there's nothing real about that, but you're glorying in metaphor and in the precise distance between the tenor and the vehicle of the metaphor. Visual metaphor in the theater creates intimacy: it is like the language of lovers, unspoken. No one says, "And that cloth, that's the blood." Yet everyone is having that same thought at the same moment, and you realize that we have a shared experience of life, a shared vocabulary, and here is a symbol that's telling us that. That creates intimacy and is a bulwark against loneliness. And that's what I think about metaphor in the theater—that it actually works to defeat loneliness.

Audience: I'm interested in something you said when you were talking about the experience you had in the woods. You came across adults playing. I'm interested in how you bring that into what you do now.

Well, it's not called a play for nothing. I said that once, and the next year it appeared on all our banners around town. If you're not playing—if there isn't the spirit of play in the room—even if you are doing Beckett or *Lear* or the hardest, deepest thing—if you're not laughing every now and then, a lot, and kind of giddy and joking around and being with each other in a kind of warm way, I don't think it's working. I mean, I might be wrong, but I'm in it for the laughs. The great richness of working in the theater is that you're working with people who are charming on a professional level. People pay to be in a room with them and watch them walk around and sing. And that's who you spend your days with.

AB: Then comes a really curious issue, both in the commercial world, and you're also about the work at the Met. As you start dealing with commercial producers, the object is not for that joy. The object is to make money.

I agree. *Metamorphoses* accidentally became a commercial production. But I've not done anything that was, from the beginning, a commercial production. Even the Met is a not-for-profit institution. But you're right. Working in opera is a whole different conversation. Your role as a director is like a zillionth of what it is in the theater. There are so many things that you are handed. But since I've been going to the Met a lot in the last year and a half, because I'm hired there now, I am floored by how it is a meritocracy. The best singer really does get the job regardless of age or body type or whatever, because there are just very few people in the world who can produce that sound at that volume.

AB: You know what I love about working in opera? It's an impossible circumstance where they've forgotten the fun about being in the small woods, or they never knew. As a director you go in and you see a stratified situation, and your job, or at least I find that it's my job, is to make an active culture out of a passive one.

That's so greatly put.

AB: You start in this little insidious way. Chorus members in opera are notoriously mishandled. They are really treated like cattle. You go up to a chorus member, or even somebody who's a lesser singer, and you say, "Well, would it be funnier to do this action on bar seventy-two or ninety-six?" And they look at you like, "Well, you're the director. Tell me how to do it." "No, you know more about music. Which would be funnier?" "Well, bar seventy-six would be the funniest." And after a while they're going, "Um, 'scuse me, Ms. Bogart! We of the chorus, we think it would be funny to do this." And this thing happens, and it starts to move through the institution. I saw that even in Los Angeles Opera, which is just as stratified as can be.

I must take a page from your book! I've only done a couple of operas locally, and none of them have I come anywhere near—I'm just scared and want them to not yell at me.

AB: At Los Angeles Opera, on the dress rehearsal, there was this really mean woman who was the production manager. She scared the hell out of me. I went backstage, and she said, "Anne, I gotta talk to you." I said, "Okay." She's a really scary woman. She said, "Well." And then she started crying. She said, "You've reminded me why I got into this business." And I thought, you know, you can—it happens. It's like a virus—that sense of humanity.

I'm going to have to so try and do that. Because the thing about it is that you're handed your cast. You have no choice. The cast is cast five years before you're hired, in my case with *Lucia*. You feel sort of compromised. The other thing with this *Lucia* is we start with our tenor for four days, then he goes away for two weeks. Then, after he has left, our Lucia arrives. The first time they're together—the first time they will in fact meet—is during tech. So the minute you hear that, you think, "Oh, I see. So it can't be any good." The temptation is to give up because, Anne, my feeling has always been in terms of rehearsal it's going to be too painful to invest in this because it's too compromised to begin with. But I'm taking a page from you. Actually, the people I've got on *Lucia* are notoriously game. So I will do my best.

There are reasons to do it. And the number one reason is that you're in a room sometimes this size with someone singing at the top of their lungs, and it goes into your body and it vibrates in your body. The notes hit down in here and shake and ravish you. It's an extraordinarily rare human experience. There are people who would pay tens of thousands of dollars to be in that room. So it's a selfish thing.

Audience: I want to go back to the first question Anne posed about this being a difficult time to be an artist. I have a lot of friends and colleagues who are wondering what they as theater artists can do in a political sense. I think you mentioned agit-prop a little earlier. Is there room in this country at all for that?

There used to be. I do not mean to be depressing or dispiriting, but I've always been extremely clear-eyed about the fact that the theater is not a popular form. Apparently, two percent or six percent of Americans have ever seen a professional play in their lives. It's not a huge form. I know the smallness of what I do, and the depth of what we do sometimes lodges in someone and has a long-term effect. Maybe it's a big copout, but I don't think my time is best spent trying to invent a new aesthetic for myself in which I write political drama. I wouldn't be any good at that.

I do think that there was a time and may come a time again when, as long as it's commercial, you can be political. *Saturday Night Live* used to be—we're talking twenty-five years ago—extremely political. Now what they make fun of are celebrities and popular culture. But that's all a much larger discussion. Theater is extremely physical and local and immediate, and it escapes and goes under the wire of corporate money and funding and influence. But that also means it's not as loud and broadcast as far. It's narrower. But also theater is extremely fleet. Theater responded really quickly to 9/11. There were plays within a year. Whereas, with a movie, the financing for that, the planning for that, the apparatus that has to be put in place, and then if it is political, it's, "Oh, well it might not make that money back." We're never going to make any money. Theater is the thing that loses money, as a friend of mine says. So we're already there. There's a kind of liberation in that. I don't mean that to be depressing. But we are small. Deep and small.

AB: I want to jump on that small—the notion of revolutions in small rooms. What is it they say? Americans imagine the French Revolution like *Les Mis*, even if they've never seen *Les Mis*. Culture is pervasive. I think *A Chorus Line* would never have happened without Joe Chaikin and the Open Theater doing these things in little rooms. As I was talking about in an opera institution, the virus or disease—disease—that you put into a culture—we can do that, and people are affected who you'll never meet. It's odd. It's interesting.

A friend of mine once said, "You know, you're up there on stage, the matinee. It's terrible. You're hating it. And someone in row XX is having their life changed." It's absolutely true.

Mary Overlie

Mary Overlie is the originator of the Six Viewpoints. But she is a lot more than that. She is a theorist, a choreographer, a teacher, a maker of communities and an avid learner.

Perhaps there are two kinds of artists in the world: the inventor and the scavenger. The inventor descends into the depths of their imaginations, uses everything learned and experienced in life, and re-emerges with a shiny new thing. The scavenger is the one who notices the shiny things and begins to make necklaces. Mary Overlie is an inventor. I am a scavenger.

I met Mary in 1979. We were both hired to teach at the newly founded Experimental Theatre Wing at New York University. We became good friends and she began to share her work with me. When she showed me her Six Viewpoints I couldn't sit still for the excitement. Ever the scavenger I thought, "Now this, is *useful!*" Much to Mary's delight and chagrin, I did use her Viewpoints and teach them and develop them in directions that interested me. I think that Mary was delighted because of the excitement that the Viewpoints engendered in the world and chagrined because of the changes I made.

Mary was born in Terry, Montana and is the first to admit that the geography of Montana continues to influence who she is, what she does and how she does it. She spent time in San Francisco working with Jane Lapiner. She met Yvonne Rainer and then made her way to New York City where she began making work as part of the Soho minimal conceptualists. She was highly influenced by the work of the Judson Dance Theater of the late 1960s and early 1970s and formed a company from 1976 to 1980. She has taught at NYU for thirty years and has spent a large amount of time in Europe, in particular in Holland and Austria, where her influence spread.

Mary is a founder of Danspace at St. Mark's Church in-the-Bowery and Movement Research, both influential and long standing institutions in New York City. Her impact on the Experimental Theater Wing at NYU is profound and longstanding. She has collaborated with artists such as Lee Breuer, JoAnne Akalaitis, Lawrence Sacharow, Paul Langland, Nina Martin, Wendell Beavers and many others. She and I collaborated on several productions together including *South Pacific* and *Artourist*. She has written a beautiful book on the Six Viewpoints which I hope will be published very soon.

November 27, 2006

AB: Mary Overlie, among many things, is the inventor of Viewpoints, and I have spent the last twenty-some years trying to say that out loud. Mary Overlie is truly an inventor. She went inside of herself and asked, "What is performance? What is this thing we do?" And she came up with this system, in a sense, a way of looking at it. We met in 1979, when both of us, much too young, were teaching at NYU. We did a number of shows together in addition to teaching. We did *South Pacific*, a play called *Artourist*, which we co-directed. Mary introduced me to this system, this approach, which pretty much blew my mind. It seemed to be addressing all these issues that I had problems with in the theater—in two words, "couch plays." The way that Mary approached the stage actually said to the actors or to the dancers, "Make work yourselves. Make it eloquent. Don't wait for somebody to tell you what to do."

Then Mary went away for ten years to Europe. We lost contact for a long time. I started bastardizing her work, adding things and changing things. When she came back to the States, Mary said, "No, they're this." I said, "No, I changed things." This has been a long process of—I guess ownership is an issue. The difference between us is that Mary is an innovator and inventor and explorer. She goes into herself and comes out with something truly original. I'm a scavenger. I look around and go, "I like that. And I like that and that, and I think I'll put them all together." What Mary had innovated made more sense to me than anything I'd ever encountered in my life—and to this day.

I was talking with Leon Ingulsrud, a member of SITI Company, about the Moscow Art Theatre. When Moscow Art Theatre first came to the United States in 1922/23, with plays by Chekhov and Gorky, these young people who came to see these productions—who had names like Strasberg and Adler—were knocked out. I used to think they were knocked out by the technique, which became an approach to acting. But what I began to understand through a discussion with Leon is that what they were knocked out by was not a technique of acting, but the way that people were being together on stage. They'd never seen people be together that way on the stage, and that changed the whole conception of what it meant to be human. It was certainly affected by quantum physics, Picasso's Cubist theories, Freud's theories of the time, but it was manifested on the stage.

I think that the reason why what you invented, Viewpoints, was so profound is that whenever you watch people doing Viewpoints it feels good. It's about witnessing people being together in a way that is unique—in a way that is lateral as opposed to linear.

MO: I have one last question about Viewpoints. I do think it is the last question. It's been hanging there—just hanging there, seeming as if I would never be able to answer it. The question was about what kind of theater is Viewpoints making—and you just answered it by that story, that parable. Viewpoints changes the way people are together on stage. That's the answer. Thank you, Anne.

You're welcome! Let's go back—because I think all of us are but the bundle of things we experience and people we meet and how we grow up. How did Montana affect you and your trajectory?

I have never left Montana, first of all. It's not a past thing. This gives me the opportunity to say something about Montana that I've been wanting to say forever. I would like to write a book about it. Montana to me is a place that propagates a Zen mind. You discover it in people you would not expect to be Zen—broad-minded, flat-thinking, deep, quizzical, assembling things, very independent. My theory is that it's because of the way Montana is geologically. The prairies start at the Missouri all the way across, so you don't even know you're climbing—up, up, up, up, up to this plain at three thousand feet above sea level, and it looks flat. The feeling you get is that you're looking over the curvature of the earth. Kate Matschullat, the theater director, is from Nebraska. She said that Viewpoints couldn't be without the West—that they are the voice of the West in some way. They're also a voice of oriental, Buddhist philosophy, which is also to be found organically in Montana.

There was also the influence of people in Montana, correct?

Yes. My mother was particularly loving. She had six children. I think her attitude to each of us was that we had all it took to do whatever we wanted.

She would just take care of the ironing and the cleaning of the clothes and the cooking of the food, and let us just evolve. I was severely dyslexic as a child. There was a clock in the kitchen. I'd try to avoid being in the kitchen so I could avoid someone calling and saying, "What time is it, Mary?" I didn't want to go to school. I always had bad stomach aches and this and that. I would get very sick in the winter—kind of fake sick because the pressure would become too much for me to be at school. My mother just got it. She'd say, "You are very sick. Why don't you go back to bed." So I could recuperate from the world and get my nerve back together to go out. During one of those periods of convalescence I got this idea. I was very much into the idea of the Greek myths, even though I couldn't read. I don't know how dyslexic people do that, but they know about it. They pick it up from pictures. I decided that I had to have baths, and the bath was like the Aegean Sea. I crawled inside the bath and thought about ancient times. One day I said, "I think I'm ready to read." So I asked my brother Eric to get some books out of the library. Mythology books. And damned if I couldn't read.

Then, I fatefully grew up across the street from painters, who are actually mentioned in *Zen and the Art of Motorcycle Maintenance*. Robert Pirsig was their friend and would visit them, and talked about Robert and Gennie a lot in the book. A mysterious thing happened to me with Gennie DeWeese. They were a nest of Capricorns across the street, the likes of which Montanans had never seen. She was a beatnik, ponytail and bright red lipstick and always a white man's shirt and Levis on—which was just not the way women dressed. People were still wearing nylons and things. Something happened where I just identified with her completely and basically took her personality. I studied her like under a microscope. To this day, we're just incredibly close.

What made you go to San Francisco? That was the next stop on the Mary Overlie train, I think.

Yes. I wanted to go to New York, because that's where the ballet and all the dancing was. But I was too afraid to go—thank God, because I think New York City would have eaten me up at seventeen. I was in a summer theater thing, and the owner of the theater, who was very wealthy, his son wanted to hop the freight train to go to California. The only person I knew who wasn't in Montana was in Berkeley, and we'd been in the theater together. She was about four or five years older, and had married and moved to California. So I got there—I can't even believe this—in 1964. You know what was going on in 1964. I just dropped into the generation as this little

Montanan. It was very, very funny: "No, I don't want to smoke grass. No, I'm going to the ballet. No, I'm listening to classical music. What are the Beatles? No."

Were you thinking of yourself as a dancer or a choreographer at that point?

Both. I met this woman who was teaching dance at a community rec center. She saw my fearless interest and my extreme poverty, and said, "You know, I have friends teaching ballet at UC Berkeley. I bet you could just come and take classes with me." So I went up to take class at the ballet. I'd only seen one dance performance ever in my life, which was when we went up to Canada to see a ballet. I was so confused by this. What I'd been taught was ballet barre and improv—floor work. That's what I thought ballet was.

That's an influence. That's big.

That's a big influence, yes. I have a theory that a dancer's first teacher is the direction they will go in. Whatever strange combination they are teaching you or how they approach dance—you will go that way. So, first of all, seeing the ballet in Canada, I was so confused as to how everybody could do the same steps. That was a major mystery to me. Then I went in to take the ballet class. I was fine doing barre. And then everybody got out on the floor, and I said, "Ooh, I wonder what improv they're going to get us to do." I already had quite a reputation for being a performer. They started all moving in the same direction, knocking me down. I was terrified.

They were doing combinations and you didn't know what they were doing?

Yes. I didn't know people could do combinations.

Was it in San Francisco that the Natural History of American Dance started?

No. It actually started here in New York. When I was about nine I started studying dance. But I was already heavily under the influence of Bob and Gennie DeWeese and the beatniks across the street. Shortly after that I started choreographing because I wanted to be an artist. I wanted to read some books about choreography: How do you do it? What's dance? Painters would talk, critique each other, exchange ideas—centuries of development: What is perspective? Where do you put the image in terms of the frame of the canvas, light? I thought I'd find out all that stuff that choreographers do. There was nothing. Nothing. I thought dance should have a technical voice like that. Performance should have that. So I decided that I, Mary Overlie, would go forth in the world. So I already had that project on my mind when I was in San Francisco. Mary Overlie is going to find out how to write this down. It seemed like a century of modern dance classes, which I hated. I had to take them. But I hated them.

What did you hate about them?

Basically that they weren't postmodern, but I didn't know what I was looking for. They were about stories. They were about emotion. They were way too visceral for me. I suffered through them. Then Margaret Jenkins, who worked with Merce Cunningham, moved away from him, moved to San Francisco and opened up her own studio. I was there. I took her first Cunningham class. I was like, "Everything's okay now."

What was it about Cunningham that made sense?

The larger question is what is it about postmodernism that makes sense to me. I think that I'm drawn to art that's elemental—because then I see it as being powerfully universal, yet specifically related. Cunningham's work was about space and time. There were no stories. There were no emotions.

What does that mean to you—art that is elemental?

A black square on a white canvas. That's elemental to me. Mary Campbell Schmidt, the head of Tisch School of the Arts, once said to me, "You're a phenomenologist." I like to see what's happening. I like to lift the lid up. I can fix Toyotas. I got a car apart. Eric had to come put it back together again, but I got it taken apart. I like to repair things. I used to have a construction company in New York City. I did all the plumbing in my own loft. Those things fascinate me.

Were you connected at all to Anna Halprin? She was really influential in San Francisco in the sixties.

I wouldn't go near her—even that side of town where she was. I never saw a performance. I just got this feeling like . . . it was too modern dance. There was lots of emotion there. It was an energy.

What was it then that brought you from San Francisco to New York?

Yvonne Rainer. Barbara Dilley had a commission from the Whitney Museum to do a dance. That was the old days when dancers got to do dances in museums and galleries. It was a really lively time. She was gathering people's work. I took her workshop when she was in San Francisco and she invited me to come to New York. Yvonne Rainer gave me a ride. She took me with her. Yvonne had just tried to commit suicide. 1970. Barbara performed in concert, then I worked with that group. We named it the Natural History of the American Dancer; lesser known species; volumes 1–25. We just had a very, very weird way of working. I don't know how it evolved, but we never spoke to each other about what we were doing—ever, ever. When we started teaching we exchanged a few words. It was very illuminating. But that was it. I think about that era as being the era of inventing the wheel backward. We deconstructed dance in some strange way, and in the process the Viewpoints fell on the floor, and I was like, "What's that?"

The other women in the dance company were much hipper than I was. They'd gone to Sarah Lawrence. They were advanced. They'd been on the East Coast all their lives. They were in Soho. I arrived late in Soho. We decided before we took the summer vacation we would do solos as introductions of ourselves to the company. I thought I was going to be the sort of hip Californian, so I decided to make the piece outside. I took them up on the sidewalk on Greene Street and did my solo, and there was a sickening silence. Things flashed through my mind: "Well, I guess I'll move away from New York. I guess I'm leaving the company." They sat there for a really long time, and someone was like, "Are you going to tell her?" One of them finally said, "Okay, Mary. Do you know where you are?" What a creepy question! I said, "I'm in New York." She said, "Well, yeah. But do you know where you are?" Someone finally said, "Well, what do you think? She's about four feet from the building?" I said, "Yeah. I'm four feet from the building." They started giving me these measurements about where I was standing. And I, in an instant, turned from an ignorant dancer. Actors are like this before they get the Viewpoints. They think space is only where they are. They don't see anything else. They don't see the room. They don't see their placement in the room. Dancers are like this. I woke up. I was like, "Help! I'm four feet from the building!" I spent the rest of the summer completely space obsessed, measuring and walking patterns, practicing walking perfect circles, and slowly accumulating space language. I can speak space. A lot of people who can do Viewpoints can speak space.

Around the same time, to contextualize a little bit, was the Judson Church move-ment. In the sixties, early seventies, people got together in Judson Church because of Al Carmines, who was the pastor who gave them the space. These young people, whose names were like Trisha Brown, Yvonne Rainer, David Gordon, Steve Paxton, took apart everything. You were around in the latter part of that period. What was your relationship to that work?

They were my gods. They taught me what postmodernism was. Also, up to the point that they started working, the entire history of dance, of Western dance, had been structured around one lucky devil who could be the choreographer. They could be the artist. There was only one per chorus. Everyone else was just the little dummy, the puppet. Dancers were never seen as creative people or artists. Part of what happened with Judson is that every dancer was seen as an artist with their own creative voice. Boy, did that shake my life up. I could be seen as an artist and take myself seriously and come up with my own statements, my own prose, my own work process.

I read in some of your writing the use of the word "nonhierarchical," which brings up the really huge word, "nonhierarchical creation," which is not only with the human beings in the room, but with the things with which you make art. It seems that's one of the principles upon which the Viewpoints stand, that it is a nonhierar-chical system. One aspect of the performance is not more important than the other. The text is not more important than the space, which is not more important than the time. That was becoming clear to you, right?

I always say this about this process. I like it more and more as it matures. I may have started out to find out the techniques of choreographing, of making performance. But that is a vastly different thing, and it has been a vastly different journey than the Grotowski journey, or the Stanislavski journey, or the Hagen journey. The character of the Viewpoints is really, really different, the way it's taught, the tone of the classroom, how people evolve themselves in it. I think where the difference originates is that Grotowski set out to create a new acting technique. Stanislavski set out to create a new acting technique. I just set out to find some rules, some mechanics. It was a hunter-gatherer mission. There have been times with the Viewpoints, a seven-year stretch where it's just me sitting there being quiet, waiting for the next part of the quest. I knew there was something missing. And then, wham—it would be clear.

I sit with the Viewpoints a lot, and I play them like a Rubik's Cube or something. If we take theater apart into six things—six voices. Taking the-ater apart . . . six voices. That means they're independent. Time is inde-pendent. That means . . . . One day I was demonstrating for class with some empty coffee cups, and I lost control of them. I was making space in between them, but they were independent. They fell out of my hands onto the floor. That means they're horizontal. Horizontal is nonhierarchical. That thought about the horizontal has turned into a lab for me that I can either physically or mentally enter. I can enter it with people. It's an exploration about what goes on in the horizontal world, which we know very little about because we live in hierarchy. Our education is hierarchical. We live in hierarchical structures. So we know very little about the horizontal structure. But certain things have been discovered in there—like the work of doing the unnecessary, and playing pool on an egg-shaped table.

Would you like to tell us about playing pool on an egg-shaped table?

It came about because I was working in the horizontal with Wendell Beavers and Paul Langland, two really old-time dance partners. We had been working on process for about six or seven years. Once a year we'd get together and put a piece together. We were trying to conquer specific problems in dance improvisation. They had been members of my dance company, so they had a tendency to continue to treat me as the leader, which was rather annoying because that meant that I had to do all the organizing. I was the disciplinarian. They also liked to pick my brain for thoughts. I discovered doing the unnecessary in Holland, and I thought, "I'm not going to throw it into the mix. I'm not going to talk about it. I'm tired of sharing things with them." I did the unnecessary and they did the old type of improv, and I started scaring the bejesus out of them. Why would I be standing over here? There's no logical reason for it. They'd make me tell them, "I don't know exactly why."

It was coming dangerously close to performance time and we couldn't get this thing settled down because they were so freaked out, and I was just like, "We'll just do a bad performance. I'm not giving my secret away." They called in a friend to look at the thing and to give them some feedback. This guy said, "I know this is the correct angular move, but actually there is an egg shape in here. Like a bowl. You're sitting in a bowl, and things are ricocheting off the sides." I put in a strange attractor, like chaos theory, that was sort of flying around, and they'd chase it, but they'd miss it, so we were ricocheting. It wasn't one of these nice, composed or proscenium, organized spaces. It was this invisible other space that had grown in there. That helped them somehow. They realized they were in a bowl, and that stopped them from getting so frightened. We had a beautiful performance.

Afterward I analyzed it because I was so thrilled by the effect. I call it playing pool on an egg-shaped table because most performance is like playing pool. An actor throws something to another actor. That actor catches it and throws it back—those prosaic theater games. It's like call and response. The problem with that is that entropy sets in very fast because it starts getting empty of any content. Then the poor actors have to pump it full of life again. They're trying to keep this thing alive as they toss it back and forth. Meanwhile, in a real pool game, the balls are disappearing and you end up with very little left on stage. If you imagine an egg-shaped table—it can't be a circular bowl because you can predict how things are going to pattern.

It's very simple to set up, it turns out. Each performer has to metaphorically face away from every other performer—turn their back and go only into their project. You may not beg, borrow, steal, playback anything from those people. You can't take their rhythm, you can't take a mood, you can't share a world. They're gone. You can only have your own material. Then the second step to that is that while you're doing your own material, you check back over your shoulder—just to see what's happening. That acknowledgement is what makes it become a unified art project. It has a way of generating energy. I swear that there's some physical physics thing going on here, because the number of strange phenomenon that will happen—

Coincidences.

Coincidences are very, very odd. Someone is like tossing their arm over their shoulder like this, and there will be somebody else who just moves their hand back, and the ball falls in your hand.

As you say, it's entropy. It's also the disease of agreement. As a species we end up in unison. As a species, we tend to want to glom and be the same. Subconsciously we gravitate toward that. So that means that the effort as an artist is to move away from that, knowing that the tendency to glom will happen by itself.

It was a cultural difference I learned the first time I ever saw Tadashi Suzuki in rehearsal. There were three American actors and about fifteen Japanese actors. I was watching, and in this inimitable, hierarchical way, Suzuki would clap, and everybody would have to stop where they were on stage, no matter where they were, and hold that position while he went up to an actor and harangued them for twenty minutes. Really vicious haranguing—and everybody just had to stand there. At one point I asked one of the Japanese actors, "Isn't that a pain, to have to stand there?" They said, "Oh, no, no, no. It's really good. Because usually he'll stop you in a moment when you're making a mistake. While he's haranguing somebody else, you have to deal with the mistake you've made." But then I noticed that he harangued the

Japanese actors, but not the American actors. I thought, "Oh, he's showing favoritism to the American actors." I asked that question. The answer was, "Oh, no. He likes American actors because Japanese actors really try to be the same, and American actors have the courage to be different." So what he's yelling at people about is being too much the same with other actors. The haranguing is about trying to get them to be more individual.

At Experimental Theatre Wing we had a visitor from the Peking Opera. They set up an year abroad study over there. He's here to pitch the studio and also to just take a look around. I was very excited to have him come in and observe my classes. I was so curious because I thought this is either going to be really good or really bad. He could take a look at this stuff and say, "Idiot Western artists thinking you are doing Buddhist practices. Ugh, chaos." Or it would work, but would he be able to recognize the Buddhist essence? And—he didn't show up. I was wandering the halls, worrying. Rosemary, my boss, saw me and she said, "What are you doing?" I said, "He's not here." She said, "He's watching the acting class." I got a terrible feeling because I know that acting teacher and she's very enthusiastic about her work and kind of forgets to share sometimes. So he stayed there. But Rosemary saw how devastated I was, and she got him to come the next day. He got so excited, and he started saying, "You can't just do everything the same. It's so bad for people. Look at the chaos up there!" But I have observed the Japanese and the Chinese also are so hierarchical. They have a hard time breaking the box.

For me, the nonhierarchical system, which seems radical, is very simple—the question of who makes the first stroke on the canvas. For me as a director, the assumption is the director makes the first stroke. "Okay, go start upstage, go down-stage, turn right, pick up the teacup." Then you assume that then the actor is going to take that and start to make it their own, and then you hope that you have a response to that. What the Viewpoints propose is to let the actor make the first stroke. Once an actor is trained in the Viewpoints, they don't wait for you to tell them what to do. The issue for me always is: When does the art start? I remember watching a director whose name I won't mention rehearsing years ago at the Public Theater. The whole rehearsal was really boring. For two hours he was giving them blocking. I kept thinking, "When does the art start?" In most situations, the art starts when there's an audience. But the question for me is why can't the director be the audience, and with the force and quality of attention, say, "Okay, show me something." So if it's true what Picasso said, that the first stroke on every canvas is a mistake and you spend the rest of the time correcting that mistake, somebody's got to make the first stroke. If the first stroke is the actors' it makes a big difference

in terms of ownership—and if it's always going to be a mistake anyway, why can't the actor make the mistake?

Because, after all, you're making it easier for the director to see.

You said at a certain point that the Viewpoints just dumped out. They fell out. You shared with a lot of people. You went off to Holland and Austria for like ten years. While you were away a lot of stuff happened. I wonder if you could talk about that a little bit.

I really wanted to give the Viewpoints to people. I wanted the world to use that language. I don't mean in a dominant way. For a choreographer to simply be able to say, "I work with space," is a huge step from what was there and what is still there. The Viewpoints were around for about ten years in New York and no one seemed to pick them up. I got discouraged. So I thought, "Well, I'll go to Europe." And I left with this thought that the Viewpoints would be discovered and used after I was dead. I had full confidence in them. I just didn't think it was going to happen in my life.

I paticipated in an organization as a part of the Vienna dance festivals. There was an experimental teaching program. And then Kevin Kuhlke called me and said, "Do you know, Anne Bogart's becoming known for your work." "Kevin, that's great! That's just wonderful." He said, "No. I think you should come back." I said, "No. That's good. That's what's happening. That's great." And then he called me again about a year later and said, "No, I really think you should come back." I said, "What are you talking about?" He said, "The theater community is getting split. There are the Bogart Viewpoints people and the Overlie Viewpoints people, and they don't talk to each other. They're angry at each other." I went, "Oh, that's not good." The idea of inventing something that would split the theater community really disturbed me. I'm a builder of communities, not a splitter of them. Bells went off. Then he called and said, "Anne Bogart is having a book come out." "I don't think I feel very good. I feel like someone is taking my life away. I feel like I'm dying. I feel bad."

It woke me up to the idea—basically I had no concept that the Viewpoints were like my flesh. I spent my whole life working on them. To lose them was to look at having devastated life. It does happen to artists. Loie Fuller was knocked off by Isadora Duncan. Well, how many people know Loie Fuller? Nobody. And Isadora Duncan just flew out into the world and became a star. So I came back, and I started asking people to help me somehow. At the Viewpoints conference, I told David Diamond from the Stage Directors and Choreographers Foundation that I needed to reestablish my name in the work in this country. He took it really, really seriously.

He's a very generous man. He started arranging—I would teach all week and then fly out to Minneapolis, Chicago, all around the country, and do twenty-four hours of work with the Viewpoints in three days. We'd be so tired. But it gave me a chance and it slowly turned the tide. After about two-and-a-half years of that I felt sure that I heard that my name was back on my work. It wasn't just going on in my head. I had almost weekly jolts of it where I would be standing in a theater lobby and someone would be talking, "Anne Bogart. The Viewpoints." And someone would look over and say, "That's Mary Overlie. I think she's attached to those somehow." I was getting erased. And then I would fight back. My brother Eric helped me a great deal. He told me, "The more corporate salesmen on your block, the more carpets are sold." He really has helped me understand this. That your working with my work has helped more people know about it.

Eric (In the audience): Jesus had his Paul. Jesus didn't get the word out. Paul did. That's the person who is capable of putting it together and getting it out.

So I'd go back and say, "What's bothering you, Overlie?" And I would grow. It's been this really interesting experience for me. It forced me to see a part of my nature that I had. I could have crumbled if I had a different personality.

Audience: I came to Viewpoints very piecemeal over several years—a workshop there, a session there. I finally got to put it all together with the publication of your book this year [*The Viewpoints Book* by Anne Bogart and Tina Landau]. I teach acting, so I thought, what the hell, I'll take this book and I'll teach the thing. I took a group of high school students and taught it to them, and had just a mind-blowing experience with them. What it did that I found so powerful was—and this is why I think you've transcended postmodern—that it broke down cliques. It broke down those social aspects. The students cooperated with each other—not just in the rehearsal hall, but at lunch and throughout the day. I have pictures of them Viewpointing after they went out to dinner in this parking lot. It really opened them up as people. It gave them so much confidence.

Also, it made me feel so good when you said Viewpoints has such a Zen aspect to it. I've been a longtime meditation and Buddhist practitioner. As I was teaching this, I was thinking this is just like a Zen meditation—or any kind of meditation—because essentially what it's doing is saying, "Stop thinking. Just do." And when myself and my students step into that place and just do we have what I can only describe as Satori experiences in the midst of doing that work.

Eric, my brother, is a huge meditator. I've had a hard time describing to him that even though I'm not a practicing meditator anymore, that I'm still evolving and I think it's because of these Satori experiences.

By the way, Anne is a good example of this because she never really studied the Viewpoints with me. She just came in contact with me. I have for years and years and years observed that if you get one little scale of them and you get that down, they will recreate themselves. If you spend time all the rest of it is there. That's why you ended up with this funny little machine—because it recreated itself for you in a system that wasn't mine. I like that about them too because it means that there's tremendous power in them and it's organic and simple—and each little part holds it.

Audience: At what point did you really feel like you were onto something cohesive—and then how did you find the strength or courage within yourself to articulate that and say, "This needs to be heard"?

The Natural History broke up because we started trying to talk to each other about dance, and the first thing I knew was that I was being strangled on stage. The next thing I knew I was in my studio and I started studying the Viewpoints. I knew there were six of them. Because I had been looking for them I knew they were there. I just removed the Natural History work from them and looked at them on my studio floor. There was space, time, shape, emotion, movement, story. It doesn't seem like courage to me, because they seemed so implicit. I would just tell people about them. They'd say, "Yeah. Wow. It's true." If I felt I had invented it I think that would have taken courage to get that out to people. I felt I'd just found them. You pull the skin back and that's what's there. The theory ended about six or seven years ago—and now I've gotten the answer to my last Viewpoints question. I'd never realized you could finish a theory. I literally could barely talk for two weeks. I'd been working on this for twenty-seven years. Obsession. I think that I'm obsessed with them. I am fascinated by them. And they keep teaching me things and that's what kept the energy up. If we start to talk to each other on that level we go off into another planet in a spaceship. We get into the Viewpoints world.

Audience: Could you talk a little about emotion as a Viewpoint? When you were talking about San Francisco, you said they were dealing with emotion. How do you see emotion as a Viewpoint? How do you talk about it?

When I go into that language I reduce it to its simplest expression to me. I call it the "dog sniff dog world." Two dogs meet on the street and within seconds they know all kinds of stuff. They know if they like that dog. I believe we do that as human beings as well, but I also believe we have guards and blockings and we don't let people sniff us and we don't go up and sniff because we don't want that much information. But we always have the ability to do that just like a dog does. If we brought some person in here from the street and had them walk in a circle and then go out, we could sit and talk about that person—their level of health, their psychological being. We know this kind of stuff about each other. If we didn't, then we would be dead. We are very, very, very sensitive. That's the world of emotion.

In the Viewpoints, the basic practice for emotion work is presence work, which is putting somebody in a chair and having them perform themselves while everybody sits and watches. There are practices about staying open and sniffable—having to do also with not letting the saliva dry up in your mouth. People actually stop saliva and retreat. Some poor actors hold the role in front of them, and they themselves are never on stage. I've actually had people come to workshops, thirty, forty years old, really top professional actors, and just walk around the space for a few days and take a look at their arm, make a few shapes, and then just burst into tears and go, "Oh, my God, I've always been so insecure on stage." That has influenced my life a great deal, this practice, because I'm uncommonly present on the stage. You can change atmospheres and events from being that open and sniffable.

But then we get to this point about, "Why doesn't Mary like Ann Halprin? Why doesn't Mary like couch drama?" Actually, it's not true. I like couch drama, but I don't like to make it myself. I sometimes think of myself as an auto mechanic. I'm a phenomenologist. I have a brain functioning and a perspective that wants to keep things at a distance. I love the interchangeable parts. You can't do that with the world of emotion. It doesn't have interchangeable parts. I'm not drawn to it. People scare the shit out of me. People who are really magnanimous and open and friendly— I'm just scared.

Audience: How does this tendency to be in unison and fight against cooperation coincide or differ from the improv world—always saying yes to everything?

AB: If I were working in a Viewpoints situation in this room with a lot of people, I would somehow be taking in everything that's happening—who's got their legs crossed, who's nodding, who's nodding off, who's sleeping, who's coughing—and all of those things would be in me and I'd be aware of them. And then I might make a choice that is none of those things. That would be an informed choice. But mak-

ing a choice without taking in or noticing all of those things would not be in the spirit of what we're discussing.

I love unison action. It actually helps to focus a lot of performances in a lot of productions. The theory is if you want to make people look different on stage, put them in the same clothes, because then you see the different people rather than the clothes. I love repetition because it organizes the stage so that you can see more. There's a book called *Moving in Time*, which is about the history of unison action. German actors are terrified of unison—because they have a history of unison that got them into a lot of trouble. Americans have less problem moving in unison. In the spirit of Gertrude Stein, the same only different. If you use unison or glomming, you want to do it with an intense awareness, so that it's the same, only different—instead of the same mindlessly. So it's not to say one should always do something different.

I'm fascinated with unison, also. I've performed a lot of unison. That was one of the forms that would come up in the Natural History. The better we got at it, the freer it would be. I think that it's in how you approach it mentally. Our thing began to be that we would even mimic each other's breathing patterns.

I like to play with particle-izing. The Viewpoints have particle-ized theater. First it was deconstruction of the six voices, and then you get closer and you deconstruct those voices and those voices and those voices. The finer the attention, the freer things are. I swear that there is a social movement in that. There's a new governmental pattern in there. Václav Havel once wrote that he felt that communism, socialism, democracy, capitalism, and all of the world government systems and corporate systems were absolutely failing, and that we needed something new. I was like, "Mr. Havel, I'd like to tell you about the Viewpoints." In some strange way there is a new way of cooperating. It affects how people are together. It's particle-izing, and particle-izing attention to detail.

You said another thing: always saying yes. I hate doing that. I don't like theater games. I think they're stupid. They don't teach you anything. They don't teach you to think. I think Viewpoints teaches you how to think. Rather than turning the mind off, I think it teaches you think, but think in different languages. One year Barney came and taught with me. We were up in these big dance studios on Second Avenue. There was a piano that had messages all over it: "Do not touch this thing. Don't even think of it." It gleamed. Here we are doing the Viewpoints and everything gets explored. The piano had a weird effect on us; the work was just stymied. So we actually started a little saying: "Don't go near the piano. Don't go near the piano." It loosened things up again. I learned something crucial: It's very important to not do things that come to mind. It sets the balances. The negative balance is really that important.

So, particle-izing: In the Viewpoints theory there's a part of a bridge. The very first step on the bridge is called News of a Difference, which comes from meditation. News of a Difference is letting your thoughts refine until they're clarified into a thought and then you transcend. The more I look at this chair, the more possibilities will come out of it. I could find a lifetime of work in this chair. It's a way of talking about what an artist does: look at something and familiarize themselves with it until they can develop a conversation and it can begin to give you ideas. That's a visual arts thing that's been applied to theater now through Viewpoints.

Audience: Anne, what's your answer to the emotion question? How does emotion play into the way you work in Viewpoints?

AB: You know, when Mary went away I forgot what her six Viewpoints were. Then I think Brian Jucha said to me, "I think one of them is emotion." I said, "No! No! It's not! It can't be!"

I think it's written down somewhere that you said that. "Viewpoints don't have emotion. Emotion's not a part of Viewpoints."

AB: Not that I don't love. My belief is that we don't own emotions; we experience them, we have the honor of allowing them to pass through us. Although my belief is changing now since I've been thinking about sniffing. I've got to take this in a little and let it alter everything. My reaction is against a lot of the American misunderstanding of Stanislavski—that the idea of a rehearsal is that somebody has a really strong emotional moment, and the director says, "Keep that! That's it." You have to keep something, and so we jump to the emotions. But any actor knows that if we're going to repeat an emotion, it's going to be false and bad and dead and fake, and you can actually never resurrect an emotion because it will always be different. But ultimately you have to set something. Much like when there's an eclipse of the sun and you can't look directly at it because it will burn your eyes so you make this cardboard thing so you can look at the reflection, the Viewpoints are a cardboard thing that you use to look at the thing you're actually interested in.

We are in the theater. We are interested in emotions, in the human experience of new circumstances that change us, that alter us, that transform us—the glorious thing of emotions. I think they are so important that I don't think we should touch them. We should create the circumstances. In this moment of the play I'm always going to be here. You have to agree on something. If you don't agree on anything, it's messy. If you agree on everything, where the body is and where the emotions are, everything, then it's anal and has no life. So you set something and let something

free. For me it's important that the emotions change. The cheaper things, the things that we could manhandle, could be set. But the reason we're in the room is for things to change. Years ago somebody said to me, "Oh yeah, Viewpoints. That's that thing where there's no face and no emotions." I wanted to slit my wrists. That's a deep misunderstanding. So it's a tricky issue.

I have for quite a long time wanted to get some people in a room studying emotion. I read somewhere that in the development of American acting techniques, way, way back, they were terrible at portraying people. They were all very stiff and childlike, with poor voices and all this squiggling around, forgetting that they were on stage. It slowly evolved. This picture I got from this thing I read is that they slowly started to study how to make facsimiles of emotion on stage, and that that is basically the history of acting techniques, all the way up to the super Cadillac of Stanislavski. I'm thrilled by Stanislavski. I think that the Stanislavski method does make it possible to develop an emotion repertory—of facsimiles. They're all facsimiles. This dog sniff dog thing isn't a facsimile—but what is it?

Wendell took me to a show on Broadway called *Tango Argentina*, a few years back. It turned out to be just very old tango partners—the top tango partners in Argentina—tangoing on stage one after another to this rinky-dink band. No glitzy costumes. They were all different sizes and different ages. By the time the performance was done the audience had been shown worlds of emotion through these tango performers that they had never experienced in their lives. Me too. People could just not leave the theater. Then we were outside and crowded around the marquee—because no one wanted to go get the cab or anything—and here were all these couples from New Jersey, who had been married for years, and it was so hot. The atmosphere was like crackling with sex. That was an emotional experience in the theater that came from just a weird source. They weren't actors. These were people.

SITI Company

Imagine my delight when the great Japanese theater director Tadashi Suzuki proposed that together we inaugurate a new initiative in the United States that could become an expression of the fellowship of theater artists from around the world. We launched the enterprise in 1992 in Toga-mura, Japan and Saratoga Springs, New York, and called ourselves the Saratoga International Theater Institute. We wanted to do nothing less than redefine and revitalize contemporary theater in the United States through an emphasis on international cultural exchange and collaboration. Although originally envisioned as a summer institute, SITI quickly expanded to encompass a company with a year-round presence in New York City and a summer season in Saratoga at Skidmore College. Although Suzuki's direct involvement in the company only lasted four years, he has maintained a benevolent, supportive stance from a distance ever since.

Recently the company joined together to reexamine our mission statement. After much discussion, the following was written collectively and I feel it beautifully defines our place in the world:

> SITI Company was built on the bedrock of ensemble. We believe that through the practice of collaboration, a group of artists working together over time can have a significant impact upon both contemporary theater and the world at large.

Through our performances, educational programs and collaborations with other artists and thinkers, SITI Company will continue to challenge the status quo, to train to achieve artistic excellence in every aspect of our work, and to offer new ways of seeing and of being as both artists and as global citizens.

SITI Company is committed to providing a gymnasium-for-the-soul where the interaction of art, artists, audiences and ideas inspire the possibility for change, optimism and hope.

June 17, 2009

AB: This past fall the SITI Company toured two big plays to the Dublin Theatre Festival. After putting them up, performing them, on Sunday we got on the plane, and on Tuesday we opened a third play at BAM. The following week we took a play to Los Angeles. That's four plays. I was talking to my friend Jocelyn Clarke, who is a dramaturg and a playwright, and I asked him, "How is this even possible? How are we doing this?" He said, "The training." I thought about it, and I think he's right. Maybe we can explore that a little bit among wider issues. But I'd like to start by asking about the pros and cons of company.

Stephen Webber: One of the cons that was articulated to me by Jefferson Mays, who was a former company member, is that in any group, one plays a role. It's true in a family, and it's true in a work environment. The other members of that group count on you to play that role. And even if it's the grumbler or the complainer or the person who always plays devil's advocate and throws a wrench in the works, you're counted on to be consistent in playing the role, good or bad. Once you're in that group and your role is defined, it's hard to change it because the brain doesn't like change. We like to get into repeatable patterns with people, so to change one's role in a group is difficult—and that can be personally and/or artistically.

The pro that comes to mind immediately is going into a rehearsal hall and being able to work very quickly on a deep level with people.

AB: That's a gauntlet to all of us to say: Who are you becoming? I'm speaking that for us together. It's a beacon for us to hear.

Barney O'Hanlon: One thing that takes work when you've been with a group of people for as many years as this, has been coming into a room and allowing yourself to look at them with fresh eyes. And I need to do something so that I can perhaps be perceived with fresh eyes." You know their quirks, you know their ticks, you know their rehearsal process. How can you work in such a way that these people are fresh to you?

Ellen Lauren: And the things that tend to rise up first that you perceive, as Jeff Mays said, are the things that you don't recognize or the things that you qualify as negative, rather than all of the amazing things that drew you to this group. You begin to make assumptions at a very, very high level of talent, of thoughtfulness, of ability, of emotional availability and deep history together—and I don't just mean history of making plays. You live a life with a group after so many years. So the things that spike out, that we tend to pick up on, being sensitive, is the thing that's wrong. I find the more the years roll by, the more sensitive the group is to anything being off in the room. It might be a glance that lands wrong. It might be somebody who doesn't say hello in the morning. It sets the day off enough that by the end of the day the trajectory is way far from where you wished it would have gotten. To bring up the image again of the brain, the tiniest firing can set off an enormous effect in the body.

Tom Nelis: I want to say something in support of role playing. Outside an ensemble you have to find your role every damn time you get every job you ever get in this industry. You have to plant a flag for who you are and get other people to recognize you for being that person. And it's tough. You spend a hell of a lot of your rehearsal time doing that. The fact that I know who I am among these people in this ensemble is a great advantage to me. I don't feel that the ensemble is so closed so as to not allow me to grow as an individual. One of the things that has happened to us over the years is that the company creates a piece, and then everybody who creates the piece is not around to do the piece next year when the piece has to happen, and somebody has to grow in that role they didn't create. It changes the company. You don't find that outside of ensembles.

AB: In designing a show for a company, Darron and Brian, how does that work well for you, and how does it drive you crazy?

Darron West: You sit so many hours with these guys, you really have to let yourself be open to every single member of the company and allow them to surprise you. It *is* incredibly hard work. Inevitably there will be tricks, things that we have learned in previous productions that we might try again. I'm usually the one who will throw the siren on and try as a designer to take the rehearsal in a different direction because I see it going where it went on a previous show.

AB: Would you say you're more aggressive with the company that you are in a free-lance setting?

Darron West: Oh, yeah.

AB: That was a leading question.

Darron West: It's really interesting, though. I spend a lot of time doing plays outside the company, and I actually feel like I have to do that because then I miss this ensemble. I have moments of sitting in the rehearsal hall at the McCarter throwing my hands up trying to explain to an actor, "Can you just wait until the cello happens to open the door?" And I just go, "I wouldn't even have to be having this conversation if Ellen were getting ready to open the door." We feed off of one another in that way, and that doesn't happen except within this group of people.

AB: How about as a stage manager who manages both in the company and occasionally outside of the company. What are the pros and cons?

Elizabeth Moreau: In this company I have an idea of where you guys are on any given day, and that facilitates how I might push through a tech, what I might emphasize, what I might prioritize time for. It takes a very small amount of information to affect a larger plan. When I'm working outside the company, I'm starting from square one. I have no idea who these people are. I have no idea how to read them as people. I don't know if their way of saying hello is how they always say hello. Maybe today is really bad, and I have no way of knowing that. It's not that knowing them or not knowing them makes it a good or bad experience. I've had great experiences outside the company also. There's a deeper experience with the company.

AB: Can I also suggest that you breathe with the company? I've been close to you. You actually breathe when they breathe.

Elizabeth Moreau: Ellen has a solo show about Virginia Woolf where she spends the majority of the first twenty minutes balancing on one leg. You'd never know that if you saw it. I realized the last time we did the show, that I call the first twenty minutes of the show standing on one leg. Mirror neurons, anyone? If I'm doing a show with the company, like, for instance, *Death and the Ploughman*, it's tightly choreographed. If Bondo's walking at this speed, then that changes how all of the light cues happen. I'm so tuned into what you guys are doing—and that is really rewarding.

AB: I'm going to open up the big can of worms right now, which is about managing a company. What are the pros and cons of managing a company, Megan Wanlass?

Megan Wanlass: I think it's helpful that we all share the same language, the same vocabulary. We've worked on the creation of twenty-five-plus shows together. In the same way that they share a common experience in the rehearsal room, I feel like we share that in the planning of how we're going to get them into the rehearsal room. Anne and I work really closely, sometimes a year and a half out, for a project. Sometimes I say, "Well, we have this grant due. Let's talk about which project." We start talking about how many actors, what do you think the set will be, what do you think the subject matter is, who's the playwright? It takes that articulation, those questions, to make those projects come to fruition. That's exciting. I also think because we are a group that's worked together a long time, we've been able to stay really nimble, really flexible. We run a really lean administrative structure underneath this group, and we've been able to do that because there's a sort of efficiency to how we go about creating, knowing that we can make a new piece in four weeks, or having the trust and faith in one another.

In terms of roles, I'm a perfect case-in-point, somebody who came into the company in a different role, as the stage manager, then had to fight like hell to become the managing director—not with the company so much, but with the board of directors. It's possible. It just meant that I had to work—and I still work on a daily basis that much harder.

What we're trying to do now in imagining the next five or ten years is say: This is our model now. Where do we see a very self-sustaining but yet growth of a model? And how are we going to get to what we need to become, keeping the things that are functioning, but blowing open other areas where this doesn't work so much? Let's pretend we're in the rehearsal room and that scene isn't right. Let's imagine and innovate something new.

Will Bond: Anne is a SITI Company member as well as being artistic director. In the spirit of this nonhierarchical and democratic company, Anne, what are the pros and cons of being an artistic director of an ensemble?

AB: In 1986 I was in Berlin, and ended up in the same room with the woman I admire the most in the world, the director Ariane Mnouchkine. I knew I had a question for her, but I didn't know what it was. So there I was on my knees, speaking French with a red face, and the question came: "What about this company thing?" And she looked at me really sternly and said, "What are you going to do without a company? Don't get me wrong. It's a pain. You lose people. It's always a problem. But what are you going to do?" In that moment, in the way that epiphanies happen, I realized that every great production I'd ever seen, with no exception, was done by a company. And in that moment it became very, very clear that this was my path. It took a while to actually find a company. I went through a false company first, called Trinity Rep. The lesson in that is that you can't inherit somebody else's company.

So the answer is the same as what Ariane Mnouchkine said. It's a pain in the ass because there are always problems. People have other things to do. There are issues of imbalance because it's not a democracy. It's actually quite an unfair situation, not totally nonhierarchical, and there are people who suffer more than others. But when you go in the room with a group of people like this, and speak a world that you imagine, and for them to get this strange look in their face and start entering this world profoundly—that feels to me like flying. They can realize things that I can only suspect. And they realize it in sinew, in muscle, in sound, in voice, in interaction. I can't do it outside of a company. Much like Darron, I think it's great sometimes to go and work with not the company because then you actually realize the magic, the alchemy that happens with a group of people that you trust, and who trust you. This is a group of people who actually trusts me. That's an amazing feeling. It's hard. But it's worth it, ultimately.

Leon Ingulsrud: If you take a jar of jellybeans and you ask a number of people to guess how many jellybeans there are in the jar, then you take the average of guesses, it's been shown across many, many different situations that the average of the guesses is always more accurate than any one of the guesses—which is just a way of saying that groups are smarter than individuals. The way the brain works, it's not one thing, it's a network of neurons. I mean, every one of the members of this company is amazing in their own way as an individual. But as a group we're actually smarter than any of us. What that's based on—and this is where it gets tricky—is that we don't always agree. If we all always agreed we'd only be as smart as whoever the person was who said it. But we don't always agree. That makes us as smart as the entire group, when we have the grace to allow that to happen. The con in it is when we don't value the diversity that's in the group and, for whatever reasons, we shut down dissent—that's when I think we get into trouble. When we're able to create an environment that's fostering a dissent that leads to a diversity of opinion, we actually make some really cool shit.

AB: Could you briefly describe our process in rehearsals?

Will Bond: I think that we don't go about any production in any one way. As you've said, Anne, you can tell the rehearsal process by what you see in the final product. You can't hide your rehearsal process in a well-acted show. It always reads.

Kelly Mauer: The only constant is that we train. And then after we train, we step into the world of the piece.

AB: One thing that is true is that we don't go out of order, except songs and dances. We start at the beginning and we don't jump. I wouldn't know what to do with scene six before I do scene five.

Kelly Mauer: When we're working on a piece, whether you're in the scene or not, you're in the room. I'm thinking of *Miss Julie*. How many weeks did I sit on my behind before I got on stage? I played Christine, so I watched Jeff and Ellen rehearse, but I was in the rehearsal room every single day. I couldn't imagine how I would make an entrance into this play if I didn't know what they were building.

Megan Wanlass: If we have an actual play with a script and a text already made before we get into the rehearsal room, the actors are, on the first day of rehearsal, already off book. Imagine the progress they can make by already being that far along in the process. They also approach each and every rehearsal with just an amazing amount of discipline, from the moment that they're there until the wee hours of the night. They are living this project. I try to reflect and mirror what I see in the rehearsal room in the administrative office.

AB: A lot of work happens in the bar. I don't go to the bar so often, so I come in the next day and it's like, "We were in the bar last night. We've decided that the first act really should be the second act." That happened once. I came in in the morning and they'd switched the order of the acts.

Megan Wanlass: I think we changed the ending once in the bar.

AB: So a lot gets done in the bar during a rehearsal process.

J. Ed Araiza: Most projects, with very few exceptions, start with an idea or interest of Anne's, and she thinks way in advance, even more in advance than how long it takes to plan the management part of it. She thinks and reads books and, as she starts getting interested in the topic more, she starts telling us about the books. We love the research part of it, so we're learning about the world. We immerse ourselves before the first day of rehearsal starts. We continue that process all the way through until the end.

There's always someone in the room who has an idea. I think it's very rare that there's not an idea or an abundance of ideas coming from the company. Anne says that she sometimes functions more as an editor than a director. She'll say, "I think it starts this way," and then she just opens the door, and we rush through the door, not even knowing what's on the other side. I find that very exciting as a member of this company.

Akiko Aizawa: The rehearsal process, if it's the scene between Kelly and me, it's not about two actresses—no: it's about everybody, including the stage manager, designers, everybody watching us—and then idea, idea, idea, idea. It's so open, and then open disagreement in a beautiful way. It's not about the two brains here and the struggle. Everybody is taking care of us—even in a solo show. It's really close, so I don't feel alone and stupid.

Brian Scott: It is good to note that often it's not just the people who are actually working on the project that are in the room. With the piece we're doing now, Stephen isn't in the piece but was there for our entire period of rehearsal. And I don't know how we would have pulled it off without that mind, that set of eyes. J. Ed has done this too. It's so hugely important to have another actor looking at you and being able to point at context or push on. That's another function—it's all of us all the time.

Darron West: We don't ever go into the rehearsal process thinking we know what this is. When you start, you've basically downloaded a whole bunch of information, and then we're all in a room trying to answer a certain set of questions. But my questions might not be the same questions as Kelly's or Akiko's or Brian's. You've got all these people trying to answer their own questions to the same end. Most of the time when you do a play, you go, "This is the play, and this is how we're going to do it, and this is what the scenery is like." But in our process it works best when we all have a series of questions and we go about the process trying to answer them as we make it.

Brian Scott: The one given agreement that we do have is that we agree to get together and do this. We never come in agreeing to agree with each other, thank God. But often, working outside the company, the agreement is to do it in a certain way. And you're all kind of castrated, and it's a little boring.

But to be in the room with the company, you're never off the hook. You're always expected to work at the highest level you can, and that's beautiful.

Ellen Lauren: Who was it who said, "Your responsibility as an actor is to direct your role, and it's the director's responsibility to direct the play"? I think we take that at face value and step up to that responsibility. As collaborative as the process is, we are all individually focused on our job, on our role, on our path in the event that we're making. Anne is directing that event, and we're just pouring stuff in. Sometimes my directing my role is going to clash with Stephen or Barney because they're doing that too, and we'll hit this place where that conflict is either exponential and explosive in a way that will move the piece to a new place, or it shuts it down. It's a very old-fashioned environment in the rehearsal room. I don't understand it to this day, but it is this mysterious alchemy that happens between people, and it happened between us. We've been together a very, very long time. That, in and of itself, in our culture, is pretty unique. We have personal relationships. We have a very strong leader who is intellectually very rigorous, who we chase after to keep up with and never can. Yet somebody will watch us rehearse and go, "Oh my God, the level of collaboration." It's all of these things that create this thing called the SITI Company. I don't mean this discouragingly, but I don't know if just doing Suzuki training and Viewpoints training and doing this play actually makes that thing. It's something else—as all good companies are.

Tom Nelis: When you say the actors are responsible for directing their role, the thing that gives us all the ability to do that is the training.

Ellen Lauren: Oh, without a doubt.

Tom Nelis: The training, ultimately, gives you freedom to know who you are on stage, freedom to have aesthetic choices about how this thing might be better. You study those techniques for a while, and then you go outside of the company and do something, and you have the technique and wherewithal to go after ideas somebody throws out at you. It doesn't feel like anything is impossible. It just feels like, "Great, there's the obstacle. Thanks for identifying it for me. Now let me go after it." The training that we share is the conduit through which we can each direct our own role.

J. Ed Araiza: And in terms of the rehearsal process, the training gives us the ability to build material very fast, which then we might keep or we might change. Dependent on how much time we have, we do as much table work as we can, but then we get up from the table with, as Megan mentioned, as much script as is available in our bodies, and we start building material very quickly. We don't do a lot of sitting around hemming and hawing. Somebody makes a choice and somebody goes. That's because of the training and also because of the freedom Anne allows in the room.

AB: I would say that in pursuing the word "alchemy," that nobody knew what putting the Suzuki training and Viewpoints training would do. I brought the Viewpoints training, which was very much from the modern dance world, from Mary Overlie, with me because it had been work that had fed me for years. Then Suzuki wanted to make sure that every actor who came to Japan the first year had Suzuki training. We put the two together and it was alchemy. That was not ever a plan. This is the combination that now a lot of training programs are doing. It's this magic duo.
      Could you describe the future of this company?

Leon Ingulsrud: A situation in which we are not project-based, but we have some kind of context that allows us to support our lives throughout the year and work together in a situation where artistic choices about projects don't have direct economic ramifications on our lives. Right now if you're not working on a project, in most cases, in the company, you're not paid—which is normal in the real world. But I think that the future of the company is to get past that. Anne has said a few times that the way that she works is a product of the environment in the States which has to do with three-week rehearsal periods. I'm interested to see what happens with us if we're not tied to that production model. Right now for a project to get going, Megan has to put an enormous amount of work into lining up commissioners, lining up presenters, figuring out how to make it work before we can get into the rehearsal hall with each other to have our magic time. I just fantasize all the time about—and I mean this in the most positive way possible—punching a clock: Going in every day and working on whatever project.

Ellen Lauren: I was so inspired by watching the Graham Company. There's the sense of a master in the room, and the company members have encoded into their bodies lessons and choreography from Martha Graham. They're a living culture. In that spirit that Leon describes, I see being in the room where we are teaching a good solid repertory that we built years ago and watching it in another generation—watching it on other bodies and personalities, and stand up against time. To me this would be an extraordinary watermark of what we put in the world.

J. Ed Araiza: The future is many more performances—and more performances in our home base. We don't perform nearly enough, and we don't perform nearly enough in New York City. I would love us to be able to get to that point—and I think it's connected to what Leon and Ellen said—where we're performing so much that we're able to pass on what we're doing to the next generation of the company. That's hard to envision now because we're not performing enough as it is. It's hard to let go of something when there's not that much, but I would love to get to the point where we're able to say that it's time to pass some of this on.

Akiko Aizawa: I'm thinking about the future, the faraway future. Even if we are aged in our nineties, we will train—with a crutch or a wheelchair, I don't know, but somehow I envision we will train. Maybe we're teaching. Yes, we are performing in our nineties.

Ellen Lauren: There's an actor in Sukuki's company who is in his late sixties, who has had triple bypass surgery. He has a pacemaker that sticks out of his chest from under his skin, about a half inch—a box. And you see it—beating. I'm not kidding. He gets up to do his stomping, and he does it with this unbelievable elegance. And you're watching this box, under his skin. There's something that I'm not elegant enough to articulate about that that leads to this idea that the real value isn't always about the speed. You have to work through that to get to the other stuff.

Leon Ingulsrud: When I look into the future, I see this as a context in which, as my artistic interests evolve, as my body degrades, I will continue that exploration with this group of people. If that means we're going to figure out how to do it on crutches, these are the people we're going to do it with.

Barney O'Hanlon: I still see a really beautiful building that has a theater in it, and perhaps a smaller space that has three gorgeous studios, with windows, and that has, perhaps—this is the really dreamy part—an apartment attached for guests or for people from other countries. I see a beautiful sign outside that says, "The SITI Company Space." It's a place that people can find us. It's a place they can come and find the training. They can find us individually, a place where they can find our work, and hopefully work by others who we've come into contact with over many years. It's a resource and a place for them to touch base and to share their work with us and with the community.

Megan Wanlass: That's possible. We had a company meeting, maybe seven or eight years ago, where we all talked about what we saw the company becoming in five years or what we wished for. We have the minutes, which were typed up on an old Apple Powerbook. We pulled them out a couple of years ago when we were starting another strategic planning process. We wished for things like heat in our office. We wished for blue road cases. We wished for windows in our office. And I'm happy to report that we have those things now. We've achieved so much together as a group—and now what? What do we see, and how are we going to get there?

AB: I remember in that list saying I want us to go to Azerbaijan. We ended up going to Tblisi instead. But we are the victims of success, which is there's a great deal of interest in what we do. Everybody wants some of the training or some of the company. We've been sending people out, so we're rarely ever together, which is why this time in Saratoga is so precious to us. My dream, and I think it reflects what everybody said, is for people to come to us. I keep reading new brain books because we're working on a brain play. The latest brain book says it's not about being able to describe something into existence; it's about feeling it. If you don't feel it, it's not going to happen. It's about visualizing and imagining and feeling what you believe in. The feeling for me is associated with a place where we are actually able to be together consistently outside of Saratoga. Outside of Saratoga we're just jets, shooting in opposite directions.

Leon Ingulsrud: This is the entire acting company sitting in a line with half of our designers and our administrator and our stage manager. This is the first time since we were with *bobrauschenbergamerica* in Boston. We just don't get to sit in a room together very much.

J. Ed Araiza: And we've never done a play with the whole company yet. That's something I would really love in the future—the whole company on stage together.

Audience: Is theater necessary, and if so, what makes it necessary?

Brian Scott: On September 30, 2001, we left New York to tour *War of the Worlds*, the radio play, which I think people thought was ill-advised.

AB: We had a lot of calls from arts centers wanting to cancel. The invasion of Martians was too close to what we had just experienced.

Brian Scott: After every performance we had a talkback. At every performance people were like, "Fuck you for doing this," or "Thank God for giving me a reason to be in a room with somebody." It really drove home this notion that there is something that television and film and other mediums can't give you, which is an organic reason for human beings to be together in a room experiencing.

AB: This book just came to me from Amazon.com, written by the philosopher Paul Woodruff called *The Necessity of Theatre*. I haven't read it yet, but his definition of theater is: the art in which human beings make human action worth watching. One of the things he talks about—and I totally agree—is that what makes us human is our capacity for empathy. To me that's the heart of the theater.

The other thing is what we do as a group is propose an alternate kind of society. When you see *Who Do You Think You Are?*, it's about a bunch of really brutal, mean people, but actually what you're watching is a group of fucked-up people played by a group of people who really function beautifully together, who listen to each other, who are kinesthetically responsive in the moment, and who have created something quite beautiful together. Every time you do a play you're proposing a way that people might be together that is alternate to ways people are in the world around us.

We're also offering alternate time signatures, which is one of the most radical things I think you can do in this day and age. We're actually proposing alternate ways of being in a room, alternate kinds of breathing and heart beating, and alternate ways the neuron system functions in the proximity of other humans.

Elizabeth Moreau: One of the major tenants of research for this new play that we delved into is this idea of mirror neurons. They've tested it on gorillas. So if you're a gorilla, and you're watching another gorilla, and the gorilla that's being watched is peeling a banana, the watching gorilla has the same neurons firing in its brain as if it were the one performing the action. One could suppose for an audience watching a play there's actually a neurological learning process going on.

Will Bond: Or theater is only necessary for gorillas.

I don't know what this story means, but on September 14, 2001, I was walking down the street in New York City and there weren't very many people walking around, and those who were were sort of dazed. I walked by the town hall, and it said that Laurie Anderson was playing tonight. I didn't go, "Oh, I've got to go see Laurie Anderson on Thursday." I just turned left and walked in. I think I bought a ticket. I don't know. There weren't a lot of people, but everyone was sort of facing the same way. And she came out and did a number. At one point she said, "We have an opportunity to see everything completely differently right now." Everyone sat up a little bit and said, "Right. We actually from now on can see everything completely differently." It struck me that that speaks to a kind of necessity. We don't always have to experience a disaster and go see a play or listen to music, but that conversation is in there.

Leon Ingulsrud: Part of what these sorts of extreme situations bring out is the need for an experience where you're sitting next to people who you may not share a lot with. Politics, religion, even education, sports—all of these things are contexts in which you are divided into clearly defined groups. Theater can be more ecumenical than that. You may be sitting next to somebody who you may not go to the same church with, or whatever euphemism you want to use. You have a common experience. You may have two totally different interpretations of what that experience is, but there's something going on in the fact that you're having that commonality of experience. In the world now, if you want to, you don't have to get any news that you don't already agree with. That's the way most people function. So being thrown into these kinds of spaces is, I think, necessary.

Ellen Lauren: The next time you're stuck in an airplane on the tarmac, remember how necessary theater is. It's the same thing, right? You're next to somebody in a communal experience.

J. Ed Araiza: I don't know if this is why theater is necessary, but every time— and I mean this sincerely—I go to the theater, before the lights come up, or the curtain, I always get very excited because it could be the best thing I ever saw in my whole life. It very rarely happens, but I really have that feeling before every show starts.

Audience: I often wonder, because I don't have a trade, what would I do in a World War III situation. And then I go back to boys in the first world war who would go around with costumes and women's dresses, and were found with those tools of the trade in their soldier's bags. I often wonder what is it about that entertainment that is necessary.

AB: I think the word entertainment defines it—which is to create a space between tensions. I think all great theater is also entertaining.

Barney O'Hanlon: Oliver Sacks in his book *Music Ophelia* describes that. There is no explanation for why there is music in the world. It's completely abstract. And why is it human beings get it? It's a very similar question, actually, in relation to art or theater.

Leon Ingulsrud: Ducks quack. This is what we do. The sum total of the performance, that's what humans do. That's our quack.

Audience: I think it's proper to describe the cornerstone of your company as collaboration. In today's society, we take so much pride in the individual and in own-

ership. Artists copyright their materials. It's hard for us as a theater, a collaborative art, to be able to take from other artists who are creating. How do you respond to people who might call your work plagiarism or stealing?

Ellen Lauren: Certainly the musical world does it—steals thematic material as well as technical material. I think it's a muscle that has to be exercised rigorously in the theater. I think it is something that should be freed up and it can get stiff and hard, and when that happens between human beings, it's not a great thing. The words—the labels "plagiarism" or "thievery"—we can change by not describing ourselves that way. It's how we use our language about what we do that sends the message or signal to people who perhaps aren't privy to how we do what we do.

Tom Nelis: Do you mean, do we see the world around us and lift them to make pieces? We do that. If text that somebody else wrote is in our work, then we get the rights and credit them.

AB: We pay for it.

Tom Nelis: I'm not sure that this company in any way is based on plagiarism.

Audience: I just wanted you to articulate that.

Audience: You've spoken about the current state of company. You've talked about the future. I would really like to know about the early stages of the company. Can you talk a little about the difficulties and the failures, especially?

Kelly Maurer: You mean in the days when we didn't have heat?

Tom Nelis: The first year was a dry run. I'll make it simplistic, but from my view, Suzuki said, "Anne, you bring some people, and I'll bring some people, and we'll meet in Toga, and we'll put two productions up and we'll see what happens." How many people came with us? It seems like there were twenty or something. Most of them did not come back. They had the experience, and it was a heck of an experience, but it was like, "This is not the rest of my life." The second year was time to—well, to start from that point. It seems to me a lot was learned going through that.

Ellen Lauren: Certainly administratively, until Megan came along, we've had a series of disastrous love affairs with managers and a variety of different ways of trying to do that—hiring consulting managers. It was a very difficult, long time—the first six, seven years.

Megan Wanlass: I think the other difficulty was that it was started with some Japanese seed money. If you were starting a company now, it would be started with not a lot of money, and you'd being trying to figure out how to raise money. We were started with money, and then due to a lot of really poor management decisions, we took a crash landing, and then had to say, "Now what? Are we going to throw in the towel and say, jeez, we're a hundred thousand dollars in debt and we have no way of figuring out how we can do this? Or are we all going to say we believe enough in each other, and band together and figure out how to get out of debt and move forward?" We all said we're not ready to quit. Again, it was a bonding thing. Those were really tough years. We all worked a lot without getting any money at all. I think we would be even farther than we are now, had really firm management been put into place in the early years.

Stephen Webber: We were already in financial straits. We weren't in debt yet, but we were having trouble paying for *Going, Going, Gone* in 1995. We were building productions that we were just at the edge of being able to afford, and then we decided to produce three of our shows in New York City—the infamous Miller season. We had a hundred thousand dollars in debt.

AB: But what a season!

Stephen Webber: It was amazing. But the result was that we were really in trouble.

Barney O'Hanlon: Also, we weren't being communicated to very well by our managers. They led us on to believe that we had the money to do a really huge thing. And we just didn't.

Stephen Webber: But we worked without a manager for a while, and the company was run out of Ellen's apartment.

Barney O'Hanlon: Three apartments, actually.

Stephen Webber: We would work for free. We would go teach workshops in Ohio or wherever, and instead of taking a paycheck, just give all of the money to the company. We did whatever we had to do. As Megan said, we pulled together. But that was a dark point.

Ellen Lauren: Also, and this is a hard one because it isn't money, but I think one of the darker times was in Edinburgh. Our first big booking internationally was at the Edinburgh Festival—not the fringe. And we were booked to do three shows in two weeks—the radio play and two very large shows. We went with our guns blasting and our crappy plywood road cases. The load-in crew laughed in our faces when they unloaded them. It was not good. I guess financially it was good. But spiritually, artistically, socially, it wasn't good, for many, many reasons. That was for me the first slam into the brick wall. We're either going to stop, because this is too painful, or we're going to get through it. And we chose to get through it. I remember that meeting, down in that green room—it literally was green—and Anne saying, "Look. This is a choice." We were freaking out, individually and as the group—the body of the group was freaking. The inability to communicate and the missed marks and stuff started to add up. And the audiences didn't like the work that much.

Audience: As actors, can you speak to bringing your training into working with artists outside the company? What's it like?

Stephen Webber: People ask this all the time, and it seems to be a burning issue. I feel strongly that as an actor every rehearsal situation I go into, regardless of whether it's with the company, or with a group of people I've never even met before, or with other friends who don't happen to be in the company, I'm bringing my training. I'm bringing what I know. That's all I can do. Even if I wanted to, I couldn't do anything but that. And even if I didn't want to bring part of that, I couldn't do that either. My training is my body—as Bondo said eloquently one time. That's what I'm bringing into the room, and that's what every other actor in the room is bringing, and on that level everybody's equal. It's just about the work. It's about making a play, and usually quickly under difficult circumstances. If I happen to see the stage in the perspective of someone who's been doing Viewpoints for however many years, or who has done a lot of Suzuki training, I'm still just making that scene.

Kelly Mauer: In a way, whatever your process is, whatever your—I hate this word—technique is, it's sort of your own little secret, isn't it? I did a play this February, and if anybody saw my work and went, "Oh, look at her Viewpoint," then I failed—miserably. They didn't have to know that.

Audience: If one day Anne were to stop existing, would SITI Company still continue to exist?

Darron West: I would like to think it would. But every one of us would make our own individual choices as to what our roles inside of that new organization might be. I would say I got involved in the SITI Company because I got involved and interested in Anne's ideas, so everything else is bonus. God forbid I ever have to make that decision, but I would like to think that company would continue.

Tom Nelis: "Whatever this *new* organization would be" is apropos. It would be new. It would be different. It would be decided if I could go forward with this new venture, but it would not exist or function the way it does.

Darron West: It would have to redefine itself because this group of people is the SITI Company, and this group of people is the SITI Company even when we're not in the same room.

J. Ed Araiza: I think we would continue to make work. We would continue to make work as a group, but without Anne it probably wouldn't be the SITI Company.

AB: I've actually been thinking about it a lot. About fifteen years ago when I first saw the Martha Graham Company, I thought I was hit in the stomach. Here were these young dancers who were doing work that she had made in her youth, and she's dead, and it was still embarrassingly bare, and exposed, and powerful. I started thinking: What is legacy? For awhile I was thinking maybe it's the plays. As Ellen said, watching younger people put on those clothes, and I still think that's valid and true, the idea of passing on repertory. But our new thinking about the future and this place we can all be together—it's actually a way of leaving a legacy of a way of being together. The legacy is not so much the human beings who inhabit the company, but proposing a different way of creating, and a way of looking at the role of theater or the necessity of theater. Unless we find a way to coalesce, we can't leave that legacy. I hope that I have long enough to live where it's something that is patterned enough for other people to inhabit, whether it's repertory or just a way of making work. But I don't think it can happen now because we're not together enough.

Kelly Mauer: But we will be.

ANNE BOGART is the Artistic Director of SITI Company, which she founded with Japanese director Tadashi Suzuki in 1992. She is a professor at Columbia University where she runs the Graduate Directing Program. Her works with SITI include *Trojan Women*; *American Document* (with the Martha Graham Dance Company); *Antigone*; *Under Construction*; *Freshwater*; *Who Do You Think You Are*; *Radio Macbeth*; *Hotel Cassiopeia*; *Death and the Ploughman*; *La Dispute*; *Score*; *bobrauschenbergamerica*; *Room*; *War of the Worlds*; *Cabin Pressure*; *The Radio Play*; *Alice's Adventures*; *Culture of Desire*; *Bob*; *Going, Going, Gone*; *Small Lives/Big Dreams*; *The Medium*; Noel Coward's *Hay Fever* and *Private Lives*; August Strindberg's *Miss Julie* and Charles L. Mee's *Orestes*. She is the author of three other books: *A Director Prepares, The Viewpoints Book* (with Tina Landau) and *And Then, You Act*.